D0916016

Voices from the Century Before

Voices from the Century Before

THE ODYSSEY OF A NINETEENTH-CENTURY KENTUCKY FAMILY

Mary Clay Berry

ARCADE PUBLISHING • NEW YORK

FIRST EDITION

Epigraph from *Requiem for a Nun* by William Faulkner. Copyright © 1950, 1951 by William Faulkner. Reprinted by permission of Random House, Inc.

Excerpt from *House of Splendid Isolation* by Edna O'Brien. Copyright © 1994 by Edna O'Brien. Reprinted by permission of Farrar, Straus & Giroux, Inc.

Family tree designed by Jeffrey Ward.

Maps of Bourbon County made by Jamshid Kooros.

Library of Congress Cataloging-in-Publication Data

Berry, Mary Clay
    Voices from the century before: the odyssey of a nineteenth-century Kentucky family.
        p.   cm.
    Includes bibliographical references and index.
    ISBN 1-55970-342-3
    1. Clay family. 2. Field family. 3. Kentucky—History—1792–1865—Biography.
4. Kentucky—History—Civil War, 1861–1865. I. Title.
    CT274.C57B47 1996
    973.7'092'2—dc20
    [B]   96-43083

Published in the United States by Arcade Publishing, Inc., New York
Distributed by Little, Brown and Company

10 9 8 7 6 5 4 3 2 1

BP

Designed by API

PRINTED IN THE UNITED STATES OF AMERICA

FOR ALL THE

GREAT-GREAT GRANDCHILDREN OF

ANN AND BRUTUS CLAY

"The past never dead. It's not even past."

—William Faulkner, *Requiem for a Nun*

"History is everywhere. It seeps into the soil, the subsoil. Like rain, or hail, or snow, or blood. A house remembers. An outhouse remembers. A people ruminate. The tale differs with the teller."

—Edna O'Brien, *House of Splendid Isolation*

CONTENTS

Author's Note

When considering how best to present these letters, I decided to look upon them as the raw material of a novel. In general, I cut the portions of the letters that did not further the action of the story, while trying to leave in enough of their flavor for the reader to savor. I cut passages that I could not decipher, passages with references that I could not track down, and gossip about people I could not identify. But I also had to cut fascinating material about homemaking, farming, child care, education, and many other subjects. Making these cuts was wrenching for me, but, had I not made them, this book would be twice as long as it is.

The letters that are presented in full contain ellipses to indicate where material has been cut. In some cases, lengthy postscripts have also been cut, though this is not indicated in the text unless a portion of the postscript is retained. I have tried to be as faithful as I could to the spelling in these letters, but, in a few cases, have added punctuation marks to make the writer's meaning clear. The letter-writers took great liberties with the spelling of one another's names, particularly nicknames. Whenever possible, I have retained the author's spelling within the letter, but standardized the spelling in the text. When I have excerpted letters in the text, I did not use ellipses to indicate cuts other than in the middle of sentences. The dates for the excerpted letters can be found in the text.

Nothing would please me more than to see a complete edition of these letters published. But until that happens, the letters themselves are part of the Brutus J. Clay Family Papers at the University of Kentucky Library Special Collections in Lexington.

Acknowledgments

Years ago, I started to edit these letters but got sidetracked into doing something else. I am grateful to the Virginia Center for the Creative Arts for making it possible for me to start this project all over again. I am also grateful to the University of Kentucky Library Special Collections for preserving the letters and for providing me with copies.

I am indebted to my father Cassius M. Clay for annotating many of the letters more than forty years ago and for identifying many of the photographs used in this book. He was one of the last people who understood the connections between the people mentioned in the letters, and his stories about these people are the roots from which this book grew.

My brother Berle Clay has traced our great-grandfather's farming activities—how many mules he bred, what his cattle were worth, what crops he harvested and with what machinery. He and I traveled together to several of the places where the writers of these letters lived. We have discussed the letters endlessly, puzzling over the characters of their writers and the mysteries they touch upon. He generously read and commented upon several versions of this book and gave me permission to use many of the photographs accompanying the text.

Many other people helped me, and I can only begin to repay my debt to them by mentioning their names. My agent Leslie Breed believed from the beginning that these letters were worth a book. Jane Kramer brought the book to the attention of Dick and Jeannette Seaver at Arcade Publishing. Jennifer Hamilton suggested a way to edit the mass of material from which the book was distilled. William J. Marshall and Claire McCann helped with the original documents and so much else. Claire Starr shared her expertise on quilts. Friends read the manuscript at different stages and I thank them all, particularly Lynne Bair. Tim Bent edited the manuscript with great sensitivity and enthusiasm.

Most of all, I thank my husband John M. Berry for his patience and forbearance as well as his support. He was always there when I needed him, even to photograph Ann Clay's glorious quilt on a sunny sub-zero day.

Voices from the Century Before

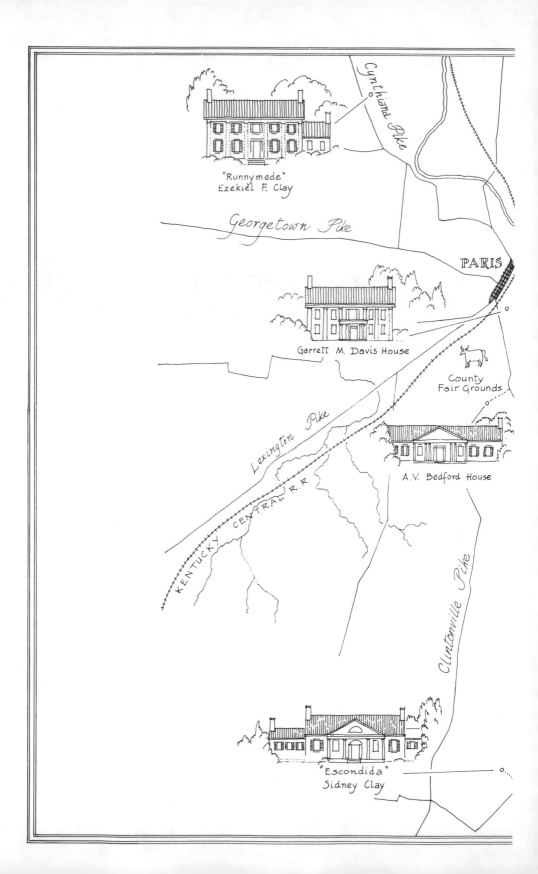

"Runnymede"
Ezekiel F. Clay

Cynthiana Pike

Georgetown Pike

PARIS

Garrett M. Davis House

County
Fair Grounds

Lexington Pike

KENTUCKY CENTRAL R.R.

A.V. Bedford House

Clintonville Pike

"Escondida"
Sidney Clay

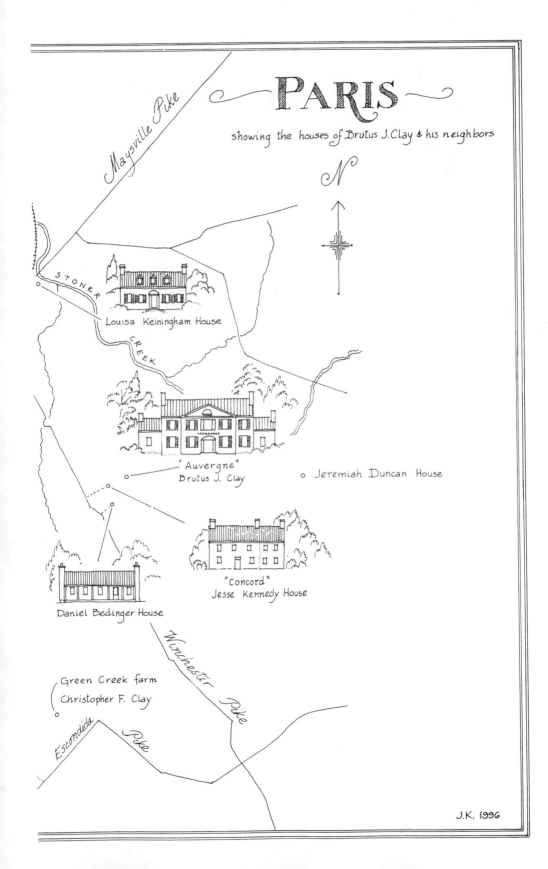

PARIS

showing the houses of Brutus J. Clay & his neighbors

N

Maysville Pike

STONER

CREEK

Louisa Keiningham House

"Auvergne"
Brutus J. Clay

○ Jeremiah Duncan House

"Concord"
Jesse Kennedy House

Daniel Bedinger House

Winchester Pike

Green Creek farm
Christopher F. Clay

Escondida Pike

J.K. 1996

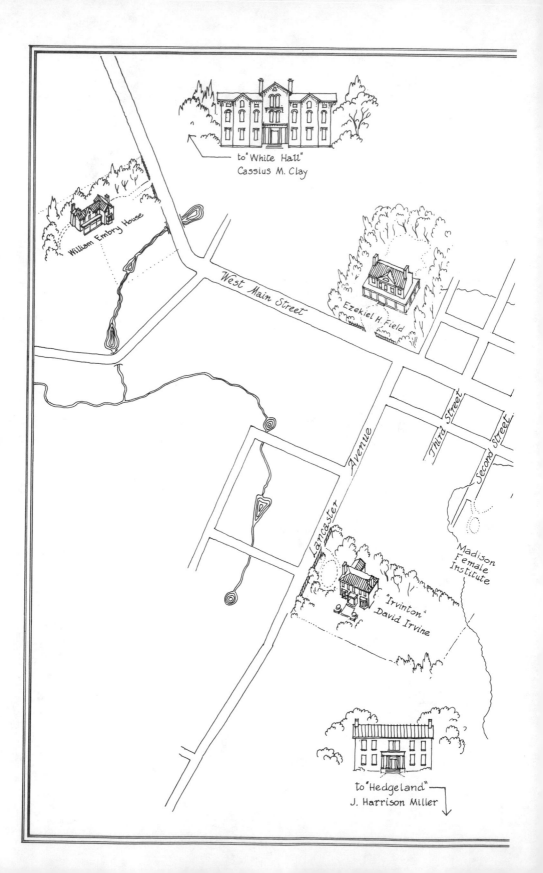

to "White Hall"
Cassius M. Clay

William Embry House

West Main Street

Ezekiel H. Field

Third Street

Second Street

Lancaster Avenue

Madison Female Institute

"Irvinton" David Irvine

to "Hedgeland"
J. Harrison Miller

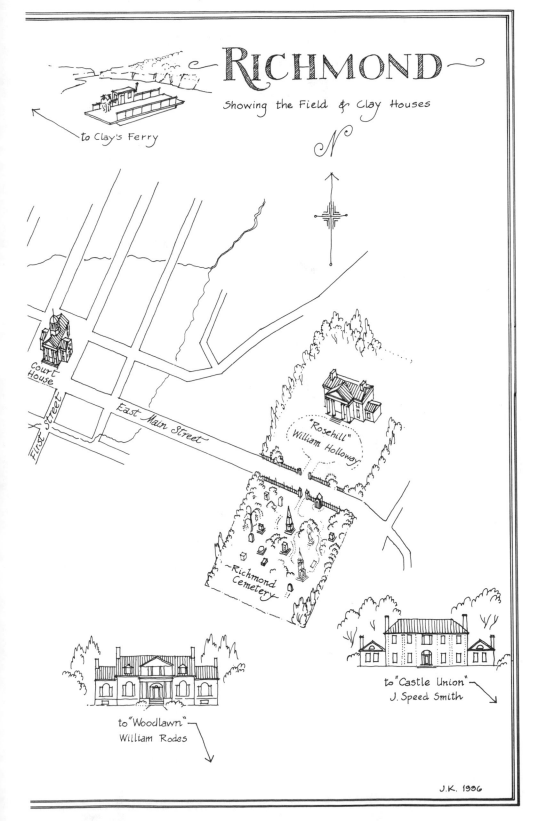

RICHMOND

Showing the Field & Clay Houses

N

to Clay's Ferry

Court House

First Street

East Main Street

"Rosehill" William Holloway

Richmond Cemetery

to "Castle Union" J. Speed Smith

to "Woodlawn" William Rodes

J.K. 1996

The Clay Family

Green Clay (1757-1828) m Sally Payne Lewis (1776-1867)

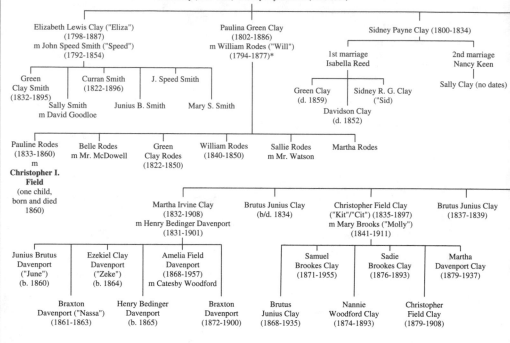

Elizabeth Lewis Clay ("Eliza")
(1798-1887)
m John Speed Smith ("Speed")
(1792-1854)

Paulina Green Clay
(1802-1886)
m William Rodes ("Will")
(1794-1877)*

Sidney Payne Clay (1800-1834)

1st marriage
Isabella Reed

2nd marriage
Nancy Keen

Green
Clay Smith
(1832-1895)

Curran Smith
(1822-1896)

J. Speed Smith

Green Clay
(d. 1859)

Sidney R. G. Clay
("Sid")

Sally Clay (no dates)

Sally Smith
m David Goodloe

Junius B. Smith

Mary S. Smith

Davidson Clay
(d. 1852)

Pauline Rodes
(1833-1860)
m
Christopher I. Field
(one child, born and died 1860)

Belle Rodes
m Mr. McDowell

Green
Clay Rodes
(1822-1850)

William Rodes
(1840-1850)

Sallie Rodes
m Mr. Watson

Martha Rodes

Martha Irvine Clay
(1832-1908)
m Henry Bedinger Davenport
(1831-1901)

Brutus Junius Clay
(b/d. 1834)

Christopher Field Clay
("Kit"/"Cit") (1835-1897)
m Mary Brooks ("Molly")
(1841-1911)

Brutus Junius Clay
(1837-1839)

Junius Brutus
Davenport
("June")
(b. 1860)

Ezekiel Clay
Davenport
("Zeke")
(b. 1864)

Amelia Field
Davenport
(1868-1957)
m Catesby Woodford

Samuel
Brookes Clay
(1871-1955)

Sadie
Brookes Clay
(1876-1893)

Martha
Davenport Clay
(1879-1937)

Braxton
Davenport ("Nassa")
(1861-1863)

Henry Bedinger
Davenport
(b. 1865)

Braxton
Davenport
(1872-1900)

Brutus
Junius Clay
(1868-1935)

Nannie
Woodford Clay
(1874-1893)

Christopher
Field Clay
(1879-1908)

The Field Family

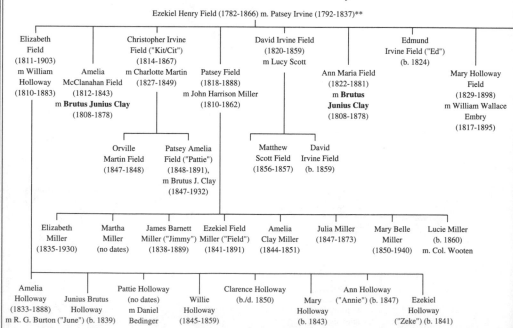

Ezekiel Henry Field (1782-1866) m. Patsey Irvine (1792-1837)**

Elizabeth
Field
(1811-1903)
m William
Holloway
(1810-1883)

Christopher Irvine
Field ("Kit/Cit")
(1814-1867)
m Charlotte Martin
(1827-1849)

David Irvine Field
(1820-1859)
m Lucy Scott

Edmund
Irvine Field ("Ed")
(b. 1824)

Amelia
McClanahan Field
(1812-1843)
m **Brutus Junius Clay**
(1808-1878)

Patsey Field
(1818-1888)
m John Harrison Miller
(1810-1862)

Ann Maria Field
(1822-1881)
m **Brutus Junius Clay**
(1808-1878)

Mary Holloway
Field
(1829-1898)
m William Wallace
Embry
(1817-1895)

Orville
Martin Field
(1847-1848)

Patsey Amelia
Field ("Pattie")
(1848-1891),
m Brutus J. Clay
(1847-1932)

Matthew
Scott Field
(1856-1857)

David
Irvine Field
(b. 1859)

Elizabeth
Miller
(1835-1930)

Martha
Miller
(no dates)

James Barnett
Miller ("Jimmy")
(1838-1889)

Ezekiel Field
Miller ("Field")
(1841-1891)

Amelia
Clay Miller
(1844-1851)

Julia Miller
(1847-1873)

Mary Belle
Miller
(1850-1940)

Lucie Miller
(b. 1860)
m. Col. Wooten

Amelia
Holloway
(1833-1888)
m R. G. Burton ("June") (b. 1839)

Junius Brutus
Holloway

Pattie Holloway
(no dates)
m Daniel
Bedinger

Willie
Holloway
(1845-1859)

Clarence Holloway
(b./d. 1850)

Mary
Holloway
(b. 1843)

Ann Holloway
("Annie") (b. 1847)

Ezekiel
Holloway
("Zeke") (b. 1841)

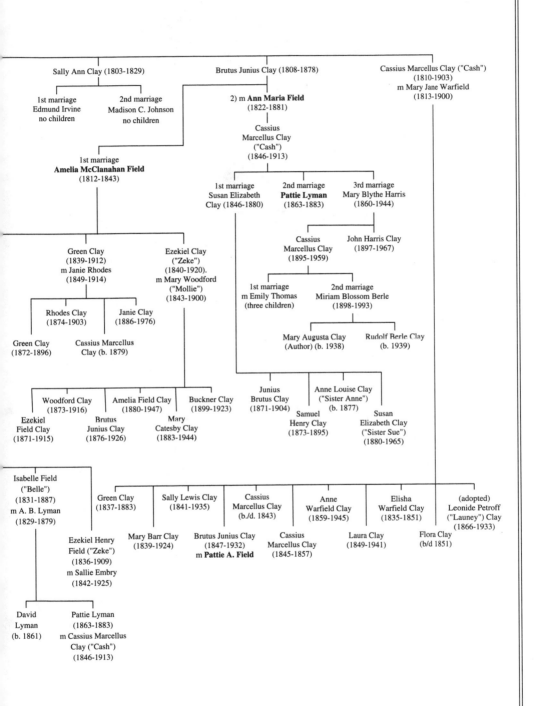

Sally Ann Clay (1803-1829)   Brutus Junius Clay (1808-1878)   Cassius Marcellus Clay ("Cash")
                                                                                 (1810-1903)
                                                                                 m Mary Jane Warfield
                                                                                 (1813-1900)

1st marriage   2nd marriage   2) m **Ann Maria Field**
Edmund Irvine   Madison C. Johnson   (1822-1881)
no children   no children
                                                  Cassius
                                                  Marcellus Clay
                                                  ("Cash")
                                                  (1846-1913)
1st marriage
Amelia McClanahan Field
(1812-1843)
                        1st marriage   2nd marriage   3rd marriage
                        Susan Elizabeth   **Pattie Lyman**   Mary Blythe Harris
                        Clay (1846-1880)   (1863-1883)   (1860-1944)

                                              Cassius   John Harris Clay
                                              Marcellus Clay   (1897-1967)
                                              (1895-1959)

Green Clay   Ezekiel Clay
(1839-1912)   ("Zeke")
m Janie Rhodes   (1840-1920).   1st marriage   2nd marriage
(1849-1914)   m Mary Woodford   m Emily Thomas   Miriam Blossom Berle
                     ("Mollie")   (three children)   (1898-1993)
                     (1843-1900)
Rhodes Clay   Janie Clay
(1874-1903)   (1886-1976)   Mary Augusta Clay   Rudolf Berle Clay
                                                    (Author) (b. 1938)   (b. 1939)
Green Clay   Cassius Marcellus
(1872-1896)   Clay (b. 1879)

Woodford Clay   Amelia Field Clay   Buckner Clay   Junius   Anne Louise Clay
(1873-1916)   (1880-1947)   (1899-1923)   Brutus Clay   ("Sister Anne")
Ezekiel   Brutus   Mary   (1871-1904)   (b. 1877)
Field Clay   Junius Clay   Catesby Clay   Samuel   Susan
(1871-1915)   (1876-1926)   (1883-1944)   Henry Clay   Elizabeth Clay
                                                              (1873-1895)   ("Sister Sue")
                                                                                  (1880-1965)

Isabelle Field
("Belle")
(1831-1887)   Green Clay   Sally Lewis Clay   Cassius   Anne   Elisha   (adopted)
m A. B. Lyman   (1837-1883)   (1841-1935)   Marcellus Clay   Warfield Clay   Warfield Clay   Leonide Petroff
(1829-1879)   (b./d. 1843)   (1859-1945)   (1835-1851)   ("Launey") Clay
                                                                                                      (1866-1933)
              Ezekiel Henry   Mary Barr Clay   Brutus Junius Clay   Cassius   Laura Clay   Flora Clay
              Field ("Zeke")   (1839-1924)   (1847-1932)   Marcellus Clay   (1849-1941)   (b/d 1851)
              (1836-1909)   m **Pattie A. Field** (1845-1857)
              m Sallie Embry
              (1842-1925)

David   Pattie Lyman
Lyman   (1863-1883)
(b. 1861)   m Cassius Marcellus
                 Clay ("Cash")
                 (1846-1913)

Children Eliza, Robert, and John died in infancy

**Children Willis Field (b. 1816), William H. Field (b. 1817), Susan McDowell Field (b. 1825),
Thomas McClanahan Field (b. 1828), and Margaret Irvine Field (b. 1833) died in infancy.*

INTRODUCTION

A Family Gathering

My brother and I straddled the lowest limb of the walnut tree that grew in the middle of the garden fence and watched the grown-ups at the Field family picnic. They were scattered across the shade-dappled lawn beneath us, among the long white tables and the folding chairs: the Atkinses from Cincinnati, the Castrillons from Missouri, the Mc-Creadys from Florida, even David Irvine Field from Hollywood.

Cousin Lucie Wooten had organized the picnic, tracking down Fields all over the country. Now she greeted them beside our trumpet vine–covered summer house, an erect white-haired woman in pale blue linen and a beribboned hat. In her hand she held a heart-shaped fan. It was a muggy day. August 1947. I was nine years old.

My mother, standing next to Cousin Lucie, wore a white dress. I thought she looked beautiful, but I knew she was nervous about the picnic. It was the first party she had given since we moved into my grandmother's house in Bourbon County, and she wanted it to be just right.

My father thought the picnic was too much fun to worry over. He enjoyed speculating with Cousin Lucie about who would come. Below me, my father was talking to Cousin Amelia Woodford and the man from Hollywood. I liked the idea of someone coming all the way from Hollywood, even though I wasn't allowed to go to the movies very often. While he talked, my father stroked the head of Rusty, our Chesapeake Bay retriever. Since we'd moved to Kentucky, my father never went anywhere without a dog.

1

I wrapped my legs tightly around the branch on which I was sitting. I could get up in the tree and Louise Atkins couldn't. I prided myself upon being able to do things most girls couldn't or wouldn't do.

On the lawn below, the guests stood in a circle while my father presented Cousin Lucie with a leather-bound book containing their signatures. Everyone clapped. Then my mother said something about this picnic being the beginning of our life in the Bluegrass. Her voice trembled, and I hoped nobody would notice.

"It was a perfect day for a family gathering," Emily McCready wrote my parents afterward. "There was a timelessness about the place as the mellow sun filtered through the trees — touching the sturdy brick out-houses, the mill and loom houses and the cabins — yet eternally young as it lighted the bright ribbons of the children who raced across the yard."

The family we were celebrating, with chicken salad and chocolate angel food cake, were the descendants of a Richmond, Kentucky, dry goods merchant, Ezekiel Henry Field, his wife, Patsey Irvine, and their fifteen children, ten of whom lived to be adults and had numerous children of their own. The house where the picnic was held had been built by my great-grandfather, Brutus J. Clay, a prosperous farmer and politician who had married into the Field family.

My brother and I and our parents had moved to Brutus's farm in Kentucky a year earlier, following my grandmother's death. In subur-ban Baltimore, where we had previously lived, our house had been spare and sunny, reflecting our mother's ascetic tastes. The Kentucky house sprawled and rambled. Its windows were covered with dusty vel-vet curtains. Some of the lamps had fringed shades. The sofa in the front hall was so hard you could only perch on it. Eight nude men sup-ported the dining room table on their shoulders. The day we moved in, my cat Tigger got lost for several hours in the vastness of our new home.

But there were wonderful things about the place. Pets of all kinds: dogs, cats, ponies, sheep, pigs, peacocks. A sleeping porch with a pseudo-Tiffany lamp that lit shadowy corners with fragments of col-ored light. A Chinese urn taller than a person into which I tossed my surreptitiously chewed Juicy Fruit. An attic full of nineteenth-century toys: Gothic building blocks, a windup elevated railway, a magic lantern, a diabolo. A velvet-and-silk quilt made of pieces of my ances-tors' clothing.

Even the ancestors themselves, still in residence, going about their everyday lives right in our midst. It seemed to me that they looked up whenever I entered certain rooms.

Lying in my four-poster bed at night, I imagined Sally Clay eloping from the same room, tiptoeing down the stairs, lifting the two-by-four that barred the front door, then running across the shadowy lawn to the lane where her lover, Oliver Keen, waited in a buggy. Sprawling with a book on the sofa in the old farm office, I thought I could hear Zeke Clay and Jimmy Miller discussing Zeke's plan to run off and join the Confederate army. Taking out a piece of paper and a pencil, Zeke wrote a note to the family. Then he pushed back his chair and went upstairs to get his gun and his quilt. In the library where my father sat night after night, working on the farm accounts and chain-smoking Old Golds, I pictured his father, an earnest thirteen-year-old who excelled in Latin and Greek, playing chess with his sister's husband, Henry Davenport. "Check," said young Cash. He had won again.

My ancestors may have lived in my imagination, but my grandmother's parrot lived in a cage on the stone porch. The big green bird spent its days yelling in my grandmother's voice for her general factotum, a black man named George Brent. Before her death, George, who couldn't tell her voice from the parrot's, invariably stopped whatever he was doing and walked up to the house to find out what my grandmother wanted. My mother hated sharing a house with her mother-in-law's voice and insisted the parrot go live with Mary White, who had come over from Madison County as my grandmother's personal servant in 1888. One day, years after my grandmother's death, my father, my brother, George Brent, and I were driving along the Spears Mill Pike when my father suggested we stop to visit Mary White. While we sat on her porch, George went around to the kitchen where the parrot's cage hung. Suddenly my grandmother's voice pierced the still summer afternoon. "George! George!" she called. "Where are you, George?"

The house was also full of letters, stored in dusty wooden crates in the attic by the same Brutus Clay who had built the place in 1837. Saving personal and business correspondence became a family habit that continued after Brutus's death.

My father knew the letters were there. As a child, he had carefully cut off all the stamps for his collection. I suppose the rest of us must have known about the letters too, but we paid no attention to them. There were too many more engaging things in the attic, a vast cobwebbed space that ran the length of the house. On drizzly days I searched for amusement there to the staccato accompaniment of raindrops on the tin roof. Anything would do: a bit of goat harness, a birdcage, a life-size plaster mastiff with glass eyes.

After my brother and I had left home for college, our father turned his attention to the letters. He would select a packet and, seated at his desk after supper, decipher his ancestors' spidery handwriting. He eventually published five articles based on a few of the letters, later collected into a small volume, *Letters from the Correspondence of Brutus J. Clay, 1808–1878*.

In 1959, our father died and the letters returned to their crates in the attic until the mid-sixties, when I took several packets downstairs. Reading those letters was like walking through the door of a nineteenth-century drawing room and sitting down among its inhabitants busily gossiping about their neighbors, exchanging recipes, and musing about politics. They describe cattle shows, a cholera epidemic, the death of a sister-in-law in childbirth, and trips on Mississippi River steamboats.

And there were more than just letters. There were also day books, bills, accounts, and ledgers, more than eighty years worth of farm records. After reading for several weeks, I persuaded my brother, who had inherited the letters, to give them to the University of Kentucky.

Since then, the collection has been a source for dissertations and scholarly works such as *Rock Fences of the Bluegrass* by Carolyn Murray-Wooley and Karl Raitz, a chapter of which is devoted to the fences on the place, who built them and when and how much they were paid. My brother Berle Clay is interested in vernacular architecture and has compiled a survey of barns and other outbuildings on the farm using information he got from the papers.

But no one has done anything with the personal letters until now. They were written by the Field sisters and their brothers, husbands, and children between the early 1840s and the end of the Civil War. Some are chatty and trivial, the equivalent of modern telephone conversations, in which we tell one another about the clothes we have bought, the meals we have served, and the parties we have attended. Others deal with the world beyond Kentucky and with matters of far greater import.

Together they provide an account of a society that rested on the backs of slaves, men and women who were bought and sold like animals, a society in which it was possible to mention in the same sentence a bull, a jack, and two girls. As I read the letters, whenever I came to a list of what certain black men and women were worth, I felt ill. Although I had always known that my ancestors owned slaves, I had not really come to terms with what that meant.

Nor had they. The letters detail the dilemma of Brutus J. Clay, a pro-Union, border-state congressman from the Seventh District of Kentucky during the Civil War. Brutus was reticent, "not much of a talker but a good thinker," as one of his Field brothers-in-law noted, so the record of his feelings is largely one of inferences. His younger brother, Cassius, was an outspoken emancipationist, and people who didn't know Brutus assumed that he was, too. In fact, Brutus was one of the major slaveholders in Kentucky.

The brothers' contrasting views on slavery provide a leitmotiv running through the letters, for their disagreement replicates in miniature the conflict in the country at large. But it never divided them. Despite Cassius's revolutionary, and sometimes quixotic, ideas and actions, the staunchly conservative Brutus stood up for him time and again.

They were, after all, family. And that is what these letters are about — family. They trace one family's odyssey across the political and geographical landscape of the mid-nineteenth century, from the halls of Congress to the battlefield at Manassas, from the swamps of the Mississippi Delta to the canals of czarist Saint Petersburg.

There was never another Field family picnic. Cousin Lucie grew too old to organize it. My father used to drive up to Winchester on Sunday afternoons to visit her. Sometimes he took my brother and me along. He would deliver a basket of strawberries or beans from our garden to Cousin Lucie's cook and give her some money with which to keep the household running for the next few weeks. Then we would go into the parlor where we sipped iced tea and looked at photograph albums with Cousin Lucie.

I wonder what ever happened to those albums. Probably they were lost or have been destroyed. No doubt they contained pictures of people and places mentioned in these letters: Uncle Christopher on the porch of his plantation house in Mississippi; Aunt Patsey weaving cloth in her workroom on Silver Creek; Martha Davenport setting out onions in Virginia; Christopher Clay grinning at the news that his

Aunt Ann is saving him some of her homemade wine; even lonely David Field sewing himself a pair of pants in his farmhouse.

I wish I had those pictures but I don't. What I do have are words, thousands of them, written by people who lived in the century before mine. Their words speak more eloquently than any pictures. They have written this book.

ONE

Tell Your Aunt Ann

On February 10, 1831, Amelia McClanahan Field and Brutus Junius Clay were married in Richmond, Kentucky. Amelia, nineteen, was the second daughter of Ezekiel H. Field and his wife, Patsey. Richmond, with a population of about eight hundred, was the commercial center of Madison County, which consisted of fertile fields bounded by the Knobs, the rugged foothills of the Kentucky Mountains. The Fields lived in a large brick house on the western edge of Richmond; their downtown establishment, "The Store," sold everything from lace to shotguns.

Brutus was twenty-three. The son of a successful Madison County surveyor and entrepreneur, General Green Clay, Brutus had studied at what is now Centre College in Danville, Kentucky, before becoming a farmer and businessman. Brutus's father had come to Kentucky from Cumberland County, Virginia, in the 1780s. The youngest child of a farming family, Green Clay saw his own future as lying on the nation's western frontier. Although it was wilderness then, Kentucky was already crawling with surveyors and land speculators. Green was both, and by his death in 1828 had amassed extensive holdings throughout the region. He also owned numerous businesses, including a ferry across the Kentucky River and shares in a toll road to Lexington. Green helped to shape the development of Madison County, though not always successfully. When he and other pioneers, including Patsey Field's father, offered the newly founded state of Kentucky 18,550 acres of land and 2,630 in pounds sterling if it would establish the capital

7

at Boonesborough, where they owned land, the state turned them down.

The same westward expansion that made Green wealthy continued to enrich his sons, Sidney, Brutus, and Cassius, as they developed the property left them by their father. In the summer of 1828, in anticipation of his death, Green deeded Brutus and Sidney more than nineteen thousand acres of land along the Licking, Red, and Kentucky Rivers. Later, through an exchange of deeds, Brutus came into possession of a 1,207½ acre tract in nearby Bourbon County, where he settled with Amelia.

Brutus and Amelia first lived in a four-room log cabin, built by his father in 1813 in order to establish his claim. By 1837, six years after his marriage to Amelia, Brutus had begun construction on an elaborate brick house combining Federal and Greek Revival styles. His mother, Sally Dudley (she had remarried after Green's death), warned him against building so large a house. "You have no idea of the expense of furnishing and keeping so large a house clean," she wrote in 1836. "It gets mouldy, spider webs, moths in your carpets." But Brutus, intent upon having an imposing dwelling, ignored her advice.

This was the house in which I lived as a child and which now belongs to my brother. It consists of a massive central hall on each floor with two large rooms on either side. A stairway descends from the second floor to the first, where an elliptical arch separates the entrance hall from the stairwell. Originally there were single story wings at either end. The east wing contained the farm office and remains only slightly altered; the west one my grandmother replaced with a Queen Anne structure, which also housed the first indoor plumbing. A covered stone porch still connects an ell, consisting of the old brick kitchen and other workrooms, with the west wing.

When it was built, the house was almost two miles from the nearest trace or path (there were few roads at that time). Brutus and Amelia had no immediate neighbors, although the lands adjacent to theirs were being farmed by three families, the Kennedys, the Bedingers, and the Duncans. The nearest town was Paris, three miles away, a county seat of about twelve hundred people.

Bourbon County is a gentle, rolling terrain crisscrossed by creeks and rivers. In early summer a bluish haze hangs over the countryside, giving the area its name, the Bluegrass. In the early nineteenth century there were forests full of walnut and hickory trees. Brutus cleared fields, of course, but left more than fifty acres of virgin forest around his house as a park, and they remain untouched to this day.

Brutus's and Amelia's new house came to be called Auvergne, after the French province, though it isn't clear who christened it this. The name first appears in an 1859 letter from a local poet, Mary McAboy. It is also used on an 1861 map of Bourbon and several adjoining counties. But no Clay used it, at least not in writing, until decades later when my grandmother ordered some imposing stationery that had "Auvergne, near Paris, Kentucky" engraved upon it.

Giving a house a name was not unusual at the time, and a fondness for exotic names ran in the family. Green Clay called his younger sons Brutus Junius and Cassius Marcellus, names he reportedly took from a Latin textbook. Their brother, Sidney, lived not far from Brutus's farm in a house he called Escondida.

Brutus's house was the largest in the county at the time it was built. His Bourbon County neighbors admired and envied Auvergne, as they were probably intended to do. One had an almost identical house built on his farm a few years later.

Brutus raised an assortment of crops, including corn, small grains, and hemp, as well as hogs, horses, and mules, but his specialty was the Durham strain of milking Shorthorn cattle, which he bred from English stock, the Seventeens, so called because the original animals were imported in 1817. Later, he and several neighbors banded together to bring English Shorthorns directly to Bourbon County. Brutus also served as president of both the state and county agricultural organizations, and in 1836 helped to found the Bourbon County Fair, where his cattle often won prizes.

The fair was a political event, too — both General Winfield Scott and Brutus's better-known relative Speaker of the House Henry Clay made speeches there when running for president. Brutus dabbled in politics himself. Like Henry, he was a Whig, a supporter of a strong national government with reservations about the ability of the masses to govern themselves. Whiggery in the United States was more than a political party; it was a way of life. Brutus personified it. In both philosophy and manner he was the quintessential Whig.

Brutus was elected to the state legislature in 1840 as a Whig and again at the beginning of the Civil War as a Union Democrat, the Whigs having dissolved as a political party by then. Brutus also spent a term in Congress during the Civil War. He had gotten there more or less by accident, as we shall see, and little enjoyed his sojourn in Washington. Brutus felt like Cincinnatus, leaving his plough to serve his country; he preferred to be at home on his farm.

He had other businesses, including a sawmill and ferry on the Kentucky River that he had inherited from his father. Brutus also operated a saw- and gristmill in Bourbon County. But his passion was land. In the years before the Civil War, he acquired property in Illinois, Missouri, Mississippi, and Texas as well as in Kentucky.

Brutus was no pioneer. It took him nearly twenty years to buy land in Mississippi, for example, despite the urging of Christopher Field, Amelia's brother, who had moved to the Delta in 1836. Brutus waited until the cotton boom just before the Civil War to acquire a plantation there.

While Brutus was clearing and developing the farm in Bourbon County, Amelia was having babies, six of them between 1832 and 1840: Martha, Christopher, Green, Ezekiel, and two other boys named for their father, both of whom died before reaching the age of two. She supervised the farm women in a series of domestic activities, including spinning and weaving and making clothes for the family and farmhands. (The room behind the old kitchen at Auvergne is known as the loom room, although no one has woven cloth there for 140 years.) She also sewed, tended the sick, and oversaw the garden. Almost nothing remains of her today — no pictures, only a few letters, and a scrapbook into which she pasted illustrations from *Godey's Lady's Book* and bits of inspirational poetry.

Amelia was a matchmaker, having helped to bring about the engagement of her younger brother Christopher to Brutus's ward, Sally Clay, the daughter of his recently deceased brother Sidney. But, to the chagrin of the Field family, Sally eloped to Cincinnati in March of 1843 with a cousin of whom no one approved. "At first I consoled myself with the belief that [rumor of the elopement] was groundless," Amelia's father wrote her soon after, "as I considered [Sally] a woman of better judgment. [. . .] If she was not disposed to marry Christopher I think I may safely say that she could have gotten released from that engagement upon much more honorable terms if she had made known to him any such wish." The whole matter was puzzling to Ezekiel Field, who continued, "These are transactions so different from the habits of our family that although probably he should rejoice that he has so narrowly escaped a communion with a woman capable of so unworthy conduct, I know he must be sorely distressed at the event." After some more musing of this sort, Ezekiel concluded, "I flatter myself that the unfortunate occurrence has not been induced by any improper course on the part of our family and that we should try to forget as soon as the nature of the case will allow. We may be permitted to complain among ourselves but should advise a prudent silence out of our family."

Not long after Sally's elopement, Amelia fell ill. A younger sister, Ann Maria, came over to Bourbon County to nurse her and help with the children. Ann had just returned from several years at Madame Aimée Sigoigne's French-speaking academy in Philadelphia, a school attended by the daughters of wealthy Philadelphians but also by southern girls from places such as Raleigh and Natchez.

In early July of 1843 Amelia's father assured Brutus that twenty-one-year-old Ann could stay as long as necessary. "I will expect her to stay with you until Amelia gets strong enough to accompany her to Richmond which I hope will not be long," he wrote. "But Mr. Shackelford [a mutual friend] says that Amelia had more company than usual on the fourth and consequently has not been near so well ever since. [. . .] She appears to be very nervous and every excitement causes a return of sick stomach & debility which if not soon relieved will certainly terminate fatally."

Ezekiel Field continued to worry, but he looked forward to Amelia's making the trip to Richmond, which involved a long day on horseback or in a buggy. "[Y]ou can content yourself in Bourbon until your sister Amelia gets well enough to come home with you," he wrote Ann a week or so later, "which we were in hope would have been by this time. [. . .] Her illness has continued longer than we or any of the physicians expected, but she must fortify herself with all the patience she can. [. . .] and must not take much exercise soon for fear of a relapse. When she attempts to come over, do travel only in the cool of the day and take two days for it."

Ann's and Amelia's brother, the abandoned Christopher, was returning to Kentucky from the plantation he and his uncle owned in Bolivar County, Mississippi, when he learned of Amelia's illness. "I would come by and see her," he wrote Brutus, "but am barely able to ride [. . .] myself, having been confined 3 days on the Boat and then in Louisville in bed. [. . .] So soon as I am stout again I will be over, hoping by that time that Sister will be better and more able to enjoy the company of her friends. [. . . .] I hope she has and will bear her afflictions with firmness and Christian fortitude. I have thought that the true Christian could bear more upon the bed of affliction than one of the world."

Amelia died three days later, on July 31, 1843, at the age of thirty-one. Brutus buried his wife in the garden behind the house. After the funeral, he sent two of his children, Martha and Christopher, back to Richmond with Aunt Ann, but kept the younger boys with him.

Brutus missed his children and wrote frequently to ten-year-old Martha. Martha found writing back hard, complaining that she had to fill her letters with news when there wasn't any. Brutus also poured out his loneliness and grief to Aunt Ann, who replied principally with postscripts to Martha's letters.

When I was a child, a portrait of Brutus J. Clay, looking quite the aristocratic young man, hung over the mantel in the library at Auvergne. Another Brutus was hidden away in the back parlor, an entirely different person with sloping shoulders, an outsized head, and a big red nose. My father said that because Brutus had refused to pay the painter the sum he wanted for this second portrait, the angry artist painted in the red nose. After my father died, one of my half brothers inherited the aristocratic Brutus. My mother hung Brutus as Prince Bulbo in his place. "I've always preferred this portrait," she said, "because he looks approachable."

By all accounts, young Brutus looked much like the earlier, more flattering portrait. He was tall, with fair hair and an imposing manner. In photographs taken in the 1860s, Brutus looks dour, but by then he was feeling the isolation of being a slave-owning Southern congressman among "Black Republicans." Back home at his beloved Auvergne, he mellowed as the years passed, cultivating a fondness for small children and cake.

An 1850s ambrotype of Ann Field shows a large solemn woman, her dark hair parted in the middle and slicked over her ears. She looks almost fierce, as if she did not want to be photographed. In a later picture, in which she wears an elaborate dress and has a fan partly open on one knee, her deep-set eyes pin the viewer with an unflinching gaze.

The correspondence begins after Amelia's death, with letters from Martha to her father, mostly accounts of the comings and goings of a large household that consisted of her widowed grandfather, three young aunts, Ann, Mary, and Belle, and three unmarried uncles,

David, Edmund, and Ezekiel Jr. Ann's married sisters, Elizabeth Holloway and Patsey Miller, lived nearby. Two of Brutus's sisters also lived near Richmond, Eliza Smith and Paulina Rodes.

MARTHA CLAY

Richmond, August 4, 1843

My Dearest Father,

Aunt Ann has just received your letter a few moments ago and was very sorry to hear that you was not agoing to bring the children [Green and Ezekiel]. Aunt Elizabeth [Holloway] says you must be certain to bring them, says she wants to see them worse than you. Aunt Ann says you will have to bring them over for her to cut out their winter clothes. They have not got any. She says Eliza can nurse the children, says she has not got anything to do, and Woodson can nurse them, too. [Eliza and Woodson were slaves.] Uncle Edmund [Field] returned home on Saturday night. I asked him a great many things about you and the children but he would not tell me anything hardly. Aunt Patsey [Miller] came up yesterday. All of us spent the day with Aunt Elizabeth today. I went down to Uncle Miller's on Tuesday before last and came up Saturday. And went out to Uncle Smith's the same day. [. . .] Uncle Smith says he is going to get you to let me go with Pauline [a daughter] to the nunnery in Lexington, says he knows you will let me, but I told him it was no use to ask you for you was not agoing to do it. Aunt Ann says she will be mad as fire if you do not bring the children. [. . .]

I remain your affectionate daughter,

Martha I. Clay

After a postscript from Martha about "yarn stockings and flaxen undershirts," Ann added, "We will certainly expect you on Thursday and hope 'ere this you have changed your mind and will bring Green and Zeke. The children are much disappointed at the thought of their not coming. [. . .] I must close hoping very soon to have your good company. Do bring the little boys. Farewell." She signed this "Ann M. Field."

Almost ten days later, Martha wrote again. "We are all going down to Aunt Patsey Miller's to eat watermelons. [. . .] I will be very sorry if you do not come over by that time to go with us. You cannot imagine how bad I want to see you and the children. [. . .] Aunt Ann says you must not bring anybody to nurse Zeek [sic], says that when he was over here before he liked for Eliza to nurse him. [. . .] She says that you must make haste and come over, that we all want to see you very much and bring all the children." She added, "I have got two new dresses, two aprons, and a pair of gloves and shoes." Then, since her father was a member of the fraternal order of Odd Fellows, "The Odd Fellows are going to march on Friday and I wish you and the children were over here to see them." And, as a final enticement, "Aunt Bell [Isabella Field] says if you will come over here she will give you an apple."

Ann added, "I intended writing a P.S. to you but Martha would not let me for fear that I would see what she had written. It seems as if the time was nearer to arrive for you to make us a visit. Do come. I will expect you next week. I am so anxious to see you. [. . .]" This one she signed "Anna." As a schoolgirl in Philadelphia, Ann had played with variations of her name, including "Anna Maria Field." In the same copybook, she inscribed a bit of doggerel: "Field is my name./ Single is my life./ Happy the man who takes me to wife."

More than forty miles separated Brutus from Ann and his older children. Starting on the plain where Richmond is located, the path — for it was barely a road — dropped sharply into the gorge of the Kentucky River. There were ferries at different points along the river, but the Fields and Clays used Clay's Ferry, the one Brutus and his brother Cassius had inherited from their father. The road then climbed through rough hilly country until it reached the rolling farmlands of Clark County. After that it crossed the forested southeastern quadrant of Bourbon, passing near Escondida. It was a long trip, but both Brutus and Ann made it often in 1843 and 1844, usually on horseback. There was a better road from Richmond to Lexington and then on to Paris, but the jolting stagecoach ride took twice as long, and the traveler had to spend the night in Lexington.

Brutus replied eagerly to Martha's letters and Ann's notes. He was, after all, a heartsick widower sitting alone in his big fancy house.

BRUTUS CLAY

Home, August 20, 1843

Dear Ann,

I am now setting [*sic*] by a big fire although it is near the middle of August. As I have read over all the newspapers I have that are of any interest and got out of employment, I have concluded to write you a few lines. [. . .] I must say to you that I feel very little like leaving home at this time upon a visit, and I could not come if I wished it, as my workmen to build my lumber house are to be here tomorrow to commence work and both of the little boys have a breaking out over their faces, Ezekiel quite bad but is getting better now. I have therefore given out all idea of coming for the present. I hope you have enjoyed yourself well since your return home in visiting your relations and particular friends after your long absence from them. I reckon you almost forgot how Richmond looked. [. . .] I shall expect the next time you write, if you should *ever think it worthwhile* to write at all, it will be a long letter and not quite as short as your last one. At least, you will give a better reason for its length than my great disinclination to read long letters. I should be willing to read and quite pleased to receive a letter from any of you and will assure you I will read every word of it. Tell Martha [. . .] she must practice her music well while she is [. . .] not going to school and whether all those little girls over there can beat her or not. I will come for her when she gets tired of Richmond. I am undetermined as yet where to send them to school but suppose it best to have her as near home as possible that she might occasionally see her little brothers. [. . .] Green is now setting by me and wants to know how I got Martha's letter & who brought it and what she says and what is the reason Aunt Ann & Martha don't come back home. He thinks they have been gone long enough and why won't I send the carriage for them. He has plenty of good watermelons and ripe peaches and if they don't make haste and come, he will eat them all up. Tell Christopher when he gets tired of Richmond I should be much gratified to have his company over here and shall look for him before long. I shall be constantly at home for some time to come, I expect.

My love to all, respectfully,

B. J. Clay

Brutus received notes of condolence from various members of the family, including his brother-in-law Christopher, who spoke of his own "constant gloom and depression." His morose state of mind may have been due to a combination of Amelia's death and Sally's elopement. "Though Providence has taken from you an affectionate wife and from us a dear Sister, it has only had the effect to cause you and your dear little children to feel nearer and dearer to all of us," Christopher wrote. "I speak the feelings of the whole family. [. . .] There was not a relation of your dear wife who did not think her happily united and was in every way gratified in the association. [. . .] We all hope and expect [. . .] that you will feel yourself one of the family still and act accordingly and that your visits will be as frequent as they were when Sister was living."

But it was from Ann who the lonely widower most wanted to hear.

BRUTUS CLAY

September 3, 1843

Dearest Ann,

I have sent to town several times during the past week for letters etc. supposing you would certainly write to me but received none from Richmond but one from Sister [Eliza] Smith until last evening. You may be assured it was doubly welcome when it did come, as I had been expecting it so long. I had almost concluded you did not intend to write. It was late in the evening when I got it. I had been quite busy all day in attending to my stock, having the workmen well attended to, until near evening when all the workmen left for their homes, being Saturday evening. I therefore seemed to be out of employment. I retired to the house. I found the windows & doors all shut, not a living soul about, the children all off at play, everything still and lonely. Dear Ann, you cannot imagine my feelings. No, no one [can] except those who have been similarly situated, no one who has not had a *Dear & beloved wife* who was always ready & willing to treat him with a warm heart and affectionate smile, one to whom he would communicate the very inner thoughts of his soul without reserve, one with whom he passed the wearisome hours with pleasure almost unconscious that the wheels of time still rolled on, one who was always willing and took pleasure in ad-ministering to his wants and comfort, one who can sympathize with him in his grief and partake of his pleasure, too. If ever a man felt such happiness in this life, it is when he returns to his home from the labour and trials of the day, fatigued, hungry, and weary, to meet a *dearly beloved & affectionate wife* at the threshold to welcome his return with a kind voice and affectionate look. O, it is then man's heart is softened down. He has a heart of flesh. It is then he feels that she was ever a part of his existence. It is then when Woman's Love shows its power and conquers the heart. Yes, the most obdurate heart must yield. Can you then imagine my feelings when returning to the house, instead of that accustomed welcome, to find all about dark and lonely? The very objects around me inspired me with a kind of dread and horror. And in casting my eyes up around the thought that the hands that [. . .] made the little pincushion hanging by the mantelpiece was [sic] now still and cold in the grave, never more to be near, and that sweet voice of welcome never more to be heard. Ah! The fate of man in what misery is it rapt. The tears involuntarily flowed down my cheeks, which after some moments gave me some relief. After setting awhile, I looked around for something to read, but found nothing that seemed to suit my taste. I gathered some of the latest newspapers and left the house and retired to a remote part of the yard under the shade of a small locust. I looked them over but found nothing in them that seemed to interest me and [was] throwing them aside when the boy I had sent to town brought me your letter. Do not be surprised if I should tell you I read it over several times before I was satisfied. I had often laughed at my wife and taken letters from her when she would commence reading them the second time. I now think I can appreciate her feelings & her anxiety about letters. [. . .] I read it with interest yet at the same time pleasure & pain, with pleasure because it was from one I esteemed highly and always admired much and from a dear Sister of my beloved wife about whom she always felt the liveliest interest. [. . .] You are entirely mistaken when you suppose I care but little about you all. Can you put your hand upon *your heart* and say candidly you think so? I know you cannot. I know that it has sometimes been thought that I had a cold and callous heart. [. . .] I think you know to the contrary, my feelings are warm and ardent to those I love and respect. [. . .]

Tell Elizabeth [Holloway] I thank her for her kind offer to take Martha but I reckon she would not be satisfied with her and it would be bad walking getting to and from her house to school in the winter time. I would rather she should remain with you if she stays in Richmond this winter. [. . .] I think you can manage her very well, with your Pa's assistance, if you will only think so and resolve to do it. I do not wish her to remain with you unless you desire it & your *Pa*. I think she is not hard to govern. She is a good child, has a high sense of propriety, and is easily content. I see from your letter which has been a long time upon the road that school has already commenced. I reckon she had as well be there.

B. J. Clay

Brutus's letters to Martha are full of messages for Ann. Martha's little brothers had been ill. "Ezekiel is quite well now and Green, poor little fellow, has broken out afresh all over his face in sores [. . .]," Brutus wrote later that month. "Tell your Aunt Ann she is the only person almost he talks about. She is all & all with him. He comes once or twice a day for some of Aunt Ann's cakes or candy and is contented with quite a small piece of either. Tell her she must not forget he was given to her and she will have to take him as soon as you and Christopher leave Richmond. [. . .] Tell your Aunt Ann I am very lonesome here by myself and want to see her very much & think of her very often & more particularly these warm sultry evenings when I am setting on the front steps and see that large bright star in the southern sky which she so well remembers. Tell her the Dahlias are all in full bloom and are beautiful. Some stalks have as high as thirty blossoms upon them and quite a variety from deep blue to deep scarlet. They are worth a ride all the way over here to see them. [. . .] Tell Ann I do hope she will pay me a visit this fall and show Amy [a slave] how to cut out and make the little boys' clothes. I know it will be some trouble to her but I know she will not mind it much."

He concluded with a postscript: "Tell your Aunt Ann she must not forget she promised to write me sometimes. She must be sure not to forget it. I shall expect one from her very soon. She must not disappoint me. I shall not write to her anymore until I receive one from her."

I felt close to Brutus when I learned that he sat on the front steps on warm nights and looked at the stars. The steps are made of slabs of limestone. In the gray rock are the fossils of hundreds of sea creatures, trilobites, mollusks, miniature clams. The stone absorbs the heat of the day, so after supper in the summertime, my father, my brother, and I would gather there underneath a panoply of brilliant stars shimmering and twinkling around the vast Milky Way.

I would stretch out on the warm stone, stare into the night, and ask my father, "Does the sky go on forever?" It seemed impossible that it did but at the same time impossible that it didn't. He said it did. Then we'd pick out individual stars, the North Star, Venus, and constellations, Orion, Cassiopeia's Chair, until my mother appeared in the doorway, with the light behind her, to tell my brother and me that it was time to go to bed. We tore ourselves away from the stars and went up to the sleeping porch, which we shared in the summertime. It had been added atop the east wing of the house after a local doctor told my grandmother that my father would die of consumption unless he slept in fresh air. As we lay in our beds, the starlight spilling through the French windows made rectangular patterns on the floor. An owl hooted in a nearby tree.

"Aunt Ann says if you are very anxious to see us indeed [. . .] maybe she will go to see you this fall," Martha replied to her father in September of 1843. "Says she reckons you do not want to see us much. She says she would like to visit you very much. You must come over and bring the children to stay while you are gone to Louisville and the mountains. She says she will take great pleasure in making the children's clothes over here and will not consider it any trouble." She added, "Tell Green Aunt Mary [Field] is knitting him a pair of gloves and he must make haste and come over and get them and I am knitting Zeke a pair."

By October, Brutus and Ann were sharing private jokes. The "dear Mrs. Keiningham" to whom Brutus refers in the next letter is Louisa Thomas, a lifelong friend of Ann's who had married Richard Keiningham, an English merchant living in Paris, Kentucky. The Keininghams had a pretty house on the edge of town.

BRUTUS CLAY

October 8, 1843

Dear Ann,

We are all (for we are but a small company at best) setting around a good fire & in good spirits this cool morning (Sunday), the boys cracking and eating hazelnuts which I chanced to come across yesterday in town and brought them out a half gallon, and told them it was a present from *you*, which I hope you will excuse me for. As they are so very fond of you I do not wish them to forget you, and, as for myself, I am reading over three or four letters I received yesterday from acquaintances and one from a very particular friend of mine and one whom *I love much*. Could you guess whom it is from? If you can't, I don't believe I will tell you now. [. . .] I did not intend writing to you until I received a good long letter from you agreeable to your promise. You certainly don't think that *poor little postscript* in Martha's letter will be taken for a good long letter from you, do you? [. . .] Your *poor little postscript* seems to have been written while in a very bad humor (although I am very thankful even for that) and I know when prejudice is once fixed in the female breast it is very hard to remove & the sooner the attempt is made to remove it the better, before it is deep rooted, therefore, if I have given cause of offense. [. . .] I wish to make amends as soon as possible. If I can therefore say or do anything that will improve your anger, consider it said and done, and that too in the very sweetest manner. How could I treat you with neglect after that sweet little *postscript* you wrote me? No, Ann, I could not treat you amiss no matter what you write. [. . .] I love you too dearly not to answer that long letter you promised if you will only send it to me. I shall wait [. . .] with a good deal of anxiety to see what kind of a reception this will get before I venture to write another & I feel certain I shall not again answer so short a letter without some better reason from you.

What would you think if I should tell you that I have not seen or spoken to a Lady since I saw you, not even your dear Mrs. Keiningham? I have not been to town except on business and then returned soon. I have been endeavoring to get through with my buildings in time for me to take a fishing frolic or hunt & I am afraid I shall be disappointed in both. My masons have not laid a single brick yet & I am very much fretted about it. I have been ready for them several weeks, nearly long enough for them to have been done & gone. [. . .] If they do not come soon I will put them off until spring which I dislike very much. We had quite a parade last week with our Agricultural Fair. We had a good deal of fine stock shown the first two days and, on the third, a fine turnout of all the Ladies in the County. I suppose something up to a thousand, big and little, old and young. Indeed I believe almost everybody was there with almost all kinds of domestics which made quite a grand exhibition and, as there was some dissatisfaction shown last year among some of the Ladies about the judges in domestics (which were men), we concluded this year to make the women judges and let them have all the quarreling (if any) among themselves. So Mrs. George Williams, Mrs. James Wright, & Mrs. Saml. Williams of Montgomery were the judges, & I believe gave pretty general satisfaction, probably more so than the men judges. There were a good many premiums distributed among the ladies & I believe more anxiety for premiums than among the men. Mr. H. [Henry] Clay, our next President, was here and was quite a favorite with the ladies. He received several handsome presents from them and I have no doubt would have received divers kisses if it had been customary, not withstanding the favors of husbands, because he was shown every attention & promised to return next year. [. . .] Adieu,

B. J. Clay

[P.S.] There is one portion of your letter I cannot close this without alluding to. It is the last paragraph written which you wrote after a little reflection and you thought you had finished your letter but afterward concluded to write another small postscript in which I hope you expressed truly and candidly your true feeling at the time. I assumed [it] was worth all the balance of your letter in at least it was much more gratifying to my feelings than everything else said. Will you be so kind as to consider the same paragraph penned and sent back in this very loved form [. . .]? I hope you will.

The Bourbon County Fair survived the economic ups and downs of the 1840s to become the premier exhibition of its sort a decade later, in large part because of the involvement of the women to whom Brutus alludes. (However, women were expected to avoid the judging of male animals, particularly bulls.) On the strength of the success of the 1843 fair, the local Agricultural Society purchased a permanent fairgrounds the following year.

Garrett Davis, a local lawyer and politician, had engineered Henry Clay's appearance at the 1843 fair in an attempt to unify squabbling Bourbon County Whigs. Despite local differences, they endorsed Clay for president in 1844. The primary issue in the presidential campaign was the annexation of Texas as a slave state, something which Clay and the Whigs opposed. Since their standard-bearer was a Southerner and a slave owner, the Whigs needed someone to convince Northern abolitionists to support their ticket, so they asked Brutus's brother Cassius, an outspoken opponent of slavery, to campaign for Henry Clay in 1844. Although Clay lost the election to James K. Polk, during the campaign Cassius made friends with several Northern abolitionists, including Salmon P. Chase of Ohio, who later served as Abraham Lin-

coln's secretary of the treasury during the Civil War, and himself began
to have intimations of a political life beyond the boundaries of Kentucky.

More than a century after Cassius and Salmon P. Chase became
friends, I arrived at a boarding school in New York's Westchester
County to discover that my roommate was a lanky blonde from
Chicago named Nancy Chase. We became friends and visited in each
other's homes. I don't remember when we realized that our ancestors
had been political allies, but when the Chase family's beagle was struck
by a car and killed, my mother sent them one of our Chesapeake Bay
retriever puppies, which they named Cassius M. Clay.

Uncle Cash's name has followed me through life. In my adoles-
cence, Cassius M. Clay the boxer was beginning to make a name for
himself, but had not yet become Muhammad Ali. For a short while, I
convinced one particularly credulous college classmate that my
brother was an Olympic boxer. Much later, when my mother visited
me in Providence, Rhode Island, a friend created a sensation by signing "Mrs. Cassius M. Clay" in the guest book at the club where he had
taken her for lunch.

As Christmas 1843 approached, there were more letters for Brutus
from Ann and Martha. Brutus's letters and Ann's messages are circum-
spect, but clearly something was happening between them.

"I am now writing in schooltime as I have hardly no other time to
do so except last night," Martha told her father in December. "And
would have written then but did not get my lessons until late and by
that time then we wanted to go to bed. Amelia [Elizabeth Holloway's
daughter] stayed all night. As she stays so seldom we want to talk and
play when she does come. Our school is out in about seven weeks. [. . .]
Mr. Smith is going to give us a week holiday, Christmas, but we will
have to make up for it and I had rather not have any then as it will be
that much longer before I get home. We have to write our examination
compositions Christmas week. I am afraid mine will be a disgrace to
me. [. . .] We have to get up before the whole audience and read them.
I should like for you to be over here at our examination very much."

She added a few words about her eight-old-brother, Kit. "Christopher is well. He stays up to Aunt Elizabeth's right now and whenever
they make him mad he comes back home again. [. . .] Aunt Elizabeth
has to tell him she will let him wear his boots to school to get him to
put on clean clothes."

Ann wrote a postscript. "Martha and the children have gone to an exhibition [. . .] so I will take the liberty of writing a few lines knowing she will tire before she gets to this page. Altho I do not think you have been deserving of my *poor short P.S.* for treating me so badly I suppose I am of little consequence, that you have forgotten your promise about writing. I was a little disappointed at not receiving a letter from you to-day and I cannot tell what I will think if I do not receive one by Wednesday's mail."

On Christmas Eve, Brutus sat down to write Ann a puzzling letter.

BRUTUS CLAY

Home, December 24, 1843

Dear Ann,

You recollect I told you I would not write any more letters to you after you refused to do what I asked you to do, and I never think about writing but I think of my promise [. . .] but you know how difficult it is to keep a rash promise when our whole thought and inclinations are opposed to it and even our happiness sometimes depends upon breaking it. I merely mention this however to give you a true index to my feelings and perhaps it may have a beneficial effect upon you. [. . .] You know how dear you are and how dearly I love you, Ann. How could it be otherwise when you have always treated me with so much respect and marked kindness? Yes, I might say with more sincere friendship than any other relation I have. I hope my love may continue for you and even increase beyond what it is now and expand to that point where it could possibly be in your power to return. I know you are capable of that deep and devoted attachment, all, all that mortal man should desire, but who shall obtain that *devoted heart*? It is not in the power of short-sighted man to tell. Do not, therefore, forget me, in the gay circle in which you move, but have a kind remembrance for one who esteems you above all others. Dearest, forever,

B. J. Clay

[P.S.] I look forward with great delight to your promised visit. You know how hard it is to bear with disappointment. Be true to your promise.

What had Ann refused to do that made Brutus promise not to write her again? It sounds as if he had asked her to marry him and she had turned him down, though perhaps not very conclusively. Maybe she demurred on the grounds that only five months had passed since Amelia's death. Or perhaps he simply refers to the fact that she had not written him a long letter as she had said she would.

In January 1844, Brutus wrote Martha that he intended to visit his mother, Sally Lewis Clay, who had married a brother-in-law, Jeptha Dudley, after Green Clay's death, and lived in Frankfort. "It was my intention to have carried both of your little brothers with me but the weather is so very cold I have concluded it would be better to leave them at home at present," he told her.

"Green was very much delighted with your present, the book of dolls. I believe he is full as fond of taking them out and then placing them back in the book and dressing them in different colored slippers as you and Bell [sic] had of making them. He says his sis is a mighty fine girl or else she would not send him so many fine things. He is promptly willing to swap Aunt Ann off now for the book of dolls and take you in her place. I fear though I shall not be so well pleased with you as he is unless you obey me better and write as often as I requested you and I am afraid you are not quite as obedient and as respectful to your Grandpa & Aunt Ann as you should be. You must recollect now you have no Mother to do for you [. . .] and you should be very thankful to your Grandpa and Aunt Ann for the trouble they show with you and do everything they tell you to do. Don't let them have to speak to you but once before you obey. [. . .] I hope you and Bell have quit doll making and have not filled your Aunt Ann's stocking full of ashes again but have been spending all your vacations from school in writing your compositions and the examination. I was glad to learn you had written so much after almost despairing of writing any. You must look it over carefully and see that you have made no mistakes with bad grammar or bad spelling. A girl does not know what she can do until she tries."

On the way home from Frankfort, he wrote Ann.

BRUTUS CLAY

Lexington, January 19, 1844

Dear Ann,

I arrived here on my way home from Frankfort on last night and shall leave in this evening's stage for Paris. As I feel a little unwell, I shall hasten home without delay.

David [Field] called to see me and said it was probable he would go to Richmond on today's stage as he was too unwell to attend [Transylvania] college, etc. He also informed me he had understood you had determined not to go to Bourbon with Martha & Christopher when their school was out. I wish you would let me know your positive determination so that I may know what arrangements to make to get Martha & Chris. However, if you are not coming and they are not very anxious to come, I have determined not to send for them as it will not be very convenient for me to come after them. [. . .] If, however, Martha is very anxious to come, I will find some means for her to get home. With regards to your coming, I suppose I have heard the probable cause and I will candidly say to you that I do not wish you to take the trouble upon yourself to come with the children to accommodate me unless you feel free and willing to do so. And, if you feel a delicacy in coming, consult and ask the advice of your Father and follow it and I shall have nothing to say. But in response to your relatives who have been so kind as to speak their opinion so frankly about me, you can inform them that if it is their desire to treat me as a stranger and not as a relative it is only necessary to so let me understand it. I am a man of too nice feelings to intrude myself upon any, relatives or strangers, if I know it. You can also let them know that their conclusions are premature and I think it would comport more with their duty if not their feeling to ascertain the facts before they express themselves so freely. The stage & David are now waiting and I will conclude. Respectfully,

B. J. Clay

Some member of the family must have questioned the propriety of Ann's visits to a single man, whether or not he was her brother-in-law. This is not surprising given Victorian decorum, but Brutus is prickly about it. Later, when in Congress, he was to respond to criticism from both Republicans and Democrats much as he responded to Ann's nosy relatives. Secure in his sense of himself, he knew his motives to be pure.

In February, Brutus was in Madison County on business (and to visit Ann). He dashed off a quick note to Martha, who was back at home, including instructions about work to be done on the farm. "Have been quite busy ever since I got here hunting cattle. Have purchased some but not quite enough yet. [. . .] Tell Mr. Wilson I shall not need him to help me over with the cattle. I will get a hand over here to assist me. Tell him I want him to run six plows this good weather and commence breaking up some of the stubble ground when he is done the sod he was about and do as much plowing as possible."

On his return to Bourbon County, Brutus wrote again to Ann.

BRUTUS CLAY

Egypt, March 1, 1844

Dear Ann,

I thought when I was over last I would go over with the girls [several nieces, including Sallie Rodes] when they went back, but I find it is very inconvenient for me to leave home so often. I have declined coming as the girls think they can get along very well without me. As I shall not be over for some time to come, I shall certainly expect you to return with Woodson in the carriage. Mrs. Holloway is now well and you have nothing to keep you if you wish to come. [. . .] I don't expect to come to Richmond again (unless on some very important business) until you come over and show some disposition to see the children & myself. [. . .] If you do not come and stay several weeks, the disappointment will be very great and I do not know when I will be in a good humor with you, probably never, for you have flattened my hopes so often. The disappointment will be too provoking and I shall try to forget you entirely. Very small matters sometimes work mighty changes, not only in individuals but sometimes even in great nations. As I have 8 or 10 miles to ride today, I must close. Adieu, dearest,

B. J. Clay

[P.S.] I would prefer you would bring someone with you who will be content to remain home and not be too anxious to return before you get your breath and one I like a *little*. Do, Ann, do come.

In the heading, Brutus uses "Egypt." Had Ann made him feel like an Israelite banished to Egypt? Brutus wasn't a religious man but he was well acquainted with the Bible. Perhaps he had proposed again while in Richmond. And perhaps, like the pharaoh, Ann "had flattened" his hopes again.

Brutus's sister Paulina Rodes had a family of girls the oldest of whom, Sallie, was his particular favorite. He seems to have tolerated banter from Sallie that he would not from someone else. She had picked up on whatever was going on between him and Ann. Evidently Ann had just returned home from a visit to Bourbon County.

The "Aunt Mary Jane" with whom Sallie's mother planned to travel to Bourbon County was Cassius Clay's wife, the former Mary Jane Warfield. Mary Jane's father, Dr. Elisha Warfield, taught at the Transylvania Medical School in Lexington and at one time owned the famous nineteenth-century racehorse Lexington.

SALLIE RODES

Woodlawn, March 17th, 1844

My Dearest Uncle,

I write to congratulate you upon the girls' brief visit. [. . .] You had better beware how agreeable you make yourself to us all when with you, or in the future you may have to complain that we give you too much of our good company. [. . .]

I did not tell Ann how you *abused* her. I left that agreeable task for you to perform yourself. But I dare say you entirely forgot all your disagreeable sayings and thoughts, too, as soon as you saw her. Didn't you?

Mother expects to visit Lexington, Aunt Patty, and yourself in about ten days. The want of a carriage and not inclination has caused her to defer these visits so long. Aunt Mary Jane [Clay] will accompany her to Bourbon. [. . .] Mr. Watson [whom Sallie married a few months later] left here a few days ago. We had a hearty laugh over your old-fashioned notions, as we termed them, about letter writing. [. . .] Kiss Green and Ezekiel and ask them if they don't love Cousin Sallie better than *Aunt Ann*. I send them some pulled candy. Don't let them forget me before I come again — you know the memories of children are short — and it is a long time before the strawberries are ripe. I suppose you feasted on ice cream and preserves whilst the girls were with you.

I am going to town soon and make Ann give me her history of their visit. [. . .]

I would write more but I expect Ann will write you one of her "*nice letters*" and this will not do to compare with hers. So adieu, with the assurance that no one loves you more sincerely than your affectionate niece,

Sallie

A few days later, Martha took advantage of an aunt's trip to Bourbon County to send a letter to her father. (Letters sometimes went by mail in the 1840s, but more often they were carried by someone going in the right direction.) Although she let Ann write a postscript, there is a hint of jealousy in this letter; clearly Martha was aware of her father's interest in Aunt Ann.

MARTHA CLAY

March 19, 1844

Dear Pa,

[. . .] Aunt Ann wanted me to write to you Sunday to let you know that they [Paulina Rodes and others] were coming but I did not feel the humor to it [. . .] and was all day fixing for Zeke's [Field] party Saturday [Zeke Field was eight]. He was sadly disappointed that [Green and Zeke Clay] did not come. He thought that of course if they were invited they would come. [. . .] You must let Green come over with Aunt Paulina. Aunt Ann says you must, too. It is of no use to ask for Zeke [Clay], as you will not let him come. Leanna [a slave] is here and I write to let you know that she is out of jail. [. . .] Aunt Ann says you must send her scissors by Aunt Paulina. [. . .] You went and give them ottomans to Aunt Ann. They were not yours to give away.

Your affectionate daughter,

Martha Clay

My Dearest Brother,

Do come and see us. I am crazy to see you. It seems like an age since I left you.

Ann

As the weather grew milder, there were more trips between Richmond and Brutus's farm. "Your Grandmother & Aunt Paulina & Mary Jane & her children have been here for several days," Brutus wrote Martha in March. "I send the scissors you wrote for by your Aunt Paulina who leaves presently. I can't send Green over with her. Zeke will be too lonesome here by himself & I think too if your Aunt Ann wanted him she would have taken him with her. He says he won't go over now, as she would not let him go with her when he wanted, and she made such a short stay here and was in such a hurry to get back."

A month later, in April, Brutus wrote a bit testily to Ann, "I have just received your letter today and, as you seem to be in such a bad humor with me, I have just stepped into Mr. Marshall's store and concluded to write you a few lines so that it may go over in Monday's mail. Do not fall out with me for failing to write as often as you would desire for you know I am no great hand to coax people when they are in a bad humor, more especially when I am not in the best in the world myself. [. . .] I don't think I can come over to Liz's wedding, as great a disappointment as you intimate it will be. You must not look for me. I don't think I can come over before the latter part of next week. I have some very particular business to do next week and I wish to accomplish it before I go to Richmond if possible. I think you had better go to the wedding and enjoy yourself as well as you can and take Martha with you for I have no doubt it will afford you more pleasure than to see me. I have been quite negligent about writing, I must confess [. . .] I hope to see you however before it will be necessary to write again."

In a May letter to Ann, Brutus described attending a Universalist meeting on a neighboring farm belonging to Jesse Kennedy. Unlike most of the women in his family, who were ardent churchgoers, Brutus had little use for religion. However, the Universalist service seems to have impressed him.

I can't help but wonder about Jesse Kennedy's church. By the time Brutus encountered it, Universalism had shed its Calvinist associations and adopted a position similar to that held by the Unitarians, with whom the Universalists finally merged in 1861. Universalist services, known for their free-thinking rationalism, were quite different from the fervent religion popular in Kentucky at the time. Bourbon County was home to the Cane Ridge camp meetings at the largest of which, in the early 1800s, several dozen Presbyterian, Baptist, and Methodist ministers preached to over one hundred wagonloads of frontiersmen and their families, winning many converts.

In 1845, Brutus, Jesse Kennedy, and another neighbor, Daniel Bedinger, sought bids for a Universalist meeting house, which they built the following year on land donated by Kennedy, using funds from all three men and lumber sawed in Brutus's mill. The church remained there until the Civil War, when the congregation dispersed. The building was briefly a store, then burned. Its tree-choked ruins were still standing on a hillside above Kennedy's Creek during my childhood, a favorite place for cattle to rest on a summer day.

BRUTUS CLAY

May 19, 1844

Dear Ann,

I walked over to Mr. Kennedy's school house today to hear a universalian preacher for the first time and must confess was much pleased with his discourse and have no doubt it would be of service to some of our warm Calvinists occasionally to hear them preach. On my return, however, I found Mr. Stone & Lady, Sally [sic] [Rodes] & Mrs. [Mary Jane] Clay all here and was very glad to see them but felt somewhat disappointed you were not with them, notwithstanding I was not expecting you. I do feel so anxious to see you. It seems like a month since I saw you. I did not get home as soon as I expected when I left Richmond. I stayed several days in Lexington & visited with Mary Jane. I paid a visit out to the Meadows [the home of Mary Jane's father, Dr. Elisha Warfield]. The whole family were quite polite and agreeable. [. . .] I saw Mr. K. [Keiningham] a few days ago and nearly the first question he asked me was when Miss Ann Field was coming over. I told him about the time I looked for you, so you know what is next. You must put on your best looks and be as captivating as possible and catch a beau this trip if you can for I think you will have a chance if you desire it. I have promised to use my influence with the same gentleman in behalf of another lady so you will not be without a rival & quite a formidable one, too. As you did not ask my aid in your behalf I have concluded to exert myself in favor of another so you see you sometimes lose your best friends because you show a lack of confidence in them. I hope however you will not cast me off on account of it but will still number me among your best friends. I shall send Woodson over in the morning with the horses & shall not come. I shall certainly expect you the day after, bring with you Miss Field, Martha & the children. [. . .] I hope you will not be in a hurry to get back home this time but will make quite a long board. I will try and make myself as agreeable as possible & go with you wherever you wish to go if that will be any inducement for you to stay. As it is late at night, I must close. Adieu,

Brutus J. Clay

By the standards of modern romance, it's hard to figure out what was going on between Ann and Brutus. He's probably tweaking her when he talks about her catching a beau. There's no evidence that Ann had or was seeking another suitor, but it's hard to be sure since only one side of their correspondence has survived. Brutus ended this letter with an unusual statement of affection: "N.B. If it is not too much trouble to you, you may bring me that palm leaf hat and a fireproof match box out of the store and as much love with you as you think proper."

Ann had not been at home long after this visit before she received a letter from Brutus containing a reference to a forthcoming duel. Duels were a common way of settling differences or slights at the time, and hotheaded Kentucky men frequently challenged one another. This letter also includes the first mention of Brutus's controversial brother Cassius.

BRUTUS CLAY

June 15, 1844

Dear Ann,

I reckon you will be somewhat surprised to receive a letter from me just at this time written at home as it is about time I told you I should certainly be in Danville. I was making my arrangements to leave home when, about near a week ago, Cash [Cassius] and John Clay came & have been here ever since, until just time enough to reach Maysville by this morning at 7 o'clock at which time there is a Duel to come off between John Clay & a gentleman from Philadelphia. [. . .] I think it probable however I will be in Richmond in a week or ten days whether I go to Danville or not. Will you be at home about that time or not? Or have you concluded not to write to me any more, once I told you I should quit looking for letters from you? [. . .] I had thought you would write sometimes to give me the news, even if you had come to the conclusion to quit a regular correspondence. If you do not answer this, however, you need not look for me in Richmond at the time I propose. [. . .] I have no news to tell you as I have been at home ever since you left, except Mrs. Keiningham sent me word Mrs. Tubman [her sister] had arrived and she was going down the next day to Frankfort. [. . .] I don't think Mrs. K. is truly pleased with you because you would not promise to go to the [Blue Licks] Springs with them when she was so very polite as to ask you several times to go with them. Maybe you had better reconsider the matter. [. . .]

Respectfully,

Brutus J. Clay

Whatever Ann wrote in response must have pleased Brutus. He also mentions a visit from Ann's brother. Christopher Field's relatives couldn't resist trying to arrange matches for him. One of the widows Brutus mentions was Louisa Keiningham's sister, Mrs. Tubman. Although she lived in Augusta, Georgia, Emily Tubman frequently visited the Keininghams and her brother, Landon Thomas, who lived in Frankfort.

BRUTUS CLAY

July 21, 1844

Dear Ann,

I did not receive your letter for several days after it was written, only the day before Christopher [Field] came over. It was very acceptable and indeed quite gratifying to my feelings to think that one whom I love so dearly should likewise have a thought for me though absent and at a distance. Oh! Ann, you cannot imagine with what delight I read your Dear letters and only wish you would write oftener and put more in them. It is the next greatest satisfaction I have next to seeing and being with you. Do write often if you feel any interest in beguiling the many tedious and lonesome hours I spend here alone, sometimes for days and not see a single white person except the little boys and they are generally off by themselves at play. Do not wonder then at my coming so often to Richmond and then remaining so long with you when I do come. It is indeed hard for me to keep away, feeling my own passion and knowing you love me so dearly. The two weeks I spent with you were delightful ones, notwithstanding one or two unpleasant incidents, but as you think I too frequently complain and you said I was unreasonable in what I ask, I will barely allude to it now and probably not hereafter. [. . .] You say you don't know what I meant when we parted last and I gave you such an answer as I did to some question you asked. I can only say that one evasion only begets another and, as you set the example, you ought not to complain: though enough of this at present. I do not wish to mar the least pleasure you may have in reading this short scrawl if indeed it should have the effect which the writer desires for I can assure you, you would never get the scrape of a pen from me if it was not for the great desire I have to contribute to your pleasures and happiness. [. . .]

Christopher speaks of leaving in the morning and I have but little time to write. [. . .] We went in to see the widows Saturday last. Mrs. Tubman had unexpectedly returned to Frankfort on business & we could not ascertain certainly when they would go to the Licks. We saw Mr. K. and the little widow and Christopher was much taken with her, thinks she was decidedly interesting and handsome & I think wants to go to the Licks with her. They were rather of an opinion they would start on the day of the Election. [. . .] I will go with you if you wish me and accompany them, but would decidedly prefer your coming and paying a visit to going to the Springs. I wish you would pay me a long visit whether you go on to the Springs or not, both before you go and on your return back. I will send Woodson over if you want him and my horses, or without my horses, as you like. I want Martha to come home as soon as her school is out & want her to remain here until her health is better. I am so anxious for you to come about that time but, if you will not, I must send for her alone. [. . .] Even if you go to the Springs, stay with me a few days before you go on. You know how much more pleasant the time would pass here than in a large crowd at the Licks. [. . .]

Yours devotedly,

B. J. Clay

[P.S.] You must excuse me for not writing such a letter as you desired and intimate in your letter I am afraid just recd. and have not courage enough for the task just at this time, but will one of these days. [. . .] I am rather suspicious of you at this time. [. . .] Woman is a very change-able creature and cannot always account for their [sic] ways.

Despite the way he begins this letter, Brutus ends it on an extraor-dinary note of caution. There is a gap of more than two months in the correspondence, during which he must have put aside his "suspicions." In October, he asked Ann to check on a new suit of clothes he had or-dered, usually a sign of an impending marriage.

BRUTUS CLAY

October 13, 1844

Dear Ann,

Edmund [Field] has just informed me he intends to go home today & I just have time to write a few lines. I was much relieved when I ar-rived at home and found Green no worse than I did. He is still unwell but I think it is nerves and will probably be relieved soon. The sick ne-groes are on the mend, I think. I left Richmond very reluctantly, as you know, as I did not want to leave you so soon, am lonesome here, more so than usual, and feel more anxious you should pay me that *contem-plated visit*. [. . .] I will come after you, regardless of some other matters. I think I will come over to see you between this & the first of next month. I will, however, write again when I hear from you. As you promised, will you ask Mr. [William] Holloway [Ann's brother-in-law and manager of The Store] to have my new suit made. [. . .] I shall ex-pect a long sweet letter with many nice things in it. In haste, your brother,

B. J. Clay

In late October, Brutus's niece Sallie Rodes wrote to invite him to her wedding. "Knowing your numerous engagements and fearing a later invitation might occasion you some inconvenience, I write this early to request you and Martha to come over by the fourteenth of next month and see the last of me as Miss Rodes. There will be a 'gathering of the clans' about that time and I think I can venture to promise you more enjoyment than you could possibly find in rowing up the Kentucky [River] as a fisherman."

Brutus's notes to Ann become terser and terser. Something had him on edge. Was Ann unable to make up her mind whether to marry him? Why didn't she let him know whether his clothes were ready?

BRUTUS CLAY

October 26, 1844

[Dear Ann,]

I have just received your letter and regret that you are so uneasy about my not answering your other letter sooner. I have not been able to say when I would come over which was my main reason. If I had written, I could not have set any certain time. I have still delayed supposing I would be able to know soon. I have been on the standing jury all last week and this, and the Court will set I expect nearly all next week and I have two or three suits in Court and none of them called as yet. I, therefore, cannot leave until they are disposed of. [. . .] I think now I will be over immediately after the Presidential Election. But do not put intense confidence in my coming at that time. I may write you before I come. Please write soon. Your Bro.,

B. J. Clay

BRUTUS CLAY

Paris, October 31, 1844

[Dear Ann,]

I had expected to have received a letter from you before this time according to promise. This is three to your two instead of six as it ought to have been, according to your promise heretofore made. I was bound to be disappointed in my correspondence *with you*, I believe, and I feel very little like writing now. [. . .] I hardly know what to say about anything, just *seeing* you have not let me know whether I may depend on Mr. Holloway about my clothes or not. I did not wish to come over but once more this winter, but I have not heard from you anything about whether you will come with me or not or when. All I can say now is I will be over on Tuesday next, the second day of the Election. If it can be so arranged for you to come over with me, I shall be gratified. If not, I will only undergo another disappointment. I have been so engaged I could not come before & I thought as I could not come we would have managed all matters and one trip would suffice, however, I am left in doubt and uncertainty about it & I suppose I can know nothing until I come over which I will certainly do on Tuesday next. I hope you will not be absent as usual. As it is difficult for me to write here in the store at Mr. Avery's, I must close. Your brother,

B. J. Clay

One trip did suffice. Eight days later, Ann Maria Field and Brutus Junius Clay were married at her father's house in Richmond. She was twenty-two and he was thirty-six.

TWO

Who Is Married and Who Is Dead?

Once married to Brutus, Ann found herself separated from her family. Her oldest sister, Elizabeth, thirty-three, lived in Richmond with her husband, William Holloway, and numerous children. Holloway, a cousin who had grown up in Paris, Kentucky, was by 1844 a partner in The Store. The next sister, Patsey, twenty-six, lived with her husband John Harrison Miller, a grandson of the founder of Richmond, and their children on a farm in a hilly area of Madison County known as Silver Creek. Ann's younger sisters, Mary, fifteen, and Isabella (Belle), thirteen, both Martha Clay's schoolmates, lived in town with their father. Ann also had four brothers: Christopher, thirty, who lived in Mississippi but spent his summers in Richmond; David, twenty-four, who sometimes worked at The Store; Edmund, twenty, who was having trouble making up his mind what to do with himself; and eight-year-old Ezekiel Jr.

I can only speculate about what the Fields looked like. Ann I recognize from photographs; with her sisters I must guess. My father found some daguerreotypes and ambrotypes tucked away in a drawer and wrote down the names of the people in them on slips of paper, which he stuck into the cases containing the portraits. The most touching is a daguerreotype of two young women holding hands that may have been taken as early as 1840. My father identified them as two of the Field sisters. If the picture was taken in 1850, they are probably Mary and Belle, who would have been twenty-one and nineteen respectively at the end of that year. Or one of them might be Martha Clay, then eighteen. However, if the picture was taken in 1840, it was probably of the two older sisters. Patsey was then twenty-two and Elizabeth twenty-nine — which seems a bit old. Perhaps the fuller-faced sister is eighteen-year-old Ann.

My father also identified an ambrotype, taken between 1856 and 1860, as one of the Field sisters. The woman in it looks to be in her twenties and therefore must be either Mary, who was twenty-seven in 1856, or Belle, who was twenty-five. Elizabeth and Patsey, at forty-five and thirty-eight, were probably too old. This sister is not one of the two young women photographed together, though there is a family re-semblance that goes beyond their severe hairdos. They all have the deep-set eyes and prominent noses characteristic of many of their descendants, including me.

Their brothers had these features, too, though I have only two pictures of them. One is a badly damaged daguerreotype of Christopher, the other an ambrotype of a soulful bearded man, who I think is David. In addition to the eyes and nose of the sister who is either Mary or Belle, he has Ann's compressed lips.

Brutus had family in Madison County, too. Although his brother Cassius and his wife then lived in Lexington, Cassius had inherited the family farm near Foxtown. Brutus's sister Eliza, the wife of J. Speed Smith, an eminent lawyer much older than she, lived with their sons and daughters at Castle Union, northeast of Richmond. His sister Paulina and her husband, hemp manufacturer and politician Will Rodes, lived just outside Richmond at Woodlawn, a graceful house Green Clay had built for them as a wedding present.

Woodlawn and Castle Union were visible statements of their own-ers' places in the Richmond community, as was the Fields' big house on West Main Street, which they sometimes called Cedar Grove. As soon as they could, the Field sisters and their husbands enlarged their own homes to make them more imposing, too. In 1850, the Millers' modest brick farmhouse sprouted a two-story Flemish bond front and was christened Hedgeland. The year before, the Holloways had converted their home, Mount Airy, into an imposing Greek Revival edifice, Rosehill, by adding a new façade with a pretentious portico supported by Ionic columns. Rosehill had a winding central staircase and silver doorknobs. Although Ezekiel Field's house and the Smiths' place have been torn down, the others still stand, mute monuments to a different way of life. Woodlawn, which recently escaped being razed to make way for a supermarket, looks across a four-lane bypass at a McDonald's; Rosehill towers above the neighboring cottages like a Mack truck surrounded by VW bugs. Both are empty.

As their houses indicate, both the Fields and the Clays were prosperous. They flourished despite a nationwide depression between 1837 and 1844 brought about by inflation, land speculation, and currency reforms imposed by President Andrew Jackson. The decline was briefly halted in 1838, but the collapse of a major Pennsylvania bank the following year led to a protracted slump.

Family life was comfortable for the Fields. The women were fine cooks and seamstresses, and they had servants to handle the household drudgery. This left plenty of time for parties and visits to friends and relatives, activities that take up much space in the letters they wrote to one another after Ann's marriage.

The Field sisters' correspondence begins with the Richmond gossip, which is its staple throughout. "Who is married and who is dead," as Martha Clay put it. Martha and her young aunts were particularly adept at mimicking the adults. Each sister had a different style. Elizabeth, the oldest, presided over family scandals and bewailed illnesses, particularly her own. In this respect, she was certainly her father's daughter. Old Ezekiel Field always thought himself at death's door.

The correspondence opens with Elizabeth's letter to Ann about an incident in which their brother David and a cousin, Will Irvine, are reprimanded for drinking at a party by the young wife of a family friend. Sarah White's husband scolded her for hurting "those gentlemen's feelings," but Uncle David Irvine felt David and Will got just what they deserved.

Kentuckians drank a lot, then as now, and most of what they drank was made locally. In the 1780s Bourbon County distillers Jacob Spears and John Hamilton had invented sour mash whiskey aged in oak barrels. It took the name of the county.

ELIZABETH HOLLOWAY

Mount Airy, January 30, 1845

Dear Ann,

Bell [sic] [Field] has come up to stay the night with Amelia [Holloway], informs me David [Field] is going to Bourbon in the morning. I will write a few lines. [. . .] I dined at Uncle's yesterday and spent the evening at Uncle David's [Irvine] but I can assure you not a very pleasant one. David and Will Irvine caused a great commotion at the Camp. We went in the supper room and enjoyed a dram before the doors were thrown open. Mrs. White went in and ordered them [David and Will] out. I knew nothing of the interruption as [I] went in to see how Willie [her baby] was coming. As Mr. White & Sarah [White] were sitting there, he told me what had occurred and how badly he thought S. had behaved, said he would not have hurt those gentlemen's feelings for 1000$. I never heard such a lecture as he gave her. [. . .] He says, Sarah, I was enjoying myself so much and now you have mortified me entirely. I cannot enter that parlor again or look these gentlemen in the face. [. . .] Whilst we were sitting there, in comes Uncle D. Mr. White says, I think Sarah has done very wrong and she has mortified me very much. He [David Irvine] says, I think she did exactly right in what she said to them and I will let them know I do not keep a tavern or tippling shop and it's not the first time David has acted so here, but I think it is the last. [. . .] I refer you to D. for further particulars. [. . .]

Pattie [Holloway] and the baby [Willie] are both sick today. I think taking the Baby out last night made him sick. I could not leave him as Lucy & Milly [slaves] were going to have company and I knew he would not be attended to. [. . .] Eggs are so scarce. Sarah could not make much preparation [for the party the night before]. What she had was not fit to eat. Maria's Emily is her cook. [. . .] Tell Martha Bell & Amelia had a pie dance last night. [. . .] Write by David. My love to Mr. Clay and the children. Also to Mrs. Keiningham. Your devoted sister,

Elizabeth

The second sister, Patsey Miller, always sounds harassed. Sometimes she has no decent pen. Other times the children are too noisy. Often half the household is sick in bed, in a time when common diseases such as measles could be fatal. The Millers were not as well off as the rest of the family, and her sisters teased Patsey about having too many babies. Patsey's letters are often full of intricate directions, as in this case, for setting up a loom.

PATSEY MILLER

Silver Creek, January 31, 1845

Dear Sister Ann,

I received your letter ten days ago but, thinking you were not at home, I have not been in any hurry to answer it. I suppose by the time you will receive this, you will have returned from Frankfort. I suppose the wedding is over sure enough, that the two young folks, Miss Jane and Mr. Turner, are married as quite a feast of good things came to me from Mrs. Stone's last night. [. . .] They sent me oranges, candies, cakes of all sorts, chicken salad and all varieties of meats and breads, but they did not honor us with a stool to sit on. Mr. T. sent an invitation to dine with them at their house today but, as Mr. Miller started bright and early this morning to the mountains on some land business, I shall not find it convenient to go. [. . .]

You wrote me something about making harness [for weaving cloth] upon the new plan. I like the plan much better myself than the old way. [. . .] You should make your weaver particular to size [starch] her harness. [. . .] If not slickened in some way, they will rub and wear out directly. Some persons have brushes for it, but I use a [corn] cob, is as good. Just hang them on the back of a chair and stretch them tight at the bottom with your hand as they are on the sticks and put on the sizing with a cob. I have my sizing made half shorts and half meal. [. . .] Make a paste, a spoonful to a yard of cloth is the rule for making it. I use the hemp thread for making the harness to weave coarse cloth in, boiled well and doubled three strands. [. . .] [Patsey explains this new method of weaving for several more pages and includes a rough drawing of the frame.]

Ezekiel [Field, Jr.] and Christopher [Clay] both had the measles and are about well. [. . .] Pa wrote me by Mrs. Turner saying that Mary [Field] had been quite sick with the measles but, as she had now broken out, she was better. I had set this time to go to town and Pa, thinking I had not heard the measles were there, wrote to me I had better not go. [. . .] I have my doubts whether you can read this letter when you get it. I have a bad pen and no knife to better it. You must be sure to get me some of Mrs. Bedford's pretty linsey and any good receipts she has. [. . .]

I shall look for a letter from you shortly. Give my love to Mr. Clay, Martha, and the little boys. I remain your affectionate sister,

Sister P. I. Miller

In spite of Patsey's labors at the loom, the Field sisters' comfortable lives generally depended upon human bondage. However, neither the Holloways nor the Millers owned as many slaves as Brutus Clay did. He had inherited his original bondmen from his father in 1828 and the following year had purchased Mingo, a black man about his own age, from his mother and brother. Brutus's ties with Mingo probably went back to their childhoods. Later, Mingo helped Brutus manage the farm. He was also paid to make shoes for the farmhands. Skilled slaves— shoemakers, masons, and blacksmiths—were sometimes paid for additional work or allowed to hire themselves out to other people, though there is no indication Brutus let Mingo do this. A lucky few were able to save up their earnings to buy their own and their families' freedom.

Slavery is immoral, plain and simple, but there was nothing simple about the web of human relationships it created. When my family moved into Auvergne in 1946, a photograph of Mingo still hung in the library. At some point in the 1840s, some of Mingo's family went to Missouri without him. It's possible that Brutus sold Mingo's children, though his carefully kept records indicate not. Perhaps Mingo's wife belonged to someone other than Brutus and, with their children, was taken to Missouri. If so, Mingo had a second family in Kentucky, since another son, Henson, is mentioned in later letters.

The slave population on Brutus's farm grew rapidly. In 1831, Brutus reported owning 19 slaves whose total worth was $4,140. In 1845, he owned 57, worth $20,000. By the time of the 1860 census, there were 130 slaves, estimated to be worth $39,000, living at Auvergne, far more than Brutus needed to work the farm. Some he sent south to clear newly acquired land in Mississippi; others he hired out as servants and workmen (in 1860, he reported $1,122 in income from slave rental). A few worked for the Fields in Richmond.

As the United States expanded westward, Americans argued over whether or not slavery should be allowed in the new states. The Missouri Compromises of 1820 and 1821 — whose principal architect was Brutus's distant cousin, Henry Clay — established a geographic line of demarcation between freedom and slavery. Kentucky was south of this line, hence a slave state. However, most whites there were subsistence farmers and did not own slaves. In 1840, 23 percent of Kentucky's population was black. Ninety-six percent of those blacks were slaves.

Due to settlement patterns and an 1833 law prohibiting the importation of slaves into the state, slave ownership tended to be concentrated in the wealthy Bluegrass counties. By 1850, the population of Bourbon County was more than half black, occasioning considerable white anxiety. The city of Paris forbade slaves to come to town without written passes from their owners, and county patrols frequently challenged free blacks. By 1860, the balance had shifted again. In more mountainous Madison County, blacks constituted only 36 percent of the population.

Despite being one of the major slaveholders in Kentucky, Brutus came from a family that seriously questioned the wisdom and ethics of the institution. His brother Cassius became an emancipationist while a student at Yale, after hearing William Lloyd Garrison give a speech there, calling for the immediate abolition of slavery. Impressed with the prosperity he saw around him in New England, Cassius concluded that a major difference between Connecticut and his native Kentucky was that the workmen were free. Later, rejecting Garrison's radical abolitionism, he argued that slave labor should be abolished not for moral reasons, but because it limited the economic possibilities of the South by preventing the development of free labor. Brutus never espoused Cassius's views, but he supported his brother, both financially and emotionally, all his life.

Brutus's older brother Sidney also had doubts about slavery. His will freed many of his slaves and their offspring following his death in 1834. As executor of Sidney's will, Brutus was responsible for setting free Sidney's former bondmen and bondwomen. Many of them went to Liberia under the auspices of the Kentucky Colonization Society. There, though free, they often suffered terribly.

It is impossible at this distance to know exactly what Brutus himself thought about "the peculiar institution," as slavery's defenders called it. Campaigning for Congress during the Civil War, he opposed emancipation, and as a congressman he defended the property rights of slaveholders in loyal states. What is clear is that he thought about slavery frequently. To this day, a scrap of paper marks page 72 in Brutus's volume of the *Revised Statutes of Kentucky*, published in 1852, the page containing Article X: "Concerning Slaves."

The residue of slavery was all around me when I was a child in Bourbon County, both that which was clearly visible and that which was more subtle. I remember we planted an enormous garden in those days — rows and rows of tomatoes and pole beans, almost a quarter of an acre of greens. We couldn't possibly eat all these vegetables ourselves, and we didn't. Many other people lived off them, most of them Brutus's slaves and their descendants.

Hamp Ayres, once the carriage man, had been born a slave in 1854. The original Hampton, his father, was one of the men Brutus inherited from Green Clay. The Hamp I knew lived in town, but once a week all summer long his nieces drove him out to the farm, and while he sat under the walnut tree in the garden fence (the same one my brother and I used to climb) smoking his pipe, they filled paper bags with tomatoes and beans. A few weeks before his death, Hamp disappeared from his house in Paris. His nieces found him walking along the Winchester Pike in the direction of Auvergne.

"Where you going, Uncle Hamp?" they asked.

The old man didn't even stop walking to answer, "Home."

It could have been a scene from Walt Disney's *Song of the South*.

That was what I saw around me: a benign, sentimental version of slavery. Yet somehow I knew that what I saw was flawed. Perhaps it was my early years in a Quaker school in Baltimore, perhaps it was my mother's stern New England upbringing (she was the daughter of a Congregationalist minister from Boston), but one day in 1954 I found myself arguing fiercely with my father about *Brown* v. *Board of Education*. He gave free legal advice to the descendants of his grandfather's slaves, but my father still couldn't imagine a world in which blacks and whites attended the same schools.

I could. For years my mother had been driving my brother and me into Paris so that we could attend the city schools, considered to be better than the county schools. At the same time she took along the children of the only black tenant family living on our farm. Their school, the "colored school," was also located in Paris. My mother would drop one brother and sister at their school, then drive a couple of blocks to drop the other brother and sister at their school. In the evening, she reversed the process. It didn't take much imagination to see that there was something horribly wrong about this.

The Clay family's antislavery activities reached a high point in 1845, when Cassius began to publish an antislavery newspaper, *The*

True American, in Lexington. Cassius was a passionate editor and had already been involved in several brawls during public appearances. Fearing interference, he armed his newspaper office with two cannon loaded with shot and nails.

As Cassius's editorials got bolder, his neighbors grew angrier. He once received an anonymous note, purportedly written in blood: "You are meaner than the autocrats of hell. The hemp is ready for your neck. Your life cannot be spared. Plenty thirst for your blood."

Brutus's brother-in-law Speed Smith worried about Cassius's safety. "Ben Warfield [a relative of Cassius's wife] has been watching two days to have a conversation with me and has just left me," he wrote Brutus in July of 1845. "He is fully impressed with the belief that Cassius will be killed if he remains here & continues his paper. He tells me that the feeling of the people is growing deeper and deeper daily. [. . .] Col. Payne tells me that Uncle Hector [Cassius's mother's brother] proposed to Nathan Payne to call a meeting of the citizens — appoint a committee of the most respectable men to wait on Cassius & urge him to discontinue his paper, & if he refuses, to tear down his office and destroy his press. *This is the course proposed by his uncle.* What are we to expect then from strangers? He is *now* looked upon here as an *open abolitionist.*"

That same July, Cassius came down with typhoid fever. A month later, still ill, he published an article urging political equality for freedmen in preparation for the emancipation of all slaves, not a view Cassius himself espoused. He accompanied it with an inflammatory editorial. "But remember, you who dwell in marble palaces, that there are strong arms and fiery hearts and iron pikes in the streets, and panes of glass only between them and the silver plate on the board, and the smooth-skinned woman on the ottoman. When you have mocked at virtue, denied the agency of God in the affairs of men, and made rapine your honied faith, tremble! for the day of retribution is at hand, and the masses will be avenged."

On August 14, a mob invaded Cassius's newspaper offices. Although Cassius eventually repudiated the editorial, he was arraigned in the Fayette County courthouse for "dangerous insurrection" on August 18. When he refused to discontinue *The True American*, a committee of sixty men seized his presses and shipped them to Cincinnati. Cassius returned to Madison County, ill and in debt but far from humbled.

My father used to say that the remarkable thing about the Clay family was its tolerance for differing points of view. Cassius's family stood behind him throughout *The True American* ordeal. His mother wrote him, "If you prefer death to dishonor, so do I."

In October, Cassius resumed publication of *The True American* but in Cincinnati, on the other side of the Mason-Dixon Line. As the excitement subsided in Kentucky, Ann and Brutus's lives returned to normal. Ann's father wrote Brutus to see if he would be interested in some cattle that were for sale in Madison County. "[T]hey are originally from the Mountains and having the very best grass all summer. [. . .] they look very nice. Indeed, 40 or 50 of them are quite large and fat. [. . .] I think you can purchase if you should attend the sale.

"Our family remains in usual health," he continued. "Mine is as usual, the last 6 months feeble. Two or three weeks ago I concluded to accompany Christopher [Field] to the mouth of the Ohio on my way to Missouri but was so unwell at the appointed time to leave that I had to decline for this reason. I am at present a little stouter.

"I hope Ann's health is now good [Ann was three months pregnant]. [. . .] Tell Christopher [Clay] we hope he has risen from his back and can move about. [. . .] He must come over with you and bring Ezekiel [Field] some of his make of suspenders to show how handy he became in his confinement."

As Christmas approached, Elizabeth wrote Ann with the Richmond gossip. Her daughter, Pattie, had had some sort of accident affecting her fingers. The doctor's advice sounds painful.

ELIZABETH HOLLOWAY

Mount Airy, December 17, 1845

Dear Ann,

[. . .] Pattie got home in the Stage today and I am happy to say her fingers are straight and she can use them. They are still bandaged. The Doct. says they must be bent backwards and forwards every day to prevent stiffening. [. . .] I was at the Store yesterday. Pa looks as well as usual. [. . .] I met with Mary [Field] there. She was complaining of being very lonesome. Ed [Field] has been on Silver Creek for several days. If he had any business habits whatever, he could get a place in The

Store. [. . .] 4 of our merchants are selling off at last. Uncle [David Irvine] is one. Some think he and the Turners are going to dissolve. Chenault says he will sell at last and throw in the sewing. The ladies should encourage him. Uncle Albert [Irvine] got home a few days ago. His last lot [of merchandise] he was holding up for $50, refused; afterwards he was willing to take it and could not get it. He rafted it up the [Kentucky] River, then it froze and he could not dispose of it, only the Hams. [. . .] Mr. H. wrote his Ma word if she and Sarah [his sister] would come over, he would meet them in Lex. this week. [. . .] I hear of no frolicking this Christmas. Where do you expect to spend it? [. . .] It is late and the children are so noisy I do not know what I am writing. They look like they will eat Pattie up. [. . .] Give my love to Martha and Cit. [The Fields spelled Christopher Clay's nickname with a C, although Kit himself spelled it with a K.] Ask Mr. Clay to let Woodson bring them over in the old carriage to spend their Christmas. The children would be delighted to see them. [. . .]

Your devoted sister,

Sister Elizabeth

[P.S.] Did you fill your ice house? We did not get ours entirely full.

In 1836, Ann's brother Christopher and Uncle David Irvine, along with several other Kentuckians, had purchased land in Bolivar County, located along the Mississippi River in the delta of the Yazoo. It was wilderness—bogs and thickets inhabited by deer, bear, and alligators—and was regularly flooded by the meandering Mississippi River, but its climate was perfect for growing cotton. Slowly the would-be planters cleared their land, girdling the trees one year and burning them the next. The Kentuckians called their Bolivar County community Kentucky Landing. When hailed from a skiff, passing steamboats would stop for passengers or freight.

Wresting a plantation out of the Delta wilderness was backbreaking labor for which the planters imported slaves, mules, and oxen from home. Both men and animals died from the harsh conditions and tropical diseases. The spring floods were torrential, often drowning the cotton crop, but the summers were worse, humid incubators for cholera, dysentery, and malaria. Planters usually went north in June, leaving their land and hands in the care of overseers until their return in mid-September.

The economics of planting cotton were harsh, too, despite the demand for the raw staple. In the mid-1840s, cotton prices had dropped to a low of 5.5 cents a pound. Costs were high. Between 15 and 20 percent of the price of raw cotton went to "factors" in New Orleans who arranged credit, warehousing, and shipping for the growers.

Life in Bolivar County was hard and lonely. In his letters home, Christopher Field often wondered what he was doing in such a place. He was a melancholy person at best, even more so after the abrupt end of his engagement to Sally Clay. His sisters hoped he would find a wife to keep him company at the plantation, which he called, without any apparent sense of irony, Content.

Mississippi is a persistent counterpoint to Kentucky in the story of the Fields and the Clays. To the young men of the family it held out the lure of wealth and adventure. Most of the women hated it from afar. No one personifies this mixture of emotions more than Christopher. His letters feature rambling recitations of the hard facts of life in the Delta side by side with philosophical and political musings, phrase after phrase strung together in a litany of loneliness.

CHRISTOPHER FIELD

Bolivar, Miss., February 15, 1845

Dear Ann,

I received your kind letter some weeks ago and would have answered some time since but for want of news to write and more. I am very busy and have been all thro [sic] the Fall and Winter. Having no overseer, I find all my time is occupied and when night comes I even am attending to something or other until bedtime. I have been looking very anxiously indeed for some letters from some member of the family for two or three weeks, having received none since yours though I received one from Amelia Holloway. [. . .] I shall have to make a substitute of Amelia in your place. Now you have the cares of a family I presume you will not find so much time to write as formerly. I hope the change you have made will conduce mutually to both you & Mr. Clay's happiness though I have thought brother-in-law & sister-in-law should never marry but in this case we all cherished the highest regard for Mr.

Clay and the memory of our dear Sister will never be obliterated and we now know her dear children will find a true mother in you and will not meet with the cold harsh and unkind treatment that we frequently see displayed by most of stepmothers. [. . .]

Miss Payne has been spending the winter with Mrs. Estill [a Mississippi neighbor]. She is in fine health and spirits and very gay & lively and seems to be perfectly happy in this dull & monotonous country. I think her a very fine girl and admire her much more than I do Miss Lydia though she is not a woman of so much sense. [. . .]

Yours truly,

C. I. Field

Christopher was a sternly upright person. Reading his letters, one begins to understand why Sally Clay ran off with another man. But his stiff backbone could not protect him from a crisis such as the one he described to his brother David in December.

CHRISTOPHER FIELD

Bolivar, Miss., Decb. 26, 1845

Dear David,

I received your letter by W. R. Estill and should have answered it by him but [he] left before I had finished one I was writing Uncle David. I now write you under as distressed state of feelings as you can imagine. A few days after Mr. Estill left us I decided to go up the Arkansas River [. . .] with a view of buying corn on speculation and pork for our place. [. . .] I had hired a young man to attend to our business until Christmas. [. . .] This young man had difficulty with Albert [a slave] and failed in whipping him and I presume called on Jim [a slave] to help him which he did not do and afterwards attempted to whip Jim. He no doubt broke to run from him and he [the overseer] shot him [Jim] dead. He was tried and swore Jim was making at him with an axe. No one saw it but two of the negro women who were off 100 yards. They say Jim was trying all the time to get out of his way. He was tried the next day and cleared upon his own statements and left the country immediately, fearing to meet me, and well he might for if I had have seen him under my feeling I fear I would have been a murderer. I only expected to be gone a week but was off 10 days. I now reflect deeply upon myself for leaving home though I feared nor thought of nothing of the kind. [. . .] He had been with me 3 weeks before I left for [the] Arkansas River and so far as I knew of had had no difficulty in any way. If money would bring the boy to life I would give any amount. I have not seen a happy or pleasant moment and do what I will this murder is in my view and thoughts. I know I have had many misfortunes and hard luck all of which I have tried to bear with fortitude but this unmans me and I cannot erase it from my memory and feelings. [. . .] I have had misfortunes all my life from the very moment I commenced trying to make a living but this affair is not connected with dollars and cents. It is the manner in which life has been taken and had I stayed at home it would never have occurred. If I had have been at home I could have convinced the jury from the circumstances that he [the overseer] was guilty of murder and had him committed, but he is gone and I presume the matter is at an end. [. . .]

The young people had some Christmas [. . .] party tonight and [a] dance at Col. Burk's about 10 miles off. All our neighborhood has gone down. I did not feel like I could enjoy it and to me now everything looks dreary. [. . .] You said something about coming down. I would be pleased to see you [. . .] and would hope by the time my present state of feelings will wear off. [. . .]

Your brother,

C. I. Field

Christopher's distress over Jim's murder went far deeper than the mere loss of property. In a subsequent letter, Elizabeth Holloway commented on the attachment between Christopher and Jim. Much as he loved Jim and grieved over his loss (and I think he genuinely thought of it this way), Christopher was unable to see that the slaveholding society in which he lived made Jim's murder inevitable. Or perhaps it was that he could not let himself see the connection between human bondage and its effects. To do so would have been to question the very roots of the society in which he had prospered.

Back in Richmond, the Fields' lives contrasted with the harsh conditions of Christopher's life in Mississippi. By New Year's 1846, Mary Field was sixteen, tart tongued, and easily bored. There was so little to do in Richmond, she wrote her older sister Ann, that she was forced to write letters. Her letter makes me think of the endless summers when I was a teenager on the farm, when the only amusing thing I could think of to do was to write voluminous letters to my boarding school roommates.

MARY FIELD

January 2, 1846

A Gloomy Day

Dear Ann,

I have just returned from Silver Creek, paying my first visit to the *Young Ladies* visiting Mrs. James Miller. I say first, but I trust not last, as I spent a most glorious time. [. . .] It is very gay on the Creek indeed, more so than in the city, as *it* is stupidity itself. I have had the blues so bad all the morning that I resorted to writing, hoping it might dissipate the gloomy and dark feelings. [. . .] I have beguiled the loneliness of the hours by knitting bags and purses but I have unfortunately used all the beads Richmond can afford. They cannot even be purchased in Lexington. I suppose we will have to send to Cincinnati. If you see anyone wishing anything done in my line of business, just recommend me. I suppose you have spent a joyous Christmas or has it become a day of as little note with you as it has with me? It does not stand as prominent in my estimation as it did in former days. [. . .]

I was begging Pa this morning to devise some way for me to pay you a visit as I am all anxiety to commence my patchwork. [. . .] I wrote to Cousin Sarah [Holloway] two or three weeks since but have received no answer. I was in hopes she would have been over by this time. In my letter, I offered a great many inducements for her to come. I frequently wished she was with us on Silver Creek as she would have had full benefit of Mr. Cyrus Miller for he did not leave us a moment. [. . .] Yesterday we were at Dr. Miller's and at the table we were all conjecturing which would be married at the end of next year. Dr. Miller concluded by saying I must try and marry Cyrus. I told him I would add in my "*mite.*" I take that as a very gross hint. I brought a letter up written to you by Patsey and I think from the length of it she has given you a detail of everything that has happened during the last year. [. . .]

Yours truly,

Mary Field

Marriage was the principal preoccupation of girls such as Mary, hence her bantering discussion of the eligible Cyrus Miller. Evidently she thought Dr. Miller, a relative of Patsey's husband, wanted her to marry Cyrus, but I'm not sure what she means by her "mite."

Later in January, Elizabeth sent Ann a letter by their brother David, who was on his way to Bourbon County. As usual, Elizabeth was preoccupied with illnesses. "Mary & Willie [Holloway] are not well. I am afraid it is or will turn to Scarlet Fever. They have high fevers and are broken out like *measles*. Mr. H. was affected the same way a few days last week." She added, "Tell Green this is Junius's [Junius Holloway was about the same age as Green Clay] birthday. I have not let him know as I know he would pester me to death. Pattie is very anxious to have a party here the 28th of next month. I told her she could not without eggs [with which to make a cake]. There was one in the hen house yesterday. I hope they have made a beginning."

By mid-January of 1846, Christopher's letter about Jim's murder had reached Richmond. Elizabeth wrote Ann an abbreviated account of its contents, which was how news from Mississippi often traveled around the family. She added, "I never felt more distressed. I could not sleep the first night. [. . .] It seems as if [Christopher] is the most unfortunate man in the world. Jim was so much attached to him. He would have periled his own life for him. [. . .] I wish he would quit the country [Mississippi]. We were invited to John Miller's Affair. He married his cousin, Miss Healy. We received this melancholy news and did not feel like going."

From his father, Brutus had inherited land along the major tributaries of the Kentucky River in Madison and Estill Counties. Green Clay had acquired this land with an eye toward commercial development, the river being the principal avenue for transportation in that part of Kentucky. Sometime in the 1830s, Brutus and Cassius constructed a steam-powered sawmill on the Kentucky River near Clay's Ferry. In 1845, Brutus bought out Cassius's interest and began refitting the mill. He convinced his brother-in-law David Field, then twenty-five, to take over its management the following year. He also secured the services of a millwright, George Weddle.

David was a restless, energetic young man who had studied at Yale and Transylvania. He is one of my favorite Field men because he writes more openly about himself than either his brothers or Brutus Clay. His letters about the mill and the Weddle family paint a picture of a world very different from the genteel domain of the Fields.

One of the first problems David encountered at the Mills was a slave named Mat. Mat's wife lived in Bourbon County and he longed to return there. Slave marriages were particularly difficult when husband and wife belonged to different owners, as in this case.

DAVID I. FIELD

Steam Mills, Friday [February] 20th, [1846]

Mr. B. J. Clay

Dear Sir,

Supposing you would like to hear what we are about [. . .] I will devote a few minutes of this boisterous night to your edification. The last ten days have been ciphers to us as it has been snowing & raining or rather pouring so that we can do no work and to see the negroes idle for ten days puts me in a very bad humor. We have been doing very well chopping wood all the time, all been well with the except[ion] of the boy Mat who is the only one that has complained or grumbled. Coming over he had to ride in the waggon [sic]. His feet was frost bitten. Had been here but a few days he must have his shoes mended. His feet were sore, then he had a pain all through his back & side, the consequence of an attack of pleurisy he had several years ago. Never been well since. [. . .] He has been at me several times recently to let him go and see his wife at Mr. Spears' [whiskey] factory. Says he loved his wife & child tenderly, was devoted to them, etc. I finally told him if I heard any more complaints from him I would chastise him. About ten days ago, he came in and told [me] he could not stand it any longer, that he could not lift his axe. [. . .] I concluded to send him up and let Doct. Harris examine him. I do not want to whip a negro or make him work when he is really sick. [. . .] Harris thought bleeding & blistering would be of service to him. I have had no opportunity of having him bled and thought that the pain would leave him. I do not think there is much the matter with him. You told me that none of them were married and I have refused to let him go to Bourbon. I thought when we need the cart & oxen I would let him go over and bring them but will not let him for I think there is some spite in his laying up so long. The other negroes are well and doing well. [. . .] I am getting out of patience with your man Weddle. I saw him about the middle of January. He told me that he would send ten of his hands over the first of February to work at the mill and would come over subsequently himself. Not a lick has he had struck. Bono was here about three weeks ago. He says he has the last lot of logs [. . .]. I told him we would not buy before spring. He said he could not wait but would bring them out [in] the dinner tide [a movement of logs on the river]. [. . .] Had Weddle come here when he promised we would have been ready to buy logs this tide. [. . .] You had better write to him that you object to his having jobs all over the county, that he must come to the mill and stay here. [. . .] Winn was over to see me some time ago. [. . .] He says Weddle is a man of integrity and cleverness but that he is a restless, discontented and unhappy man. He gave me a gloomy account of his domestic affairs. His wife is crazy, lost her mind. He has a great awkward overgrown daughter, only one or two [steps] removed from an idiot. I get along so well alone that I dread their coming. I have got clear of Mrs. Thompson & family and have rented the ferry to a Mr. Igo, a very clever industrious man. [. . .]

I received a letter from New York from Mr. Whittesey informing me of the death of his sister, my old sweetheart. She died with consumption. It would have distressed me very much had I not been going to Mr. Barclay's wedding which dispelled all melancholy feelings. There was a large and grand party at Col. Miller's in his new house last Monday. I went back to it. I had been very sick for 10 days with these very large boils on the back of my neck. Will Irvine came and stayed with me a week and through his agreeable society and tender nursing I was made well enough to go to the wedding. I felt like an uncaged lion. I am distressed about my fine clothes. I have worn nothing but the pantaloons Ann gave me, the green blanket, and a pair of brogues since I have been here. [. . .] They would stare at you if you looked decent down here. The negro girl I had of Mr. Irvine I sent back to town. [. . .] If we should need another have you one that you can let us have? One large enough to set tables, churn, clean up my room. I have fixed up this room very comfortably and shall expect yourself & family to stay with me when you pass. [. . .] Mary [Field] I believe has concluded to go East with your friend Madame Jones. I wrote to Papa today urging him to countermand his permission already given [. . .] some of Mary's friends to whose opinion she should pay great deference do not consider Mrs. Jones a fit *companion du voyage* for her. [. . .] I can't say anything myself as Mrs. Jones says she is the best friend I have and that I always make myself sociable and that I am one of the most elegant gentlemen of her acquaintance. Of course I am mum. [. . .]

With great respect your old friend,

D. I. Field

As an unmarried woman, Mary Field could not travel alone. Her father must have heeded David's warning about the unsuitability of Mrs. Jones as a traveling companion, since when Mary went east it was with Christopher, not "Madame" Jones. I'm not sure who Mrs. Jones was other than a friend of David's. Several years earlier she had given a birthday party for her son to which she invited all the other two-year-olds she knew and had employed David and his friends as "waiters."

Brutus's mill was in poor shape. "The furnace draws very well but upon getting out the bands to make some repairing and patching we found [them] [. . .] very much damaged," David wrote him in April 1846 from Lexington, where he had gone to get materials with which to make repairs. "One of them (that runs the saw) almost entirely ruined. The other one is not so bad. [. . .] The bands were about in the same condition with the whole mill. It was very much out of repair, full of sand and dirt, patched up with old pieces of staves."

By late April, George Weddle had moved his family into the mill. "Mr. Weddle reports to me that the machinery runs as smooth [. . .] as he ever saw it," David told Brutus, "the saws cut well, furnace draws, in fact everything about the mill works as well as he could expect. We have been running about 10 days but have never done a full day's work. We are dependent at present upon the spring for water [for the boiler] and that is not sufficient. Weddle has not had time to fix the pump as it is very much out of repair, pipes leaked, rods nearly all gone, Cassius having taken them up to his farm and worked [on] them up in his shop."

David found life with the Weddles difficult. "[Weddle] has had a hard time of it for a week past, sick himself and his wife crazy as a bed bug. She has been on a high horse, preaching, praying, shouting etc. She is getting over it for a day or two past. She has fits or spasms every day and these crazy fits of a week every three or four months. It is the most hopeless family I ever [saw]. The mother and ten children combined hardly have two respectable ideas. I shall have to get married to get clear of their annoyance."

In May 1846, Christopher wrote Ann that he planned to marry Charlotte Martin of Louisville, whose relatives also had a plantation in Bolivar County.

CHRISTOPHER FIELD

Frankfort, May 20, 1846

Dear Ann,

I have come to Kentucky to consummate marriage on the second day of June which is Tuesday week next. The lady is Miss Charlotte Martin of Louisville, the granddaughter of Mayor J. L. Martin here. Father and mother both dead. [. . .] I reckon I am told it will be an affair in high life, though I would have preferred a plainer affair, but they all seem proud of me and suppose they will make it a grand affair under Episcopal ceremony. They say I have to present a ring [. . .] and put it on the fourth finger of the left hand and repeat a verse as long as my arm. From your knowledge of me, you will infer I will think this all stuff. My lady love is a plain woman not handsome but fair looking, rather low in stature but good size, 19 years old. She says she is wild and childish but I don't think so, at least you know she has got the upper hand of me. My only regrets about the affair [are that] she is a delicate woman and I fear never will be stout. Her Grandmother wishes me to take her to [the] sea shore this summer and bathe in salt water. Her physician recommends it also. I reckon we will go East pretty soon after marriage. Tell Mr. Clay a trip to Louisville will be pleasant. You must write us at Richmond. I am taking them on surprise there and will not have time I fear to come over and see you before our union. [. . .]

Your brother,

C. I. Field

Certain of these letters I cherish above others, and this letter of Christopher's is one of them. Despite his unvarnished description of his "lady love," he seems pleased with his wife-to-be. Although he doesn't say so, Charlotte Martin was extremely wealthy.

In Richmond, the whole family was titillated by news that a slave woman named Lean had attempted to poison Patsey Miller, as Ezekiel Field wrote Brutus. This Lean is probably the Leanna who Martha mentioned earlier as having been in jail. It's easy to imagine the simmering resentment of Kentucky's slave population. Crimes against masters were probably common. Cassius Clay always believed that his namesake had died from arsenic administered by a nurse, Emily, one of the servants he could not emancipate because of the terms of his father's will.

EZEKIEL H. FIELD

Richmond, July 13, 1846

Dear Sir,

Mr. Harrison Miller came up from home today with your negro girl, Lean, on his way to your house with her. His family have undergone a very severe and trying time. During last night, after they returned from preaching yesterday with considerable company, having had some fresh fish, their little daughter Amelia was picking some bones and her mother was fearful she would get choked and directed Lean to take the plate from her which she neglected to do and consequently the child was badly choked and Patsey slapped Lean in the face and it appears that Patsey had directed the girl to hand her some water to wash her mouth after supper. The girl brought her a very small quantity, saying it was all there was. Patsey drank a mouthful of it and immediately discovered the poison and was almost intensely very much distressed and had Doct. Miller sent for as soon as possible and by severe remedy got relieved of the effects of the strychnine poison which the girl by some means had procured.

Mr. Miller says he can leave home now with considerable inconvenience and the extreme warm weather in addition. I have said to him that I will send the girl down to David [at the mill] and get him to keep her until an opportunity offers to send her elsewhere. Think it probable you would not like to take her to your house so that probably she will remain at the mill until you can give some directions what you wish done.

On the way up today Lean confessed the crime to Mr. Miller. Patsey objects to having any steps [taken] lawfully to punish her and insists on her being returned to you or to your order. You will please write to David shortly your wishes on the subject.

We hope Ann and the family are enjoying good health but we fear you have had so much electioneering to perform during this extreme hot weather that you do not enjoy yourself under the circumstances. [Brutus was running for a seat in the legislature.] Our friend Col. Irvine is in your predicament but does not stop for weather and I now think will be elected.

Christopher, wife, and Mary Field left Cincinnati last Monday for Pittsburgh, Brownsville, and [. . .] Washington City. [. . .]

My love to all the family.

Yours respectfully,

E. H. Field

Brutus sent Lean to live at the mill while he looked for a buyer for her. Sometime late in the summer, David mailed Brutus another installment of mill life.

"Misfortune never comes singly but in battalions," he wrote. "Bright & early Monday morning Dick cut his foot very badly with an axe and as we were filling a large bill for a church in Athens I took his place which has nearly prostrated me. It was too violent & severe. For three days I was [. . .] off the mill only to go to my meals. Yesterday Malvina took [to] her bed with her breast. It is rising. Lean & Levi are our cooks etc. Also Mrs. Weddle is crazy, her daughter has a sore foot and is sick in every way. I much prefer risking the wickedness & mischievousness of Lean to old Mrs. Weddle & daughter's filth."

A prospective buyer had come to look at Lean. "He says she is too small at $380. I told him I was looking for you over in a few days. He says to you that he would give $300 for her and that if you would take that that I must send her to Lexington about the 1st of September."

The family had heard from Brother and Charlotte, who were still on their honeymoon in Canada, David added. (Although it seems an odd thing to do, Mary Field accompanied them.) They expected to be back in Kentucky by the beginning of September.

In August, Brutus lost his election. "I am sorry to hear of your defeat," Cassius wrote him in October, "but such is the fate of war and sooner or later all politicians meet the same fate; but as you have philosophy enough to bear all those things easily it is unnecessary for me to say anything."

Cassius was en route to Texas to fight "Mr. Polk's War" against

Mexico, as the Whigs called it. President James K. Polk had been elected on a platform of enlarging slave territory, and the war's chief object was to acquire Texas, with California and New Mexico thrown in for good measure. Cassius had raised a regiment principally to recover his dignity and reputation after the *True American* affair. He was not in favor of expanding slave territory, but this was only one of many quixotic and paradoxical things Cassius did during his life.

"The more I see of slavery in the south the less I like it," he told Brutus, "and I think the annexation and war of Texas will not strengthen the 'peculiar institution.' I am sorry you have so much invested in slaves as troublesome times are ahead. Would it not be well to lighten off the vessel somewhat for the rough sea?"

He didn't think much of the territory they were fighting for either. "Texas is a miserable country. The Eastern part pine and hickory and sandy — the western, prairie, muddy and quicksands and mesquite. The whole state is not worth six cents an acre, as the climate is warm and sickly and enervating and must ever be inhabited by a semi-civilized and degenerate people."

Many Madison County men, including Edmund Field and one of Cassius's and Brutus's nephews, Green Clay Smith, had also volunteered to fight. "Ed Field and Clay Smith are well and in fine spirits and seem as if they would stand the campaign very well," Cassius assured Brutus.

Back at the mill, David Field was still preoccupied with Mat, as he told Brutus.

DAVID I. FIELD

Mills, Sept. 22cd, 1846

Mr. B. J. Clay

Your wife will have informed you of the deportment of the boy Mat, that he ran away from me on Thursday last upon my calling him to the mill to chastise him. We have not been able to catch him yet. You know the natures of negroes. They would take a whipping before they would tell on another. He came to Milburn [a slave] on Saturday and asked him to get his clothes for him. They were in the woods. Milburn did not let Mr. Weddle know it until Saturday night. Eli [a slave] saw him at the ferry Saturday night & still wanting his clothes & Eli did not let anybody know that he had seen him till Sunday morning. He crossed the river that night. He was seen at Mrs. Rogers' Sunday morning & at a negro meeting near Burkley in Clark [County] that day and that is the last I have heard of him. As soon as I heard of his being at Rogers' I went over there and told Rogers he had been there and employed a trusty servant of his to watch for him. I have done the same thing with several other negroes. They are only to inform me where I can find him. When he came home Sunday (the first time he run off) [. . .] he told them [the other slaves] that he did not intend to live with me and that if I went to fooling with him when I got home then he would run off again where I never could hear of him, that he would go to the Spears' in Bourbon and some white folks about the factory would hide him and give him a free pass. By his great anxiety to get his clothes, his best ones, I fear he intends to execute his threats. [. . .] I have done all in my power to have him caught, offered a reward for him, and have told the negroes to send him over, that if he would come in I would not whip him. He may have got some clothes and is making for your county. He told the negroes that he had been doing bad for some time, as bad as he could so that he would not be sent back next year, that he wanted to live on a steam boat, be a waiter. Mr. Weddle could have caught him while I was in town and also at the time he was running off had he have exerted himself. I think he [Weddle] is taking very little interest in our affairs. He is at present absent, gone to Bush's Mill in Clark [County]. [. . .] Yesterday his wife had one of these prostitutes in the neighborhood spending the day with her, a Mrs. Creed. I will not say anything to Weddle about her conduct for he is foolish enough to pack up & leave on account of my complaints. Melbourne [Milburn] reports himself this morning with one of his short ribs broken. While in the act of throwing out a stick of wood his foot slipped and he fell upon the wheel that was down yesterday and he did not find it out till this morning. I have not examined him and I suppose it is only very sore, bruised. [. . .] I do not know what to advise you to do about Mat. I have no idea where he is and I do not know whether any reliance should be placed upon his conversation as reported above. If you should get hold of him don't let him get out of your sight until he is locked up in jail. If I catch him, I shall do so. [. . .]

With great respect,

D. I. Field

If ever there was an argument for Cassius's free-labor theories, the situation at the mill was it. Never mind the moral issues involved;

forced labor wasn't getting the work done. However, the predicament of Mat and David, like that of Jim and Christopher, poignantly under-lines the impossible human dilemma of slavery. Brutus must have caught up with Mat, for his records show that a short time later he sold a thirty-six-year-old man named Matt.

Ezekiel Field wrote to Brutus in September to tell him that he was sending a check to him for Ann, part of the inheritance that he was distributing to his children during his lifetime. "Christopher and Char-lotte speak of going to Lexington on their way home in the morning and will leave Louisville [for Mississippi] about 1st Oct.," he added.

David wrote from the mill, "I have heard nothing of Mat since I wrote you last [. . .] & I am well satisfied he is in your county. Whether he is trying to get out of the state [to freedom] or not [. . .] I do not know his character & disposition well enough to determine. Do you not think it would be advisable to employ Hutchison of your place to examine Spears' establishment & send your trusty boy up to your brother's farm & among the free negroes about there?"

George Weddle was away more than he was present. "I thought we would have started the mill this week," David wrote, "but Mr. Weddle has gone up with Jonathan Bush. [. . .] I believe I mentioned to you [. . .] he intended leaving us at the end of the year. [. . .] He told Ship-ton last week he was going up to Red River to build a steam establish-ment up there with Mr. Jackson. That is [the] last notion. I suppose he will have another one when he comes home from Bush."

David was thinking about marriage, probably in reaction to the loneliness of life on the river. "I have for some time felt the importance of perpetrating matrimony," he wrote Brutus. "Your injunction for me to do so shall be attended [to] at an early opportunity. I do not consider it difficult to marry but to get some[one] to consent to live at the river I find rather difficult though I am in earnest when I say I want to marry this winter. [. . .] Mr. Daugherty White marries Miss Walker tomorrow evening. They [will] have a very large wedding. I shall go over though not as an attendant this time. I just did escape. I was talked of as one."

In spite of his comments about wishing to get married, David's verb tags him as a confirmed bachelor. The idea of "perpetrating marriage" is revealing, particularly in light of his "escape" from having to serve as one of Daughterty White's groomsmen.

Life at the mill was devolving into melodrama. I try to picture Bru-tus reading one of David's letters. Was he annoyed by the chaos and inefficiency there? Because of a fierce photograph of him taken nearly twenty years later, I tend to imagine Brutus with a scowl. Or did he see the humor in David's accounts of the mill's vicissitudes?

DAVID I. FIELD

At Home, Sunday 1st Nov. 1846

Mr. Brutus J. Clay

To while away a part of this dismal blues-giving day and as well to divert my attention from the discordant gabble of vulgar fury and idiocy of Mrs. Weddle, daughter & [. . .] maniacs quarrelling in bedlam, I have concluded to keep you advised of our doings, etc. I am [with] the blessings of Providence restored to health and I believe with the exception of Melbourne [Milburn] there is no sickness here. He last week in lifting a log hurt himself again, brought on a return of his disease, the running of the veins (or range as the negroes call it). He is laid up & will probably stay so for some time. He has been of very little service lately, sick nearly all the time, a well disposed boy but no judgment. He on the mill [sic] frequently does more harm than good. And as we are sawing a great deal of plank now we are very "weak handed" as the farmers say. So if you can spare us some more force that will do on the yard we can use them profitably. For the last 2 weeks we have sawed constantly & done fine work sawing every night late, 9 o'clock. [. . .] [Mr. Weddle] is [a] restless, discontented man. While I was in town sick his wife got mad with him & all the family, cursed the whole posse. Malvina [a slave] was hanging out clothes. As fast she would hang them out, Mrs. W. would take them and array them about the mill yard, Mr. W. looking at her but afraid to say anything to her. That night she got out of bed, went to a drawer, got a knife, sharpened it, supposing Mr. W. to be asleep and started into the room where her daughter was. Weddle made some noise which stopped her. W. says he did not sleep very satisfactory then all night. She was getting out of bed all night, roaming about the house. He expected that she [would] also burn up the mill. Only his imagination I suppose having had his mill on Muddy Creek burnt up by a crazy man (Christmas). The next day he sent for Doct. White to consult with him about sending her to Lexington. [. . .] His wife suspecting something ran off and stayed all night across the river. [. . .] It would be useless for him to send her to Lex. for as soon as she should get over one of those crazy fits she would [be] pronounced cured & sent back to him. [. . .] His daughter is the most depraved abandoned creature not to be a public prostitute I ever saw. Persons tell her she ought not to be running about the house as she does she says, "She does not care doing just as much as she pleases," all such talk as that. Igo has gone away & has left two young men, strangers, here to attend to the ferry and she goes up frequently after breakfast & stays all day with those men. Thurman told her the other day that he understood that [. . .] a young man whose house she goes to frequently pulled down his britches & run all over the yard & she laughed, did not deny it. [. . .] The only thing that has prevented these rowdies about here from seducing her is that she is such a simpleton. The negroes have become almost ungovernable since my confinement. I have had to inflict very severe punishments upon Dick & Eli. They have left here twice & gone to town Saturday nights, returning Monday morning. Dick works very well. I have so far favored him, but this morning I gave him [a] "severe flogging." They are all very afraid of me. [. . .]

Yours,

David I. Field

As the end of the year approached, David was still having problems. "Mr. W. has requested me to send to you by him," he wrote Brutus, "hoping I suppose that my information in regard to his destitute condition pecuniously & his very unpleasant situation domestically would appeal to your sympathy & compassion. [. . .] Yesterday he talked very freely to me in regard to his wife. He says his patience is completely exhausted, that no man can live with such a 'devil' (his own words) as she, that he has no peace no pleasure when she is about. [. . .] This recent outbreak with him was occasioned by the bacon I brought from your house last week. She said it stunk, that I had picked out the rotten pieces for them to eat. Mr. W. reproved her for it and that made her mad & she abused him very much. This is Mr. W.'s report to me for I have not eaten at the same time with Mrs. W. for several months."

Weddle hoped that Brutus would help him buy a mill on Muddy Creek. He told David that he would remain at Brutus's mill, but his family would live at Muddy Creek. David was doubtful. "I told him that this arrangement would suit me very well, that I was desirous that he should remain but that his family could not stay in the same house with me & where the negroes stayed, that they could occupy the ferry house till a new house could be built, that all I [wanted] was that they should be removed from all *contact* & intercourse with the negroes."

In early December, Elizabeth Holloway wrote Ann that two slaves, Lucy and Nelson, would be "going over to pay you all a visit." Lucy and Nelson were not Brutus's slaves, but they may have had relatives living on the farm. Elizabeth hoped Ann would give Lucy lessons in cooking venison. "I told her when she cooked our saddle, I thought she had forgotten how. She has had no experience in that way this fall. She used the Liquor of the Venison. Mrs. Breck does not. She makes butter gravy. Puts in a great many spices, brandy, etc. I do not like it. Some of the gentlemen admire it. I told Ezekiel [Field] to go there today and get her receipt."

The rest of the letter consisted of tidbits, including news from the Mexican War. "Several of the sick Volunteers have returned. They give Ed [Field] a fine name, say he would share his last cent or piece of bread with any of them. [. . .] Mrs. [Cassius] Clay has returned to the farm. She went over to purchase a Market Wagon. Cousin E. said she was thinking if she went to see her perhaps she would have nothing to eat. [The Cassius Clays were in bad shape financially.] [. . .] Pa rode every step of the way from Lex. in the rain on Wednesday; he says he is very stiff. I wonder it did not kill him. I never saw as hard a rain in my life."

Brutus's 1846 accounts with Field and Holloway, as The Store was then called, show that on February 3, someone purchased half a bushel of dried apples for fifty cents. On April 18, either Ann or Martha bought a bonnet ($5.00), four yards of bonnet ribbon, one-half yard of bonnet lining, a French flower ($1.25), as well as cambric, whalebone, and hooks and eyes. On May 9, linen, gingham, sateen, and numerous buttons. On May 15, more whalebone and ribbon, calico, lace, and a pair of rose clippers ($2.25). Among the more expensive items purchased during the year were a French cape ($18.00), a fine shotgun ($42.00), twenty-four yards of Clermont plaid ($15.00), and sixteen yards of silk ($20.00).

At Shackelford's, a similar establishment in Paris, Brutus's family bought fifty pounds of coffee for $11.50, castor oil, ginger and other spices, raisins, cambric, a kitchen knife, an ax, a hairbrush and a comb cleaner, and numerous buttons, nails, and pins. Occasionally the notations are personal, such as "1 soda for Mr. Field" on January 1 (most likely David, who had come over to talk to Brutus about operating the mills). The soda, probably taken for medicinal purposes, cost twenty-five cents.

David continued to have problems. "Our gangway is nearly all rotten," he wrote Brutus early in 1847. "We will put up gunnels of old boats in their stead. The shute is rotten but if I tell you all the rotten things about the mill I could fill this sheet but the repairing of the gangway is all that keeps us from starting the mill Monday."

He became convinced that Weddle would not last much longer. "I am now well satisfied that he never intended to comply with the contract he made with us," he told Brutus, "and that all his talk about getting away from his family was only a pretext to get where he is & there to stay. After you left here he went home & *told* me he would return in a few days. It was two weeks before he came back. After he came from Cincinnati (where he has been to purchase a fire front & shafts for the log housing wheels) he left immediately for home & told me that he [would] be back about the first of this week. A few days afterwards I received a message from him saying that he did not know when he could come, that his wife was *about to die* (all stuff) & today his son brought this note [now lost]. [. . .] I told him I should immediately inform you of his failure to comply with his contract."

In February, Elizabeth wrote to Ann via Martha, who was returning to Bourbon County, taking her cousin, Pattie Holloway, with her. Pattie appears to have been a difficult child, although her relatives were fond of her. She had trouble reading (dyslexia?), thus did not attend school. "I tell her [Pattie] Eliza [a slave] must learn her how to sew and knit and you must make her keep house," Elizabeth told Ann. "She is so wild it will be a difficult task."

The principal family news was from Christopher in Mississippi. "We got a letter from Brother. He has lost 2 valuable men with cholera. Said C [Charlotte] had got home 6 days before in worse health than he had ever seen her, was confined to her bed. I hope she will soon recover. He wrote very downspirited." William Holloway was leaving soon on his annual buying trip for The Store. "Have you any commands to Phil. [Philadelphia]?"

She concluded, "I will refer you to Martha for the balance of the news. She and Amelia are in the dining room, entertaining some Beaus. [. . .] Tell Mr. Clay Mr. H. says he must come over the last week in March and go to the Narrows [to fish], also Mr. [Charles] Garrard."

David wrote Ann from Lexington, where he had gone to buy tools, that their father was sick again. "I went up to Richmond Wednesday intending to return then. Papa was taken very ill. I remained till Saturday on his account. He was very sick indeed though better when I left. He was taken with a chill, having walked about in the rain for a day or two. He says he never suffered so much with his head, has been taking medicine which had a desirable effect. I would not be surprised if he did not have one of his spells. Sister E. has also been very sick with pneumonia."

A few weeks later Elizabeth and her father were still unwell. Simple illnesses, which were such a large part of people's lives then, were complicated by the fact that there were few medicines with which to treat them — no penicillin, no sulfa drugs, no antibiotics. A cold could easily become pneumonia; an infection could turn septic.

ELIZABETH HOLLOWAY

Richmond, March 5, 1847

Dear Ann,

[. . .] The week after you left I was entirely confined to my bed and the Doct. visiting with insistent cold which severely affected me. I had a violent pain in my head which came on at particular hours. Pa was taken the same day, but more violently, at The Store with a chill. [. . .] The same is going through the town & county. All the ease I had was someone would set by me and apply hot cloths to my head, as hot as they could bear in their hands. [. . .] I have not seen Mary [Field] for 10 days. Sarah Burnam was here this evening, said Pa was there this morning, and she [Mary] had her foot propped up on a pillow, said she could not tell what was the matter. The Doct. thought she had sprained it. She herself thought that there was a needle in it. I asked S.B. if she knew whether Mrs. [Cassius] Clay had been confined. She said yes, several weeks ago, had a son [Brutus Junius Jr.], that there was no one there except Doct. Walker. I feel very much for her. You no doubt have heard the report that Cassius has been taken prisoner by the Mexicans. [. . .] I had received a letter from Charlotte saying she had the idea of coming up immediately to Louisville to see a physician who helped to cure her once [. . .], that she was going alone on a boat, the next day to arrive at her Grandpa's. [. . .] Liz Irvine was here yesterday, says whilst she was in Danville, she picked up a Louisville paper and saw the arrival at the Galt House of C. I. Field & Lady & servants. We have not heard one word and do not know what to think of it. [. . .] I received a letter from Patsey last week. She was staying with Mrs. Miller. They do not think she [Patsey's mother-in-law] will live but a few weeks. [. . .]

Your Sister Elizabeth

News traveled slowly from the war in Mexico. Earlier, David had written Ann of a rumor that Cassius Clay had fought a duel with another Lexington man. This rumor turned out to be true (neither hit the other), but because so many proved false, Mexican War stories were greeted with a certain skepticism in Kentucky. However, the report that Cassius was taken prisoner was also accurate. He and thirty companions had been captured by Mexican cavalry forty-five miles from Buena Vista. They were being held in a monastery in Toluca.

In March, Ezekiel Field sold a farm he owned just outside Richmond to the Whites. The first account of the sale comes in a letter from Martha to Ann. This letter also contains the first reference to Ann and Brutus's only child, my grandfather Cassius Marcellus Clay Jr., born on March 26, 1846. Martha was fourteen years older than her half brother.

MARTHA CLAY

Richmond, March 28, 1847

Dear Aunt,

[. . .] I suppose you have heard Grandpa has sold the farm (on the right hand side of the road coming this way) to Mr. White. The whole family are in arms about it except Uncle David [Field]. [. . .] Cousin Sarah White is very much pleased with the farm, says she had no idea it was such a good-looking place. They are going to build. She says Mr. White is going to get her a yardman to lay off the yard and garden but I reckon it is all talk. They will get possession in May. [. . .] Will [Irvine] has been trying to buy the other part of the farm but he and Grandpa cannot agree as to the price. Liz Stone has got home. I heard she said she had been so much with the aristocrats that she would not know what to do now she has got home with common folks. [. . .] She brought Mrs. W. a box of oranges and lemons and a beautiful net bag.

Liz S. was at church today with a new Leghorn bonnet on that looked large enough for the whole family to get in. [. . .] What is the news in Paris? Who is married and who is dead? I never was more surprised in my life than when I seen [sic] Mr. Alexander's wedding announced in the paper. I did not know he even knew Miss Butler. I suppose he had a fair opportunity then for showing his fine vest Mrs. Spears bought him. Oc-tavius Goodloe died last Friday, was a week [ago] though so I suppose you have heard it. He was buried at his father's. [. . .] David Goodloe [husband of Eliza Smith's daughter, Sally] came over in his rockaway with the corpse. [. . .] Everybody is busy gardening. Aunt Mary planted her peas a few days ago. Mrs. White's are up. Goods wagons are coming in every day. A good many of the merchants have got back. I got me a bonnet off that piece of yellow calico in The Store like Cash's coat. No news from the army that anybody credits. There are a great many ru-mors afloat that our volunteers have had very bad luck. [. . .] My love to all. Write soon.

Martha

[P.S.] You must send Cash and Zeke [Clay] over in my carriage for me to see. I have forgotten how Cash looks. Can he walk? [. . .]

Young Cash grew up to be a precocious little boy but lame, a con-genital handicap no one ever mentioned (I don't think Martha's ques-tion is related to this). The only reference to his lameness I've ever found is an irreverent comment about his lurching gait that his third wife, my grandmother, made in a letter to her mother. As an adult, Cash walked with a cane.

Elizabeth also wrote Ann about the sale of the farm. She was ex-pecting a baby soon, nevertheless entertaining numerous callers.

ELIZABETH HOLLOWAY

Mount Airy, March 29, 1847

Dear Ann,

I have been wanting to write since Mr. Clay was here and have scarcely felt well enough. I would have written by him but had a ner-vous headache the evening before. I suffered a good deal with it just as I did before Mary [Holloway] was born. [. . .] I had 12 calls [visitors] one day, six the next day, I think. None of the ladies thought I had been confined but heard I was very sick. I never felt more benefited in my life. [. . .] I have not seen Pa since you were here. I never was more improved than I was 10 days ago when I heard he had sold his farm to Mr. White. I did not know he had an idea of it. Mary [Field] says he cares nothing about selling it, but Mr. White & Will Irvine was [sic] always urging him to do it. Says David [Field] had a hand in it. He got a fine price. [. . .] I received a letter from Mr. H. yesterday, saying he would not be here before Friday, a few days over 4 weeks. [. . .] He had just returned from New York. Said he found great advantage in going, found the style of dress goods for ladies much handsomer & lower, said I could write you he had bought you there a beautiful dinner sett [sic], very low but you would think it cost a plenty. [. . .]

Pa walked up here this evening [. . .] Pa only sold one side of the wood, 150 acres. [. . .] Will Irvine wants the other side, is not willing to give the price. Or rather Pa wants to exchange with him for some woodland and he is not willing to give the difference. [. . .] I have filled out my parlor if Sarah & her Ma [Holloway] are to live with you. Give my love and tell them I will certainly expect them. Only can't you come? Of late, you write me so short.

Your Sister Elizabeth

Everyone worried about the fate of the Kentucky volunteers. The Fields clearly were more concerned about Edmund than they were about Ann's brother-in-law Cassius. After all, Cassius was in the relative safety of prison, while the others were still fighting battles.

"You mentioned you were so uneasy about Uncle Edmund [Field] that I have concluded to write and give you all the news we have heard," Martha wrote Ann in April. "Uncle Edmund and Tom Turner were in the battle but were not hurt. Mrs. Turner was so uneasy about Tom that Squire Turner sent William all the way to Louisville to get the news. [. . .] It is reported that Vera Cruz and the castle have surrendered but few believe it. I suppose we will hear something today as the stage comes over." Her grandfather had sold the rest of his farm to Will Irvine, Martha added.

She also reported that her uncle had returned from his buying trip. "He brought some beautiful lawns [dress material made of cotton] in his trunk. They are very thin like that one you got here last summer with those beautiful wreaths of flowers. [. . .] He says he bought you a handsome set of china, white, with a wreath of different colored flowers around the edge, I believe. He said there was [sic] 275 pieces. It cost 250$."

Ann thought the set of china William Holloway had bought for her too expensive. Unfortunately, the bill for it has not survived. Nor can I identify the china, though a few plates that might be described as having a "wreath of different colored flowers around the edge" still sit in the cupboards at Auvergne. Obviously, the china was important to Ann, possibly because most of her household goods had belonged to her sister Amelia. This china would be all hers.

Many members of the Field family thought William Holloway lived beyond his means (he was soon to install those silver doorknobs in his renovated house), and Ann's quibbles about the cost of the china may reflect this. Martha advised her to stop complaining.

MARTHA CLAY

Richmond, April 10, 1847

Dear Aunt,

[. . .] Aunt E. said Uncle David [Field] was up the other day. He has received your letter saying you were very much distressed about the cost of your china. I was mistaken in the price. We all misunderstood Uncle William, though I suppose you know the exact price now as he sent you a list of the pieces and prices the other day. Uncle William says he is sorry he bought it now as you are so much dissatisfied. Aunt E. says you kept telling him you wanted a fine set and every time you wrote you would say something about it, so he thought he would get a handsome enough one to suit you. If I was you, I would not say anything about it. Uncle William says it was a very cheap set for the size. He thought he made a great bargain. He brought some lawns. [. . .] There was a beautiful one in The Store that I wanted so bad. I have just found out Martha Whesert got it Saturday. I don't care now what sort of one I get. [. . .] Uncle W. brought beautiful bonnets. They are very thin. Two of them are the most beautiful ones I ever saw. The ribbons are very pretty. Martha Whesert is going to be married Thursday to a Taylor named Halsey. I heard he was going to sell a pistol. He had to raise money for the occasion. I will send you a sample of the dress she got.

[. . .] Aunt Elizabeth sent her watch by Uncle William to swap for some spoons. He got 69$ worth of silver forks for it and bought a good many spoons besides. She made out like she was very mad about it, said she always said she never would use such things, but I think she is very much pleased as a good sign is whenever she talks about them, she can't help from smiling, she is so overjoyed. But I don't want you to go and tell her. She says you must make Pa drive you over in the buggy and sends her love. [. . .] Cousin Sarah [Holloway] says if you come over you can make your nurse [for Cash] ride her horse if you want to, as she promised Cousin Amelia [Holloway] and me the use of it if we would contrive some way to get it over here as we have no horse to go anywhere [. . .] My love to all.

Martha

Even Ann's friend Louisa Keiningham knew about the china. "I beg that you will not open the cask of china until I come out," she wrote, "and then we will make Mr. Clay find time, or rather he will be glad to do it that he may be relieved of the *clatter* of our tongues."

Mary Field sent Ann an account of a recent dinner party, also news of Elizabeth's pregnancy. Giving birth was always a public event.

MARY FIELD

Richmond, April 22, 1847

My Dear Sister,

I have made up my mind to write after waiting so long. [. . .] Patsey has gotten up at last. She came this even. as Mrs. Miller seemed at a stand[still]. [. . .] They do not expect her [Patsey's mother-in-law] to live but a day or two. [. . .] Our town was enlivened by two or three strangers. (Mr. Helm & Lady, also a Miss Breck, a cousin of Pattie White's). I dined out at Mr. Stone's with them on last Saturday. She gave one of the most elegant dinners I ever sat down to. The first course being a new fashionable soup. The next vegetable, the next the cloth was removed for cakes & cream. The next raisins and almonds. Wines of all descriptions. Her napkins were rolled round and tied each one with a different colored ribbon. I was the only one violet of my age. [. . .] After dinner, the waiter [urn] of coffee was lit on the center table, poured out by Lizzie. After we went upstairs to come home, they brought some nuts and candy she made herself the Monday before, the most delightful I had ever tasted. She had finger dishes at every place with orange leaves to flavor your mouth with. Tell Mr. Clay I wish all the time he had been there to enjoy the good things. Coconut pudding and other things. [. . .] We are trying to make up a party to go to the Mammoth Cave the last of this month or the first of next. Won't you and Mr. Clay go with us as we will want someone to keep us straight? [. . .] But we do not think of anything else but the Volunteers coming home. Their time will be soon out. [. . .] We have not heard anything from Ed [Field] lately. He was *not in the Battle*. [. . .] The next time you hear, Sister will have been confined. She keeps up astonishingly. Martha is well, but I rarely ever see her now. I have sent her word to come down here and stay until Sister gets rid of her house full, 4 workmen [the conversion of Mount Airy into Rosehill had probably begun], Aunt H., and her children. I send my love to Mr. Clay and all the children. With love,

Your Sister Mary

Martha wrote to tell Ann that the new baby had been named after her. "They all say it is like Mary but I can't see any resemblance. I have not seen its eyes open yet, no hair on its head. Aunt Elizabeth is tolerable well." Patsey Miller had come up to Richmond to be with her sister. She was still expecting her mother-in-law to die any day.

William Holloway had bought Ann a dress, also trimmings. "The lace is to trim your cape and caps on the sleeves," Martha explained. "Have them made straight and very short, dress very low in the neck and the cape very high, broad round point, cape pointed before, no seam on the shoulder."

The Holloways were still unhappy about Ann's reaction to the china. "Amelia is such a favorite with you I will tell you what she says. She says she would like to know why you always send by her pa for things [. . .] when you never like anything he brings you. She says she expects it is some trouble to her Pa to walk all over the cities to buy the articles and then can't suit you. She made me mad by saying Cash was an ugly flat-nosed thing. Don't you say anything about it. After I went to school, her Ma asked her if she wasn't ashamed to say that about you, said I gave her such a look that she expected I would tell you." Martha concluded, "For gracious sake, don't you say anything more about anything Uncle William brought you."

Word of the china even reached David at the mill. He sent along some gossip about William Holloway, who was sometimes called the Colonel, in a letter to Ann.

DAVID I. FIELD

Lexington, May 2, 1847

Dear Ann,

Dick [a slave] has just got in with our letters, etc. Some 2 or 3 Sabbaths ago, I concluded [. . .] to drive up to town &, on the next, I received your letter. I perused it with my usual care & attention. I must confess saw nothing in it to give offense to the most fastidious & delicate. Had I have discovered anything like[ly] to offend Brother Holloway & his wife, I certainly should not have handed it to him to read. He read it & mentioned who had told you that the plate cost 250$. He said it had not cost so much. I told him that I did not know for it was the first [I had heard] of his having bought anything for you. It is the only time I heard of your fine sett, its cost, and your letter spoken of. I handed the letter to Papa at dinner & have not seen it since. The Col. I suspect was in a bad humor as usual. He has bought too many goods, so Papa says, & I suppose someone has told him so. He and James Hagen concluded to speculate in corn, bought 500 barrels at $1.60. Hagen sent to Louisville & engaged it at $3.25. Corn fell & the men flew. Hagen is now in Louisville with his corn and I suppose would be glad to get the first cost as I believe it is very low. Someone asked Papa what was the Col. staying in Phila. so long for. "Oh," he said, "William he reckons now buying some pretty things to set on his desk & counter." He has bought in Cin. [Cincinnati] some 2 or 3 cast iron urns for holding balls of twine. When they came, no one could tell what they were intended for. [. . .]

[. . .] Your suggestions in your other letter in regard to my marrying were sensible & I fully appreciate them, but I do not think I shall accept them. I do not at present wish to marry. I do not say I *never expect* to marry. I certainly never will bring a wife to this place. My *pride* must have a *fall* first. I intend now to devote myself assiduously to the mill, the engine more especially, & make myself acquainted with [it] so as to be more independent in the carrying on of the establishment. [. . .] Should I ever meet with a lady whom I can & do love, that lady I will make my honorable intentions (maybe I am different from most young

men). I can live to enjoy myself without a helpmate. My disposition &
habits are such that her absence does not inconvenience me in the
least. I do not expect to be an old man [. . .]

D. I. Field

In March, Cassius had written his wife that he hoped to be released
from prison soon. He described his life there as hard, though in his
memoirs, written when he was an elderly man, Cassius viewed his imprisonment through rose-tinted glasses, describing his visits to an eighteen-year-old Indian girl called Lolu and her parakeet, Leta. In order to
visit Lolu, Cassius claimed he disguised himself in a serape and som-
brero, thus passing unnoticed through the streets of Toluca to her house.

Mary Jane Clay sent the letter to Brutus that May, since she worried about discrepancies between her husband's optimistic predictions
and events that had happened since he wrote. "I want to know what
you think about the prisoners being detained," she begged Brutus. "I
cannot think, think for me."

A month later, Brutus himself heard from Cassius. "We are on parole, confined by the bounds of the City, and, except that we are
continually liable to assassination by the 'greasers,' or common people, we spend our time very agreeably. Living in this City is higher than
in any place in the world and, in consequence, we are somewhat
troubled to get the means of support. [. . .] I suppose the country now regards this war as no trifle — ruinous — if not infamous. Can any man
tell me why all this expenditure of blood and money? Have we not
land enough? Do we want eight millions of revolutionary Indians and
half breed[s], to increase the difficulties of the elective franchise and
the stability of the Union? Surely this administration will have a heavy
load of responsibility to carry. I hope they will everywhere be defeated."

In August, Brutus took Ann to the Blue Licks Springs, the popular
spa to which they had considered going with the Keininghams during
their courtship. The Licks in nearby Nicholas County had been a
source of salt for men and animals since prehistoric times. Daniel
Boone had been captured by the Shawnee while gathering salt at the
Licks in 1778 and with other early white settlers took part in a major
battle there four years later. The resort, which straddled a horseshoe
bend in the Licking River, included two salt wells, a white sulphur
spring, and a frame hotel capable of accommodating six hundred

guests. Board for six days, three baths in the spring, and quarters for a servant and two horses cost Brutus twenty-four dollars.

Meanwhile, in Mississippi, Christopher's wife had given birth to a child, Orville Martin Field. At the end of a November business letter to Brutus, Christopher wrote, "My wife's health is better than when in Ky. but not good. Our boy is fat & hearty generally. We would be pleased to have a visit from you all this winter. Our crop is not good and prices here declined nearly 1/2 in 6 weeks from 11 to 6 cents with a downward tendency. It makes a man who is in debt have the blues. My wife joins me in love to you all."

David finally got rid of George Weddle and hired a new millwright. Whatever Weddle's shortcomings, by 1861 he had come up in the world sufficiently to be listed in a Lexington business directory as "Geo. Weddle, Millwright and Miller."

"I succeeded in seeing Mr. Shiddell this day," David wrote Brutus. "I [. . .] hired him for 2 weeks at $2 per day at the expiration of which time we will make some arrangement for the balance of the season. [. . .] I succeeded Tuesday in hauling one log up into the mill & that was all I could do as the Band was too loose & would not stay on the drums. Shiddell came out the next day & found several things out of fix & not right. The Cylinder was not in line & the cogs were not adjusted. Weddle I think had not known how to do it."

In late September, Cassius Clay and other prisoners were sent to Tampico, where he and two other captains were exchanged for two Mexican generals, but he did not reach Kentucky until December. Mary Jane wrote urging Brutus and Ann to come to Lexington to meet him. A few days later, on December 9, Brutus's stepfather, Jeptha Dudley, wrote, "With the brightest degree of pleasure, I announce the arrival of Capt. C. M. Clay at my house at 12 o'clock this day, where he met his wife and four sons."

Cassius's Mexican War experiences won him considerable goodwill in Kentucky. He was widely eulogized and treated to numerous congratulatory dinners. With the presidential campaign of 1849 coming up, Cassius hoped to capitalize upon his newfound support. The first thing he did was to attack the local Whig Party, turning on his kinsman Henry Clay. He was not the only Whig to do so, either in Kentucky or nationwide, and the party soon split into those who wanted to nominate Henry Clay for the presidency and those who feared Clay could not be elected and thus supported Mexican War

hero General Zachary Taylor. Taylor eventually won the party's nomination, but somewhat surprisingly, Cassius did not take much of a role
in the ensuing campaign.

In Richmond, politics were far from the minds of the Field sisters.
Elizabeth Holloway was worried about Martha Clay's health.

ELIZABETH HOLLOWAY

Mount Airy, April 18, 1848

Dear Ann,

[. . .] I was at Mr. Miller's last week. [. . .] Went down on Saturday
and stayed until Monday. I was nearly dead when I got there. The roads
were so bad. She [Patsey] has a fine large baby [Julia]. [. . .] Martha has
looked very badly for some time. Last Tuesday, a week tomorrow, she
came home from school sick. Headache, fever. I gave her an emetic.
She thought it would relieve her head. She has not been to school
since, has a wretched cough, no appetite. Yesterday, I got so uneasy I
sent for the Doct. Before I sent, I inquired of her as regards her Monthly
Courses. She has not been as she should be since she came home
Christmas. Doct. McKee says she must not go to school until she is well
and must go through a course of Medicine. I think I shall send to Mrs.
Gentry to make her Medicine. Emma & M. Turner have taken it from
her. I know there are a great many girls who are often as Martha is, but
her cough is alarming. She rode out yesterday and this evening she rode
to her Grandpa's. I have borrowed Harry for her to ride every day. She
has just got home. I asked her what to tell you. She says she will be well
in a few days. I hope she may. She was in bed nearly all last week. [. . .]
You want to know about my party. I was saving cream for several days
before Mary [Field] came home, intending giving her a party. Me and
Mr. H. came on Friday and he heard in Paris [the] Col. would be here
on Monday. I postponed it until he came. I invited all the girls in town
and my married friends. There were not more than 12 ladies and a few
more gentlemen. Some were sick, others afraid of the mud holes,
etc. [. . .] The girls helped me make the Cake and Martha iced the
Cake. She is certainly the most handy neat girl of her age I ever saw.
Your centerpiece was beautiful. [. . .] Mary [Field] has a very devoted
Beau, Lieut. Walker, who is stationed here on recruiting service. Very
fine looking, agreeable, etc. He calls about twice a day. He got here the
next stage after she did, will be here a month. [. . .] Several young men

of this place went to College with him. [. . .] Edmund [Field] said when he came Lieut. Walker was more for recruiting a wife than volunteers. [. . .] I have put nearly all my seed in the ground. We will have a quantity of fruit. Patsey has the finest strawberry bed I have seen for a great while and the cleanest of weeds [. . .] I wish you were here to have your miniature taken. [. . .] Everybody is going deranged on the subject. Mr. H. wants me to go down and have mine and the three youngest. I tell him I can't afford it. Cousin May Turner and Cyrus [Turner] have had them on the same plate. Emma has had taken 2 different ones and can't get a good one. [. . .] Martha had made you some very pretty [quilt] squares and would have made more the first of last week, but I thought it made her head ache. In haste,

Your Sister Elizabeth

Martha did not get better, so the Holloways wrote the Clays a joint letter.

WILLIAM AND ELIZABETH HOLLOWAY

Richmond, April 24, 1848

Dear Sir,

All have felt much concern for the last 8 or 10 days in account of Martha and yesterday I had determined [to] write for you and Ann to come over immediately. She remains very much as she was when Elizabeth wrote, no worse and no perceptible improvement. Yesterday Dr. McKee who has been waiting on her for the last 10 days told me he thought it was possible her lungs were affected; today I took up Dr. Letcher to see her and he assures us such is not the case and thinks he can relieve her. He will alter the course of treatment on some measure and I hope we will in a few days advise you of a change for the better. She is quite weak yet has agreeable pulse and some fever at night, with an ugly day cough. [. . .] I will leave the balance of the sheet to Elizabeth to fill out.

With regard,

Wm. Holloway

Dear Ann, I tell Mr. H. he will alarm [you] much from [. . .] his [account of] Martha's illness. She has been very sick. I have not considered her ill. If I had I should have certainly sent for you and her Pa. [. . .] She has never been in bed but one day. She has no appetite. She has not eaten enough for the last week to keep her alive I think. I told the Doct. I thought she ought to force something down. He said no, if she does not want to eat it would do her no good. [. . .] I told her I was going to write to you and must I tell you and her Pa to come. She said no. I think she is afraid if you come now you will not [come] to the [Emma's] wedding. [. . .] She is no trouble to me. I find it a pleasure to wait on her and I infer her staying here she is more convenient to the Doct. He does not give her but little medicine, pills at night and [. . .] some drops for the cough. [. . .] I will write by the next mail. [. . .]

In haste, your sister,

Elizabeth

Whatever was the matter with Martha, she must have responded to Dr. Letcher's treatment, since her sickness is not mentioned again. In an age when women frequently complained of "spells," Martha had a remarkably robust constitution all her life.

On a happier note, A. V. Bedford, a Bourbon County neighbor, sent Brutus word of a fishing trip he was planning. Fishing was a favorite pastime for the men of the family. Brutus belonged to a Bourbon County fishing club, formed in the 1830s, whose charter members included William Holloway, Brutus's cousin Charles Garrard, and several neighbors.

In one of my grandmother's photograph albums, there are pictures of my grandfather, Cash, and one of his sons fishing in the mill pond at Auvergne. Cash wears a frock coat and an odd straw hat resembling an inverted salad bowl. The little boy is barefoot. Cash's patient horse dozes between the shafts of the buggy.

The barefoot boy may be my father. He said he liked fishing, though I was never convinced of this in spite of seeing many snapshots of him as a grown man standing triumphantly beside marlins he had caught. He took my brother and me out into the Gulf Stream on deep-sea fishing trips, but there wasn't much joy in these excursions, just sunburn and seasick children. I don't remember fishing in one of the farm ponds with him, as he and Uncle John did with my grandfather.

Outside my bedroom door at the farm stood a curio cabinet containing, among other oddities, the jaws of several "clever sized bass." A tag attached with a piece of blue ribbon identified one as "head of big mouth bass caught by CMC Jr. in the mill pond June 1912 [. . .] the largest bass ever caught on the place." My favorite was a Goliath of a fish head. "This catfish," the tag reads, "was caught by Hon. B. J. Clay at the Rapids of Rockcastle River, on a small hook and line, while fishing for suckers for bait. He ran across river & stopped under a big rock and it required an hour or more to land him. He weighed 90 lbs. CMC Jr."

"Edwin came by this evening on his way home and learning from Matt Clay that we were to start in the morning to advise against going up to the mouth of Holly," A. V. Bedford wrote Brutus in 1848. "He says the hole at Brush Creek is as deep but not so long as at Holly; the water was so clear he could see his minnow & could see clever sized bass come up and pinch at the bait and not take hold. They caught some few small fish. Charles is here and says we will meet you at the meeting house at sunrise and he advises and expects you to carry a gun; and the subject of a change of destination will be the subject of a general consultation."

In the fall, Mary sent Ann all the Richmond gossip. "I have been greatly grieved at a piece of intelligence received a few days since that the handsome friend [Lt. Walker] was to be married to Miss Matthews. I suppose there is no doubt of it. [. . .] I spent the day at Col. White's last week in connection [*sic*] with Belle Rodes, Pauline Smith [both Brutus's nieces], Mary Turner, Amelia White and Mrs. Bean. If you had have seen Belle Rodes that day you would have been struck with her beauty. [. . .] Curran Smith [Brutus's nephew] is in love with Mary Turner. I met him coming out of there dressed more beautifully than I ever saw him and I spent the night with Mary Wednesday and who should be ushered in but C. Smith. Mary looked for him in the even. [. . .] I told her I would leave them alone so as to give her a chance but lo! he brought Will Stone over. I had to stay to entertain him. [. . .] Cyrus Turner walked home with me yesterday from Church." Making fun of her headlong style of letter writing, she concluded, "I know you will laugh immoderately at this letter but have sat down with the quite determined notion of giving you the news *en masse*."

Belle Field was seventeen, a little older than her cousin Martha. In November, she wrote her sister Mary, who was visiting in Bourbon County, a letter full of giggly news about beaux.

BELLE FIELD

Monday Evening (Nov. 7, 1848)

Dear Mary,

I am just upon the eve of starting for Silver Creek with E. [Elizabeth Holloway] & Martha. Patsey came up with them to have her teeth operated upon by Doctor Brown on Friday. [. . .] Shelby [Irvine] has not received one word of intelligence from Walker [Mary's "handsome friend"] since you left as I told you I knew he would. But suffice it to say he is enjoying *matrimonial bliss* at this time as word reached Richmond he was married. I have thought so little of it myself & scarcely thought it worth my while to write to you. [. . .] We attended a delightful dance at Mr. Stone's Friday. Everybody you could think of was there. You were invited. [. . .] Tell Ann I will answer her letter when I get back. I will be gone only a day or two. She must be sure to come over to the venison feast. [. . .] It is getting very late and Mr. Miller will be ready to start in a few minutes. You must be sure to answer this by return mail. [. . .] You must present my respects to Mr. Sidney Clay [Brutus's nephew] and my love to Ann. [. . .] Shelby says he does not care if Martha never writes to him. [. . .] Write soon and do better and be more communicative. [. . .]

Belle Field

Four years after Ann's wedding, the Field family remained much as they had been. The married sisters had a few more children. Ann had a son. Christopher had a wife and child. The rest of the Fields continued to be based at the family home on West Main Street. Martha Clay lived there most of the time, too, although her younger brothers remained in Bourbon County. Her father, Brutus, is a bit shadowy during these years, mentioned in letters but seldom heard from directly and overshadowed by the exploits of his flamboyant brother.

THREE

Everything Looks Gloomy

In 1849, an epidemic of cholera broke out in central Kentucky. In the nineteenth century, cholera was a periodic threat wherever there was poor sanitation, which was almost everywhere. Not until 1883 was the organism that causes it identified. Before then, no one understood that the disease was spread by tainted food and water; people blamed a variety of causes, including an excess of fresh vegetables. (Elizabeth Holloway cautioned Ann Clay against eating potatoes.) Because of its short incubation period — two or three days — cholera spread quickly. There were frequent epidemics.

Cholera still kills. Its victims die from dehydration caused by violent bouts of diarrhea and vomiting. Although today the disease can be treated by the intravenous replacement of body fluids, and the death rate can be as low as 5 percent, untreated cholera during epidemics can still kill as many as 90 percent of its victims. While I was working on this book, people were dying of it in the refugee camps just over the border from Rwanda. I would see their emaciated faces on television and think of Isham, the Fields' coachman, who collapsed and died in a stable at Estill Springs.

These letters begin with another potentially fatal disease, scarlet fever. Patsey Miller was worn out from nursing even before the cholera epidemic began. Things were not going well in Mississippi either. In July Christopher's son died. Charlotte returned to Kentucky, where she gave birth to a daughter on November 22, 1848.

A few days later, David Field wrote Ann from Louisville about the baptism of his newest niece, Patsey Amelia Field. By this time, David had given up the management of the mills and was helping Christopher in Mississippi. "I have just got here from Miss.," he told Ann, "Charlotte still very low. Her friends would not be surprised at her death at any hour. They have thought she was dying several times but has revived and is generally very cheerful. When I took leave of her she said she would like to see you all. The baby was baptized yesterday afternoon. She also took the sacrament and I suppose considers herself a member of the Episcopal Church. A few of the relatives were present & myself." He concluded with a bit of family news. Their brother Edmund had been toying with the idea of going to California to pan for gold but had decided not to do it.

Belle wrote Ann that she hoped to go to Frankfort to see President-elect Zachary Taylor, who was visiting there.

BELLE FIELD

November 1848

Dear Sister,

As Martha [Clay] will start so soon in the morning, I will write you a line or two. [. . .] We all were very glad to see Zeke [Clay], but much disappointed that the other boys [Kit and Green] did not come with him. [. . .] He has not looked well since he came but says the cause of it was riding in the carriage. They were so very unfortunate as to lose one of your very valuable carriage horses. I know it will be a great loss to you all. I regret very much indeed that Martha has to leave as she has been with me for so long, but she will be so much company for you. I tell her I will make her a visit in two or three months, provided she will return with me. [. . .] I presume you would like to go down to Frankfort & to see *General Taylor*. I thought I had succeeded in getting Pa in the notion of going down and taking me, but he says he thinks he cannot go as there will be such a vast concourse of people assembled there to behold the President Elect. Pa has been complaining for a day or two past. He remarked that he was afraid he was going to be sick as he felt so bad and lost his appetite, has looked very bad today, but I do hope he will be well in a day or two. I persuaded him not to go to The Store this evening. [. . .] We received a letter from Brother [Christopher] the other day. There was only one case of *cholera* on his plantation at the time he wrote, he said. Charlotte's health very bad indeed. [. . .] Tell Cash [Clay] I sent him the crackers. Martha told me it was not worthwhile as she would stop in Lexington and get some, but I was afraid she would forget so I sent him a *Bunch*. [. . .] The Methodists have been carrying on in protracted meetings for several days but they were not very successful. The Presbyterians also had [a] meeting which lasted two or three days. [. . .] I have a very nice piece of satin and I told Martha I intended to trouble you a little to make me a pin cushion when you were at your leisure. [. . .] I had a hint the other day that a wedding would take place soon and I always intended to make the Lady in question a Bridal present whenever it did occur. I believe there are no other contemplated weddings spoke of as yet. Well, I must close as I have well nigh consumed my paper. And moreover I will refer you to Martha and Pa for the news. Make Martha write to me as soon as she gets home. She's so good at promises but rarely performs. Yours affectionately,

Bell [*sic*]

Belle wrote Ann again a short time later. She had been left behind while Mary attended a wedding in Frankfort.

BELLE FIELD

Jan. 4, 1849, Cedar Grove

My Dear Sister,

As I am very lonely, I will while away the dull tedium of an hour by writing to you though I am at a loss to find what to write at present as the town is well nigh deserted owing to a great many having gone down to Frankfort. [. . .] However, I will endeavor to make myself as entertaining as possible, as you will know I am never at a loss for gab or gossip. For you must remember [. . .] Dame Nature has lavished the gift of gab very profusely upon me. Cousin Sarah [Holloway] & Mary [Field] made their departure on last Wednesday and rather promised to return on Monday. At least Aunt Holloway wished Cousin S. to come back at that time. We will expect them on Monday as Mary officiates as bridesmaid to A. Miller. [. . .] *The young people are anticipating much pleasure.*

(Monday morning) [. . .] I again resume pen, ink, and paper (you have doubtless observed that this was commenced last week) for the purpose of detailing to you the proceedings of the past weeks. It will prove of some interest to you as you cannot be among the many participants. Had the bridal party. [. . .] Misses Pendleton, Logan, Graham, and Mrs. Bacon, some of them can boast much of beauty. It is true Miss Graham is rather fine looking and is said to be remarkably intelligent and agreeable. The young men have it whispered among them that they have come for husbands. Mrs. Bacon I understand is smitten with David [Field]. But I see he is perfectly indifferent to her *many charms and attractions*; as you know he would require a great deal of *perseverance* [. . .] *Shelby Irvine* is perfectly carried away with Miss Graham. Miss Pendleton said to be sighing for John. [. . .] In the midst of all the gaiety & jolliness Mrs. Turner's death occurred on last Monday. Doctor Harris assured them that she was in no danger whatever and I suppose they never expected such a tragedy [. . .] the family thought she was much better that morning and one of them went to her and she was just taking her last breath. [. . .] We have had our dresses made up. They are begging me to have two flounces and I saw how beautiful Martha's looked. Her dress was much admired indeed. It was white tarleton with two flowers each flounce, with red ribbon. Her body is black velvet, the prettiest velvet body I ever saw. Red velvet's all the rage. Amelia [Holloway] has three flounces with no ribbons and I have two with red ribbon. We all came out in them at the Grand Ball, also Uncle David's dance that he gave [. . .] Miss Mary [Field] says she went to Frankfort for the express purpose of catching Mr. Thomas [brother of Ann's friend, Louisa Keiningham] but failed entirely. [. . .] I hope Mr. Sidney Clay is not yet married. If not [married], present my respects to him. [. . .]

I will close as I have told you all. [. . .]

Belle

By February, Martha was back in Bourbon County. Belle wrote Ann a chatty letter full of speculation about young men, her principal interest at the time. Ann and Martha had both been to Frankfort for the president-elect's visit.

BELLE FIELD

Feb. 19, 1849

Dear Ann,

I have at length arrived at the conclusion that you do not intend responding to my poor and unworthy note so I will write another. [. . .] Martha has treated me in the same manner. When she left, I extorted a promise of her that she would write immediately after she reached home. But so much for her promise. Richmond has been quite gay for several days past on account of Mrs. Gilbert's marriage. Mrs. Bourne gave a large party last Monday evening. It was very delightful. She had a beautiful table and everything to please the eye and delight the palate. [. . .] The young gentlemen gave a dance at the tavern. The Ladies of the Presbyterian Church design having a fair Thursday night though I fear there will not be many in attendance as the young gentlemen declared when our fair came off, that that was the last fair they would ever attend. [. . .] Pa received a letter from Edmund [Field]. He had resolved to go to California, the gold region. He wrote he would bring the negroes to Louisville and perhaps he might bring them on home. David says he has no notion of going. It is just an excuse to get home. I do not know what in the world will become of him as he will not stick to anything for any length of time. [. . .] And so you and Martha went down to Frankfort. Mrs. Addison White said she seen Martha when she left here. I was extremely anxious to go and thought that I had succeeded in obtaining Pa's consent to go down. His excuse was that the weather was too cold for him, consequently I was prevented from making the anticipated trip. Well, I suppose General Taylor came up to your expectations or that he far exceeded them! Tell Martha she must write to me and give me a full description of his visit and tell me who she seen [sic] and above all who she fell in love with. Ask her if Mr. *Moore was there*. Tell her Mr. White *my old beau* and the one I gave her has been to see me several times since she left. He tells me to present his very best respects to her. [. . .] I have been begging David to take me over when he goes but he says he will take *the churn* so there will be no room for me. [. . .] You must write me that receipt for making ginger cakes. Pa says he never has tasted any to match the one you sent him so you must send it. [. . .] And I understand Mr. T. Bedford is soon to be married. That is not very cheering intelligence to me. But I know that, if I am invited, I shall certainly accept so, if they do not want me, they must not invite me. Ask M. if she is making any friends for my behalf in another quarter. Tell her I am doing lots for her. I reckon you think I had better write to Martha myself and not send so many messages through you. [. . .] There is a young lady visiting Judge Breck's from Versailles, Miss Isetta. She has created a tremendous sensation. She dances beautifully and is extremely wild and Mischievous. I dare say Mrs. Breck will be very much mortified when she returns home as she has been guilty of a great many imprudences during her absence. Belle Rodes is at home for the winter, looking as transcendentally beautiful as ever. She is half crazy to go down to Frankfort. She has a white bonnet and beautiful blue feather boa and muff. [. . .]

Belle

In March, Elizabeth wrote Ann that Patsey's youngest baby, Julia, was ill with scarlet fever. "Patsey was very unhappy about her. She and Mr. Miller had lost a great deal of sleep. Lizzy [another daughter] was very unwell, was taken with the disease. I expect it will go through the family."

Elizabeth was also worried about Christopher's wife and daughter. "I wrote to Mr. Martin [Charlotte's grandfather] that we had not heard from Brother and if the babe was living. We did not hear from C. for 2 weeks before she left Louisville. I thought the child might have died in that time. I hope it is living. It might be a great comfort to Brother tho I know he can't keep it and I don't know who will." Elizabeth assumed Charlotte, whose health had been precarious before the baby's birth, was already dead. "I sympathize with Brother from the bottom of my heart. I could not feel more grieved at the death of any relative. [. . .] She [Charlotte] had as few faults or fears as any of us. I would like to see the person that has no faults. I always said there should be allowance made for her, her health was so bad and she had nothing else all her life and it was enough to make any of us fretful and ill-natured. I don't say she had a bad temper. I think she was very affectionate."

Before Elizabeth could mail her letter, word arrived from Charlotte's grandmother that Charlotte, alive but ill, had insisted on rejoining Christopher in Mississippi. "She said when May Martin came up from there [Mississippi] there was a number of deaths from the bout of cholera and they were afraid to go, but go she [Charlotte] would. [. . .] Her grandpa scolded, her friends reasoned. She said if her husband died with cholera she wanted to die, too. She said they made every effort for her [Charlotte's] comfort. [. . .] Said he [Christopher] was such a devoted nurse. She was afraid he would injure himself if she continued ill for a length of time. She said Brother had become very dear to them as she thought there were few such men in this world of Sin and Temptation. She said when she last heard of the babe it was doing well with its black Mammy."

Elizabeth continued the same letter the next day. David Field had left for Mississippi to see if he could help his brother. The Fields clearly feared Christopher might have cholera even though Uncle David Irvine had gotten a letter, dated February 12, saying that, while Charlotte was "low," Christopher and the slaves were well.

Finally the Fields got a letter from Christopher, too. "I will write you what he says about C.," Elizabeth told Ann. "Says she returned home [Bolivar County] 4 weeks ago quite weak and feels worse every day, is not able to turn herself in bed, has had bowel complaint for 8 weeks and it has now become chronic. I fear she will never recover from it. She is very low spirited and weak. And has no one to nurse her except myself [Christopher]. [. . .] In the last of the letter he says a few days ago I received a letter from one of Toffer's [a Mississippi planter] neighbors and informed me he had been murdered by the boy he got from Mr. Boyce last Sunday and in attempting to take off, he [the slave] jumped in the river and drowned. He said it was the worst county in the state to live in and he had thought since he would rather live in Illinois on 40 acres and earn his bread from the labor of his own hands."

Belle also sent Ann a letter written over a period of several days. It includes an account of a practical joke played on an admirer of Brutus's beautiful niece, Belle Rodes.

BELLE FIELD

March 3, 1849

Dear Ann,

[. . .] I determined immediately after breakfast to sit down and write as I fear you are already fretted at me for not sending those pieces of muslin you wrote for. But I came home from Silver Creek and found Green [Clay] here. I felt so fatigued and *sore* that I could scarcely move myself. It was really such a task to ride over those dreadful roads. [. . .] Green, the moment he ate his dinner, was impatient to make his departure. And this morning, just as I had prepared my writing materials to write you a right nice letter. [. . .] I heard the knocker. Mrs. Payne Turner & Will Stone were announced. I still continued to write a line or two, not thinking *Miss Belle* was called for. But Lucinda [a slave] soon assured me to the contrary and then I had just got into a mood for discussing Miss Belle Rodes' numerous charms, attractions, and accomplishments as I knew full well what kind of conversation would delight Mr. Stone. [. . .] Before Mr. Stone left, Lt. Dunlop was *ushered* in and, after they made their departure, Doctor Green Miller and [. . .] Ann Williams came to return Mary's call. [. . .] I was asking Mr. [Henry] Grady if he seen Martha. I told him this was her first visit to Frankfort though still a *school young lady* and expected to resume her studies again in a few months. I told him she was quite young. [Martha was seventeen, only a year younger than Belle.] He said she did not look so and that he would have supposed she had turned out 2 years or three ago. I think I will let her get out of this first before I make my debut into the gay world. Thompson Field was to see us the other day. He came home expecting to obtain his father's and mother's consent for him to go to California. [. . .] He says he knows Ed [Field] will not go without him [. . .] I think he is very much pleased with Belle Rodes. When Henry Grady came, Will Stone told him he had a formidable rival in Richmond. He asked who it was, he told him it was Doctor *Peacock*, a talented young physician of much promise, and that he was decidedly the most elegant and refined gentleman in the town, that he was dandy of the day and leader of the fashion. The joke was carried on for a day or two, he not dreaming for an instant that he was duped. He mentioned to every lady he called on, and they understood it directly. [. . .] I was quite lavish in his praise. He then went out to see Belle and began to talk to her about her devoted beau. She at first laughed at it, but in the end she became very mad. He then found out there was no truth in it. [. . .] Mr. [Cyrus] Turner has returned home. He has been to see Cousin Sarah [Holloway]. He told Cousin Sarah Cousin Robert [her brother] was desperately in love with a Miss Wood from Frankfort. Aunt Holloway hoots at the bare mention of such a thing. She says he must not think of the girls until he graduates. [. . .] Sister says she thinks she displayed so much courage in going over those dreadful Silver Creek roads that she and me must get on our horses and ride over to see you. [. . .]

Belle

David Field wrote his father from Mississippi that Christopher was not ill, as they had supposed.

DAVID I. FIELD

Mississippi, March 19, 1849

Dear Papa,

A young gentleman, Mr. Offutt of Shelbyville, is here waiting for a boat and I will avail myself of the opportunity to write you. [. . .] I was agreeably surprised to find Brother perfectly well, had not been sick, and says he has written to Richmond every week since Charlotte has been sick. [. . .] Brother left here yesterday for his plantation and expects to return today or tomorrow and will start up with Charlotte [to Kentucky] and I will remain on the plantation till he returns. The river is very high [. . .] the whole lower country is overflowed. It is rising here one inch in 24 hours. If Brother's levee breaks, I will not stay here as he will make no crop in that event. It has been so wet that he has been unable to do much work on the plantation and is about six weeks behind hand.

Charlotte is very low and I do not suppose will ever get well. She is [. . .] very irritable, has fallen out with everybody and everything, says she does not mean to get well and threatens sometimes that [. . .] she will destroy herself, gets mad with Brother and tells him that she wishes he would go away and never come back. I have been out of patience with her myself at hearing her talking to him. [. . .] I think she is better since she has been here, is more cheerful, is stronger and eats more. She is very helpless, has no use of her feet or legs, can sit up while her bed is made up. She had a bad cough and has copious sweats at night, followed by chills.

[. . .] Brother will stay in Louisville only a day or two, is anxious to return. [. . .]

He lost his best boy, yellow Dan [. . .] a few days before I came. Although he was at first of the opinion that the negro died of cholera but has his doubts now. If a negro has a bad [. . .] complaint it is called cholera though it matters not what they call it. In some instances it kills very suddenly. This is a desperate country at Brother's. [. . .] In going home yesterday, he had to ride up to Col. Perkins', 4 miles, then take a skiff about 5 miles, and get on a levee and walk the balance of the distance, 7 miles home. Charlotte has fallen out with the baby, says it looks like the Fields and is ugly, hardly ever notices it, and says I am [. . .] proud of it because it is named after Mama, is like the family. It looks like Orville [Anderson, a relative of Charlotte's], is a remarkably good child. It is now suckled by one of May M.'s women. I have promised her to adopt the child and it shall inherit my fortune. When I found that Brother was not sick, I expected to return in a short time and that is the reason I have not written home in regard to my own plans. I will go up to the plantation in a few days and, if the river is down so I can ride through, I will return here when Orville Anderson and wife return. Yours affectionately,

D. I. Field

[P.S.] Charlotte has just waked up and sends her love to you all and says that she does not feel as well this morning as she has done for weeks and that she had a very bad night last night.

In late March, Patsey wrote Ann about her family's protracted bout with scarlet fever.

PATSEY MILLER

March 21, 1849, Silver Creek

My Dear Sister,

I received your letter sometime since and would have answered it sooner but for the continued sickness of our family. [. . .] Julia was the first one that was taken with something like scarlet fever and was the last to get well. They were all sick but Martha. Several of the negroes have been sick with the same. Mr. M. was very sick for a week, he is now well. Julia was very sick for three weeks, has made her first attempt to walk alone today. The swellings have not gone from her throat yet. Her throat had to be lanced on one side which hurt a great deal. What a distressing disease scarlet fever is. I thought for some days she would not get well. There was [sic] three weeks I did not know what it was to sleep two hours any night. [. . .] Martha and Elizabeth are giving me a great many messages for Patty [Pattie Holloway was staying with Ann Clay]. They say they would have been delighted to have been with her to see you. We have not been so fortunate yet as to procure a teacher.

M. and E. are quite anxious to start to school. I do not know what we will do with them if we do not get a teacher. [. . .] Tell Cash [Clay] Amelia [Miller] talks a great deal about him and [it] still affronts her very much when she calls him Brother for the children to tell her he is only her cousin. She is begging me very often to let her go to see you. She wants to go to school when the school begins but she is too small [she was five]. [. . .] Tell Cash Amelia has now a little pet chicken in the house. She thinks as much of it as if it was gold. It is a busy time now with housekeeping, turkeys to attend to, hens to set, gardening, spinning, etc. etc. I feel as if it had been a long time since I was in town, but I don't see much prospect of getting there shortly. The roads are almost impassable. [. . .] You speak in your letter to Sister of Eliza's [a slave] not being well. She will be a considerable loss to you as a seamstress. [. . .] Cousin E. Jones gives Eliza such a name that I would like to own her if she was not so old, as Edmund [Field] has so soon gotten out of the notion of needing a servant. I was very sorry to hear that he had become dissatisfied and had an idea of going to California. He will be sick of that trip. We have various accounts of that country, gold not near so pretty as represented by some. I suppose you have never got your [. . .] churn Mr. M. started to you. I see a glowing description of a new one just imported to Lexington. I was so much amused at the representation at the head of the advertisement to see the little old drawn-up negro [. . .] his coat and hat laid off as if for hard work and a chair by as much as to say he should have to rest and no butter in three hours and at the same time there sits the little white girl showing her plate of butter gotten in 5 minutes. [. . .] I was very sorry I forgot that rose bush you gave me. You must send it to me if there is any way. I expect now it will get to Richmond before I do. [. . .] Give my love to Martha. I was sorry for her to leave Richmond without coming to see me. If she goes off to school, I may not get to see her for a great while, but I suspect the beaus will tell Martha that she is smart enough with[out] a New York school. [. . .]

Patsey I. Miller

On April 24, Charlotte Field died. She was eventually buried in the Field plot in the Richmond cemetery. The baby, Pattie, went to live with her grandfather and unmarried aunts. "The Baby is not very well," Mary wrote Ann Clay in May. "She kept me awake all last night. I suppose she is teething [. . .] Pa helps me nurse a great deal. He came up last night and got her to sleep. I could do nothing with her. She

ought to have the best kind of management — someone that under-
stands attending to children."

It's strange to me how people such as Charlotte die with almost no
mention in these letters, and others become the subjects of a litany of
love and regret. I suppose Charlotte's in-laws had been expecting her
to die for such a long time that the end may have been something of
an anticlimax. Death was an accepted part of the continuum of life. In-
fants pass in and out of the Fields' lives with almost no mention: Charlotte's first baby, and several of Elizabeth Holloway's children. It was
not that they were not mourned; they were, often quite elaborately. A
photograph album at Auvergne contains a picture of a nameless baby,
its eyes tightly closed, who died in Texas. But everyone accepted that
a certain number of people such as Charlotte and those babies would
not live long. Other deaths, particularly those of young vigorous men,
were unacceptable. One such death occurred in Madison County on
June 15, 1849.

In June, Brutus's brother Cassius set out on an antislavery speaking
tour. The Kentucky legislature had repealed an 1833 law restricting
the importation of slaves into the state, then issued a call for a constitutional convention to write a new proslavery constitution. Cassius
and other emancipationists foresaw the possibility of an alarming increase in the state's slave population and campaigned against the constitutional convention. Before setting out on the campaign trail,
Cassius armed himself with a bowie knife and a brace of pistols.

At Foxtown, a small settlement in Madison County not far from
his home, Cassius followed a proslavery speaker named Squire Turner,
a neighbor of the Fields', on the podium. While he was speaking, a
young lawyer who had his own grudge against Cassius, a matter concerning some school bonds, pushed his way forward. Cassius misunderstood what the young man was saying and accused him of being Squire
Turner's "tool." At that point, Turner's son, Cyrus, hearing his father so
insulted, stepped out of the crowd and called Cassius a liar. Cassius
drew his bowie knife and they began to fight. When the melee ended,
Cassius was stabbed in the chest, but he had mortally wounded Cyrus
Turner in the abdomen. Both men were carried to a nearby house
where, after ten hours of agony, young Turner died. Cassius recovered
slowly, nursed by members of his family.

Because of episodes such as this, Cassius Clay became a folk hero in Kentucky. His explosive behavior was the subject of a whole literature of stories circulated (and embroidered upon) by a Lexington raconteur, William H. Townsend, during the 1950s. A record of Townsend's recounting the bloody deeds of Cassius Clay was a best-seller throughout Kentucky. An awkward teenager, I often entertained dancing partners at cotillions by recounting ambitious embellishments of my own, thus solving the problem of what to say to strange boys.

Many of Townsend's stories were drawn from Cassius's old age, during which he divorced his wife, adopted a Russian boy generally believed to be his illegitimate son, married a fifteen-year-old country girl, and defended his home against a sheriff's posse by firing on the men with a cannon loaded with horseshoe nails. Why was he so violent? No one else in the family behaved that way. David L. Smiley published a biography of him in 1962, but the book doesn't really address what was going on inside Cassius. The public man was loud and pugnacious, causing Henry Adams to call him a "noisy jackass" after meeting him in England.

During the Civil War, President Lincoln named Cassius United States Minister to Saint Petersburg to repay him for campaigning for the Republican ticket in 1860, an appointment that would affect Brutus's family, too. I think a clue to the puzzle of Cassius's personality may lie in a photograph of him taken there. It shows a handsome middle-aged man whose face is riven with lines of pain and disillusionment, not a face Cassius often allowed people to see.

My father remembered driving over to Madison County in a buggy with his father to visit Cassius shortly before his death in 1903. By this time, Cassius had quarreled with his own children, and my grandfather Cash was the only member of the family he would see. I heard the story several times as a child, but all I remember of it now is that my father, who was six or seven at the time, took several little terriers with him in the buggy and lost one somewhere near Escondida. I suspect that the loss of a precious dog was more important to him then than the conversation of a querulous old man.

Patsey Miller wrote Ann a few days after the Foxtown incident. The Turners were friends of the Fields, particularly Patsey and her husband. Mary Field had mentioned Cyrus in letters written in 1848. Belle told Mary how polite he had been to her at a party. She also described a visit he had made to William Holloway's sister, Sarah, who seems to have been in love with him. The "occurrence" at Foxtown shocked the entire family.

PATSEY MILLER

June 20th, 1849

My Dear Sister,

Your very welcome letter was received by us on last Sabbath evening and, if I could have compelled myself sufficiently to have written, I should have answered you immediately, but two or three hours before I had heard of the awful and unexpected death of Cyrus Turner, one of our best friends we had on earth. I cannot find language to express my feelings and in so many respects what an awful ending. [. . .] Our neighborhood has been stripped of one of the cleverest men. I have never seen so many people regretting the death of another and mourning his loss to society. [. . .] He always showed more pleasure in a visit to our house than any brother I have. We feel indeed that we have lost one of our truest friends. [. . .] I wish Cassius Clay's destroying knife had have fallen on some more worthless character. [. . .] We heard that Mr. Clay is recovering rapidly but does not know, I believe, that poor Cyrus Turner is dead. His mother asked him if he was willing to die, he said yes, also if he could forgive Mr. Clay, he said he had the night before. I hope he was better prepared for his very sudden departure from this world than another of his friends supposed him to be. He was learned upon the subject of religion some years ago, but always said he was not fit for any church. [. . .] I went up on Monday morning, supposing the funeral would take place as we had heard, but they were compelled to bury him Sabbath evening. I called to see the family. I came home the same day. David [Field] for a rarity came and stayed two nights with us, left here early that morning.

I commenced this letter a day or two ago and have had for two days such a spell of jaw ache that I could not finish it. [. . .] Mr. M. has heard today that Belle has got home. I am very anxious to see her as she has not been to see me for some months before she left your house. I heard Mary say Monday when I was in town that she was very anxious for Belle to come home, that she meant to leave for a long visit to you as soon as Brother came which he thinks will be by the fourth. I think his situation quite a critical one, coming through all the cholera. It will be a miracle if we ever see him alive. Little Patsey [his daughter] looks better than she did when she came, is an interesting sprightly babe. I told them they ought to send it to me these sickly times as I do think the trouble of it on Pa all the time in his old days is too much. Being kept awake at night does not suit him at all, you know [. . .] and then it is confining on Mary and will be now on Belle.

Well, Ann, this is the third or fourth time I have made the attempt to finish this letter. I have been suffering so much with my jaw I could not finish and in the time I have been writing some of the children have tried to see how much they could blot it and really I am ashamed to send it [. . .] but I am really afraid if I attempt to write another I never will get it to you. Tell Mr. Clay he must not be a candidate [presumably for the legislature]. It is a dangerous business in our days to be a public character. [. . .] I feel very unhappy for them [other members of the family] these cholera times in town. I have wrote [*sic*] to them all to come and stay with us. [. . .] We are talking of moving out to some springs. I want Pa to come and go with us if we go this fall [to] Lick Springs in Garrard [County], about ten or eleven miles from here. I am very sorry you cannot get over to see us all. We heard that Mr. Clay is at his brother's, helping to nurse him. [. . .] Patty [*sic*] Holloway has spent several days with us since she got home, but she would get so lonesome while they were all at school. [. . .] Elizabeth and Martha and James and Field [Patsey's children] [are] only going to Mr. Duff. Martha has prevailed on her Pa to let her take lessons on the piano from Mrs. Duff. She is very much taken up with her music. We sent up and got Pa's old piano for her to practice on, but it is almost of no use. [. . .] Elizabeth has been complaining all summer the walk [to school] of a mile and a half is too much for her [. . .] we shall have to board them somewhere this winter [if] they are to go to school. I don't know what we will do with them as Mr. M. has now his building on hand and more than he has the means to go through with and cannot afford to pay the high board they ask in town. [. . .] Mr. M. some two or three months ago, by hard scraping and paying the last cent he had, made his last payment for his land. [. . .] Field went to town with David. He came home today. Junius Holloway came with him. [. . .] Amelia [Miller] says tell Brother Cash she loves him more than two or three others put together and that she wants to see him. [. . .]

Patsey I. Miller

A couple of days later, Elizabeth wrote Ann that cholera was all around them.

ELIZABETH HOLLOWAY

June 22, 1849

Dear Ann,

[. . .] Everything looks gloomy. We have such awful accounts of cholera and see so many passing as if for their life. Two men that passed through here died at Estill, had cholera, I suppose, when they left. I have not been down that way visiting for some time. May was here yesterday, says you scarcely see anyone on the street, no ladies. [. . .] No business going on, we are not making our expenses. A large stock of goods are left on hand. We should be thankful that we are not scourged. [. . .] Ezekiel [Field] has just come in, says Mr. Toffer has died with cholera. He was a poor widowed man. [. . .] Pa received a letter from Brother Monday. He had returned from May Martin's [Mississippi neighbor] place. He had lost 15 negroes. [. . .] He was there 10 days, said the Overseer could not attend to all and he assisted him. Milly's [a slave] babe was dead. I did not know that children died with it. Before this were 4 that had died. We will be lucky if alive this 4th of July. [. . .] Maj. [Squire] and Mrs. Turner sent a request to Sarah [Holloway] to come over and stay all night Tuesday. I went over with her. I feel greatly for them. It will be the means of making us all perfectly friendly. Mr. H. went over yesterday. There never was any difficulty. Mr. H. never liked him [Squire Turner] and would not go there. He has his sympathies now. [. . .] Maj. T. said he regretted the occurrence and hoped he [Cassius] would get well. It was too late when the deed was done. I felt for Mrs. Clay when I heard it. [. . .] The impression was he [Cassius] would certainly die, the other would recover. You speak of the election, I have heard it is scarcely spoken of. I was interested in it a week ago; I feel perfect indifference now. [. . .] There has been several cases of it [cholera] in town. Will Irvine has it. Mrs. Jones' family have recovered. I hear she is very much offended with her friends for not going to see her. I should like to know who she thought would go there. [. . .] I hope by the time Brother comes the alarm will all be over and we will have some pleasure in a visit from you. Sarah [Holloway] wishes to be kindly remembered to you, she thanks you for your invitation. She does not know when she will feel like visiting. [. . .] My love to Martha. Why don't [sic] she write to Amelia [Holloway]? She takes it very hard. She is devoted to her Aunt Sarah [Holloway]. She had promised herself much comfort and pleasure in visiting her at her own home. Alas all things are uncertain. We are convinced daily of the uncertainty of life and the certainty of death and shown we should try and prepare for a change. Your affectionate Sister

Elizabeth

Two weeks later, the cholera epidemic continued to rage.

ELIZABETH HOLLOWAY

July 4, 1849

Dear Ann,

I wrote you last Monday and sent Cousin William the letter, thinking he would leave the next day. He is still here and says he will not go soon if the Cholera increases in Paris. He was going to take the girls. The accounts are still alarming from Lex. Yesterday from daylight up to 12 o'clock there were 11 deaths. It is very fatal in the neighborhood of Walnut Hill. [. . .] We have none as yet, are daily looking for it. A great many have threatening symptoms. Sarah Turner was quite ill a few nights ago. She had diarrhea for ten days, had eaten no vegetables for weeks. That day she indulged in eating 2 potatoes. That night she was vomiting and had every symptom of cholera. Potatoes are considered very bad indeed. 2 Irish at Walnut Hill died from eating them. If Brother does not come today, we will be very unhappy. [. . .] Sarah [Holloway] has just left this morning for home [. . .]. She is very well now, looks much better. You and her Ma must go and see her. [. . .] When Mr. Stone came up for Sarah, he said Liz Irvine was very ill. He did not say what was the matter, flux, I expect. Will and Lucy [Irvine] has [sic] had it. [. . .] Mr. H. heard yesterday Mr. [Cassius] Clay was worse and very low spirited. He is going to see him in a few days. Amelia and Bell was at Mrs. Miller's last week. Patsey was suffering a great deal with her teeth and looking very badly. She ought to have them taken out. Our Night Blooming Lilies bloomed one night this week. [. . .] After supper Mr. H. was passing the fire house and discovered it. We were not looking for it for several days. We gave the word out down the street. There were a good many as late as it was. It was very large and fragrant. [. . .]

The mail has come and no tiding[s] of Brother. We cannot imagine why he has not got here. I fear very much he is not living or sick. There were 15 deaths of cholera in Lex. yesterday, on Tuesday 250 in Cincinnati. There has been 4 or 5 deaths in Irvine. It was a judgment sent on them. An Irishman from Lex. went up there, passed through, been sick, he died up there. They did not put him in a coffin and scarcely covered him in the ground. The citizens could scarcely stay in the town, it was so offensive. The tavern keeper where he stayed was the first to die. A man died at Charles Town yesterday. He assisted in burying a friend who [died] a few days ago. Mr. H. saw Mr. Rodes today. He was from Mr. [Cassius] Clay's, said he rested very badly last night, was very low spirited, and he thought was weakening. [. . .] Mrs. Dudley [Cassius's mother] is still there. My garden looks beautiful now. I have a bed of phlox, all colours of red from the darkest crimson to the lightest pink. [. . .]

Elizabeth

A joint letter to Ann from Amelia and Elizabeth Holloway recounted yet more horrors of the cholera epidemic, though Christopher Field had arrived safely from Mississippi. Amelia's portion of the letter makes a startling switch in midstream, from "death and pestilence" to "beautiful tableaux," reminding me of the medieval nobles who partied in locked castles while the black death ravaged the countryside around them. *Tableaux vivants*, in which people depicted famous paintings or scenes, were still popular in Kentucky when I was a child. My mother lent clothes from Auvergne's closets for one such production in Paris, Kentucky.

AMELIA AND ELIZABETH HOLLOWAY

July, 1849

My Dear Aunt,

[. . .] As Ma is away, all the responsibilities of her post revolve upon me. She and Grandpa have been at Estill Springs since Monday.

Though she was conscious of the fact that she needed the waters, yet it was with the utmost difficulty we could prevail upon her to start. She left with great reluctance as at that time the relentless scourge Cholera was threatening us. There has been 8 deaths from that source, 1 last week and 7 during the 4 days of the present. [. . .] In its sudden sweep one of our most respected & esteemed neighbors has been removed from us, Mrs. Lee. [. . .] She was one of the most respected members of society, especially to the *poor*. Her family are truly in pitiable condition. She left five children on the bed of sickness, without a single relation to soothe their woes. [. . .] She and another lady had been the only cases amongst the whites. The remainder were negroes. We received a letter from Ma today. She was perfectly unhappy about home, has heard of the cholera, & could not possibly remain but a day or two longer, thought she had in measure begun to feel the beneficial effects of the waters. She has a distressing cough. Grandpa has been complaining for some time before he left of a continual dizziness in the head. [. . .] The stage driver from here to Estill being sick this week, Uncle David [Field] voluntarily took his place. We have suffered great uneasiness concerning him as it is such a long, tedious drive with the addition of the great heat of the sun. [. . .] Uncle Christopher [Field] has proven the most useful & active individual in attending the cases of cholera here. Had it not been for his experience, the physicians should have been at quite a loss. They were guided entirely by his suggestions. Whenever there is a case ascertained, he is immediately sent for. He remains with them until all is over. All are loud in the praise of his merits & worth. With death and pestilence in our midst, pleasure continues its career uninterrupted. [. . .] There was a beautiful tableaux at Mrs. Stanton's. [. . .] She, Aunt Mary & Belle & Laurie Walker were the actors, together with I. D. Smith, Mrs. Walker, and Uncle Ed [Field]. It passed off admirably to the infinite satisfaction of Mrs. Robt. Stone who, of course, was the mistress of ceremonies. After the tableaux we had a dance. The greatest compliment we could pay Mrs. Walker's beautiful table of most delightful refreshments was to stand aloof & admire. We dared not indulge to the full extent of our wishes. [. . .] Laurie Walker has just returned from Estill, she and her cousin having spent a week there, and was a *great* belle, and is now on the eve of starting to Harrodsburg. She will not feel much like going East to school after figuring in the Beau Monde so extensively. [. . .] The cholera was greatly on the decrease. I suppose ere this it has entirely spent itself. There is a kind of epidemic fever prevailing here. [. . .]

Sunday evening. I commenced this, thinking it would be sent by

Saturday. Well, there have been some great and serious changes since then. The cholera is raging with redoubtable fury. Uncle Christopher was attacked Friday morning with it but, before I proceed further, let me assure [you] he is now relieved for four hours. His life was despaired of, there was not the slightest hope entertained even by his physicians. Only by the unremitting attention of his friends he was rescued from his critical situation. It is indeed truly marvelous how he survived such extreme agonies. Ma was down to see him this morning, says he looks quite natural, and is evidently much better. [. . .] Throughout he maintained the same coolness & intrepidly giving his counsels with the utmost deliberation. He told them he knew his situation and they would have to use the boldest remedies. It was deemed expedient to send for Ma & Grandpa. Uncle Isham [a slave] left about 9 o'clock Friday morning, reached Estill 1 1/2 o'clock, was immediately seized with cholera and died about dark. Uncle David did not wish to send him and he was so anxious to go. It is quite probable he did not receive attention. He was taken sick in the stable and died there. Ma and Grandpa reached here about 10 o'clock that night. They are both very well though Ma has a touch of the Diarrhea. [. . .] Zeke Field had the symptoms but, by being taken care of in time, he is now as well as usual. Aunt Belle has been an invalid here for a day or two. We have given her so much Physic that she is relieved. She had the premonitory symptom, Diarrhea. There is greatest panic here. It appears like Sabbath. The only passing is to and from the sick. Mr. Lewis has suffered a deep affliction from cholera. It has removed from him three daughters in about 36 hours, one fifteen years of age and a schoolmate of Martha's, Sarah Lewis. There was an adopted niece, Miss Stevens. She died a most affecting death. [. . .] They lost another daughter, 3 yrs. of age. They have another daughter ill with cholera. John Lewis has been ill with flux for the week past but never entirely recovered. He was taken with cholera last night and died this morning. Up to today, there has [sic] been 12 deaths during the past week. [. . .]

Amelia has left her letter and I will finish it. My Dear Sister, words cannot express what I went through on last Friday. I had no idea of seeing our dear Brother alive. The Lord for some wise purpose has spared his life. So far he is relieved of Cholera but left very weak and pale. I was there this morning. He looked like himself. The night I came I went there. He was vomiting all night and in the greatest agony. He was heard plainly at the Goddins' [next door]. He exposed himself waiting on the sick down by Mrs. Lee's all the time. She was very heavy, had to be raised up very often. He assisted in shrouding. He also sat up with

Mr. Cooper. I reckon there never was so much interest taken for his re-covery in anyone. The house was crowded. I was taken with Diarrhea, then came home immediately, have lain in bed all day, am taking med-icine and feel quite weak. Bell was taken sick here, has been in bed for 2 days. I hope she is relieved. [. . .]

[no signature]

In August, Ann received still another cholera report, this one from her father.

EZEKIEL H. FIELD

Aug. 1, 1849

Dear Ann,

[. . .] The cholera has not abated any with us and, from present indi-cations, I fear will not very soon, but this is all guesswork as we can make no certain calculations about it, but we should summon up all fortitude and do our duty to the utmost of our ability as it appears that dread and excitement always proves injurious. I am pleased to think that your Brother Christopher is now improving and we have hope of his recovery which is mainly owing to his strong constitution and the bold and powerful remedies used from the first. Your Sister Elizabeth is now very feeble &, were it not for the great excitement now prevailing, would soon be well. She has been threatened with flux but is not now [in] danger.

Isabella was very cheerful yesterday and our expectations were raised high of her speedy recovery but today many symptoms are unfa-vorable. She is kept warm with great exertion and much protected and we consider her situation extremely critical, but we hope for the best. There has been many cholera symptoms in all our family, but are not now dangerous.

Mr. Lawrence's family have been truly scourged, having today lost a grown daughter & small son, since the death of John and another daughter very low. William M. Stone has had the cholera but is thought now out of danger.

I am sorry to learn from the papers that it is alarming in Paris, but hope sincerely your neighborhood will escape.

David [Field] has looked badly a long time but still keeps up. He, Edmund [Field] & myself can do what nursing Christopher requires. [. . .] Patsey [Miller] is very unhappy. She cannot well come up. [. . .] We do not wish any of you to come until we get well. [. . .]

E. H. Field

Ezekiel Field wrote Ann later in the month that the epidemic seemed to be abating. "You will learn from the papers that our town has become healthy yet all have every few days some deaths to report. Two on Saturday night, Mr. Rodes Nelson and a negro child at Mrs. McClanahan's, and today are two deaths, John F. Burby and a negro child of Jane Embry's, and there [are] still some cases under treatment. William & Thomas Stone are both sick, but not dangerously. We have now but few inhabitants in town. They have scattered to all quarters, a number to Lexington and different watering places and all business suspended, but we every day hope that no more cases of cholera will appear."

Bourbon County had apparently escaped the worst of the epidemic, although one of Ann's neighbors, a Mr. Duncan, had died of cholera. Ann's brother Christopher was better, and Ezekiel Field added in a letter to Ann in August, "if he does not eat too much, [he] will soon regain his strength."

Christopher was making preparations to return to Mississippi. He wrote Ann in September, "It was fully my intention to have spent some time with you [. . .] but I came up late, was sick in Louisville ten days, and remained so here until the cholera broke out. For the last two months I have spent a gloomy time and one of much anxiety about my friends and relatives. I consider but few persons who have had cholera are ever cured. Still several cases have been cured here, my own amongst the rest. If you have escaped up to this time, I think you will have no fears but I would still be prudent in diet & etc. etc."

With Christopher's departure, the family's troubles subsided. They had survived Charlotte's death, Cassius's fatal fight with Cyrus Turner, and the cholera epidemic. Little Pattie was settled at her grandfather's house. The coming years promised to be happier. Mary and Belle Field, twenty and nineteen respectively, and Martha Clay, almost eighteen, were approaching the ages when they might be expected to marry, as was Amelia Holloway. The Holloways had completed the transformation of Mount Airy into the imposing Rosehill, and the Millers, not to be outdone, were making plans for Hedgeland. Everyone looked forward to the return of normal life in Richmond with its rounds of visiting and gossip, interspersed with parties and new dresses, as well as more letters from their friends and relations.

FOUR

Rather an Uphill Business

Although life returned to normal for the Fields and the Clays in 1850, the balance had subtly shifted. They were at the beginning of a decade when all aspects of American life raced toward the cataclysm of the Civil War. With so many people questioning its morality, slavery could no longer be taken for granted. As the family became more and more involved in cotton plantations in the Mississippi Delta, the ugliest fact of slavery, the buying and selling of human beings, increasingly impinged upon their lives.

Congress passed a Fugitive Slave Law as part of the Compromise of 1850, requiring runaway blacks to be returned to their owners and penalizing those who helped runaways. Since the law worked against fugitive slaves and freedmen, it upped the ante for both fleeing slaves and abolitionists. Feelings about the issue in Kentucky reached a fevered pitch. Predictably, Cassius Clay's knife fight at Foxtown had had a negative effect upon the antislavery cause: Cyrus Turner had become a martyr and Cassius a "damned nigger agitator." Not a single antislavery candidate won a seat to the convention that wrote Kentucky's 1850 constitution. But Kentucky emancipationists made plans to field candidates in the 1851 state elections.

Cassius announced that he would run for governor. "I candidly believe," Brutus's brother-in-law J. Speed Smith, then a state senator, wrote Brutus in February, "should Cassius be a candidate for either station, the probability to be great that he would be *killed* before the election."

The 1850s were also a period of tremendous economic growth, spurred by the influx of foreign capital and the discovery of gold in California. It was an era of railroad building. By 1856, Bourbon County had not one but two projects that Brutus, with a Whiggish interest in internal improvements, supported. With the coming of "the cars" to Lexington and Cincinnati, the tempo of life there accelerated. Richmond, which did not get railroad service until after the Civil War, remained a sleepy little town.

Early in 1850, Patsey Miller wrote Ann a harried letter.

PATSEY MILLER

Feb. 10, 1850

My Dear Sister Ann,

I have put off writing so long that I feel I owe you an apology. [. . .] But I must beg you excuse me upon the score of the want of time for really, since I saw you, I have thought sometimes that certainly no other human ever had so much to devolve solely upon their own hands or such an accumulation of work for a great many reasons as I have had this Jan. [. . .] I have had for four weeks a Miss Baugh sewing with me. We made 6 coats, two quilted skirts, about twenty-eight shirts and chemises, comforts and quilts, gowns, etc. etc. [. . .] The young lady went home yesterday. I have got a good deal done but did not succeed in getting through, have two shirts yet for Mr. M. [. . .] and I shall not have time to blow before I must commence spring work. [. . .] The workmen will at last make a completion of Mr. Burnam's house in a week or two. They are then coming here [to build the new addition to their house]. I have a quantity of sheets and pillow cases and other articles to [. . .] make up for their beds. You are quite made up, no doubt, now that you have the good company of Belle [Field] and Amelia [Holloway]. The girls made themselves very agreeable to me for a very short time this fall during Mr. Miller's absence to Cincinnati. I should like to see more of them but our almost impassable roads and weather of winter [. . .] prevent them. I have not seen Mary [Field] since I saw you. I suppose she now has to stay at home more closely on Little Patsey's account. I am sorry Brother has never had confidence enough in me to consent to my taking the child. I should have been pleased to have relieved them at Pa's and will do it yet if he is willing. Mr. M. went up on Thursday to attend the examination [for the Millers' oldest children]

that day and Friday. It rained so and the Creek [was] so high they did
not get home till late yesterday evening and then had to swim their
horses and cross in a boat at Moran's. [. . .] Mr. M. was very well satisfied with their examination and, as we cannot send them from home to
school for a great many reasons and a good education being what we
greatly desire they shall have above everything else, we wish to continue them there. But Mr. Miller says he will not sponge upon Pa's lib-
erality and great kindness to us in the privilege we have had of their
staying at his house any longer, that he will get housing for them at
Fayette's. [. . .] They think it quite against what is due them that they
have never had the privilege of a visit to your house and I do think myself, as Elizabeth will enter this summer her 16th year, she shall not
have it longer to say that she had never crossed the river, but I will do
all in my power to enable them to pay you a visit this summer. [. . .] I
have never had the politeness to write and thank Mr. Clay for his present of such a handsome sheep. Mr. M. praises him very highly. He frequently speaks of his short but very pleasant trip to your house and says
he has great reason to thank you for the bountiful supply of cake that
you provided him with as he made three dinners of it. [. . .] Sister [Eliz-
abeth Holloway] frequently of late enlivens some of my dreary moments this winter with a long note or letter but her theme at present is
her great trouble with Cousin William again, concluding he is dissatisfied [presumably with his work at The Store and life in Richmond generally — William Holloway was a restless man]. E. and M. tell me their
Aunt E. occasionally cries over it as she says she wants to bury her
bones in Richmond. [. . .]

P. I. Miller

In April, Elizabeth wrote Ann of bonnets and recipes. "I went to
The Store this evening and sent over for your Bonnet. [. . .] Mrs. B. [a
seamstress] made the strings too short. Mr. H. [Holloway] was quite
provoked. As usual, I have returned here with the headache." Her slave
Lucy was going to Auvergne for a visit again. "Those Ginger Cakes you
sent were so good. Send me the recipe. If you make any whilst Lucy is
there, let her learn. I tell her I want her to learn a great deal in a week."
She continued, "Monday I made the nicest Lemon Puddings I ever
made. I did not put quite three quarts butter into a pot of lemon. I did
not cook it any, at least I put it on the fire, scarcely got it warm." Her
newest baby, Clarence, was sick and slept in her room at night.

Field family picnic, August 1947. In the foreground, Lucie M. Wooten. Just behind her, Miriam Berle Clay. *Photograph by Cassius M. Clay.*

The author, Mary Augusta Clay, age 6, and her brother Berle Clay, almost 5, on the back porch at Auvergne with Blueberry and Johnnie. Summer 1944. *Photograph by Cassius M. Clay.*

Auvergne. October 1995.

Ann M. Clay, in Washington, D.C., in
1864 when she was 54.

Brutus J. Clay as a young man.
Photograph reproduced from
Antebellum Portraiture in Kentucky
by Edna Talbott Whitley
(© The National Society of the
Colonial Dames of America in the
Commonwealth of Kentucky).

Cassius M. Clay, the author's father, age 59, on the limestone steps in front of Auvergne, with Rusty and Brownie. September 1954.

Two Field sisters (Patsey and Ann at 22 and 18 or Mary and Belle at 21 and 19). Daguerreotype, ca. 1840, 1850.

One Field sister (Belle at 25 or Mary at 27). Ambrotype, ca. 1856.

Field brother, probably David I. Field shortly after his marriage, about 36 years old. Ambrotype, ca. 1856.

The Holloways' house, Rosehill, seen from the Richmond cemetery. In the foreground, the tombstone of Eliza and J. Speed Smith and family, behind it the Gothic pillar marking the burial plot of Green Clay and his family. *Photograph by Berle Clay.*

Mingo, Brutus Clay's head man.
Tintype, ca. 1865.

Hamp Ayres with his dog, Shep,
ca. 1895. Green Clay's 1813
cabin in the background.
*Photograph by
Mary Harris Clay.*

Cassius M. Clay Jr. fishing in the
Mill Pond at Auvergne with one
of his sons, ca. 1900.
Photograph by Mary Harris Clay.

Cassius M. Clay, age 54,
in a photograph taken in
St. Petersburg, Russia, ca. 1864.

Ann Clay's medicine kit.

Christopher F. Clay with his hunting dogs, probably taken not long
before his death in 1897 at the age of 62.

In early August, the Clays went on a shopping spree in Philadelphia. No correspondence exists describing the trip, but the bills run up by "Mr. Clay & Party" have remained among Brutus's business papers all these years. The "party" included Brutus and Ann, Belle Field, and the Keininghams. They stayed at the United States Hotel on Chestnut Street for five days, costing them $52.75. On the 2nd, Ann purchased from L. J. Levy and Company ("Importers and Jobbers of Fancy & Staple Dry Goods") two pieces of silk, one twelve yards long and the other fourteen. She also bought embroidered muslin sleeves, chemisettes, collars, and caps. Later that day, at Bailey and Company ("Importers and manufacturers of watches, jewelry, diamonds, silver ware and fancy goods"), she bought a set of flat silver for $475, a $50 bracelet, a $30 gold chain, and other items, including a turquoise pin and a silver card case. Also included on the bill was a $4 pin for "Miss Field." A few days later, at E. Brinton, No. 122 Chestnut Street, the Clay and Field women bought more material and trimmings. Richard Keiningham bought two dozen blue band finger bowls, two dozen gold band coffee cups and saucers, and two dozen gold band teacups and saucers from William J. Kerr ("Importer of all kinds of china, glass & Liverpool ware"). He paid $28.50, but it must have been intended for Brutus, as the bill from Keiningham and Shackelford ended up among his papers.

Back in Kentucky, Ezekiel Field reported to Brutus that the women were savoring their memories of the trip. While they were gone, little Clarence Holloway had died.

"We are in hope that we have favorable weather for your Bourbon Fare [sic]," Ezekiel Field concluded in September. "Mary and Isabella are anxious to go over and probably will succeed. Christopher had intended to go to your house about this time, but having fixed on Saturday next to leave for the South, and wishing to close up David's stage business [one of the things David Field had been doing since leaving the mills], he finds it will occupy all his time here."

As Christmas approached, Martha went to Richmond. She spent much of her time visiting relatives, as she told Ann. "Amelia [Holloway] and I, Belle Rodes and Field [Miller] are about ready to start down to see Aunt Mary Jane [Clay]. She was up at Uncle Rodes' over Tuesday and here Wednesday and extracted a promise from us to spend tonight. [. . .] We were to see Aunt Patsey last week and were waterbound there almost five days though we had a delightful visit. Spent one evening with Cousin Lucinda. We walked all the way over rocks. [. . .] They paraded me off with a pair of boots which carried me much faster downhill than I wished, far to the sorrow of my head and back. [. . .] We spent yesterday with Belle Rodes."

"Uncle David [Field] is as quarrelsome [and] fault-finding as ever," she continued. "I told him he ought to have stayed [in Mississippi] as he was appreciated whilst absent. He has no confidence in the country [Mississippi]. Bob Stone [. . .] says if he had been David Field, he would have been there yet, without wife & children and with a good constitution."

Finally, she had news about several of Brutus's nephews. "Clay Smith has recovered from his horse fall, I believe. Davidson [Clay] has gone home. He was to see us Monday. The girls all send Sidney [Davidson's brother] word to come over Christmas."

Martha remained in Richmond for Christmas. "I went down street this morning to buy the children some presents as George expects to go over this week," she wrote Ann on December 23. She planned to return to Bourbon County soon, accompanied by her cousin Amelia Holloway. "Uncle William [Holloway] heard of my Furs today. I expect they will be here next mail. They were very expensive. I don't suppose I can have my cloak made until I am on my way home." Meanwhile, the visiting continued. "Tell Pa after this week I am at his command. I shall then probably have seen all my relations. I have seen none of the Smiths, but suppose June and Curran will be in this week to the parties. We were invited to an oyster supper this evening but declined as we did not care about it, concluding to take our oysters at home." She ended with a few comments about Edmund Field, then in Louisville (he never did make it to California). "Aunt Mary [Field] says, as he is to prove the flower of the flock, she intends to go down and call on him."

Although there is no mention of Martha's "very expensive" furs in Brutus's 1850 account with Field and Holloway, among the other items listed are eleven yards of "rich silk for Martha" ($24), twelve yards of "rich" black lace ($21), and two dozen sterling silver forks ($85). Most of the items are small: fifty yards of fishing line, several pairs of kid gloves, envelopes, a fruit gatherer, a pair of spurs, a toothbrush, and twenty-eight pairs of yarn socks.

While Brutus was buying these things, his brother Cassius was going bankrupt, the result of debts incurred by the *True American* and during the Mexican War. When his possessions went on the auction block in 1850, Brutus bought back many of them for him, including a $270 "gilt dinner set." Their stepfather, Jeptha Dudley, bought back statues of the four seasons, an assortment of farm implements, and more than 2,200 acres of land.

In 1851, Cassius launched his campaign for governor on the anti-slavery ticket. He canvassed the state tirelessly, speaking in eighty of its one hundred counties, sometimes to empty rooms. There were no more incidents, although he was attacked verbally by both Democrats and Whigs as a vile Disunionist. Mention of Cassius's activities began to creep into the Fields' letters.

Ann, who was visiting in Richmond, described to Brutus an attempt by the abolitionist John Fee to preach there. Cassius later gave Fee land in Madison County for a church and a school that was to become Berea College, still in operation today.

ANN CLAY

Feb. 21, 1851

My Dear Husband,

[. . .] I have had a pleasant visit indeed but almost regretted coming at this time as, on Monday last, your Sister Smith & Col. Smith came over and said they were just ready to start to our house when they were told by someone that I had come over here the day before. [. . .] And, as Mrs. Rodes and family were spending the day there, I promised to go there the next day. [. . .] Mary Jane [Clay] has spent two days with me, Monday at Sister's and Wednesday at Papa's. [. . .] Mary Jane has ordered so much finery from Philadelphia that I expect she will have no objection to your paying her expenses. [. . .]

There has been a good deal of excitement in town for several days about an *abolitionist* that came here from Cassius. He said he was a Baptist preacher and wanted to speak on Emancipation on Sunday in the Baptist Church. The members would not permit him. He then tried all of the other churches and no one would permit him, and at last he went to the negro church and preached and some of the young gentlemen, 4 boys, went there and drove him out of town, threatening him with a dunking, etc. etc. He went to Cassius and told him of it. He wrote an account of the treatment he received and sent it [. . .] to Tom Goddin to publish [in the Richmond newspaper] and, as soon as some of the gentlemen found he was back again, they followed him out of town and dunked him 11 times until he consented to leave the state. He was going to go to the Big Hill [a community near Richmond] and, I think, as he did not intend stopping here, that they treated him badly, but a great many of the citizens think he was not treated half bad enough. [. . .] I never seen anyone so enraged as Mary Jane was when she heard how he was treated the second time. [. . .] I hope that Cash & Zeke are doing well. Tell Cash I will take him a hat and no boots as his Sis wrote me that she would get him a pair in town & tell Zeke & Green I will take them some nice sugar. [. . .]

Ann M. Clay

Cassius was badly defeated in his gubernatorial quest, but antislavery ballots split the vote, so that the Democrats won by only a slim margin. Less than a month after the Kentucky election, attracted by the vitality of the Free-Soil movement, Cassius met with Northern abolitionists, including his friend Salmon P. Chase, to explore the possibilities of the national political arena. For the next couple of years, he toured the North, lecturing on the evils of slavery to people already excited by the publication of Harriet Beecher Stowe's novel *Uncle Tom's Cabin*, which appeared first as a serial and then, in 1852, as a book.

In December, Davidson Clay, one of the three sons of Brutus and Cassius's late brother Sidney, died suddenly in Lexington. Another nephew, Green Clay Smith, sent Brutus word of Dave's death. "Sidney [Dave's brother] wishes me to request you to attend to having the grave dug. He wants it dug by the side of his Father's *leaving space enough between for another*. If there is no suitable ground on the side the foot he next suggests. He also wishes a square box made to receive the coffin — 6 feet 4 inches long — 16 inches wide, made of two inch plank. He leaves here tomorrow morning at 7 1/2 or 8 o'clock. He hopes you will be ready by the time he reaches home."

David Field was working in the dry goods business in Lexington at the time. "Your silks & canopy have been here 3 or 4 days," he wrote Ann. "I learnt D. Clay was dead and at the time I intended to go down with the corpse and got up this morning with that purpose, but Mr. Irvine reported himself sick this morning and I could not well leave today and I should have sent the silk with some of the company, but I deem it improper."

The year 1851 had not been a happy one for Patsey Miller. Her adored daughter Amelia, seven years old, died and many members of her family were sick, as this letter to Ann explains.

PATSEY MILLER

Dec. 21, 1851

My Dear Sister,

[. . .] Ezekiel [Field] just left here since breakfast, the first time he has been out to stay any time for several months. He came out Friday evening and brought Charley Walker's hounds and his gun. He and James and Field [Miller] had great sport yesterday after rabbits. [. . .] He grows very fast and is a manly well-behaved youth so far as I can see or know of him, but Sister says she is very uneasy about him as he is not at The Store half his time at night and indeed if he escapes with good morals and steady habits through the many temptations of so wicked and immoral a place as Richmond he will deserve much credit and I do sincerely hope that he has gladdened Pa's declining and old days by his moral and industrious course of life. [. . .] Pa looks thin and pale and is frequently complaining of his head, but he thinks the dieting course he is pursuing is a great benefit to his health. Belle and Mary both really deserve great credit for their great attentions and love for Pa and his comfort, also for Patty [*sic*] [Field]. She is being raised as well as any one could do it and I agree with you in feeling towards them. They are more confined than most girls. [. . .] I received a long note from Sister yesterday. [. . .] I fear greatly for the future for her. She says in her note that Cousin William is very uneasy about her health and unbeknown to her consulted Doc. Letcher and he directs her to put on Flannel next [to] her skin, flannel drawers. [. . .] She says she is cold night and day from her knees down. You speak of a number of your servants being sick. I do not envy your situation in that respect owing to the number you have to attend to [. . .] Field's [Miller] arm is yet a source of suffering to him and trouble to us. During the time of his spell of flux [. . .] his arm for the first time reduced to its natural size and seemed to be about well but so soon as he recovered his strength and appetite it got back to the same old thing and we started him to school. He got very wet some weeks ago coming from school. [. . .] After that it inflamed and swelled very much and discharged a great deal. [. . .] We had to stop him from school which I feel very sorry for. I feel sometimes of late that our diffi-

culties [. . .] is [sic] more than I can bear. The loss of so dear a child as
Amelia is a source of deep grief and distress with me. She was an un-
common good child from her birth, so affectionate and considerate towards black and white. She frequently in the last year or two since she
got old enough to know the right relationship between her and Cash
would laugh and talk to me about her having called him Brother and
continued to have a warm attachment for him. I think sometimes that
I have less to look back upon that is consoling to my feelings from the
time she was taken sick till her death than any other distressed mother.
The day after she was taken, Mary Belle [Miller] was taken sick. At that
time Field and black Martha [a slave] required constant attention.
Field's arm has so impaired his nervous system that when he is sick his
nervous system is so easily excited that it is every thing [sic] that we can
do to keep very distressing nervous spells off him. He can't bear any
noise. For the first few days of Amelia's illness I had to pack Mary Belle
in my arms continually so that I could not stay in their room at all on
account of her crying and I was [. . .] debarred of the very great pleasure
I should feel [. . .] now of having administered to her [Amelia's] little
wants *which were few* the few short days she was sick. [. . .]

[no signature]

Patsey's lament makes one acutely aware of the primitive state of
medicine in the mid-nineteenth century. The wooden medicine kit
with which Ann Clay treated family and slaves alike is still at Auvergne. It contains scales, bottles of medicine, lancing tools, glass
leeches, and a book of directions for their use. Only when the treatment failed did Ann send for Doctor L. D. Ray, the family physician.

Brutus and Ann were improving Auvergne. A January 1852 letter
from David Field mentions both a refrigerator, or icebox, and a bathtub, "about 5 1/2 ft in the bottom, it flares considerably to the top."
The refrigerator probably sat on the stone porch outside the kitchen,
but I cannot imagine where they put the bathtub, which would have
had to be filled by hand.

David also sent the Clays linseed oil, white lead, sugar, a teakettle,
and some window shades. David seems to have been in Lexington acting as some sort of agent, perhaps for The Store, perhaps for his uncle,
David Irvine. E. H. Field Sr. had retired, for by early 1852 The Store
was called Holloway and Watson. The following year it had become

"Wm Holloway, Dealer in fancy & staple goods, Hardware, Iron, Steel & Building Mat."

The children were growing up and going off to school. Both Christopher (Kit) Clay, who was almost seventeen, and his sixteen-year-old uncle, Ezekiel Field, attended the Kentucky Military Institute near Frankfort during the winter of 1852. Kit's board and tuition there from January to June cost Brutus $140.22. Kit studied arithmetic, Latin, and algebra, and his general progress was reported to be "very good." Zeke Field wrote thirteen-year-old Green Clay in March, "I am now at the K.M.I. and I am very well and doing well at present but I do not know how long I will be so for it is a tight place but I like it a great deal better than I expected to."

In the fall of 1852, General Winfield Scott, the Whig candidate for president, spoke at the Bourbon County Fair, an event immortalized by a daguerreotype of Scott and local dignitaries standing next to a shorthorn bull. Brutus is at the far left of this unusual picture, an official's sash over one shoulder and a top hat in his hand. Arrayed around the natural arena are the county's most important men, many of them cattle breeders: Charles Garrard, Jeremiah Duncan, Samuel H. Clay, Charles Brent, Garrett Davis, and several Hutchcrafts. Scott, who stands beside a small stepladder from which he must have addressed the crowd, mostly women in sunbonnets, rallied local Whigs for a final campaign.

The photographer took a second daguerreotype a few minutes after the first. Scott remains rigidly erect beside his stepladder, but, as it was a hot day, the other men have put on their hats. The female audience has turned away, raising parasols. And the single shorthorn is replaced by a ghostly parade of pale cattle and their black handlers moving across the ring while the shutter remained open.

The fair was a particularly splendid event that year, with a ball at the Bourbon Hotel, P. T. Barnum's Chinese family and Hercules the Strongman on the midway, and an exhibition of patriotic quilts made by local ladies. According to family legend, Scott spent the night after his appearance there at Auvergne. Brutus, a delegate to the state Whig convention earlier in the year, campaigned for him all fall. In November, Scott carried Bourbon County but lost the election to Franklin Pierce.

Brutus's sister, Paulina Rodes, wrote in December to invite him to the wedding of her beautiful Belle. "As this is the fourth daughter I will have married, all of whom leave the state except one and she located in a distant county, I feel as I advance in years a strong desire to cherish the fraternal ties of our family. Ma has promised to be here and has expressed a wish to see all the children present."

Once at boarding school, Kit Clay began to cultivate a forthright style, as well as a fondness for cigars. Kit was a fine shot, with an eye for a good hound, as Uncle Christopher later said, "a perfect Daniel Boone." By his own account, Kit was happiest when out in the woods. The only picture I've ever seen of him, probably taken not long before his death at the age of sixty-four, shows a robust man with a long white beard surrounded by bird dogs.

"The session will close here the fifteenth of this month," Kit wrote his father in June. "We expect to have a large Ball here that night. I sent you a ticket, not expecting you to come, but only to honor you with one and to let you see our nice ticket etc."

He enclosed a letter to his brother Green in the one to Brutus.

CHRISTOPHER CLAY

June 3rd, [1853] K.M.I.

Dear Green,

As I was writing to Pa and did not write as much as I expected I concluded to make out this letter with a few lines to you. The time is passing off very rapidly and my school is very near expired. I am only waiting for the fifteenth to come to pass. I will then come to Old Bourbon. [. . .] The squirrels are now large enough to kill. I suppose that there is a great many this spring. Green there is one thing I want you to be certain to do without fail. And it is this. I want you to take my gun to the gunsmith and have a globe sight put on. And if it is rusty in the least, you must have the saw run through it, and cleaned out smooth and nice. I don't want it to be made any larger, whatever you do. And if the ramrod is broke or hurt in any way, have another made. I hope when I come home that I will find my gun in order, nice and clean [. . .] leave a few squirrels for me to try my hand on when I come to Bourbon. Give my best respects to Judge & Jimmy and all inquiring Friends. [. . .]

Your Brother Kit

P.S. Green I have concluded to write a few more lines. I see that a long letter is no harder to write than a short one. My motto is when you start to write a letter let it be a good long one. It only takes no time to write a letter, and when you have that time, why not make good use of it. You know that time that is once lost is lost for ever. You can't call back the time that has passed to judge the future. Green let me tell you one thing; always take a good advice, matters not who the Author may be. You are now growing up to be a man. And you will soon have to leave home and go to College to fill your young and feeble mind with good and useful knowledge which will be of use to you hereafter. It will seem hard to you to be drove off from your home sweet home. But my dear sir you do not think you will get a good and useful Education by staying at home. I know when I first left home, I thought that I was treated very bad. But I now see that it was for my own good. When you have to leave all of your sport at home and go off to school among one hundred or more strangers, where every man for himself, you won't have Pa to go to if you are imposed on by others, you will then see and feel the difference from home and at home. If you get a little hungry before it is time, you can't go to the kitchen and get something to satisfy your want.

Yours truly,

Brother Christopher F. Clay

A few days later, Ezekiel Field invited Brutus to his daughter Mary's wedding to a local widower twelve years older than she, William Wallace Embry. Ann was already in Richmond, and the family hoped Brutus would join her there. "Mary and Mr. W.W. Embry have made arrangements to get married on the arrival of Christopher [Field] and go on East with him immediately," he wrote. Mary had gone with Christopher and Charlotte on their honeymoon; now Christopher would accompany her on hers.

By 1853, the Holloways' daughter, Amelia, had married R. G. Burton and moved to Perryville, Kentucky. Amelia wrote in June to thank Brutus for his wedding present, a cow and her calf. "I take this opportunity of sending for her," Amelia said. "Mr. Burton has secured the services of a safe and careful man."

That same year Brutus and several local men formed the Northern Kentucky Importing Association and sent representatives to England to select pedigreed cattle. (Brutus's shorthorns, descendants of the Seventeens, lacked pedigrees.) On August 18, 1853, the Northern Kentucky Importing Association held its first sale at Auvergne, netting $47,860 on an investment of $11,780. Family legend has placed the cattle sales near an Indian mound in the parklike field behind the house. Several generations of Clay children dug into this mound in search of arrowheads until my brother, an archaeologist, excavated it in the mid-1970s and found a single individual buried there, feet toward the setting sun.

Brutus's Durhams were his treasures. While his bulls had names such as Locomotive, Napoleon, and the Duke of Bourbon, his cows were often named for female family members. He owned several Pattie A. Fields, for example, named after Christopher's daughter. Some were named for Ann's sister Belle. Others were Butterfly, Misfortune, Diana, and his prize winner, the imported Lady Caroline.

Cattle must be in our blood. When I was twelve, I raised Hereford steers for a 4-H project. I showed them at the Paris stockyards, where I was the only female of any species. I still remember how it felt to stand there under the scrutiny of the beefy buyers for Swift and Armour, a skinny girl in a plaid dress and saddle shoes leading a well-coifed calf named Ferdinand (I had curled his fur and back-combed his tail in preparation for the show). I was having misgivings about the undertaking. So was Ferdinand. He put down his head and tried to run from the ring.

In 1853 Brutus also set out on an ambitious plan to improve the orchard at Auvergne. He expanded the existing orchard, a square plot east of the house, by planting almost two hundred more trees, mostly apples, pears, and cherries, each identified on a map: two Summer Rose apples, two Fall Pippins, four Ladys Sweet, one Jersey Sweet, and one Maidens Blush, also some dwarf pears on quince stock, both White and Gray Doyenne pears, and an assortment of cherries including Yellow Spanish, Early Purple, and May Duke. The cherries evidently didn't do well; many Brutus recorded in his daybook as being "killed" in 1856.

By the time my family lived at the farm, Brutus's orchard was overgrown with mock oranges and blackberries. On hot August afternoons, my mother used to send my brother and me out with tin pails to collect blackberries. It was cruel work and we would return a couple of hours later covered with scratches. Eventually the rock fence between the orchard and an adjoining field fell down, and my father's steers roamed the thickets. I used to entertain them by dancing in the clearings. While the white-faced cattle jostled one another to get a closer look, I whirled around and around, dancing both Marge and Gower Champion's parts from *Showboat*.

In January 1854 Kit was back at K.M.I. and wondering what he was doing there. "I am now far from my parents' home and my friends that are dear to me," he wrote his father, "placed in a high college for the purpose of acquiring a good education for the benefit of my future happiness. [. . .] Pa, when I reflect upon the past and calculate the years and months I have spent in the school room and on the blackboard for the purpose of acquiring an education, and several more yet to spend before I graduate, it seems to me that the best part of man's life is spent and he hardly knows what he has learned. [. . .] I don't see what inducement there is for anyone to get the best education in the world who expects to spend his life on a farm. [. . .] I am getting very tired of going to school but hoping that I may have enough perseverance to complete my education."

Only Ann's packages of "eatables" consoled him. "Tell Aunt Ann I am very much obliged to her for her pity and kindness to me in sending that good box of provisions which I partake of with the greatest honor of a well starved soldier," he added. "When I eat of that old ham and them good biscuits made me think of home once more. I can imagine the good hominy etc. you all partake of every morning at breakfast."

Patsey Miller wrote Ann of their father's illnesses, imagined and real. She worried about him sleeping alone on cold nights at a time when most people shared beds for warmth, sometimes even with their slaves. Belle's friend Mr. White is probably the "old beau" she mentioned in an 1849 letter, the one she had "given" to Martha.

PATSEY MILLER

Jan. 22, 1854

My Dear Sister,

[. . .] I have stayed at home till I have no inclination much to visit except to see my relations and, as Pa is now so often complaining of getting old and has not long to live, I would be delighted to get to see him a day or night every week or two, but I very seldom get up. Every now and then of late, he seems to be arranging his matters and his mind all the time upon that subject. He told Mr. Miller two weeks ago when he was in town that he did not expect to live long. [. . .] I have thought a great deal about Pa lately in the extreme cold night. We have had two or three of us in a bed here sometimes. [. . .] Pa, being so thin and sleeping alone, I fear he suffers and he is so afraid of troubling a negro or somebody. [. . .] Mr. Embry and Mary at last paid us a visit two weeks ago. She seems to be quite happy and he as attentive and clever as ever. [. . .] I think he is so kind and seems to be doing everything in every way to make Mary's time comfortable and happy [including building her a large Italianate house on the edge of town], purchasing good servants so that she ought to be a very good wife, and be as kind and treat his children as well as she can, [. . .] for, if he loves his children as he should do and Mary does not treat them well, it might and will tend to estrange his love for her. I have thought it a little strange that Nannie [Embry] has never been taken home. He must certainly wish her to be with him. [. . .] I too often perhaps have this subject on my mind for my own happiness [. . .] if I die and leave my little children, how horrid the idea that, for the sake of a young wife, they should have to be kept out, my little girls in strangers' houses. [. . .] Mary must not hear what I say. Still I have wished that I could talk to her without making her mad with me. She has no mother to advise her. At any rate, she is and will be watched with Hawk's Eyes. You are a stepmother, but take nothing I have said to yourself as it lays not at your door. [. . .] I suppose you have your excellent ice house full as we have had two or three good spells. We have filled ours. But the labour is thrown away about as, by the time we need it, it is gone. [. . .] I have felt quite sorry for Cousin William and Sister at Ezekiel's [Holloway] conduct. I have not seen Sister or been to town. I hope, at any rate, that I have exaggerated accounts that he was in a spree with other boys at Christmas. I suppose it is true, the report that he is spreeing frequently at night. [. . .] I feared his joining the church under the excited circumstances and being armed up by the old members would not result in real good, but would wear off. [. . .] Mr. White is renewing, I believe, his visits to Pa with some zeal. Well, as long as he has been visiting Belle, she never has said anything at all to me and I have heard more from his Brother Will than anyone else, that he had loved Belle for seven years and was heartbroken as she did not return his love [. . .] his mother and family lays his bad habits and dissipation to that cause. Well, in all my life I never heard of such constancy for if any other man had have been put off and treated as he has been they would have courted and married some one long ago [. . .] but it seems it was his first love. [. . .] I do not know how Belle has managed the matter at all, but [. . .] if she did not intend to marry him she should have given him a positive denial long ago [. . .] if Belle still suffers the engagement to exist and could believe him reformed and worthy of her, she ought to marry him or by all means not suffer his visits any longer. [. . .] I though fear a man who has taken his dram to drown sorrow or anything else. He will expect to do it again. [. . .]

Patsey I. Miller

Among Brutus's 1854 papers is a touching letter from Mingo's son in Missouri. It is not clear whether Dudle wrote it himself or dictated it.

DUDLE ALLISON

January 31, 1854 from Boonville [Missouri]

My dear father,

Many long years has elapsed since I heard from you and was of the impression that you was dead but was informed better a few days ago by Mr. Tivis. I am now living in Boonville belonging to a Mr. Frederick Houx and he is a very good master, too. I have also one of the best little wives you ever heard of. She is both kind & indulgent and we live as happily together as anyone could. Oh I wish you could see her. Aunt Malinda is well and doing well. Brother Hardin is living at a Mr. Elliot's. He is also married. I do not know much about his wife but she is not as sweet as my wife. Me & my wife are both members of the Methodist church. The season is very dry. There are some farms out in the Prairie from 250 to 350 acres that will not produce one gallon corn. How do things seem to come on in Kentucky? Do you think you will raise enough corn to make bread. [. . .]

Love to all, Answer as soon as you can. Here in Boonville I go by the name of Dudle Allison — What do you go by, I mean by what name?

Write soon,

Your devoted son,

Dudle

The same year Dudle wrote Mingo, Ann Clay began what she called her Negroe Book. In it she listed the winter and summer clothes distributed to every man, woman, and child on the place for the next twelve years: lindsey dresses, shirts, and undercoats for the women; shirts, jean pants, vests, and coats for the men; shifts for the girls, shirts and pants for the boys; socks for the men and boys (two pairs each), and hanks of yarn for the women's stockings. The summer outfit was similar, but of lighter material. Most of the garments were made by Ann and the slave women. In the early days, they wove the cloth as well. Up until the Civil War, Mingo made the shoes.

Ann listed all the recipients by name — Mahala, Bid, and Caroline, Leo, Harrison, and Blind Tom. Combined with Brutus's list of slaves, which gives their ages, mothers, and dates of death, it is possible to reconstruct some of the black families at Auvergne between 1846 and the end of the Civil War.

For example, Biddy, one of the women Brutus inherited from his father, was the mother of John, Peter, Augustus, Jacob, Simeon, James, Caroline, Nancy, Louisa, Amelia, Henrietta, and Harriet. John was living on the farm at the end of the war; Peter went to Mississippi with Kit; Augustus, having taken the name of Augustus Waters, enlisted in the Union cavalry in 1864; Jacob, Simeon, and James all died before the war began. Biddy's girls were not very lucky. All but Harriet had died by 1865, though Biddy herself was still alive.

According to his records, Brutus sold only ten of his many slaves, including two David Field took South with him a year later — Wesley, twenty-one, another of Mingo's sons, and a fifteen-year-old boy named Dudley. The other slaves Brutus sold were Matt (the runaway from the mills), Leanna (the Lean who tried to poison Patsey Miller), Pressley, King David, Dillard, Harriet (not Biddy's daughter), Eliza Ann, and Jane. He did give some slaves to his children, thus separating them from their families.

In February, nineteen-year-old Kit sent Aunt Ann one of his curiously worded letters. "With a determination I have seated myself to write you a few lines to let you know that I have a deep interest and respect for a mother." He continued, "I at present have something to undergo that is not as pleasant as hunting or fishing. You may judge what it is [. . .] *Hard Study*. I am studying Descriptive Geometry, Analitical [sic] Geometry, Shades & Shadows, and French." He was also studying surveying, but his father had not sent him his surveying instruments, and Kit asked Ann to remind him to do so. He concluded with a request. "I hope you will send down a box of refreshments soon. They will be expected with the greatest pleasure."

In May, Kit sent his father his account for the session, along with his report card. He had received ten demerits, though his general deportment and progress were considered "excellent." He needed money to pay his bills, he wrote Brutus, and for a trip to Mammoth Cave in south central Kentucky.

By the spring of 1854, his brother Green was also away from home, at Professor B. B. Sayre's preparatory school in Frankfort. Green's school account shows he spent 65 cents for Goodrich's *Fifth Reader*, $1.90 for a dictionary and a pen knife, $2.50 for a history of Kentucky, $.25 for indelible ink, and $1.05 for a comb and brush. At fifteen, Green was far more sophisticated than Kit. Judging from a picture made when he was a college student in the late 1850s, he looked a lot like the painting of young Brutus Clay that once hung at Auvergne.

The early letters Green exchanged with his siblings at home reveal interesting aspects of Brutus's fathering methods. Brutus taught his boys farming by "selling" them livestock, then encouraging them to trade with him and among themselves. Young Cash apparently owned both cattle and a horse. Cash in turn encouraged his sons, my father and Uncle John, in similar ventures involving chickens and bees.

Brutus's methods were passed on to a third generation. My brother and I owned four ewes, Fluffy, Giblet, Chocolate, and Caramel, which ran with our father's flock and produced lambs for sale every year. We had raised Fluffy and Giblet on bottles. (We had selected Chocolate and Caramel, both black, because we could easily spot them in the field.) Fluffy, who was mine, ate all the blooms off my mother's crocuses the spring she lived in our front yard, but she more than repaid us for this during her long productive life.

"Cash says he made swaps with you," Green wrote his father in April. "He says he gave you his colt which was rather stiff in the legs for a fine blooded calf. Tell him I think he cheated you."

He then asked about Brutus's recently imported bull, Locomotive. "I suppose you don't like him as well as Diamond." Diamond, purchased the year before by the syndicate for $6,000, later proved to be impotent. "Cash says that you have so many imported cattle that you are building another stable for them between the yard and barn lot." This was the first mention of an elaborate cattle barn Brutus was building.

Green concluded with an exotic note, "Have you heard from the buffaloes? I expect they are all dead," a reference to a livestock experiment his father began in 1850. Brutus's buffalo paid no attention to fences and soon scattered. The same thing happened with a recent attempt to raise buffalo in Bourbon County, and several semiwild animals roam the wooded banks of Stoner Creek today.

In an enclosed note to young Cash, Green remarked, "You say in your letter you have sold your peach trees to Pa for the whole calf which I think is a very good price for them, but if you don't mind Pa will sell him, but as you were so smart in taking his note for it, maybe he will not claim him. You say also you have swapped off your horse for a fine calf, which I think is a much better bargain than the other."

Always a bit of a clotheshorse, Green added a postscript to Aunt Ann. "I send my white pantaloons back for you to make me another pair or two, as I have not any summer pants. They fit me very well, as good as I would want them to fit me. You can make me some kind of striped pants for summer as I have not a pair of summer ones. You must not make them any larger or any smaller than the white ones. Do not make the legs a bit larger than they are. I had my coat cut yesterday. You can make me an alipacher [alpaca?] coat by it for a Sunday coat and if you have time you can make another striped every day coat. [. . .] You must send my clothes as soon as possible as nearly all the boys are beginning to dress in their summer clothes."

Belle, now almost twenty-three, was the only unmarried Field sister. Parties and dresses were foremost on her mind, judging from this letter to Ann.

BELLE FIELD

May 4, 1854

Dear Sister,

[. . .] The girls [Elizabeth and Martha Miller] came Monday to attend the May party. They have all just gone to The Store to finish their shopping so I shall take advantage of their absence in writing you. We had a very brilliant and grand time at the party, both old and young turned out, and the house was crowded, a very nice supper was prepared, and, of course, was enjoyed. In the forenoon, the girls formed a procession and marched around the public square. It being court day, of course, they created some stir as I noticed a good many of the county codgers following them some little distance as I presume they were lost to *wonderment and amaze*[ment].

[. . .] Mary Smith [Brutus's niece] was at the party, looking as beautiful as ever, said her father was much better. Owing to Ezekiel's [Field] carelessness, he neglected to tell you the morning you left what Mr. Rodes said. He told him to tell you that Colonel Smith was much better and that he was *not calculating upon dying* any time soon. [In fact, John Speed Smith died a month later.] [. . .]

Amelia and Mrs. Burton [Amelia's mother-in-law] left Tuesday morning. Sister as usual is quite sad and is looking forward to a trip this summer. Mrs. Burton attended the party, said she never saw as many beautiful girls together in all her life.

Pa is still annoyed with his cold, said he slept none last night on account of it. He distressed me to death to see him breaking himself down at The Store. When he can scarcely lift his arm, he is measuring heavy cotton cloths and such like. Cousin William [Holloway] went to the river yesterday and he [Pa] was necessarily detained at The Store all day long as the press was so great. [. . .]

Pa says he has scratched the blankets off and you will get them. [. . .] The edging has been charged. I must bid you goodbye. [. . .]

Belle

In mid-July, Brutus took possession of a fancy carriage he had ordered for Ann and Martha, a coupé rockaway made by George C. Miller and Sons of Cincinnati. Not only the bill for $495 but also architectural drawings of the carriage are among Brutus's papers. The rockaway, which was pulled by two horses, looked like the carriage in which Cinderella rides to her ball.

In May 1854, Congress passed the Kansas-Nebraska Act, establishing Kansas as a slave territory and Nebraska as a free territory. Its passage led to violence in Kansas as Free-Soil settlers and proslavery men from Missouri battled it out for control of the territory. The civil unrest in Kansas continued for more than two years, culminating in the Pottawatomie raid led by John Brown in May 1856. Meanwhile, Cassius Clay toured the Midwest, denouncing the Kansas-Nebraska Act and laying the groundwork for his future activities in the Republican Party.

Brutus was also thinking about slavery. He had promised, as executor of his brother Sidney's estate, to free certain slaves and their offspring when they reached the appropriate ages. At the beginning of 1855, two women, Cassy and Rilla, were approaching twenty-five, the age at which Sidney's will freed them. However, the 1850 Kentucky constitution forbade newly freed slaves from continuing to live in the state. Brutus needed to find a way to carry out the intent of his brother's will without violating the letter of the law.

On January 1, 1855, he arranged with Christopher Field and Sidney's surviving sons, Green and Sidney, that the young women, plus Cassy's small child, were to go to Mississippi to live with Christopher. When Cassy and Rilla were old enough to be freed, Christopher would take them to New Orleans and arrange for passage to Liberia for them under the auspices of the Kentucky Colonization Society. Brutus had a legal agreement drawn up, which all the principals signed.

In February, Christopher Field wrote Brutus from Mississippi inquiring about two slave women, a jack (a male donkey), and a bull. The livestock was intended for his plantation. The women were Cassy and Rilla. Christopher invited twenty-year-old Kit to accompany the girls and animals to Kentucky Landing. This would be Kit's first trip south, where he would join not only Christopher, but also David and Ezekiel Field. Christopher hoped to interest all three young men in becoming planters.

Of Cassy and Rilla, Christopher wrote Brutus in February, "I have a neighbor, Mrs. Cook, who is a very clever lady, and says she will take them on your terms and will treat them well and keep both in the house, one as a cook, the other as a house servant. I would consider it [a] much better home for them than either my own or O. M. Anderson's. We both have to keep overseers and they have the management of all during our absence, but Mrs. Cook keeps no overseer and never leaves home. If you was [sic] willing to this arrangement, Mrs. Cook & myself would pay the expenses of Christopher or some other person to bring all down. David said you had sold the Bull. Perhaps Sidney has one that would suit and you could give him as good a one hereafter. I think there would be no danger or evil in sending Kit down with them. David will give him all the information how to come and would come to Louisville. Boats know my landing. Kit could stay a while with me and hunt and I will go his security for good conduct in his absence."

David wrote to urge Brutus to let Kit come. "The arrangement Brother speaks of in regard to the Negroes is a good one. They will be better off with Mrs. Cook than hiring (generally) in Ky. I will pay to you if it is any inducement to let Cit [sic] go (as Ezekiel remains with the hope that C. F. Clay will come down & hunt with them). I will go down with him. Bro. seems exceedingly anxious to get the Jack & Bull & would like to hear whether they can be sent soon. The river is most too low now to ship stock well. It will certainly rise soon & I would much prefer going down on the best Louisville Boats (Shotwell say). They are much the safest. [Steamboats often exploded.] Shotwell will likely be leaving in about 2 weeks."

Brutus let Kit go. "I received a circular from Louisville stating that they expected the Shotwell up tomorrow & she would be there in 2 days," David wrote Brutus in March. "Suppose you send up the Bull & Jack by Wednesday morning train & I will take charge of them & send next day to Louisville. Christopher & the negroes can come [the] next day & go to Louisville in the afternoon. The Boat will not leave before Thursday night if that soon."

Judging from Kit's letter to his father after he arrived, he did not immediately fall in love with Bolivar County. Cassy and Rilla were not happy to be there either.

CHRISTOPHER CLAY

Steam Boat Empress, March 26, 1855

Dear Pa,

I arrived at Uncle C. I. Field's at last and all right. We got to Louisville in time to get on board the Shotwell. I found it to be a very fine and accommodating boat. We got the stock on without any difficulty. We went to Louisville on the morning train and the stock on the evening train. We got the Captain to wait for them. I find Miss. to be a very fine and warm country, but it is one of the hardest places for work I have ever seen. I find the people to be thinking about nothing but buying Negroes and making cotton. I like the country very well for a visit but not for a home.

The first day after my landing I killed two fine deer. [. . .] I saw all sorts and kinds of game, all sorts of squirrels. I am now on my way to New Orleans with Uncle Christopher. I have had but little trouble with the two girls. We did not give them a chance to escape. They were not at all satisfied with the country. Rilla has been sick ever since she left home. She was unwell all the time on the boat. Cassy stands the climate very well and don't seem to care where she is going. Rilla wants to come back home. She says she will kill herself before she will go to Liberia. She came up to me the other day and asked me what I was going to do with her. I thought it was no use to keep her in distress and I told her she had to go to Liberia. She seemed to take it very hard. I don't think you will catch me in such a scrape as this anymore. If it was some of them trifling scoundrels as that devil at the house, I could take them as far as wind and water could carry them with the greatest pleasure. But, as these two are such good Negroes, I have a feeling for them. [. . .]

Uncle Christopher thought that you intended for Mrs. Cook to keep them. He did not receive your letter that you wrote to him before I left home. He did not have any place for them without putting them with the plantation Negroes. But I told him they were both good cooks and house servants. So he has made arrangements for them very well. He has put one of them cooking and the other to wait on the table and tend to the house.

You must excuse this bad written letter as my pen is bad and you know how hard it is to write on the boat. [. . .]

Your Son,

Christopher F. Clay

When it came time for Kit to go home, his uncle sent a letter to Brutus.

CHRISTOPHER FIELD

Ky. Landing, April 21, 1855

Col. B. J. Clay

Dear Sir,

As Christopher is now thinking about returning home, I write you. He and David brought the negroes and stock all safe. The calf is a very fine one, indeed too valuable to come to our swamps. He fell off considerably and is yet thin though I am taking care of him. Sh. he live, he will be much advantage to our longhorns. The Jack is in fine health and vigor and I am much better pleased with him than when I saw him last summer. I presume 300$ is about the price you expected me to pay for him and I enclose you my note for him which I can settle almost anytime. The negroes seem very well satisfied so far, but say their hopes are that they will never have to go to Liberia. They say nothing about freedom and don't want it, that they had good homes and were contented. I have said to them when the time comes if they have to go they must do so. I concluded after they came that I would keep them myself, in fact, I thought the article of agreement bound me to do so. Your letter did not come for two weeks after they came. I have put Cassy to cooking for the negroes, only one meal, dinner. She will have an easy time. Rilla has taken the place of a small boy I had in the house, in the balance of her time serving. I consider both well situated for acclimation. Rilla has been sick, but not serious. [. . .] I think Christopher has enjoyed himself very well and I hope the trip will be of service to him. He went to N. Orleans with me, but I had to stay too long and he got tired of such constant gaiety as we had two young ladies in our party. He came home 3 or 4 days ahead of us. He has had fine sport hunting and is a very fine shot indeed. He has killed 7 deer, I think missed but once or twice, and is a very fine woodsman. Indeed a perfect Daniel Boone, fond of the wild woods and its game. He killed an alligator 6 or 7 feet long and a variety of other small game. He is a little singular in his disposition but not hard to wean over. He says he wants to go to Texas to see the country and live, if he likes it. I have tried to dissuade him from that and said to him if you thought it was not necessary for him to go to school anymore, that if he would show a disposition to go to business you would start him on a Ky. farm. I have seen no disposition on his part to dissipation in any way. [. . .] We have had a remarkable winter and spring, indeed not rain enough for stock water. [. . .] Ever since our levee system has been in operation, we have been planting quite successfully. A well managed place can clear about 10 percent on the capital invested beside the improvement of this property annually in value. [. . .]

Yours truly,

C. I. Field

While Kit was in the South, Green returned to school in Frankfort. He was already thinking about college. "I wish you would tell me whether you intend to send me to college or not and what college so that I may prepare those studies which are required to enter," he wrote his father in February of 1855.

Although Brutus did not answer his question about college, Green had an idea of his own, Yale. Since Uncle Cassius was a graduate, it was a natural choice. "I think I can enter the sophomore class at Yale this session," he wrote his father in March, "or at least 5 months in the next session with Mr. Sayre, excepting my Greek, which I could make up for as I just started Greek this session."

In April, E. H. Field wrote that he was sending David's sorrel mare over to Brutus's farm to be bred. "Probably David [. . .] said something to you about his wishing you to take charge of the mare until his return from Mississippi," he wrote.

A short time later, David himself arrived in Kentucky. "Got here last night," he wrote Ann from Lexington, "and found my sky as brilliant as when I left, not overgrown with clouds of disappointment. [. . .] I suppose I will be married about the middle of next month."

In May of 1855, thirty-five-year-old David Field, the self-proclaimed bachelor, married Lucy Scott of Lexington. Ann described the wedding to Brutus, who did not attend.

ANN CLAY

Richmond, May 14, 1855

My Dear Husband,

We reached Lexington about 3 o'clock the day we left home and I was a good deal surprised to find so many of our relations there. Mr. E. [Embry], Mary, Mr. H [Holloway] & Sister, and many others of the relations. [. . .] Great disappointment at not seeing you. David had told them all he expected you & I do wish you could have felt like going as it would have been a great gratification to many of us and you had many friends at the wedding who inquired particularly why you were not there. [. . .] They had a large and elegant wedding but I can assure you I felt but little like enjoying it. I had seen Mrs. K. in so much distress that it was with great reluctance I went to this wedding. [Mrs. Keiningham's husband had just died.] I do not think that I ever left home with a sadder heart. I regretted much that you did not come to the house to see us off. We came here [Richmond] the next day after the wedding & since Martha & me have been assisting Belle in her preparations for the party on Tuesday evening. Sister gives a large one on Wednesday next. David & his wife come over here on next Tuesday and will stay a week or 10 days. [. . .] We found in Lexington he [Green] and Ezekiel Field, being diffident, stood and leaned against the wall. David Irvine went to them and told them he heard a young lady say they were wallflowers so they were so much ashamed they left before getting their supper. Tell Zeke [Clay] he must write and plague Green about it. The supper was so fine, nice & good. I regretted Green did not get some as he would have enjoyed it much. Belle & Sister send you & Cit [sic] pressing invitations to their parties. Tomorrow evening Martha & me are going out to see your Sister Smith and will stay until Monday and we wish to make Patsey a visit, also Mary Jane, so I do not know certainly when we will get home. [. . .] Tell Cash to be a good boy and I will take him the book I promised him. Yours,

Ann M. Clay

[P.S.] David has bragged so much to all about you pressing him to make us a visit when he was married and said he had a great mind to ask you if you would not give him a party. [. . .]

David confirmed with Ann the plans for bringing his new wife to Auvergne. "We propose going to your house Thursday next & you might send the carriage in the afternoon. [. . .] Ladies carry a good deal of Baggage. Perhaps you had better send the one horse cart along with the carriage. If you do not hear from me you can make the arrangements. I told Bell what day we would go to your house. I will [not] bring anyone with us but will wish some friends to meet us there if we conclude to have a fishing-picnic etc."

Toward the end of the school year, Green wrote his father for money to pay his bills, $320 "as Mr. S. has raised upon his price." He had also borrowed fifteen dollars from his grandmother to purchase a coat.

That summer Brutus's nephew, another Green Clay, decided to go to Texas to look over land there he had inherited from his father, Sidney. Before leaving, he invited Ann and Martha to "come up tomorrow night and *grease a plate* with us." Rumor had it that the occasion would be a fancy party. "I can not imagine how such a report has got out as it was only at the solicitation of some of my friends to have a dance, that I concluded to have one, telling them that as I would be so busy preparing to start that they must be satisfied with what Louisa [his cook] could prepare to eat. I expect to have nothing except what

Louisa can get except a bowl of cream, but would like for you to come up during the day if convenient & bring some common plates with you, & assist here by your orders."

On the back of this invitation, Ann scribbled a list of things to do, perhaps in conjunction with Green's party: "Send Sid table cloth & towels, plates & spoons. Bone beef. Parch coffee. Make bread. Oysters, vinegar. Egg whites. Parch coffee (again). Stem apples. Make cake. Cook beef. Turkeys & Chickens. Make Jelly. Charlotte Russe. Send waggon to town. [. . .] spoons, Mrs. D [. . .] & Williams. Coffee pots. Brown cups & saucers. Lard in lamps. Trim candles. Wash apples."

On reaching New Orleans in early July, Green wrote to Kit. "I arrived here yesterday in company with Burnet & Fremont, two of the K.M.I. boys. We had a pretty gay time of it last night but I have had a severe diarrhea all morning attended with a good deal of pain. I was fearful at first that it was Cholera but I took some medicine & I feel very well now. I leave for Texas tomorrow. [. . .] Tell Judge [Bedford], Jim G., & all the boys that promised to write to me I will expect letters from them at Goliad. If you see Dave Richardson, tell him I will not sell him Billy Moore [probably a horse]. I have determined to take him to Texas. [. . .] Tell Sark T. not to fail to save them pups for me. What sort of a time did you have on the 4th? I took a drink at 11 o'clock in memory of Old Kentucky & swore off until my return to Bourbon."

Now that David Field was a married man, he bought a Mississippi plantation near his brother's. The 1850s were boom years for cotton. More and more land was under cultivation. The price of cotton had more than doubled. David hoped to cash in on this prosperity.

Just how real it was is debatable. Traditionally, historians considered plantation agriculture a decreasingly profitable enterprise, but revisionists have analyzed the available data and concluded that slave agriculture yielded as great a return on capital as many alternative investments. Others are not so sure, concluding that whatever the reasonableness of individual planters' reinvestments in agriculture the economy of the South as a whole was living on borrowed time.

Reinvestment in cotton country primarily meant the purchase of slaves. David didn't own any, so he wrote Brutus, inquiring if he had hands for sale. "My wife will go down with me in about a month and at her suggestion I have concluded to propose to you to sell us Eliza as Lucy thinks she will suit her and aid her much in fixing up and keeping house, sewing clothes, etc. I make the proposition also because I heard

you say that you had a notion of selling her. [. . .] I have heard Ann &
Martha say that they could not manage her on account of her temper
& I therefore suppose they would not object to her being sold to me."

He added a bit of family news. "Ann & Cassius [young Cash] &
Patty [sic] Field started to Estill [Springs] Saturday morning. Martha
with the others' company go to Mr. Miller's tomorrow afternoon &
then start to the [Mammoth] cave Wednesday morning. Lucy is to
meet them in Danville Wednesday. I cannot go as I am busy trying to
buy some negroes. [. . .] Should you have any other negroes that you
wish to sell you can let me hear from you & I will come down. My first
arrangement was to open a place on the ridge above Field & Irvine between their places & Lake Bolivar & did not expect Lucy to go down
with me & would not need such a girl as Eliza, but going on an improved place such a servant will help us very much in starting housekeeping etc."

E. H. Field wrote Ann in Estill Springs that the party had left for
Mammoth Cave. "Our friends for the cave got off directly after dinner
on Tuesday and reached Mr. Miller's in safety. Lucy will join them at
Perryville and from present appearances will have good weather for the
trip. In order to insure more comfort and [to be] certain in reaching the
cave, Christopher [Field] concluded to take Lawson [a slave] who rides
a work horse in case any accident should happen to the carriage or
buggy horses and also takes Mitchell [a slave] and a side saddle for the
girls alternately to rest themselves."

Ann wrote Brutus that same day.

ANN CLAY

Estill Springs, Thursday morning [postmarked August 30] [1855]

My Dear Husband,

I came up here on Saturday last in the stage and though we have
had rain every day & night untill [sic] yesterday I find I have improved
much. The water agrees with me well & I bathe twice a day which I
think is of great benefit to me. [. . .] Cash is getting along very well,
much better contented than I expected and would be delighted if it
were not for the little girls [Pattie Field and some of Patsey Miller's
younger daughters]. There is no company here except 4 southern fami-

lies and I do not feel so badly about being here without a gallant as I know the Chiles and they are all very polite to me. [. . .]

When I reached Richmond I found Sister Elizabeth in bed sick [. . .] & to make her worse Zeke [Holloway] had a few days before gotten into a drunken spree, behaved outrageously, and gone off to the Midway Springs and the night before I came up here he came back and went to Lexington in the night and left word with some one for his trunk to be sent to him, that he never intended to come back. His Papa sent money to pay his expense to Illinois & his trunk. The next day Sister was almost crazy about him.

Cash spent some time yesterday in writing to you untill he used up all of his paper and none of it was written well enough he thought to send to you [Cash was nine years old] so he requests me to say that he tacked up 3 of the Bills [probably political posters] at Richmond, one here, and when he can make up his mind to go he expects to take one to Irvine and he has concluded that Foxtown will be a suitable place for the other one.

[. . .] Green told me he intended to ask you to let him come to Richmond. If you are willing I would prefer his coming next week as I have to get him a good many clothes. He has none to commence school with. If he comes let Zeke [Clay] come with him, but make them come on horse back as it is so expensive through Lexington stage, fare $2 to Richmond. I intended to ask you if you were willing for Maria [a slave] to take some of Cash's chickens to town to sell the next Court Day. I want them out of the yard and he is not willing for them to be eat [sic]. [. . .]

Ann M. Clay

Like his father, Cash, my father raised chickens as a boy. He had a business selling fertilized eggs, which he shipped to their purchasers via the railroad, in boxes with labels of his own devising. "EGGS FOR Hatching. Keep From Extreme Heat and Cold. From CASSIUS M. CLAY, JR. Breeder of Latham Strain Barred Plymouth Rocks. Paris, Kentucky. HANDLE WITH CARE!" On the labels is a picture of his prize-winning hen, Biddy.

David was busy outfitting himself for plantation life. Although Brutus did not sell him Eliza, he agreed to part with Mingo's son Wesley and a young slave named Dudley. The man to whom they were rented, named Gaines, took them to Lexington, where David met them.

DAVID I. FIELD

Lexington, Ky., Sept. 30th, 1855

Dear Sir,

Gaines reached here yesterday afternoon & I was very much provoked to find he had Wesley so tied up. It was scandalous. He was hand-
cuffed, his arms tied behind him, a cord around his neck & that
fastened to the front part of the waggon [*sic*] & his feet chained and fastened to [. . .] part of the waggon. He had then put locks on him. The
negro's arms are very sore this morning. Gaines is an old fool not fit to
have anything to do with negroes. I was ashamed to own them. He
drove through the streets, came to the Bank inquiring after me with the
negroes in the waggon & fastened as they were. Of course I was not in
very good humor to appreciate the purchase of Dudley. I am very much
[. . .] [disappointed] in his appearance. He is very small, small boned,
not a good chest, weight about 80 lbs., is low stature, with about the size
of a 12 year old boy. I can show you boys 11 years old that I gave $875
for 1 foot taller than he, black & likely. I assure you I consider $600 a
big price for Dudley but I agreed to give $800 and shall fill up the note
at the figure but if on reflection you are satisfied that 600 is plenty you
credit the note by deduction of 200. I am well satisfied that you do not
want more than the negro is worth & that you as well myself did not
know what he was worth & that neither of us had seen him for some
time. [. . .] Gaines was telling me about Dudley, that he was 11 years
old, stout & likely, well grown, do as much work as a man, but did not
know what he was worth. I asked if he was worth $800 & he said yes.
[. . .] Had I have seen [him] I would not have bought him, but I do not
complain of you. My conversation with Gaines fixed the price. [. . .] I
expected to ship all the negroes tomorrow but have deemed it best to
defer it a few days on account of yellow fever. C. I. Field went to
Louisville yesterday, telegraphed me from Louisville last night I had
better wait a few days. Wesley says he told his wife several days ago that
he expected to be sold & she said she would like to go with him & that
her master would sell her that she has several children but they are not
here & she is willing to leave her children & go with him. Can you see
Mr. G., and if he will sell at right price, I will come around and look at
her. I am willing to accommodate negroes & buy their wives if I can at
fair prices. [. . .]

D. I. Field

Not long before I first saw this letter, I had been reading David Livingstone's descriptions of the slave caravans he had encountered in East Africa at about the same time. I felt a shiver of recognition. The cotton boom had increased the demand for slaves in the deep south, and Lexington was one place where dealers assembled their coffles — processions of shackled people — before heading south.

In October, Brutus was in Frankfort. Ann wrote him that a cattleman from Virginia was in Paris. "He came here on Friday night and said he had left three, Mr. Remmick & two young ladies, in town who wanted to visit us and the state, and probably would buy some stock of you. [. . .] Christopher says you did not tell him even that you were going away, says if you had have told him what stock you had for sale & the prices, he thinks he could have sold some. He took Mr. Rogers to see the calves and he thought you had saved the lightest roan one for him, but Rogers preferred a dark red that is in the stable with the light roan. [. . .] Rogers says that Mr. Remmick wants to buy a fine Jack and he had told him he expected you would supply him so if you want to sell you must let us know the price."

By 1855, Kit Clay had his own account at what was now Shackelford and Hoverton's in Paris. On it are recorded frequent twists of tobacco ($.25), pipe tobacco ($.75 for a half a pound), and two "papers of smoking tobacco" ($.20). He also bought a red saddle blanket ($2.75), various kinds of cloth and trimmings for pants, coats, and vests (Shackelford's charged one dollar for making up a pair of pants), spurs, and riding gloves for a modest total of $42.56.

Kit was growing up in other ways, too. By 1856 he had returned to Mississippi, where he and Ezekiel Field Jr. were toying with the idea of acquiring a plantation. Christopher Field had offered to help them go into business together on partially cleared land he had first offered to David.

CHRISTOPHER CLAY

Bolivar, Jan. 4, 1856

Dear Pa,

[. . .] Uncle Kit has made a survey lately of the land he proposed to sell me and found about six hundred acres of good land that can be cultivated without any difficulty [. . .] on the Kentucky Ridge, the same ridge that his plantation is on. And we think the land as good as his or better. The six hundred acres is stiff cane land. That sort of land we consider the best, as that is a good sign of being above the over-flow. But I think the country is leveed so well now that there is no danger. [. . .] I think about two hundred acres of this land has been deadened [the trees girdled], some for several years, and the balance last year. I have been through the part that has been deadened and I find all of the trees dead and falling down. I think one hundred acres is now fit for cultivation after the cane and logs cut and burned. I think this tract of land as good and cheap as any land in the swamp that has no im-provements. Col. Manley, a neighbor of Uncle Kit, offered to sell me his place for fifty dollars per acre. He has three hundred acres in culti-vation. He has a nice house and splendid gin and everything that is necessary. He says he has been offered $50 per acre and of course he won't take any less. I told him I would like to have his place, but his price I could not stand. [. . .] I am satisfied with the land and price of Uncle Kit's. [. . .] Uncle Kit is willing to go in with me and I think by his assistance we can clear out a little place in a few years. [. . .] I have made up my mind, if I can't do better, I will make a start next fall, if you are willing and I have luck. [. . .] I will look for an answer as soon as convenient.

Your son,

Christopher F. Clay

Meanwhile, Christopher Field and Brutus's nephews, Sidney and Green Clay, had worked out an arrangement whereby Green would take the slave women, Rilla and Cassy, with him to Texas, in contra-diction of their agreement with Brutus. They justified doing this on the grounds that the girls did not want to go to Liberia.

The proposal must have originated with Christopher. "I have just read your letter to Sid," Green wrote him, "and have concluded to take the negro girls with me but I do not wish Uncle B. to know anything about [it] [. . .] have the negroes in readiness to start at any moment and I will stop the boat at your place and get them. But should I fail to get them, you can ship them to Indianola, Texas [. . .] & I will of course pay all expenses incurred."

Sidney added, "For the proper control of Green's slaves it would be best that the girls should believe they are to remain & be slaves also.

Therefore I think you would do well to tell them that they go to Texas as such."

Kit had no part in this deception, though he must have known about it. His mind was on the land he hoped his father would buy for him.

CHRISTOPHER CLAY

Bolivar P.O., Miss., Mar. 10, 1856

Dear Pa,

[. . .] The land I have been thinking about settling the other day Uncle Kit and I surveyed or rather ran the outlines of the whole tract. We both have come to the conclusion that it is a fine tract of land. Uncle Kit thinks it worthy of settling as well as myself. We found the outlines most of the time a stiff cane break, a few dry sloughs, which is no objection. We infer, after finishing the outside lines [surveyor's lines] thro cane, that the interior must be likewise. You stated you could give me a few Negroes if I liked the country well enough to settle here. If you expect me to settle the ridge, you will have to give me a strong force. If not, I could never clear enough land to make bread. I must say before we go any further, I am not anxious, neither have I made up my mind to be content with the swamp. I am pleased with the country, provided I have an improved place. You will see in one of my letters to you the proposition I made to Col. Manley. I had a conversation a few days ago concerning the trade; he says he can't trade so I think [there] is no chance to get his place at a reasonable price. [. . .] Uncle Kit will write to you by this week's mail and give you his views on and about the whole arrangement. It seems from your letter and all I have received from home [you] are anxious for me to settle here. [. . .]

I am getting quite lonesome here and I will start for home about the middle of next month. [. . .]

Yours sincerely,

Christopher F. Clay

In mid-March, Green Clay passed on his way to Texas. As Christopher told Brutus, he was glad to get the women off his hands.

CHRISTOPHER FIELD

Kentucky Landing, March 22nd, 1856

Dear Sir,

A few days since Green Clay passed my landing on the *Belle Sheridan* and hailed one of the negroes as she passed to send Cassy & Rilla on to New Orleans by the 1st Boat. After much reflection, hesitation, and doubt what I ought to do [about] the strong and urgent appeals of the negroes, I concluded to let them go and you never saw two more joyful negroes in your life. If they had been sentenced to be hung on a given day and had just heard of their reprieve, they could not have depicted more joy. I feared Green & Sidney had made no satisfactory arrangement with you tho if Green had any letter to me from you, he had no chance to leave it as the boat did not even stop her steam. You nor the heirs will never have any difficulty so far as the Negroes are concerned. They said they did not want their freedom, never had wished it, that they never intended going to Liberia, that they were perfectly willing and desirous to go to Texas with their mother, brothers, & sisters and forever remain slaves of Green. I may not have acted right towards you in giving up these Negroes without having your written permission but I have erred on the side of feelings towards the Negroes. I could not have had the heart to have forced them to New Orleans and given them up to the Colonization Society. They came to me some time ago much dissatisfied and earnestly but respectfully told me they would never see Liberia. I then suspected they had come to some desperate determination and asked them, but they would not tell me, but the day they left, they voluntarily told me they had agreed to drown themselves when they found they would certainly have to go. They are much better off as the slaves of Green with their kin with the views they had. They were both delicate and would never have supported themselves in Liberia. Had there been males going along with them from the same family it would have been different but two helpless delicate females alone with the men & feeling [as] they had would have done no good and freedom, instead of a boon, would have been a curse. My anxiety to get clear to them may have made me act hastily. They had both so far as I know of acted properly at my house, but when I was away from home [white] men was [sic] prowling about. This to me was annoying in the extreme. Their failures in succeeding heightened their desires and caused renewed efforts. I did not intend them [the girls] to have remained another summer on my place and I had heard that some of my neighbors were accusing me of being guilty of the success in which they failed. I was not guilty and do abhor such a practice and could not reconcile it to myself to be in such a situation when not guilty of the act. [. . .] I have been this lengthy knowing I have acted hastily, hoping you will appreciate my motives in the matter and I wish you to write me on the subject as I wish to know upon what ground I stand. [. . .] No news. Had a terrible winter. [. . .] Love to all.

Yours respectfully,

C. I. Field

N.B. I ordered my merchant to send Cash some Tobacco seed. Did he get them?

What Christopher is talking about here are sexual relations between white men and slave women, a taboo subject. They occurred frequently, though no one in the South would admit it. Some of Christopher's neighbors or their overseers evidently had designs upon Cassy and Rilla, and, unable either to seduce the young women or force them to have sex with them, had started rumors that they were Christopher's mistresses.

I wonder if Rilla and Cassy understood what was happening to them. I can't blame them for not wanting to go to Liberia, but, by setting off for Texas, they were closing the door on freedom. Green died in Texas a few years later and Rilla and Cassy were no doubt sold at auction to help pay his debts, even though they were free women.

In April, David and Lucy Field and a baby born two months earlier, Matthew Scott, were ready to leave for Mississippi. David wrote Brutus to accept Ann's offer of "a pair of *Cass* chickens if the boys can fix up a coop for 1 pair. [. . .] They can come on the freight train [to Louisville] with the calf."

In June, Brutus's son Green wrote for money with which to pay his bills at Professor Sayre's: $290 for board and tuition, "including two or three other fees due to outside teachers," plus $60 for a trunk and books. Green was still debating whether to continue to study with Sayre or to enroll at Yale. As he decided to do the latter, his next letter came from Connecticut.

GREEN CLAY

Fontaine House, N. Haven, Conn., July 21st, 1856

Dear Pa,

After a long & dusty [train] journey we arrived here last Saturday morning. I was much fatigued & thinking "you all" were somewhat concerned about my safe arrival, I sent you a dispatch soon afterwards, but, as I am now rested, I will congratulate upon a more lengthy scale.

I have found New Haven to be a very beautiful City & perhaps will find Ct. to be very pleasant afterwhiles. [. . .] I notice the manners and customs of the people here are different than those in Ken. While I have not now time to speak I will leave until another time.

I find favorable Circumstances for entering College. I have seen my tutor and will talk more with him tomorrow upon the subject.

Looking over the Catalogue, I see the Amount of Money to be secured in advance is $200 which you can attend to anytime between now and September, the time for entering College. I will send you a catalogue in a day or two.

Yours truly,

Your affect. Son Green

A few days later, Green wrote his father again. "I wish to ask you what class you would prefer for me to enter under the following Circumstances viz. After consulting my tutor, I find by 'Close Cramming' (as we here term it) I can get into the *Junior Class perhaps*. But will be somewhat behind my classmates therefore can take no *considerable* stand[ing]. I now propose to you that I give up all my aspirations for Junior and turn my attention to Sophomore, which class I can enter with some merit upon my part and more satisfactory to you."

Brutus advised his son to enter as a sophomore. Green thanked him, then asked for additional money. "You will please send an amount at my disposal as my Check in Bank is getting rather low, having to pay for some furniture etc. Also I shall have to pay a large tutor fee being at the rate of 75 cents per hour.

"It will require a good deal more money now at the beginning than at any other time after I get my room etc. fixed up. [. . .] As to the amount it will be as is convenient with you. $100 or $150. It will not be wasted or spent foolishly."

That fall the Kentucky Agricultural Society, of which Brutus was president, held its first statewide fair on the Bourbon County Fairgrounds. A new circular exhibition pavilion was built for the occasion, and the Lexington and Maysville Railroad laid double tracks between the fairgrounds (on the southern end of town) and downtown Paris to make it easier for people to get to and from the exposition. Brutus must have felt pleased with this visible proof of economic growth. Furthermore, the imported bull Locomotive, standing at stud on his farm, won first prize.

The following November, *The Country Gentleman*, a magazine published in Albany, New York, printed an article entitled "A Day or Two Among the Bourbons," which included an account of a visit to Auvergne. The author, Lewis Falley Allen, was an agricultural journalist with whom Brutus had had correspondence.

"Brutus Clay lives on a farm of two thousand acres, or more, four miles south of Paris," Allen wrote. "The road leads over a beautiful, undulating, and well-cultivated country. For near a mile before you reach the gate leading into his premises, his buildings are in sight, and between them and the highway lies a very considerable farm. Entering a gate, and by a carriage road through the open pastures, another gate or two is passed, which puts you on to Mr. C's own grounds, and a ride of a hundred rods places you at a gate leading into his home park of sixty or eighty acres, to which a well-wrought carriage way takes you into the lawn in front of his house, a spacious brick mansion in all its appointments fit for such an estate and the residence of a wealthy country gentleman."

On the left as you approach the house were barns, stables, and cattle sheds, including a stone barn 160 feet long and 40 feet wide, "with convenient yards arranged about them, having water at command, and separated by substantial stone walls," continued the author. On the other side were horse barns and paddocks.

"The foreground of the dwelling is filled with a variety of luxuriant exotic shrubbery and trees; in the rear a large garden, and beyond that, a noble woodland pasture, where under the great oaks, walnuts, maples, ashes, beeches, and hickories, grazed his forty or fifty Short-Horn cows and their female progeny." (That pasture, virgin forest, looks much the same today as it did one hundred and fifty years ago.)

"Adjoining this woodland park, in the rear of Mr. Clay's garden, are the laborers' cottages, a dozen perhaps in number, white-washed, clean, and comfortable, with a garden for each family attached, everything in *order*, and abounding in plenty." The "laborers" presented Allen with a bit of a problem. He never once referred to them as slaves, and he made their dwellings sound as hospitable as possible.

"Stretching away on the north, east, and south [. . .] lie the corn and wheat fields of the farm, intermixed and surrounded by the great pastures. The farm is chiefly devoted to grazing. Mr. Clay's herd of Short-Horns with one or two exceptions is the largest in Kentucky, and one of the best. He breeds horses largely, rears a great many mules; and produces many of the finest jacks and jinneys that Kentucky can boast, as well as all the swine he needs. [. . .] In short, this is one of the finest and most systematically managed stock farms in the State, and a day's ramble over it, together with the hospitalities which are extended to the visitor by the refined and cultivated family residing upon it, mark it as one of the most agreeable in the journey of his life."

Although *The Country Gentleman* article is a puff piece, an example of what my brother calls "progressive agriculturalist rhetoric," it gives a good idea of what Auvergne looked like in the mid-1850s. Allen also described Brutus's new cattle barn. Brutus's barn burned in the 1920s, and all that remains of it are its limestone foundations and photographs taken by my grandmother and my father at the turn of the century.

The barn, which was the last word in agricultural innovation at the time, had a central aisle that my father remembered as having metal tracks along which a feed cart could be rolled. On either side of this aisle were bays that went the length of the barn. The complex included a large cistern/well at the western end and a small stone structure where my father said the cattle feed was cooked. The barn was surrounded by stone-walled paddocks, The Lots.

My brother and I used to play in The Lots, building dams on the branch that ran through them and climbing all over the timber and cement roof of the old cistern. We ignored the huge cracks in its roof. One morning at breakfast, George Brent, our handyman, reported that the cistern roof had collapsed during the night. We all walked down to The Lots to look at the splintered locust posts and pieces of wire fencing covered with cement which hung haphazardly above six or eight feet of dirty water. I stared at them a long time, riveted by the thought of our narrow escape.

Traveling between Kentucky and Connecticut was costly, so Green spent the Christmas holidays at Yale. "Spending my Christmas in a manner never before," he wrote his father, "lounging in my room, having no fun at all, what we might term fun but nevertheless very agreeable to myself, hearing instead of Crackers and 'big guns,' slay bells by the hundred; instead of being troubled by 'Christmas Gift! Christmas Gift!,' saluted with 'Merry Christmas! Merry Christmas!' [. . .] I did think that I would go to N. York, but upon taking a second thought I concluded not to go, knowing that a good many of the students were going down, and of course I would have to join them and have a 'big Christmas spree.' So I may set down one wise movement of my own during the college course and I hope I may make many more such."

Green was enjoying himself. "If Cash had awoke a few mornings back in New Haven he would have been very much surprised at seeing the deepest snow on the ground he ever saw. And in a few moments would have raised a great laugh seeing me, the first one from the door, in a snow bank, nearly up to my neck." He admired the sleighs he saw on the streets of New Haven, noting the rugs in which travelers wrapped themselves. "They are some kind of fine fur, very nicely lined so as not to soil the ladies' silks. Just the thing for Aunt Ann and Sister to use in the rockaway these cold days."

Negotiations to acquire a Mississippi plantation for Kit proceeded slowly. After David bought a developed place, Christopher Field offered the Kentucky Ridge property to his brother Ezekiel. Zeke Field was slow to take him up on the offer, so Christopher approached Kit. By January 1857 he was talking about a partnership, as this letter to Zeke explains.

CHRISTOPHER FIELD

Kentucky Landing, Mi., January 10th, 1857

Ezekiel

Dear Sir,

[. . .] I have with Mr. S. Cook [a neighbor] made a partial survey of the ridge land and find it even better than I had thought when you were here. Your declining to go into partnership with Christopher has placed me in an unpleasant attitude. I invited you both down to settle the land thinking if both were pleased that it would suit very well for *you*, particularly, to have a partnership with Christopher as you would not be able to start on your own hook as well as I would like to have seen you done and I felt like I could help you but little as I was compelled to put my means with David. I am aware that I invited you first but at that time I did not know what amt. you would be able to commence with as Pa had said nothing to me. When I went to Mr. Clay's I had no idea of Mr. Clay having any desire for C. to come here. He proposed to buy my interest with David. I told him David would not be willing. I then remarked to him I had this land. At the time it did not occur to me that you would be very likely to come here to live and if you did I saw no reasons why you & Christopher could not plant together but I now see the dilemma I have got myself in. I of course would prefer giving you a bargain to Christopher. He is through his Pa able to commence anywhere but he was willing and proposed to you to go in together. You refused. He then said he would take the land himself. [. . .] I confess I am sorry I named it to both of you at the same time. I should have waited until one had backed out. I still think the best thing for you would be to join Christopher. I could sell the 1350 acres for 20,000$ in a month. I proposed to sell it to you both at $6750. If C. takes the land, I shall sell him but 1/2 interest and will form a partnership myself but I now propose to you this: if you will plant with him I will sell you 1/2 on 5 year credit and will loan you the amt. that Christopher will owe me on same time. This amt. with what Pa will give you will start you with 12,000$ and I would consider your land worth full 6000$ more than you owed for it. Well, plant a year to two with Christopher. If you then found you could not get along, propose to buy or sell. If you had to buy I could help you. If you sold you would sell at the true value of your interest not what you have paid for the land but its real value. I don't want you to lose this difference between what I sell at and what it is worth. [. . .] I am aware that Christopher is contrary and self-willed and will be hard to get along with & is domineering but you can have an article of agreement stating what part of the planting interest each is to have charge of and I think he will improve some, in fact I think I have already changed him very much since he has been here. [. . .] Show this letter to Pa and Mr. Holloway or Mr. Embry and get their views. I have no interest further than wishing to aid you. If Christopher leaves here before I hear from you, I will say to him I will plant with him and that you may change your mind etc. but write

me nothing in answer that I cannot show your letter to him if he is
here as he will of course expect to read it. [. . .]

Your brother

C. I. Field

Kit wasn't thinking about partnerships. "Since I wrote my last letter, I have made a proposition to Col. Manley for his plantation containing about five hundred acres," he told his father in January of 1857,
"about four hundred acres clear. The proposition is this: I agree to take
20$ per acre for the land Uncle Kit sells me, laying back of Col. Man-
ley's upper plantation, we think about five hundred and sixty acres. I
am to give him $45 per acre if I sell him 560 acres. If not, I pay him $40
per acre. [. . .] Col. Manley is willing to take $25,000 for his home-
place. That you see would be $45 per acre. By me selling him five hun-
dred acres or more at $20 per acre, which Uncle Kit sells me at five,
will do very well towards paying for Manley's homeplace.

"I will sell Col. Manley five hundred acres. [. . .] That would be
$10,000 towards paying for the Manley place. I would then owe him
$15,000, five thousand the first of January, 1858, and the balance in 1
and 2 years without interest. I would owe Uncle Kit $2500 but he says
I could let that stand until I could pay it. [. . .] If you could give me
twenty five hands, I could pay the one and two notes, $5000 each, by
the time they would be due. If not, Uncle David would rent the land I
would not be able to cultivate.

"I told Col. Manley when I made the proposition, if we concluded
to trade, you would have to sanction it before it could be closed. Uncle Kit and David think it is a good bargain if we should trade. Uncle
Kit thinks it rather an uphill business starting a new place with all un-
climated [sic] Negroes. But, if I can't trade with Manley, I am willing to
try and start the Kentucky Ridge place."

The Holloways' son-in-law, R. G. Burton, wrote Christopher in
January that he had purchased the Richmond residence of Squire
Turner, the man whose son Cassius Clay had killed at Foxtown. The
Turner house still stands, somewhat altered, on North Second Street.

Burton had moved to Richmond in order to become a partner in
The Store. "We finished taking account of stock on the day preceding
New Year," he wrote Christopher. "I was fully aware that the stock was

large but thought it would not exceed $25,000. It reached $31,700. Col. H. [Holloway] says that he will not buy largely this spring as the stock is certainly very large. I shall encourage him in his determination."

He concluded with news of holiday parties and a mention of David's son. "Col. John A. Duncan gave a party which would have been largely attended had it not been for inclemency of the weather. Notwithstanding he had a respectable turn out. Those that attended [. . .] drank champagne and danced nearly all night. Clifton Estill not feeling inclined to be surpassed by any bachelor of the nation gave an entertainment a few evenings afterwards which was also spoken of in very complimentary terms. [. . .] Please remember me to David, Wife & Master Scott. Ezekiel [Field] says Scott can beat in sprightliness & good looks all Ky. boys of his age. Amelia thinks Johnny [Burton] is hard to take and Ma thinks Bobby is not surpassed so we will try to get them together next summer and let you decide the *nice* point."

In March, Christopher Field sent Brutus a map showing the land he intended to sell.

CHRISTOPHER FIELD

Ky. Landing, Mar. 9, 1857

Col. B. J. Clay

Dear Sir,

[. . .] On the opposite page is a plot of our immediate neighbourhood, including the land which I proposed to sell jointly to Christopher & Ezekiel or to join Christopher myself if Ezekiel should decline. How they will determine time will tell. I have examined the land with chain & compass. [. . .] I think there is fully 600 acres behind Kentucky Bayou on and adjacent to Ky. Ridge which is mostly cane land. All of this 600 acres can be cultivated. You will then perceive from the plot that about 500 acres in Sec. 9 is represented as being in front of Ky. Bayou & ridge. This is a level slough formerly overflowed [. . .] but can now be cultivated as well as the ridge, tho it is 5 or 6 feet higher than the slough. This 500 acres is the land which Manley wants. [. . .] I a month ago thought there was a strong probability of Manley offering to take this 500 acres at 20$ in exchange for his home place at 45$, but I

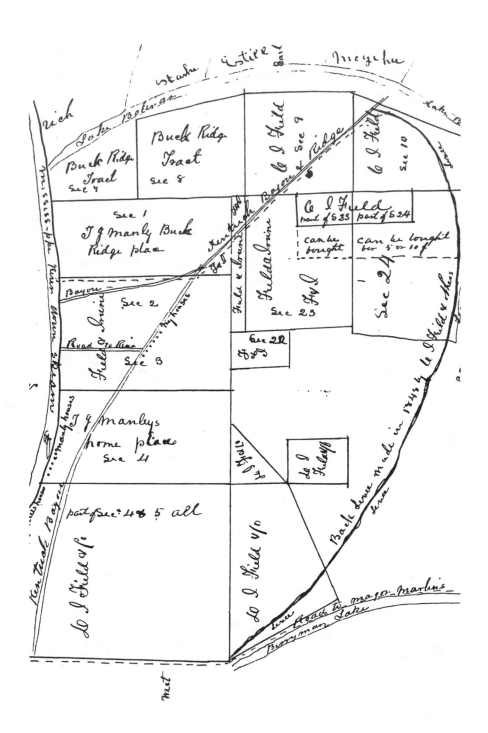

now doubt whether he will accede. [. . .] As to the value of my 12 or 1300 acres of land I have no hesitation in saying I could have sold it repeatedly this winter for from 15 to 20$, but I was and am willing to give C & E a great bargain in it. If E declines, I will join C and put as many hands on it as he does. I believe he is very well satisfied with the country and has made up his mind to try it. I have let him come to his own conclusions without any aid of my own, in fact, I have shown him the dark side for I think he is foolish in preferring to live here when you could fix him up in Ky. [. . .] It will be very bad for him if he settles here next fall not to get the negroes in the fall. If he did so, he could build houses & get land enough cleared by spring for them to cultivate but not if he got them the 1st Jany. as you propose. If he comes, you must make some arrangement to release those that are hired and you put some at home in their place until the end of the year. [. . .] There is about 200 acres well deadened land on the tract and will make a good crop the lst year when cleaned up. As to the value of the land, if the two take the land, I shall feel that I have presented them with 7500$ each. The dotted line along Ky. Bayou & Ridge and along the line between D. I. [David Irvine] and the Back Ridge place will be their nearest road to the River. [. . .] The round dot on Sec. 9 is where they will build which is the front of the ridge & 6 feet higher than the slough. [. . .] Christopher has killed some 20 deer, wild geese, pidgeons, partridges, coons, opossums, & nearly everything our country abounds with. Has met with no Bear. [. . .]

C. I. Field

The river is very high upon the Levee.

N.B. [. . .] If any chance should offer to buy young likely negroes in your county, Pa will advance the money for E or myself or if you saw proper to do so the interest will be paid you. [. . .]

En route back to New Orleans in March, Christopher Field learned that a relative of his late wife had died. News that the dead man's sister proposed to marry an infamous gambler threw Christopher into a fit of depression, similar to the one that followed the murder of his slave Jim years earlier.

CHRISTOPHER FIELD

Mss Ingoma March 26th 1857

Dear Ann,

I am on my way home from New Orleans having left home ten days ago and have truly had a trip of grief and sorrow. I heard when I got on a Louisville Boat on my way down of the death of O. [Orville] M. Anderson which news I was unprepared to receive tho I had heard of his sickness in Rome. [. . .] He was truly a gentleman in all of his conduct and acts and we were truly companions. [. . .] Then to add to my sorrow and grief on my arrival in New Orleans I saw a paragraph in a freight letter that the marriage of Miss Anderson of Louisville, Ky. was deferred in consequence of the death of her Brother and who do you suppose she was or is married to? [R.] Ten Broeck, a high gambler and horse man, the former owner of Lexington [a famous racehorse]. He is said to be a good looking man, very smart and plausible. Orville, poor man, in an unthoughtful moment introduced him to his sister never dreaming of such a thing as marriage for he must have known who he was. Orville was taken sick and Ten Broeck went to his house and remained with him until he died (Orville was keeping house in Rome) and I presume it was his attention that has brought about this thing. My only hope is the marriage will be deferred until she returns [to Kentucky]. If so it will never take place as she will then find out who he is. I telegraphed three times to Geo. Anderson from N.O. One answer said they did not believe it. I then asked him if anyone had gone for her. His answer was they were waiting to hear from her. I then answered lose not a day and go immediately. I would rather go to [. . .] [my] grave than it should happen if my Pattie is to thus throw herself away. I want her to die before she is grown. I am weighted down with grief, sorrow, and mortification and it seems my responsibilities are yearly increasing. He made a will before going to Europe and left George and myself his Executors. Tho I had as much business as I could attend to I do not feel I can refuse to act. I know he would have done so for me if I had have been in the same situation. Say but little about this marriage. If it can only be prevented. [. . .]

Your brother C. I. Field

Green continued to study at Yale. He had an active social life and was often short of money. "I know you are somewhat displeased at the amt. of my expenses," he wrote his father in June of 1857, "yet I am compelled to ask you for $250. I had concluded to ask you for none or not more than $100, and borrow the rest from some of my relatives or friends, but thinking that this might be unpleasant to you and it would be extremely so to me, I have asked you for the full amount that will cover my expenses and leave some $40 in hand for my vacation. You may think I am extremely extravagant, but Messrs. Brown and Burnley's sons have each spent over $1000 since they have been here." He added that he hoped to spend his summer vacation traveling through Canada and western New York State.

Brutus was slow to respond to his son's request. "I write to remind you of my letter. [. . .]," Green wrote in early July, "I hope that this will cause an answer from you, whether you grant my favor [. . .] or only drop me a line or two, that I may feel I have one in this world who cares something for me and above all a father." Brutus did not send him money, and Green spent his vacation in Kentucky.

During the summer, Brutus decided to buy half the land in Mississippi himself. Christopher would give Zeke the rest. In September, Kit and Zeke prepared to go south as partners. "I think Christopher and Ezekiel ought to be ready to leave Louisville on the 1st Oct.," Christopher Field wrote Brutus, "at least leave home on that day. All the articles they will need such as axes, tools, etc. had better be bought at Louisville. [. . .] All they need start from home with will be their bed clothing, such as sheets, comforts, towels, etc. and their Negroes. If you could spare C. two of your broke mules it would be very well. I will make you a short visit between now and the time they will leave and we can arrange the deed to the land."

He then addressed their financial arrangements. "Ezekiel will invest about 8000$ in Negroes. I will loan E. say 4000$ which will be near the amount that C. will owe me for the 1/2 the land and the cost lately paid for deadening 400 acres and 200$ worth of plank purchased for them before I left home which would make them start equal, etc. etc."

In September, Green had a perilous trip back to college. "I left Cin. that evening, traveled all night and arrived in Columbus, O. next morning several hours after the due time," he told Brutus. "Luckily our train was behind time at Columbus, for there was an accident on the road just beyond Columbus a piece. A large tree had blown across the road and [the] train from New York had run into it doing tolerable fast speed in the night with considerable smash. If we had made our right time likely [we] would have been first train along where the tree was fallen."

He had also had money problems en route. A dozen years of growth and prosperity suddenly crumbled in the summer of 1857, when the failure of an Ohio investment house touched off a financial panic. "Tell Sis [Martha] she was smart getting rid of her N.Y. bills (although I laughed at her)," Green told his father, "for I find they would not [take a] check on [a] N.Y. Bank at Paris or at least did not like to and at Cincinnati at railroad office did not like to take N.Y. money (as below par), preferred Ky. money."

In October, Kit finally got his Mississippi plantation — though his prudent father held on to the title. One hundred and thirty-two years after Christopher Field drew the map he sent Brutus that October, my brother and I used it and an earlier one to locate the Field and Clay lands in Bolivar County. Superimposing Christopher's drawings on a U.S. Geological Survey map of the area from Catfish Point to the hamlet of Bolivar, we could see exactly where Content and the other plantations had been. The river had cut through the shore opposite, making it an island and bypassing what had once been Kentucky Landing. Before the river cut through, it had undermined most of the riverside plantations so that the land the slaves had laboriously cleared at Christopher and David's places was carried downstream. By 1995, what was left of those plantations was largely outside the levee, a tangle of canebrakes and cypress swamps. Brutus's plantation, being inland, was intact.

It was a glorious May day, hot but with a steady breeze. We sat in the grass on top of the levee. Below us, flat as a tabletop, lay several thousand acres of dusty gray fields. The cotton was only an inch high and we could easily pick out a slight rise angling northeast from the levee. "Look," said my brother, "Kentucky Ridge." Following a gravel road along the crest of the ridge, I could see a clump of buildings, a house, a barn, and six smaller houses. They were right where Christopher had put the dot to indicate where Kit should build his house.

We drove over to the compound and knocked on the door of the main house. There was no one home. Then we noticed a man working on a tractor in the barn. We waved and walked over to him. My brother explained that our family had once owned land there, and we were trying to locate it. "Do you know what this place used to be called?" he asked. Green, the last of the Clays to live there, had called it Isole, French for "isolated," a comment on how he felt about finding himself in Bolivar County.

"This here's Isole Plantation," the man replied, pronouncing it "eesolay," which is correct. "I rent it from the Prudential Insurance Company."

"This is what we're looking for," my brother said.

"The house burned twenty years ago and they brought this one over from another place. You all look around all you want."

I walked to the front yard, sat down under a pecan tree, and looked out across a little slough in front of the house on which a pair of mallards paddled. How strange to be looking over a landscape Christopher, David, and Kit had scanned so many times. It wasn't the same landscape, of course. Today Bolivar County is so intensively cultivated for cotton, rice, and soy beans that it seems scarcely habitable for human beings, and certainly not for deer, alligators, and bears. But there in the distance were the low wooded shores of Lake Bolivar. And to my left, beyond the levee, the great muddy river itself.

In October 1857, old Ezekiel Field was again ill, and Ann hurried to his side. In her absence, Martha was in charge of the house at Auvergne. "You must make your visit and stay as long as you feel inclined," she told Ann. "There is nothing to bring you home except these troops of mean negroes & they do not deserve any consideration." Cash had been to the circus, she added, and one of Amy's [a slave] children had the flux.

At Yale, Green had apparently failed to attend "the religious and literary exercises of the college" often enough and had received demerits. "He has I am sorry to say over sixteen unexcused marks against him for absence from college exercises for which he has been placed upon the 'course of discipline' in accordance with the enclosed regulations," Green's tutor, a Mr. Chapin, wrote Brutus in December. He added that Green was "manly, gentlemanly, and kindly disposed," although in scholarship he had done only "moderately well."

"These marks are not at all connected with our studies [. . .] but are merely marks of observers from excuses such as rising early to morning prayers, etc.," Green explained to his father. "So I hope you will not overestimate the import of such a letter. I am not peculiarly fond of early rising. Hence, the accumulation of my marks."

Kit was finding clearing a plantation in Mississippi hard work. His letter to his father mentions that Lucy Field had lost a baby, presumably a miscarriage. Poor Lucy's first child, fifteen-month-old Scott, had died the previous spring.

CHRISTOPHER CLAY

Bolivar P.O., Mississippi, Dec. 8, 1857

Dear Pa,

[. . .] I arrived here soft with every thing and been hard at work all the time. We have been getting along so far very well. We have had but little sickness among our negroes. Mary had been quite sick [. . .] but she is now improving and without she has a backset [relapse] will soon be well. She was threatened with pneumonia and other female complaints. We have built four quarters, have [corn] crib, cut about sixty acres of cane and made about two thousand rails. We will commence building our house next week. We have got out all the logs and boards for our house and kitchen. [. . .] I have been all the time with the negroes and I find an overseer's life quite tiresome and disagreeable. [. . .] I think by close attention to your negroes and hard work we will get all of our necessary buildings up by Christmas. I have had no difficulty in managing my negroes except Levi. He rather resisted me but I made an example of him that all will recollect. I had to use the lash very often for some time but now I think are all well trained to the Miss. rules and regulations. Zeke and I together have twenty-one negroes, eighteen hands. [. . .] Zeke and I are getting along so far very well and hope to continue. Two partners living on the same place can never get along well or give good satisfaction to each other. I think it useless to say any more on this subject. [. . .] You can say to Aunt Ann Aunt Lucy has been quite sick, lost her child but now well. Aunt Lucy received a letter from her mother stating that Martha expected to make us a visit this winter. We will be glad to see her and she *must* bring the flour Aunt Ann expected to give us. Uncle Cit [sic] says he will take her to New Orleans and fly around there awhile. [. . .]

Your son Christopher

A short time later, Martha set out by steamboat for Kentucky Landing. "I left Frankfort Monday morning," she wrote Ann. "I was quite provoked when I reached Louisville and found the boat would not leave until Tuesday evening. [. . .] Today is Wednesday and we are no farther than Evansville & will remain here until evening. The boat received no freight at Louisville and the consequence is we will be very much annoyed by stoppage. I am almost sorry I left home."

Kit and Zeke were already thinking of breaking up their partnership. "Ezekiel Field and myself have come to the conclusion that one or the other should own the whole place," Kit wrote his father in January 1858. "He does not feel able to buy my interest. [. . .] He has made me a proposition which I have accepted, provided you think it best and will lend your assistance. He proposes to take $21,000 for his interest, seven Negroes, six mules, and 917 acres. The value of his 7 Negroes at $700, mules six, $850, land at $15 per acre. The amount added makes the above. He wants 1/3 now, the balance in one and two years with six percent interest. The first payment will be $7,200, the two last $7,432 each. I think if I owned the whole I would be better satisfied with the swamp." He added, "Martha is now at Uncle David's waiting for a boat from New Orleans."

When Christopher Field returned from New Orleans, he learned about Kit's offer to buy out Zeke. He wasn't happy about it, as he explained to Brutus.

CHRISTOPHER FIELD

Bolivar, Miss., February 25th, 1858

Dear Sir,

Christopher showed me your letter in answer to one he had written you during my absence. [. . .] I knew nothing of these propositions from one to the other until my return home. [. . .] When they told me of it, I told them it was very bad treatment to me to say the least of it, that I had given them about 15,000$ when I sold them the land, that my object was to give them a home and occupation. [. . .] [Now [. . .] one wanted to sell out to the other and that in 12 months the other might become dissatisfied and he would perhaps sell out at 20$ or 25$ per acre and then I would certainly feel nice seeing them selling property in less than 12 months for 5 times what I had sold it at to them. [. . .] They have had a very bad winter for clearing. Now have about 140 acres cleared, ready to burn when the weather will permit. This will give them plenty to do the 1st summer. They have a good double hewn Log

Dwelling, Kitchen & 2 good double cabins, all with brick chimney & very comfortable houses their negroes use well. Martha is thinking about home. Yours etc.

C. I. Field

Christopher included a list of what both Kit and Zeke had put into their places. Kit, or rather his father, had contributed eleven slaves plus three small children, two mules, and $1,030 in cash. Zeke's share was seven slaves, seven mules, and $550 in cash.

In Richmond, the Holloways' son, another Zeke, was again a problem, as Mary Embry told Ann.

MARY EMBRY

Spring, 1858

My Dear Sister,

[. . .] I have been to town this afternoon, found [. . .] Sister in great distress. Ezekiel H. together with some boys had gotten into a drunken frolic last night and Tom Stone and E. had started last night at 12 o'clock running off, said he had disgraced himself and he intended to leave. They were riding up and down the streets all the even., behaving very badly. [. . .] I believe I never saw Sister so distressed. You know how hard she takes trouble, says it always comes upon her when Mr. Holloway is absent. Pa went over to Lexington today to see if he could hear anything from them as Sister seemed so unhappy. To crown all, he [Zeke] took 500$ out of the drawer of Miss Martha Williams, entrusted to Pitt's care. [This must refer to cash kept at The Store.] He is very careless about the key and is to blame for not putting all the money in the safe at night. I cannot think E. knew how much there was. But do not say anything about that as that was rather disgraceful. Mr. Embry and myself went up to see Sister a few days, indeed, the very day Amelia came. Before she got there I asked Sister what trouble next. [. . .] She said there would be sure to be something to come on. Cousin William [Holloway] said, yes, she hunted them [troubles] up, but it seems she does not have to wait long or go far for them. [. . .] We have been quite busy laying off a flower garden. Mr. Embry laid me one off the plan of Sister's. And you cannot imagine how much I wish I had some of your pretty flowers, as I know you would so freely divide and probably would like to get some out of way as they increase in size. [. . .] I am crazy to get some of your varieties of strawberries as I want to set out a bed the first of next month and thought if it would not be too much trouble I would get you to put me some, as well some of your surplus flowers. [. . .] If you think it best to send me those things, you cannot imagine under how many obligations I will feel to you. [. . .] Farewell!

Your sister,

M. H. E.

[P.S.] We will look for Ed [Edmund Field was in Arkansas] in June as he has written to Pa. [. . .]

In his next letter to his father from Yale, in May 1858, Green commented on recently passed legislation admitting Kansas as a slave state. "This will doubtless be of great damage to the Northern democracy & widens the breach already made in their ranks." He had heard from Mississippi, he added. Kit was determined to stick it out there in spite of the spring floods.

The floods were the principal thing on Kit's mind when he wrote his father. "From newspaper accounts you would suppose we were all drowned. [. . .] We all had a little strip of dry land on the front of our ridge. The balance was under water from six inches to six feet. We have had the highest water ever known to the West[ern] settlers. But I have consoled myself that those are the liabilities of this country we cannot always control. [. . .] I have planted my corn and cotton over and thus hope to make a fair crop without we have more water."

The floods continued into June. "The river is [. . .] still rising," Kit told Brutus. "If the reports about the upper river are true, we are fearful of another overflow. If we should have six inches more water here, we cannot keep up the levees. We have had a trying time this year, with water and insects eating and cutting down corn and cotton. As for my crop, I am not yet injured by them. I have a splendid stand of cotton and fine corn."

A day later, Christopher Field also wrote Brutus. Clearly Brutus had sent Kit to Mississippi hoping that his association with his industrious, upright uncle would be good for him. Evidently he did not feel Kit had improved enough to own the Kentucky Ridge plantation by himself.

CHRISTOPHER FIELD

Bolivar, Miss., June 8th, 1858

Dear Sir,

[. . .] We have had a terrible high water and now have it within 5 inches of the flood we had two months ago. [. . .] This season at the commencement of the high water many of our levees had been rode on, hauled on, and some were not as high at no time as we had been led to think. All these levees had given us much troubles. One of them broke in Major Martin's neighborhood, one in the upper end of the county, and one 3 miles below us which overflowed generally about 3/4 of our places [. . .], remained over about 10 days, then fell 5 feet and, with the energy only characteristic to our River people, we stopped all the breaks and have kept all the whole levee in the county up from that time to the present, but a time have we had of it who live on the River &, being the head commission[er of levees in Bolivar County], I have had more than should often fall to the lot of one man to do. [. . .]

I will make the deed you speak of, have it seconded, and bring it up but I am sorry you did not permit me to make the deed to Christopher. [. . .] I have no fears whatever that he will or would make any disposition of the property at any time without your or my consent and he is very attentive, free from any dissipation, and now seems to fully appreciate that he is a man and acting for himself. He ought to own the property alone. [. . .] It would be a very difficult thing for anyone to plant with him and have anything to say or do with the property without very frequently having his feelings wounded. [. . .] I am sorry this is the case for I wished Ezekiel to have lived in the country and the arrangement he had with C. suited remarkably well as he had not the means to do anything alone. [. . .] E. & C. have had no outbreak and E. has not complained to me or anyone that I know of but, knowing C. as I do, and E. much preferring to remain at my house than home, I am fully satisfied as to how they stand to each other in the matter. I mean, as I have said C. is very attentive, industrious, and taking great interest in his business, had no bad associations whatever and I consider the change from Ky. to Mi. the most fortunate circumstance of his life. [. . .]

I think you had better write him immediately. He will not go up until late, if at all. [. . .] C. talks of staying as well as D., but it is foolish in both of them and I have so said to them, but they are both alike, go their own way. [. . .] I cannot say when I will be up. Not until this River goes down. [. . .]

Yours truly,

C. I. Field

As summer neared, Green asked for money to travel, this time in New England. "I would be most glad to visit the White Mountains etc., perhaps higher north if I then feel disposed," he wrote Brutus in June. But Brutus did not send money, and Green had to spend his vacation at home.

By midsummer, the cotton planters were all back in Kentucky. Christopher Field wrote Brutus shortly after his arrival. "I reached here last Friday, having left home on Sunday. The River was within its Banks and had fallen 3 1/2 feet and by this time is down 10 or 12 feet. I left the country very sickly. I think it will soon be over, think it was caused by the seep water drying up too quick with a green scum on it which was drying up from a very hot sun. There was much sickness on my own & David's places. C. & E. place had several convalescent cases but none seriously sick. Still I have my worst fears for these unacclimated negroes this season. [. . .] I am sorry to hear C. is having chills but that is better or less dangerous than a spell of bilious fever having originated in the South. He was entirely well up to the time he left home, but was very thin."

He enclosed Brutus's deed for the Kentucky Ridge property. "Christopher does not know anything about the deed [. . .]," he told his brother-in-law, "and you had better say nothing to him about it tho I am sorry you did not let me make it direct to him. His residence in Miss. has made a happy change in him. He is entirely steady and is thinking about his business and wishes to know how every dollar goes that is spent and will I think make a safe and reliable man."

That summer Belle Field was twenty-seven — a spinster by the standards of the time — who lived with her aged father and a ten-year-old niece. Belle must have found this life confining, though she never complained. In early August she wrote Ann an oblique letter.

BELLE FIELD

August 3, 1858

Dear Ann,

No doubt you have been expecting a letter from me for some days. Well, it has been my desire to write, but we do not always act as we know we ought and I may have felt that I had some good reasons for delaying.

I had a note from Martha yesterday. She writes that there is a delightful company assembled there [Estill Springs] and that she was getting along very pleasantly. Brother, Cousin William [Embry], Mary [Embry], and Pattie [Field] went up yesterday. Pattie [now nine years old] has not thought of anything else but her trip. Mary E. said she was thinking more about her dresses than half the grown girls. [. . .] Will Irvine came down yesterday [. . .] said he had never seen more clever and pretty girls together [. . .] but I guess there will be quite a delegation coming this week. And there will be no scarcity of beaus. I was very sorry you did not conclude to come over. You would have enjoyed it. [. . .]

[. . .] Mary and I spent a day and night with Patsey last week. She is looking very thin and pale [she had just had another baby] [. . .] seemed to be very much gratified to see us, said she was glad we had come, that Martha had told her no wonder we did not come to see her, that we were ashamed of her for having so many children. I can assure Martha that she does us gross injustice for I sympathize so deeply with her to feel that way. [. . .] We will look for you over and I am going away the last of this month, so if you have any desire to see me, I will be gratified to see you.

Yours truly,

Belle

Belle was planning to marry, doubtless her "good reason for delaying" writing Ann and for "going away" later in August. Soon E. H. Field invited Brutus to his last daughter's wedding. "Isabella is about to marry Doctor A. B. Lyman, who came from Ohio to this county some years ago and for the past 3 or 4 years has lived in Richmond. His habits are industrious and moral and [he] seems to be disposed to take care of his property. We are not acquainted with his family as we would like to be but as now a days [sic] nearly all the young men are disposed to be drunkards and wasteful, I have set up no objection to the match, thinking he will take care of what he acquires, and being of age and habits calculated to make a prudent companion."

By now, Zeke Clay was a student at the school where Green had prepared for Yale. Zeke's letters are so few and terse that it's hard to form any impression of him. Evidently he had a great deal of personal charm, but it doesn't come through in his adolescent letters. Zeke was not the only member of the extended family to study with Sayre. The professor wrote Martha to thank her for telling him that Patsey's son (probably Jimmy) would be attending his school that fall. He was also glad to hear that Green expected to pay him a visit. However, Green did not get to see his old teacher before he had to return to Yale. "He [Zeke] must mention to Mr. Sayre my great disappointment in not seeing him at the Bourbon fair," Green wrote Brutus in September, "& to tell him nothing less than a letter from him will be satisfactory."

In November, Martha purchased $125 worth of pearls from a Louisville jeweler, John Kitts. Martha also had her own account at Garrett Spears and Company in Paris, where she charged lace, crinolines, dress material, kid gloves, and two corsets.

In New Haven, Green had been running up bills, an old story by now. "No doubt my expenses have been such as to make your complaint a just one," he admitted to his father.

The eve of 1859 found Brutus contemplating his children's extravagances. The Field sisters were all married, but Martha Clay, now twenty-six, remained single. The Mississippi colony had expanded to include Zeke Field, twenty-three, and Kit Clay, twenty-four. Green Clay, almost twenty, was at Yale, and Zeke Clay, eighteen, at Professor Sayre's school in Frankfort. Only twelve-year-old Cash still lived at home.

FIVE

Mournful Intelligence from the Sunny South

The availability of slave labor was always an important consideration on the cotton plantations in Bolivar County, and it became increasingly so as the Fields and Clays expanded their holdings there. In February, Christopher Clay wrote his father about a slave named William who had escaped while Kit was taking him south to work on the new place, which Kit had christened Hard Scrabble. Ann and Cash, almost thirteen, accompanied him.

CHRISTOPHER CLAY

Galt House [Louisville], Feb. 5, 1859

Dear Pa,

I suppose you have received Aunt Ann's letter long before this [. . .] and [she] informed you of William making his escape before we got to Frankfort. I had kept my eye on him all the time except the time he got off and the cars were underway all the time.

I think, when he thinks I am gone, he will go to Frankfort. I left word with several men to get him if possible, but I have heard nothing by the cars of interest except they are still on the lookout and think he has not yet come to Frankfort. I wish you to get him as soon as you hear where he is and send him to Miss. if possible. If you write to any of those traders in Lexington, you can hear when they will start Negroes south and I know they would take him safe. I am fearful he will take a notion and go to a free state and we will never get him. [. . .]

Nothing More.

Your Son,

Christopher F. Clay

William was quickly caught and sent on to Mississippi, but tragedy awaited the Clays there. One of the Holloways' sons, Willie, who was visiting at Kentucky Landing, was killed in a hunting accident on January 29. Willie was thirteen, less than a year older than Cash, and his death made an indelible impression upon the boy, as Kit explained to Brutus. Willie was buried in the Richmond cemetery beneath a carving of a pensive boy holding a book.

CHRISTOPHER CLAY

Ky. Landing, Miss., Feb. 16th, 1859

Dear Pa,

[. . .] I drop you a few lines now to inform you that William landed here today safe and well. He was under the charge of Mr. Collins of Lexington, who was taking some Negroes south. I was not at the river when the boat landed and, as there was no bill presented, I suppose you had made arrangements in Kentucky to pay his way here. If so, I hope you will inform me as soon as convenient. [. . .]

The death of Willie Holloway has distressed Cash so much that he will not enjoy his trip and as his Ma talks to him so much about his gun he has come to the conclusion to hunt but little. We are all well among the whites. I still have a good deal of chills and fever at my house with the Negroes. They all have had a hard time of acclimation.

Aunt Ann and Mary [Embry] are now at Mr. Estill's spending a few days. [. . .]

We are all plowing and will commence to plant as soon as the weather will admit. [. . .] All my new Negroes seem to be very well satisfied, Fanny in particular, and all are glad to see William as they thought he would not come until next year.

Nothing more I believe at present of interest.

Your son,

Christopher F. Clay

In spite of Willie's accident, Cash did go hunting and wrote Martha about his exploits. "I have killed one duck, two geese, and one deer of which you have heard of," he related proudly. "I have stayed the most of my time at Uncle Kit's and Kit's. Kit has a good pack of hounds. They are in a better condition than when you was [sic] here. So they have not run much. I have not hunted much since I have been here but intend to take a deer drive in the morning."

In early March, Kit wrote Brutus that Ann and Cash were preparing to return home. "I don't think they enjoyed their trip under the unfortunate accident that happened a few days before our arrival. Cash has not had much sport hunting as I was busy all the time and could not spend my time in that way at present. But I think he is satisfied as he has killed a large *buck*."

Most of the letter is devoted to the value of his field hands. Christopher and David Field estimated that eight of Kit's slaves were worth $6,050. Henry at $1,100 was the most valuable; William next at $1,050. Fanny and her child Aggy were worth $250 each.

In New Haven, Green, as usual, needed money. He had again spent the Christmas holidays at Yale. "Quite different are the Christmas holidays here from the same in Ky.," he wrote Brutus.

He was somewhat more expansive to his sister. "Last night our class was handsomely entertained at the President's — being the first of three levees given by him to each Senior class," he told Martha. "I enjoyed myself very much. There were many ladies present — the beauty and intellect of New Haven — As to beauty, in quality there was a sad deficiency. With but one exception I saw none whom Kentuckians would pronounce pretty or beautiful. One particular young lady with whom I was much taken is the exception. There is also an entertainment soon to be given by one of the professors."

Green enjoyed the social side of Yale and was successful at it. In his senior year, he was elected to Skull and Bones, the secret society. Like Green, my father was a member of Bones. Once, while on a family vacation in the Great Smokies, my brother and I tried to get him to tell us about it. "Heavens," he said in mock horror, "you don't expect me to tell you anything in the presence of your mother, whose whole family went to Harvard." Later, when my brother was at Yale, our father would arrive in New Haven for vague and unspecified purposes. We decided he must be attending meetings of Bones.

Green wrote Brutus about his time at Yale and his plans for the future.

GREEN CLAY

Yale, Feb. 8, 1959

Dear Pa,

Soon will be my 20th birthday and it is also no great measure of time till my graduation at Yale. Hence it is none too soon to be considering what I shall do after leaving college. But I preface a remark or two first.

You no doubt think that I have thus far been too extravagant (perhaps I have; I have tendencies to such faults). And that it is high time I was doing something for myself — that I have been spending money all my life and making none; but especially that I am extravagant, and therefore you do not look with much favor upon my proposition for extending my studies farther before commencing practical life. All this I admit, and this anxiety of yours, of course I am not so foolish as not to know, has been for my own good; preeminently I am aware this has been your only motive. But I have always believed that those who are so fortunate as can afford themselves an education of the highest stamp, it is their duty, the neglect of which their folly and shame, to seize upon the opportunity and make it good. Your money thus spent is infinitely to a much nobler and better purpose than when devoted to living a life of luxury and comparative ignorance. This especially is a proverbial fault with young men of the South, who waste large estates that might have placed them amongst the crowned noblemen of Thought, in luxurious and unprofitable living. [. . .] Whereas, a good education is an ever-unfailing source of wealth; the possessor of which is rich though he have nothing else beside. [. . .] I do not plead entire innocence to expenses that are strictly unnecessary. Still I do plead not guilty as regards my excess. You know at college there is always a certain amount of this to be done — at least by those who are thought able to afford it — as such one's reputation for closeness and stinginess is not at all enviable. With Southerners here at Yale, to this element of college life it is especially hard not to conform to. [. . .]

These things, I have candidly written in consequence of your message in Aunt Ann's letter which, with others alike to it, have been a source of mortification to me since at college. [. . .]

Now, to the real object of this letter. I have two considerations to submit to your perusal. The first is whether you think it advisable that I should study two years in Germany and are willing to let me go. The second is: I think I would be pleased to study law for a year or two with Rufus Choate of Boston [a lawyer who served out the unfinished Senate term of Daniel Webster]. [. . .] I can obtain, I think, a situation with him. [. . .] There will also be the advantage of being able to attend the lectures at "Harvard," which are about the best in the country. Going to Germany, of course, would be the greater sacrifice in one respect to me — the leaving of home, etc. — considerations which would lead me to choose rather the latter plan though the advantages might not be so great. [. . .]

This letter I hope will meet with your favor: if not, it can't be helped. One of the strongest motives I have [. . .] has ever been to please you. [. . .] You have most generously given me the opportunity of a good education and your own indulgences to me have been many. Base then it would be if I should abuse them all and be ready to offer nothing in return. [. . .] Your son,

Green C.

The spring of 1859 was a difficult one in Mississippi. "We have had a great deal of high water and more rain than ever was known before in one season," Kit wrote Brutus in April. "The levees are broken in many places in our neighborhood. Uncle David's levee was entirely washed away and everything afloat. The water was in his house. We have had so many storms during the high water it was impossible to keep up the levees near the banks of the river. The waves would wash a man off the levee in five moments so we had no chance to do anything to save the levees. My land on the ridge is still dry, but in front of my house is six feet water. [. . .]

"We are at this time quite low-spirited. I am sick with chills. I have been close at home for sometime, hard at work when able. I have no overseer and I have all the business to attend to. After all my hard work the water I am fearful will bust my fine prospect for a crop."

While most of his family was away, Brutus plunged into politics in a way he had not since the early 1840s. Disturbed by Democratic inroads into their old constituency, former Whigs met in Paris in January to form the Opposition Party. After considerable debate, they chose Brutus as their candidate to represent Bourbon and Bath Counties in the state senate. It was a nasty race. Brutus's opponent, John A. Prall, of Bath County, claimed that Brutus would use his wealth to buy the election.

John M. Harlan, then state attorney general, wrote to offer Brutus assistance. Harlan was the opposition candidate for Congress in the district. He later became a Supreme Court justice and wrote the sole dissent in *Plessy* v. *Ferguson,* the case by which the Court declared racial segregation acceptable under the Constitution. Despite his later views, in 1859 Harlan was no more of an emancipationist than was Brutus.

"[Y]ou will find that much of the valuable matter contained [. . .] has been condensed and put into the 'Campaign,'" he told Brutus in May 1859. "I have, therefore, taken the liberty to put your name down as one of the Subscribers to that paper. The 'Campaign' is a private enterprise of Col. [A. G.] Hodges [a Frankfort publisher] though it is published under the supervision of the State Central Committee. [. . .] I suggest that you might assist yourself materially in the canvass if you will have a number of the 'Campaign' papers placed into the hands of the people."

A bit of sunshine changed things in Mississippi, as Kit wrote his father.

CHRISTOPHER CLAY

Lake Bolivar, May 20, 1859

Dear Pa,

I drop you a few lines to inform you how matters and things generally are in the "sunny south." We Kentuckians are all getting along very well at present. Our crops are doing well, weather at present quite hot but the very sort of days we want for cotton. The river is still very high and today rising slowly. But news from above [upriver] are [sic] rather favorable. [. . .] Uncle David is still behind in his crop and quite unfortunate[ly] has lost four Negroes in the past month. Uncle Kit lost a valuable man not long ago since. All died with "pneumonia." The disease has been quite common and fatal in the bottom. Clay and Field hands are all getting healthy, and new hands are all still healthy at present. [. . .] Most of our county is still under water and will remain some time from present prospects. Col. C. I. Field and Ezekiel will leave for Kentucky on the 8th of June, will be in Louisville about the 12 or 14th. [. . .] I suppose I will leave here in July. [. . .]

Your son,

Christopher F. Clay

P.S. I would like to know if my name has a Col. or not.

C. F. Clay

The title "Colonel" was honorary, not hereditary. A number of members of Kit's family were called Colonel, including Uncle Christopher and William Holloway, but never Kit.

A few days later, Ann Clay received a soul-searching letter from her brother David, in which he told her that he had decided to remain in Mississippi during the summer in order to rebuild his plantation, even though Lucy had just given birth to another son in Kentucky. In letters home, David left a vivid account of the summer he spent in Mississippi. He was a blunt man, in some respects similar to his nephew Kit. I imagine them as having an earthy sense of humor that must have bewildered both Brutus and Christopher Field.

In this letter to Ann, David refers to ill feeling between himself and his wife and Mr. and Mrs. Rodes Estill, Mississippi neighbors who were relatives of Brutus's brother-in-law, William Rodes. The Estills apparently brought a black child with measles to the Fields' house. The Fields' son, Scott, contracted the disease and died.

DAVID I. FIELD

Content, May 25, 1859

Dear Ann,

I received your letter a few days ago for which I thank you very much as well as for your visit to Lucy. [. . .] Lucy labored under an apprehension or presentiment that she would not survive the confinement. I did not think there was any ground for her apprehension, but feared it might have a very bad effect if she had any difficulty. [. . .] The birth of the boy & her good condition is about the only good luck I have had lately. I suppose I should except my own good health. We have buried four negroes since she left here, 2 young babies & 2 healthy Blk. M. dead of bilious pneumonia. [. . .] John lived 2 weeks & took no nourishment except water in that time, could not or would not eat. He was a very valuable negro, good to work but hard to manage, required much whipping. With every overseer I had he had difficulty. Poor fellow, when he was first taken sick, he saw it was a judgment upon [him] that he had been doing bad, had fallen from grace. He said that if he got well he intended to do better. He had among other offenses been riding the mules at night. [. . .] His wife has been laid up over three months with dropsy. She, I think, is getting well, is up at Brother's [Christopher Field's] was taken there when we were overflowed. The other, Wesley, died of typhoid fever, lived only a few days. [. . .] [This was not the Wesley who arrived in Lexington bound hand and foot.] His color being nearly white made the chances against him [a reference to the widely held belief that blacks were not as likely to contract diseases as whites]. He was the son of Mary Saunders, our cook. He was an excellent boy, truthful & correct. These deaths and the high water discouraged me much & I may say depressed me though it is my philosophy not to grieve over evils & accidents that I cannot control. I [had] done everything I think to save those negroes, had physicians & the overseer was untiring, slept in the quarter when they were sick & they were well nursed. [. . .] By the overflow, I lost I guess the use of 100 acres of ground which ought to have produced 100 bales of cotton [. . .] the prospect of cultivating & making a crop was gloomy. All our houses surrounded with water. [. . .] I saw new houses had to be built, gin to be moved. I told Brother that I had concluded to let somebody else do all these things, that I wanted to sell out. It seemed to annoy him & [he] tried to discourage me. Said his object & wishes would not be realized if I left, that he had joined me in the purchase, not for profit or desire to increase his possessions here, but that we might be here together. Another reason I had was the debt I was incurring which annoyed me more than most people & we would have to incur more in making these improvements. He replied that was a small matter, that he would pay my balance with the merchants, build a dwelling house & advance me as much money as I wanted, not to let that disturb me. There was another consideration that influenced me to want to sell out though I did not tell him. I had become satisfied from many things I had seen that he was going to marry Miss [Pauline] Rodes [Brutus's niece] & I was fearful we would not get along so well & amicably & that I had better get out of the way before there was any alienation of feeling between us two which I would deeply regret. [. . .] I have built new quarters & had a great many yards of ditches dug. The land or rather the growing crop, however, has not recovered from the effects of the transpiration (seepage they call it here) waters. I am still occupying the house. We have had to pass by skiff for over 2 months. [. . .] I suppose next year I will build a new house. I tell Bro. I will build for him that his young wife *will have* a new house. [. . .] It is a little singular he yet denies he is engaged to marry, never has given me the slightest intimation of his intention one way or the other. When I have been in the humor, I say some pretty hard cute things to all three of them [Christopher, Zeke, and Kit]. All three have been corresponding with young girls & they all deny it. All are in love. It is the custom with us who is at the office first to receive all the mail. It is taken to Brother's, being the central point. It seems that all three, when they expect a certain letter, have maneuvered & step off to get there first, but the boys generally go there first & they occasionally saw the Col.'s letters &, as we annoyed him some, he directed the P'Master not to give out certain letters to us until he reenvelopes them. We caught him at that. [. . .] Then I would open out on young ladies that would write to gentlemen. Ezekiel, he would get mad, he is very sensitive & easily plagued. Kit would join in the laugh against the others as well as him. I tell E. it has given him the consumption being in love. He says now he has been rejected, is down on the sex. When letters are received from Ky., we have all been in the habit of showing them. Recently Bro. has not done so, but read portions of general news. A few days ago, he handed me Mary Embry's. [. . .] From remarks in that, I inferred Mary had been posted [of Christopher's intentions]. [. . .] I do not know Miss Rodes, but from all I have heard I think she will make him a good wife & he will be happily married. It would be most foolish [. . .] & mean in me [. . .] to wish him not to marry a woman because she was related to a woman I did not like.

[. . .] I do not think Mrs. E. [Estill] is clever, but, mind you, I do not think hard of anybody else for thinking different. I could not expect relatives or anyone I know [. . .] to agree with me because I have cause & they have none. I know that families generally do not appreciate & sympathize with the sorrows & trouble & heartaches of a sister-in-law as they would of a blood relation & sometimes of a near friend. That is human nature & I do not condemn it. But such is the temperament & disposition of woman generally that I am much afraid that this alliance of Brother's will not be pleasant for me. Miss Rodes is a clever girl & it is very natural, being a relation, that she should feel more congeniality & more pleasure in Mrs. E.'s society than ours [his and Lucy's]. Nor do I think she will say or do anything to wound our feelings intentionally. I do not often speak of Mrs. E. & I will [be] very guarded & not say anything that will give offense to the young lady if she comes among us to live. I have heard Bro. say often that Mrs. E. was not clever & he did not like her, but I perceive now he likes to go there & don't care about anyone saying anything against her. I have discovered that & never mention her name. [. . .] I am satisfied Mrs. E. has not acted clever to us &, if I choose, I could tell you something else different from what they told you in regard to that little negro's measles. I know Mr. and Mrs. E. had no idea of that negro's having fever for if they had they would [. . .] [not have brought] the negro to our house. I do not complain of that. It was Mrs. E.'s conduct and actions since. [. . .] It is my intention to spend the summer here. It behooves me to economize & save, losses being great and family increasing. I would like to see my wife & child, but, being human, when they are well off and in good hands with kind friends, I can forgo the pleasure. If I get sick, I shall leave (if I am able) though I have no apprehension. I wrote to [R. G.] Burton a few days ago & told him I had some peculiarities, one was that I did not think women with young babies should be traveling about on account of the mother, the baby, & the friends they were visiting, therefore, if Lucy did not get over to see them, not to blame or impute blame to her, that it should be my fault. [. . .] If she could go to one place & stay, it would do, provided she did not have to go in public conveyance, particularly stages. Now going to your house is different, that is in the country & plenty of room. [. . .] Mrs. S. [Lucy's mother] writes me that the baby is not named & [they are] waiting to hear from me. I had told Lucy if it was a boy I wanted it called for Pa, if girl, Elizabeth for her Ma & Sister E., or Lucy for herself. She has got some highfalluting frenchified notion & wanted it called Lilla or some such, an outlandish name, but was perfectly willing to call [it] for Pa & he objects to his name, it being so hard to pronounce & easily nicknamed &, there being so many of that name, I thought I could call him Henry. [The baby was named David.] I at one time determined to let Bro. name it, be what sex it might, if he would consider it a compliment as he has been so clever & good to us. But, if he is to be married, he may have a lot of his own & would not appreciate the compliment. I also intended to tell him he could name & adopt it & make it heir to part of his estate, but if he is to have a quiver full of his own that would not do. [. . .] How it will interfere with our arrangements if the Col. gets married it is hard to realize. [. . .] If we wanted advice, money, assistance in any way, all went to him. His young wife will put a stop to all those things. What a fool it will make of him I am afraid & so tell him. [. . .] I tell him she will have new house, furniture, fine carriage, other servants, etc. She will tell him he can afford it, that Mrs. Manley, Mrs. Estill, & others have all these things & she might as well have them [. . .] & maybe cry a little & he cannot resist that. We plague him some & talk in this strain to him, says we are fools & think he is a fool. I tell him he will do just like most old widowers, as soon as he realizes fully that he is married he will get right old. There is in truth too much disparity in their ages [Christopher was forty-five and Pauline twenty-six]. [. . .] You can say to Mr. Clay that if it will do him any good he has my wishes that he may be elected [to the Legislature]. I do not see much use in running "opposition" Democrats & Republicans, for or against Slave Trade, North & South. That, however, does not apply so much to the state elections. [. . .] Here I should vote for an ultra Southern man. Were I in Ky., I suppose I should vote for an "opposition" man.

Well, I have written you a long letter, most of it I fear tiresome, but I cannot write any other sort. [. . .] When I set down, I put down whatever I think [. . .] I failed to go over in the skiff at dinner & so am waterbound in the house & I have had nothing else to occupy my attention, no newspapers to read & no sewing to do. I turned in a few days [ago] & cut out & made myself a pair of drawers out & out, worked button holes & all. They are pretty rough but do very well. I suppose if Lucy was [sic] to see them, she would give them to one of the negroes. You will please remember me very kindly to Mrs. Keiningham, Mr. Clay, Martha, etc.

Your brother,

D. I. Field

Green was about to graduate from Yale. In May, he wrote Brutus for additional money and asked about his campaign. "The fight will be a hard one I presume on all hands. [. . .] Cash, I suppose, is now a greater politician than ever and is anxious about the result. Parties at present, as far as I can see, are none of them thoroughly principled or organized. There seems to be a general revolution and breaking up of all parties. And the political world in a state of bankruptcy to anarchy. What will be the result no one can tell!"

Brutus was away from home a great deal that spring, campaigning. "It was my intention to have went [*sic*] to Flat Rock on tomorrow," he wrote Ann from Owingsville on June 14, "but now Prall came here yesterday morning, it being County Court and we both spoke and I got a complete triumph over him so say my friends. [. . .] My friends are much elated and Prall very much cowed and some of them have come out for me. They are working well and I wish to keep the advantage I have gained.

"Prall at the commencement of his speech read [. . .] appointments [for appearances] in the hilly part of the county, which he made without consulting me [. . .], evidently with the design of getting clear of me, thinking I would return home and leave him to himself. I have determined to follow him and will not be able to get home before the 27th or 28th of the month."

Among Brutus's papers are notes he made for these campaign appearances, some written in pencil and now almost unreadable. In Millersburg on July 2, he talked about education and land grant colleges, also about agriculture and funds for a new penitentiary. In other places, he was less parochial. He discussed slavery in the territories — a burning issue ever since the civil disturbances in Kansas — President Buchanan — who had proposed purchasing Cuba to increase the number of slave states in the Union — and the Black Republican, or abolitionist, Congress. His notes for an appearance in North Middletown include the comment that "he [Prall] endorses the administration of Mr. Buchanan." As an Opposition Party candidate, Brutus opposed both the Democrats and the Republicans, and supported a middle-of-the-road position once espoused by the Whigs.

During the summer, Christopher Field married Pauline Rodes, as David had predicted. Edmund also married, planning to take his wife, Anna, to Mississippi. During a stay in Arkansas and Kansas, Ed had become a doctor and he hoped to practice in Bolivar County.

In Mississippi, David stayed at Christopher's house while rebuilding his own. He wrote his brother Zeke about the shooting of one of the Estills' slaves by an overseer.

DAVID I. FIELD

Content, July 24th, 1859

Dear Ezekiel,

Your letter of 9th instant has been received & I take pleasure in answering it. [. . .] Till within a few days past we have had intensely hot & dry weather. For a day or two we are having rain. [. . .] I had planted my front in corn & the rain will be of great service to it. [. . .] It will start the cotton to growing again. There was [sic] plenty of bolls but this will make them grow larger. [. . .] I have been quite well except a little debility from the excessive heat & I am satisfied if one will not exert himself in the climate during the summer he can have as good health here as anywhere. [. . .] When I heard of Edmund's leaving Kansas I thought about his coming here but I see no chance for him. You know his wife will remain in Tenn. I do not see how he could settle here with her & it certainly would not do to leave her there. When I heard he had gone to Tenn., I was in hopes he would find out I was remaining here & he would come down & spend the balance of the summer with me & he could then see the prospect of getting practice. From all we have heard in regard to his wife I would not like to see her coming among us to live. I think she would be hard to please & seeing the difference with the other wives she would give trouble & keep E. or some of us in hot water. I wrote to Lucy a week ago in which I mentioned that Davison [an overseer] had shot one of the Estill negroes. I had heard he was one of Mrs. E.'s negroes but I was mistaken. E. purchased him in N.O. several years ago. The jury of inquest said he was justified. I was not there nor have I talked with any who was & it is likely when all the facts are known he was not justified. The negro ran from him. He caught him three times & he got away. That does not look like he was resisting. The third time the negro cut him, only cut his clothing, but of course D. did not know the extent of the cut, then he shot him and the worst thing about it is he shot him in the back. He was a bad negro, I believe, as I heard he had resisted & fought McFadden [an overseer] once. The impression among the overseers is that Mr. E.'s negroes have got the impression among them that the master permits them to judge how far an overseer shall go with him [them]. Now I do not believe Mr. E. has any idea of such a thing & if he thought any negro had such an impression he would whip it out of him, but he is lenient & places great confidence in many of his negroes & I suppose they know it. [. . .] This affair is one of the consequences of planters leaving home in summer. If Mr. E. had have been at home his negro would not have been killed. [. . .]

I like to have forgot & not mentioned the Col.'s name. From your letter & what I had previously heard from Sister E. I hope his honeymoon will be over before they come down here. I expect to be with them some but if he continues as loving as I hear I believe I had as soon be *shit upon* as to witness that billing & cooing. [. . .] I have not been anywhere & seen no one *hardly*. [. . .] As George [a slave] is so poor a carpenter I have to stay & oversee him. We have built a new house in Carroll field for the Cooks. Another house one I will use as kitchen. In a day or two I will move Mary [his cook] out there. [. . .] I will continue to sleep at the old house but expect to move soon. [. . .] If I cannot have it moved, I will pull it down by sections. I am going down to Galloway to see a house mover & ask him if he can move it across the slough. [. . .]

Yours affectionately,

D. I. Field

Back in Kentucky, Brutus lost his election by twelve votes (a total of 3,426 were cast). He carried Bourbon County, but Prall carried Bath by a larger margin. The Democrats swept the state, electing Beriah Magoffin governor and winning a majority in both houses of the legislature. Brutus's ally, John Harlan, lost his race for Congress to William E. Simms of Paris.

David wrote Kit that things were improving in the Delta.

DAVID I. FIELD

Content, Sept. 4, 1859

Dear Kit,

Your letter was received some time ago. [. . .] I can communicate the usual information. Crops promising, health good, & weather seasonable & pleasant. [. . .] For a week or two past, the weather has been delightful, cool nights & morning (fine for sleeping) & warm days. How I could hold forth extensively on the comfort, conveniences, & *economy* of spending the summer at home, but for fears that such exposition might make many of you "summer boys" to spend the summer here. In a few days, I suppose, I can record the fact that I have remained on my place twelve months, have not been out of the neighborhood during the time, only rode on a steam boat once & that from my landing to Bolivar when I was shipping cotton seed for myself and C. I. Field, one night at your house last fall, & a few nights ago at Mrs. Cook's place. [. . .] I have not prospered as well as many others who acted different & have not given the same attention to their affairs. The mortality has been so great since I have had charge of the place that I am tempted often to resolve if it continues to sell out. [. . .] Unless we can judiciously increase our force largely this fall, I shall look around for some other occupation & prepare to change. I suppose you have heard of Lovell's [a neighbor] death. Like too many people in the country, he was too imprudent & had too much confidence, did not pay sufficient attention to the premonitory symptoms. It seems though that he has had [a] diseased liver & enlarged spleen for some years. Let his overseer, old Bryant, go to Virginia in July & he oversaw, hunted, & fished. [. . .] I have been running both of my waggons for some time, hauling brick, rails, & logs for smoke house & my old house. After some trouble & inconvenience, using only my own men, about 7, have torn down & set up the old house. Not yet completed, but a portico can be occupied by me if it don't rain hard. I have 12 chimneys to build, 2 cisterns, any quantity of fencing, smoke house to build, shops & sheds, etc. I think I could employ all my men till Christmas doing things that ought to be done, but I have them picking cotton, except teamsters & one man working on house. [. . .] I received a letter from the Col. in which he stated he would cheerfully take charge of Lucy in coming home. I shall expect you to aid him, but maybe you will have *baggage* enough of your own. I see by the papers the Ohio River is in fine boating shape. If so, you can come that way easily. Should that be the case, I will expect your Aunt Ann to send me two barrels of flour. [. . .] I will also trouble her to put me up a few strawberry and raspberry roots, not many, & any other things of that sort she may have. Now these things are to come if you come by boat & bring freight yourself. I hear Mr. Estill has gone to Ky. When he left, he expected to return with Bro. & you. If so, it may not be very pleasant either to her [Mrs. Estill] or Lucy to be of the same party & perhaps Lucy had better shift for herself. Bro's wife, of course, will much prefer Mrs. E.'s company. It is natural she should & the Col.'s inclinations now must be to his wife & her wishes &, to prevent any feeling of dissatisfaction, perhaps Lucy had as well return either with you a different time or some other friend. However, you can all fix up to suit yourself. I would much regret if Lucy should be so placed that she would feel as if she was not welcome or in a situation to have her feelings hurt, etc. From letters I have received, I had expected Edmund & wife would be here before this. I consider it unfortunate that he should determine to come here, anyhow to bring his wife before he came to see the prospects which I fear are gloomy. We have 4 doctors at Bolivar, either [sic] of whom I suppose have had more experience than he. [. . .] I think it will be unfortunate for him & us, his coming here to live. He is a fickle poor manager & I much fear his wife. [. . .] We all know that she lacks many of the commendable qualities & will no doubt get up a big fuss before she gets through. [. . .] What is to become of E. I cannot tell. Pa will eventually, I fear, have to set him up about Richmond & I suppose all the family will object to that on account of his wife. But, as I am about most things, hope for the best. As I expected, the Democrats beat you fellows. I have noticed all along that your papers wrote too much to what Mr. [Henry] Clay [who had died seven years before] said & what he wanted. [. . .] Now the people are tired of Mr. C. They have repudiated him [and the Whig Party] long ago. [. . .]

[no signature]

A few days later, David wrote his brother Zeke again, detailing abuses by Christopher's overseer, Mr. Overton. Christopher was recuperating from a painful carbuncle.

DAVID I. FIELD

Sept. 7th, 1859

Dear Ezekiel,

[. . .] I thank you for your proffering to attend to anything I may wish brought from Ky. A few days ago I wrote a note to R. G. Burton asking him to put me up a few articles I enclosed in Overton's letter to Brother. I wrote to Brother some ten days ago in which I jested some with him & was a little saucy. If I had known he was so bad off, I would

not [have] done it. [. . .] I suppose he has not been in proper condition
to enjoy or humor my fun. So I now offer him the *amende honorable*
through you. [. . .] I do not know that there is anything particular requiring Bro's presence here. His negroes have complained once or twice
to me that Mr. O. [Overton] has killed a beef & that they do not get
any of it. [. . .] I think O. has done wrong about negroes. I went up several times to get peaches & tomatoes & Amelia [a slave] would tell me
that the people from Bolivar got [them] as fast as they were ripe. I got
no peaches & tomatoes. Only once he has killed the beeves & most of
it has gone either to Mr. Van R. [Renslar] or [Doctor] Shelby. I of course
have said nothing about & have not encouraged the negroes to talk to
me. [. . .] O. is a good manager generally but [. . .] [a] sneak in some
things. Shelby has a sister & Van R. a daughter & O. goes about them
a good deal & I think they flatter him & puff him up & he in return furnishes them [with foodstuffs]. [. . .] In Bro.'s letter he proffered to take
charge of Lucy home which will suit her & myself very well & I so
wrote him. Since then I hear at the store that Mr. E. has gone to Ky &
as usual will wish to return with you all. [. . .] Now I take it Bro.'s wife
is like all women. She thinks Mrs. E. is clever & thinks Mrs. F. foolish
to continue her prejudices & hostility to Mrs. E. [. . .] Maybe when she
has a baby of her own & loses it by the thoughtlessness of another, Mrs.
E. by bringing in useless servants who will communicate measles,
whooping cough etc., she then may have some patience with such as
Lucy. [. . .] I have heard nothing of Edmund. He is so fickle & unsteady.
Maybe he has concluded to stay in Tenn. [. . .] Well, I have got along
very fine in the swamp this summer but a good many things worry me
but I have kept in a good humor, not fretted or got angry. I expect it
would have been to me as hard work if I had spent it in Ky. [. . .] Don't
you get very tired riding about doing nothing & *courting*. Any little or
big thing you see laying [sic] about that you think will suit me pick them
up & save them. With kind regards to everybody, I am most affectionately,

D. I. Field

Before the Field party could leave for Mississippi, Christopher received a chilling letter from one of his neighbors there, W. S. Cook.
"Your brother David, after a short illness, died today [Sept. 11] about
half past 12. He was taken Friday with purging and vomiting. Drs. Russell & Allen were sent for. Saturday Dr. A. found him very ill, congestion of the stomach & bowels. [. . .] However, Dr. A. went to work and

did all he could till Russell came, then Shelby and Scott were called in. They all concurred in one treatment and his friends were soon collected in and no [one] in our midst has received more attention or died more regretted. We thought of sending [his body] up to Louisville to be buried with his friends and relations, but, on consulting with the doctors, we think it extremely doubtful of reaching Lexington with the body at this season of the year. Mr. Van Renslar told me of [an] instance in his own family where it was impossible for salt and charcoal to save [a corpse] on as long a trip. I would have gone up and was making my arrangements to leave, but it is unsafe. You can remove him in the winter and no risk will be seen. I regret we have to come to this [. . .] yet it seems to me safest."

Patsey Miller copied out this note and sent it on to Ann Clay, along with a letter of her own.

PATSEY MILLER

Richmond, Sept. 21, 1859

My dear sister,

O how can I pen the very awful mournful intelligence of the death of our dear Brother David. A letter came in last night's mail to Brother Christopher from a Mr. Cook, a neighbor, very unsatisfactory as regards any particulars. [. . .] O how sad, no wife, no sister, no relation near to soften those last awful moments. I cannot realize this heavy stroke of providence, but, dear sister, should it not be a warning to us all to think of and be better prepared to meet the monster death. [. . .] Brother came in an hour ago from Mr. Rodes', so let down, so distressed, says he did all in his power to get him to come away. Brother, Mrs. Rodes, and Pauline spent last Thursday and Friday with me and Mrs. Rodes was complaining of the insociability of Brother's sisters, said she wished us all to spend a day with Brother and Pauline before they left [for Mississippi], and would not leave me till I would set a time to be in town this week (as they would leave next week). So I told her [. . .] that I would drive with them today and all were invited out there today, but o how different the day is being spent with us, in grief for a Brother who was laid now 12 or 13 days ago under the clods away off from us. [. . .] Poor Lucy, oh how awful and heart rending the many conflicting feelings she will have to contend with [. . .] Ezekiel [Field] went out to our house yesterday evening about some mules. Brother proposes as soon as he returns to start him to look up Lucy as none seem to know whether she is in Frankfort or Louisville. [. . .] I have seen so little of poor Brother [David]. I only saw him twice last summer for a short while. Although he was a little eccentric, quite a noble-natured man as ever lived. [. . .] Pa is in good heath, but looks this morning so bowed down. As white as a cloth. Brother is in deep distress, shedding tears like a child. [. . .] It will certainly craze Lucy. To think poor fellow, he has not seen his wife for six months nor never [sic] saw that sprightly interesting boy. [. . .]

Patsey Miller

Elizabeth also wrote Ann.

ELIZABETH HOLLOWAY

[September] 25, 1859

My Dear Sister,

How heartrending to think this day 2 weeks ago our dear [. . .] Brother breathed his last with only strangers to close his dying eyes. It rends my heart to think of his sad fate, had been down all summer and striving for the perishable things of this sinful world. [. . .] He was having everything made comfortable for his wife. Poor Lucy, how can she ever live under it. Pa wrote to Doct. Dudley as soon as Mr. Cook's letter was received. Brother came in, said he would be better satisfied to send Ezekiel over, thought it would be showing her more respect. Doct. Dudley told him she [Lucy] had just come up from Frankfort. [. . .] Her Ma was in Lex. when she heard of it. She had one of her spells. They sent a message for her [Lucy] that her Ma was very sick. She will get her wish now to leave the South but in a different way from what she wished. My heart is rent once more this year. How sadly his fate and my poor Willie's were alike. No kindred heart near to see the last breath. [. . .] Brother received a letter from Ed [Field] at Memphis, saying he would reach Bolivar the next day which would be the day after he [David] was buried. [. . .] Pa wrote him not to take Anna. He wrote back he had no place to leave her. [. . .] Brother will leave on Thursday. When he first heard of it, he thought he would leave P. [Pauline] until he came up in the winter with the remains. She is not willing to stay. [. . .] I do hope Lucy will not object to his being laid in our cemetery with the rest. Poor fellow. Lucy told me when here he said he was not coming up, he had nowhere to stay. I sat down and urged him to come, said everything I could to induce him to come, spoke of his interesting boy. The letter he wrote back was very interesting. I said David writes like a Christian. It was passed around through the family. I hope it is not lost. [It has not survived.] [. . .]

Since I wrote the above, Ezekiel Field has come. Poor fellow, he is much distressed. [. . .] Ezekiel says Pa received a letter from Ed, said he was shocked to find he [David] died a few days before he got there, with congestive chill. His mind was in no condition to [. . .] make a will. Ezekiel said he only wrote a few lines. [. . .] Ezek thinks he may go with Brother. [. . .]

Your sister,

Elizabeth

"We all seem to have given up but Pa and it is astonishing the control he has over himself," Belle Lyman wrote Ann in September, "but his grief is silent but deep. He remarked that morning that it was just 16 years ago since Amelia [Clay] died, seemed to console himself in that way, that he had not lost his children very fast." Christopher and Zeke Field were leaving that day for Mississippi, accompanied by Christopher's wife and her mother.

Christopher wrote Elizabeth as soon as he got to Mississippi, and a version of his words soon reached Ann.

ELIZABETH HOLLOWAY

Sunday (Fall), 1859

Dear Ann,

[. . .] Last night I received a letter from Brother. I will just write his words.

They had been there a week. He says our neighborhood has been much afflicted during September and I see its mournful effects upon the countenances of nearly everyone I have met. It has been my intention to have written you or some member of the family ever since I got home, but I have not had resolution enough to do so. David's death I feel very hard — and will do so for a long time. Nothing but time will eradicate the gloom from my feelings. I have but little to add to that which you have heard. Judge Murry and his wife came to see us two days ago and was [sic] with David for 18 hours before his death and saw him breathe his last breath. Mr. Cook was also with him from morning until his death at 12 o'clock. They say he was perfectly calm and entirely rational and retained his mind up to the last moment. He had but little to say [. . .] was entirely conscious of his situation and remained perfectly calm. When Judge M. told him he had to die, he replied he was fully aware of his situation. [. . .] Said his wife would be the greatest sufferer and she would miss him most. Said as to his affairs he had no preparation. [. . .] I see he says he came to my home [Content] on Thursday, was quite sick with something like cholera morbus, returned home on Friday morning relieved. Mary his cook says when he came home that morning she asked him if he was not sick. He said he had been sick at my house, but was then relieved. She says he ate a rather hearty dinner and drank too much buttermilk. That evening he walked to the overseer's house. At night, he told Mr. Vaughn [the overseer] what had occurred at my house. He gave him a pill. He [. . .] slept none but did not complain. Next morning, Saturday [. . .] during the day he had a chill and was very bad from that time up to 12 o'clock Sunday, when it terminated. Mortification had taken place, I have no doubt from what I learn was the situation of his body the next morning. I have not examined all his papers. I have no idea he made any will. I have consulted with Edmund and [. . .] [Doctor] Offutt. Both say his body cannot be taken up until spring. He was buried in the usual manner and they say decomposition will go on until that time. We are so remote from any town that it would be difficult to make the preparations necessary to carry it up sooner. I have not fully determined what I will do about it. Nor have I determined what is best for his estate to be done. Edmund and Anna have been up to see us. Both I believe are very well satisfied. As yet Ed has had no practice off of Mr. Anderson's place and I fear he will do but little off of the 2 places. [. . .] I believe Pauline is very well satisfied. So far she has been much engaged fixing up our cottage house and will be contented. I would hate for her to take up Lucy's prejudices against the country. I have no very high opinion of the country myself, but, while I am here, I wish to be contented and have all around me so. I have not had a gay and mirthful thought since I heard of the death of David and am in a poor condition to enjoy the company of any one. [. . .] Here he ends.

Poor fellow, died as he lived. [. . .] I do wish David had made a will. [. . .] You say you thought I would say something about where David would be buried. I broached the subject to Mrs. Scott, asked her if Brother did not say he would bring his remains up this winter. Oh yes, she says. She says it nearly killed Lucy to think he is buried down there. I was afraid to say a word. I tell you I measured my words. I am not sorry I went [to see Lucy]. I thought I owed my brother that much. [. . .]

E. F. Holloway

I am moved by David's death, since so many details of his life are available to me: his battles with the millwright's crazy wife; his anger over a mistreated slave; his homemade pair of pantaloons. I have no idea what happened to his lone descendant and namesake, "little Dadie" as Lucy was to call him, a child of boarding houses and rented rooms. Perhaps the David Irvine Field of Hollywood was his descendant.

Despite their mourning, the Clays were in the midst of preparations for the January 5th wedding of Martha to Henry Bedinger Davenport of Charles Town, Virginia (now West Virginia). Henry, only a few months older than Martha, seems to have sprung full-blown into her life. I have no idea where she met him, though some Bedingers had a farm adjoining the Clays in Bourbon County.

Martha's wedding was to be an elegant evening affair unlike the simple marriages of the Field sisters. Her engraved wedding invitation reads:

Mr. & Mrs. B. J. Clay

AT HOME

Thursday, January 5th

at 7 o'clock, Auvergne, Ky.

and included the cards of "Miss Clay" and "Henry B. Davenport."

Surprisingly, the bills for Martha's wedding finery no longer exist, although there are bills for numerous ribbons of velvet and satin, as well as some material that Martha charged at Garrett Spears and Company in Paris late in 1859. The bills for the wedding feast have survived, however, and quite a feast it was. Brutus paid $90 to a Paris purveyor of groceries for 8 cans of oysters, 200 meringues, one cake pyramid, one temple, one candy church, one coconut pyramid, a pound of cream, a pound of rock candy, and other delicacies. From B. Cavagna and Son, a family bakery and grocery in Cincinnati, he purchased two baskets of Charles Heidsieck champagne and a dozen bottles of Longworth's sparkling catawba, as well as a dozen oranges, a dozen lemons, and some crackers. It cost him $1.45 to ship these items from Covington (across the Ohio River from Cincinnati) to Paris on the Kentucky Central Railroad (the two railroads reaching Paris had merged).

I feel a proprietary interest in Martha's wedding, since I was married in those same double parlors a little more than a hundred years later. There had been one wedding at Auvergne during the intervening years, the April 1902 marriage of my father's half sister Sue to an English doctor she met while visiting Cairo, Egypt, before World War I. (He followed her to Greece and proposed on the steps of the Parthenon.)

I never knew Martha, but I did know her daughter, Amelia Woodford, a strong-willed old lady who I suspect resembled her mother in many ways. She had married her uncle Zeke Clay's partner in the horse business, Catesby Woodford, and, by the time I knew her, had been a widow for several decades — a wealthy childless woman who lived in a dark house full of Troy paintings of her husband's horses.

My father had inherited his father's job of being confidant to the family's elderly members, so Cousin Amelia often came out to our house to consult him about her affairs. She could be quite terrifying. On one occasion she arrived in her chauffeur-driven navy blue Oldsmobile at a time when only my brother and I were at home. Dreading a confrontation with this fearsome person, my brother and I climbed out a window and fled to the woodshed, where we found George Brent, the handyman, who was also hiding. The three of us huddled by the woodpile, giggling nervously, while Cousin Amelia circled the house, accompanied by her chauffeur, a sinister-looking man named Clarence. Sounding just like my grandmother's parrot, she shouted, "George! George!" Finally George could stand it no longer and gave himself up.

Sister Sue I remember well. She and Dr. Cyril Goodman, a surgeon with the British army in Egypt, returned to Kentucky in the 1930s. He died before I moved there, but Sister Sue lived on into the 1960s in a cottage full of mementos, a curious combination of central Kentucky and the British Empire that puzzled me as a child. It was only much later that I learned how deeply disturbed her father, Cash, had been at the prospect of his beloved daughter marrying an Englishman and moving to North Africa.

My father and his younger brother John were to be attendants at Sister Sue's wedding, dressed in black velvet Little Lord Fauntleroy suits with lace collars, but at the last moment my father refused to go through with the performance and Uncle John had to march across the parlors with a girl cousin. For years, the suits were packed away in a trunk at Auvergne. My children and their cousins tried them on one rainy afternoon in 1978, then posed for photographs.

Martha was twenty-seven when she married, an old bride by the standards of her time. In April 1966, I was a year older, a newspaper reporter in Rhode Island. I left most of the details of the wedding to my mother but insisted that she hire a string ensemble. One of my clearest memories of my wedding is of standing at the top of the front stairs as the trio played a piece by Telemann. "Doesn't baroque music sound great in this house!" I exclaimed to my maid of honor, Salmon P. Chase's great-great niece. Then I gathered up the train of my dress from Bendel's, sprinted down the stairs, and married another Providence *Journal* reporter, John M. Berry, in front of assembled relatives, assorted friends from New York and Providence, my childhood nurse, Virginia Hughes, and Hambone, the last of our Chesapeake Bay retrievers.

No one attended all three weddings, and only a handful were present for more than one, so the only continuity was the location and three long white dresses. I know from a newspaper account that Sister Sue decorated the house with Easter lilies and American Beauty roses. I cut boughs from the magnolia tree outside the sitting room window. I don't know if Martha tossed her bouquet from the landing on Brutus's elegant stairway, but Sister Sue and I did.

Preparations for Martha's wedding began in December. Mary Embry offered Ann her help.

MARY EMBRY

[December, 1859]

My Dear Sister,

[. . .] Tell Martha if she does not feel equal to the occasion to let me know and I will try and sustain her in the trying hours and, if you want any of us to assist you or need any of our servants, you are perfectly welcome to them. I feel as if I would be in the way and we all would dirty up the house for nothing, but, if we can help you any [. . .] Mr. Embry has been away all week, went to Cincinnati Monday. I expected him back tonight. He did not come. He went to get a pair of horses and buy me a new waggon as you well know I am crazy on the subject of vehicles of that kind. [. . .] James Miller has returned [from Mississippi]. Mr. Burton was out yesterday even. He said all was well, that Zeke Clay [who was visiting in Mississippi] would come about Christmas. [. . .] Pauline is *fat* and fine, he reports, from appearances will not hold out long. [Pauline was five months pregnant.] [. . .] Pa has been complaining. [. . .] He had a chill last week from imprudence but is going about now. He says it will depend on the weather if he gets over or not, but I think he will go [to Martha's wedding]. Mr. Burton was telling a great tale that Jimmy [Miller] had said Lucy had written Bro., she had heard he was going to sell everything, her Bridal presents and all, and she wrote she wanted what was hers. So Jimmy came up, loaded with *hers* and more, too. I have not been in, and do not know the particulars. [. . .] It will not do if Lucy intends to cut up. She has enough to think about and brood over without thinking about what she is worth and how much she will be cheated out of everything. [. . .]

Your affectionate sister,

M. E.

Belle Lyman also offered to help.

BELLE LYMAN

Richmond, Dec. 20, 1859

Dear Ann,

I was thinking all day yesterday that I would write to Martha as I felt an apology was due her from me for my [neglect] in not sending her the black lace as soon as I returned home, but I heard her say that she needed some corsets. I was thinking she would write every day for those or something else, and they could all be sent together.

I was sorry to hear through your letter of Jackson's [Ann's slave gardener] death. He will indeed be a loss to you. George [a relative of Jackson's] had not heard he was sick. I called him in this morning and read that portion of your letter to him. He said not a word except that he wondered if Milly [also a relative] knew he was sick, looked very much distressed. He could have gone over very well if you could have written in time. [. . .] James Miller has returned [from Mississippi], brought a long letter from Brother to Pa, said he never was at such a loss to know what to do about David's estate. Sometimes he thought it best to sell out and then thought on the child's account it would be best to keep it, said he did not desire the guardianship but, at the same time, would like to see the child's portion well managed, said she [Lucy Field] of course would receive a widow's portion, but that at some future day she would marry again, which was all very proper, but in case the child should die, David's brothers and sisters were heirs to her portion and would like to see them get it, etc. [. . .] said poor David was never out of his thoughts, he missed him in every way, and that he did not know when he would get over it, and that is the way I feel, too. He had set the 1st February to bring his remains [. . .] and he thought Richmond the proper place to bury him, but had said nothing to Lucy on this subject. [. . .] James says Brother received a letter from Lucy before he left there, saying she wanted him buried in Lexington, just what we expected. If you receive this letter before you see her, suppose you allude to it if she broaches this subject. [. . .] Brother sent his watch up to her, thought at one time of keeping it for little David but Lucy might have thought strange of it. Zeke [Field] packed her things up and sent them by James. The Overseer said he [David] talked so much about Lucy and the baby, said he had been writing begging her so much to come up after her. Said he told the physician to feel and see if he had any pulse. He told him yes. David then replied so calmly that life was almost extinct. Did you ever know such composure and calm resignation? If he had only then Confessed a hope (though feeble) of pardon and acceptance with God. How consoling it would be to his bereaved relatives and friends. I never saw anyone who feels it so keenly and deeply as Brother. James says there never lived on that country a man more popular and more sincerely loved than he was, said a gentlemen told him that they would take his and Brother's *word* before they would take most men's notes. And yet notwithstanding all this, Lucy was so unhappy and discontented there and, on the contrary, he so happy and well satisfied. [. . .]

Tell Martha her commands will be attended to by every letter. Pa says that he will certainly turn out if the weather is favourable. As for Dr. Lyman, there is no counting upon him. He is out today some distance in the country and was last night. Some days he is riding for 8 or 4 hours in succession. [. . .] I believe every other member of the family will be in attendance, however, as to Patsey, I cannot answer. [. . .]

The people of the county have been in a great state of commotion and excitement in regard to Fee [John Fee, the abolitionist to whom Cassius Clay deeded land for Berea College] and his comrades. A committee of 90 share holders have been appointed to visit them on tomorrow at Berea and invite them to leave the country. [. . .]

I was in hopes you and Martha would come over Christmas and spend a quiet week with us. We wouldn't have made company of you. [. . .]

Belle

One member of the family who didn't make Martha's wedding was Green, by then a law student in Cambridge, Massachusetts. "You all are so indifferent about writing I had almost concluded to give you up," he wrote Ann in January of 1860, " — but *Cash* came to the rescue (no pun intended). His letter was a very good and well-written one tho rather grotesque and highly seasoned with flattery. Its principal feature was the foreshadowing [of] a grand event — or at least he put on one of his most knowing smiles & whispered to me that great preparations were going on at home which he did not exactly understand. I suppose by this time he is no longer in the dark."

The Fields in Mississippi, Christopher, Pauline, and Ezekiel, and Kit Clay also missed Martha's wedding, so Belle Lyman obliged them with the only description of it that exists. Zeke, to whom her letter was addressed, apparently had marriage on his mind, too. He was almost twenty-four.

BELLE LYMAN

Jan. 11, 1860

Dear Zeke,

[. . .] I thought I would have something to write about that would interest you during this Christmas week, but I was sick in bed for several days but I have been told the week was [. . .] dull and quiet. There seemed to have been a marked change in the whole community, even the servants were more quiet and there seemed to be less confusion among them than was ever observed before. Perhaps the expulsion of John G. Fee and party had something to do with it. [Cassius's abolitionist colleagues had once again been forced to leave Madison County.]

At last, the long-talked of wedding has been consummated. Pa, Pattie, and I went over Wednesday and returned Friday. Sunday and Monday was [sic] so extremely cold that I was fearing Pa would not consent to go, but on Tuesday there was a favorable change in the elements and we concluded to go over one day in advance. [. . .] Martha had one of the most magnificent entertainments I ever saw, everything that you could call for and in the greatest abundance and everything so deliciously and elegantly prepared and I never saw Martha looking better. She was dressed so becomingly and at the same time so elegantly. She was married with a ring and stood in the folding doors [between the double parlors at Auvergne] with the most beautiful swinging flower basket over her head. As for Mr. Davenport, he always looked well in my estimation. His friends and his brother-in-law accompanied him. I presume they will leave for the South in a few days. She had a number of beautiful bridal presents. His was a watch with chain and a set of jewelry [made] of lava. The nearest relatives and a few of their most particular friends from Paris were invited. [. . .] I received your letter when I returned from Bourbon. I do not know whether I was surprised at its contents or not. You remark that you presume I have heard something about it. No indeed I have not. If you have ever mentioned it in your letters to Mary [Embry], I have never seen one of them, but I know that Sallie was always very free to talk about you. [Zeke was in love with Sallie Embry, one of W. W. Embry's daughters.] Dr. Lyman is always joking her about you and always contended that you both were very much in love with each other. [. . .] All that I can say is I hope it may be consummated without any difficulty and we are glad to see you at any time, the sooner the better. I was gratified to learn that you were making such arrangements, for I am most violently *opposed* to young men setting up *bachelor* establishments. There are too many temptations to do wrong. You know Sallie was a favorite with me and I trust that it will be productive of much happiness to all parties. I think everyone is happier married, at any rate such has been my experience. I have never regretted it for one moment for [I] have married a man who is in every way worthy of me and who has proved himself so, one who is sincerely attached to me and who has ever sympathized with me in all my afflictions and cares and troubles and what more can we ask. I acknowledge it is a serious responsibility, but when two parties start out with the determination to discharge their duties faithfully towards each other, I apprehend no difficulty, but, of course, you have thought of all these things. [. . .]

Yours truly,

Belle

[P.S.] [. . .] What has become of my saddle of venison?

Eighteen years later, on November 9, 1878, Martha wrote Ann, remembering "the night I was married when we were all so happy." Many terrible things would happen during the intervening years, of which John Brown's raid on the federal arsenal in Harpers Ferry, Virginia, several months before Martha's wedding, was a harbinger. As a member of the local militia, Henry Davenport commanded the guard that took John Brown to and from the jail in Charles Town during his trial.

SIX

If the Union Survives the Election

In the fall of 1859, abolitionist John Brown led eighteen men into Harpers Ferry in an attempt to seize the federal armory there. Less than thirty-six hours later, U.S. marines captured Brown. He was hanged on December 2, and those of his companions who survived the raid were executed a short time later. Documents found at Brown's Maryland headquarters linked him to six Northern abolitionists, including young Franklin B. Sanborn, a protégé of Ralph Waldo Emerson and his children's tutor.

Frank Sanborn was a friend of my mother's father. My aunt remembered him as a Byronic hero. In her apartment in Washington, she had a picture of Sanborn in Greek native dress, commemorating his involvement in that country's struggle for independence from Turkey. In her late nineties, my aunt recalled Sanborn describing how he had traveled down to Harpers Ferry from Boston to make sure Brown was properly buried. This sounds unlikely, since Sanborn fled to Canada once his connection with Brown was discovered. However, my aunt remembered in great detail how he missed his train in Baltimore and had to stop off there before he could get to Harpers Ferry. Nothing about John Brown or the hanging — just the details of a long-ago travel snafu.

Frank Sanborn's layover in Baltimore en route to Harpers Ferry is like the dog my father lost near Escondida while driving over to visit

Cassius Clay. In a child's perception — for both my father and my aunt were children at the time — the irrelevant detail becomes more important than the event and, as the story is told and retold, eventually replaces it. What lives on is a collection of trivia in which lie clues to the past.

After John Brown's raid, the slave question paralyzed the country. For nearly two months at the end of 1859 and the beginning of 1860, the House of Representatives was unable to elect a Speaker. Through forty-four ballots, the members remained deadlocked. Congressmen armed themselves; so did their partisans in the galleries. The political system was stretched to its breaking point.

1860 was a presidential election year. The first of the political conventions, that of the Democrats, was scheduled to begin in Charleston, South Carolina, in April. Although Senator Stephen A. Douglas seemed the likely nominee, many Southern Democrats preferred a Republican president in order to bring the crisis to a head. When, after fifty-seven ballots, the Democrats were unable to pick a candidate, they adjourned to try again six weeks later in Baltimore. There the Southerners deserted the party, organized their own convention, and nominated John C. Breckinridge of Kentucky, then vice president, as their presidential candidate.

The Republicans were set to meet in Chicago in early summer. Cassius Clay had great hopes for that convention, seeing himself as the perfect compromise candidate, so at the beginning of the year he set out on a speaking tour of the Northeast.

Meanwhile Martha and her new husband departed on a prolonged honeymoon in Mississippi, New Orleans, and Cuba. At Kentucky Landing, they visited Christopher Field and his new wife as well as Kit Clay and Zeke Field. The Fields planned to return to Richmond in mid-February with David's remains. Ann, Brutus, and young Cash spent the winter on the farm in Bourbon County, but the older boys were all away. The first to write home was Kit. He needed more field hands.

CHRISTOPHER CLAY

Bolivar, Miss., Jan. 12, 1860

Dear Pa,

I write a few lines to inform you all is well and moving at a slow gait. [. . .] On last Monday, we shipped forty-five bales of cotton, and I suppose I have yet sixty bales to Gin. Our crop is very good and splendidly picked. And I hope to get a good price for my cotton. Cotton at present in New Orleans is on the decline. [. . .] But I hope to pay expenses this year which will be rather a large item with a poor man and small planter. This year or now I would like to increase my force six or seven hands. I would want three young women, the balance young healthy men. If I could buy them on 12 months' time, I could about pay the debt from the present year's crop, provided I am not overflowed and make a fair crop. My calculations are to plant for 200 bales. If you intend to give me any more negroes, or wish to sell any of your negroes, I would be glad to hear from you on the subject. The proceeds of the crop for several years belong to me and, if I am going to stay in the South, I have no use for the money but to invest in negroes. We now have six hundred acres of land ready for cultivation and we have too much wild land for our force. [. . .]

Nothing more at present. My love to one and all.

Truly yours,

Christopher F. Clay

Kit included a note for Cash. "I am glad to hear of your good success in shooting on the wing," he wrote his brother. "In hunting you must be very careful with your gun unless you might accidentally get shot. I must tell you of a sad accident which happened a few days ago in our neighbourhood. A young man was out hunting after a rain when everything was slippery. He was on a fence, looking for a deer, the Gun fired and killed him dead. He was shot thru with twenty-four buck shot. So, my Dear Sir, you cannot be too careful with your Gun at all times."

Martha wrote Ann that she and Henry had arrived at Kentucky Landing.

MARTHA DAVENPORT

Bolivar, Jan. 20, 1860

Dear Aunt Ann,

When we reached Lexington Saturday, we received Mr. Carroll's dispatch saying the boat would be waiting. On our arrival, he was at the cars to inform us the boat was at the city and would not start before the next day so we went to the Galt House and found a room on the first floor waiting with a good fire for us. He called to see us next morning, accompanied us to the boat, and we found there also he had the nicest room for us, one of the end rooms in the Ladies cabins. As usual, it was well known there was to be a bride on board so every eye was turned upon us. I had the satisfaction of hearing that it was the unanimous opinion of the company, as I was about leaving, that I was so well behaved no one would suppose I was a wife of less than ten years standing, and Mr. Halliday pronounced me of all the brides he had ever seen the most dignified and agreeable to other people. [. . .] Mr. Davenport won the hearts of all the married ladies and girls by having been so generous as to present me with such a magnificent diamond ring which I wore at his solicitation. They all intend to sett [sic] their caps for him if he ever becomes a widower in order to have the ring. He was perfectly delighted with the boat and begged me not to stop here as he disliked to leave such agreeable company, etc. Kit had just gotten my letter and was reading it to the family here when they looked out and saw the boat landing on Thursday morning. He & Zeke [Field] came down full tilt and soon Alfred [a slave] on a horse with a side saddle for me. Pauline and Uncle Kit were delighted to see us. The boys were just preparing for a hunt so Mr. Davenport joined them, but it was so late in the day they found no deer. This morning they all started out again and brought back a few deer and Mr. D. very near killing another. [. . .] Uncle Ed [Field] and Anna came up this morning. She is looking well, but faded very much and is very homely. Uncle Ed the same as ever, had scarcely taken his seat before he expressed a wish that he was at home again. [. . .] I think we will remain here a week, spend half of the time here and the rest out at Mr. Estill's. Mr. D. does not seem to think we will have time to remain any longer. I want to go down to Uncle David's tomorrow and out to Kit's one day. Uncle Christopher looks very well, but so sad he does not seem natural. He scarcely ever smiles and his countenance indicates much mental suffering. There will be a sale of a few things [of David's] tomorrow. [. . .] They sent Aunt Lucy everything that was worth sending, much more than she wrote for. She did write she heard Uncle Kit intended selling everything and she wished her bridal presents all reserved. From what Pauline says, I guess Uncle Kit did not like it. She has consented to let Uncle David be buried in Richmond. [. . .] She was very cheerful and agreeable when we called [in Lexington, en route to Louisville], stayed about an hour. She had the baby brought in immediately. It looked very sweet and smart and is like Mrs. Scott. [. . .] Kit is so delighted at hearing that you have put away some wine for him. His mouth is stretched from ear to ear. [. . .] I will not comment upon the perfections of Mr. D. until I have tried him a year for fear I will want to retract. [. . .] Pauline looks very pretty and not bad. She is fixed very nicely and has a very nice table with cut glass & china and fine linens. Her bridal presents have come in good play.

Affectionately yours,

Martha Clay D.

There is no record of the sale of David's possessions to which Martha referred, but in mid-May his executor, Zeke Field, sold an assortment of David's personal things. Christopher bought a table for $20 and four parlor chairs ("two injured") for $10. Zeke bought a bay mare for $150, the sale's most expensive item. Kit picked up a saddle for $6. A stranger got David's shotgun for $25.

David's widow wrote Zeke that her trunk had arrived in Lexington.

LUCY FIELD

Lexington, Jan. 21, 1860

My Dear Brother,

I did not intend that so long a time should pass before answering your kind letter, but circumstances and not want of inclination has prevented until now. A few days after I wrote to Brother, little David was taken quite sick, and I was constantly occupied with him. [. . .] I am so anxious about him all the time, feeling that he is my all, and the measles and scarlet fever have been prevailing here for some months. I do not allow him to go out of the yard for fear of his taking the disease. He is now the picture of health again, weighs 90 pounds [sic]. He is a general favorite in the house where we are boarding. On Christmas night, they had a tree full of presents for the children and sent into my room for Dadie to come and secure his. To my surprise, he came back with a dozen or more, some of them very nice indeed, and the next day he received a letter from his cousin Pattie [Field] and a nice little present accompanying it. For such kindness I feel very grateful, more as a remembrance than the value of anything received.

I was so glad to hear that you were living on the place and that the servants were contented and getting on well. I know that overseers very generally need to be watched as much as servants themselves. Brother did not mention whom you had for the present year. I would like to know and do sincerely pray that you may get a kind good man and one that will at all times discharge his duty conscientiously to the poor slave who is so much his power. [. . .] I did not unpack the trunk containing the china until a few days ago. All the glass things were broken, but I know it was unavoidable. It is so difficult to pack things of that kind to come so great a distance and handled so roughly as they must be. I was sorry they had not been disposed of down there. The rest of the things came safely and I was very much obliged to you for attending to them. [. . .]

Remember me to all the servants. And give my love to Brother & Pauline and all other relatives and friends. [. . .] I hope you will write soon and give me all the news of the place. Your sister,

Lucy Field

In Cambridge, Green was looking for an office in which to read law since his first choice, Rufus Choate, had died. "I had hoped by this time to have obtained a favorable situation in the office of Mr. Caleb Cushing [former U. S. attorney general]," he wrote Brutus in January, "which arrangement I was confident would meet with your approval. Mr. Cushing, now as Choate is dead, stands perhaps at the head of the profession in this country, and his advice would be of great advantage to a young lawyer. But, on acct. of continual absence from his office, he thought he would be of little advantage to me, his practice being principally in the Supreme Court. [. . .] He himself studied 5 years before touching the practice. However worthy of imitation so exalted an example may be yet, of course, I expect practicing long before that. His advice to me was to stay at Cambridge two terms longer or rather 6 mos. at least."

Belle Lyman wrote Ann from Richmond that she wanted Zeke

Clay to make her a picture frame. Ambrotypes and tintypes were all the rage, and Zeke and Ann specialized in making frames for them decorated with nuts and seeds. Unfortunately, none of the frames still exist. However, the photograph to which Belle refers may be the ambrotype of the single Field sister taken between 1856 and 1860. "Pattie Holloway was asking me how those frames were made," Belle wrote. "I told her to tell Zeke that I had not received the Photographs and could not tell the size [. . .] but I guess Zeke has started for school before this [Bacon College in Harrodsburg, Kentucky]. I was afraid he would think me troublesome, but I admired them so much and was well aware that I could never make them half so nice. The photographs would have been here sooner, but Dr. Lyman forgot to give them the colour of my hair."

Belle also told Ann that Christopher planned to leave Mississippi between the 15th and 20th of February with David's remains and would bury him in Richmond. Some member of the family would have to send a carriage over to Lexington for Lucy.

Green wrote to thank Ann for sending him goodies from Martha's wedding. "The box I have [. . .] received. A receipt is worth it for manipulating the cotton from the cake & would have been of use, however, fortunately the cakes were iced and were easily shelled or hulled. And, together with the redeeming bottle of 'Heidsick [*sic*],' make up a gift for which I am much obliged."

In late January, Ann discovered that Kit had ordered a new suit from a local tailor and wrote her brother Zeke to twit Kit about it, since ordering a new suit of clothes, as we've seen, usually meant an impending wedding. Wedding or no wedding, the Clay men dressed well. Before setting off for Harvard, Green purchased several pairs of pants, some shirts, a silk vest, a silk scarf, and a linen duster from John B. Talbott of Paris. Late in 1859, Zeke had bought himself a cashmere coat and pants from S. E. Tipton, "Merchant Tailor," perhaps for use at college. Brutus got a six dollar hat from Joseph Porter, "Fashionable Hatter," as well as a $1.50 cap for Cash. He also paid $30.87 for nineteen wool hats ordered by Mingo for the farmhands.

ANN CLAY

Auvergne, Jan. 29, 1860

My Dear Zeke,

I want you to go to see Cit [sic] and give him a whipping for me. I was in town ten days ago & Tipton the Taylor [sic] told me that he had expected Cit the night before, & supposed he would certainly come that day. I asked him why, that I knew he had no idea of coming as I had just received a letter & he said he had not the time or money to come to Ky. this winter. Tipton remarked there was no mistake, that he had his letter telling him to have a fine suit of clothes ready by the 17th, that he wanted them to visit a friend, but, of course, everyone thought he was to be married and I suppose it caused some excitement in town, but I knew there was nothing of [sic] it and told Tipton that Cit had only done it for a joke. I knew he had no idea of marrying so soon as he had never mentioned it to his Papa and then Miss [Mary] Brooks is yet at school. I have believed for a year that there was something between them, but I have thought that Cit did not know his own mind on the subject. [. . .] I do dislike to see young men treat young ladies so, for I thought last summer that Cit was trifling with her. I never have been very well pleased, but still it provoked me to think of his trifling with her. I expect she is a very clever girl but she does not look smart though I have never been in her company. I suppose that Cit intended to marry next summer & concluded to order the clothes for a joke & they would be ready, but I hope he will have to pay for his joke.

I suppose that Martha has left you before this as it has been two weeks since she left here. She promised to write as soon as she reached Bolivar so I have been expecting a letter for a day or two. She declined stopping, but I found Mr. Davenport was so anxious to stop that I told her she must stop. [. . .] I am sorry that Ezekiel [Clay] came home so delighted with the South, says he wants to live there. I tell him, no, one is enough to be in that country. He starts this week to Harrodsburg to college. I did not want him to go there, but he proposed it to his Papa and he agreed and I really did not know what other school to recommend. He tells me that, if a letter comes from you, I must send it and not let anyone see it as there will be some secrets in it. [. . .] Belle wrote me that Brother would start up with David's remains the 15th or 20th of next month and that he would be buried in Richmond which I was very glad to hear. [. . .] If she [Lucy] had shown more love for him by staying more with him, I would have been glad to have seen her wishes carried out, but, as it is, I cannot feel half the sympathy for her that I should. [. . .] I don't know how she is ever to forgive herself. But she does not seem to reproach herself, but only abuses the country. She told me when I saw her just before Christmas that Brother had written her and that he was more ready to leave the country, but I understood it and knew that Brother did not mean it as she construed it. [. . .] I want to have David's likeness painted in some way this spring and I intend to make the frame myself so I want you to save me some gum balls off of some of his trees. Please select the best and bring them to me when you come. And, if you have any acorns growing there, please get me some of those. I have used up the balls Zeke brought and made me some beautiful frames, but, for his likeness, I wish them off his place. You would be surprised to see how nice a frame I can make of the nuts. Zeke got him & me both to make them, one apiece, so he has made the hard part & I have had to do the balance so it has been my employment since Martha left & we have now 6 ready to send over. He got so tired of it that he declared he would not make another, but yesterday I wanted one and I had to promise him $2.25 to buy a knife before he would make it. He and Cash have been for two days attending a [maple] sugar camp, Cash complaining very much that Zeke will not work. They are equal partners. We had quite a nice stirring off today & I hope will have some more as they have about 40 trees tapped.

[. . .] Tell Cit to write us how he is going to wear these fine clothes. [. . .]

Ann M. Clay

There is no record of how Kit explained the suit. He wrote his father in late January that Martha and Henry Davenport had left for New Orleans, "both looking well and [. . .] quite devoted to each other."

He continued, "I am now ready to raise my Gin and will commence Monday morning. And I suppose in three weeks will have the Gin completed. I find building a Gin quite a heavy job. I have shipped 45 bales of cotton and will commence Ginning the balance next week at Col. Field's Gin. I suppose I will make one hundred bales. I will take in about fifty acres more land if we have dry weather so I may get a good burn. I am now ready to commence plowing my corn ground and will start two plows next week [. . .] for the past two weeks, I have had none in the field but my *chop shot* gang. I will have a splendid Gin house when completed. The timbers all heavy and sound. The house is

82 by 42, but two story high [. . .] will cost about 1200 dollars. I hope and think my cotton will net about $3500."

Christopher Field's daughter Pattie was eleven. She loved to tease, and prickly Zeke Field was a perfect victim.

PATTIE A. FIELD

Richmond, Feb. 1, 1860

Dear Uncle Zeke,

In your letter to Aunty Belle Lyman, you asked her what [had] become of me. I am still in the land of the living. [. . .] I will now entertain you, something about Miss Sallie Embry [Zeke's fiancée]. You had better look sharp or Field Miller will cut you out. Him and Cousin Sallie are carrying on quite a flirtation. She and Cousin Pattie Holloway not long ago went down to Silver Creek and Uncle Miller was in town and told them to stop at the mill and get Cousin Field and Cousin Sallie spoke up and said it would not be a visit without Field. When Aunt Patsey went over to Bourbon, Cousin Sallie went in the carriage with them and, from what I hear, they were making love all the way over there. And the next morning Cousin Zeke Clay, Field M., and Mary H. [Holloway], and myself were standing in the parlor and I was telling Cousin Zeke Clay about what love they were making coming over and Uncle Embry came in in the midst of it. Cousin Field told me to hush, but I kept on until I got through and his face turned crimson. I presume you have heard of the [literary] club parties. They were to meet at Cousin Amelia Burton's and Cousin Curtis was to read and he was on a spree and could not go. He told Aunt Mary [Embry] that he had a beautiful piece to read. [. . .] Aunty got your letter, but I was deprived of reading it. I concluded there must be some secret in it. [This was probably the letter in which Zeke told Belle he hoped to marry Sallie.] So when you write, please write me a long letter. [. . .]

Pattie Field

Martha and Henry made their leisurely way to New Orleans, where they planned to embark for Cuba.

MARTHA DAVENPORT

New Orleans, Feb. 4, 1860

Dear Aunt Ann,

[. . .] We left Uncle Christopher's just a week ago, after remaining there a week. [. . .] I never saw Kit so polite. He came down with his gun and dogs every morning to go on a drive with them. They ran deer every day, but only killed 3. Zeke and Uncle Christopher always went with them. Kit stayed all night the morning we left and saw us on the boat. Mr. D. was delighted with his visit and seems much inclined to live down here. I went down to Uncle David's, but everything appeared so strange I did not feel at home. He had fixed the house so nice, set the yard out full of trees and roses and would have had a beautiful place in a few years. We rode over to the old place. The yard is nearly all gone in the river and his orchard is all thrown outside of the new levee. I saw his grave far out in a desolate spot in the cotton field by the side of some overseer who had died there. [. . .] Mary [David's cook] keeps the house very nice. His willow chair sits just where it used to and the sewing machine with the old piece of bagging over it. Uncle Christopher seemed so sad and unhappy. His appearance shocked us whenever he was laughing & talking. Uncle Ed seems perfectly contented and happy. [. . .] Anna [Field, Ed's wife] seems very sad. And I think her afflictions have made her a different woman. [. . .] Anna says Cousin Pattie White told her that the Fields made a great deal of fun of her and the way she dressed when she came to Ky. as a bride. [. . .] We are going to Havana tomorrow, quite a pleasant party of our own, Henry Buckner, Mr. Givens & Mattie, and a Miss Green [. . .] who came down on the *Pacific* with us. Her father has placed her under Mr. Davenport's protection. [. . .] We anticipate a very pleasant trip after our seasickness is over. I do not think Kit knows what he wants to do. I heard him tell Mr. Halliday perhaps he would go up to Ky. the next trip, but I do not believe one word of his marrying that girl [Mary Brooks]. [. . .] [The rest of the letter is missing.]

Martha signed her next letter to Ann "Martha Clay."

MARTHA DAVENPORT

New Orleans, Feb. 11, 1860

Dear Aunt Ann,

Much to our surprise we are still here. The steamer we expected to sail upon went but a week since. Mr. Davenport, contrary to my advice, would not take passage upon her until he found out if we could have a party consisting of Mr. Givens & mother, Mr. Buckner & Miss Green. They were so long making up their minds that when he went to engage rooms they were all taken so we have been compelled to remain here another week. The vessel we go on tomorrow is the best on the Gulf. And we will have a very large & agreeable party, mostly from Mississippi. It is well we did not go out on the first steamer as she encountered a severe gale so that we should have been very cold. The ladies wore their velvet cloaks & furs with comfort. [. . .] We made arrangements to go over to Mobile this week, but Henry Allison persuaded us we would be very sea sick and I was afraid it would put Mr. Davenport out of the notion of going to Havana if he was made acquainted with the disease so soon.

I suppose Uncle Christopher will be going up soon on the *Baltic.* When I left there, I thought it quite probable we would be ready to go up also, but we will scarcely be able to be here in time. I guess we will return on the *Pacific.* [. . .] I had the finest view yesterday I nearly ever saw from the top of the Custom House. We counted 50 steamboats and 1,000 ships lying in port. The appraiser of liquors took us into his apartment and treated us to the finest bottle of champagne I ever tasted. [. . .]

Martha Clay

The Davenports finally reached Havana. It was Martha, not Henry, who was seasick en route. "I could not lift my head up for ten minutes after we entered the Gulf until we sailed into the still water of the harbor," she wrote Ann. "I really believe if I had have been out two days longer, I should have died. You can have no possible conception of what a loathesome mean sickness it is. I am not well now, cannot touch meat or bananas, etc. It gave me a distaste to almost everything I used to enjoy in the way of eating. I tell Mr. Davenport this whole world could not induce me to go to Europe. He was not at all sick. We had about 25 ladies and they were every one deathly sick, yet the Captain pronounced the voyage very smooth. I cannot enjoy my stay here for the dread of returning."

In mid-February, the sad little cortege from Mississippi, consisting of Christopher, his pregnant wife, and Ezekiel Field, arrived in Kentucky with David's body. "I write to tell you that a dispatch has just been received tonight from Zeke, saying they would be for [sic] Lexington Saturday night," Belle Lyman informed Ann. "You must certainly come over Saturday, any way you prefer. Oh! Isn't it too sad. I can write nothing more."

David was buried with his little son Scott in the Field cemetery plot, a few feet from the bas relief Christopher had placed above the graves of Charlotte and her baby. Christopher then returned to Mississippi, leaving Pauline at her mother's house to await the birth of their child. Zeke also remained in Kentucky, where he married Sallie Embry. In April, Kit wrote his father that they were having an unusually dry spring.

"The River at present quite low, about 25 feet in banks. [. . .] My Gin is now completed & Gin stand at hand. We have made 98 bales of cotton the last crop & all sold except 27 bales. When I was in New Orleans, Mr. Black (my merchant) thought he would sell the 27 bales in a short time at a good price. He thought our crop would average 110. Our expenses for the year has [sic] been enormous & I am fearful after expenses paid will only have about $100 to our credit. It seems to me at present my prospect for making money is hard to arrive at."

He added that he hoped Martha was feeling better. Like Pauline, Martha was pregnant, although she didn't know it. She thought she was still suffering from seasickness when she left for her husband's home in Virginia. Pauline, however, was truly ill.

On April 13, William Holloway telegraphed Ann, "Pauline died today at eleven & half o'clock A.M., leaving an infant girl. To be interred Sunday two o'clock P.M. Come over."

E. H. Field wrote Ann a few days later. "We have again been deprived by death of another dear relative. It has fallen heavily on us and Col. Rodes' family but much more so on Christopher, who is very poorly prepared of late to undergo further misfortunes. His melancholy since the death of poor David has been constant.

"Pauline had suffered from Monday until Friday at 11 o'clock, when she had a daughter, and during Friday evening and night both seemed to be doing as well as usual. But, about daylight following, she began to sink rapidly and died soon without a struggle. [. . .] The child did not survive much longer and both [were] put into the same coffin and buried in Col. Rodes' lot on yesterday at 2 o'clock."

Christopher had been notified, but his father hoped he would not come to Kentucky. "The circumstances that surround us will be nothing to content him." He was sorry Ann and Brutus had not gotten word of Pauline's death in time to come to Richmond for the funeral.

It was very important then for women to know what they called "the particulars" of a female relative's death in childbirth. This wasn't just morbid curiosity. Childbirth was a dangerous undertaking; Pauline's dying wish that her daughter grow up to be an old maid was not unusual. Elizabeth sent Ann a lengthy account of Pauline's death.

ELIZABETH HOLLOWAY

[undated]

Dear Ann,

What a disappointment you did not come over. [. . .] You ought to have gotten the dispatch Friday. Everyone that came in at the door at Mr. Rodes' this evening I watched to see if it was not you. We had a fine sermon from Cousin E. and the largest procession I ever saw in Richmond, about 50 or 60 vehicles, and, when we got to the Cemetery, we found as many people on foot. She was buried in her father's lot. Mrs. R. said she hoped Brother's feelings would not be hurt. She felt as if she wanted to be buried by her sister. [. . .] You want to know all the particulars. It would take me all night to do that as I was with her from Monday morning 8 o'clock until Thursday night. [. . .] When I got there, I found both [Drs.] Walker and Smith. She was taken in labor Sunday evening. Her Ma wanted to send that night for them both, but she objected. She sent before day. She had pain all the time, none to do any good until Wednesday night, suffered violently. The doct. never began with the chloroform until 6 that morning. It killed the pain very much. Towards the last she could not inhale it very well. She was so much exhausted. Whenever she felt a pain coming on, she would beg for it which was every few moments. [. . .] Between 3 and 4 o'clock Thursday evening she was delivered of a daughter, very good size babe, a smart perfect image of her. The whitest creature, it looked very well, I thought, as much like living as any infant. The next morning its breathing got very quick, seemed in great pain. About dark, it died. It was a perfect beauty. It was laid in the coffin with her, its face touching hers. She was buried in her wedding dress. Mr. R. sent to Lex. and got the finest coffin that could be had. Now, as to her death. About 6 that evening I was suffering so much with headache, having lost so much sleep for 3 nights, I told Mrs. R. I would come home. She said [. . .] that she and M. K. [Mary Keen, a relative who lived with the Rodeses] would stay with Pauline. The baby would be taken in another room. After the babe was born, I took it in [. . .] [Mary Keen]'s room [. . .], went back in Pauline's room. She says Sister, you told me the child was born. I would be easy, but I don't see one. [. . .] Nell took it to her. She looked at it, in a cheerful tone, says, Miss, you will be an old maid. Well, [Pauline] says, it is my baby and I have named it. [. . .] The babe was laid on the bed with her that night. Mr. Rodes says he determined she slept only occasionally, talked some little, about day he said he did not like her breathing. He had Dr. Smith come. As soon as he examined her, sent off to Dr. Walker. [. . .] Doct. S. remained. The carriage came for me. I found her dying. She said to her Pa at day, Pa, put your ear down. I am too feeble to speak loud, Pa. I am no better. I am worse and most gone. He says he shall never forget that last look she gave him, as though she wanted to say something. Those were the last words she said. She died as calmly as she was all the time of her illness. She never had a frown on her countenance although she suffered so much. She was the most patient creature and most thankful to black & white. [. . .] She looked more beautiful when sick than well. Her Pa thinks she thought the day before she would die. [. . .] Mary Keen thinks she was conscious all the time. I do not think so. Nell made several prayers over her. She would say, Pauline, open your eyes and look at me. It made no impression on her. She did not move a muscle in her body from the time I went in at 7 o'clock until she died at half after eleven. I performed the sad office of closing her eyes. [. . .] She went off very easy. Her breath just got shorter and shorter. [. . .] As to cause of death, no human knows. The Docts. say she may have ruptured a small blood vessel. They did not like the looks of the afterbirth. [. . .] They also say there was an over portion of water in her chest. [. . .] They had to give her opium several times [. . .] to give her rest. She was so much exhausted. She has been sick ever since she came up, suffered with neuralgia in one side. [. . .] Brother was telegraphed. I saw no sense in that as he could not get here to see her burial. He will be in the greatest anxiety, will think as you do it was Chloroform. [. . .] He wrote to Mr. R. if he apprehended any danger to write him and he would come up, that she was dearer to him than any other thing on earth. I think he ought to have been here and Mr. R. ought to have written to him how much she was suffering. It made no difference to his business. He has enough money if he never makes another cent. [. . .] We can't tell whether he will come right up or not. There is a letter from him to her in the office. Came last night. [. . .]

Now, about Mrs. Rodes' distress. [. . .] She kept up very well, never left the room day or night scarcely until Thursday morning she could not stand it any longer. She [Pauline] had a spasm just before the babe was born and at least a day since she begged to die. Said she [Paulina Rodes] had no religion, she could not say the Lord's will be done. Says all the time I want my child back. Before the babe was taken sick she prayed to be spared to raise the little Pauline she called it. Mr. R. has more fortitude now than he had whilst she was sick. They are both heartbroke. Says their idol has been taken from them and she was truly one. [The rest of the letter is illegible, including signature.]

Chloroform was a new drug in 1860, having first been used as anesthesia in Scotland in 1846. It is doubtful that a Kentucky doctor would have been skilled in its use, so Ann and Christopher may have been justified in thinking it deadly — though the thought of poor Pauline being in labor for several days without pain-killers of any kind is ghastly.

It was the custom for friends and family to gather at the house of a dying person. Among those at the Rodeses' house during Pauline's confinement was her stepdaughter. Pattie also gave Ann the details of Pauline's death, details all the more vivid because they are seen through a child's eyes.

PATTIE A. FIELD

April 15, 1860

My Dear Aunt Ann,

I have just returned from poor Ma's burial. You have no idea how bad I felt and particularly as my Dear Pa could not have been here to see the last of his dear wife, first and last of his infant daughter. As Aunty Belle Lyman is not well enough to write, I will try to tell you the particulars of Ma's death. [. . .] She was very sick 3 or 4 days before the child was born. It was the perfect image of its mother. After it was born, Grand Ma Rodes dressed it and brought it to Ma and Ma laughed and said, I am going to make an old maid of you, Miss. It was white as marble and looked as if it had no blood in it. Friday, it was very sick and groaned and breathed very hard. They put it in hot cloths and, between 6 and 7 o'clock, they told Mary Keen to see if it was breathing and the poor little thing was dead. That day Grand Ma had it brought to her and named it Pauline and she told them not to bring it to her again for she felt like it was going to die, for if they did, she would love it so that it would break her heart if it died. It lived 30 hours. The poor little thing was laid in the casket with Ma. Aunt Belle sent for me about ten o'clock from school that Ma was dying. When I got there, it was very hard for Ma to get her breath. [. . .] They all said she was doing very well the night before but about daylight they saw she was getting worser [sic]. [. . .] Ma was dressed in [her] wedding dress and looked beautiful when first laid out, but she soon began to get black and they had to put cotton all over her neck and face except her forehead. When she was laid out, she looked as if she was asleep. Aunt Belle was very low spirited about herself and said that she would never get well again [she was pregnant], but her friends and relations encourage her and tell her, if she will go by Uncle Lyman's direction, which I think she is doing, and take medicine whenever Uncle wishes her I think she will soon be well. She still keeps her bed, but was very much disappointed that you could not come over. [. . .] I am so much obliged to Cousin Martha [Davenport] for the breast pin, but, as I am still going to stay in black, I expect it will not do to wear. [. . .]

Monday morning, April 16

Aunty is very sick indeed this morning, worn down from excitement but hopes when the medicine acts will feel better. She says as soon as Uncle Clay gets back, you must come over. [. . .] I received a letter from Aunt Sallie [Zeke Field's new wife, who had returned to Mississippi with him]. She seems very much pleased indeed, but will be greatly shocked to hear of Ma's sad death. [. . .] Your niece,

Pattie

As Pauline was being buried, Martha arrived in Virginia. There she met Henry's family for the first time.

MARTHA DAVENPORT

Jefferson Co., Va., April 20, 1860

Dear Aunt Ann,

We reached here on Saturday night after a very circuitous and tiresome trip. [. . .] I was so sick I could scarcely raise up my head, but have been better since I came though cannot find any liquids to agree with me yet. I have been received very kindly by the family and find them very pleasant. Mr. and Mrs. Gibson [Henry Davenport's sister and her husband] are still here. [. . .] They have two of the prettiest children I ever saw, but the little girl is totally blind. It is truly pitiful to see her groping her way around. She knows everyone by their voice. The place is very pretty, but everything is greatly out of repair except the house which is very nice and comfortable. I feel every day as if I wanted to take the negroes and go around cleaning up the trash and digging up the bushes out of the yard and filling up the chicken and dog holes. The garden is so small I fear I cannot find a place to sow even a few seeds, so I do not know how I can interest myself during the summer. [. . .] I have just received a letter from Amelia Burton telling me of the sad death of Pauline. [. . .] I have so often thought how happy and cheerful she seemed when we saw her and how proud Uncle Christopher seemed of her. It seems his cup of affliction is never full. [. . .] Tell me how Aunt Belle was and if she is as low-spirited as ever. I never think of being in Ky., without regretting I was not well enough to see all my relations for there are many I may never see again. Mr. Gibson says his fellow companion to Europe was so sea sick that he was affected just as I am for three years afterwards. Mr. Davenport wants me to send for Dr. Mason but I have no faith in medicine doing me any good, but I believe if I was housekeeping the exercise and diversion of mind would restore me. [. . .]

M.C.D.

Martha soon wrote again, lamenting the fact that she did not have a house of her own.

MARTHA DAVENPORT

Jefferson Co., April 30, 1860

Dear Aunt Ann,

[. . .] The weather still continues cold and the season is very back-ward. The farmers are just beginning to plant corn and nothing in the garden is growing. I walked out to the woods a few evenings since and never saw such rich earth in my life. The leaf mould was six inches deep. I could but wish you had it to put around your roses, and that I had some to put it around. The greatest quantity of young forest trees, so many one could soon improve a place. I brought home an armful of sassafras, so had some tea to drink. I suppose I have made the acquain-tance of nearly everyone in the county, judging from the number of vis-itors I have had. Even all the young gentlemen have called on me. I find the ladies very refined and agreeable and the nicest people all liv-ing in the county which is very thickly settled. [. . .] From all I have seen, I think I can live very happily if I only had a home of my own, but here I take no interest in anything, feel nothing is mine, having noth-ing to employ my time in, feel a mere boarder. [. . .] Indeed it makes me very unhappy to know and realize my dependent situation, not that the family are unkind to me, for on the contrary, I have been received with the greatest kindness [. . .] and find the servants very obliging, atten-tive, and polite, and have a nice comfortable room, but with all this I do not feel like being dependent upon Mr. Davenport's father for every mouthful I put in my mouth. [. . .] Mr. Davenport certainly deceived me, for I had positively made up my mind not to marry him if he told me he intended living with his parents (you know I have always had a horror of such things). On the contrary, he told me it was not only his wish, but his Mother's and Father's also, that he should keep house. So I never was more surprised to hear him at home suggest such a thing. I did not say much, but I knew I could not be contented then. I think it perfectly ridiculous the more I think of it that, because his Father in-tends giving him this place at his death, he is unwilling to go anywhere to improve another, for he may outlive us both and then my whole life will have been spent in inactivity and have enjoyed none of the plea-sures and comforts of a home of my own. [. . .] Another thing, if the im-provements here were handsome enough to be an object and the grounds also, then there would be some sense in talking about wasting time on another place, but that a very good barn and two negro cabins should be an obstacle to my happiness seems very hard to bear. In five years we could commence even a new place and make it more desirable than this. The house is merely good, inconvenient, and one half of it frame. The yard has some pretty forest trees, but no evergreens that have not been planted in the last two years except two arbor vitas, a good match for ours, one old cedar that the chickens have broken to pieces [. . .], and one pretty balsam fir. Wherein consists the great attractions I do not know, but suppose because Mr. Davenport was raised here it is better than anybody else's to him.

The garden is about the size of your flower square and nearly half of it is taken up in trees and grape vines. [. . .] He [Henry] says he has no place for an orchard so will not have any. [. . .] Just think of people living without any orchard.

[. . .] The country is very pretty and on the farm there is [sic] several beautiful locations for a house, commanding a view of the whole county with the mountains in the distance, and I understand there is a very pretty place at the upper end of the farm. I should be willing to go into a log cabin, however, if it were the only hope.

I deposited the money in the Bank that Pa gave [me] and there it shall stay until I can have a place to put what I buy with it in. Mr. Davenport frequently asks me why I don't ask Pa to buy Zeke Field out [in Mississippi]. That is the greatest investment he knows. And make Kit and me partners. I tell him no, I want no more divided interests. [. . .] Just to think every relation I have can have a home of their own. Even Mr. Burton, who told me he was not worth $5000, has a nice house and all the comforts Amelia wants. [. . .]

Yours affectionately,

Martha

Meanwhile, the Field sisters busied themselves with plans for a visit to their father's sister in Illinois. Ann, Mary Embry, Elizabeth Holloway, and Pattie Field hoped to go, but Mary thought she might not be able to make the trip because she, too, was pregnant, as she explained to Ann.

MARY EMBRY

Friday morning, May 1, 1860

My Dear Sister,

I received your message through Belle. I have not seen Mr. Clay yet and was so provoked he did not get my invitation to dine with me yesterday. [. . .] If I had have thought he was coming I would have sent to the toll gate for him but in strawberry time I was so busy stemming. [. . .] I can't think or get anything else done. I had a big dinner and [. . .] had just laid [*sic*] down to rest when six or seven came to eat strawberries. I had a freezer of cream and the strawberries were on the ice so they soon got what they came for. [. . .] The Reform Ladies had a strawberry feast last night but I fear without much success. As tired as I was I went in to see the table and see them go over to the Court House from Miss Webster's. She was here and insisted so much on my going. I had company all day long and really felt sick. Mr. Hutchinson came along and treated us to another bottle of Mrs. Clay's wine which helped me exceedingly. [. . .] I am so much afraid I will have to decline my Illinois trip as I feel there is something the matter with me. I would have told you when you were here but I could not tell. [. . .] But I have missed twice and have been very sick. [. . .] But this is all confidential, as I have not breathed it to a soul. There is so many to talk and some have so little else to do that I never tell them anything. [. . .] Of course if it is so these things show for themselves soon enough and we are objects of talk and to look at long enough to keep it concealed as long as possible. If Belle had her dresses made I could wear them. [. . .] I remember *before* I did not know how long it would be. I could wear dresses and had some made and before I knew it I had to lay them aside [. . .] and if I stay at home they are the very dresses I will need, for I do not visit around a lot and have not done so since I put on mourning since Pauline died. [. . .] You must write to me and let me know what you are going to do. Expect you are all ready to start. If I had the dresses and thought I was well enough I would go at all lengths [to go] but some days I feel badly. [. . .]

M.E.

In Mississippi, Kit really was thinking about marriage.

CHRISTOPHER CLAY

Hard Scrabble, May 3, 1860

Confidential

Dear Pa,

[. . .] I have at present but little news of interest to report. [. . .] Uncle Kit has not yet returned from Kentucky. [. . .] When he left, he remarked he was going to Ky. to mingle his tears with Pauline's distressed mother & over the grave of his dear wife & babe. We all were sad & much distressed & surprised to hear of Pauline's death. But she is now no more & I hope gone to a better land that this.

[. . .] Zeke Field & lady [his wife Sallie][. . .] will start I suppose for Kentucky the middle of this month. As for myself, I had not set any time for leaving & in fact thought but little about Kentucky. Sickness & the hot weather will be the only inducement for me to leave the Sunny South. My notions of the South are very different from many of my Kentucky friends. I have thought I would be better off here than in Kentucky. If I was a man of family, it would be very well for me to go to Kentucky during the hot summer season, but as I am *alone* I think it a matter of no moment. In the first place, I have not the money to be going away on expenses. The present year has come as near breaking me as I should wish for. [. . .] But I will never give up. I will still stick to the cotton. [. . .] If we have usual good luck this crop with everything generally next year, we are bound to make money. But Zeke F. is yet unsettled and *don't* know what to do. If D. I. Field Plantation is sold next year, which place he is now living in, he will have no home & then there must be a change or division some way. [. . .] Ezekiel & myself had a long talk recently on the subject. I said to him this: Ezekiel, I will sell my interest to you, you paying me what land joining us is worth & price of negroes here at present on three years time. [. . .] This proposition would not suit him. He has not the money. I then made him another as follows: We will still remain equal partners. I give you full control & management of the Plantation. You live on the place. I will live in Kentucky or somewhere else. [. . .] This proposition is left for his due consideration. [. . .] Well, Pa, I will now give you my views on the subject, particularly in regard to the plantation. I think it fine land for cotton & corn & some day may be valuable. I don't consider the property worth a hundred thousand dollars or even half of it. I am not willing to buy Ezekiel's interest at any price. [. . .] This is too uncertain country. We are liable to many misfortunes which might cripple us for life. In fact, I would rather own half than the whole. [. . .] I think I look farther ahead than Ezekiel &, if he would let me alone, I will some day make him a fortune. [. . .] The three years I have been here I have made expenses each year, commenced in the woods, only lost two grown negroes & two mules. I have not had a negro killed by an overseer or brutally punished. Everything has generally went on [sic] well. I have been saving in everything & starved nothing. Had a good deal of hard work done & but little whipping. My books give an account of every dollar. I have not swindled the place out of a dollar or made any bad purchase or bargain *neither extravagant or penurious*. [. . .] I am ready to do anything with Ezekiel that is right, honest, and equally fair. But, if he thinks he can make ten or fifteen thousand dollars out of me, he certainly is mistaken in the man. [. . .]

Pa, I wish to say something to you about a subject I have thought of for some time, but as I had not [. . .] yet come to any conclusive determination, I had never mentioned the subject. I have been thinking of getting married, but always thought I was too poor to support a wife. But I might think the same twenty years hence. I thought next fall I would marry, if then entirely agreeable to my feelings & suitable all around. [. . .] I have thought if I ever intend to marry I should marry while young. I don't think it a good plan to put such things off so long, especially a wild man like myself. This letter is strictly confidential. I hope to hear from you at your earliest opportunity. My love to one and all of the family. I am yours very truly,

Christopher F. Clay

Christopher Field stayed in Kentucky for a while after Pauline's death. After he returned to Mississippi, Elizabeth wrote Ann, "A Letter came from Brother to Pattie [Field] tonight. I opened it. Poor man, he is so unhappy and heartbroken. He wrote a long letter entirely filled about Pauline. He said she was so perfectly happy. [. . .] He says in one of her letters to him she had [said] all that was [needed] [. . .] to complete her happiness was to see him join her in Christian Love, said he never had a doubt of her Christianity. Said he had not attended to any thing since he returned. [. . .]"

Martha was still homesick. The desserts she was served at a luncheon reminded her of Aunt Ann's, particularly something called "transparent pudding," a concoction of sugar, butter, and eggs.

MARTHA DAVENPORT

[undated]

Dear Aunt Ann,

[. . .] Last Thursday, we spent a delightful day at Mr. Lewis', about ten miles from here, just on the river and at the foot of the mountains. There are three brothers living together, two of them are young married men and Mr. D's intimate friends. [. . .] I was so forcibly reminded of home on that day as the house and table were loaded with flowers and she had the same desserts you always have, ice cream and lemon sherbet, very nice cakes, iced, lemon and transparent puddings, delicious preserves, oranges and nuts. Mr. William Lewis tends to the flowers and the garden entirely. He took me out to show me his tomato plants with nearly full-sized fruit and eggplants, cabbages & celery, all of which are much more forward than anyone else has. I told him when I had a house & garden I would not allow everyone to say he had the best & earliest of everything. His strawberries were just turning. He has all the fine varieties and thinks he has found the best of all in some new plants he has just gotten, the Triumph de Grande [sic]. It was a perfect treat to me to be with him. [. . .] Mr. Davenport went to Baltimore a short time ago to have a place cut out of his arm which the physician advised him to let alone. He was really angry because I would not go. I told him I would go on no such foolish errand, that it was all his imagination about the place being dangerous. Tell Cash if he & Zeke were here I would make them rich in clothes as Mr. D. has the greatest quantity which he cannot get on, he is so fat. He says I must save the best and take them to Cash when I go. [. . .] He promises me he will go to housekeeping sometime within the year, but is at a great loss to know where to go, says he sees no arrangement except to go to town which will suit him and there is no house there he is willing to buy, that he is not able to build yet such a house as he intends to when he does commence. He is putting up some corn houses & an overseer's house and wants to stay here until they are completed and pull down some old buildings, stables & etc. which are just in front of the house. I tell him it is the first time in my life I ever knew anyone to find the hogs at the front door. He says it annoys him [. . .] and he does not know why his Father ever put the shed where it is. [. . .] I expect he has had a great deal to contend with in changing the old ways of the place [. . .] but his Father & Mother, like all old people, [. . .] don't like to see anything changed from the old-time way they have been used to all their lives, which you know are very far behind the times to anyone who has been used to as nice buildings as Pa has. Mr. Davenport is ambitious to have everything in the same order & style as Pa and I am sure I will do my part. [. . .] I tell Mr. Davenport he must never for a moment think I will be contented to live here, that I feel no interest in anything [. . .] while I am so situated, and that is no way for young people just commencing life to live, so we will leave here sometime within the year.

[. . .] I regret so much to hear of Uncle Miller's ill health. I was in hopes he was well. I hope Aunt Belle is improving. I would write to her, but dread to write to Ky. as I always have a cry when I do. [. . .]

Martha

Kit decided to return to Kentucky for the summer, but found himself short of money. "Our crops all looking finely & the hottest weather I ever felt," he wrote his father in early June. "We at present want rain very much for our corn is sickening. [. . .] One *good* rain will make our corn crop. Cotton don't want rain at any time. All cotton wants is hot & dry weather the whole season."

In Harrodsburg, his brother Zeke also needed money to get home. "Our examination commenced on last Tuesday," he wrote Brutus, "will close on the 27th."

In January 1860, Cassius Clay had begun his campaign for the Republican nomination for president on the steps of the capitol in Frankfort. He kept his audience standing in a cold drizzle for three hours while he defended Republican principles in a slave state — no mean feat. He went on to campaign in New York City and elsewhere, arguing that as a Southerner he had the best chance of defeating the Democrats in November. At the time Martha moved to Virginia, he was still hopeful about getting the nomination, but when the Republican Convention met a month later, Cassius was doubly disappointed. The successful attempt to deny William H. Seward the presidential nomination weakened Cassius, whose only chance of winning lay in the possibility that Seward and Abraham Lincoln would cancel out each other. Nominated for the vice presidency, Cassius polled 101 and one-half votes to Hannibal Hamlin's 194 on the first ballot. But after Hamlin picked up a number of favorite-son votes on the second ballot, Cassius's floor manager moved that Hamlin's nomination be made unanimous.

A week before the Republicans met, remnants of the old Whig Party convened to form the Constitutional Union Party, which nominated a wealthy slave owner, John Bell of Tennessee, as its candidate. Thus the election devolved into two separate contests: Lincoln versus Douglas in the North, and Bell versus Breckinridge in the South. Brutus canvassed Bourbon County for Bell.

Green wrote Brutus that he hoped to tour New England during his summer vacation. "I am again on the begging list," he said in June, requesting $350. "I have allowed myself in the amount above sufficient to carry me on a trip to the White Mts. and among the lakes of New Hampshire, as I propose to spend the summer vacation in that way, but will make it also useful (by continuing my reading) as well as pleasant."

Politics was on his mind, too. "Bell and [Edward] Everett will undoubtedly get a handsome vote in Massachusetts," he told his father. "The two heads of the Democracy place many of the party in a dilemma. Breckinridge & [Joseph] Lane though will be *the* ticket. The wisdom of the secessionists in their selection completely flaps the sails of Douglas. It is doubtful whether he will get a single state. The race eventually, if I may be allowed to predict, will be between Breckinridge & Lincoln, notwithstanding Bell & Everett will obtain a most respectable vote in every state of the Union and Douglas will slice thickly into Penn., Illinois, & Missouri. In any event, the present administration will be ousted [. . .] [necessitating] an entire change in the government agents and confidentials."

Martha remained preoccupied with her own situation. When she wrote Ann in mid-June, she thought they had found a house to rent and was busy planning her garden and servants.

MARTHA DAVENPORT

Jefferson Co., June 13, 1860

Dear Aunt Ann,

I was very glad to hear from home through your last letter, and must answer it immediately to tell you the joyful news that we are going to housekeeping in the Fall although Mr. Davenport has not yet bargained for the place. I kept at him until he has spoken to the gentleman who has charge of the place. It is a very nice new brick house [. . .] with a pretty yard & good garden that [. . .] will be for rent for at least three years. [. . .] I tell Mr. Davenport I do not much fancy the idea of putting all my labor & improvements on rented property, but he says he prefers renting to buying. He does not think he could be satisfied in town and says he is not able to buy a place without going in debt. [. . .] He says he does not know what we will do about servants. He has a man, girl, & boy to take there and I have been thinking about what Cousin Margaret said about Sophia and think, perhaps as you do, she will suit me for a cook — better than any of the others. The difficulty is about her being hired out. I wish Pa could let the woman have someone else in her place. He told me to select a boy. For present I would rather have a large one for his services, but, when I remember it is so much better to train a little one for the dining room, house, etc., I think perhaps I had better select a little one. I have always fancied Amy's Will and think I would rather have him than anyone on the place. I guess Pa will not like to spare him and Amy will make a great fuss about having her children all taken from her. It would be better if I had an old woman as I will be a new housekeeper, but they are all so spoilt at home. I could never put up with their laziness and backaches. As for Laura, I guess I will make a seamstress of her. [. . .] I wish Sophia was at home so she could stay in the kitchen and let Milly learn her to work, as I know little about it, especially to make waffles & biscuits, as I have seen none fit to eat since I left there. We have very nice light bread, but that is the only bread Mother's cook knows how to make that I can eat. One reason is the flour is so mean. [. . .] I tell Mr. Davenport he need never brag on wheat when the greatest wheat country furnishes the meanest flour I ever saw. You must save me a barrel of yours and not send it all to Kit. I will pay willingly the freight to have white bread and cake occasionally. The Episcopal ladies had a strawberry supper & dinner last week. I made a white cake which was very nice and, had the flour only been whiter, it would have been beautiful. As it was, it was the nicest cake there. [. . .] I had it iced at the confectioner's and I reckon you never saw such a nasty botch in all your life. I was so mad I told him our confectioner would not allow such a daub to go out of his house. Everyone had told me what an elegant confectioner he was. [. . .] He told Mr. D. I was wrathy [sic] afterwards. [. . .] The Manning house [which they hoped to rent] is 1 1/2 miles from here. Mr. D. will come here every day and attend to the farm. The kitchen is in the basement and the storeroom, a nice cellar, and common dining room so I shall have a nice place to keep my preserves and canned fruit. [. . .] I kept such a fuss about going down there and putting in some cabbage and celery plants and beet seed (I suppose it is too late for anything else) that Mr. D. is having some ground ploughed today for the purpose. [. . .] There is an ice house, stable, and negro house to the place. We will have to put up something for the chickens. A very nice cistern just at the door, a nice porch in front and back, and ventilation door as Cousin Charles [Garrard] has. Indeed, I had no idea of finding so nice a place to live at. It is about the best place and newest of any I have seen. I will have my flower beds in the yard as there is a small circular carriage drive just in front for the purpose. There is also a small young orchard. [. . .] I do not know when we will buy the furniture. He [Henry] says he wants handsome while he is buying and it will take [. . .] so much money I dread to commence, especially as he will not have it unless the wheat crop turns out better than it now promises. I am so perfectly delighted at the idea of going to myself that I do not consider anything the least trouble. I feel like going down there and taking the hoe and working all day. [. . .]

I wrote the above several days ago, only waited to see if we would rent the house. Much to my surprise and disappointment, Mr. Butts, the boys' guardian, wants the house himself. [. . .] If Mr. Davenport had have spoken to him when he first came home, he would have had no difficulty about the thing, but he seemed to think I would & must be contented to live here. As soon as I discouraged his idea, I just let him know he need never expect me to be contented for that was impossible and he had no right to bring me here under false pretenses and [. . .] that the result would be I should spend just half of my time in Ky. for here I would not stay. I do not know what we will do now as I want to move in the Fall. [. . .] Tell Cash I have been most heartily rejoiced at the split-up of the Democrats, but fear, like themselves, they will all flock together again at Baltimore rather than give up the spoils. The Democrats here were all very low down, but are brightening as now that they believe Douglas will concentrate them all. Mr. D. said after the convention he would not support Douglas and never had been for him heartily. I told him I did not think he would verify Pa's prediction quite so soon, that for consistency he should have kept dark a little longer. He is again a supporter of Douglas. There is no doubt but what they would cast their votes for the old Devil if he were the nominee. I never heard such abuse & bitter feeling as pervades the Democrats here for the North. I am the continual defender of the Republicans. They all say & believe Lincoln should be massacred sooner than be allowed to occupy the presidential mansion. They buy as little from the North as possible and think no one should go there from the South. [. . .]

Martha C. Davenport

In July, Green finally got his chance to travel to the White Mountains. He asked Brutus, "Aunt Ann wrote something of White Mts. 'mosses.' How does she wish me to send them?"

Later he sent Ann an account of his journey. I wish Green had said more about the White Mountains, as I have often looked up the Conway Valley at Mount Washington and visited the ruins of the old Crawford House, one of the earliest big frame hotels in the area. Almost nothing remains of it now, but the graded bridal path to the summit of Mount Washington is a favorite of modern hikers. I like to imagine Green on the porch of the Crawford House, gazing up at the steep sides of the spectacular notch in which the hotel stood. He is wearing his linen duster, of course.

GREEN CLAY

Conway, N. H., July 22, 1860

Dear Aunt Ann,

After a tiresome journey by stage I arrived at this place yesterday. Have been compensated however by the splendid views & scenes of to-day. Conway Valley thro which you approach the mountains is beyond expectation, rich in picturesque scenery of the most attractive style. The surprising manner in which the winding road reveals the many beautiful lakes & ponds that lie on the one side & the other was particularly noticeable, in which they say pickerel & trout are abundant. I am tempted to remain here two or three days to fish, but, being alone & fishing a lonesome occupation, I will probably leave tomorrow morning for the Crawford House which is at the foot of Mt. Washington, some 35 miles from this place. One might linger the whole summer in Conway Valley, but would not feel comfortable until he had visited the greater attraction, Mt. W., which he is constantly beholding in the distance. This anxiety put at rest and one could not find a more agreeable summer retreat than in Conway Valley. The only thing to detract from the enjoyment of a trip of this sort is the being alone, without any pleasant company with whom to converse. You have to admire in silence which only artists have learned to do and the tedium of one weary hour is to be worn away only by the tedium of the next. [. . .]

Yrs.,

G.C.

In August, Belle gave Ann all the Richmond news. She was looking forward to a trip to the New Jersey seashore.

BELLE LYMAN

Aug. 5, 1860

Dear Ann,

[. . .] I intended to have written by Mr. Clay but was sick in bed the evening he left to go out to Mr. Embry's. I know he laughs and tells you how scrawny and poor and ugly I look. I have been talking about going to Cape May. [. . .] I wish you would go with us, if we should go. Pa laughingly asked me how it would do to go the day after the [local] election. If it were not so [. . .] dusty traveling I would look forward to a trip somewhere with much pleasure as I have been confined at home so long. [. . .] I am perfectly delighted to hear you are coming over to the Fair. Don't you let anything prevent you and bring some of your nice work to exhibit. [. . .]

No doubt Ann [Holloway] is getting along very pleasantly with you, as I hear nothing of her being homesick. Give her my love.

Patsey was up when I received your letter, said she felt thankful that you were so willing to take Junius [Holloway]. Mr. Miller is in Rockcastle, thought he was very much benefitted from his first trip. Patsey is getting ready for her trip, had two girls sewing for her. [. . .]

Amelia [Burton] is getting along very well but the baby's eye[s] still continue very sore.

[. . .] Brother [Christopher Field] is here and seems much more cheerful than he was. [. . .] Must close with my love to all.

Yours truly

Belle Lyman

Green wrote Brutus from Portland, Maine, that same month that he would soon be back in Cambridge. "I have been most of the time among the White Mountains where I found the fishing very good," he said. "The air bracing & healthy. And altogether I passed the time very pleasantly. I was at Lake Winnepesaukee several days where I met ex-Pres. [Franklin] Pierce & family, found them exceedingly pleasant. Gen. Pierce is one of the most agreeable men I ever met with [. . .] far from being the man deserving of the many hard things that have been said against him." But he was short of money. Could his father send him $150?

In a subsequent letter, Green explained to Ann, "The white beard mosses of which you spoke I saw in all their magnificence and could have easily procured any quantity of the choicest but, knowing I would have no way of sending them to you except thro the expense of express, I left them to still longer adorn their native trees until some poor fellow's ruthless hand shall snatch them in the exercise of a more exacting gallantry."

In the fall, Christopher Field returned alone to his plantation, Green resumed his law studies at Harvard, and young Cash went off to Professor B. B. Sayre's school in Frankfort. But Kit got a late start for Mississippi, Zeke decided not to continue college, and Martha returned to Auvergne, where Junius Brutus Davenport was born in October.

Meanwhile, the presidential campaign of 1860 was in full swing: torchlight parades, emotional speeches, cheering crowds. Cassius Clay was in the thick of it. He crisscrossed the Midwest tirelessly, making more than a hundred speeches for Abraham Lincoln and the Republican Party. His aim was to convert Southern Democrats to Republicanism, so he played down any connection between the party and radical abolitionism. Because of the split in the Democratic Party, the Republicans had the upper hand during the campaign; however, Senator Stephen A. Douglas still toured the South relentlessly, pleading to Southern Unionists to support him.

As the election day neared, Green wrote Aunt Ann about politics.

GREEN CLAY

Cambridge, Oct. 21, 1860

Dear Aunt Ann,

[. . .] Your question as to when I will be homeward bound I think to answer. If the Union survives the election, I can obtain my diploma in January. Will however — as my own expectation is — remain until next summer or fall. What then is yet to be consulted. [. . .]

In this district all — Bell, Douglas & Breckinridge — men are combined upon one candidate against Mr. Burlingame, the Republican nominee. Would that in other sections the same lesson might be learned. I may probably address a meeting on behalf of the Union candidate (Mr. Wm. Appleton) soon. Mr. [William Lowndes] Yancy [an Alabama secessionist] made a most telling speech in Faneuil Hall a few evenings ago, a copy of which I send to Pa hoping he will find leisure *to read it.* [. . .]

Zeke, I regret to hear, has concluded his education is completed. I shall then have to write to Mr. Sayre that he has in Cash the chief hope of the family as we shall look to Cash to uphold the double responsibility that Zeke has imposed.

Well, Junius Clay Davenport. My regards to this young man. I can only say that must certainly be his name. However, as this advice is unsolicited, tell Sis she need not consider it obligatory.

Yrs. truly,

G. Clay

On November 6, Abraham Lincoln was elected president. In the North, the Republicans celebrated lustily. In Charleston, people greeted the impending revolution with fireworks and illuminations. The palmetto flag of South Carolina flew in open defiance of the Union.

"Persons are getting very excited here over the election," young Cash wrote in an undated fragment of a letter, probably intended for his brother Green. "There has been more betting than ever before." Predictably, John Bell carried Bourbon County.

A short time before the election, Brutus's nephew Green Clay, the man who had taken Cassy and Rilla to Texas, died there. His brother,

Sidney, went out to settle his affairs. Sidney was now his father's only son still alive and heir to most of his estate. A favorite of Brutus's and Ann's, he lived at Escondida.

Sidney wrote Ann from Texas in November, "It has ever been to me one of the saddest spectacles in life to witness the sale of property of one who but a short time before had been engaged in collecting & improving that property & extending the hospitalities of that very home to those persons who even then, in a few yards of his freshly made grave, forgetful of their former friend & neighbor, [are] eagerly striving to appropriate at the lowest possible price his goods to themselves, indulging in the low jest, the boistrous laugh, & the loudly spoken oath. You may judge of my disgust when that dead person was my only Brother, & every article, exposed to the avaricious scrutiny of the vulgar herd, was associated with some recollection of him. His secretary bought for its *beauty!*, the purchaser perhaps unable to write. His favorite horse, never mounted by any but himself, rode off by a drunken overseer. The handsome *cradle*, by which he had so often stood & looked with all the pride & admiration of a young Father upon his first-born babe, knocked off with a ribald jest to a half-clad cow driver."

He added a postscript to Brutus. "I hope there will be no invasion of negro territory in consequence of Lincoln's election before I return."

From Frankfort, young Cash thanked his mother for candy made from "my homemade molasses," one of his business ventures. He added, "I am getting along first rate in my studies. [. . .] I have got about half as much studying as I can do, but I reckon after Christmas I will have as much as I can do. Mr. Todd's eating is good, etc. etc. etc. I go to see Grandma very often as she always gives me some good apples."

Now that Lincoln was elected, Cassius Clay hoped to be named a member of the new president's cabinet. His mind was full of details, including the kind of entertainments he would need to give in Washington.

"If Mary Jane goes to Washington, she would like to have the dinner set," he wrote Martha Davenport, who was in Bourbon County. "In that case, we would pay you the difference between the cost I now allow Brutus and the new set for you. But if she does not go to Washington, she would prefer you to keep it as we would have no use for it here. Please number the pieces and pack it carefully; and it will be ready for either of us." Could this have been the china Brutus bought at Cassius's bankruptcy sale in 1850?

Meanwhile, Green asked his father to help him find a place in the office of Madison C. Johnson, an eminent Kentucky lawyer, once the husband of Brutus's deceased sister, Sally Ann. "Such a situation since I have thought more of it will have great advantages and I hope it will be in yr. power to obtain it for me. Upon application, I can obtain my diploma here at the Law School this term. I had intended to remain another term, but events that are developing compel me to change my plan and continue my reading with some good lawyer in Kentucky."

On December 20, South Carolina seceded from the Union. "Still a good deal of excitement in southern country," Kit wrote his father on December 27. "Too sad to think of at present."

As the year wound to a close, Cash, fourteen, sat down to write his brother-in-law, Henry Davenport, a letter. Cash was intensely interested in politics ever since he had nailed up political broadsides for his father on a visit to Estill Springs in 1858. He had grown up listening to discussions of the very questions that now were tearing the country apart, and his letter eerily foreshadows arguments to come.

CASSIUS CLAY

Paris, Dec. 31, 1860

Dear Sir,

With many apologies for not writing sooner, I will write with the motto better late than never. I have been for two weeks enjoying the beauties of home after an absence of two months. I will start back to school in one day, but, before going I have concluded to write you a letter, not on politics exactly for I have long given up my interest for the political world, but the sacred topic of the Union, whether by our exertions it will last, a grand monument for us to hand down to our descendants, or by our neglect of duty plunge our country into the midst of civil war, the only two alternatives. South Carolina has already seceded from this Union, therefore, we should be more active in the cause of the Union. Buchanan has acted infamously. *Firstly*, he has not the nerve to send reinforcements to Fort Moultrie & other forts around Charleston. Secondly, he has ordered all the cannon at the Pittsburgh arsenal to be sent to Galveston and the mouth of the Mississippi so the Disunionists can get them (thus acting traitor). Thirdly, he has not dismissed certain Federal office holders who have come out for disunion and the rascal and coward during the last year.

Your letter to Sis said that Buchanan acted with great *bravery* in not sending reinforcements to Fort Moultrie and otherwise acted the part of a patriot. If that be your model of bravery & patriotism, [Andrew] Jackson was a coward, [Benedict] Arnold a patriot, Gen. G. Washington a traitor, & Catiline an honest man. With the President & cabinet wielding the force of the Government we will have to contend with [sic]. If your [William Lowndes] Yancey ever wins the name of great, he will win by the ruin of his country and heaped up bodies of his countrymen. Truly great against this host will the Union men contend. An appeal to the God of battle who alone can give and take victory is all that is left us. What has brought this on our country: the ambition of [Robert A.] Toombs [a Georgia secessionist], Yancey, & others. We, the Union men, call upon them to deliver up their ambitions on the shrine of their country's welfare. If they will do so, we will honor them with our trust and the name of patriots. If not, may the destructive elements of God concentrate around devoted heads and his curse be on their descendants for destroying the tranquility of thirty millions of souls and extinguishing the bright light of liberty in the western continent. If any one of them attain the golden crown of a king, may a Brutus's stabs send him to the judge of judges and God of Gods.

But enough of this. Pa has laid up the Constitution of the United States for you when you come. Sis & the baby are well. Kit killed 16 bear in two weeks. The rest of the family are well. I am very sorry I will not be at home when you arrive from Vir. to play chess with you.

Yours respectfully,

C. M. Clay Jr.

Martha added a domestic note to her little brother's letter: "I hope you will put on your yarn socks before coming to Ky."

It was going to be a cold winter.

SEVEN

The Momentous Crisis Is upon Us

On New Year's Day 1861, Christopher Field sat down to write his friend Brutus about the state of the country. Delirious enthusiasm spread throughout Mississippi as the state prepared to follow South Carolina by seceding. There was also great excitement in Kentucky, where Governor Beriah Magoffin, who was sympathetic toward the South, had called for a conference of border states.

CHRISTOPHER FIELD

Bolivar, Miss., January 1, 1861

Col. B. J. Clay

Dear Sir,

I have been thinking for several weeks I would write you hoping to elicit an answer from you. You are not much of a talker but a good thinker. What do you think is to be the result of the momentous crisis that is now upon us? There is no getting around it, we have got to act and meet the consequences. I am as good a Union man as any one but it is now too late to shriek for the Union. The Southern Country is wild with excitement, we talk about nothing but secession, disunion, revolution and now confederacy, and to stop this boistrous current down here is impossible. To save the union we have to go with the current to some extent, and the few conservative men here are advocating a convention of all the slave states, [. . .] for that convention to set forth our wrongs and grievances, then make reasonable demands demanding our rights under the constitution, repeating all personal liberty bills, enforcement of the Fugitive Slave Law, our rights guaranteed to us in the Territories, and present these to the North as an ultimatum: Now will you grant all these, if so we remain in the Union, if not we all leave you together. Then we may be respected and might stand some chance to support a government, but I would hope by this course we would get our rights in the Union, for I would hope there is yet conservative feeling in the North to grant us our just rights. I have no sympathy with South Carolina. She has been disloyal ever since the days of nullification and has been waiting for just such an opportunity as has now presented itself, and she has a willing tool in that old Granny Buchanan. He has opened the door wide for her to walk out. [. . .] I ask you what is to become of the border states when the cotton states all go out of the Union which they will do in 60 days from this time. That is a determined and settled fact. If you remain in the Union, you must give up your slaves. You will be forced into this. You could not live even as poorly as you now do in the Union. You must go to the North or come to the South. I am aware who has been agitating this whirlwind that we are now in. It is demagogue Politicians. [. . .] They have got but little to lose and all to gain by this revolution, but as I have said in the onset the momentous crisis is upon us and look which way we will it is staring us in the face, and we must meet it but what is the best way? If we had a Clay or a Webster in Congress [we] would have some hope. [Representative] John J. Crittenden [of Kentucky] is a pure statesman but his advice has never been listened to as it should have been. I hear Magoffin has called your Legislature together and I think it is right, hoping that some such proposition as I propose may come from Kentucky. I see no other chance to save this Union under which we have prospered so long. I hate to give it up as bad as you do, but something has to be done to save it. [. . .] it will not do to fold our arms and look on. [. . .] You have got something to lose and it behooves you to come forward and throw yourself into the breech and lend a helping hand to calm agitated waters. Our [secession] convention meets on Monday next and I have not a doubt that we will be carried out of the Union in double quick time. We send a conservative man from our county who is not for haste and is for cooperation of all the Slave States, but he is in a hopeless minority and will be powerless. You all in Ky. have but a faint idea of the intense excitement in all the Southern States and they will all go out I am sure before the 4th March. Christopher [Clay] is well. I have sent him up to Memphis with a runaway negro from David's place to try to exchange him for another. Thought such a trip would be of service to him. [. . .] Our crops are not good this year. I made 500 bales. Christopher 100. We have sold but a small portion of each crop. Money was never scarcer in N.O. [New Orleans]. Many suspensions. Cotton has been very dull for two months but it is thought it will revive. [. . .] I have declined selling David's place for a while. In fact it would not now bring 1/2 what it would have brought 12 months ago. [. . .] I hope you will at your leisure write me.

Yours truly,

C. I. Field

He was right about cotton being dull. After a discussion of articles Christopher had ordered from him, including oysters for Belle Lyman. ("As the weather has been too warm to warrant sending oysters from here, we have taken the liberty of sending Baltimore oysters instead. They are equally as good as ours & being put up in freezing weather they *will keep sound.*") New Orleans merchant George P. Black wrote, "We are still of the opinion that cotton will go considerably higher in the spring but we fear that between this & then, there will be a good deal of trouble & we may shortly have another period in which it may be impossible to sell cotton at any price on account of the difficulty that may exist of negotiating exchange after Louisiana secedes which we feel confident she will do this month. We thought it best therefore to sell now when we could get a good price than hold any longer especially as we knew that the necessities of the owners would not permit the cotton being held till April or May."

No one in Mississippi had any money. When Christopher scheduled a sale of some of David's personal property, no one came. However, life in Richmond continued much as ever. There even was talk of Pattie making a trip south. No one seemed to realize what the secession of the Southern states would mean.

Pattie had been sick, Belle wrote Ann in January. "She coughs incessantly and almost as bad as Pa did and looks wretchedly. [. . .] Sunday Dr. Lyman drew a blister on her breast but as soon as it began to burn she became so impatient to have it off that it did not draw deep enough so he will draw another and I do trust it will benefit her." Belle blamed her illness on a visit to the Millers' house. "Their rooms are so cold."

Then she told Ann of Pattie's invitation. "Pattie received the most loving and affectionate letter last night from Pattie Ten Broeck [the sister of Christopher's late friend Orville Anderson], begging and teasing for her to go south with her to spend 2 or 3 weeks at Port Anderson [the Anderson plantation] and probably a few days in New Orleans. [. . .] Pa seems to regret that she is sick, says he would be very willing for her to go if she was well, that it would be a fine trip for her." Only the day before they had heard from Christopher that "he supposed the next thing we would hear that Mississippi would be trotted out of the Union with South Carolina."

She concluded with news of Sister Elizabeth. "Cousin William's spiritualist was to be here last night and it made her mad every time she thought about it." William Holloway had begun experimenting with unconventional healers.

Young Cash returned to school in Frankfort after the holidays. School was fine, he told his father, but Sally Dudley had had an accident. "Grandma fell down and hurt herself very badly Monday. I am afraid she will never walk again."

Brutus's brother Cassius still hoped for a cabinet appointment. "There is an attempt to induce Lincoln to believe that my appt. to the War Dept. would be very offensive to Ky.," he wrote Brutus. "I believe that my course in war and peace warrants the belief that I am loyal to the state and that in my large relationship here I give security for fidelity to Ky. which no Northern man can give." He asked Brutus to get several Paris citizens to write letters to the president in support of him.

Christopher Field continued to ruminate on the state of the nation. In the meantime, Mississippi had seceded.

CHRISTOPHER FIELD

Bolivar, Miss., January 27th, [1861]

Col. B. J. Clay

My Dear Sir,

I have received and read your letter with much interest and profit and I had come very much to your conclusion in regard to the cause which had precipitated us into our present difficulties, that is, I charged it to the Democratic Party. True I cannot say I have that hostility that you feel! [. . .] I myself have undergone no change. I look upon it as the most dreadful calamity that could befall a nation. It has nearly occupied my whole thoughts ever since the election. [. . .] We will have mob law, vigilante committees, and our situation in the swamp will be a very critical one. Our white population is so small and negroes so numerous, it would take very little to bring about an insurrection particularly if we should have war. One abolitionist could start the flame. I have counseled prudence and caution amongst my friends and not to be carried away by the excitement we are now in but to be men and not children and to engage in nothing like whipping or branding white men without positive evidence of guilt. When Lincoln was elected I gave way this far, I thought now was the time to stop this agitation, that the Republican Party had denied us our rights in the territories, annulled the Fugitive Slave Law, and when fully in power I thought they would go further and I thought now was the time for us to set forth our wrongs and grievances and to make reasonable and rightful demands. And when I saw the extreme South going off I wanted a convention of the slave States and could we have kept this hasty precipitancy party back, I think we would have got our rights in the Union, and could have gone on to further greatness and renown. As to a middle confederacy, I must confess I had thought but little about it in that now looking at Kentucky I could but think she must come to the South as all her feelings in trust and sympathy run with us. [. . .] It had pained me to see the course pursued by the South in Taking the Forts, Arsenals and other government property while they are in the Union. I say they had no right. But as to coercion, this I am utterly opposed to. I would have sustained Mr. Buchanan in any thing he would have said or done to have kept S. C. in the union but he in his message opened the door wide to her and the others to go out, and now he must let them alone, not one drop of blood must be spilt in such an attempt. Should it be done I fear

I might become a Secessionist which I much depreciate for I love this Union and will hold on to it as long as I can do so with honor. This Secession feeling is like a rolling Ball of Snow every turn it increases. [. . .] We had but 15 conservative men in our convention out of 100 and they at last signed the ordinance. I think that Ky. has so many of her sons in the extreme South that when your son is fighting for the same principles, the same interest that you wanted, that your sympathies would be aroused and you could not withstand the temptation to come and help us, at least you would not be willing to see the Genl. government mowing us down. I am [in] no way responsible by vote or act for our present position but I cannot stand coercion and you may whip Americans but you can never make them submissive. [. . .] I fear you will think I am a pretty good Secessionist but I do not find things as I wish. [. . .] And if you are correct in your views we are bound to have civil war and it will be a Bloody one. [. . .] May God in his wisdom and goodness arrest such a calamity but my hopes are very faint. [. . .] We are busy preparing for another crop, cleaning up and clearing. My regards to all the family.

Yours truly,

C. I. Field

The rhetoric all this activity spawned seems curious now. While talking secession, Christopher protested how much "I love this Union." One can only guess what Brutus had said to him. Brutus was then rallying support for the Union in Bourbon County with the assistance of several men who were to become his allies in the coming years, including former Congressman Garrett Davis and W. C. Lyle, editor of the *Western Citizen*.

Young Cash absorbed the words he heard all around him. Writing to urge Kit not to join the Secessionists, he regurgitated the florid prose of the moment. This letter is unsigned; it probably was never sent.

CASSIUS CLAY JR.

February 23rd, [1861]

> Never give up the ship
> While hope is life

Dear Kit,

I received your letter two days ago and hasten to answer it. I am surprised to hear you say that there is no hope for the Union because eight states have seceded. [. . .] Why sir that is an argument that the Union men should double their exertions. Why sir are you going to give up a Union which has cost thousands of lives & under the most God-like prosperity has taken one century to be built to its present greatness to the first strain that she receives because the tempest is at hand. Are [you] going to lie down and be crushed and [are] you going to cut a hole in the ship & sink us. Why sir this is the time that the orders of the captain should be obeyed, the pumps in readiness for a leak, and the men to work like tigers if you wish safely to outride the storm. [. . .] You have received many blessings from this Government and now you are for giving her up without an effort, without a stroke on her behalf. You say that [in the] South are a brave breed of people, but does that show manliness to desert your country on the least stroke she receives. Dam not without hope for she still has flocking around her standard 20 million Union hearts to defend her stars and stripes. [. . .] While old Kentucky's heart & hand is offered to the Union I will not despair. [. . .]

[unsigned]

Kentuckians struggled with their dilemma. Should they support the Union, secede, or try to find some middle ground? Both John Crittenden and Senator John C. Breckinridge addressed the Kentucky legislature on this subject in March. Crittenden was conciliatory and cautious, but Breckinridge's sympathies were openly pro-Southern. (Soon after, he left the Senate to become a Confederate general; Garrett Davis took his place.)

In Washington, Lincoln did not want a loose cannon such as Cassius Clay in his cabinet and to get him as far away as possible offered him a diplomatic post in Spain. Cassius accepted primarily because of the salary (as usual, he was broke). When the position was later given to Carl Schurz, who had headed an effort to get German-Americans to vote for Lincoln, Cassius agreed to an appointment as United States minister to Russia. He decided to take his family with him, as well as two secretaries, Brutus's son Green, and another young relative, William Cassius Goodloe, known as Willie. "Let me know at once if Green accepts," he wrote Brutus in March.

From his school in Frankfort, young Cash commented on his brother's new job to his mother.

CASSIUS CLAY JR.

Frankfort, March 24 [1861]

Dear Ma,

[. . .] You say that Green has accepted the appointment to Spain. I thought he was a disunionist. I am glad he has done so although if I was in his place I would have some scruples in accepting an office from the hands of a Black Republican whose principles aim at the destruction of the rights of our section & who in his wild ardour for freedom has dismembered this once glorious confederacy & banished Peace from our midst. But then on the other hand, the appointment affords a handsome chance to both acquire knowledge of language & to become acquainted with diplomacy. [. . .]

The Legislature has been in session here for several days. The Secessionists had a meeting here two or three days ago. It was a complete failure, there being only I suppose 100 delegates present.

Mr. Buckner of our country was present. He seemed greatly disappointed. Mr. Crittenden had a reception here a few days ago. There was a great crowd in attendance. [. . .]

Mr. Sayre has come down upon us pretty hard lately. I get seventeen lines in Virgil every day & write two thirds of a page of Latin syntax.

[. . .] Tell Pa the Union men have a majority in the Legislature.

Write soon. Your son,

C. Clay

In Virginia, Martha was so preoccupied with the acquisition of a home of her own that she scarcely noticed the turmoil around her.

When she wrote this letter to her father, she thought she had located the perfect house for him to buy for her.

MARTHA DAVENPORT

Jefferson Co., Va., Tuesday, March 27 [1861]

Dear Pa,

[. . .] The only desirable residence here for sale is Mr. Andrew Hunter's. I visited the place yesterday and found it so complete and pleasant I feel inclined to purchase it although it will be investing more in a home than I would wish. [. . .] Mr. Davenport visited Mr. Hunter today to learn his terms which are as follows: He proposes selling to you his house, yard, garden and stable lot, consisting of 4 1/2 acres for $8000. [. . .] At the same time selling Mr. Davenport 25 acres for about $140 per acre, which he agrees to buy, if you buy the house. The advantages of the place are these: a new nice brick home with 8 rooms, large dining room, with pantry attached, store room, a large kitchen, 4 nice cellars, 2 good cisterns, good brick servants rooms, ice house, stabling for 4 horses & 3 cows, chicken house, corn house, meat house, nice fencing, a good sized garden, a quantity of fine budded peaches, fine cherries, pears, plums, quinces, grapes, apricots, many shade & evergreen trees. [. . .] If you approve of the purchase, I suppose you will write immediately about the deed, etc. [. . .]

Aunt Ann spoke of your giving Mr. Davenport a Bull calf. He says if you wish to send me some cows & the calf, he will send a man out for them. Have you any Cleveland Bay colts you are willing to give away? I should like to have one. [. . .] The baby has taken up completely with his new relations as he is petted very much by them. He keeps well & still grows fatter. I hope to hear from you very soon.

Affectionately your daughter,

Martha C. Davenport

[P.S.] I made $16 on my N.Y. check.

She enclosed a letter to Aunt Ann, much of it devoted to the glories of the new house. But Martha also was having servant problems. "I am completely out with Laura," she wrote of a slave she had brought with her from Kentucky. (Laura was fifteen, scarcely more than a child.) "Had I known how no count and hard to manage she is, I would not have paid her expenses from Ky. here for her. She is filthy, pays no attention to what I say to her, throws her clothes & every thing else under her feet, slips out of my sight every time my back is turned. The negroes say she strews hers and their clothes all over the cabin floor and if they tell her about it, tells them to shut their mouths. She won't keep Junius clean two minutes after he is dressed and a hundred other things I might name she is guilty of. She does not remember 5 minutes where she put anything. I sent her Saturday to wash her linsey dress & she spotted it with soap from the body to the last. It is not fit to look at. [. . .] Junius cannot bear her, so I do not know what I will do when Sophy goes to cooking, as she is too filthy to attend to my table & let Sallie nurse who is devoted to children. [. . .] Tell Sallie [Laura's mother] I had not an idea she would raise such a mean negro & so disobedient as Laura is. I told her yesterday when I went to Ky., I meant to take her and ask her master to send her to Mississippi if she did not do better."

Kit wrote to reassure his father that he was still a loyal Union man although many Southerners regarded President Lincoln's inaugural speech, with its carefully worded vow to "hold, occupy, and possess" federal property, such as Fort Sumter in Charleston harbor, as a declaration of war.

CHRISTOPHER CLAY

Confederate [States] of America, Bolivar, Miss., March 28, 1861

Dear Pa,

[. . .] I know of little news of any importance except civil war which now threatens our common country. The traitors of our country unfortunately have the great mass of the people with them in trying to break up this government. [. . .] Our trusty pilots are beneath the cold sod. & our great ship so badly [. . .] wasted upon the rock of disunion & I fear may be lost forever. But [when] the clouds look gloomy and the storm more threatening one will stay with the *ship* until the last plank is lost in the mighty deep. The more I see of the movements of the Traitors the more firm Union man I remain. I am now for the Union let it cost blood & money. But I will give you my views in regard to the seceding states. I think the most powerful dagger Mr. Lincoln could use towards the South would be let them alone. They are going to the dogs fast enough & will soon break their own necks. [. . .] Our taxes are at present out of all reason & what they will be if [this continues] *God* only knows. [. . .] I hope to leave the South this summer much sooner than usual. I am tired of being sick all summer [. . .] so, soon as I see my crop safe, I will start for the Union [Kentucky]. But if in case of war I must change my ticket. [. . .]

In great haste,

Yours truly,

Christopher F. Clay

Fifteen days later, the bombardment of Fort Sumter began. Knowing that a Union relief fleet was on the way to bring reinforcements to the beleaguered fort, Jefferson Davis, who had been chosen president of the provisional Confederate government in February of 1861, and his cabinet had ordered General Pierre G. T. Beauregard to destroy the fort if its commanding officer refused to surrender. Federal Major Robert Anderson refused, and in the early morning of April 12 the Confederates opened fire. After thirty-three hours, the garrison surrendered. Lincoln promptly called for 75,000 troops to put down the insurrection in the South.

The entire country pulsed with excitement, but in western Virginia, Martha had no stomach for any of it, as she wrote Ann. Unable to buy the Hunter place as she had hoped, the Davenports had rented another house.

MARTHA DAVENPORT

April 17, 1861, Virginia

Dear Aunt Ann,

[. . .] I am very much afraid Green will not come to see us [on his way east to join Uncle Cash]. If I had any idea he would pass Harpers Ferry today, I should go down, notwithstanding the great excitement about here. The biggest set of fools I ever saw. Last night we heard Virginia had seceded and 2500 troops were sent from Richmond to take possession of Harpers Ferry and that Lincoln had sent 8000 to intercept them. You never saw such a set of fools here. Scared to death, they assembled (mostly boys) in Charles Town last night. Sent riders out to all their sympathizers, the disunionists, and kept watch all night. They sent here several times for Mr. Gibson [her brother-in-law] & Davenport. I told Mr. D. just to stay in his bed and act like he had some sense. He is expecting his company to be ordered out every hour. I tell him his is the party that has raised all the fuss, & they are the very ones to fight it out. I never listened [. . .] to such treason, such traitorism as since I have been here and long to hear a loyal man with some dispassionate sensible sentiments. If I had have come here a secessionist, I should from complete disgust have been made a Unionist. It is the first time in my life I ever heard the advent of civil war hailed with pleasure. I and my whole family are regarded as abolitionist. I am afraid yet we will have a blow up before I get away from here. Tell Pa if he had been living with other people as long as I he would be impatient to get away. Tell him he must use the money [he had intended to give her]. I want none of my property in Jeff Davis' dominion among such a set of insane people. They may take a notion to burn my house down. [. . .] I tell Mr. D. as Pa told me, there is no knowing what his political sentiments are to bring me to yet. I have at last got him in the notion of making improvements, painting, papering, & building so we can live very comfortably at this place we will go to. [. . .] Mr. Davenport will not want me to leave here [his parents' house] if he is ordered on military duty but I shall not adhere to such a thing for a moment. I am tired of living off other people. I shall either go by myself or to Ky. This horrible secession move. There is no telling what we are to look for so near Washington, as Jeff Davis' big brags to attack that city are met here with great rejoicing. I am so rejoiced to hear from Kit & Zeke. Mr. D. has been bragging on them being secessionists. *Now*, they have no patriotism and worship money more than their country. I never saw such efforts as have been made to influence the convention in Richmond. All kinds of sensation[al] dispatches were sent to influence them. Our man from here went down to the Ferry and finding some arms boxed up to be sent off (as if Lincoln had not a right to order the government property to be transferred when it was needed) came back, got up a sensation among the idlers & vagabonds and got them all to sign an appeal to the Gov. & convention to issue an order for them to be seized. They misrepresented this county, all good citizens were at home, tending their business, and these idlers alone were raving. [. . .] Tell Pa as soon as Junius is old enough I want him to take him. I want him raised and also to live in Ky. He is as smart as he can be. He has just learned to pat his hands & hold them out. He is exactly like Zeke. I have just finished him seven dresses. I embroidered the yellow up the front, made a beautiful pattern for it. [. . .] Mr. D. says I can have full sway at this new place, so you may know I will use my opportunity. My first move was to set out an ivy and rose on the end of the house. [. . .]

Yours in haste,

Martha C. Davenport

Tempers flared everywhere. Brutus's good friend Charles Garrard had a run-in with an outspoken Bourbon County secessionist, Captain Richard Hawes. As Cousin Charles wrote Brutus, "I accidentally was passing along the street on yesterday and in front of the Citizen office Capt. Hawes [was] talking to a crowd [. . .] urging [. . .] that the people should refrain from every *kind* of excitement, [urging] as [a] project of settlement [of] the difficulties now before this country 'that the people should as soon as possible vote for delegates to a convention and let it come together in the *best of spirit* and in its *calm* judgment *decide* upon *what* course Kentucky should take in our present troubles.' I listened silently to him until he was through and then said to him, 'Captain I approve of your plan and would only suggest one amendment, and that was: Whatever the convention did decide upon, let it be submitted to the people for their approval.' He replied certainly, he intended *that* as a *part* of his *plan*. He then turned around and said, 'He had heard a sentiment attributed to me that he was astonished to hear as coming from a man of my sense.' I said to him, 'What is that, Captain?' He then repeated that I should have said, 'I thought it a great blessing to Ky. that she was not armed at this time.' I told [him] that it was my candid conviction and [I] believed it to be true. He then flew off the Handle and used language and manners that I feel from a sense of *duty and self-respect* to *demand* an explanation of."

In the letters written throughout this period, it is possible to trace shifts in opinion by various members of the family. By April, Kit and his uncle had found out that it was not easy to be Delta cotton planters and good Union men at the same time, as this letter from Kit to his father indicates.

CHRISTOPHER CLAY

Bolivar Post Office, Bolivar Co., Miss. April 23, 1861

Dear Pa,

[. . .] At present, our people to the man seem desperate & all arrangements for war are fast progressing. Cannons & munitions of war duly received. We all think [. . .] Mr. Lincoln [. . .] [is] trying all means under Heavens to muster an army strong enough to crush out the South to the man. But I hope before he can possibly get ready to invade the South, which I have no hesitation in saying are his intentions at present, we may be well prepared to meet him in war both by land & sea. Pa, I now think the time has come when we in the South are in great danger. Both our lives & property. [. . .] I am a Union man yet, but Lincoln's proclamation has forced me to share my fate with the South, my present home & salvation. [. . .] I think myself at this moment the whites are in much danger of being killed by his [*sic*] own slaves during so much excitement & talk of war. I have talked to my negroes about Mr. Lincoln & war & impressed it upon their minds the war was about territory & not for freedom & they would be killed as well as myself if we should have war upon our soil. But in regard to my own negroes I would not fear them if every ax & hoe on the place was drawn. [. . .] I am taking everything cool & deliberate. If war seems like[ly] to come I cannot stop it. [. . .] If about the middle of May there is prospects for peace & Plantation affairs going on well & quiet, I expect to start for Kentucky. [. . .]

Yours very truly,

Christopher F. Clay

Cassius Clay's family and his two secretaries gathered at the Saint Nicholas Hotel in New York to await the arrival from Washington of the new minister to Russia. "After paying for my uniform," Green wrote Brutus from New York on April 26, "& some other clothing I find I have not enough money. So I telegraphed to you yesterday to send me $150 more." He added, "*The whole North is bristling with bayonets.*"

Uncle Cash finally turned up. "We leave this place tomorrow morn. (Tues.) for Boston from wh. place we will sail the next day (Wednesday)," Green wrote Ann three days later. He had been unable to stop and see Martha on his way north, he added, because "the train we went thro on was the last regular train that passed Harpers Ferry."

Green next wrote Ann from Boston. They were to sail on the *Niagara* on May 1. "Mr. [Charles Francis] Adams and family [his son Henry] go upon same vessel." Green was pleased with his new title, administrative secretary of the legation.

Henry Adams, who was serving as secretary to his father, the new minister to the Court of Saint James, later took sarcastic note of the presence of Uncle Cash and his party on the *Niagara*. He wrote in *The Education of Henry Adams*, "Secretary Seward had occasion to learn the merits of Cassius M. Clay in the diplomatic service, but Mr. Seward's education profited less than the private secretary's [Adams himself], Cassius Clay as a teacher having no equal though possible some rivals."

I can't help wondering what Green and Henry said to one another. They were about the same age. Though a graduate of Yale, Green had spent the previous year in Henry's bailiwick, Harvard. Henry probably snubbed Green the way his father did Uncle Cash.

It was my mother who urged me to read *The Education of Henry Adams*. She loved Adams's work and thought the best possible treat would have been to be conducted through Chartres Cathedral by Henry himself. While I shared her admiration for Chartres, I never could work up much enthusiasm for *The Education of Henry Adams*. Now I wonder if this was due to his supercilious remarks about Uncle Cash, remarks I spotted as soon as I thumbed through the book. Adams was right, of course. Uncle Cash did behave badly in England, where he stopped en route to Saint Petersburg, attacking the British government for its pro-Southern sentiments without checking with Ambassador Adams first. The diplomatic service was not his milieu, though he seems to have gotten along fairly well in feudal Russia, which resembled antebellum Kentucky in some ways.

In the new Confederate States of America, life was growing increasingly difficult. A Saint Louis merchant advised Christopher Field that he could no longer draw on his account with them. "We are very sorry to inform you," wrote George W. Banker, "that in consequence of a perfect stagnation in business (caused as you are aware by this terrible civil war which threatens to engulf all in one common doom) we shall be unable to meet the two small drafts which we sent you last month promptly."

Kit wrote Ann that he had joined the local militia.

CHRISTOPHER CLAY

C.S.A.

Bolivar Post Office, Bolivar Co., Miss., May 5, 1861

Dear Aunt Ann,

[. . .] I know of but little news of any importance except civil war which will soon be on our border & it may be at our homes. Times are indeed dark & gloomy. What will become of us God only knows. Every man in the South old & young must shoulder his gun & march to the field of battle. Mr. Lincoln's course has thrown all Union men in the South bitterly against him. He has acted a scamp & scoundrel from beginning to end. [. . .] He possesses but little what I call in a man noble, brave or honorable, he and his party are beneath the notice of all gentlemen.

The only voice, the only hope & only expectation & determination with one & all in this country is to stand & die in defense of the Confederate flag. Col. Field, Mr. Estill, & all those dear lovers of our once glorious Union are strong [. . .] for secession. Col. Field is now the greatest secessionist now in the South. I was the last of the family in these parts to give up but very recently I have taken sides with the South, formed a company, & [am] ready for war when ever it comes. I am determined to defend my county, my interest, & my home, let come what will. Mr. Lincoln & his scoundrels say in emphatic words we are going to wipe out the South & free the blacks. Can we or will we stand any such infamous course. No, no, we will all die on the field of battle. [. . .]

Yours devotedly,

Christopher F. Clay

In Kentucky, Junius Holloway, Elizabeth's oldest son, joined the Union cavalry as a second lieutenant. "Pa says if I can find a horse to suit me, he will pay for him," June wrote his Uncle Brutus in May. He wanted Brutus's Cleveland Bay stud, Young Lord, but, like many of Brutus's nephews, June presumed too much. Brutus didn't sell him Young Lord.

In mid-May, Kit wrote that he would be home in a few weeks. "Our climate is beginning to get unhealthy," he told his father. "I think it is time for all who leave for north should be off."

Although surrounded by secessionists in Virginia, Martha remained a Union supporter of sorts. Actually, Martha was remarkably indifferent to both sides; she wanted to be left alone to "improve" her new residence with trees and flowers. Anything that got in her way annoyed her.

MARTHA DAVENPORT

Charlestown [*sic*], Va., May [1861]

Dear Aunt Ann,

I [. . .] was sorry to hear you were sick, but suppose it is one of your usual spells and it is now over. [About this time, Ann began to have regular attacks of a chronic illness, some kind of "female complaint."] I hope Belle [Lyman] may have luck with her baby [her son David]. It would be a great pity after all her suffering to lose it. And I know she is just now beginning to feel an interest & love it. I find Junius occupies more of my thoughts and attentions every day as he becomes more sprightly & interesting. Indeed now that Mr. Davenport is away [he had been mobilized into what became Stonewall Jackson's Brigade] I could not live without him. He is the only pleasure I have. For I am so heartily tired and disgusted here, I stay to myself as much as possible. Nothing but secession is talked of & nothing but abuse of all & everybody who does not agree & join with them. I wrote to Mr. Davenport yesterday he must come & make some arrangement for me. I must either go to Ky, go to this place we are fixing, or else board in town. He is violently opposed to my living alone, but [if] I have to sleep on a straw tick on the floor & eat bread & water, then I shall go. [. . .] Blanton Duncan's regiment [a Confederate regiment from Kentucky] are now at Harpers Ferry, consisting of 600 men. He says 1000 more are coming and that 50,000 Kentuckians are ready to fly to Southern aid. They are terribly disappointed here at the position of Ky. & Mo., they thought when Va. led, they would all follow. [. . .] Mr. Davenport believes they will have a fight at the Ferry before many days. There will be 10,000 troops there the last of the week. You can't make them believe but what Lincoln is thirsting for the blood of every Southern[er]. They only judge him by themselves. [. . .] Such people as these you cannot argue with, they ought to be just knocked in the head & be done with it. [. . .] Tell Zeke if he wants to go to the wars, just come here. He will get plenty of it, enough to disgust him. If I just could get to myself, I do not think I would want to look out of the door or hear North or South mentioned.

In that pudding recipe of Aunt Mag., she says nothing about butter. Is it right?

Yours affectionately,

M.C.D.

Some Kentuckians, such as Representative Crittenden, continued to try to find a way for the state to remain truly neutral. But, while the legislature debated resolutions, the governor, expounding on something he called "armed neutrality," placed Southern sympathizers in charge of the state militia. At the same time Union men began to organize a "home guard." A federal naval officer, Lieutenant William Nelson, procured five thousand muskets and bayonets in Washington for distribution in Kentucky. Three hundred of them reportedly were passed out in Bourbon County. One, an 1816 Springfield musket, wound up in Brutus's possession.

When Brutus learned that Kit had joined the home guard in Mississippi, he was furious. Christopher urged him not to be too harsh on Kit.

CHRISTOPHER FIELD

Bolivar, Miss., May 24, '61

Col. B. J. Clay

Dear Sir,

Christopher was here waiting for a boat for Ky. and received your letter [. . .] he seems hurt at the tone of its contents. I told him he had used epithets that were harsh and grating to your feelings that he should not have done, you know how young men frequently run on. [. . .] Until the coercion policy was pursued by Mr. Lincoln, he was very strong for the Union. When Lincoln changed, as we of the South considered, he saw no other course to pursue. His all was here in the South. Mr. [Salmon P.] Chase said this was a war between liberty and freedom & slavery. The northern papers said go down and cut their levees and drown them out like rats. Now if you had your home and your all here and had noticed the encroachments on the South from the North by these conspiratorial acts, your feeling[s] & your interest would have been powerfully acted on. As to C. volunteering, it was for a home guard to keep down mob law, vigilance committees, and to keep internal difficulties away from us at home. Every citizen in our county joins it for that purpose. I was looking ahead a little & wanting to prevent mob law, etc. and consulted with several of our citizens who all had the same object in mind that I had, to protect our home & property at home, and we came to this conclusion, that a home guard would [. . .] have the desired effect. I think the position of Ky. is a noble one, that of neutrality, but it [. . .] seemed to me in this matter all the states must be for or against. [. . .] If Lincoln's army comes among us, I fear the worst consequences as it regards our property. If I try to stay here, it is hoping my presence will have some influence at home. I hope you will be conciliatory in your course with C. as he seems hurt.

Yours truly,

C. I. Field

Finally the war hit home. Forced to flee before advancing Union troops, Martha wrote Ann that she had reluctantly become a secessionist.

MARTHA DAVENPORT

Charlestown [sic], Va., June 8th [1861]

Dear Aunt Ann,

I have been for the last six weeks like a "drowning man catching at straws," hunting some avenue of approach for a letter to Ky., and have only within the past few days gathered even a hope of letting you hear from me and hearing in return. I met in Winchester young Arnold who lets me [. . .] enclose my letter to the Louisville Courier, Nashville, Tenn. They will tear off the envelope & send it on. I pay five cts. on the first envelope & 3 on the second, so you must remember this when you write. Just on the eve of writing, I see the Nashville road has been seized, so I know not if you will now ever receive this. [. . .] So many things have transpired here I do not know where to begin. After the

Confederate Army deserted Harpers Ferry, we fell in a very unprotected condition, at one time concluded to leave the farm, take all the negroes, horses & silver and go down the [Shenandoah] valley. At last, Mr. Davenport urged us to take the house servants alone & go somewhere as we were in daily expectation of the Ferry being occupied by the Federal Army and as has been done elsewhere the houses would be searched, the silver all stolen, and furniture & other things destroyed. [. . .] I was opposed to leaving and taking the servants but had to go with the rest. I packed up, intending to stop in Winchester and remain so long as Mr. Davenport was encamped in the suburbs of that place where I could see him every day. Just as we started (Sophy, Junius, and myself in the Buggy, Father on horseback, and the rest in the carriage, except the negroes and baggage which was in a 4 horse wagon) we learned the Army had all left to meet the enemy near Martinsburg. There being no other alternative, I went on with the others to Orkney Springs about 70 miles from here. [. . .] After spending ten days there and hearing from Mr. D. that the enemy had left Va. and crossed the river [. . .], I concluded it very foolish to be away from home on expenses among entire strangers where I could not hear a line from my friends in Ky. [. . .] So I packed up and came back alone, intending if I had to leave home again and Mr. D. was willing to have started for Ky. before this. When I got to Winchester, I there learned the enemy were in large force at Martinsburg only 18 miles from us on the Baltimore railroad (we can hear the cannon from there [. . .]). A grand battle was hourly expected, the most intense excitement prevailed in the community and everything I could hear was against us. The heights of Maryland opposite the Ferry is [sic] occupied also by a large force. [. . .] A most bountiful crop of wheat is now cut in the country, but no one feels he is to secure it for if Charlestown [sic] & the Ferry are occupied by the Federal forces it will be all destroyed. There is nothing now to prevent this occupation as our army have retreated on yesterday to Winchester. [. . .] Where they were last encamped no enemy could come into Jefferson without great risk, so we are now unprotected & would not be surprised at any hour to hear Charlestown is occupied. In that event all secessionists will fly. Mr. D. wrote to me yesterday urging me to leave again but I do not feel inclined until a more urgent necessity compels me. You cannot imagine in what a dreadful condition we are, feeling that at any moment we must leave our homes, not knowing when we can return, or that we will find anything but ruins when we do return. Mr. Gibson has just come in & says the enemy are at Shepherdstown, only 8 miles from here. I am having my clothes washed today to be in readiness to leave. My silver is all at Orkney, except my waiter, should I leave again I will take it also.

In the last skirmish, two companies of Mr. D.'s regiment were engaged and his company was waiting in reserve should the enemy advance. [. . .] I shall not think of leaving Va. in the event Mr. Davenport will be wounded so I will be near. I see the Union party again triumphed in Ky. Tell Pa all along I have been a sustainer of the administration, advocated Lincoln's policy, and really felt no sympathy with the seceders, depreciated everything they had done, abused them, and incurred the reproach & suspicion of every one with whom I have conversed. But now, since reading Lincoln's message, and seeing the avowed object to subjugate, a thing which will never be accomplished, I am no longer his supporter, & I think Ky. can alone do one thing now, go with the South. [. . .] I shall never regard secession right, never feel less bitter toward this vile Democratic party upon whose shoulders rests all this trouble [. . .], at the same time can no longer approve Lincoln's course. If Buchanan had whipped in South Carolina, I should have approved and acknowledged the right of subjection, but not now when this sentiment has such strength, such power. You cannot conceive of the silent determination & deep desire for vengeance which pervades Va. and the South now. [. . .] I never believed up to this message of Lincoln's that he intended to try to conquer the South. I believed he was trying to secure the government property which he held and regain what had been seized. [. . .] But now he is overleaping his prerogatives. [. . .] These propositions in Congress to confiscate property has [sic] made the secessionists very sad. Mr. D.'s father is selling off everything on the farm he can, only saving enough bacon to give the servants to keep in their houses in the event he leaves the county. He [. . .] says he is 70 years of age, and does not know but what he will have to commence toiling for his bread again. [. . .] Mr. Gibson says he believes Duncan's men [Kentuckians] are the [. . .] meanest in the whole army. I tell him I knew that when I heard they had come here. They are now perfectly ragged, the seats of their breeches are all out. I should not be surprised to hear of their disbanding. There is already great trouble about provisions. Sugar, coffee, & tea. [. . .] So much has been sold to the army there is now none in the country for private families and the merchants say they do not know if they can get any more, everything they have for sale is very high. [. . .] Mr. Davenport was to see me yesterday for 2 hours. He is so thin & sunburnt you would not know him. [. . .] Mr. D.'s whole company lost their tents in one of the 1st fights. They are now without shelter. [. . .] Junius is well, has cut two teeth without my knowing it. He eats green apples & everything he can lay his hands on. He is very pretty & very smart. He would be a great amusement for the boys [her brothers] if he were at home. He is so self-willed and scolds so much if you don't please him. I do hope you are well again and felt so anxious to get to Ky. and just see you all for a few weeks but would not be willing to leave Mr. Davenport now as I suppose the war will have just begun after Congress acts. [. . .]

Yours affectionately,

Martha C. Davenport

Lincoln handled Kentucky with kid gloves, understanding all too well his home state's pride in its traditional role of mediator between North and South. Representative Crittenden tried to put together a compromise after the pattern cut by Henry Clay three times before. Governor Magoffin called a border state conference in Frankfort in June, but as only Kentucky and Missouri sent delegates, its activities proved futile.

Many Kentucky Unionists wanted to remain neutral, and Lincoln did the best he could to respect their wish. In April, he told Garrett Davis that while he had the right to march U.S. troops across any state in the Union, he did not then intend to do so in Kentucky. In accordance with this policy, he allowed an immense amount of trade with the Confederacy to continue until after a strong Unionist victory at the polls on August 5. The voters elected a legislature with a Union majority of 76 to 24 in the house and 27 to 11 in the senate. Among the newly elected Unionists was Brutus Clay, who had narrowly defeated his Democratic opponent to represent Bourbon County in the house.

Martha continued to send letters to Kentucky whenever an opportunity offered itself. A surprising number made it.

MARTHA DAVENPORT

Va., June 9th, 1861

Dear Aunt Ann,

Not reading the papers I did not know of Mr. Lincoln's proclamation to discontinue all mails into seceded states until too late to write you before the 1st of June. Since then I have made many inquiries to find out some route to Ky. [. . .] My only way is to send this to Mr. Davenport, hoping he may find some one either going to Baltimore or Frederick, Maryland. Then I cannot hear from home for I know no one to write you to direct to in Maryland and I suppose it is some risk to the person who forwards the letters. I tell Mr. D. so far the evils of secession are far greater than those of Union, and they are but commenced, hence I can't see what they are fighting for. He has just left after a furlough of two days. The first in a month. Two weeks since his regiment were ordered about 55 miles from here towards Grafton. We then felt very uneasy but suddenly one night we heard of their sudden immediate departure from their camp to the Ferry again. He sent me word to come down the next day as he feared they would be ordered to Alexandria, so I went and took June for the first time. The place is nothing now but a military encampment, every house & vacant ground is covered with soldiers & tents; in the evening I saw all the troops in dress parade, a very beautiful sight. There are two Mississippi, Tennessee, Kentucky & several Virginia regiments. Some 7 or 8000 men in all. The trains are now bringing great additions as they arrive in Richmond from the South. Mr. D. heard a rumor last night his regiment has been ordered off. He thinks if true it is towards Manassas Gap. They think here there will be a great battle at that point unless a compromise is made, as it would be a death blow to the Southern cause to have their troops driven from the point. It would cut off all supplies or troops to Harpers Ferry, Grafton, or Western Va. Mr. D. made me feel very sad the day I spent at the Ferry. He said it was believed there, which he did not doubt, that Harpers Ferry would be deserted and the troops retreat up the valley. [. . .] He told me to draw my money, get all my jewelry, silver, etc. together and be ready at a moment's notice to leave if we heard of the desertion of Harpers Ferry, that it would be safe for no one to remain in the county, especially females. And his Father must also get his negroes all ready to take with him. In the town every preparation was made to remove the bank deposits and burn the poll books. You can well imagine the excitement & fear that was created in our community. Andrew Hunter took down his secessionist flag. I told Mr. D. I would never be so great a coward as that; if I had a flag up, no enemy would make me take it down. He said he was afraid they would burn his fine house. I guess he was sorry enough he had not sold to us and we were rejoicing over it. I would not have Mr. D. in debt and own valuable property here for anything. He also told me to stop all improvements for it would be just as it was in Maryland, private property burned, houses robbed under pretense of searching for arms, and females violated constantly. [. . .] I never saw anything like the ladies & people here. They do nothing but sew, cook, wash and follow up the soldiers. The carriages are going by the hundreds to the encampments every day. The best men of the county are in the ranks and more volunteering every day. Some ladies have three & four sons in the army. I tell Mr. D. the Va.'s are making fools of themselves, that in no other state are the first young men in the ranks as privates, that these troops from the South are mostly idlers & lower classes of the country, especially those from Kentucky. I do not offer my services for anything. I tell them that I have no heart nor hopes in the secession cause and think when I perform my duty to my husband, supply his wants, and add to his comfort and my child and servants my last is done and nothing more is required of me. I have been making flannel and calico shirts and drawers for Mr. Davenport. [. . .]

[. . .] You must not feel uneasy about me for so long as Harpers Ferry is held by Va. there is no molestation to persons here. Should the troops be repulsed there, we will immediately leave for the lower or interior part of the state. I hear today all persons are forbidden to visit the troops [. . .] it is supposed to guard against spies. Every man here who voted the Union ticket is under suspicion and closely watched. I tell them it is already a military despotism when men are constantly insulted for their opinions. Some arrests have been made of the most respectable men in the county for merely expressing disapprobation of the secession cause. [. . .]

It is very distressing to the people that Ky. is not with them. They tell me she will be scorned upon by the South. I tell them she will have just as much to do with the South as she has a desire to and that the Southern Confederacy does not constitute the world by any means.

My garden is looking very well. The season is so favorable, every thing grows rapidly. I went to Winchester last week and bought me beautiful flowers, about 25 large fine roses [. . .], a good many geraniums

[. . .], verbenas [. . .], a large pretty oleander [. . .] and several other things. I have made me fine pretty flower beds and have them all filled. [. . .] I have had a poultry yard made and summer house over the well and a million of weeds dug up. The house is yet unfinished. It will be so nearly done except painting that I will send the negroes up this week and get my chickens home and try and raise some for late [sic] use. [. . .] Junius is the sweetest thing you ever saw, as white as a lily, deep blue eyes, and fat as he can be. I have put on his short dresses and dress him very prettily. I trimmed him a beautiful little straw hat and also my bonnet, prettier than it ever was before, with yellow. He never cries, sleeps all night, and has weaned himself. [. . .]

Yours affectionately,

Martha C. Davenport

She wrote Ann again a few days before the Battle of Manassas, in which her husband's regiment played such a flamboyant role. Martha herself was surrounded by the enemy.

MARTHA DAVENPORT

Charlestown [sic], July 18th [1861]

Dear Aunt Ann,

[. . .] The divisions of Genl. Patterson's army are now quartered around us in every direction. We had heard for 3 days they had left Martinsburg, were marching towards Winchester, but [. . .] no one believed it until we saw them coming upon us, instead of marching upon [General Joseph E.] Johnston. It is a maneuver of [General Winfield] Scott's, I suppose, which I fear will be injurious to the Southern cause. We suppose this column will march simultaneously with one from Washington towards Manassas Junction & will cause Beauregard to retreat from his position and thus give up the important military position in the state. Perhaps the most so. However, before you receive this, the papers will report what the plan of this movement is. [. . .] We have no idea how long they will be quartered here although the discipline is very rigid, the penalty being death to injure private property, yet they are running all over your yard, garden, taking your vegetables, and every few minutes begging for something to eat. I had gone up to Sunnyside [as she called the house they had rented] yesterday morning to make the negroes clean up when the army came just along by the yard, I guess 500 at least came in to get water & something to eat. They did no harm nor offered any insult, except to ruin one of my flower beds by walking over it & pulling up the flowers by the roots. The first one who touched one was a negro. I was so indignant as to step out & tell him he could not pull any more on my premises. A good many took my onions, some asked for them. They are generally a fine body of men & well clothed. I saw their great man [Major General George] Cadwalader. He rode by to the well on a splendid horse & trappings. I think now I had a great deal of courage to stay there all day with no one but my negroes & encounter all these soldiers & all enemies. They would have ruined the place if I had not have been there. I talked with many of them. I find they are very sanguine of whipping the South. Some were tired and anxious for their three months [enlistment] to expire. I have no idea how many troops there is [sic] but they were passing from 10 o'clock until the same hour at night in one close mass. I never conceived of so grand a sight. The negroes have nearly gone crazy with excitement. I do not know what effect it will have on them. I hear about Martinsburg they were very unruly. Mrs. Faulkner's all refused to go with her away, and her carriage man left her going towards home with carriage & horses without a driver and returned to the enemy. We feel anxious about our troops. I fear they will move from Winchester towards Beauregard & Richmond & we may not see them for six months, even longer. Wherever they go, if it be practicable, I shall follow Mr. Davenport. While he was at Winchester, I would see him often & heard from him every day, so felt very well satisfied by his being in the army altho at first I was violently opposed to it. Last night a gent. from Penn. and Capt. Ahern who married Miss Taylor of Newport, sister of Mrs. Tom Jones, came in to offer us a guard, and offered to send a letter to Ky. for me, so I will give this to them. [. . .]

My neighbors, the men, when they heard the army coming, all took to the woods and cornfields and left the women to guard the houses. But they sent men through the fields in every direction to guard against [ambush] on their march and scared the hiders up. [. . .] You see I can think or talk of nothing but the war. And I guess it is just now begun and from this [time] out, our anxiety & trouble will be upon the increase. [. . .] Write me about Kit & Zeke, Green & Cash, all the Richmond relatives, how Pa is & Mrs. Keiningham & every body. How are all the babies? I wish you could see June, he is so sprightly and playful.

Is equal to Mrs. Thomas' little girl, has his mouth spread as soon as you speak to him. He knows his Pa whenever he comes home. [. . .]

Yours affectionately,

Martha C. Davenport

Having arrived in Russia, Green wrote his father in late July. He didn't think much of Saint Petersburg, finding it oppressively warm. He did not even mention being presented to Czar Alexander II, along with Uncle Cash and Willie Goodloe, on July 14. The principal object of his uncle's mission to Russia was to win support for the Union, which Cassius did, in part by giving lavish Kentucky-style entertainments at the legation. But Green was unhappy and talked of spending the winter in Germany or Italy. Most of his letter was devoted to his own plans.

Only an undated fragment of Green's next letter home has survived. "To one abroad oh how heartrending it is to see so noble a govt. so seriously endangered! It is almost like beholding the sun of day going down for the last time, never more to bring good cheer with the dawn of morning. But enough of politics to which I have probably been led by the news we today received of the dreadful battle of Manassas Gap." He found the long summer days in Saint Petersburg "wearisome," welcomed the lengthening nights in August, and felt cut off from his family in Kentucky. "I appreciate the difference in my situation & yours. For my part, I can imagine pretty correctly how things move on at home, what you all are doing, etc. While on the contrary you all find a difficulty even in locating me."

In August Patsey wrote Ann about a family scandal. The letter, however, was never sent, and an 1863 letter was written upon the same piece of paper.

PATSEY MILLER

Hedgeland, Aug. 17 [1861]

My Dear Sister,

[. . .] Yes, how I do feel for Pa. He is so troubled over this ridiculous and outrageous affair of Patty's [Pattie Field]. As I believe he says in all his afflictions he has never had any thing to so weigh him down as this. When I look at him, I feel that it should be the aim of his family that his few days on this earth may be quiet and as free from care as possible [. . .] but oh this turbulent wicked world. I did not see your letter but [. . .] anticipated your feelings in the matter, have myself always felt a great attachment and preference for her, did not conceive that so innocent and high-minded a girl, and one of her bright prospects and her many opportunities, could or would be so led astray or stoop so low. But Ann I cannot, do not feel towards Patty as some of them do. [. . .] I lay the whole blame upon him that every day of the world that poor innocent child should be thrown in the music room entirely alone (as he gives a short lesson every day) and do we not know that many girls of many more years, of 16 or 20 make foolish engagements, fall in love with trifling characters [. . .] this poor unfortunate thing of 13 years being so led astray [. . .] [by] a vile immoral foreigner [. . .] would you believe he says he is coming some night and is determined to have her and worst of all that, after all they had all gone through [. . .], Belle has been told that she wrote another letter to him and Louisa [a slave] took it the evening that Belle went to the Big Hill [. . .] for peaches and Dr. Lyman as soon as he was told took the poor wretch and whipped him very severely [. . .] oh, what would her Poor Pa say or do. It is very well he is ignorant of it. [. . .] Last January when I came home, Elizabeth [Miller] was here with me for two weeks. She told me at the time that she was very uneasy and felt Aunt Belle ought to know of things, telling me that whilst I was gone that Patty, Paulina Breck, Mary Keen, Ann Holloway all came out to see Julia and Mary Belle [Patsey's daughters]. She gave them a Candy pulling. She said that Patty and Mary Keen would be out pulling Candy and together in very close Chat in the porch and that every other word nearly was Professor and that not long after that he overtook her on the way to Sister's (below the store out of Pa's sight) and walked up there with her. [. . .] Well, said I, Elizabeth, your Aunt Belle [. . .] must know it. So that very day Sister and Amelia [Burton] came out to stay all night. I told them with tears in my eyes begging them to go to Belle as soon as they got back. [. . .] It did not seem to strike them with the force it did me. As Sister replied, why he goes to Mr. Rodes'. But not long after Belle came here. [. . .] Elizabeth was still here, took Belle out and told her all she knew. She was perfectly furious and went to town and *Pa* had her to stop taking lessons but without Belle's knowledge she began again. [. . .] [The letter ends here.]

Pattie at thirteen was remarkably like the woman she was to become. Scandals of this sort swirled around her all her life. She was bright and precocious, but headstrong and a bit spoiled. And thanks to her mother she was also an heiress.

Kentucky's delicate balancing act was put to its greatest test with the August 5 elections. When the legislature met in September, one of the principal issues before the members was the presence in the state of armed men from both sides. As a member of the legislature, Brutus got plenty of correspondence about the "home guard" camps that had sprung up during the summer.

His brother-in-law, William Holloway, writing to urge him to support a nephew for assistant clerk of the house, added, "This infernal Secessionist Party are [sic] never satisfied. [. . .] I think it is highly probable we will have to fight them on the soil of Ky. Just now the encampment in Garrard County [Camp Dick Robinson] is a great boogaboo [sic] with them. I trust the encampment will never be abandoned."

Another issue was whether Federal troops should be allowed to gather in Kentucky. Charles S. Brent, a Paris banker, wrote Brutus, "I consider it the settled policy to retain the Fed. troops in Ky. [. . .] Now the next step should be to increase their numbers to 30 or even 40,000 as *quietly* and rapidly as possible."

By leaving home in early September, Brutus missed the annual fair. Still, his stock did well, winning firsts in classes for aged bulls, three-year-old bulls, one-year-old cows, and the sweepstakes for both sexes. Ann sent Brutus a detailed account of the fair.

ANN CLAY

Saturday morning [postmarked September 6, 1861]

My Dear Husband,

The Fair is over and after the first was very well attended and the people seemed cheerful and interested in the show. [. . .] The most of the time the most of the rings were well filled. Nothing to show against The Duke [Brutus's bull, the Duke of Bourbon] in the first ring, but about 8 in the sweepstake ring. I concluded that I would not go or take dinner the last day as Brother [Christopher Field, up from Mississippi] and the girls left that morning, but went in the evening to get my articles from the Fair. [. . .] Brother came on Tuesday, attended the Fair two days. Field Miller came on Wednesday to meet his Uncle Cyrus [Miller]. [. . .] I understood the principal topic outside was how you were going to vote about this camp [Camp Robinson]. Zeke [Clay] says the secessionists are claiming you will vote against it. I say yes, abuse & vilify you all they can and then want you to make laws to suit them, but Brother says he saw Troutman and he says you have great influence in the Legislature and that you will vote for the camp to remain. [. . .] I judge from several hints given me by your friends that if you do not vote against it that it will give great dissatisfaction. Volney Bedford said to me that the Union men here voted, many thinking they [you] were for neutrality and would vote against any troops being in the state so you are watched by both sides. I was asked at the Fair till I was tired how you would vote. I told them I did not know, but felt very certain you would do what you thought was for the good of the state. [. . .] As you are not fond of reading long letters I must close. Do write to me. Everyone I meet wants to know when I heard from you.

> Yours devotedly,
>
> Ann M. Clay

[P.S.] Mrs. Tubman [Mrs. Keiningham's sister] will go to Frankfort on Monday or Tuesday and will only be there a day. Call to see her. [. . .]

Kentucky was on the brink of war. Confederate troops under Major General Leonidas Polk had occupied Hickman and Columbus. General Ulysses S. Grant countered by moving Federal troops into Paducah. Although soldiers from both sides now occupied portions of the state, the Southerners had moved first, thus were viewed as the aggressors.

"We are here in a fretful state of excitement," Brutus wrote Ann on September 8. "We have reliable information of our state being invaded by the Southern confederate army taking possession of many points in the south[ern] part of the state. *War seems inevitable.* We shall take strong measures in the Legislature on tomorrow. Call for troops, etc. & General [Robert] Anderson [of Fort Sumter fame] will take command. He is now here. I had hoped we would have been able to keep out of this war but all hope is now gone. We must prepare for the worst. Say to Ezekiel for me to stay at home every night & not leave you alone."

On September 9, General Polk offered to withdraw the Confederate troops if Grant would withdraw his army. The legislature adopted a resolution calling for the expulsion of Southern troops. There was no mention of Federal troops, since from the Union point of view they had a perfect right to be there. Governor Magoffin vetoed the resolution, but the legislature overrode his veto on September 18. The resolution did not please all of Brutus's constituents, as Ann warned him.

ANN CLAY

Bourbon, Friday, Sept. 1861 [postmarked Sept. 13]

My Dear Husband,

I received your letter on Monday last and was delighted to hear from you but have felt quite sad & dispirited ever since. Before receiving it, I had felt that fighting in Ky. was all *talk only* of secessionists. We are getting along as well as usual. Henry still quite busy sowing the wheat. [. . .] We have not heard a word from Cit [sic] & Cash [who had gone hunting] but I think they will certainly be at home in a few days. So Zeke and me are entirely alone. Have had no company and he has remained very close at home except one evening this week, went to town and there heard a great deal of news. Says I must tell you that all of your friends are leaving you. That they cannot see why our friends from the South are driven out and not an enemy, the Lincoln men. He is so strong a secessionist I will not let him talk to me. He says he will go heart & hand to drive out both sides and that is the way the Bedfords, young & old, a good many of the Clays, John Hickman [a neighbor], and a host of others talk. He says if the vote of Bourbon was taken today the Southern rights men would get 500 majority, that there has been a great many changes and that they all say that they will not stand it to see one side ordered out and the others invited in. [. . .]

You must write me what is to be done about the negroes' shoes. I expect the sooner they are bought the better and I was thinking it would be advisable to send Mingo to Lexington to get them. Everything much higher here. [. . .] if you will want any more salt before next spring would it be advisable to buy that now for fear of the [rail]road being torn up which will I expect be the case if troops are sent here from Ohio & other free states. No letters from Martha yet. [. . .] Do you think there will be any prospect of Cit getting his negro clothes south?

Yours devotedly,

Ann M. Clay

Kit and his uncle planned to return to their Mississippi plantations, war or no war. Brutus advised them to set out as soon as possible.

BRUTUS CLAY

Frankfort, Saturday, Sept. 14th, 1861

Dear Ann,

I have just received your letter of yesterday. I think it would be wise maybe to buy the shoes as soon as the merchants bring on the new supply. Also let Ezekiel see how many barrels of salt we have in hand and buy enough to make up 25 or 30 lbs. including what we have for fear the road may be broken up. Let him go do it at once. Things here not changed much from what it was when I wrote last. We are bound to have trouble & that soon. Your brother Christopher & Mr. Miller passed here yesterday from Louisville for Richmond. Mr. Miller had gone down to see this new doctor at Louisville who has been writing so much of late in the Journal. He seemed to be in good spirits considering [Patsey's husband had been ailing for some time]. [. . .] Your Brother is anxious to start South & wants Christopher to go along. I advised him to go & think Christopher had better go. He can carry his negro clothing. I have written [. . .] for a permit [from the home guard], but have received no answer yet. [. . .] If you have any news that the boys will not return soon & intend to stay any great length of time, they must be sent for. Ezekiel probably knows something about it.

[. . .] As to my votes in the Legislature, I shall vote as I deem necessary for the welfare, honor, & integrity of my state and the pledges I made to my county before I was elected. If some of my friends have changed since I was elected, I have not, and shall pursue the course my judgment shall dictate. To drive out both parties when we were but invaded by Tennessee is nonsense. [. . .] How can Kentucky drive out both parties without a man to do it? It is the duty of the federal government to do it. They are our friends & not enemies. The mail is about to leave & I must go.

B. J. Clay

BRUTUS CLAY

Frankfort, Ky., Sept. 15th, '61

Dear Ann,

I wrote yesterday to you but since then I have received a letter from Collector Cotton & he informs me [. . .] that Christopher cannot carry his negro clothes south, that he cannot give a permit. [. . .] Tell Christopher I suppose he will not be allowed to take anything but his own clothing & I suppose not even the gun which he brought up to have mended unless they take [a route] through the country and get into Tennessee by some other road. I reckon he had better go and see C. I. Field and make these arrangements. What money he wants to take with him let him write & I will send him a check on the bank for it. The town is all quiet here. No news.

Brutus J. Clay

Ann wrote Brutus that Kit and Cash had returned from their hunting trip.

ANN CLAY

At Home, Thursday night [postmarked Sept. 19]

My Dear Husband,

I have been to town today and the news that I heard there of the troops at Muldrow's Hill [where Confederates had burned a railroad bridge] made me feel sad indeed as it is probable there has been some fighting in Ky. and we know not when & where it will end. I hear that some of the secessionists in this county have already gone with their families and negroes to the south for protection. [. . .] When I came home this evening I was so relieved to find Cit and Cash had come home [from their hunt] quite well, had enjoyed the trip much, killed 3 deer, and caught a few fish. Cit said he could not persuade Cash to come any sooner. Cash said he did not see a Secesh while he was gone [. . .] . He says he wishes there was [sic] 10 times as many Union troops at these camps. I only received your letters last night as I did not send to the office on Monday and I read them to Cit. He seemed so surprised to hear of the difficulty of his getting home that he has gone to bed without saying a word. [. . .] The good Union men here are very warm & do not think you have hardly been severe enough in the Legislature. But those that were on the levee before the election have gone over and are very abusive. [. . .] I know that Sam Clay [a neighbor] is seething about these Union camps. And quoting Frank Kennedy on all occasions. I have not seen Mr. or Mrs. Bedford and do not want to see them as I know how they will talk. I wish Frank Kennedy had stayed in St. Louis. His speech here did a great deal of harm, telling of *extreme* cases of cruelty in Missouri to work upon the feelings of the people. Zeke heard him speak and came home like some one crazy. And frequently quotes him. We only have 8 barrels of salt so Zeke will go today to get some. Zeke says he can hear of no hogs to buy. He has been inquiring in every direction. [. . .] I saw Sidney [Clay] in town yesterday, said if he was detained in Lexington tonight he would go to Frankfort to see you. I promised Mrs. Tubman that when she called for Mrs. K. the last of next week to go to Frankfort if you were still in Frankfort and likely to be there longer that I would go down with them to see you for a few days. But now as things are I do not wish to leave home though I would like much to see you. I feel that you and me both would be better satisfied for me to be at home. [. . .]

Yrs. in haste,

Ann M. Clay

Armed bands roamed the countryside, and everyone was suspicious of everyone else. A Clintonville resident wrote to warn Brutus of a secessionist uprising. "For my own part I of course am not in their secrets but it is nevertheless believed that they intend to make a demonstration of some sort. Amongst other things it is believed that they intend to try and take possession of the arsenal at Frankfort. [. . .] I will further say that your life [. . .] is threatened."

While secessionists plotted insurrections, pro-Union Kentuckians wondered why the Federal government didn't step in and protect them. "Don't you all think it's high time to make a call for Union troops in old Ky.," Thomas T. Vimont, a Millersburg grocer, wrote a member of the legislature, John W. Campbell. "Tell our representative, Mr. Clay, his friends here are *firm* and have every confidence in his action and wisdom."

In the midst of this confusion, Kit went to Richmond to see his un-

cle, then returned home to pack for his trip south. He wrote his father
that, since there was no time to get a check from him, he had borrowed
$105 from Ann. "I find a good deal of excitement in Paris today," he
added. "Andy Johnson of Tenn. [the future president] speaks this
evening in the Courthouse yard. A large crowd to hear him."

In Virginia, Martha was desperate to hear from Kentucky. She had
become a full-fledged secessionist, as this letter to Ann indicates. She
was also pregnant again.

MARTHA DAVENPORT

Charlestown [sic], Va., Sept. 21st, 1861

Dear Aunt Ann,

I was very glad to hear from you again a few days ago. [. . .] I began
to think I would not hear again from home. [. . .] Lincoln's despotism
has interfered very materially with our pleasure in this way and he truly
seems about to accomplish his threat on this portion of Va. to starve us
out. I went to Winchester last week to buy the negroes clothes and get
Junius a crib. The cotton for the negroes' chemises I had to pay 25 cts.
for [. . .], spool cotton is 62 cts., white sugar 35 per pd., brown 25, coffee 45, salt $4 per barrel, indigo $3.75 per pound. [. . .] Shoes very high,
all woolen goods just double the old prices. We have all begun to economize in the shortest manner and find there are many things we can get
along very well without. Every one uses rye for coffee and what preserving is done is with molasses. Honey is used in place of sugar. [. . .] I
suppose [Jefferson] Davis [. . .] [considers] men more necessary now
than eatables and luxuries and we are willing to put up with it in order
to keep Lincoln's raiders from destroying our homes & our liberties.
Tell Pa he does not understand my position. It is merely a defensive
one. If I endorse Lincoln's administration I am encouraging & leaguing
with those who are trying to destroy [. . .] my property, taking my liberty from me, trying to hang my husband, & degrade my children by
convicting the Father of treason. I should be insane to endorse such enemies as these and be a traitor myself. I am for Virginia & the South
now, ever since the hour I read Lincoln's message and found he intended to whip the South into his support. [. . .]

I hear from Mr. Davenport every few days. He has been stationed at
Centreville ever since the battle [at Manassas]. He has moved in the

last few days near to Fairfax — seven miles nearer Alexandria. I do not know what it intends, but I fear a dreadful battle there soon. [. . .] Mr. D. belongs to the 2cd Reg., Va. Volunteers, [General Thomas J. "Stonewall"] Jackson's Brigade. They were in the thickest of the fight, just in front of [Colonel William T.] Sherman's battery at Manassas, were ordered to lie upon their faces for nearly two hours, concealed from the enemy but their shells were falling among them all the time. 27 were killed in this time by shells bursting over them and they not permitted to move. They were, after finding out the enemy had flanked them, ordered to charge bayonet, but there being some misunderstanding [. . .] the order was not obeyed & the regiment thrown in great confusion. Mr. Davenport having his Capt. badly wounded endeavored to rally his men but, failing to do so, he & a dozen of them jumped into a Georgia regiment nearby to & fought through the battle. [. . .] He wrote me many interesting incidents & some horrible ones of the battlefield after the fight. [. . .] I did think something of going down to see Mr. D. but the horror of going near that battlefield [. . .] prevented me. [. . .] I have not seen him since two weeks before the battle and then for a few hours only. They tell me he has volunteered for 3 years. I don't know what will become of me if the war does not cease. [. . .] Tell Cash I reckon he will have to come here & be my protector. I know he would want to go in the Army after staying a little while. There are many youths from here & elsewhere no older than he [fifteen]. [. . .] I have been housekeeping nearly a month and am perfectly delighted. I have improved my place so much it is scarcely recognized. [. . .] I do nothing but work, scarcely touch a needle, or take time to eat, and knit for Junius only at night. I am so tired when night comes I can scarcely sleep. Sophy cooks. Ellen attends the milk, chickens & the table, and Laura nurses, so I have to nurse a great deal myself to enable her to work in the garden, gather the seeds, peas, pull weeds & I sometimes wish very much I had another hand, as I have so much work to do. I have filled up so many chicken, hog, & horse wallows, and done so much sodding. I am as successful at the business as you are. I have set out so many shrubs, flowers & berries that one would scarcely believe it a new place but begun in the spring. I have quite a supply of fowls, about 60 chickens, 16 chicks, and a dozen turkeys to commence the winter with, the most of which I have bought while little for a small price and raised since the negroes came here. I have had to buy everything in the world I have (even my bacon) except a few pieces of furniture of Mrs. Gibson's. I wrote to Mr. Davenport there was a wide difference between going to housekeeping near my parents and his. I believe his Mother intends to give him a feather bed. I bought some feathers which were full of moths and have had the greatest time scalding & drying them you ever heard of. [. . .] I have made soap by those recipes we have & succeeded very well, except in changing a barrel of lye soap. It yellows my clothes but I think it was owing to its being in an old beer barrel. Junius has had a present of one tin cup since he came to Virginia and that was stolen by Lincoln's men. I have just bought him a buggy with which he is perfectly delighted. He is very smart and like a piece of lead he is so fat, has six teeth, and crawls everywhere. [. . .] I [have] no doubt you will be much surprised to hear I expect to be sick [give birth] again about the middle of Oct. I do not know what I am to do with not a white soul near me and no negro that I will allow to come near me. I will try and hire a monthly nurse and get the overseer's wife to be with me at the time. Mr. Davenport is much distressed at my not being willing to go to his Father's. I tell him that is just the reason I left there, for it is a liberty I would not take in any house but my own Father's. [. . .] I have been so busy all summer, have never realized my situation until now and the thought of having two babies is very mortifying and distressing. I had better had twins at once and then I could have perhaps had some time to rest. [. . .]

Affectionately,

Martha C. Davenport

Ann wrote Brutus that Kit and his uncle had left for Mississippi, planning to take a route through Tennessee.

ANN CLAY

Sunday night [September 1861]

My Dear Husband,

[. . .] Poor Cit, I felt so sorry for him. He went to Richmond on Friday, found Brother ready to start on horseback but he agreed to wait till this evening for him so he came back yesterday morning, said he must go to town and try and get 100$ from the bank. I told him I could let him have my premium money [from the Fair]. [. . .] He went back to Richmond early this morning and they were to go as far as Mr. Miller's this evening. [. . .] He looked quite sad. His Uncle Cit told him he must take not a paper or letter and only a clean shirt in his pocket. It looked hard that he could not even take his clothes and I do not think he was very well. Cash had been quite sick but I think it was from overloading his stomach. He vomited all one night & had some pains in his bowels & side but he is going about today and I hope will soon be quite well.

I went to town yesterday evening and was persuaded to go to hear [Andrew] Johnson speak. I found a very genteel, quiet crowd of our best people, both gentlemen and ladys, he commenced speaking in the court house yard but it soon commenced raining & they had to go into the house, and as I felt uneasy and feared a mob, I concluded not to go in but to come home & Sidney [Clay] tells me today that the secessionists made fools [of themselves] after the speaking. That John Talbott [a Bourbon County politician] and Clayton saw Garrett Davis, Johnson, & George Williams [a Bourbon County politician] walking up street with their arms linked, Talbott and Clayton walked through separating them. He says altho it was disgraceful that he is glad it happened as it will be the cause of 500 Union soldiers being sent to town. He says there are no Union men in the County that are any account. I saw Issac Wright [a local farmer], he told me when I wrote to you not to fail to give you his love. He approves your course and says he feels perfectly satisfied that you will do exactly proper. Says he regrets much these Tennesseans find us with so few camps, and so badly prepared for them. I wish I could hear of a few more of them being arrested. I think it would frighten them a little more.

I tell Zeke [and] it has quieted him and I believe he is frightened. Cit informed us there were a great many troops at Boonesborough and Foxtown. [. . .] You will be provoked and surprised to hear that Green is coming home the last of next month and he says *on leave of absence* and that Mary and Sally [Clay] are coming with him, but Sidney says they are all coming except Cassius and Will Goodloe. I sincerely hope Green will get your letter in time to stop him. He says in his letter to me that he does not know whether he will go back to Russia before Spring, but if he comes he will not go back I expect. He certainly is a great simpleton, a crazy one. [. . .]

Yrs.,

Ann M. Clay

Amelia Burton described the departure of the two Christophers in a letter to Ann. "This has been a sad, sad evening in our family. Uncle C. & Cit left us this evening amid tears & sobs. I did not see them. I felt as if it would be a long, long farewell. They were much affected. What a horrible state of affairs when in this community [people] are flying for their lives. We know not what a day may bring forth. I fear Uncle C. & Cit will have some difficulty in passing. They are such splendid looking men and riding such fine horses, they will be suspected of going to join the Southern Army."

Amelia was right to worry. Ann soon received word that Kit and his uncle had been arrested and taken to Camp Dick Robinson. She immediately sent this news on to Brutus, writing atop Kit's letter, "Try and do something for them, especially Brother, as I can't think they can tell ought against Cit."

CHRISTOPHER CLAY

Camp Robinson, Friday morning 1861

Dear Aunt Ann,

This sad morning I have concluded to drop you a short note to inform you Col. C. I. Field, Charly Breck & myself are prisoners at this camp. We were taken by the Home Guards of Rockcastle County & brought to this camp as prisoners of war. I hope this may not alarm you and we think after next Tues., which day our trial comes off, we will be permitted to go South. I find a good deal of excitement here. James B. Clay [son of Henry Clay] is here a prisoner. When I am released from here I will come to Bourbon. I think Charly & myself will get off without difficulty but the Col. I fear will not, but I hope you will not be alarmed.

Yours in great haste,

Christopher F. Clay

Ann's letter crossed with one to her from Brutus. Once the legislature passed the resolution calling for the expulsion of the Confederates, Senator John C. Breckinridge went over to the Confederacy. Many other Kentuckians followed suit, including Simon Bolivar Buckner, whom Brutus mentions.

BRUTUS CLAY

Frankfort, Sept. 24, 1861

Dear Ann,

 I received your letter on last evening. I am sorry Christopher had to leave so suddenly but I reckon it was best and I am now afraid they will be apprehended upon the road before they reach Tennessee, as the highways are watched in all directions & all suspicious persons arrested. I hear that three members of the Legislature who were starting for Louisa [. . .] were arrested near Harrodsburg and are now in confinement. This country is in a dreadful state of commotion in every direction. But the Legislature is fine & will do what they believe to be right no matter what may turn up. We are endeavoring to arm the state as fast as possible. The war is now upon us and we will either be subjugated or the state overrun with the confederate power. As we must whip & drive them back, I am for driving them out of our state and for putting forth our whole strength for this purpose. [. . .] The vile *Traitor Buckner* is at the head of the invading force who was at the head of the State Guard under the Governor. The whole of them are a vile lot of Traitors and would cut our throats if they had the power. We had [a report] here on yesterday evening that H[umphrey] Marshall & some men [. . .] would attack this place last night to take the Arsenal, rob the Banks in the place, & upon the strength of the rumor, we telegraphed to Lexington & brought down 300 soldiers from that place last night [. . .], but he has not made his appearance as yet and I suppose it is all a false alarm. The U.S. is moving troops very fast to Louisville & other parts of Kentucky. [. . .] We will soon be in a situation I hope to [drive] the men into Tennessee.

 The Legislature will adjourn, I think, about next Monday. We shall leave here as soon as our business will permit. We are all anxious to get home. Stay at home at night & keep the boys there with their guns loaded, ready for use, & be sure and have all the doors fastened at night.

Yours,

Brutus J. Clay

[P.S.] When the day of adjournment is fixed I will write again.

 Before Brutus could get home, Zeke, who was almost twenty-one, left the following note on a table in his room.

EZEKIEL CLAY

Sept. 24, 1861

B. J. Clay and family,

I leave for the army tonight. I do it for I believe I am doing right. I go of my own free will. If it turns out I do wrong I beg forgiveness.

Goodbye to you all. You will hear from me soon.

E. F. Clay

In Frankfort, Brutus received a message from the sheriff of Bourbon County. "I think I owe it to you as a friend to advise you that it is told and believed that your son, E. Clay, is going to the Southern army. Whether it is true or not I think it becomes my duty as your friend to advise you. Now, Brutus, this is strictly confidential as you know I would incur his everlasting displeasure if it be known I have written you."

Ann also wrote Brutus of Zeke's departure.

ANN CLAY

Bourbon, Wednesday night [1861]

My Dear Husband:

I feel that the only relief to my sad feeling tonight will be to write you. I suppose you have received Mr. Scott's letter saying Zeke had gone off last night to join the secession army. On Monday Aunt Holloway, Cyrus Miller, and Jimmy Miller [Patsey's son] came here, the two former on their way to Illinois. Yesterday Dudley, Zeke and Jimmy went to town and to see Judge Bedford [Volney Bedford's son], came [back], sat through supper and then went to the office. At bedtime Jimmy came in the house. I asked him where Zeke was. Said he would be in in a few moments, and as it was bed time they were soon asked to [go to] their beds upstairs, and Zeke did not make his appearance. This morning Isham went around for him to come to his breakfast. Said he was not there, he had slept in his bed and he expected he had gone coon-hunting this morning. Jimmy said yes that Judge had asked him to go hunting with him this morning but that Zeke remarked he could not leave him, so we ate our breakfast and concluded he had gone hunting, and directly after breakfast we went to town as Aunt Holloway wanted to see the Hickmans and some friends before she left today for Illinois, and I thought no more of Zeke till I went to the depot and Scott told me he had gone last night. I remarked that I did not believe it, but if he had, he had disgraced himself. He told me Judge Bedford and Wash Clay [a neighbor's son] had gone with Zeke and that Volney Bedford knew all about it. I felt so provoked I determined to come by there and give him a piece of my mind. I remarked to Mr. Bedford that I had heard he knew of it, but I did not believe it, that if he was a friend, as I supposed he was, that he would have sent me word so that I could have written to you. He looked confused and evaded it. I asked him the second time if he knew anything about it. He remarked Judge had not confided in him and he supposed I knew as much about it as he did. I told him I felt that he and all that had gone with him had disgraced themselves and that I hoped that they would be arrested and kept in jail, which speech I was severely reproved for. I told them I hoped they that had induced a boy to take sides against a father who had left everything in his charge whilst he was away striving and exerting himself to do all he could for his state would suffer for it. Cousin Margaret Bedford was there and I never heard anything so violent as she and Volney Bedford were against every one who was in favor of these camps and said no one had brought on the trouble here but them and they had destroyed the neutrality of the State, etc. etc. I told them I only regretted we had not had 10 times as many all the time and then we would be better provided for the traitors. So I left them making a more violent speech. I believe they are all violent secessionists and I do not wish to see anything more of them. Last week in town I heard that Zeke had joined a secession company and they had promised him some office. I told him of it and he denied it and said he would die or find out who told me, so I concluded there was no use in troubling you with it [. . .] and I did not believe it till I came home this evening and Cash had found a note in his room, directed to you and the family. [. . .]

Zeke rode his brown mare, took a comfort and blankets off his bed, your Sharp's rifle and a few shirts. Ever since you wrote to me about his having his guns ready, he has been busy making cartridges and I gave him the credit of making them for you, but Cash tells me he did not leave a load of powder on the place. He will go to town in the morning to get some, do not be uneasy about us at home. I do not feel afraid and do not suppose I will be troubled. Sidney and Mr. Hawkins both have offered to stay or attend to anything that is necessary. [. . .] I have been very particular about the doors and have always had the windows down as I did not consider the shutters secure. James Miller lied to us and knew all about it, and Mr. Bedford thought he was going with them. Aunt Holloway was hurried off by the troubles in Ky. Mrs. Keiningham went to Frankfort today so I suppose Mrs. Tubman came. Do try and get to see them. [. . .] Cash is about well. My love to you, Ma [Brutus's mother], and Sally [Watson].

Yrs. devotedly,

Ann M. Clay

Zeke had left with other Bourbon Countians to join Humphrey Marshall's forces in western Virginia. Their outfit eventually became the First Kentucky Mounted Rifles, CSA.

I try to picture that night of September 24. I imagine a wind in the cedars behind the house. The door of the office is open and the lamp within casts a rectangle of wobbly light across the lawn. The last cicadas of summer strum insistently. Zeke and Jimmy sit around a circular table, drinking whiskey. They argue, their gestures monumental in the lamplight. What makes Jimmy leave? Something Zeke says? Perhaps until this moment, he hasn't realized that Zeke is serious. After he goes to bed, Zeke pours another glass of bourbon, then takes a piece of paper from his father's desk and begins to write. This note seems the most important thing he has ever written, a declaration of selfhood. The urgent slanting letters run together. "I do it for I believe I am doing right."

Brutus's immediate response to Zeke's defection hasn't survived, but he was furious. He is supposed to have said that he intended to disinherit Zeke.

Kit and his uncle were still imprisoned at Camp Robinson. The Fields worried about their safety. "[A] gentleman past [sic] from Camp Robinson informs me that the trial of our friends and James B. Clay takes place today," Ezekiel Field Sr. wrote Brutus on September 27, "and the impression at camp is that J. B. Clay will be sent to New York and probably our friends may get clear, but that is doubtful. [. . .]" He added, "I am distressed to hear of the conduct of Ezekiel Clay."

Brutus was finally able to free Kit and his uncle.

A rockaway carriage in front of Auvergne, ca. 1900. *Photograph by Mary Harris Clay.*

Brutus's cow house, ca. 1895. *Photograph by Mary Harris Clay.*

Bourbon County Fair, October 1852. From left to right: Brutus J. Clay, Charles Garrard, William Alexander, Captain John Cummingham, Jeremiah Duncan, Surgeon-General Lawson, General Winfield Scott, James Hutchcraft, Reuben Hutchcraft, Jack Hutchcraft, Samuel H. Clay, Charles S. Brent, Garrett Davis, Samuel Brooks. Daguerreotype.

Grinding feed at the cattle barn in The Lots, ca. 1905.
Photograph by Cassius M. Clay III.

Hamp Ayres pumping water
from the cistern in
The Lots, ca. 1895.
*Photograph by
Mary Harris Clay.*

Ann M. Clay and Cassius M. Clay Jr., ca. 1859.
Ann was about 36, and Cash 12. Ambrotype.

Isole Plantation, Bolivar County, Mississippi. May 1995.

Willie Holloway's tombstone
in the Richmond cemetery.
Photograph by Berle Clay.

Cassius M. Clay III, age 19,
the night he became an editor
of the Yale *Daily News*.
Winter 1914–15.

Green Clay, age 19, at Yale. Engraving from a daguerreotype, ca. 1858.

Cassius M. Clay III, age 7, in the velvet-and-lace suit made for the wedding of his sister Suc Clay to Cyril Goodman in April 1902.

Clay Berry, age 7, in the same velvet-and-lace suit. Summer 1978. *Photograph by John M. Berry.*

Mary Clay Berry tossing
her wedding bouquet in
the front hall at Auvergne,
April 9, 1966.
*Photograph by
Bradford F. Swan.*

Martha Clay Davenport,
probably in her early fifties.
Cabinet card, ca. 1880–90.

BRUTUS CLAY

Frankfort, Sept. 30th, 1861

Dear Christopher,

Mr. [R. G.] Burton left for Louisville this morning, carrying a Petition from a large number of Union members of the Legislature [. . .] requesting Genl. Anderson to release Col. Field, Mr. Breck, & yourself & I feel assured he will do so. As Mr. Burton will return on the evening train & will not stop, I shall hand him this letter, & have to write before I know the result of his mission. We have also requested him to provide you with a permit to go South. Mrs. Tubman is here in Frankfort & is anxious to go South [to Augusta, Georgia] & we think it is unsafe for Mr. Thomas, her brother, to go with her. I should like therefore [if] you would come and go with her & Col. Field also might go this route, as it is probably the safest now with a passport. You might take your own luggage along. I shall leave here for home on Wednesday, dine in Lexington at the Broadway Hotel. If you can go this way you might meet me there and go home with me & give Mrs. Tubman two or three days to get ready to start. [. . .]

Yrs.

Brutus J. Clay

[P.S.] Show this letter to your Uncle Christopher.

Once freed, the two Christophers made their way south. It isn't clear whether they took Mrs. Tubman with them, though she somehow did manage to get to Georgia. Meanwhile, Martha sent the family a letter from her husband, who was stationed near Washington, at Munson's Hill.

When my son Michael was in the sixth grade in Alexandria, Virginia, Irene Rouse, a poet and the parent of a classmate, and I were invited to talk to the class about writing. Irene and I conferred beforehand about what we were going to say. I decided to talk about the use of historical documents. I selected several letters I thought would interest sixth graders, one of them Henry's letter from Munson's Hill. I thought the boys would be interested in his account of picket duty and everyone would find the soldiers' speculations about the Munson family amusing.

Irene looked at me incredulously when I told her this. "I'm a Munson," she said. "The house on Munson's Hill belonged to my family."

I let her read the letter. Irene already knew from family stories what had happened there.

"The family was furious when they got back to their house," Irene told me. "The soldiers had written messages to Lucy and her sister all over the walls. They'd even dressed up in the girls' clothes. The place was a wreck."

HENRY DAVENPORT

Camp near Fairfax C.H. [Court House], Sept. 25th, 1861

My Dear Martha,

We have just returned from picket duty down at Munson's Hill some twelve miles below this and within sight of Washington. We were absent just one week and all returned safe and sound except young Berry of Capt. Moon's company of Charles Town who was killed by the enemy. [. . .] Let me tell you something about picket duty, its labors, and then you will understand it is not a very grand employment. When we reached Munson's Hill, which in a direct line is about 5 miles from Washington and in full view of the dome of the Capitol, we found our pickets about a half a mile beyond the Hill behind a fence and the enemies' pickets on the opposite side of the field behind the other fence, a distance apart [of] about 400 yards. There they lay, watching each other, and every time a man accidentally [exposed] his gun, he was immediately fired upon and almost every day a man was killed. The first day I was there, our pickets had agreed not to fire on each other and there was no firing, but every day after that they were continually shooting at each other. [. . .] We were relieved every 24 hours and then rested 24 hours before going on duty again. We could only be relieved at night, as it was too dangerous to approach the posts in daytime. We were compelled to crawl for some distance on our hands and knees. [. . .] Just below Munson's Hill there is a now vacant house until recently occupied by a man named Munson who it seems had a very pretty daughter named Lucy Munson. Appeals to her affections are written most profusely on the walls by many soldiers who have heard of her beauty. One had written her name and then under it written an affectionate [note] whether she could love a brave Rebel soldier. I found one of her skirts and hung it on the sword belt of Lt. Meade who is a young man and whom we tease a good deal about the ladies. Miss Lucy and her Father have however retired to Washington on our approach (being Northern people and consequently sympathizers with our enemies). [. . .] Our headquarters when on picket duty was Falls Church, an old English church said to have been built in 1692 of brick brought from England. All around this old church the Yankees had settled and built quite a pretty little town. They have deserted their homes on our approach, leaving their gardens full of fine vegetables off of which we feasted. [. . .] Why they should have run away I can't imagine unless they thought we would force them into service, a thing we had no intention of doing. The Yankees have improved this and Alexandria county more wonderfully, and land that sold fifteen years ago at 5 dollars per acre is now selling, or was last spring selling, at 50 dollars. Every farm here is a garden of vegetables and fruit trees. [. . .] The Virginians living here all have negroes. The Yankees of course had none and spoiled those that they lived near, and I think the Virginians [. . .] hope they will never return. We are still accumulating troops here but what our movements are to be we cannot tell. I do not think we will attack the enemy's positions between here and Washington. [. . .] They have one continual line of fortifications from Washington for five miles out, and if we carry one they can fall back upon another. If we make any forward movement here it will probably be to go around the enemy's position and enter Maryland somehow. [. . .]

I hope Father received my letter written on the 18th Sept. [. . .] In this letter I wrote for my gray coat made of Porter's gray with a velvet collar. I also want the vest made of the same material, the pants I already have here. The two blankets for which I wrote I hope will be sent soon. [. . .]

I hope you are doing well. You must be careful of yourself. Take a moderate degree of exercise. You know how much good it always does you to walk. Do not fail to heed my recommendations in my last letter to you. Secure a proper nurse and also secure the services of a physician. You must not be backward in doing these things and make all proper arrangements. Let me know when you expect your confinement. I must say I do not think you have *selected* a proper *season*. It is too near winter to have the care of a young baby and it will be very apt to keep you in the house all Fall. [. . .] Kiss little Junius for me. How I would like to see him now. [. . .]

Affectionately your husband,

Henry B. Davenport

A late September letter from Cassius Clay probably reached Bourbon County about the same time Henry Davenport's did.

CASSIUS CLAY

St. Petersburg, R[ussi]a, Sept. 25, 1861

Dear Brutus,

Green returns home for three months of a leave of absence and I send the two girls home, Mary and Sally, and Brutus [his second son]. [. . .] I want Brutus to go to Sayre in Frankfort till he is ready for Yale College and then go there. [. . .] I am glad to hear that Ky. stood for the Union. But the rebels are not to be trusted. You must all be ready. Spend your money freely in the cause of the Union law and order or you will be ruined entirely. The only safety *is* in the government of our fathers. [. . .]

I am sorry so many of our friends have joined the enemy but like Dr. Franklin in the Revolution we must know no kindred but our country, and all who are not for us are against us. I rejoice in your election [to the legislature] for the country's sake. All send their love to all.

Your brother,

C. M. Clay

On November 18, pro-Southern Kentucky delegates met and passed an ordinance of secession. They formed a provisional government and were admitted into the Confederacy on December 10. The Confederate state of Kentucky consisted of the southwestern corner of the state. There, 35,000 Confederate troops squared off against 50,000 Union troops. After much skirmishing, war had finally come to Kentucky. Green, who had by this time arrived home, talked of joining the Union Army.

In late November, Cassius wrote Brutus from Russia. He was principally concerned with his own finances, which were as usual in disarray (his children, who had returned with Green, were all dependent upon Brutus for funds). He added, "I heard that Green has joined the army or thinks of it. I hope he will not do so as he is in a fine place here for improvement and seems well adapted for the post and does himself great credit by his steady and observant conduct and business habits. I hope he will return, as our family are very much pleased to have him with us and do not expect to find his equal. [. . .]

"I am sorry to hear of Ezekiel's and Christopher's joining the Rebels. I trust at least Cash will stand with Green for the country of our fathers. [. . .] I was greatly rejoiced at Ky's stand for the Union. Let her now show her ancient valor in the field and save her beautiful fields from ravage and ruin and eclipse her militant glory in arms and patriotism!"

Green went to Washington to make arrangements with Secretary Seward to allow him to fight in the Union Army during his leave of absence. In early December he wrote Ann for a servant to accompany him to war. As usual, Green was preoccupied with appearances. "The boy that goes with me I want him to have one good suit of jeans, the coat of tolerably good length, & the pants sufficiently long, not like those Isham wore to town with me the other day, 6 or 8 inches too short. He had better also have a round-about of some sort of heavy 'cassimere,' and probably pants too, if convenient. I would prefer Isham, or if it suits you better, I will take 'Hancin' [Henson], Mingo's son."

Green's letter crossed with one from Ann to Brutus, who was in Frankfort for another session of the legislature. Her letter filled him in on what the slaves — Tom, Henry, Isham, John, and Hamp — were doing on the farm

ANN CLAY

Paris, Dec. 4, 1861

My Dear Husband,

[. . .] Cash & June [Junius Holloway was on leave from the Union Army because of an injury to his toe] came on Saturday [from Richmond], reported the river high & dangerous to cross. I was getting along so finely eating in the kitchen, keeping up but one fire and getting a good deal of work done, that I was not very glad to see them. Cash is still crazy about hunting, says he only had one good day to hunt whilst in Madison and that he would not have been willing to come home had I not been alone. I have not sent for the sheep. Tom was ready two mornings, but it was raining and then the boys reported the river so high I concluded to wait till tomorrow. We have not had a pleasant day since you left on Monday. Henry killed 28 hogs and yesterday morning [they had] to be put in the cellar to thaw, so hard frozen could not be cut out till this morning. When Green left [for Washington] he requested me to get Isham ready to go with him. I told him I knew that you preferred his taking John. I am not willing for him to take Isham & shall not consent to it as I know of no one that can take his place. [. . .]

June says that a rumor reached town yesterday that the fighting had commenced in Ky. somewhere & that [Confederate General Felix] Zollicoffer had come back [the Confederates had in fact occupied Cumberland Gap] so I hope we will hear by the papers today.

The regiment left town Sunday evening and on the strength of it I hear there were 10 fights in the streets in town on Monday but the rest of Matt Clay's [a neighbor's son] company had come to make their farewell visit home so they gave the Secesh a good whipping. [. . .]

Mrs. Patsey Clay's son Sid bid Hamp goodbye a week ago and told him his mother [had] said we [the Brutus Clays] were too good Union and that she was afraid he would be arrested if he came here, that she could send no longer to our [grist] mill. So yesterday the waters all being high & cold, she sent [Sid] back for Hamp to grind for her. He [Hamp] sent Sidney back, telling him he must go to some of his Secesh friends. I was glad he did so. [. . .]

Yrs. devotedly

Ann M. Clay

On receiving Green's letter, Ann again wrote Brutus. "I wish you as soon as you receive this letter to write me word whom I must get ready to go with him. [. . .] As you gave him the liberty of selecting from the plantation he will not expect to be opposed in his second choice, but I did not expect you would consent for Henson to go." She added, "We are all well and all hands shucking corn. Tom went to Madison [County] today for the sheep."

While Green was preparing to leave for the war, Belle Lyman wrote Ann a letter, dated December 11, about quilts. "I send you the skirt to line the log cabin [quilt] and by the time Eliza is through with the other, I will be through with my old black mousline delaine [mousseline de laine, or wool muslin] that I am now wearing which will do to line it. I have a beautiful gray mousline delaine that I got just before I went into mourning. I was thinking what a beautiful quilt it would make but I have gotten so stingy I was thinking I must wear it a while longer. [. . .] As to the yard of crimson delaine, when I was looking for some little remnants Pa remarked that there was so little of it, that I had better take it along with the other little pieces so you could do with as you liked. Pattie has just brought down one of her old last winter dresses that she had turned up to wear Saturdays, says I must have it, but it seems to be so thin that I do not know whether it will do with the other two pieces. As they were her dresses I tell her after I use it a while she may have it. I will see some day what progress I can make toward begging some silk pieces but I am afraid the chance is pretty slim."

Since people used quilts instead of blankets, women were expected to have a baker's dozen on hand when they married and to continue to make them all their lives. After reading this letter, I rummaged in Auvergne's blanket chests, looking for what my mother called "the wedding dress quilt." When I found it, I spread it out on the floor in the library. It is more of a decorative throw than a quilt, consisting of fifty-one silk rosettes on a field of dark velvet, an ornate hexagonal mosaic, glowing with patches of magenta, sapphire, and gold. The heart of each rosette is white or off-white and is signed, leading my mother to surmise that they were pieces of wedding dresses.

I wanted to see whose dresses were included, but after sitting beside the quilt for some time, I came to the conclusion that it has nothing to do with weddings. Some rosettes bear men's names. Some clearly predate the Civil War (there is one for Amelia Clay). Others were probably made later (Martha has two, the first signed "Clay," the second "Davenport"). The pattern is Grandmother's Flower Garden, but this is an Album or Friendship quilt, a collection of squares made either by the people whose names they bear or by Ann of remnants of their clothing, the "silk pieces" Belle begged from members of the family.

In the center is a wreath of needlepoint flowers. Later, in a book about quilts, I located an early 1860s quilt from Bourbon County with a similar central motif. This one had been made for Elinor Branham by her sisters. I don't know who Elinor Branham was, but I would be willing to bet that Ann Clay saw her quilt, perhaps in a display at the Bourbon County Fair, and noted the needlepoint wreath.

*   *   *

Green arrived in Kentucky late in the year, having obtained an appointment as an aide to Brigadier General Albion Schoepf in General George H. Thomas's army, which was advancing southeast across Kentucky to confront Zollicoffer. He did not see his father before he left for the field. June Holloway, who was still visiting at Auvergne, wrote Brutus of Green's departure.

JUNIUS HOLLOWAY

Paris, Ky., Dec. 15th, 1861

Brutus J. Clay, Frankfort, Ky.

Dear Uncle,

[. . .] Green left on Friday. He has by this time reached his brigade. He was fortunate in getting off so early, as he may have the pleasure of witnessing a battle this week. It is rumored that Gen'l. [Humphrey] Marshall is now in possession of Prestonsburgh. I hope Gen'l. [Don Carlos] Buell will at once impede his progress. The Secessionists about here are again getting very bold. I have been to Paris once or twice since you left. You can see them assembled in cliques all over the town. I think it would be advisable to send another regiment over the town. [. . .] One of them bid Green good-bye. Wished him "Every *Personal* success, but his brigade a thorough drubbing, and himself a very fleet horse in the first engagement." I have concluded not to accept the transfer but to join my company at Washington as soon as my toe admits of it. I will have a better chance at distinction with the Army of the Potomac. My leave of absence has been extended until I am able to walk well. [. . .] Should anything of importance transpire I will inform you immediately. Hoping to hear from you soon, I remain

Very Respectfully

Your nephew,

Junius B. Holloway

Green enjoyed himself in the army. "There is no chance of a fight for some days yet," he advised his father on December 17. "Whenever it may come on we feel quite confident as to a favorable result. [. . .] The Gen'l. [Schoepf] is a stirring man. When he does move you may expect success tho there is no doubt the enemy outnumbers us at present. There was a little picket skirmish a day or two ago. I rode out this evening with the Gen'l. to our advance pickets."

In Frankfort, Brutus was anxious to get back to the farm. "I think I will not come down on Saturday," he wrote Ann, "but will come on Monday, the day of adjournment. Send for me on that day. [. . .] We have heard of no fighting at Somerset yet where Green has gone but there is no telling how soon there may be fighting."

Green spent Christmas slogging through southern Kentucky in dreadful weather. Four thousand men slowly marched into the roadless Kentucky Mountains through winter rain and sleet.

GREEN CLAY

Hd. Qrs. 1st Brigade, Somerset, Ky., Dec. 28, 1861

Dear Pa,

[. . .] We are in no fix for an advance as yet without reinforcements, especially cavalry in which, tho the most advanced brigade in the field, we are greatly deficient. Still we must soon either advance or fall back, for forage etc. is becoming very scarce. I go tomorrow to Lebanon to see Gen. Thomas on official business. [. . .] Zollicoffer I believe will not attack, tho we are always ready for him. His cavalry sometimes make a very bold dash close into our lines, which we find ourselves unable to return in the absence of cavalry of our own. We however paid our compliments to him the other day in force. Drove in his pickets, & confounded him considerable as to the object of our movements. So with the exception of an attack of the enemy on us, there is I think no very great probability of a battle soon. [. . .] Yet we can tell but little more about it than you. The order of today may be countermanded tomorrow & so it goes.

Affectionately,

Yr. Son Green C.

June Holloway returned to Richmond, still nursing his toe, as he explained to Cash.

JUNIUS HOLLOWAY

Richmond, Ky., Sunday, Dec. 30, 1861

Cassius M. Clay Jr.

Dear Cash,

I reached home on Friday evening and found the family all well. I forgot to bring Zeke's sabre with me, the one Green gave him. You will please send it over by Uncle Brutus when he comes. There is no news here. [. . .] I don't think I'll be able to attend to duty as soon as I expected. My *toe* is still very tender. I expect to hunt all this week. I wish you were here to hunt with me. Tell Aunt Ann I will have my Carte-de-visite [photograph] taken this week and send it to her. I will also send one to each of the "Hickman girls." Pa has not yet received his commission as commissary of subsistence. [William Holloway was trying to get a position with the Union Army.] I think it is very doubtful whether he does. The indications are apparent that a concerted effort is being made in influential Abolition circles to suppress Gen'l. McClellan and remove him from his important command [head of the Army of the Potomac]. We will never succeed in our glorious cause when this is done. [. . .] General McClellan will doubtless move when our army is ready for its appointed work and it would be folly for him to do it before. He has accomplished a great deal since the never-to-be-forgotten "Manassas Races" in converting an undisciplined mass into a powerful and well-disciplined army and you are unreasonable if you expect, in the winter, when the Virginia roads are impassable for artillery or baggage waggons, that an active campaign should commence. [. . .] The attacks upon Gen'l McClellan, in my judgment, spring from the fact that he is a Constitutionalist in politics, and not an Abolitionist. It is a part of the game of the latter to get the war into their hands, to be changed from a struggle for the Union and the Constitution to one of abolition. [. . .] Pa still thinks "the Rebellion will be put down in three months." He says the Confederates have never gained a battle. He really believes they were whipped at Manassas. He says Schoepf will *bag* Zollicoffer in a few days. Pa, I think, is almost a Republican. He believes in freeing the slaves our government takes. It is reading those vile Spiritual papers that has produced the change. Republicanism and Spiritualism go together, both Species of Insanity. There was a man here from Eastern Kentucky not long ago. He says he saw Zeke [Clay] and his company. They were well armed and equipped. Zeke said he thought he was right and intended to fight it out. A man told me in Lexington that 200 men had left Bourbon County for the Confederate States. I laughed at him and told him exactly how many had really gone. [. . .] I have a very fine setter pup, the one Zeke Holloway gave me. If you don't go to Frankfort [Cash's school had been suspended between September and December because of the threat of war], come over and hunt. [. . .] I have just received a letter from Washington City. [. . .] "The Grand Army of the Potomac will not move before the last of March." This news will cause me to remain at home until my wound is entirely well. I expect to join my company as soon as the army moves, well or unwell. My foot got very cold coming from Lexington and caused the *toe* to swell a good deal. [. . .] Pa has received a telegram from Washington saying his appointment is certain. I am expecting a letter from Green this week. He has promised to give me all the news of his Brigade. His relations here think he is in love with Mary Clay [Cassius Clay's daughter]. I tell them his sweetheart lives in Yankeeland. [. . .] Miss Nannie Embry sends her love to you. Richmond is very dull, most of the young men having joined the army — fed. and confed. [. . .] Wishing you all a Happy New Year I remain

Ever Your Friend,

Junius B. Holloway

Letters from Green came at regular intervals. Both armies were gearing up for what became known as the Battle of Mill Springs, at which the Confederates attacked General Thomas's troops at Logan's Crossroads, Kentucky, but were repulsed and eventually routed by them.

"The roads are becoming almost impassable," Green wrote Brutus on January 6, "& action now is not only our desire but to a great extent our existence. Gen'l Thomas, if this weather does not prevent, will allow us a programme in two or three days. He had sent to the General a very *strange* dispatch in contemplation of movement. But as yet no concert of action is arranged. There is no doubt but what Zollicoffer has been reinforced by [General George B.] Crittenden with very few troops however." He wondered if he could exchange Tom, the slave Ann allowed him to take, for the more presentable Isham.

Four days later, the army was still waiting to advance. "Gen. Schoepf has submitted 2 or 3 times a plan," Green told his father on the 10th, "for himself to cross the river & get in the rear, let Gen. Thomas advance from Columbia & thus make a sure thing of entrapping Zollicoffer & his entire command. But tho meeting with the approval of Gen. Thomas, Gen. Buell objects to it. So the plan that is now to be pursued is for an advance on this side of the river, & I have no doubt it will but result in driving him across, & *that is all.* [. . .] Gen. Thomas is now this side of Columbia in force, and in a few days will decide the result. But remember if Zollicoffer escapes by recrossing the river it will not be the fault of Gen. Schoepf." He marked the envelope "For *your perusal alone.*"

While Green prepared for battle, Cassius wrote from Saint Petersburg that the rest of his family was returning to Kentucky. He was full of plans for a new house he and Mary Jane wanted to build around his father's old farmhouse and asked Brutus to get the work started. He concluded, "I am glad there is no war with England so far. I hope the rebellion will be soon closed up forever!"

In January, Patsey Miller's husband, who had been sick for some time, died. Dr. Lyman sent word to Ann. "Mr. Miller arrived here on Saturday evening last at 4:20 o'clock, very much prostrated, remained here till Sunday 10 a.m., and then left for home and lingered on, manifesting the greatest difficulty in getting his breath till 8 o'clock last night when he suddenly expired. As yet we do not know when he will be buried."

In a letter written to Ann a short time later, Patsey relived his death in great detail. They had been visiting the Clays a couple of days before it occurred.

PATSEY MILLER

Hedgeland, Wednesday 29, '62

O my dear Sister,

How hard, too hard, for me to realize that my dear Husband is dead, is gone from us forever, that I am left alone, as it were, in this cold uncharitable world with a heart overflowing with grief and sorrow. I write to you whose tender sympathies I know I have, and if there is anything that could console me so [. . .] it is the assurance of the sympathies of kind brothers, sisters, relations, and friends. But oh to give up one who was every way so calculated to make this life happy and cheerful. It is hard to bear [. . .] when I look back upon that day [of his death] I feel that I must have been as it were blind. Now when I think of his appearance and stupor all day that I could not see death but [was] lulled into [a] sort of security that resting at home he might rally from his fatigue and be better and even at 3 o'clock when Dr. Lyman left and I discovered he was cooler than I had ever felt his flesh, a trembling came over me and I went to rubbing and rubbing his feet and hands in flannel, I did not want to, indeed, could not think it was death. [. . .] I could not get up the Fortitude to talk of death to him, wishing to keep him as cheerful as possible. [. . .] And I have thought, Ann, O why was it that Dr. Ray should be fixing up for me to bring home so many bottles of medicine and with directions to send back for more. [. . .] Could he not see that he was prescribing for a dying man? I would have thanked him to have so advised me, warning me to get home with him, and I started once to stop him in the dining room and get his opinion but I had not the fortitude. [. . .] Dr. Lyman told me he hoped he might rally and be better, but if not he would sink rapidly, so that false hope blinded me. I can now see it but too late. [. . .] [Most of the rest is illegible.]

Patsey Miller

The nightmarish Battle of Mill Springs finally took place on January 19, after a week of cold rain that left the Cumberland River and its subsidiary creeks swollen beyond their banks and the roads in the vicinity quagmires. The Confederates attacked in shin-deep mud, blinding rain, and winter lightning, but they were quickly discovered by General Thomas's pickets. In the rain, General Zollicoffer, who was wearing a white rubber raincoat, lost his sense of direction and rode toward a Union officer, mistaking him for one of his own. When the general shouted an order, the Union colonel turned and shot him. Seeing their general dead, Zollicoffer's troops fled in disarray.

Although the battle was a Federal victory, General Thomas could not follow it up with an advance because of the condition of the roads. Thus the eastern part of Tennessee, a hotbed of pro-Union sympathy, remained under Confederate control.

Green wrote his father an exuberant account of the battle.

GREEN CLAY

On the cars from Nicholasville, Wednesday [January] 22 [1862]

Dear Pa,

I have been on the spur ever since the battle & for two days before. So have not had time to write you until this opportunity. A *complete* victory on our side. The enemy showed great weakness in anticipating our movements by his own move, leaving his entrenchments & marching out 8 miles to meet us. Gen. Thomas' column met them first & repulsed them with considerable loss on both sides. [. . .] I suppose such a complete rout never was known to *any army.*

They fled [. . .] panic stricken for 8 ms. to their entrenchments, leaving knapsacks, guns, wagons & 2 pieces of artillery on the road. We came up in close pursuit, shelling them 2 or 3 times, until we finally commanded their entrenchments & shelled them from 2 points. They only replied with 6 guns. The night closed upon us & we lay upon our arms under their entrenchments until morning & at daylight threw a few shells into their entrenchments, receiving no reply. We marched up & were soon in possession of their entire works.

They had crossed the river during the night, leaving every thing, 10 pieces of artillery, several hundred head of cattle and horses, besides several 100s wagons. Left everything, their private baggage & all. They had winter qrs. for 15,000 men, log huts.

We took positions in their encampment & shelled some tents on the other side of the river but found no one there.

Their last order was by their Comd'g Officer for them to disperse & save themselves as best they could.

So this army was scattered to the winds and will not be again organized.

[. . .] I myself was not in the first & severest engagement but came up soon afterwards & participated in all the rest.

I am on my way to Louisville by order. I have in my possession the enemy's flag captured which is to be presented to Gen. Buell. [. . .]

I expect to be in Lexington Friday night & will leave for Somerset Saturday morning.

If Aunt Ann can spare Isham I wish she would send him to the Broadway Hotel Friday night, with *one suit* of good clothes & my *valise.*

Will send Tom home. The General may ask for my appointment as his Adjutant General (not certain however & you must say nothing about it). In such case must I accept & resign my position as Sec. of

Legation? I see Uncle C. is to be recalled [Cassius Clay was recalled from Saint Petersburg in January 1862, then reappointed the following year] & I have heard nothing from [Simon] Cameron [Cassius's replacement].

I hope you will make this out (written on the cars).

Write to me at Lexington Broadway Hotel by Friday night.

Yr. Son,

G.C.

In February a short letter arrived from Mississippi, the first since Kit and his uncle had headed south the previous summer.

CHRISTOPHER FIELD

February 8th, 1862

Dear Ann,

Having heard a gentleman was at New Madrid, Mo., from Ky. I have concluded to write you, hoping it may reach you. We, the whites, C.E.A. [Kit, Edmund, and Anna] and myself have had fair health during the fall & winter. C. has had some chills but he hunts so much he exposes himself to rain and bad weather but I now think he is clear of them. We have had a warm wet *winter*, very changeable and cold for a day or two only, but those sudden changes have produced much sickness with the negroes. Dudley, Amy's son, died from cold brought on by his own fault, had a fight and run off without waiting to see whether he would be corrected for it, took violent cold while out. I lost a man at home in the fall from congestion. Money is very scarce amongst the cotton planters [. . .] we use our crops all at home on the plantations, not shipping any. We had all some few hogs and beef enough to last until hot weather and there is pork for sale in many portions of the South but at very high prices. [. . .] But all these seeming difficulties in the South only gives us the [. . .] willing determination to try and succeed. Our defeat in Crittenden['s] Army [the Battle of Mill Springs] will be of great service to us. We had had so many victories that we had got to risking too much and thought we could not be whipped regardless of our numbers. [. . .] How I would like to see Mr. C. now and ask him if the South could do otherwise than what we are doing. And how any *slave owner* in Kentucky can now sustain this war or administration is a mystery to me. We in the South feel that it is *victory*, *death*, or *exile with us*. [. . .] We all expect to be called into this fight before it is over. And what a spectacle will it be for me & C. [Kit] to be on the same field of battle and to see G. [Green] on the other side. Oh, it is too unnatural to think about! My regards to Mr. C. & all.

[no signature]

The Fields and Clays emerged from the first year of the war unscathed but divided. Christopher was right: it was unnatural.

EIGHT

Do You Think They Will Ever Be Whipped Out?

By late February 1862, Brutus was back in Frankfort. One of the first acts of the legislature was to issue a declaration of thanks to Union generals for their victories on the perimeters of the state. Federal troops under Ulysses S. Grant had seized Fort Donelson, Tennessee, on the Cumberland River, just a few miles from the Kentucky state line, while Thomas's army took control of Nashville on February 25. But Confederate troops still threatened southwestern Kentucky.

June Holloway, back in the army again, served as Brutus's eyes and ears for military matters. "There is nothing new here," June wrote in early March, "except that Buell is beyond Nashville. You may expect to hear of a bloody battle very soon, either at Columbus, or Murfreesboro. Columbus is not evacuated by the 'Rebels,' but they are reinforcing very heavily. If they remain at Columbus 10 days, their entire command will be bagged by ours." In fact, Federal troops took command of Columbus the day June wrote this letter.

June had seen Green recently. "He spoke of resigning his position in Russia. But I advised [him] to hold on to it, knowing that you are opposed to his going into the Army permanently."

In March, Green prepared to return to his post in Saint Petersburg, even though his uncle was no longer minister there. "I have all my baggage with me & find it inconvenient for me to stop over at Frankfort to see you," he wrote his father. "Can't you come up home next Friday?"

The next day, Ann wrote Brutus that she was not well.

ANN CLAY

Monday evening [March 11, 1862]

My Dear Husband,

As I wrote to Cash [. . .] I have been sick and in bed the most of the time since Friday [. . .] now I am a good deal better and hope in a few days to be well. I am not suffering any more but feel weak and good for nothing. I did not intend to send for the Dr. but, on Friday last, Dr. Ray came to see Leander [a slave] and then came to the house to tell me about her. She gets no better & he tells me cannot recover. [She died a short time later.] He told me I must keep very quiet, take quinine and bathe in cold water. [. . .] I feel very anxious to get out and get some work done but as have come to the conclusion that as *big and fat as I am* that I am not very stout and that I will have to take better care of myself. Sidney [Clay] spent the day with me yesterday, told me Mary Jane [Clay] had come home [from Russia] and would probably be here this week. If I was well I would be delighted to see her. Mrs. Keiningham was here on Friday. She was quite cheerful and full of fun! Dr. Ray told me Mrs. H., Mrs. Rogers, and Miss Anderson stood on the street all day Court Day with the men, begging money to send clothes to the Fort Donelson prisoners and bragged they collected 700$ and I was quite mad yesterday to hear Sidney say he gave them $1.50 when he has never given me that much for the Union soldiers. [. . .]

Yours,

Ann M. Clay

As it turned out, Brutus was able to spend a few minutes with Green as he passed through Frankfort. He wrote Ann that he hoped to be home before Green left for Washington.

"Our glorious Union victories are flowing in regularly," William Holloway gushed to Brutus from Louisville. "For one I must say first now I would make a pretty good Methodist *Amen* man just now, for this [. . .] gratifies me to the very depth of my Soul." As his son June had remarked earlier, Holloway was an incurable optimist.

Cassius Clay remained in Saint Petersburg awaiting the arrival of his replacement. At home, his wife was having stone quarried for their new house. As usual, she had money problems. "You told me you had no money of Mr. Clay's but you would furnish me if I needed it," she wrote Brutus in March. "Now if it inconveniences you at all, do not send it, I beg of you." She added, "I get frequent letters from Mr. Clay. He is enjoying himself highly with the Imperial family, Princesses, etc. etc. etc."

When Green arrived in Washington, he discovered a change of plans. "I called upon Mr. [William H.] Seward last evening," he told his father on March 23. "Mr. [Simon] Cameron [Cassius's replacement] had desired to select his own Sec. of Leg. The Dept. refused to remove me for this purpose, without it was my wish. Mr. C. got a little 'crusty' about it, & said he would not go then. Mr. Seward thinking it might be more agreeable to me concluded to vacate a position of same rank & salary & so, if I desire, will transfer me to the Court of Turin where I shall have greater advantages of climate & improvement. But he says I can retain the other position if I want to, Mr. C. notwithstanding. Of course I have no hesitation about choosing Turin to St. P."

He had discussed remaining in the army with Seward. "Mr. S. also said if I desired to remain in the Army longer, I could do so & resume my position after another campaign, but this will be too much trouble and expense now. I am *grateful to Uncle Cash, beyond measure*, but must say it is more honor to be free from the favor of nepotism in any *public* position."

A day later Green wrote Brutus again. "Have been transferred to *Turin*. But as it will require the confirmation of the Senate, my papers will not be ready by the 26th, the day I expected to sail. So I shall have to await the next Cunard steamer & sail from Boston Apr. 2nd. In meantime I will leave tomorrow morning for Harpers Ferry to see Sister Martha." He was looking forward to his new post. "Mr. Marsh, the minister, is a man whom I will find at once agreeable & improving. He is no politician, but an excellent scholar & fine linguist."

Green got through to Charles Town and saw Martha, who now had two babies, Junius and Braxton, who was born on October 20, 1861. The Davenports called Braxton "Little Nassa" after the Battle of Manassas. Green mailed a letter from Martha to Ann.

MARTHA DAVENPORT

Jefferson Co., March 27 [1862]

Dear Aunt Ann,

I was very much surprised to see Green on Wednesday. I supposed he was still in the Army. He leaves for New York today and will sail from Boston on Wednesday next. I have but time to write you a short letter. The children are both sick with colds, and threatened with croup, so I am constantly engaged nursing & watching them, but have endeavored to enjoy Green's company every unoccupied moment. [. . .] Poor Zeke was to see me just a month ago. He stayed but five days and the enemy came in and he had to leave with but ten minutes' notice. Poor boy, he is now an outcast and an exile from home. But so long as I have a roof or clothes to wear, I will share them freely with him. There has been a hard fight at Winchester between the Federals & Jackson's army, resulting in the grand slaughter of the enemy, and but a small loss on our side. [She refers to a clash between Stonewall Jackson and Union forces near Kernstown, a tactical defeat that turned into a strategic victory for the Confederacy.] I was so miserable about Mr. Davenport that Father sent Mr. Littleton to the battlefield, & not finding him among the dead or wounded we feel satisfied he is safe. Would that I had time to write you of the insults & thievery, etc. of these demons who have come here under [General Nathaniel P.] Banks, an as infernal scoundrel as God can let live. Negroes have been run off by [the] hundreds. Father has lost 4 negro men and they are still going. Those that are left are so impudent and ruined I do not know how we can live with them. You can't conceive of the horrible state of affairs here. The army place themselves entirely on an equality with the negroes and have made them tell them everything about their masters & families and are begging and offering every inducement to them to go. They have even driven their waggons [sic] up and packed up the women & children and carried them off. Some gentlemen have had every Negro taken from them. Oh! Would that I had the time just to tell you what they have done, and what they intend to do. And how I despise them. I would rather become a province of England or France than ever live with such demons again. My only regret is my two boys cannot go and shoulder the musket by their father's side, and kill some of these infernal devils. [. . .] Tell Pa he is trusting in the Union but I fear he has a frail trust. What does he think of the incessant nigger question in Congress. If I were cowardly enough to be a Unionist, I should be ashamed to let it be known. I have not heard from Zeke, do not know when I shall, but he is dearer to my heart than ever before, and come what may, he shall never be cast off by me. I am sorry his step is so regarded by you and Pa. I suppose however you look upon the rebels just as we look upon the Union traitors, as being disgraced and despised. I wish I had time [to] write such a letter as I wish but I am afraid to send a letter through the military mail, as I know it will be opened and perhaps myself arrested for treason. Not that I am afraid of them. No, I defy the whole set from Lincoln down, but I cannot be separated from my little babies when I have no confidence in my servants. Well! Green has told me about everybody, so I feel that I have paid a visit to Ky. I am obliged for your desire for me to go there, but would never leave Mr. Davenport now that he is in constant danger. He was at home on a month's furlough when Zeke came. [. . .] We have met with terrible reverses but are not dismayed, nor discouraged. We will hold out until we are all killed, and then the women will defy them still. Green says the Army of Ky. and Tennessee have not behaved as they have here. They are a different set of people. What could we expect when Banks rode down from Winchester a few days ago with two negro wenches setting [*sic*] up by his side. Well, goodbye. My love to Pa & all friends. Mrs. K. Cousin Margaret. Also to Cash. I don't know when I shall write again.

Affectionately,

M. C. Davenport

Martha's letter traveled to Kentucky with one from Green. In it he told Ann that Martha seemed much better off than many of her neighbors. "There is no doubt the vandalism of Banks' Army in that region is a disgrace to the service," he wrote. "I pity those people from the depth of my heart. The insolence they have been & are almost daily subjected to. Even what *negroes* they have left are insolent beyond control so I understand." Little June was a "very fine looking boy," he added, and Martha was hard at work in her garden.

Somehow Martha managed to get another letter through to Brutus a few days after Green left.

MARTHA DAVENPORT

Charlestown [sic], Va., March 31, 1862

Dear Pa,

I write to you in a great hurry. [. . .] Prudence suggests that I shall not say many things to you nor tell you many facts which would astound you until I have some assurance my letters will not be opened & myself imprisoned for telling the truth. [. . .] Would to Heaven the eyes of the Union people of the Border States would be opened to the real object of this war. [. . .]

Last night, the government waggons drove up to Father's and loaded up the plunder & children of 11 of his negroes & drove off with them. He had previously lost 3 negro men. He knew nothing of it until they were gone. The soldiers told the negroes they were to take some more belonging to another member of the family, meaning mine. Laura told me something this morning that made me believe Ellen is arranging to leave. [. . .] I do not know about Sophy and Laura. I have always despised Ellen so that I am very sorry I ever was persuaded by you to bring her. She is a black rogue and every thing else that is mean. I have known for some time that her head was full of freedom & white men. You must write me word what I shall do to recover them, for they are virtually yours. Whenever they come for them, I shall endeavor to defend them with a weapon, so there is no knowing what may be the result. [. . .]

I have written to Mr. Garrett Davis on the subject. I shall doubtless hear from him before you receive this letter. Hundreds & hundreds have been run off from this country in this way, and when application is made to the Provost Marshall here, who is a slave-holder in Maryland, he replies he must obey his orders, which are they cannot be restored to the owners unless they are willing to return. [. . .] It is now known that two families belonging to Mr. Dick Washington are to be carried off this week. Tell Mrs. Bedinger they have taken every one Mr. James L. Ransom has, and broke into Mr. Bolt's home and destroyed all their furniture & even tore up Mrs. Bolt's dresses, broke her china, and used her parlor with an elegant carpet on the floor for a certain purpose, too low life to mention. [. . .] I have not time to write more. My love to all.

Affectionately your daughter,

M. C. Davenport

June Holloway continued his reports to his uncle, writing in this case from Federal headquarters in Nashville on the eve of the Battle of Shiloh. Like the fight for Fort Donelson, that battle, which took place April 6 and 7th, was an important step toward Federal control of the Mississippi River.

JUNIUS HOLLOWAY

Headquarters Department of the Ohio

Nashville, Tenn., April 1, 1862

Dear Uncle,

[. . .] Our armies are still on the advance, except a part of Halleck's which is in status quo. Buell and Halleck are cooperating together. Gen. Grant with all his available force has gone up the Tennessee River to destroy connections at Corinth, Miss. Buell and Halleck are trying to cut [General Albert Sidney] Johnston's line with Memphis for Randolph & Island No. 10. [. . .] We will take Corinth very soon. The enemy are strongly entrenched with 10,000 men. A big Battle will be fought during next week which will decide the fate of the South. [. . .] We have but few friends in Tennessee. We are keeping 15,000 men in the city [Nashville] to keep the people down. John Bell [the former presidential candidate] is with the Southern Army at Jackson. Gen. Buell wrote to him to come back, but he refused, saying he was no submissionist. We took a 1000 sick rebel soldiers here and most of them have applied to take the Oath of Allegiance. I suppose they will all be released. Gov. [Andrew] Johnson has formally taken charge of the state affairs. He is very unpopular with the citizens. [. . .] I suppose the Rebels in Bourbon County are looking despondent. We will see the War closed in 90 days. [. . .]

Affectionately your nephew,

Junius B. Holloway

Meanwhile, Green reached Europe. In a letter dated "Mai 7," he wrote his cousin Sidney Clay, "Sid, Paris is the greatest place in the world." However, he was leaving the next day for Italy, where he wrote his father from Turin. "I have just moved into my rooms & feel now quite at home. The city is all that one could wish for [in] a residence, the air invigorating tho a mild climate, etc. And Mr. Marsh, a man at once agreeable & improving. All things tend to make my position a pleasant one, & your wandering son a more contented man."

He had arrived in the midst of the unification of Italy. The previous year, Victor Emanuel II had become a constitutional king over lands that included the former kingdom of Naples, given him by the revolutionary Guiseppe Garibaldi. Garibaldi had in turn been elected to represent Naples in Parliament. The government was based at Turin until the Austrian provinces of Venetia and Tirol and the remaining part of the papal states could be added to the new nation.

"Turin is like a democratic city," Green continued, "the greatest freedom of opinion is allowed, [. . .] upwards of 20 papers are published & discuss freely all questions of state policy. In fact, Italy is the seeming anomaly of a Republican Kingdom & a Republican King. [. . .]

"This is all very gratifying to an American & contrasts widely with the political situation in St. Petersburg, as does the climate of the two places.

"To feel the warm life blood of a growing nationality & to watch the settlement of this great continental question is no ordinary privilege."

In Mississippi, the Confederate army seized and destroyed the cotton stored on the riverside plantations. The soldiers left behind them receipts: "This is to certify that I have this day caused to be burned on the Plantation of Messrs. Fields [sic] & Irwin [sic] by authority of the Confederate States of America in the County of Bolivar and State of Mississippi Three Hundred & Forty (340) Bales Cotton Ginned & required & supposed to be that quantity by estimate. Given under my hand this the 16th day of May 1862. O. R. Lyles, By Order of Gen. Beauregard." Destroying the cotton was intended to reduce the supply reaching British mills and thereby convince the English to enter the war on the side of the South.

June Holloway wrote Brutus from the occupied South on May 26 that he had become engaged to a woman he had met in Nashville. He wanted Brutus to lend him $350 with which to get married, and Brutus did. June added, "I, in a few days, will be appointed Captain in the Quarter Masters Department upon the recommendation of Maj. Gen. Buell."

Green wrote Ann, begging for news from home. "I scarcely see much less read any English papers at all now, except a bundle of old

ones the Dept. sends us every now & then, & most of the legation papers are French & Italian. Tho I am glad of this, for it is such a great
advantage to me in having the languages yet I must depend upon my
letters from home [for] news [of the war in Kentucky]."

He was excited by events in Italy. "The Italian House of Parliament opens next week & they have quite an exciting question before
them, the late Garibaldian project to invade Austria [the Austrian-
controlled provinces of Venetia and Tirol]. Garibaldi himself is now in
town & being a deputy will himself speak. I am very anxious to see &
hear him."

In fact, there was little war activity in Kentucky that spring,
though Colonel John Hunt Morgan's cavalry had been harassing the
Louisville and Nashville Railroad, a harbinger of things to come. For
the moment, Union men remained in control of most of the state. In
late April, a grand jury in Bourbon County indicted twenty-four citizens for joining the Confederate army and another twelve for invading
the state.

On June 1, Brigadier General Jeremiah T. Boyle was named U.S.
military commandant of Kentucky. A few days later, he issued "instructions for the guidance of provost marshalls" from his headquarters
in Louisville. The marshalls were to arrest anyone aiding either the
Confederate army or guerrilla forces and require these "rebels" to take
an oath of allegiance to the Federal government. The penalty for violating this oath was death. "The arrest of your Secesh candidate has
kept the Rebels in Madison from bringing out Candidates for County
Offices," June Holloway wrote Brutus on June 1. There was little regard for anyone's civil rights.

Another letter from Martha made it to Kentucky, this one written
in June though misdated 1863. Ellen had run away, and Martha hoped
Brutus would be able to get her back.

MARTHA DAVENPORT

Charlestown [sic], June 11th 1863 [sic]

Dear Pa,

I wrote to you several days ago a long letter [now lost] which I hope
you have received as it will be explanatory to this. Presuming you have

read it, and your business and inclination will allow you to come to Va. for myself & negroes, I will proceed. [. . .] I hope if you can come you will come with the determination to get Ellen back. Mr. [Senator Garrett] Davis wrote me word you could reclaim her but I suppose now it would require permission from Stanton to do so. Hence a trip to Washington. [. . .] I think the more suddenly you could come upon Ellen the less trouble you will have, for there are hundreds of negroes at the Ferry who would secrete her were it known you were in Virginia. Father has one there who hides every one that is hunted by the Union. Not only do I not wish to lose the value of Ellen, but I think the example in reclaiming her would do much good to the remaining ones both here and at your house. For I anticipate when these go to Ky., you will have some trouble with yours. I have told mine all the time you could get them back, and know that Matt and Laura have only been waiting to see the result before they started. I understand Laura asks every time she goes down to Father's when the negroes are going from there, that they must let her know, as she would rather die than go back to Ky. You have no idea how much they know. Many of the negroes here can read & write. We understand they buy the daily papers, the rankest abolition sheets you ever saw. They read all the appeals for them, see all the proceedings of that vile abolition Congress now in session, see where they are supported by the government, where they are declared free in the south, where they are arming & drilling them, and also where they are stimulated to even the killing of the women & children who own them. They then tell all this to those who cannot read, and hence their whole soul & mind is filled with freedom. When mine tells yours all this, I fear you will have trouble at home. [. . .] Even the religious tracts that are given the soldiers are filled with exhortations to the negroes to leave, that they are the only things under Heaven in bondage, that this war is for them, now is their time, when Lincoln and the government is for them, & should they not accept the invitation, it may never be offered again. The Chaplains are the worst men here. They are the ones that circulate all this matter, and slip them in wherever they find a negro that can read. Hence those who would stay are worried with inducements & provocation until they have to go. Everyday I find some of my clothes that Ellen had stolen, fixing to leave. [. . .] I think after I told her you could get them back, she had given up going, but Sophy says the soldiers who she was feasting in my kitchen from morning till night told her that was all stuff, you never could get her back. The morning she left I told her you should know it [that she had run off]. She told me that she cared nothing for you & was not afraid of you and said if her

Father came for her, she would have him arrested. She frequently bragged she was exactly like Wesley, no body could manage her, told the soldiers her daddy was a white man, and she never intended to have anything to do with negroes, had made all arrangements to educate her child, etc. I must say I would rather run the risk of losing the other three by staying here than go to Ky. without this one. Mr. Davenport's father does not want me to go to Ky., but as I see no hope of Mr. Davenport coming home, I am willing to go, and think it to our interest to do so. This part of the valley can never be held by the confederate troops, hence will be under the enemy until the war terminates. [. . .] I can go now or a month hence. I have secured a tenant for my place. I only wish after you determine, write me word in time to break up housekeeping before you come. [. . .]

Affectionately your daughter,

M. C. Davenport

How combatants should treat women on the opposite side was a troubling question. Of General Benjamin Butler's May 15 order that any New Orleans woman who insulted a Northern soldier should be treated like a prostitute, Green wrote Ann in June. "Gen. Butler's New Orleans proclamation, a disgrace to the man & the army if genuine as reprinted, is published in all the European journals, mostly severely criticized as having a very deleterious effect here. How any genl. [. . .] could make such an order, even its effect upon the discipline of his army, I can't well see. If there is such an order, I hope the Prest. will immediately recall the general. If true, I am confident he will do so. Mr. Lincoln has shown considerable nerve. I have much confidence in him & believe he will remain true to his conservative policies & serve the nation." Not long after Green wrote this, General Boyle ordered the arrest and imprisonment of "disloyal females" in Kentucky.

In July, John Hunt Morgan led a brigade of horsemen on a raid through Kentucky and Tennessee during which he captured 1,200 prisoners and tons of supplies. Morgan's men disrupted the legislature. They threatened Richmond. Security was tightened. Brutus's papers include a pass issued by the office of the provost marshall in Lexington on July 15: "The guards and pickets pass J. Brutus Clay Esq. [sic]."

On July 18, Morgan and his men camped in Paris, but they were driven out of town by the arrival of volunteers under Brutus's nephew, Green Clay Smith, a flight the Unionist *Western Citizen* labeled the "Great Skedaddle." The following day Morgan was in Winchester, and the day after that Richmond. He never stayed long in any one place. Smaller bands of guerrillas also threatened towns and individuals. On July 29, two hundred men, reported to be on their way to join the Confederate army, demanded the surrender of Mount Sterling.

In early August, Eliza Smith wrote Brutus from Lexington that their mother was still suffering from the hip she had broken the year before. She wrote, "We heard they had a battle in Richmond Saturday. Mr. Bob Stone and young Breck shot badly, & M. Miller and Shackelford kill'd. etc. etc. They brought *Old* [Squire] Turner, Jim Caldwell, and Francis over as prisoners. I am afraid we will have a great deal of Trouble in Madison. There are so many *Secesh* there. I am going over in the stage this evening. Mother wants me to stay longer, but I must go home. [. . .]"

She added a postscript: "I wish so much I could have seen you and we could have talked over all about Morgan's Raid, and the excitement we have had. I suppose you heard they searched *my house, and Curran* [her son] *had to hide out for several days.*" But the real battle of Richmond had not yet begun.

Far from Kentucky, Green suffered the anguish of an exile.

GREEN CLAY

Turin, Aug. 16, '62

Dear Pa,

Of course it is with more than usual anxiety that I look for news from America. For now it seems the war is hot to the very heart of Ky. and the homes of the loyal are invaded by guerrillas.

Our state, I saw from the beginning, through much trial would have to pay for her loyalty. But clearer still would have been the price of disloyalty. As soon as all hope of winning us to the cause of the rebellionists should disappear, it was natural to expect that we should then become the object of their bitterest hate! A border state, we would suffer from their injuries, their barbarities, and their vindictiveness. On the other hand, too, we were prepared to endure suffering and unjust abuse at first, and even afterwards, some hard licks, from our *loyal* sister states. Patriotism was beset by the peculiar circumstance in which almost every home found itself — divided against itself. [. . .] In regard to slavery: [. . .] the institution must melt away before steady and constant enmity in the operating forces of the government and by the attrition of a war carried on for the most part by free states against slaveholding states. It was probably wiser for Ky. to adhere to the old Union even at this sacrifice & retain the benefits in other respects of a good & beneficent government, than by violence in war to turn the whole North against an institution which so thoroughly permeated the social organization of the South. [. . .]

Now the question is, I think, will Ky. stand by the realization of this conviction which was given in her pledge when she gave herself to the Union cause? Will she make the sacrifice in reality? Or continue to occupy an anomalous position, suspicioned by her own government & subjected to the constant arrogance of brigands & conspiracies from the other quarter? [. . .] At a distance, an observer, and not a participator, [. . .] I feel the interest of a passenger in our destination. And if my writing will do nothing more than to get your views on the state of things, I shall be satisfied. [. . .]

My love to all.

Affectionately,

Green Clay

On July 28, the governor summoned the legislature into extraordinary session to help him cope with the chaos in the state. Brutus was deluged with constituent requests for commissions and appointments. R. Patton of Moorefield wanted an appointment as first surgeon in a Kentucky regiment. White W. Forman wanted to be a notary public in Paris. Matt Layson of Millersburg needed a pass in order to go to Ohio on "important business." And Lewis Stivers was annoyed that he had not yet received a commission as major. Men rose quickly in the volunteer army. Brutus's nephew, Green Clay Smith, was already a general.

In the midst of the excitement, Kit arrived at Auvergne from Mississippi by way of Georgia and Virginia. He was sick and frightened. As a one-time member of a Mississippi Home Guard unit, he was in danger from Union military officials in Kentucky. Ann wrote Brutus to tell him the news.

ANN CLAY

Saturday morning [postmarked August 18]

My Dear Husband,

You will be surprised to receive a letter from me so soon. Knowing it would be a great gratification, I write to say that Christopher came home last night at 12 o'clock. Says he came very near being taken by home guard, had to draw his pistol on the negroes. He was so much fatigued he went immediately to bed and is not yet up.

Cit says when he left home about the 15th of July he could scarcely walk. He had been sick all winter & spring, but the traveling & excitement has improved him much. He is thin & has now gained his strength. He went first to Mobile & Georgia, Virginia, & Tennessee & has come through the mountains on horseback. Says he was not well & felt that he wanted to come home & to see and talk to you some, but if he knew of the troubles here, he would not have come. That after getting into Ky. he heard of the arrests being made all [over] our country & then he regretted having come & now does not feel easy here, as he is a decided southerner in his feelings, and if he is arrested that he can never take the oath, as he lives & his property is in the south. He has had some trouble & made a very narrow escape, so he will I trust know how best to act. But I feel so uneasy about him. [. . .] So you had best write to me to advise him what to do. He says feeling now as he does, he thinks it would be best for him not to stay very long here.

He will not tell me much. Says that he & every other southerner are sworn not to tell anything they know. He burnt 175 bales of cotton and they are not raising any. Says he has 300 acres of corn in and his 125 hogs to fatten & that they are doing very well, but all the negroes were pressed to make that canal at Vicksburg & he gives a most dreadful account of how the Union army acts in the south. He says since in Ky. he has had to travel altogether at night. He left Brother at home on plantation, but ready to go in the army when necessary. I shall be miserable all the time about Cit and am sorry that he has come. I tell him if you were at home I know he would be safe. Do write to me tomorrow. [. . .]

Yrs. devotedly,

Ann M. Clay

Union Admiral David G. Farragut had captured New Orleans in April and steamed up the Mississippi, conquering Baton Rouge and Natchez, but his ships were unable to get past the gun batteries at Vicksburg. Meanwhile, Union gunboats captured Memphis and continued three hundred miles downstream until they found themselves on the other side of Vicksburg. In July, Union soldiers, assisted by blacks from plantations such as Kit's and his uncle's, began to dig a canal across an oxbowed neck of land near Vicksburg. The idea was to divert the Mississippi River, thus bypassing the Confederate stronghold, but the river did not cooperate. Numerous men lost their lives from typhoid, dysentery, and malaria.

A day after she sent word to Brutus of Kit's arrival, Ann wrote again. Confederate General Kirby Smith had entered Kentucky through Cumberland Gap and was marching toward Richmond.

ANN CLAY

Sunday morning

My Dear Husband,

We are in the greatest distress about our friends in Richmond. Papa, Belle, and Pattie [Field] came last night & Uncle McClananhan will be here this morning and perhaps others of the family, as Mr. Holloway was with the Union Army & sent them all word to leave town. You have heard of the desperate fight 5 miles the other side of Richmond. Commenced Friday evening & was resumed yesterday morning at 7. When they left at 2, they were still fighting on. At least they heard the cannon louder than in the morning & concluded they were nearer town. And, as usual [Colonel Leonidas] Metcalfe's men there fleeing in the greatest disorder & the impression was when they left that our troops were cut all to pieces & the rebels would soon be in Richmond. One small band completely overpowered by the large numbers of the rebels. I feel now that it will not be many days before they are here. And as anxious as we are for you to be here, I write to beg of you not to run any risk in coming. Christopher seems very anxious about you and has told me if the rebels get near here that he would not have you at home for anything in the world. That they are so desperate, there is no telling what they would not do to you. [. . .]

Let what happens I shall stay at home & try to protect every thing unless I should hear the women & children were being murdered, which I do not suppose will be the case. The negroes are watchful & seem to be doing their duty. We will all try to do the best we can & only regret you cannot be with [us] but for God's sake run no risk & stay where you are safest. Cit has visited a little more than usual but I have seen nothing out of the way. He is very anxious for your safety. I shall send this to town hoping some one may go to Frankfort.

Yrs. devotedly,

Ann M. Clay

Ann wrote Brutus again the following day. She had had her valuables buried in anticipation of the arrival of Confederate troops. Years later, my father told me that Cash and Mingo lowered Ann's silver into the cistern in The Lots.

ANN CLAY

Tuesday night [postmarked August 20, 1862]

My Dear Husband,

[. . .] We were all delighted to hear from you, especially Christopher. I suppose you heard from Mr. Holloway that Papa, Ezekiel & wife, Patty Holloway & some other of the children had come here for safety. Reached here at 12 o'clock on Sunday night, saying from all information they supposed by that time Morgan had possession of Richmond. Of course, I was much alarmed and supposed by the next day, he would be here. I have had my silver & bed clothes buried. Christopher thought it advisable. Our relations in Richmond sent me a waggon load of valuables & Papa had intended them to [go to] Cincinnati tomorrow, but the last news is that there are no rebels in Richmond yet and Papa thought he would wait a day or two longer & hoped he would hear from you whether you thought it advisable. He insisted on me [. . .] sending [my silver] with them but Cash & Mingoe thought it [better] buried in a safe place. If I hear of the rebels being near us, I shall have a good deal of bacon buried.

Christopher seems much relieved at your letter. He has not left the place or seen a soul since he came but Sidney [Clay]. He persuaded him [Kit] that he would have to take the oath & I believe he has agreed to do it but if you think it is not necessary, he would prefer not taking it. [. . .]

Zeke F. [Field] says he [Kit] is decidedly south but is very conservative, & he & Brother were both much opposed to burning the cotton. They attempted to hide 300 bales but Mr. Estill informed on them & they now despise him. I think that C. knows that the south intends sending a tremendous army here. Says they are determined to have Ky. [. . .]

[I]f the enemy are to take possession here, I do not want you to come home. Cit says it is well known to them that you are the strongest Union man in the state and that if they do come, they will do you a great deal of harm. [. . .] Write just as often as you can for we are afraid to leave here & are glad to have all the news.

Yours,

Ann M. Clay

[P.S.] We have a watchful guard. They stopped Papa & Co. They told them they were Union friends. [. . .]

Brutus, still in Frankfort, tried to reassure Ann, but even as he was writing, the Confederates were marching through southeastern Kentucky unopposed.

BRUTUS CLAY

Frankfort, Aug. 21, 1862

Dear Ann,

[. . .] I suppose you were a good deal alarmed upon the report of Morgan's second raid in Ky. & more particularly upon seeing your family flying from Richmond. It turns out however they did not reach Richmond & I believe not nearer than London. I think they cannot possibly again reach our section from the direction of Richmond. We now have some 12 or 15 regiments from Indiana & Ohio in Ky. and [more] coming every day. We will soon have a very large force in Ky., such a one that cannot be drawn out by the Rebel forces, & every day's delay will weaken their ability to come into Ky. I suppose they are now making an attack upon Cumberland Gap. But that place is so strong they will not be able to capture [it] very soon. [. . .] The troops are pouring in upon the Covington, Louisville, and Lebanon roads, all in the direction of the Gap. I don't think it necessary to send off any thing to Cincinnati, at least for the present until we see the result of the Richmond battle, & see what course the Rebels will pursue from there. I at this time feel perfectly safe. [. . .] I should like very much to come home on Saturday and will do so, if I can. We have a very important military bill that will come up in the House soon and if there is a probability it will come up on Saturday, I cannot come. [. . .] We are straining every nerve here to meet the Crisis. The Rascals have never had much back[ing] in Ky., and I feel certain they will be soundly whipped whenever they attempt an invasion of Ky. in larger force.

Write often. Let me know what is going on at home. I am glad your family is with you in my absence. I hope they will not be in a hurry to go back to Richmond since they have heard there are no rebels there. Wait until our armies advance beyond Richmond & they will be safe. Tell Cit not to neglect to keep a guard out against house burners & horse thieves.

Yours,

Brutus J. Clay

Ann sent Brutus a letter she had received from her father in Richmond. E. H. Field's letter was dated August 24, five days before the actual Battle of Richmond. "I feel that we are all in the greatest danger," Ann wrote in the margin, "& hope you will soon be at home. I am miserable about Richmond friends, could not sleep last night, I am so weary, because our troops are not drilled & I fear they will all run and do us but little good."

"We arrived at home safely 3 o'clock Friday," Ann's father wrote, "found all well but more excitement than war. Yesterday Col. Metcalfe and the rebels met on the big hill and had a battle. Metcalfe badly defeated. Metcalfe's men last evening running in the utmost disorder until dark.

"At 11 o'clock here last night the rebels were near Richmond on the State Road, sent a flag of truce to Town, demanding a surrender in one hour, if not surrendered the Town was to be burned. Fortunately at that moment, the Indiana Infantry had arrived within two miles at the toll gate and the citizens declined to surrender. We remained in the utmost dread, expecting the shelling, but we think the rebels were informed of the near approach of the Union forces and did not come in. The women and children all left Town. Isabella, Patsey, Wm. Mc-Clanahan, and myself went to Ezekiel's. The county is full of Rebels in every direction and what will be our ultimate fate we do not know."

The first skirmish occurred on August 29 at Big Hill, southeast of Richmond. In ninety-six degree heat, Union troops pulled back toward the city. The Madison Female Institute, which Martha and her cousins had once attended, became a hospital, as did the Holloways' home, from the portico of which the battle must have been clearly visible. Routed, Federal troops withdrew across the Kentucky River.

On August 31, the legislature adjourned because the Confederate army was approaching Frankfort. Its members fled first to Louisville, hoping to reconvene there on September 2, but soon moved on to Cincinnati, as Louisville was threatened by General Smith. Among Brutus's papers are his bills from the Burnet House in Cincinnati, where he stayed during the crisis. A week's board was $14; washing cost 75 cents, as did an extra dinner. By the time Ann wrote him, Union troops had evacuated Paris and the Confederates were in control of Bourbon County.

ANN CLAY

Paris, Sept. 6, 1862

My Dear Husband,

Mr. [W. W.] Embry met on the pike Col. Chiles of one of the Temple regiment, one of the paroled prisoners, & brought him in to rest & he is leaving this morning to try to get into Cin [Cincinnati] & has offered to mail a letter to you. We are doing as well as could be under the circumstances, be there so many rumors. But I am happy to say that we have not yet been disturbed by the rebels, and if we could only hear that you are safe & get a little advice from you, we would get along very well. I would not have you come home for anything in the world. About 4,000 strength in Paris night before last & went on to Cynthiana. But I suppose we have no troops anywhere & are just to be murdered by the rebels. I am miserable about Cash. Cit says he will soon have to go into one army or the other & I want you to think seriously about sending him to Europe to Germany to school. [. . .] Zeke Field came from Richmond last night, says so far they have not been molested but there is the most awful smell there & advises Papa & Mary's family not to go back yet. They have been with me one week. [. . .] Mr. E. came here with his family & fully intended getting with the Union Army but could not & [. . .] expects to leave here today. Cit went to town yesterday to see the rebels & has not come home. I suppose he got to town after they left. They say that Marshall's forces are [with]in two days march of here. Cit says as you are not at home they only arrested Judge Samuels. They hold ten of the Richmond citizens as hostages. [. . .] Write & let us hear from you & do not come home. I will not leave if it is possible for me to stay. Cash has just told me they have taken the Union men [. . .] in the neighborhood. I see nothing amiss in Cit. All are well.

Yrs. devotedly,

Ann M. Clay

A week later, Ann wrote Brutus that Zeke had returned home for the first time since joining the Confederate army.

ANN CLAY

Sept. 10, 1862

My Dear Husband,

Mr. Thomas was so kind as to send me your letter today, as soon as received. I had written twice, thinking you were at Louisville. We are all well, doing as well as we can in your absence & have not been mo-lested or troubled in any way. The evening of the battle at Richmond a good many of my relatives came on, fearing the town would be shelled. But on Monday last they all went home as Papa was so anxious about Mrs. Holloway's affairs. Sister E. remained at home and had a house full of wounded & sent me word. She was nearly crazy with trouble & wrote to know if I had heard anything from Cousin W. [her husband]. Please write if you know anything of him. [. . .] When I heard from Richmond, none of the houses had been disturbed but they had arrested C[urran] Smith, fined him 700$ & held him as a hostage as well as others. [Humphrey] Marshall's cavalry came in on Sunday, the next day Zeke called to see us. Altho I would have preferred his not coming, I was kind to him. He seemed sad, said he was sorry you were not at home, that if you were here you would not be disturbed but, after questioning him, he said they would probably make you take the oath. As anxious as we are to have you here, I would not have you come for anything. [. . .] E[zekiel] said he heard you intended to disinherit him but he would like to have his watch & one of his horses. That if he was not killed, he was strong and able to work. He behaved so well & was not boasting & abusing the Union as C. [Kit] is always doing so I have much more confidence in E. than C. He says we will not be disturbed and that if any of the soldiers should come & demand a horse or any-thing, we must try & find out who they are & they will be punished & the horse returned. He came again today & eat [*sic*] dinner with Cash & me. I told him you have not forgiven him & I hoped whilst here he would do nothing to offend you so he has just left I suppose for good & took no horse. Cash & me have lost confidence in C. He is, I suppose, getting up a company for the army, though when I asked him he said he had not joined & did not know that he would, but I do not believe any-thing he says. E. told me he was getting up a company & I fear when he leaves here he will take what he wants. He is here but little & if he has joined the army, the sooner he leaves here the better. Judge B. [Bedford] & another soldier came here on Sunday & I felt so insulted I could not hold my tongue & though I knew it was imprudent in me I did not want to see one of them, & C. was insulted by my chat to Judge & he has been in a bad humor ever since, says the Union people are mad because the rebels have stole [*sic*] nothing. [. . .] I had the stock all scattered 10 days ago & we are attending to every thing as well as we can but do not know for how long we will be undisturbed. I can't think our gov. in-tends to let us be harmed but still I hope to see the day they are driven back. [. . .] Do not be uneasy about us. But go to some safe place & don't let them get you. [. . .] I do not leave home or send to town. [. . .] So I suppose you know more that is going on than I do in Paris. [. . .] I have seen 3 rebel soldiers, just as many as I want to see. Not knowing the rebels were expected, I went to Paris with Belle [Lyman] to the Dentist and was so completely disgusted with the women that I do not feel like going back. [. . .]

Yours,

A.M.C.

[P.S.] Henry [a slave] would like to hear from you about the wheat. [. . .] Please write to Green. [. . .] He is so anxious about us.

In early September, Green wrote Ann. Although he could scarcely comprehend what was going on in Kentucky, the little news he had gotten made him feel sad and useless. "The latest is that our armies of Va. are all in retreat and many new points in Ky. are occupied by strong forces of guerrillas. Even one report makes them within 25 miles of Lexington. Is it not possible to put the entire state on a defensive footing? Why does not the legislature move in the matter? The state has remained loyal, do they expect by this, to lean on the Federal arm for *home defense?* I was much surprised and I may say mortified to hear that our best citizens must abandon their homes and hide from guerrilla barbarities. [. . .] And I sometimes feel that this is no time for a Kentuckian to be sporting in the courts of Europe."

A Maysville friend, H. G. Bush, wrote to tell Brutus of the Confederates' recruiting activities. "The Rebels are behaving well, only they are pressing young men into Confederate service & holding recruiting meetings all over the country. D. Waller Chenault of Madison is raising a regiment; Joseph T. Tucker of Winchester and T. Brent of Paris are also raising regiments. It is reported that one of your [sons] who has been in the confederate service [Kit] was tendered with a barbecue & dinner at North Middletown yesterday."

Like Martha, Ann made use of every passing traveler to get letters to Brutus.

ANN CLAY

Sept. 13, 1862

My Dear Husband,

Last night about 11 o'clock 5 wounded soldiers came from Richmond, sending me word they were requested by Mrs. Holloway to call. I did not see them and they are not yet up, but thinking perhaps they are going across the Ohio I will write you a few lines. [. . .] Marshall's cavalry went out to the Maysville road yesterday & Cit says to have a fight with [Colonel William Henry] Wadsworth. Perhaps in my other letters I have done C. injustice, as he told me last night he had not joined the army & would not unless forced to. We have not been molested in any way and are getting along as well as we could under the existing times. Please write about the wheat. Henry says he thinks there was too much rye in the oat field to sow the wheat there. C. says you had better get away from Cin. soon as there will be tall fighting there before many days. We are all well but Linden [a slave] expected to die every day. Amy's youngest boy got his hand mashed in the cutting box so badly the Dr. had to cut it off. [. . .]

I hear there are no rebels in town now but passing through about every day. [. . .] One of the gentlemen, Mr. Carey, who is here will take this letter to Cincinnati & if you can tell him anything about Mr. [R. G.] Burton, do so, as Amelia has requested him to try & find out. [. . .]

Yours,

Ann M. Clay

Ann worried about where to get clothes for the servants and urged Brutus to buy himself a new suit.

ANN CLAY

At Home, Sept. 17, 1862

My Dear Husband,

Hoping Mrs. K. [Keiningham] will have another opportunity of sending you a letter, I will write a few lines. We are all in usual health and doing very well considering the time. I am in constant dread of the soldiers coming to steal & demand something but thus far they have not molested us. They have searched the most of our neighbors' houses and, as we have no Lincoln guns [apparently Ann didn't know about the ancient musket], I hope they will not trouble us. Papa & Patty [*sic*] Field came back yesterday to see us. Papa says to get some fresh air. He left all well in Richmond & the air was improving. Indiana sent the day before yesterday 40 ambulances over for the wounded which would be quite a relief to the Citizens. But Papa said Gen. [Kirby] Smith would not permit them to go back by Covington but have to go by Maysville. I am getting quite impatient to hear of our troops driving them back before they get any stronger, as I believe that is the only chance of your getting home. Cit hints they are quite anxious to get you & does not want you to come home. Says they would certainly hold you as a hostage if not worse, says they are very anxious to have the Legislators. He still says he is not getting up a company but will have to make his escape with the army if they are driven back. He stays but little here.

I fear that Metcalfe will prove a great curse to us. Sidney [Clay] re-marked last night that he had made more rebel soldiers than everything else. Judge B. [Bedford] told him if they [the Confederates] were driven back they would take every negro you had. I do not know where E. [Zeke] and his company are.

I can't tell where our negroes are to get clothes & shoes from. There are but few in town & they enormously high & Mrs. K. writes me the merchants do not intend to buy 1 [cent] worth of goods of any kind. You had better go to the tailors on Main Street that made Cash's clothes & get you a common suit of grey or mixed goods to wear at home if you are ever permitted to get home. You have never paid for Cash's clothes. $20.50 cts. [. . .] Do try & write to me. I have only heard once and that was Mrs. K.'s letter. I have written 4 times since. I hope you have received some of them. Linden died on Sunday.

Yrs. devotedly,

A.M.C.

"I hear from our section of the state every few days," Brutus's Union friend wrote from Maysville. "The rebels are generally behaving pretty well. But if they are forced to evacuate Ky., they will devastate our State. I hear they have taken 3 horses and two negro men from me and that they are hopeful they will be able to capture me. They de-nounce me roundly and have sworn eternal vengeance against me & say if they don't catch me they will make me feel their prowess."

By late September, Ann finally received a letter from Brutus. Only Ann's response has survived.

ANN CLAY

At Home, Sept. 25, 1862

My Dear Husband,

Mrs. Keiningham has just sent me your letter dated the 20th, the only one I have received since you left home more than a month ago. I have written to you often but suppose you have received but few of them. We have paid the strictest attention to your wishes, & consider-ing the time I think we are getting along very well. Henry & Mingo are striving to do their best, take a great deal of interest & we have frequent consultations & will do our best to keep things straight. Today a rebel soldier came and asked for something to eat, the first time we have been annoyed since the two of E.'s men came and I gave them such a talk & I do not regret it now as I think it has kept them and others away. Cit says I gave them such a fright that they will be afraid to return here again something wonderful. C. has been very quiet at home for 5 days, threatened with chills & I believe too he is quiet for fear of having to join the army. I do not believe he wants to join & thinks too if they are driven back he will have to go home then. [. . .] He & E. say that you will yet be indebted to your rebel sons for saving your property & everything else before this war is over etc. etc. The latter [Zeke] I believe is at Mt. Sterling though we have had various rumors of Marshall's forces being in Paris yesterday & today. C. says they are going to before many days make some wonderful strategic movements that will astonish the Yanks. You can't imagine what a time Cash & me have. No news but the most favorable to our enemies. I am in constant dread of soldiers coming to search this house, have only left the place one evening for more than a month, & then Papa remained to take charge of things. He was anxious when here last to leave Patty Field so she is now here and I find her a great deal of company and is a good girl. C. & me wish often we were in your place long enough to read the daily paper. I am glad to hear that you are well and in good *spirits* but we cannot feel very cheerful here when we have had nothing but bad news. [. . .]

Cousin A. Bedford sent me word she was coming here this week. Her two sons have joined *the army.* James the one that joined Matt Clay's company & they sent him off to Illinois, came home a few weeks ago a good Union boy but says his mother told him how *dreadful bad* the Union people have been behaving & he determined immediately to join the other side. I would prefer not seeing such people at present. Cit has no visitors of any kind. They are all in the Camp drilling. What a shame that they were ever allowed to come here and get such additions to their number. Do you think they will ever be whipped out?

You have no idea how dry it is here, no rain yet, and Henry says the water is very scarce & the grass dead & short. He is & has been feeding the hogs the old corn on the creek [Brutus's Green Creek farm] & here [. . .] *the stock is yet safe.* No deaths since you left. It is so dry we are *rushing* to get the corn cut up & have been at it for 10 days. As the fodder is wasting, he [Henry] is sowing the wheat in the big field, 55-60 acres. The ground is so hard & dry he is ploughing & harrowing it in and takes as much pains as possible, has sowed the field of rye, but not finished. The army have [sic] pressed all the mills into service, say they must have 200 barrels of flour a day.

From all accounts, I suppose there is nothing in the town to buy. Salt enormously high. I have forbid the stock being salted some weeks ago & keep the key myself but I fear our negroes will suffer for shoes before they can get them. I hear that tea is 3$ a pound. I thought by way of giving you some employment (if you had room in your trunk and any chance of you getting home soon) that you could call on Mr. *Cavanaugh* & get me some tea & a pound of *Indigoe* that I am out of [. . .] & by all means get you some every day winter clothes. You have nothing at home to wear of any kind. Cit says we are now getting a taste of the way the poor Southerners have lived for the last year. I hear nothing from Richmond. I believe Sidney [Clay] went there on Monday last. Hope he will bring me a letter. Do you know any thing of Mr. Burton or Col. Holloway? Papa hurried down to aid in The Store. They were ordered to take their script [Confederate money] there. Suppose they were to come here and order our wheat cleaned out. What could I do? If they stay here much longer they will, I expect, take all the stock. I understand they are paying 1$ of their trash [Confederate money] for that. I shall write every few days to you & hope I shall have a letter often from you but rest satisfied that we will take the best care possible of everything.

Yrs.,

A.M.C.

Ann's letter to Brutus of October 2 contains the first mention in the correspondence of President Lincoln's September 22 Emancipation Proclamation, issued five days after the dreadful battle at Antietam. The proclamation freed only those slaves in the states in rebellion on January 1, 1863; it did not free slaves in Kentucky. Lincoln's interpretation of the Constitution was that he had no power to end slavery in the loyal states. Even so, the proclamation would have long-reaching effects in Kentucky.

ANN CLAY

At Home, Oct. 2, 1862

My Dear Husband,

I hear that Mrs. [Elizabeth] Kennedy is going to O. [Ohio] to see her husband so I will write you a few lines by her. A few days ago, we were a good deal troubled hearing the troops had taken your young cattle on Stoner [Creek], but Henry went over & found the 4 missing ones in with Mr. Lewis', had gone through the Water Gap. As it was reported in town that you had lost 100, I suppose you have heard it before this, but I am happy to inform you that so far we are all safe & nothing taken. C. says all our neighbors have been called on for corn, etc. but us and that you are indebted to your two sons for not being disturbed in any way. But I expect if we had been in their way we would have had to furnish a full portion [. . .], & I have been a little uneasy last night & this morning as I heard M's [Humphrey Marshall] forces camped at G. Bedford's last night. [. . .] They are all moving & concentrating somewhere & from the numbers they have on the border of T. [Tennessee], I fear much our gens. are not prepared for them. Can't you write something to comfort us? Zeke Field spent yesterday here, and as he wanted me to get some medicine from Dr. Ray for Eddie Burnam I went to Mrs. K.'s [. . .], it was a great pleasure to see Mrs. K. I there saw several ladies. All wanted to know what you wrote, said Major W. wrote such doleful letters that they all had the blues & that they would have more confidence in what you said than anyone they knew. I told them you wrote quite cheerfull [sic] & said you were in fine spirits. E. Hickman said she had been crazy to see me to hear from you, that there was no one living whose opinions she would put more confidence in than yours. So if you can possibly, do write something that I can tell them, but then every letter I write I am hoping that you may get home before you receive it. The corn on the place will be finished today but the field on Green Creek is to cut. We are through sowing wheat but not quite the rye. Have had one frost that has reddened the leaves on the sugar trees & then we have had a nice shower of rain this morning that I hope will revive the grass. [. . .] The rebels I understand now [have] 200 sick in town. Mr. Bacon has just commenced a school in the room the loyal ladies held our aid society meetings in & they have taken it from him for a *kitchen* for the sick. [. . .] E. [Zeke] Field heard as he came through Winchester that Groves & Duncan had both changed their views on account of the late [Emancipation] proclamation which is causing some changes everywhere. What a pity to have so little judgment. They always come off at the most improper time.

Cit is better & gone hunting today. [. . .]

[no signature]

On October 4, as Ann was writing Brutus much of the same news she had written two days earlier, some Confederate soldiers arrived at the door asking for food and a place to camp. Greatly agitated, she could scarcely finish her letter.

ANN CLAY

At Home, Oct. 4, 1862

My Dear Husband,

I have just sent a letter to Mrs. Eliz. Kennedy, who I hear will go on Monday to Ohio to see her husband, but for fear she may not get there, I shall write you again & send to Mrs. K. to send to you. [. . .]

When are you all [. . .] to get home? But then you are just as impatient as we are. C. is better. He has gone today to hunt with Mr. [David] Gass [a neighbor]. I do not think he has any idea of joining the army himself, but I suppose has induced all he could to go. [. . .] There has been a good deal of concern about J.B.H. [Junius Holloway]. He was coming from Nashville a few weeks ago, was taken prisoner, 5 other officers with him at the time, he the only one taken [by] the rebels. When he got to Richmond [everyone] was very polite & gracious with him, provided a bigger guard & sent him to Knoxville. From there he will go to Miss. to join his wife & says he does not wish to be exchanged. But he has been offered a Lt. Col. position if he will join them. I, hearing this, sent him word if he did leave the U.S. Army I never wanted to see him. He requested [Ann Holloway] to write me word it was false & he had no idea of it, but his conduct is certainly strange. Says it is only a *Nigger* war.

[. . .] Several soldiers just came up [. . .] to say they are camping in the front pasture & I must cook for 140 & corn for their horses & I have said all I can but they are determined to stay. [. . .] I am so agitated I can scarcely write & have sent to Mr. Gass for Cit. [. . .] I tried to be as polite as I could but some of the vile neighbors have done it. I told them I had not the meat to spare. [. . .]

[no signature]

Despite Ann's fears, the Confederate encampment at Auvergne did little damage. I think I know where they camped, based on my father's story of their visit, as told him by his father. Ann's letter says first that they camped beside the dam on Kennedy's Creek and later "in front of our house." My father told me the soldiers tethered their horses and pitched their tents in a grove of walnut trees along what was then a lane that wound between Brutus's farm and the Bedingers', halfway between the creek and the house. Cash's job was to hide the horses from the soldiers, since they were always looking for fresh mounts. He took them back to Stoner Creek where the land was forested and hid them there until the Confederates left.

Although more and more Union troops were pouring into the state, the Confederates felt secure enough to inaugurate a provisional governor, Richard Hawes of Bourbon County, the man who had insulted Cousin Charles Garrard at the start of the war. After he was inaugurated, Hawes announced that the Confederates would hold the state at all costs, but four hours later he and his government fled Frankfort.

ANN CLAY

At Home, Oct. 9th [1862]

My Dear Husband,

Hearing the town was quiet & no soldiers there, I ventured in since dinner to see Mrs. K. & to hear the news, if any, & there found your letter dated Oct. 1. [. . .] I hope you have received my letters telling of Grove's men camping in front of our house last Saturday night. The next day I rode around to see what damage & it was difficult to tell where they had been. A few rails taken off of [. . .] part of the fence. They opened a gap at our gate at the lane & camped principally on [the] Dam for the convenience of the water. Henry hauled them 6 barrels of corn & some hay but they were so quiet and orderly that I feel very thankful. [. . .] I hope when our army get in they will behave. There was all sorts of bad news in town this evening, that Buell had been cut all to pieces, had 17,000 prisoners taken [the Battle of Perryville, where there were tremendous losses on both sides, but Buell drove the Confederates back]. McClellan been whipped in Virginia, too. But I have got so I do not believe anything I hear. [. . .]

Hearing the troops & all had left town on Saturday I could not help but look for you for the last two days. But there was 150 cavalry came to town whilst I was there & I hear it will still be dangerous for you to come as I hear Maj. W.'s house was searched three times for him. [. . .] [D]o not run any risk & stay away till you can come back open[ly]. Cit is at home & says he will stay here as long as he can, has no more desire than I have to go into the army. There is a very happy change in him since the troops left, quieted and pleasant. But seems to fear that when our troops come that he will have to run. What do you think about it? Please write word; he would prefer staying if he can. He is better but still as yellow as a pumpkin [jaundice?]. I called at Mrs. Kennedy's gate. She told me a handbill had been sent there signed by Jim Clay [a neighbor] saying the state was to be conscripted. What am I to do about Cash? He hunts some with Cit but remains very close at home, has not been to town & did not even go where those men were on Saturday night. Two stayed at the house & did not allow their men to come here so we did not even lose a chicken. C. has taken possession of G.'s [Green's] horse and the sorrel as he said several had their eye on them. I have not seen E. [Zeke] for three weeks. Then he left two broke down horses here & rode off one of the work horses. C. says when his rests [he] will return it. I regretted that he took it but could not help it & I expect we are indebted to him for not being disturbed in every other way. He acted very well. We are all doing the best we can & trying to watch & take care of everything & Mingoe [sic] & Henry are doing their part. I forbid the men going to town except on Saturday night, and all seem to be attentive to their work. [. . .] I was so glad you were willing to get the *shoes* as I feared the negroes would suffer for them, & I will send you a list in this letter as Mingoe is making out a list, & I would be so glad to get some jeans & linsey but I fear you have not seen any of the kind that I buy as in the best times I give 65 cts. for the jeans. Please inquire at the *wholesale stores* the price of Eastern-made linsey. [. . .] I feel that I have a good deal to begin on as I shall use C's box of clothing [the one that never made it to Mississippi] when necessary. C. bought some negro jeans to make himself a suit as he could get nothing else, gave 3$ a yard, what I usually give 65 [cts.] for. If you buy our negroes shoes, Mrs. K. wishes you to buy some for her & will send a list in this letter. [. . .] I am almost barefooted myself but as I stay at home so close am wearing the old cast-off ones. [. . .] These are awful times. The Union men running for fear of the conscript. The Secesh also running for fear of the Lincoln troops. I hope you will soon have the liberty of your own home. I am always anxious & uneasy in yr. absence but would hate to see you at home to be carried off south, but do not believe any report you hear about us as I know already a great many have been stated here that were not true. [. . .] Sidney [Clay] was here Sunday, very low down, would give a good deal to see you, regrets he did not go to see you when he went with Mrs. French to Maysville about the proclamation, etc. etc. etc.

[no signature]

She enclosed Mingo's list of 69 pairs of shoes, plus his request for a special pair for himself.

As the Confederates withdrew, life became more tranquil. Brutus's sister, Eliza Smith, wrote Ann in October, "We were much disappointed that you did not get up to see us again. I intended to send Speed [her son] down with the carriage for you, but he had rode one of the horses out to the *drill*. [. . .] We all went out to the Drill Saturday. Mother enjoyed it very much, would shake hands with some of the Soldiers, went to Clay's [Smith] tent, said the ride and looking at them helped her and intended going again. [. . .] Mother says give her love to you all. And tell Cassius she thanks him for the birds, that she always enjoys them very much."

Finally a letter arrived from Brutus.

BRUTUS CLAY

Maysville, Oct. 14th, 1862

Dear Ann,

I met an Irishman today who has promised to take this to you & who will start soon. I arrived here several days ago, intending to go right on home, but upon reflection I concluded to remain a while until it may be entirely safe. [. . .] Your letter about the shoes I received here since my arrival. I do not expect to go back to Cincinnati. I purchased while there a suit of clothes for myself, four dozen pairs of negro shoes, 200 yds. of negro jean, 200 of linsey, and 200 yds. of negro cotton which will be sent up as soon as the road is safe. I did not know what you wanted, but concluded to buy such items that I knew you used a good deal of. The shoes I had also to "guess" at as to sizes. As I do not know what letters you have received I urge again the propriety of keeping watch over my Horses, both day & night, to prevent groups of two or three men from stealing them. Let some of the negroes do nothing but watch. Tell Christopher to shoot any rascal who may be caught stealing. Tell him all the protection I want from my rebel son is to shoot the rogues who come to steal either day or night. The Rebels will not have much longer to stay there & I understand it is the new recruits for the rebel army who are stealing horses. As to Christopher staying when the Union army comes, it will depend upon his acts since he has been there [. . .] if he has followed my advice, there will be no danger, but it seems my sons are disposed to follow the advice of every *scamp* in the country [. . .] in preference to that [advice] given by me. Just as he has acted he will be dealt with. I sent word to you by Mr. Kennedy to keep Cash out of the way for fear they might want to put him in the army but I do not think there is much danger, [and] yet it is best for him to be on his guard. [. . .] We have been generally successful everywhere lately. The Rebels have been badly whipped in Maryland, Missouri, & lately at Corinth, Mississippi [. . .] and our news from Buell & Bragg near Perryville, by way of Louisville, is that Bragg has been beaten badly & is retreating to Camp Robinson. There was a fight in Versailles. The rebels took the county and 150 prisoners, & our Army is on the march from Covington to Paris & Lexington, & I suppose is about two thirds of the way up. You may look for them in a few days at Paris. [. . .] You might send John frequently to town at night and learn all about the movements of the Rebels, also when our troops arrive there. I do not know when I shall come home. It will depend upon what I learn from Paris as to when our Friends think it safe for us to come. [. . .]

B. J. Clay

In addition to shoes for the slaves, Brutus purchased a number of other items in Cincinnati. From R. M. Bishop, "Wholesale Grocers and Commission Merchants," he bought a bag of choice coffee for $16.25, two barrels of different kinds of sugar for $26.01 and $18.67, respectively, and $1.75 worth of currants. From A. McDowell, a dealer in carpets, oilcloths, and matting, he bought 41 yards of carpet for $45. Earlier in the year, he had bought more than $80 worth of salt from a local representative of the Kanawha Salt Company and $14 worth of machine parts (probably for his mills) from W. W. Mitchell Sr.

Ann was still looking for a letter from Brutus or, better still, Brutus himself.

ANN CLAY

Tuesday at Mrs. K's [no date]

My Dear Husband,

I came to town this evening to see if I could hear anything of you, as I could not help but look for you ever since I heard you were in Maysville. [. . .] We have been so disappointed that our troops have not come as yet. Mrs. Keiningham sends her love & says she is very anxious to see you at home but that you must not come yet. That she was talking with some Union men this morning & they say it would be madness for you to come yet. Of course you will know when the army will get in. Cit is quite anxious for you to come but he says he knows it will be dangerous yet, as he says the rebels are still scouting about. He is quite uneasy and says he does not know what to do and must see you. Said if you cannot come soon he must try and go to see you. He says he must have some money [and] that his southern money will not pass. What ought he to do? He is now very quiet & I know he does not want to join the army & if he goes home, I suppose he will have to do it & he is afraid to stay here when our troops come in. [. . .] He says if he is taken and paroled he is considered a soldier & if exchanged would have to go into the army. [. . .] We are quite anxious to see you but I feel that you have been away too long now to be caught as soon as you come, & of course we are getting very impatient for our troops to come in and think they are a long time getting here. I want to hear of the Secesh flag being [taken] down in town. I have never been in town on the street since it has been there. [. . .]

[no signature]

Slowly the rebels retreated from Kentucky through the eastern mountains. There was heavy snow throughout the state in late October, as much as twelve inches, and the poorly clad soldiers suffered horribly. The provisional Confederate government also fled; Governor Hawes's house in Paris was seized by Federal troops and turned into a hospital. Skirmishes continued into November, but the state was once again under Federal control. Treason trials began immediately; there were 195 indictments in Bourbon County alone.

In Washington, President Lincoln met with border-state legislators and urged them to support the Emancipation Proclamation when it went into effect on New Year's Day 1863. It was, he said, a war measure against the states in rebellion. Although the proclamation exempted the border states as well as those portions of Tennessee, Louisiana, and Virginia that were controlled by the Union army, it opened the door to the enlistment of slaves in the Union forces, a liberating force no one in Kentucky had anticipated.

The first year we lived in Bourbon County, I came home from school one day and told my mother that Lincoln had started the Civil War. She turned on me angrily. "Is that what they're teaching you in that school?" I had never seen her so furious. I demurred. "Not exactly." Her violent response had frightened me.

To this day, I don't know why I made such a remark. We were studying Kentucky history, but I don't remember my teacher telling us that Lincoln had started the Civil War. Perhaps I was testing my mother. I knew she hadn't wanted my brother and me to go to the local school and had talked of teaching us herself at home. I may have overheard someone say Lincoln started the war. Or perhaps it was something more subtle, a reflection of the betrayal many white Kentuckians felt over the Emancipation Proclamation. Most of them hadn't understood what the war was really about until 1863. Then they discovered that it had nothing to do with their high-flown rhetoric about the Union. It was a war for the freedom of their slaves.

"A Nigger war," June Holloway had said when he was considering changing sides.

NINE

A Hurrah for Clay

After the uncertainty created by the Confederate raids during the summer and fall of 1862, people in Kentucky settled into the long slow slog of life characteristic of a country at war. Some things changed very little.

Brutus's cattle continued to multiply. Emily Tubman calved on the twenty-third of August, Speculation on the twenty-ninth. On the same day, Pearl was bred to Kentucky Duke. On September 4, Napoleon served both Julia and Fanny.

So did his slaves. Returning a rented servant, a neighbor wrote Brutus on Christmas day, 1862, "I send Lotty, Rilla [not the Rilla who went to Texas before the war], & the children home today. If you want me to have them the next year send me the price by *Bill* this evening. Rilla, if I am not mistaken, is likely to increase your number in a few months."

But slaves no longer behaved like slaves, as Patsey Miller complained to Ann.

PATSEY MILLER

Sunday, Jan. 4th, 1863

Dear Ann,

[. . .] It seems dear Sister my troubles are never to end. Ben [a slave] walked himself off on Friday. James [Patsey's son] was in town at the

Ball Thursday night and did not get home till late Friday evening. [. . .] James concluded he [Ben] would be hid at his wife's house that night so got a man to go there as soon as he got home from town, confidently expecting he would be there but had only gone by and got a bundle of clothes and went on. James then went yesterday before day to town expecting to find that Andrew's wife [a slave] was secreting him or that he was in the Camp but no Ben. Instead of keeping on as I urged him as fast as he could go to Paris, he came back home last night, and this morning (Sunday) [. . .] he started for your home and on to Paris, I fear he is too slow. He has let him get the start of him too long, two days and nights, and will never get him. I reckon they will never do us much more good and need not so much regret the loss but I shall dislike it so much if he does not get him. [. . .] And I dislike it the more as I must bear the blame or gave [sic] him a very slight excuse. He [Ben] went off Christmas eve to his wife's house and stayed eight nights successively. When he came in New Year's morning to make my fire, I was taking the matter very calmly [. . .] [said] how badly they had all behaved [. . .], no one to make me a fire, he began to talk very short to me. I told him not to give me any impudence or I would send for James Miller to make him know his place. The next morning he went off. [. . .] I went to town Tuesday to meet Miss Brown [a new teacher], and although nearly all the troops from Richmond passed us on a forced march to Danville yet I had no idea of the excitement ensued by Morgan till I got to town. [Morgan's cavalry was skirmishing in the southeastern part of the state.] [. . .] I hope Miss Brown may be all and even more than Cousin Eliza says and that Pattie [Field] and all may do well with her. Martha [Miller] still seems so little like getting well that boarders will be quite a handfull with the servants I have, but my children must be at school and I turned it over many times in my mind and no other way presented itself to me that would suit as well for my own family. [Patsey was taking in boarders in order to pay for her children's schooling.] [. . .] I hope James may not get into trouble over Ben. I tell him his mother being free he has gone right there [Bourbon County]. [. . .] He [James] was going by to get Cit's help. [. . .]

Affectionately yours,

P.I.M.

There were political changes, too. Pro-Southern Governor Magoffin had resigned; Lieutenant Governor James F. Robinson reconvened the legislature on January 8.

As a member of the legislature, Brutus acquired numerous correspondents and advisers, one of them Judge William Cassius Goodloe. Judge Goodloe was related to Brutus by several marriages, and his son, Will, had served with Green as one of Cassius Clay's secretaries in Saint Petersburg. Kentuckians such as Brutus and Judge Goodloe opposed secession, but they also questioned the legality of the Emancipation Proclamation. They wanted the slavery question to be set aside until after the war against the Confederacy had been won. This letter, though found in an envelope addressed to Brutus in Frankfort, seems to have been written to someone else.

WILLIAM CASSIUS GOODLOE

Richmond, Janry. 11th, 1863

Dear Osborne,

In visiting town on yesterday I was very much surprised to find the Union men down upon Gov. Robinson's message. They thought we had nothing to do with the President's Emancipation Proclamation as it did not affect Slavery in Kentucky & the only influence of the message was to strengthen the rebellion. Not a few of them charged him as being half rebel. In the common mind there are but two parties — the Union Party and the rebels. [. . .] This unreasoning view controlls [sic] public opinion & action & must be heeded in all of our political moves. [. . .] It is best for the Legislature to give the subject the go by. [. . .] We have a Governor, Lt. Governor [. . .] to elect on August next. Is it not time we were moving in favor of a 22cd of Feby. convention to nominate candidates? The last time I conversed with Gov. Robinson he expressed a fixed purpose not to permit the further use of his name. I presume the party would prefer [Joshua F.] Bell anyway as he was our last standard bearer. [. . .]

This is not intended for publication. [. . .]

Very truly yours,

W. C. Goodloe

Another adviser was Brutus's brother-in-law Madison C. Johnson, now president of the Northern Bank of Kentucky. "In regard to the State Stock in the Banks, I would say this," Johnson replied to Brutus's inquiry, "that I regard Bank Stocks as precarious property in war times. It would not be difficult to ruin any Bank during war. It is true all property is precarious but as all the assets of the Bank consist of debts due it and money, they are being put in jeopardy by all destruction of property, all robberies, and all bankruptcies and confiscations. I think therefore a solvent individual would do well to discharge his debts with his Bank Stock. Considering the state in the same light as a solvent individual, the same remark would apply to it."

Brutus was in Frankfort from January 8 until March 3. His board at A. G. Hodges's Capital Hotel there cost him $100. From there, he wrote Ann about work he wanted done on the farm.

He added, "We are doing but little as yet in the legislature. Our members are not all in of yet. Tell [Emma] Hickman when you see her that I think they will go on well here. She need have no fears, we shall disapprove Lincoln's Proclamation in *moderate tones* & that will be all. We will not do it in such a manner as to give offense but we will do it as a matter of *principle* as the proclamation is not aimed at Ky. It is a matter more between Lincoln and the Rebel States. And we will leave the quarrel between them."

Now that things had calmed down in Kentucky, Cash went back to school. His first letter home, written to Kit in late January, consisted of unrelated sentences such as "Keep Sid the dog and don't let anybody from Madison have him" and "The Vicinity of Frankfort poorest place for game in Ky." He added, "Don't suppose you will go to Mississippi soon."

Instead of going to Mississippi, Kit took charge of the farm for his father. His letters to Brutus about life on "the Plantation" fall into a category of letters from home that my brother and I used to call "the bull died and the horse broke a leg." These letters were usually written by my mother, a recitation of rural disasters including animal deaths, droughts, and crop failures.

Reading these nineteenth-century letters, particularly Kit's, I am reminded of the ones from home I used to open in the living room of my college dormitory in Northampton, Massachusetts. They were like missives from a foreign country, as unreal as the communications an

African exchange student might receive from home. There I sat, surrounded by girls from suburban Connecticut who were planning their weekends at Yale, reading that the sheep had developed maggots. Often I simply folded up the letter and stuck it in the pocket of my jeans, unread.

My college friends had discovered to their vast amusement that my father signed his letters "Affectionately Your Father." I never thought much about this before arriving at Smith. It was simply the way my father signed his letters. But I began to wonder how a father could be so verbally distant from his only daughter. What was the matter with him? It wasn't until I started reading the Clay-Field letters, years after his death, that I understood why my father had signed his letters that way. His father had signed his letters that way.

CHRISTOPHER CLAY

Bourbon County, Ky. Feb. date forgotten, 1863

Dear Pa,

I have sit [sic] down to write you without anything of interest to communicate. As usual we are doing but little on the Plantation, working about two days a week, weather to [sic] disagreeable for farming. We are plowing here & at the upper place when we possibly can which for the past three weeks is not worth notice. Stock of all kinds doing tolerably well except the sheep. We have lost a good many. Two of the fine sheep in the calf pasture died, from what cause we don't know. We have about 1/2 dozen lambs. They seem to look well so far. We have been cribbing corn when the weather suits. [. . .] Negroes in good health while they have nothing to do but eat and sit in the house. We are still feeding all the poor cattle fodder & feed. The fat cattle what[ever] they will eat. We have six of the jenny mules working very well, two yet unbroke, and one of them very badly horned in the breast by one of the work oxens, done by carelessness while hitching. I believe nothing more of interest going on on the Plantation. The troops at Mt. Sterling had a little skirmish on last Saturday with the *rebs*, captured 11 *rebs* & horses. The federals had one man wounded & five missing. Nothing more from that quarter as yet. [. . .] I can see nothing from the papers [about what] you are doing in Frankfort. I suppose but little. I see [sic]

Col. [John] Prall [state senator from Bourbon and Bath Counties] in Paris yesterday but suppose will return to Frankfort soon. Nothing more at present. All in usual health at home.

I am in haste
Yours truly,

Christopher F. Clay

"I am again on the wing as a refugee," William Holloway wrote Brutus from Lexington in February. "1000 Rebel Cavalry were reported marching on our Town this morning and I fear they are backed by a larger force, probably [General James] Longstreet's Command." Since business at the The Store was poor, "owing to our national troubles," he had applied for a job as a paymaster with the Union army. "I have been nominated by the President and probably confirmed by the Senate before this. [. . .] Mr. Field will be one of my Securities and I will ask the favor of you to be the other. [. . .]"

June Holloway had returned to active service with the Federal army. He owed $350 to his Uncle Brutus, promising to "send [him] the money from Nashville."

Writing Brutus about financial matters, old Ezekiel Field remarked on March 7, "Our friends who had so many servants and horses so long at your house lately regret very much the necessity for that stampede. I hope you have escaped any further damage from the traitors and thieves. We are measurably quiet here now. The Rebel General [. . .] [Kirby Smith] did not stay long enough to do much damage except taking all the good horses near the road they went over." As an afterthought, he gave the usual gloomy assessment of his health. "I have been confined a week with weakness in my back."

Another of Brutus's political correspondents was David Goodloe, Judge Goodloe's brother and the husband of Brutus's niece, Sally Smith. He wrote urging Brutus to attend a meeting prior to the Union Democracy Party's state convention. Earlier, the Democrats had attempted to hold a convention, but Union military officials disbanded it, the first of many acts of high-handedness that were to alienate Kentuckians from the Lincoln administration. "The Buckner-Wickliffe party [Democrats] has called a meeting to consider the resolutions we have laid on the table on next Saturday 11 o'clk," Goodloe told Brutus on March 11. "And many of our friends have urged me to write you to be there at that time and address the meeting. [. . .] Think you could be of service to us and promote our political intent."

Meeting in Louisville on March 18 and 19, the Union Democrats nominated an old Whig, Joshua F. Bell, for governor. Brutus was also a candidate but got only nineteen votes. A little more than a month later, Bell withdrew and Colonel Thomas E. Bramlette, who had recently resigned from the Union army, took his place.

In March, Brutus's stepfather, Jeptha Dudley, died. E. A. Dudley, a relative, urged Brutus to come to Frankfort to help his mother with her husband's estate. "Aunt Sally has been quite feeble, I believe. [. . .] I think your presence and advice would aid in *our material efforts to promote in all things her comfort & her wishes.*"

June Holloway was having trouble repaying Brutus. "The Paymasters of this Department have gone to Washington to draw funds and on their return will forward you the amount," he wrote in April. "I have not drawn any pay from the Govt. since last November."

He also sent news from army headquarters. "I fear [General William S.] Rosecrans will have to fall back on Nashville as a heavy force of the enemy have appeared on his right flank, with the intention of cutting his line of communication and supplies. The enemy have been largely reinforced from the Potomac. I do hope the Govt. will abandon the idea of attacking Vicksburgh and reinforce this Army with Grant's troops. [General Green] Clay Smith is winning considerable notoriety here. He has had several successful skirmishes with the Rebels. Several Kentucky officers were arrested today, charged with smuggling goods to the Rebels. The wife of a U.S. officer was arrested yesterday on the Louisville & Nashville Railroad with $9000 worth of quinine for the rebels. She was put in the Penitentiary and heavily ironed."

Sally Dudley continued to be frail. For the rest of her life, she remained in the care of her widowed daughter, Eliza Smith. "Sister [Paulina] Rodes and myself have just got here and expect to go to Frankfort this evening," Eliza wrote Brutus from Lexington on April 7, "and want you if you *please* to come down to Frankfort and try to persuade Mother to leave there at once. [. . .] We think you have more influence with her than we have."

June Holloway was in and out of trouble throughout the war. In June of 1863, he was arrested for "uttering treasonable language." The amazing thing about June was that he always seemed to emerge from these scrapes with a new and better military appointment.

JUNIUS HOLLOWAY

Nashville, Tenn., June 30th, 1863

Dear Uncle,

I have been intending writing to you for some time in regard to the note you hold against me. I have had a good deal of trouble for several weeks past with the authorities here. I was arrested on the 1st June by two Detective Police for uttering treasonable language. I was taken to the Penitentiary by them and kept there for several days. Through the influence of Gov. [Andrew] Johnson [of Tennessee], I was released from the Penitentiary and kept in close confinement until today. I refuted the charges brought against me and have just received orders to go to Washington. I have drawn no pay from the Govt. for several months but will be able to draw my pay when I reach Washington. I am exceedingly sorry that I was unable to liquidate the note when it became due. If the Govt. does not pay me, I will dispose of some property I have and pay you at once. One charge against me was for being in Nashville for the purpose of taking my wife's negroes South to sell, all of which was a falsehood. My wife has some very insolent negroes and I advised her to let me take them to Louisville and sell them. The negroes heard of it and reported to the detectives I was going south with them. I will write you as soon as I reach Washington. [. . .] I have been appointed Col. of an East Tennessee Regiment by Gov. Johnson, but will not take the field until the first of August.

Affectionately your nephew,

Junius B. Holloway

In Kentucky, Unionists were involved in an exciting campaign to elect a governor and congressmen. Although their opponents, the Peace Democrats, and their candidate, Charles A. Wickliffe, had practically been driven underground by the Union army, Unionists felt it important to carry the state by a large percentage of the vote. On July 10, Governor Robinson banned alleged secessionists from voting.

On July 26, a little more than a week before the vote, John J. Crittenden, the congressional candidate from the Seventh District — Henry Clay's old bailiwick — died. The Union Democrats replaced him on the ballot with Brutus Clay. Brutus was not the convention's unanimous choice. His friend Madison C. Johnson won on the fourth ballot but declined the nomination. Brutus then won on the fifth, defeating his opponent by ten votes. Brigadier General Jeremiah T. Boyle, the head of the military district of Kentucky who had political ambitions, refused to abide by the convention's choice. Five days before the election he announced that he, too, would be a candidate, making it a three-way race.

Despite this less-than-united front, many Unionists, such as L. B. Todd of Lexington, wrote Brutus to congratulate him and offer their support. "When our greatest Statesman has been called from the Arena in which he has performed a past so noble, glorious, distinguished and useful, it is fitting that his place should be filled by one worthy and Capable and equal to the emergency, such as our Community believe you to be," he told Brutus. "Our party are perfectly united upon yourself. I think your opponents will receive but few, very few votes. We are ardent in your support, and by *promptness, vigilance and industry* at the Polls entertain not a shadow of a doubt concerning your election."

Brutus had but a few days to put together a campaign organization. On July 29, he issued a declaration of principles, containing a clear statement of where he stood on slavery.

To the Voters of the 7th Congressional District

In accepting the nomination by the Union Convention as candidate for Congress in the Ashland District, in place of the lamented Mr. Crittenden, it may be proper that I should make a short statement of my political principles in regard to the present crisis.

I am, and always have been, for the preservation of the Constitution and the Union, and for the vigorous prosecution of the war to subdue the Rebellion, which threatens their overthrow. If elected, I will vote for the necessary measures to carry on the war to the extent of the national power and resources. To my mind, it would be far wiser, at once to acknowledge the success of the Rebellion, and make a treaty for separation, than to insure it triumph, and the degradation of the loyal States, by refusing to vote the means of sustaining the military strength of the nation.

At the same time, I am opposed to the policy of the Administration, as to the abolition of slavery, and the enlisting of slaves as soldiers, and while in the State Legislature, I voted for the various resolutions which were passed, condemning those measures.

But I do not regard Revolution, or Secession, or a submission to the Rebellion, as the remedies for that evil policy, they being evils, incomparably greater. The remedies are in the Union, and under the Constitution and laws, through the Legislatures and Judicial Tribunals. Should the Union be restored, it would be for the courts of the slave states to decide upon the legal effects of the President's Proclamation of Emancipation.

Until the Union shall be restored, the rebels, while depredating upon the commerce of the loyal citizens, on the Ocean, and upon the property of the citizens of Kentucky, Missouri, and other loyal states, in their predatory raids, cannot rightfully complain that their property in slaves is not respected more than other property, by the armies of the Union. I am not and have never been in favor of emancipation, either gradual, immediate or compensated.

I was a member of the Union Convention which assembled in Louisville, in March last, and voted for the platform of principles they adopted, and intend so far as they apply, to be guided by them should I be honored with a seat in Congress.

I should hail with joy any disposition manifested by the people of the Rebellious States, or any of them, to return, in *good faith*, to their lawful allegiance, and in that event would support all measures to facilitate the resumption of all their rights and privileges under the Constitution.

In the short period before the election, it will be impossible for me to visit the various Counties in the District, or to see but few of the voters; but if time allowed it would afford me pleasure to defend and sustain my position before you in public discussion. As this cannot take place, I thought it better that you should fully and fairly understand my principles than the argument and reasons by which they are sustained.

BRUTUS J. CLAY

July 29th, 1863

Among Brutus's papers are notes made in preparation for appearances during the brief campaign. The most concise are points to be refuted, written by his friend and supporter John L. Scott, a Frankfort lawyer: "1. They say you was [sic] not friendly toward Mr. Crittenden, 2. That you will probably vote for a Black Republican speaker of the House of Representatives, 3. That you are an emancipationist etc., 4. That the Convention was gotten up in haste, & was unfair. You would do well to answer these charges."

On the eve of the election, General Ambrose E. Burnside declared martial law throughout the state, ostensibly to preserve order during the election and prevent disloyal men from voting. Anyone wishing to vote who could not establish his loyalty would be arrested and required to take an oath that he had never been in the Confederate army or in any way aided the rebellion.

Brutus won the August 3 election handily, with nearly twice as many votes as either of his opponents, Boyle and Democrat Richard A. Buckner. Unionists swept the state, electing a governor, Thomas E. Bramlette, and nine congressmen, one of whom was Brutus's nephew General Green Clay Smith. However, the election was seriously tainted by military intimidation. Many people were afraid to vote.

Letters from Brutus's lieutenants in various counties capture the campaign's flavor. Reading them I am reminded of the campaigns in which my father was involved when I was a child.

In the early 1950s my father helped to defeat a call for a new constitutional convention. The issues were complicated and difficult to explain to the voters, particularly in mountain counties where many had little or no education. Letcher County, at the time one of the poorest in the state, was a particular problem, so my father hired the father-in-law of one of our tenants, Old Man Rogers, to travel through the county in which he had been born and tell people why they should vote against a constitutional convention. The opponents of a new constitution won, nowhere more handily than in Letcher County.

Old Man Rogers came by the following Saturday afternoon to tell my father about his part in the campaign and submit his expense account. My father was at his desk in the Queen Anne sitting room, which he used as an office, and Old Man Rogers, a wiry little man who spoke with a mountain accent (a mare mule in Mr. Rogers's lingua franca was a "mar-mule"), was seated in a rocking chair. I was curled up at one end of the leather sofa in the corner, reading *My Friend Flicka*, a book I reread at least once a month in those days.

Old Man Rogers had hired a mar-mule and ridden into all the distant hollows, stopping at each house to give his spiel on the new constitution. My father pressed him for details. What had he told people about the constitution? I looked up from my book to see what Mr. Rogers would say.

"I told 'em if they voted for a new constitution the Roosians would come over," Old Man Rogers replied. "And then I said," he lowered his voice dramatically, "and you know what the Roosians does to wimmen."

The first letter to Brutus is from his Frankfort ally, John Scott.

JOHN SCOTT

Simpson & Scott, Frankfort, Ky., Aug. 5, 1863

Hon. Brutus J. Clay:

As you was [sic] here last Friday and learned something of the character of the split in the Union party in this county, especially as between yourself and Gen. Boyle, [. . .] I must tell you how the two wings managed the short campaign from Friday until Monday evening. The whole of Friday, Saturday and Sunday, the Boyle men had their runners throughout the county denouncing the convention, declaring that you was not secure on the slavery question, and winding the harangue up by pulling out a few hundred dollar bills, and offering to bet that you would not get 50 votes in Franklin County, as that you would be the hindmost man in the race.

Col. Hodges, Wm. A. Gaines & myself & others saw the necessity for meeting and counteracting these movements. On Saturday morning we learned that the Hutchinson family at Bald Knob (the controlling influence there) had been secured for Boyle. I knew a man of whom the whole Hutchinson family stood in fear — he had whipped one or two of them some years since — so I employed him to take several hundred of your circulars & tickets and ride day and night through the Bald Knob precinct and place them privately and quietly in the hands of every voter in the precinct. He started about 11 o'clock on Saturday and rode until 2 o'clock on Monday morning, when he laid down and slept until 5 & then started for the polls at Bald Knob to see the result. The 4 Hutchinsons walked up and voted for Boyle as soon as the polls opened — then some 5 or 6 Boyle men came up and voted — indeed I believe the Boyle vote run [sic] up to 10 or 11 before you received a single vote — then the men commenced coming in with your cards and tickets — one voted for you, another, another — the men we had sent there kept up such a hurrah for Clay that I believe Boyle did not get another vote during the day. Indeed the excitement in your favor run so high that by noon it is said that one or two of the Hutchinsons who had voted against you early in the morning were working for you with all their might.

We pursued nearly the same course in every precinct in the county, and the result is a majority of 499 for you. Considering the character of the split in the Union party here — the monied men and other influences brought to bear against you, I think we did nobly in this county. At one time we almost trembled before the faction that opposed your election, but we felt that we were right and must prevail, and went to work with all our energies, and have triumphed gloriously. [. . .]

Very respectfully,

John L. Scott

The next letter is from Brutus's kinsman David Goodloe.

DAVID S. GOODLOE

Lexington, Ky. August 5/63

Hon. B. J. Clay

Dear Sir,

The loyal heart of this Community is rejoicing over your election. There never was [the] same amt. of *Villainy* resorted to in same length of time to defeat you — A dispatch from Gov. Robinson to C. A. Wickliffe — saying I leave for Georgetown to vote the Union Ticket and elect Buckner for Congress — was printed and circulated in Clark County and other points. Also Woodford and Jessamine. Dispatches from Boyle saying he would get *two thousand* 2000 votes majority on the other side of the river was extremely circulated. In Harrodsburg a dispatch was received signed *H. Shaw* saying B. J. Clay was no longer a *candidate* — vote for Boyle — was circulated. All of which *was false*. We have a copy of the dispatch and have written for the original. Never was a party so badly used upon before. [. . .]

I have not got in all expenses but will have considerable funds left for you — will advise you when completed.

[. . .] Mr. Vance has just arrived from Harrodsburg and says Genl. Boyle had it announced by friends that you was the nominee of a *bogus convention* and that he was the nominee of the regular convention. Yet you ran ahead of him until the dispatch arrived stating that you was no longer a candidate, to go for Boyle. Then Boyle got nearly all, that his majority will be about 200. [. . .] Boyle was boisterous and threatening. Denouncing [. . .] Vance and Judge Goodloe & myself for our agency in this matter. Saying that he would have had no trouble but for us. Vance is taking depositions to prove Boyle's threats to the judges of the election. I know some of them and think Boyle will not hold his *Commission long*. When will you be up? Your friends here will be glad to see you.

Yours truly,

D. S. Goodloe

The next writer, A. G. Hodges, edited the Union Democracy's newspaper, *Commonwealth*.

A. G. HODGES

Frankfort, Aug. 5, 1863

B. J. Clay Esq.

Dear Sir:

I take great pleasure in congratulating you upon your very successful race for Congress in this district. I doubt not, if your life shall be spared, you will so discharge the duties of your high position, that you will reflect honor upon your country and upon yourself.

The official vote of this county is as follows:

Brutus J. Clay	596
Gen. J. T. Boyle	97
R. A. Buckner	176

[. . .] We have succeeded in our own county greatly beyond our expectations, considering we had some of our most able electioneers doing what they could to advance the cause of Genl. Boyle. However, on the day you left here, we employed some 6 or 8 active, energetic men, and sent them into every part of the county, and caused your address to the People to be placed in the hands of almost every voter. We treated the friends of Genl. Boyle with great kindness and consideration. Let them do the bragging, and all that sort of thing, whilst we worked quietly, and as the result has proved, with great efficiency.

The one hundred dollars left with me by you has been used. [. . .] Any additional expense, we intend paying it ourselves.

Yours truly,

A. G. Hodges

P.S. I feel it due to Col. John M. Harlan [later Supreme Court justice] to say that after his arrival at home on Saturday, we were greatly aided by himself, personally, in securing the majority for you in this county. He went, on Sunday night, about 1 o'clock, to one of our most important precincts, and remained there until nearly all the votes were polled for you. He remarked to Mr. Gaines, one of your most active friends, that he owed you a debt of gratitude for your exertions for himself when he was a candidate for Congress, and he was glad of an opportunity to reciprocate for it.

A.G.H.

A. G. Hodges wrote three days later with further congratulations and added, "As far as heard from there are but three *no-more-men-and-no-more-money* men elected to the Legislature — and upon my veracity as a man, if I were either of them [*sic*], I would resign my seat and go home, and ask some genteel Union man to kick me out of the county, and if practicable, out of the State."

Cassius Clay, back in Saint Petersburg, was overjoyed to learn of Brutus's election. Cassius was still anxious to be president; this letter presents a highly colored version of what happened during the 1860 Republican convention and afterward.

CASSIUS CLAY

St. Petersburg, R[ussi]a, Sept. 2, 1863

Dear Brutus,

I rejoice to hear that you are elected to Congress from the Ashland district. The influence of the border states in the next presidential election will be great, and you and Clay Smith will have much to do in its direction. You are aware that I was the highest candidate for the vice presidency at Chicago and would have been nominated but that Seward was to be propitiated by giving his friends the choice of the vice president, and they agreed upon Hamlin who even then could hardly beat me. I was then promised the place of Secretary of War by the President and the party, and again I was pushed out of my place for supposed public reasons. In consequence of the ambition of the same men I was recalled without consulting me from this court, to give place to others. And when I proposed to [do] duty in the field, I was refused a command by the same influences. In consequence of all this, my friends are anxious to run me for some office where the people shall decide upon my merit. I have had a frank conversation with Jas. L. Rollins upon the whole matter [Rollins, a childhood friend of Cassius's, was a Missouri congressman] and I wish you would put yourself in early communications with him in *person*, to determine what is best to be done in the premises. I shall be governed by what pledges you and he may give *except as to political principles*. Those I will define myself. I need only now remark that I have not changed my views so often enunciated in regard to slavery. I was for the President's Emancipation Proclamation as a *"war measure,"* but because I would not go along with the radical [Charles] Sumner doctrine of the overthrow of the state organizations to reach slavery, that faction made war upon me in the Senate. But I beat them and can do it before the people. I hold that slavery is a state and constitutional institution and that there is no power in the national government to touch the subject; in times of peace all the powers of the states *revive*. Under the proclamation all the slaves made *actually free* would remain so. But those only theoretically free but still in the possession of the citizens of the several states, at least the loyal masters, would be subject to their exclusive control as before. I think upon this ground I could carry almost all of the Republican Party, and most of the Democrats, all the loyal ones. And that ground would be all the southern border states, or even the rebel states, under a restoration of the Union, could ask. I think my popularity as an earnest antislavery man cannot be shaken by the miserable faction of which Sumner is the head, whilst the south could rely upon me as a firm defender of all their constitutional rights. [. . .] I take it for granted that you will promote my interests most cheerfully so far as you can, consistently with your public views. Can you do better than sustain me upon that platform? [. . .] If Mr. Lincoln is a candidate, I should not be, and that you are authorized to use as you think best. I believe him a patriot and deserving of a reelection if he desires it. I am getting on well in my political associations here. And shall be able to pay you at least $2000 on my debt this year. Give my love to all, to Cash, and to Anne [*sic*].

Your bro.,

C. M. Clay

P.S. In breeding my cattle have regard to the red color which I admire and the *Best Stock*. C.M.C.

Cassius had returned to the United States from his mission in Saint Petersburg in the summer of 1862. In August, he opened his campaign for leadership of the "radical" wing of the Republican Party, made up of those determined to abolish slavery, with an attack on the president for not doing so immediately. But he was careful not to break completely with Lincoln. Lincoln, on the other hand, wanted to get Cassius out of his hair. He thought up a task that would get Cassius out of Washington, sending him to Kentucky, where he had not been for fifteen months, to test the waters for the Emancipation Proclamation.

Cassius arrived in the state in the middle of the tumultuous summer of 1862. General Kirby Smith's troops had just invaded through the Cumberland Gap. Cassius, who held a commission as a major general of volunteers, offered his services to the Union army and was given some raw recruits to march from Lexington towards Clay's Ferry. Relieved of his duties two days later, he traveled to Frankfort to speak to the legislature about the forthcoming Emancipation Proclamation. Then he rushed back to Washington to tell the president that Kentuckians would accept a proclamation freeing slaves belonging to rebels. When Lincoln issued the Emancipation Proclamation a few weeks later, Cassius praised it as "immortal," thinking he had shaped the president's thinking. Lincoln had cleverly co-opted him into becoming a supporter of his administration.

The Emancipation Proclamation took the rug out from under Cassius's feet, since he had no further program to propose. Unable or unwilling to take up another issue, he became a man whose time had passed, even though he still longed to be president. When Simon Cameron's tour of duty in Saint Petersburg was up, Cassius reminded Lincoln of his promise to send him back to Russia. He returned in the spring of 1863, this time without his family.

This is the Cassius Clay the Saint Petersburg photographer captured, a lonely middle-aged man sheared of his bombast, as naked before the camera's lens as the emperor in his new clothes. Lincoln and many others thought Cassius too obtuse to know what was happening to him, but, looking at this picture, I think he knew all too well.

Cassius's second tour of duty in Russia did not go as well as the first. Although he made money on various telegraph and railroad schemes and facilitated the purchase of Alaska by the United States, scandals involving women undermined his effectiveness as a minister. At first they were no more than whispers and innuendoes, then a British woman tried to blackmail him for attempting to seduce her. When the Russian courts refused to hear her suit, she petitioned the U.S. Congress for relief. Congress did nothing, but American newspapers ridiculed Cassius, particularly in Kentucky, where an anonymous pamphlet entitled A Synopsis of Forty Chapters Upon Clay, not to be found in any treatise on the Free Soils of the United-States of America heretofore published circulated.

Poor Uncle Cash. He should never have left Mary Jane at home.

Meanwhile, his one-time secretary, Green, wrote Brutus giving his opinion of Uncle Cash as a diplomat and offering his views on the diplomatic life. Apparently Green had not yet heard of his father's election to Congress.

GREEN CLAY

Turin, Augt. 1863

Dear Pa,

It has been a long time since I wrote, knowing incidents of Turin life would be of little interest to you and my impressions of events that are passing at home of no use.

[. . .] I have not heard from Uncle C. since his return. [. . .] You know he is no diplomat, but must always enjoy that influence belonging to a straight-forward, honest, able man, who however acts from impulse more than from consideration of politics and must have strong prejudices. He is just the opposite of the crafty Russians. You remember on his arrival in Europe, his first act was to speak to the whole British nation in the tone he would to a conclave of asses. [. . .] Of course then he was not admired by Englishmen. The first question I believe the English ambassador here asked me was were I related to the Minister at St. Petersburg. This may account for a certain coldness I experience on the part of the Eng. Embassy. [. . .] The Ambassador himself is very cordial. I think I have to laugh & tell him he has spoiled forever all chances of the Clay name in the field of diplomacy. Strange how well he [Uncle Cash] anticipated what we have come to: he was the first to put in print, even against [Horace] Greeley & the rest, that no one, nor 7, nor 15, states would be allowed to secede from the Union without war: he was the first to announce that emancipation of the slaves of the South must enter into the aim of the government. [. . .]

I like the people I encounter here but must confess don't enjoy diplomatic life. I should have much rather stuck to the law. But you know the circumstances of the time. War has broken up my plan. There is this disadvantage in our system of appointments: a man, however completely he may have turned his attention, & with whatever success, to the requirements of the foreign service, learning the languages etc., he must in general show his certificate of home service to party before receiving an appointment that is, I mean, of any importance. And just the time one may be qualified to fill such a station, the 4 yrs. wheel of political fortunes makes a revolution & out he goes. [. . .] This brings our appointments abroad into ridicule. Think of a minister serving at Paris without knowing the language of the Court!

Again the salaries are inadequate [. . .] to live in the style of the exigencies of the position: which is a great element of a minister's influence. As Tallyrand once said, A good dinner goes a long way in a diplomatic discussion. [. . .]

Tho I like the place well enough & especially the country, I think I should prefer after the coming winter to return home & live a life more within my means. If I intend to again take up the law to stay beyond that time would be so much lost, and as I have said in our country there is no such thing as the profession of diplomacy. However qualified a man, party is King. One who sits at his little farm-table, however humble it may be, can at least feel he is independent.

Thus I have given you my general ideas. I must say there isn't any *resolution* there, they are merely [. . .] thrown out, and I don't know if you all wouldn't say that I hardly know what a resolution was. So it may be.

Remember me to Aunt Ann & all. For Cit, I expect I am to find him an account of a chamois hunt in the Alps.

Ever your affectionate Son,

G. Clay

At home, Brutus basked briefly in the pleasures of political success. But it also had its chores. Everyone wanted favors from him. His friend David Goodloe wanted his son, Green Clay Goodloe, to go to West Point. "Young Swigert was rejected and there is a vacancy from this *district at West Point,*" Goodloe wrote in August 1863. "Clay will leave for Washington Monday afternoon to get the appointment and go on to West Point. Your *nomination* will secure *the appointment.*" This was only the first of many such letters.

On September 3, the provost marshall's office in Paris received from Brutus three "abled bodied negro men to work on Government fortifications at Camp Nelson and elsewhere [. . .] to be returned to owner after the completion of the work for which they are impressed." Although the impressment of slaves was to become a big issue among his constituents in the coming year, Brutus sent John, Will, and Augustus to Camp Nelson. John and Augustus were Biddy's sons; Will was "Amy's Will" whom Martha had considered for a houseboy.

In preparation for his arrival in Washington, Brutus ordered himself new clothes, a fine cloth coat with doeskin pants and a silk vest, a "cassemere" coat with pants and a vest, and another suit with two pairs of pants. All this cost him $101. At the same time, he also bought new shoes for everybody on the farm from George Doehrer, the Paris shoemaker, including an $11 pair of boots for young Cash.

Thinking about living quarters in Washington, he wrote to ask where Clay Smith planned to live. His nephew replied, "I have secured boarding at a private house, a good place. My wife will go with me. [. . .] I understood all the desirable rooms at Hotels are engaged, but when I get there will see to it for you. You will find unless you get a certain class of rooms at the Hotel it will be much more agreeable at a private House, but if one can be had I will secure it for you either at Willard, Browns, National or — (forgotten name, all about alike). If either of these will do let me know."

In mid-October, word reached the family in Richmond that Zeke Clay had been killed in the fighting around Chattanooga, perhaps at the battle at Chickamauga on September 20, perhaps later in the defense of Chattanooga itself. Patsey immediately wrote to Ann.

PATSEY MILLER

At home, Oct. 15th, '63

[Dear Ann],

Having just received my Dear Sister the sad news of poor Ezekiel Clay's death at Chattanooga, I write offering you and Mr. Clay my deep heartfelt sympathy. [. . .] It is a sad affliction to lose our beloved ones when we are around them and able to administer to their comfort and wants, but how afflicting and distressing to have them die on the battle field, no friend, no relation by to hear a last word — Poor fellow — the last I saw of him was near a year ago. He took his dinner here as the Southern army retreated. As I shook hands and bid him good-bye I said to him I hoped all would be well with him. He looked sad and replied he would not be sure of it. Field [Miller] went over to Lexington yesterday and returned today. He said a young Graves of Montgomery County had seen a soldier belonging to Ezekiel's company, who told him he was killed instantly on the field. We however hear so many reports that turn out to be utterly false, I have a faint hope to hear it is not so, but Field seems to think there is no doubt of it. [. . .]

Yrs.,

P. I. Miller

The report of Zeke's death went unconfirmed for several weeks and the family was not convinced he was dead. In the meantime, Martha wrote that she was more determined than ever to come to Kentucky. She and the children would come alone. Although Henry had been honorably discharged from the Confederate army following the Battle of Gettysburg, he refused to live with his Unionist in-laws.

Unfortunately, only one of Henry's wartime letters to Martha has survived. Henry's service differed from that of his brothers-in-law. Green's participation amounted to little more than a flirtation with war. Zeke, a lieutenant colonel in the First Kentucky Mounted Rifles, fought under Nathan Forrest at Chickamauga. Later his cavalry served as an advance guard for Confederate armies in western Virginia and eastern Tennessee, as well as in Kentucky. In one memorable incident, Zeke's horse was shot from under him. Commandeering another, he was injured but remained mounted and took charge of his battalion. But Henry was a foot soldier. As a lieutenant in the Second Virginia Infantry, he slogged up and down the Shenandoah Valley with Stonewall Jackson in the early stages of the war. Later, as part of Robert E. Lee's Army of Virginia, he participated in the Confederate invasion of the North, culminating in the decisive and bloody battle at Gettysburg in July 1863.

MARTHA DAVENPORT

Altona, Oct. 17th, 1863

Dear Aunt Ann,

[. . .] I have rather unexpectedly received a permit to go to Harpers Ferry tomorrow to purchase some goods for the family. [. . .] I embrace the opportunity of again writing to you as I have not heard that you have received either of my [previous] letters. I have determined to go to Ky. this Fall if I can get anyone to come for me (of course I do not ask so much of Mr. Davenport as to accompany me). I thought perhaps Kit would not object to taking a trip, or even Cash, if he is not too busy with Mr. Sayre. I wrote to you to that effect in my letters. [. . .] Presuming you can dispatch one of the Boys for me sometime soon, say to Pa, please give them money to pay expenses to & fro for the whole party. I have not despaired of my former letters not reaching you and look a little every day for one of the Boys. I have made all my arrangements so shall be ready at any time to go. I was last week engaged at Sunny Side, my former home, in replanting grape vines and budded trees all of which I have raised since I came here, trimming and staking roses, removing bulbous roots etc. to a safer place during my absence as the place will be rented to laboring people who spend no time upon the beauties of nature. [. . .] I have also dined around with all my particular friends in adieu so you see we are not all starving in Dixie, although the Yankees have all filled their pockets off of us. The children are both well, talk a great deal about going to Ky. although June thinks he must soon return on his Pony to stay with his Pa to whom both are perfectly devoted. Mr. Davenport seems quite blue at the idea of being left alone and for me to sojourn with such Unionists. It is late. I leave very early in the morning. My love to all.

Affectionately yours,

Martha C. Davenport

Cash could not go for Martha as he was at school in Frankfort, where he boarded with Mary Embry's stepson, Joe. In a letter to his mother in late October, he included a list to show how he had spent the $13 his father had given him on October 10: passage, $1.50; hotel, $1; books, $3; knife, $1.50; stamps and ink, $1; cost of getting his trunk from the hotel, $.25; "other things," $2; the Flag Association, $1; leaving a balance of seventy-five cents. He concluded, "I am getting along very well in my studies, etc. Mr. Sayre says if I will study hard this session that I can enter Yale College next year. Send me a box of eatables as soon as you can conveniently do so."

On November 1, William E. Simms, the Confederate senator from Paris and one-time congressman from the Seventh District, wrote Brutus, "Your son, Lt. Col. Clay, was reported in the newspapers of the day as being amongst the killed at the late battle at McMinnville, Tennessee. This report may have reached you. Under the circumstances, I feel that it is my duty to inform you that this report is incorrect. Col. Clay received only a slight wound in the shoulder. He is now doing well and will be restored to health in a few days. I hope you will appreciate the motives that induce me to write this note. Whatever may be our present political relationship, these I hope may never be sufficient to make us forget the kindly remembrances of other days, of the claims of humanity."

In November, Ann received a letter from her niece, Pattie Holloway, asking for advice.

PATTIE HOLLOWAY

Richmond, Nov. 2cd [1863]

Dear Aunt Ann,

[. . .] I was up to see Aunt Belle [Lyman] a few days ago. She is doing very well, has not named the little girl yet [her second child, Pattie]. I suppose will give Dr. Lyman the privilege of selecting a name. She wish [sic] me to thank you for the nice wafers and says you must come over this fall as soon as she can enjoy your company. Ma & Amelia [Burton] spent the day with Aunt Patsey [Miller] yesterday. She has been quite sick, has a risen [swelling] under her arm which has been very painful. [. . .]

Ann [Holloway] has not returned from Nashville [where she was visiting her brother June]. We looked for her last week with Judge Embry but she declined coming with him, will come home with Pa. [. . .] Capt. Van Ness spent Saturday night at the Webster House on his way to Lexington from Tennessee. I think he & Aunt Lucy [Field] will

marry. [. . .] I hope it is not so. I understand he is fond of a glass of
liquor, gets very bad off very often. You wish to know if I have heard
from Mr. [Daniel] Bedinger. Yes, I have, several times. I desire a free and
undisguised expression of your opinion as regards your neighbor and
myself. I am now reflecting upon a very serious and important step. I
ought to act cautiously and therefore desire the counsel of Uncle Clay
and yourself. In taking a step of this kind, I above all things else would
wish to obtain as large a share of happiness as falls to the lot of mortals.
I do not know that he possesses the traits of character essential to a
woman's happiness. I have heard he was remarkably stingy. A person so
remarkably close I do not think they can possess a very good heart. You
know I have been brought up in a liberal manner. My desires have always been gratified. At the same time, they have been of a reasonable
nature. Please give me your advice in an unrestrained way. I would not
be surprised to see him in R. any day. The family send their love and
hope you will be in Richmond soon.

Yours truly,

Pattie Holloway

Dan Bedinger, whom Pattie married a short time later, was the son
of the Clays' neighbor. The Bedingers lived in a small frame house that
still stands near the entrance to Auvergne, overlooking a dammed-up
portion of Kennedy's Creek, now inhabited by a lone swan, a refugee
from Claiborne Farm down the road. Out behind the Bedinger house
is a separate building, built in the 1840s as a school for slave children
(the Bedingers were dedicated emancipationists). An educated black
woman taught there, thereby earning both her freedom and passage to
Liberia.

In a letter from Frankfort sent in November, young Cash remarked
to his mother that he supposed Kit had left to bring Martha and her
children to Kentucky. He also mentioned Brutus's purchase of the farm
belonging to another neighbor, Jesse Kennedy, which gave Brutus
frontage on the turnpike for the first time. (Brutus later bought out the
Bedingers, too.)

Cash was having problems with his teeth. "I will go to the dentist
tomorrow. Since writing the above I have had my teeth examined and
one of them plugged. [. . .] The whole cost of fixing my teeth will be
about fifteen dollars. I am having a pair of shoes made so I cannot help

to pay the dentist from the surplus of money you sent. So you must send me 5 dollars to pay the dentist with."

Later that same month, Martha arrived from Charles Town with her little boys, June and Nassa. It could not have been an easy trip for Martha, who was again pregnant.

In Italy, Green fretted about his country and family but had to content himself with advising Cash on the best way to enter Yale. "You ask me about Cash's schooling," he wrote Ann on November 21. "I think he had better stay with Mr. Sayre during the winter at least, devoting his extra time to reading at his room. Mr. Sayre can tell him about what class he can enter at Yale and if he thinks he could enter the *last term* of *Freshman*. [. . .] If not so far advanced, then he must go on early in the summer and prepare himself for the regular examination. At New Haven, one can take lodgings & employ a tutor (connected with the college). [. . .] Mr. Sayre, however, is a good counselor in these matters except that he wishes to place his scholars in an advanced class at Yale, the benefits of which I doubt. As Cash must be the scholar of the family to have the full advantages of a studency in college, he should commence with his class & grow with it.

"As for my own individual notion: in Cash's place I should much prefer to come to Germany and study. The advantages of a European education (costing little, if any, more) with the languages & a wider scope of observation amidst different peoples & governments certainly would be appreciated by one of Cash's good mind. [. . .] The Germans, you know, are celebrated for their universities, the thoroughness with which they teach, and Germany [has] one of the finest schools for gathering political knowledge. Now that our country has become the scene of civil war and the breaking up of institutions & political changes, this great duty of resettling & reforming institutions & laws will devolve imperviously upon the young men that are saved from the war."

As Brutus prepared to leave for Washington to take his place in Congress, he received invitations to a last-minute meeting with his supporters. "I shall invite fifty or more good Union Gentlemen to meet Genl. Green Clay Smith and you at my house on Tuesday evening next," David Goodloe wrote on November 22. (His wife was Clay Smith's sister.) "I expect Governor Bramlette and others from Frankfort. I shall rely confidently on seeing you Tuesday evening. Your numerous friends here are very desirous of seeing you before you go to Washington."

Judge Goodloe also urged Brutus to attend. "I desire to see you again a last time before you leave for Washington & this is perhaps the only chance."

However, Brutus did not make the reception at the Goodloes', as Martha's Little Nassa died the day before. Perhaps he became ill on the trip from Virginia. On November 30, Brutus paid a bill from George W. Davis ("Manufacturer and Dealer in Furniture, Chairs, Mattresses, Window-Shades, Blind Trimmings, Picture Frames, Etc., particular attention given to the undertaking business in all its branches") for a No. 4 Burial Casket, with Hearse, costing $45. The same Davises handled my father's funeral ninety-six years later.

A letter from Judge Goodloe explains what the men at his brother's house were anxious to tell Brutus — that he should vote with the Lincoln administration for control over the House of Representatives. The Republicans had done poorly in the 1862 elections and needed a majority of the 183 members to push through the president's plans to wage an all-out war against the Confederacy. Brutus, as a member of the Union, or Conservative Union, Party, was an independent, but his vote for Speaker of the House was crucial to the Republicans' success. The Goodloes and their friends urged him to support Indiana Republican Schuyler Colfax rather than Ohio Democrat Sunset Cox.

WILLIAM CASSIUS GOODLOE

Lexington, Ky., Nov. 25, 1863

Dear Sir,

We were disappointed last night at not meeting you at D. S. Goodloe's as your Union friends desired to have a conference with you before you left for Washington, with a voice to a full Harmony of views. We are satisfied at this end of the District that we are to have a battle next year between a moderate Republican & a [. . .] [Peace] style of Democrat & we are [. . .] on the side of the former— [. . .] We think here [. . .] that you should attend the Union caucus for Offices of the House & vote for the [. . .] [Republicans] & let the *conservative alias* copperhead caucus go to the Devil. We would not touch Bob Mallory with a forty foot pole. We are satisfied that it is our duty to support the President, whenever it can be done without violating the conscience, & when it cannot be done object respectfully & kindly & not attempt by denunciation to aid the rebels.

Bramlette was here last week & met our Union friends at my house & agrees with us all around & I think you will find his message [to the legislature] all right.

I think you, Clay Smith & [William H.] Randal [a Kentucky congressman] ought to address a respectful note to the President & request him to send Genl. Boyle out of Ky. [. . .]

I will write you occasionally during your absence.

Very truly yours,

W. C. Goodloe

During the fall, June Holloway resigned his commission in the army, despite the promotion he had written Brutus about earlier. His family was unhappy about this, but he wrote his cousin Green the full story of his marriage and resignation. Green passed this along to his father in hopes Brutus would be able to do something for June once he got to Washington.

GREEN CLAY

Legation, Italian States, Turin, Nov. 30, '63

Dear Pa,

I suppose June Holloway's conduct has been much blamed by his friends but when his motives & situation are known, don't think they would criticize so severely. In a letter to me—written to me of course in a feeling of close friendship and not intended for other eyes—he says, "I regretted giving up my commission in the army but my wife and her family were bitterly opposed to my remaining in service and to satisfy them I resigned. But shall always regret it. But I was so troubled and my wife being such a rebel I began to be suspected. My marriage was a very unfortunate one. My wife's family opposed the match & still dislike me & have poisoned the mind of my wife against me. They told her I married her only for her money. She is now at Nashville and separated from me by mutual agreement. I have been to her a dutiful & kind husband. She is a beautiful & accomplished lady but very high tempered. Her family has been influencing her for more than a year to leave me. She has repeatedly told me she thought when she married me that I was immensely rich, though I had told her I had nothing but my pay to live on. I would like to say more on the subject but I leave it off."

I thought [it] best to take the privilege with June of giving his own statement that you may appreciate the annoying circumstances under which he was forced to resign and may more appreciate his sincere regret. So, if you should think proper, when you go to Washington, you may try and get him restored. [. . .] There is no other life will ever suit June. He would make a valuable officer. If you should see fit to apply for his restoration, you would while promoting the interest of the service do a kind act for a relative & namesake. [. . .] And Ky. ought not [to] lose her officers & just part & influence in the war. I have been expecting you would write to me but have received no letter.

Your affectionate son,

Green

Shortly after Thanksgiving, Brutus departed for Washington, leaving Ann and Kit to run the farm. Martha was there as well, awaiting the birth of her third child. Green was in Italy, Zeke in Virginia with the Confederate army, and Cash at school in Frankfort.

TEN

An Unconditional Union Man

One of the treasures yielded up by Auvergne's attic is Brutus's memorandum book for his term in Congress. This pocket-sized book is as succinct as the man himself — a list of accounts, visitors to his office, and prisoner of war petitions, enlivened by an occasional personal note. "Get the gloves from Miss Mason," he wrote in early March 1864, referring to gloves he had agreed to pick up for his niece Sally Clay, Cassius's daughter. "Distance from Home to Washington 840 m.," he wrote in May when life in the capital had gotten particularly grim.

Brutus left for Washington on December 1, 1863, carrying with him $400 in cash and high hopes for his country's and his state's future. He was optimistic that he could make a contribution to the welfare of both. He was fifty-five years old, intellectually and physically vigorous, an Unconditional Union Man.

He traveled in the company of his nephew Clay Smith, the newly elected congressman from Kentucky's Sixth District. One of the first entries in Brutus's little black book records the addresses of his own room (he boarded with a Mrs. Choate at 471 Sixth Street) and that of General C. Smith (402 Thirteenth Street), as well as the number of his own post office box (177). I picture him sitting in his room in Mrs. Choate's house at night, writing down his expenditures for those first days in Washington: a nightgown, an umbrella, and his room at the Metropolitan Hotel, where he stayed until locating a boardinghouse.

The first order of business in the House of Representatives was the election of a Speaker. As his supporters in Kentucky had urged him to do (though he had made them no promises), Brutus voted with the Republicans to elect Schuyler Colfax, thus declaring himself in support of President Lincoln's determined prosecution of the war. For his vote, Brutus was rewarded with the chairmanship of the House Committee on Agriculture.

Brutus's vote for Colfax pleased many of his fellow Unionists in Kentucky. "The news of your vote for Speaker reached here today," Judge Goodloe wrote on December 8, "& gave your friends the highest satisfaction & created dismay amongst the copperheads. [. . .] We know the issue is coming in Kentucky between Mr. Lincoln or some other moderate Republican & copperhead Democrat & we are preparing for it. [. . .] If the residue of the State will stand as firm as northern Kentucky we shall carry the Presidential election as decently as we did the Governor's election."

Brutus was deluged with requests almost from the moment he arrived in Washington. One of the most common was for "passes" through Federal lines. "I want a 'permit' from the war department to visit my husband in Richmond, Va. & to *return* here at a future time," wrote Martha Jones of Versailles. "He is in delicate health and afflicted with an alarming disease of the eye, threatening blindness. [. . .]"

Robert Peter of Lexington wanted agricultural reports. Since Brutus had been attacked in some newspapers, particularly the Louisville *Journal*, for voting for Colfax, Peter added, "*Unconditional* Unionism is growing in Kentucky and such papers as the Louisville Journal & Democrat & our Observer & Reporter are far from representing the sentiments of the Union Party here. On the contrary much indignation has been excited against them in consequence of several of their 'coppery' articles."

Writing to congratulate him on his vote, A. G. Hodges of the *Commonwealth* apologized for his own lukewarm editorial support. "I would have defended your course in my paper, against the attacks in the [Louisville] Journal, but for the peculiar position in which I am placed just at this time. I am a candidate for the State Printing, and so is Mr. Prentice of the Journal. Some of those who will vote for me are opposed to the course of yourself, Smith, Randall, and Anderson in voting for Mr. Colfax for Speaker. Hence I cannot afford to lose their votes, or I shall be defeated." He was financially dependent upon the printing contract, he told Brutus. The *Commonwealth* made so little money that he was forced to supplement his income by running the Capital Hotel where Brutus had often stayed.

"I wrote a day or two ago saying I was coming home at Christmas," Brutus told Ann in mid-December. "Our house passed a resolution to adjourn on the 18th & meet again on the 9th of Jan. but since I wrote the Senate disagreed to our resolution & thereafter defeated it. It is probable we will now adjourn for a few days only, not giving me time to go home. After we fix the day, I will then determine whether or not I will go & write again saying what day I will reach Paris."

It was not the holiday but business that was on his mind. "I received a few days ago a letter from John Martin, the Shaker, saying he wished to purchase some more cattle from me. I wrote I would probably be home New Year's Day & asked him to meet me at that time. Should I not come, tell Christopher to sell him any of the 2 yr. old heifers at Midway. [. . .] Henson can tell the mothers of them all and if any one [is] sold, set down the calf & dam, to whom, & post office address & I can send pedigrees when I get home. Tell Christopher I wish him to stay at home as much as possible & see the stock well attended to."

Brutus continued to receive congratulatory letters from Unionists. In one, David Goodloe raised the issue of the draft. By 1863, most of the men who were likely to enlist for patriotic reasons were already in the Union army, but the government needed more soldiers. As a result, the Thirty-seventh Congress had authorized a draft, to be enforced by a provost marshall bureau within the War Department. The provost marshalls' task was to enroll every citizen between the ages of twenty and forty-five, also every immigrant who applied for citizenship.

The draft was a lottery, but if a man's name were drawn, he didn't necessarily serve. One-fifth of those whose names were drawn fled, usually westward. Three-fifths were exempted for various reasons. The remaining draftees could serve in the army, hire a substitute from a pool of eighteen- and nineteen-year-olds and immigrants, or pay $300, which exempted them from that particular draft but not a future one. A system heavily weighted in favor of the well-to-do, the draft was unpopular in Kentucky. In order to encourage enlistment, many local governments offered bounties to volunteers. In December, Bourbon County increased its taxes in order to pay larger bounties.

DAVID S. GOODLOE

Lexington, Ky., Dec. 18/63

Hon. B. J. Clay

Washington, D.C.

Dear Sir:

[. . .] Your friends are not only pleased but *delighted* at your vote for Colfax thereby giving evidence that you would unite with the Union and War party and show no quarters to the opposers of our Government. [. . .] We are glad to see that the Speaker has [. . .] [succeeded] in placing you at the head of one of the *Committees*. You are now in position to truly represent your district and get anything for them that is just and right. Had you have united with the other party you would have been powerless to do good for country & friends.

Yesterday being county court day a meeting was called (after due notice being given through the *papers* and *posters*). The court house was filled to its utmost capacity (Many leaving that could not get in). I was called to the *chair* — the object of the meeting being to raise funds to assist volunteering. Speeches were made and resolutions passed unanimously (not a dissenting voice) instructing our representative in [the] Ky. legislature to have a law passed taxing Fayette County an amount that would give each volunteer 300 and thus escape the draft. I never saw a more intense or more unanimous meeting. Kentuckians have a great aversion to a *draft*. And I will here remark that you should by all means vote against the repeal of the $300 exemption clause. There is not one in ten of those I have seen in favor of the repeal. [. . .] Give my regards to Clay [Smith] and say to him that his friends here endorse his vote [for Colfax] fully. All well.

Yours truly,

D. S. Goodloe

When Brutus returned home just before Christmas, he found letters about his brother-in-law waiting for him. No one had heard from Christopher Field for more than a year. His Louisville friend and agent Thomas S. Kennedy wrote Brutus that Christopher was trying to get the field hands to return to his plantation (and those he was managing for their absent owners such as Brutus) so that he could plant a cotton crop in 1864. These blacks, known as contrabands, had been freed by the Emancipation Proclamation. Many of them had attached themselves to the Union army or were living in camps behind Union lines. Kennedy wanted Brutus to get Christopher permission from the Union authorities to hire contrabands.

"The object is only to trust him with the negroes and afford protection to him in working the plantations," Kennedy explained on December 30. "It does not debar investigation into his past conduct, absolve him from any just penalties or even reinstate him in his citizenship. But it places him on an equal footing with hundreds of planters, who having been out of reach of the Army, have retained all their negroes and by quietly giving into the 'new system of hiring' are now reaping large prices for their cotton. Notwithstanding many of these men are arrant rebels and not one of them half as loyal as Col. Field or those citizens of Ky. who have been stripped of their property in the South." He added that he had sent a letter to Christopher by David Field's widow, Lucy, saying that he would meet him in Memphis.

On the heels of Kennedy's letter came one from Christopher himself.

CHRISTOPHER FIELD

Memphis, Tenn., Janry. 1st, 1864

Hon. B. J. Clay

Dear Sir,

I was quite astonished here today to meet with Lucy Field. She showed me your letter for which I thank you very much. Lucy has gone on to Helena, Ark. to try and get her former cook to go home with her which I think she will do as the negro was very anxious to get back to Ky. I came up here and have been to Cairo, Illinois looking after 17 bales of cotton of Christopher's, 56 bales of my own, and 11 bales of Lucy's place which was taken by a Gun Boat last spring. I got a receipt from the Gun Boat for the cotton at the time it was taken but could not follow the cotton from the fact no one was at that time permitted to come out of our lines. In fact, I could not find out until this fall what had become of the cotton. I now find it was carried to Cairo, Illinois, turned over to the Government, and condemned under the Treasury Act and sold by [the] Martial [sic] of the state and the proceeds by him paid into the Treasury of the U.S. I called on Rear Admiral [David D.] Porter, commander of the Mississippi River Squadron. He treated [me] with great politeness and is in every way a perfect gentleman. He has examined into the case and has given me a letter of all the facts as I have stated, and tells me to go to the Marshall of Illinois and get from him a statement of the sale and the amount and then to take or send my papers to you, and he sees no reason why I should not get my money & that of others. [. . .] I see from your letter to Lucy you have not understood my position and course during this war. In the first place, I opposed Secession. [. . .] After the State had gone out, I quietly agreed and said nothing and was disposed to make the best of a bad thing, determined to remain at home a quiet citizen, trying to attend to my business and have in no way been engaged in any army movements against the U.S. [. . .] I expected Christopher had told you of the views I entertained and how unpopular I was for those views with the Secessionists, and I really thought that fact made him leave the South. I will now inform you as to the situation of all the places. There has been no burning upon any of them, except the cotton. The houses, buildings and fences are all standing. No mules or stock has [sic] been taken from any of them. The places are all grown up with grass & weeds and I fear if they are not cultivated this year will all be burnt up by accident. The negroes are all gone of C., save 2 women & 2 children; all of Lucy's except 3 women & 5 or 6 children. I have about 25 — 10 women and 2 men, balance children. [Of] [t]he negroes that have gone off, many have died, particularly children. All the young men used in the army. The balance are at Lake Providence, mouth of [the] White River, Helena, Memphis, Island No. 10 & St. Louis. All of the women [. . .] and old men I would like to get back with others and go to work and make a crop this year, if the negroes will go, which I have some doubts about. They have been taught since they left us that it is death to anyone who goes back into Secesh as they call it. [. . .] I have suffered dearly, have been often robbed, and have lost nearly everything about my house at one time. [. . .] Horses, Saddles, Bridles, Gins, Potatoes, Corn, Silver, Bed clothing, in fact nearly everything. Mary [a slave] when she went off took everything C. [Kit] had in his house, bed clothing, towels, sheets, pillow cases, etc. His mules were all there when I left but raids are yet being constantly made. What has occurred since I left home I can't say. [. . .] I wish the Federal lines were closed up so as the people in the Valley could go to work and plant. I think it is very important for us to make cotton during the balance of the war. We could then afford to lose our slaves, but I do think Mr. Lincoln is pursuing and has been all the time [on] a very suicidal course to restore the Union. I think he is severing it further & further [with] every act and Proclamation he issues, and I cannot approve of it tho I desire a reconstruction. [. . .]

Yours truly,

C. I. Field

Christopher had barely sealed this letter when he thought of more he had to say to his old friend. Words flowed from his pen after months of solitude. His second letter describes a proposal by a Mr. A. Lewis, a Northerner, who wanted to raise cotton with Christopher. "He can make a fortune if he will manage it right between now and the 1st of June," Christopher told Brutus. "He has offered to me to join him and I could be of great mutual advantage but the Southern people generally being Secesh they are very unfriendly to any man who goes trading for cotton or joining in with the Federals in any way and, as my home and my all is here and may remain in the South the balance of my days, I do not wish to be marked out as a man who would not fight for the South [. . .] while others having much less at stake than he had was [sic] fighting and he joined over to their enemies and went to making money."

He gave a further account of the damage wrought by Union gunboats. "Christopher [Kit] has sustained no other injury except the taking of 12 or 15 of his negroes by a Gun Boat. [. . .] My own place & Lucy's lost negroes at the same time and same manner. My place being on the River and the Landing for both C.'s & Lucy's place, I have been the greatest sufferer. Perhaps as many as a dozen times. [. . .] The Plantation of the Estates of G. L. Martin & O. M. Anderson [deceased relatives of his daughter, Pattie, whose estates Christopher ran] they made a clean sweep of, negroes, mules, oxen, cows, farming utensils, and everything on both places they could pack away, and what they could not take away destroyed, broke the engine and gin stand and set the gin afire but fortunately it went out. I have charge of G. H. Merriman's Estate. They put 16 cannon balls and shells through the house and took off 42 negroes."

He hoped to work these plantations with contraband labor. "I am willing to pay them. I only ask for the women, children, and old men, not in the Army, and in addition I want as many more formerly belonging to others to make up the deficiency for the men in the Army and deaths which have occurred, and I can say to you humanity requires something should be done for the creatures for they are and have been dying like sheep around these posts."

In his letter, Christopher makes the same kind of financial calculations he made before the war as if the old rules still applied. "Christopher's place if cultivated and a good year ought to make 175 or 200 bales of cotton which would bring I think 40,000$." He had unrealistic expectations about what the Federal government would do for him, such as replace his mules. And he concludes, in a remarkable exercise in denial, "We are a ruined people any way. My conscience is clear that I have had no hand in bringing this about."

Meanwhile, Green had become restless in Turin. When I first read these letters, I identified with Green more than any of the other Clays because of his restlessness. I could imagine him hitchhiking through Europe or spending a year in an ashram. Now that my hitchhiking days are over, the trait with which I most identify in Green is his detachment. He invariably looked at everything from afar (partly because he was far away), seeing all sides of every question, as if life were an academic exercise rather than a passionate partaking.

After reading these letters the first time, I decided to name my second child for Green. Regardless of its sex, I decided to call the baby Green Clay Berry. When she turned out to be a girl, my husband prevailed upon me to give her a female name as well, so she became Elizabeth Green Clay Berry. Her brother Michael, age four, used to ask guests if they knew his little sister's full name. When they shook their heads, he would shout, "Elizabeth *Red* Clay Berry!" at the top of his lungs, then burst into spasms of laughter that lasted until he was led from the room. The guests were mystified.

GREEN CLAY

Turin, Jan. 4, '64

Dear Pa,

I received your letter of Dec. 10 and was very glad to hear from you directly. The late events may have given hope of an early termination of the war, but I fear our miseries [have] just commenced. The military problem even solved, there remains a very difficult political one. [. . .] I thought some of returning home this spring tho may wait until fall. I have applied for a leave of absence. If granted, I want to make the trip of South Italy, Rome, Naples, etc. In this case I will need some money & wish you would send me $700. [. . .] If I return this spring, I may have the probability of returning in the fall, if there shall be any chance of a new appointment. You know it is time I was thinking of some profession or employment for life. I would have liked to remain abroad during the war. If I should neglect the opportunity of seeing the ancient cities & most interesting parts of Italy while I'm here, I know I should regret it afterwards. [. . .]

You can transmit the money by depositing it with a well-known banker in W. and I can draw for it at will through our bankers in London, Baring Bros., or by *a bill of exchange on London*. Whichever you find best. [. . .] I'm in no great hurry for it. Please let me know soon on the subject. [. . .] I wrote you [a] letter about wanting to come home but you did not answer me.

G. C.

Brutus returned to Washington shortly after New Year's. Ann planned to join him later, accompanied by Cassius's daughters, Mary and Sally. In Kentucky, New Year's Day was bitterly cold with sleet, snow, and high winds. The temperature at 8 a.m. in Lexington was 8 below zero.

"Did you ever see such weather?" Ann asked Brutus on January 7. "I fear you had some trouble in getting on & must have suffered much at night. We got no mail yesterday as they say the river was frozen over and no crossing & it is now snowing hard. I do not know what is to become of the stock but Christopher seems quite attentive & I hope will remain so. Frank [a slave] died yesterday & several others complaining but I suppose mostly colds. [. . .] I have not heard from the [Clay] girls. I suppose every one is frozen stiff."

Two days later, Martha gave birth to a third son, Ezekiel Clay Davenport. His delivery could not have been easy. Martha had been more than seven months' pregnant when she made the journey to Kentucky from Charles Town, and her second child, Nassa, had died shortly after they arrived at Auvergne.

A few days following young Zeke's birth, Mary Clay got in touch with Ann about the sisters' plans to accompany her to Washington.

"We will go with you with great pleasure, and are delighted that you will go, as our chances for any other company are quite shadowy, and we would so much rather go with you. We will be ready to start any day you wish us [. . .], so if I don't hear from you, I'll come the last of this week if we can cross the river. Shall I write to Cousin Belle for your bonnet to be sent with mine to Washington and for gloves and how many?"

Ann's friend Louisa Keiningham wrote Brutus from Paris to request a pass through the Union lines for her brother's widow, Emeline Thomas, who wished to get to New York from Georgia. At the end of the letter, she added, "Your wife was in town yesterday, all were well and Martha and the young stranger doing as well as they could do."

Brutus was still smarting from criticism for having voted for Colfax, and Judge Goodloe sought to buck him up. "Your vote for Speaker of the House explained itself. It was a vote for a Union man against a rebel. [. . .] It was the only way to redeem your pledge to the people to give the War to put down the Rebellion a fair support. Union men here such as supported you would have been disappointed & dissatisfied with any other vote."

Brutus warned Ann that there was smallpox in Washington and suggested she and the girls get vaccinations before leaving Kentucky. The technique of vaccinating people for smallpox was well known by the middle of the nineteenth century, but this would indicate that one got a vaccination only when traveling to a place where the disease existed. In a subsequent letter, Brutus comments upon the fact that his vaccination "took," indicating he could have caught smallpox without it.

ANN CLAY

Jan. 20, 1864

My Dear Husband,

I received your last letter a week ago about our trip and the small pox & the girls here much disappointed that I did not go with them last week. [. . .] I wrote to them that I would be ready to go to Cincinnati on next Monday so as to start to Washington on Tuesday morning, so if they are still so anxious and I do not hear any thing more discouraging from you, I suppose we will leave Cincinnati on Tuesday next. And you will know what time we ought to get there so I hope you will be at the Depot to meet us. [. . .] Mr. Martin the Shaker came last week, bought of me the Premium young bull & said he would probably take the other one. He was quite anxious to buy a young heifer in your select herd. [. . .] But of course I did not sell as you told me not [to]. He wanted and offered me 5$ for some of the mixed blood common sheep, but I told him I would write to you about it. He did not like the young fillies except one & said it was bred to the jack [Brutus's stud donkey, Republic] which would be a great objection so did not agree to take any. [. . .]

Papa has been quite ill so of course I made no preparation to go to Washington till I heard he was better so on Monday morning I went to Cincinnati [she means Richmond], came back yesterday. There is still some difficulty in crossing the river.

The sick are all better but the weather so bad that we get no work done and no one wants [to rent] the other negroes left on hand which gives me much trouble. I received the seed & will distribute them. [Throughout his tenure in Congress, Brutus sent free seed and agricultural pamphlets to his constituents, often asking Ann to distribute them for him.] Martha & child are quite well. [. . .] If the girls decline going for the present, I will write to you, but if you do not hear again, you will know we will be there. [. . .]

Yrs. affectionately,

Ann M. Clay

[P.S.] Christopher has been staying home ever since you left.

While in Congress, Brutus ran his farm by letter, sending Ann or Kit or Martha precise instructions about what to feed the animals and which fields to plow.

BRUTUS CLAY

Washington, D.C., Jan. 22, 1864

Dear Ann,

[. . .] I am glad to hear Martha is doing so well. Her confinement was quite unsatisfactory to me. Frank [a slave] I did not expect would live long when I left home. He was a good fellow. I am sorry for his loss. When I first got here I was vaccinated against the small pox. It took well and my arm is very sore now [. . .] it taking so much shows my system was in a good condition to take the disease but presume the danger is now over. [. . .] Did you get my letter directing you all to be vaccinated before you started here? I think it very important it should be done. [. . .] Tell Christopher & Henry that the little field next [to] Duncan Spring, where they are now feeding the fat cattle, might as well be kept for a feeding lot for the whole winter. [. . .] Tell Henry not to feed in waste, but regulate the feeding according to the weather, let every thing have enough and no more. In bad weather they eat more, in good, less. Tell Christopher to write to me about matters at home. [. . .]

B. J. Clay

Charles Garrard wanted to know if Brutus could get his son an appointment to West Point. He included in his January 22 letter a photograph of a handsome teenager, looking absurdly young in his cadet's uniform. Cousin Charles prefaced his request by poking fun at Brutus. "I have no doubt you have a great deal of business not very congenial to your taste or feelings but as you have undertaken to be the 'Servant' of the 'dear people' you will have to stand it."

Desperate for additional soldiers, the Union hoped to recruit Kentucky slaves, a course of action that excited opposition on the grounds that it violated the property rights of the slaves' owners and would be bad for the morale of white soldiers. In response to a letter on the subject from Brutus, Governor Bramlette stated, "It is an outrage that these recruiting brokers seek to enlist slaves in Kentucky and [they] will be promptly met and summarily punished." He included a copy of a letter he had written General Boyle in which he said, "No such recruiting will be tolerated here. Summary justice will be inflicted upon any who attempt such unlawful purpose."

From Europe, Green wrote on January 30 that his leave of absence was likely to be approved, then added, "Always loyal to my government & my position, yet I must confess when I search for any *probable* result of this war that will be consistent with our form & principles of government, I find little cause of congratulations. [. . .] Criticism, today, is I know a dangerous weapon, it brings upon the wielders suspicion. [. . .] My fault is then that my patriotism is not *blind,* and my crime frankness to those I know to be *friends* of my country."

On January 25, two days before Ann and the Clay girls arrived in

Washington, Brutus defended his vote for Colfax on the House floor during an exchange between the Kentuckians Clay Smith and Robert Mallory, over whether Kentuckians supported the Emancipation Proclamation. Mallory claimed Clay Smith had said during his campaign that the proclamation was constitutional and that he approved of it. Clay Smith hedged, replying that the question of its constitutionality had never arisen, a remark that was greeted with laughter. All this, including the laughter, is recorded in the *Congressional Globe*, the predecessor of today's *Congressional Record*.

Brutus must have grown impatient with the fencing going on between Mallory and Smith, particularly when they started talking about promises made to constituents. He rose to ask if Mallory meant to include him in his remarks. Mallory assured him that he didn't.

Brutus replied he was glad to hear that, adding, "as I am upon the floor I wish to make an observation or two, so that I may stand fair before my constituents and the world. This very question as to whom I would vote for as Speaker of the House of Representatives was put to me on every occasion in my State, and I replied emphatically that I would make no pledges [. . .]; that I intended to do what I thought right and proper under all the circumstances when I got here."

As if this weren't succinct enough, he continued, after a bit of taunting by Mallory, "I have never attached myself to one side or the other. I am independent; I mean to vote for measures as they come up, according as it seems to me best and for the interest of my country, disregarding all party ties and party feelings, for I cannot say that I cordially agree with either side of the House."

And, a minute later, "I intend to act here for myself, not to be governed by anybody, to exercise my best judgment on all these questions, and to go home and face my constituents like an honest man, and tell them that I have done my duty according to the dictates of my own judgment."

Two months after the vote for Speaker, Brutus was still taking intense political heat. For a man unused to criticism, this must have been hard. His allies wrote to rally him.

"It is true that there is a class of persons who call themselves Union men here in Kentucky who dislike the course you have pursued," wrote John L. Scott from Frankfort, "but they are mostly those persons who are very tender-hearted toward the rebels, and very tender-footed in support of the government."

John Anderson of Montgomery County worried about Lincoln's plan to enroll blacks in the armed forces and its effect on the Union Democrats in the next elections. "I should be glad that the Pres. adhere to his position about recruiting negroes in the State. To wit, until the Member of the district in Ky. asks to have recruiting in his particular one that he will take no action. This is about right unless there is an overpowering necessity, then every body will say Amen except Rebels and they have no rights except to be shot and really I think old Abe is one of the best men, means always to do right, no matter however much we differ as to the fact [or] as to results flowing from it."

At the time, the House was discussing legislation permitting the Union to confiscate slaves, land, and other property belonging to the Rebels. On February 10, Brutus rose to inquire of Massachusetts Congressman Thomas D. Eliot if the proposed legislation included Kentucky. He was assured that it did not.

No doubt thinking of himself, Brutus then remarked, "I will say that the gentleman goes so far as not only to take all the negroes in the South, but he is disposed to seize all the lands in that country, under the idea that they are abandoned. I have many constituents who hold property in that country who are all loyal men, but who are living in the State of Kentucky and never have lived in the South. I wish to know whether the lands of residents in Kentucky are to be considered as abandoned, and hence to be seized and disposed of under this bill?"

Representative Eliot of Massachusetts replied that any plantation that was not abandoned would not be seized. "If those plantations are abandoned, I think the honorable gentleman's constituents are rebels."

"I go further, and say that I am the owner of a plantation there myself," Brutus said to general laughter. "Because I am attending to my duties here on behalf of my constituents, is my plantation there to be considered as abandoned and to come under this law?"

"The gentleman is constructively upon his plantation," Eliot replied.

A day later, the subject on the floor was drafting black soldiers. Brutus rose to defend the property rights of their owners. He also warned that such a draft would alienate Kentucky Unionists. "It will create a civil war among us. It will lead one neighbor to shooting another neighbor [. . .] it will crush out the Union sentiment which is growing up there."

Brutus had gotten Christopher Field's permits and was pursuing his cotton claims as well as those of other members of the family. But some of the Fields, particularly Ann's brother Zeke, didn't want anything more to do with the South.

EZEKIEL FIELD JR.

Richmond, Feby. 14, '64

Dear Sister Ann,

[. . .] To Mr. Clay I am much indebted for procuring the Permits to carry on our Plantations upon the free labor system. I desire to be as agreeable about the matter as I *can be*. I know I am as much interested as Cit and should be willing to do my part but, Sister Ann, the facts are these. I have abandoned the idea of ever trying to do anything in the South any more under any circumstances. As you are aware, Pa gave me a start there and now it's all gone. I came to Ky. and by strict attention to business there accumulated something more and to invest it in the South, to be lost probably in one night I can't think of it. I know if a crop of cotton could be raised and saved there, it would bring us a good deal of money but the risk is too great for me, besides I have rented a farm at a large price, hired 200 negro men, and am preparing a large crop of corn for my force and the place largely stock[ed] for one of my means, and now to sell out to get money to go upon [a Mississippi plantation] is more than I can do.

I owe Cit and Brother and if my land there will pay them both, I would be more than glad to do so. [. . .] I will say this to Cit, if he is willing to try the South or will get a man to go for him, that my interest there in land or anything else he can have and use without compensating me. Bro. wrote me I would have to come down. I replied to him I could not do so. [. . .] If it was not for Pa, I would go West because I do not want to be in Ky. at the close of this sad War. I know it would have been gratifying to Mr. Clay if I had consented to go but under all the circumstances must decline. [. . .] With the love of myself, Sallie & all, will close.

Yours truly,

E. H. Field Jr.

Brutus had gone to President Lincoln himself to obtain the Christophers' permits. Everything in the Washington of 1864 was done in person. Christopher received the papers in mid-February, but he was not happy with them. He was then engaged in some sort of collaboration with Mr. A. Lewis, the Northerner mentioned in an earlier letter, to reestablish Delta cotton plantations. The details aren't entirely clear, but the plan had something to do with granting amnesty to planters such as Christopher, to allow them to get on with the business of planting cotton. Christopher made some extravagant demands, considering his situation: changes in the wording of his permits and a full regiment of Federal soldiers to protect the planters in his part of Mississippi.

CHRISTOPHER FIELD

Memphis, Tenn., February 14th, 1864

Honl. B. J. Clay

Dear Sir,

Since I wrote you last, the letter & documents which you kindly obtained for me & C. [Kit] came to hand for which I thank you. The only objection I have to Mr. Lincoln's document is I think it makes me acknowledge individually the freedom of the slave. I wish that sentence left out. If it cannot be, then I wish it changed or altered so as to place me in the position you advised in your letter to Lucy which is now before me, and you say this, which I fully endorse and sanction: Hire the negroes leaving the question of the Freedom of the Slaves in abeyance until the war is over, not considering the hiring of them will destroy your right to them hereafter if the courts should decide the Proclamation void, and I presume this was the intention of the President as I consider it such in his amnesty Proclamation, but I do not consider the permit granted to C. & myself so reads. I asked Mr. Lewis to point this out to Mr. Lincoln and ask the extinction or modification. [. . .] If Mr. Lewis accomplishes his wishes with the President on his return, none will be offered this amnesty as I will call it but those who we think are worthy. [. . .] But now to aid in the successful carrying out of this conciliatory project [. . .], we must have some military protection on the East side of the Miss. River to drive out marauders, deserters, and scouts who infest the swamp and are now as great a curse to us as we thought the Federal Army was when they were securing us. [. . .] The Gun Boats are powerless to do any good to prevent this thing, for they cannot even stop their men [Confederate raiders] from swimming their horses across the river with dispatches or any other purpose. The Boats pass backward and forward through their Beats. A Guerrilla or any other person wishing to cross is standing on the bank of the river concealed, is out of sight; as soon as he sees a Gun Boat pass, he drives his canoe into the river and in twenty minutes he is across the river with or without his horse as the case may be. The same is equally applicable to the marine fleet they land, a Guerrilla or soldier sees them land & knows by the appearance of the boats and the smoke of several boats together an hour before they land. They send out their cavalry along the main roads back for a few miles. The soldier knows from the landing what road they will go out. He rides out in the cane break. They pass. And as soon as he wishes he can go in, burn a gin, take a horse or anything he pleases. No, this is what we want, a full regiment of cavalry stationed by companies on the East bank of the River or back from it. Let them scout and [. . .] you will rid the country of all such. Crops will be made. The people will feel the Government is protecting us. The Government will be protecting itself by cutting off communication between the two armies. A large amount of cotton will be made which produces revenue. This cotton will take the place of Gold for shipment. The Government will be relieved from supporting a large number of those poor creatures who have died up like sheep in the last year at these camps [the contrabands]. [. . .] I am very well aware the Government cannot attempt to protect every planter but this is protecting in a large and considerable part of the only country that will grow any cotton [. . .] and in doing so the Government is accomplishing a military object, that of cutting off communication between the Army East & West of this River. [. . .] If you coincide with me in views and can aid Mr. Lewis in any way, I will feel I have done something towards a restoration and helping myself and other ruined people to try and make a support for them and their families, who have not made a dollar during this war but have suffered beyond the imagination of anyone who has not been an eyewitness.

Yours truly,

C. I. Field

Enclosed in this letter was a second that covers much of the same ground. Christopher wanted Brutus to continue to pursue his cotton claims against the federal government. A Union officer, Colonel D. L. Phillips, was bringing transcripts of proceedings in the District

Court of Illinois to Washington and would deliver them to Brutus in person.

Christopher had additional demands. "What I want *now* . . . ," he told Brutus, "is the privilege of going to any Government corral, and [. . .] getting 180 condemned horses, mares, or mules in place of 90 fine young mules generally near 16 hands high and very valuable. These mules were taken off last April and I presume taken to Vicksburg as the Army was surrounding that place and [in] great need of waggons [sic] to haul across the cut off from above & below Vicksburg."

He accepted Brutus's offer of a loan, adding, "If I make crops and succeed in all these matters, I will make Christopher & Ezekiel whole again as to their hopes. I will either pay you interest or if I should take an interest in any of those places as you suggest which I have had charge of, and use your money in making the crop, I will make you a partner with me."

Finding himself the only person on six plantations who had remained in the South during the war, Christopher remarked, "I have worked all my life more for others than for myself. I was once very forcibly struck with a remark of an eccentric bachelor neighbor I had. He stopped me once when I was in a full lope by his house, says he, '[S]top a minute,' and said, 'I have known you for 15 years, been in a hurry all the time, ride a horse down every year, and you have not got along any faster than any body else. I would go a little slower the balance of my life.'"

Louisa Keiningham wrote Ann to thank Brutus for getting her sister-in-law a pass through Union lines. In Brutus's memorandum book, there is a cryptic notation, "Sent paper from Pres. to M. Keiningham." Mrs. Keiningham was anxious to secure a second pass for her sister, Emily Tubman. "A gentleman told me the other day I had better ask Mr. Clay for Sister's passport," she told Ann in mid-February , "that he had heard it on the street that Mr. Clay had already more influence with the President than any man at Washington. Is not that a compliment, for this is his first session? I want you to ingratiate yourself with the 'Powers that be,' so that you may assist also."

Mrs. K. also had news of the family at Auvergne. "I went out and spent Saturday with Martha. She certainly has one of the finest children I ever saw & she says he grows daily. She calls him after Ezekiel. She is looking very well, said two weeks ago her breasts threatened to gather, but now she is as well as she can be. She said she felt very lonely after you left but was getting somewhat used to it now. And I will not say how much I missed you, only that everything looked very quiet & lonely but Junius. He was as bright and cheerful as ever, talked about his Grandpa and his *young* Grandma."

She concluded on a self-deprecating note. "Dear me, dear me, what a scandalous letter I have written to the *Hon. Mrs. Brutus J. Clay Washington City*, the grand lady flourishing at all the grand receptions in her silk velvets, moiré [. . .], sattins [*sic*], and silks. What will she think of the *hen scratched* country epistle. But do pray do not forget us all way back home in this far off unfashionable land. I have some idea of going to Cincinnati to get a *new bonnet* to meet you in for fear you won't know me in my old one."

In Brutus's absence, Kit was in charge of the farm. He wrote his father regularly.

CHRISTOPHER CLAY

Paris, Ky., Feb. 23, 1864

Dear Pa,

I will attempt tonight to write you a letter giving all news of any interest here. I will give all bad news at first. About a week ago, I had put Joe & Milburn to work in the stone fence. [. . .] I sent Mingoe [*sic*] over to fix the frame and plumb the work. Mingo went over to fix as he was directed. Joe drove him off & threatened to kill him. I was out on the place with the hands. Mingo came out & told me what had occurred. I came to the house & sent for Joe to come to the house to me. He came in rather a bad humor. I said a few words to him & told him to cross his hands as I wanted to tie him. He very soon let me know he would not. I gathered a stick close by & we had a general fight. In the scuffle, he took the stick from me and struck me several times. As soon as I found he was getting the advantage of me, I drew my pistol, fully intending to kill him. When he found I had a pistol, he ran off & shooting five shots at him without effect, I then got my shot gun & dogs as soon as I could & followed him nearly to Mr. Gass' before I caught him. When I came up to him, he had his pockets filled with rocks & a stick in his hand & defied me to come near him. I run my horse on him, he trying his best to knock me off of my horse. I told him several times more to drop the stick & he would not do [it] & trying every chance he had to hit me. I could stand it no longer & shot him down. I thought for several days he would die, but he is now getting better. I suppose will get well. Before this occurred, I had to give 15 a general whipping to get them out to work at all. They have been free so long & you putting guns in their hands they are very near ruined. I intend to make them toe the mark so long as Lincoln will let me. On last Sunday night, some of them killed & skinned one of your fine Southdown sheep heavy with lamb. I have not yet found out the scoundrel. If I do I think I will tan his hide right. They have got the devil in them but I will try to keep them straight. The stock generally looking very well. I will follow your directions in regard to the farm. About the clover seed, Ficklin did not buy the seed as you directed & now it is worth $9. When the time comes to sow, do you wish me to buy at such prices? I have sold the Rye. [. . .] We will finish cribbing corn if we have a few days good weather. [. . .] I am pushing everything as well as I can, as I think nothing very safe at present. [. . .]

Yours Very Truly,

Christopher F. Clay

When I first read Kit's letter, I envisioned the scene between him and Joe as a tableau from *Uncle Tom's Cabin*, the white man on a horse with a gun and baying dogs and the black man on foot with a pocketful of stones. I still struggle to understand it. Kit was not a cruel man. I've read enough of his letters to be certain of that. But Joe was behaving in a way that threatened the already disintegrating relationship between master and slave. The enlistment of blacks into the Union army had done more than anything else to destroy it. As W. C. Lyle, editor of the *Western Citizen*, observed to Brutus, "It has affected very much the conduct of our slaves."

When Ann got home from Washington, she talked to Joe and determined that at the root of the matter was some sort of quarrel between Joe and Mingo. Mingo was the head man, but Joe was the master mason. Mingo gave Joe an order which, for some reason, Joe refused to obey. But none of this exonerates Kit. I can imagine Brutus scowling with displeasure as he read Kit's letter.

Young Cash wrote from school that he had bills to pay: his board at Mrs. Chiles's and his tuition, plus the cost of his washing and a new hat and shoes. "I have 14 of the 20 dollars I left home with remaining," he told his mother. Could his father send him a check for $90?

In Richmond, business at The Store slowed. In hopes of augmenting his income, R. G. Burton wrote Brutus seeking an appointment to a commission to assess damages to loyal citizens' property caused by the Union army. When Ann received a letter from him later in February, he had decided he would prefer a different appointment with a higher salary.

He added a bit of family news. "Your Pa has fully recovered and looks quite well, very regular in his attendance at the Store but yields to my persuasion not to work as heretofore and business is very small, doing very little owing to the fact that we have had small pox in town and the Country People are afraid to come to Town. Indeed I'm not much inclined to do much business this spring as we cannot tell when we may have a Rebel raid, and I well know that if they do come in to Richmond that we are to suffer in every way. Therefore it is better that we should have a small stock on hand until this outrageous rebellion is put down. Goodness knows we have suffered enough already on account of our devotion to the Government & it behooves us now to keep our bark close to shore for fear we may be sunk by some Rebel cruiser."

He concluded, "I hope you & the girls are having a nice time. Give them my love & say to them not to marry this trip. [. . .] Say to the girls they must attend all the places of attraction so the Washington folks can see the sort of folks we have in Ky."

Despite his earlier refusal to go to Christopher's aid, Zeke Field continued to worry about what he should do. "I have been trying to make up my mind to go South," he confided to Ann on March 8, "and had about done so but I rec'd. a letter from Bro. saying I must not come down unless he wrote to me and he did not think he would do so [. . .] [since] it seems guerrillas are still very troublesome. While they infest a country I would judge it would be money thrown away to try and stock a plantation."

Zeke reported that old Ezekiel Field was ill again. "He went down to the Barber Shop one cold windy day and had his hair cut which gave him a dreadful cold & cough." The family continued to worry about the cotton claims. "Uncle David Irvine asks me daily if I have heard how Mr. Clay was getting along with the cotton claims. If you have the time and it's convenient, please drop me a line upon the subject so as to satisfy Uncle David."

Whatever Christopher had told Zeke, he was clearly planning to restart the Bolivar plantations. Among Brutus's papers are bills for goods Christopher had purchased from Rice, Stix and Company, Memphis dry goods dealers that spring, including material for "negro clothes," oznaburg (coarse cotton cloth), calico, and shirting and a half pound of flax thread, as well as a pair of pants and a vest, presumably for himself. In March, he had the wholesale grocery firm of Lacey, Able and Company send him two barrels of flour, $45 worth of coffee, salt, sugar, a coal oil lamp and some oil, a dozen buckets, several bits for horses and mules, and an assortment of ropes. He also ordered drugs from W. A. Thorpe, a Memphis apothecary: a half gallon of castor oil, four boxes of mustard, a pint of diarrhea cordial, camphor, heartshorn, and sulfur quinine.

He wrote Brutus to inquire about his cotton claims. The "Sherman's March" he refers to in this letter probably refers to General William T. Sherman's role in the successful Federal assault against Vicksburg in the summer of 1863. By the time Christopher was writing, Sherman's troops were laying waste to central Mississippi from Vicksburg to Meridian, but small bands of Confederate troops still roamed the state.

CHRISTOPHER FIELD

Memphis, Tenn., March 10th, 1864

Honl. B. J. Clay

Dear Sir,

Since I arrived here I have seen Col. Sharp who made your acquaintance in Washington. He said you had not received my papers from Col. Phillips, the [Provost] Marshall of Ill. [. . .] This astonishes me very much as he, Col. P., voluntarily offered to take my papers to you and said he would do all in his power to aid me. If you have not yet heard from Phillips, call on Judge Trumbell, the Senator from Ill. Ask him if Phillips is still in Washington City. If so, see him. If he, P., has returned to Springfield, Ill. without your seeing him, please write him and ask him to mail you all my papers *immediately*. I am here waiting for A. Lewis. He has not arrived as yet. He has lost so much time that I fear nothing can be done with his project. Since Sherman's march through Miss., the Confederates have come back in the swamps along the river in small squads on both sides of the river from Memphis to Vicksburg to annoy and watch the boats. Also they say to keep the citizens along the river loyal to the Confederacy, to prevent them from planting. [. . .] I have been trying to get the negroes back, but I find between death, those in the army and scattered about, I can get but very few. [. . .] Nearly all of C's negroes are dead or in the Army. Those few I have seen say they will go home with me. [. . .] I am glad the Government refused to let me have condemned stock. It is of no value to work this season. I bought 27 head here, 6 of them died before reaching home. [. . .]

Yours,

C.I.F.

He wrote again the next day, enclosing "a statement of the larger injuries I have sustained from the Federal Army." "I fear I am troubling you too much and that neither will be rewarded for the trouble, but if you can do anything I will be gratified. [. . .] I learn from Mr. Lewis you had received my papers from Phillips which I was much pleased to hear. I hope with this claim, backed as it is, and the Government having had the use of our money for 8 or 9 months, that you will have but little difficulty in this matter. I think with my present arrangements if I am prudent I can yet make money this year. [. . .] Hold on to the money you have a while longer. I will keep you advised."

One notarized statement indicates that during the spring of 1864, the U.S. gunboat *Conestoga* had taken fourteen black men from Kit's plantation without whose labor Kit could not raise a cotton crop and whom Christopher had estimated to be worth $20,000. A second statement of losses on the O. M. Anderson place provides more details: "[T]he entire plantation force amounting to one hundred and twenty-four negro persons were marched down to the Steam boats and with their clothing, beds, bed-clothes and household and kitchen furniture were carried off; thus forcibly seizing and dispossessing the said owners of the means of availing themselves of the hired free-labor system, depriving the negroes of the kindly care and the comforts which they had been accustomed to and for the want of which, I have learned on investigation, forty out of the one hundred and twenty-four negroes, have died in less than the short period of one year since their removal; thereby clearly proving that both the interests of the negroes and humanity would have been advanced by having allowed the negroes to have remained on the plantation." Christopher claimed that these field hands represented a $75,000 capital investment.

Few letters still exist from the family at home to Brutus and Ann in Washington. By the time Martha wrote this one, Ann was already on the way home. Ann never said why she didn't stay with Brutus in Washington. Perhaps they both decided she was needed on the farm.

MARTHA DAVENPORT

Bourbon Co., March 10 [1864]

Dear Pa,

[. . .] I shall write [so] you may hear from home, as Aunt Ann writes you are always anxious to hear. Kit is away, I suppose nursing his friend Hillery Bedford who, in coming from town Monday evening, was thrown and dragged some distance by his horse which became frightened at something in the road. Kit was with him when it occurred. He was carried to Mr. Gass', but has since been moved home. The horse was found at home, having jumped all the fences. He sent 4 head of cattle yesterday to Mr. Martin, who was to meet them in Cincinnati upon Kit's telegraphing him. He remarked to me he had sold two more to the Indiana man who bought them from description. They were sold for $250. I suppose Kit claims the $50 as you authorized him to sell them for $200. He ordered Henry to kill the beef today, but as it is raining I suppose he will not do it. Mingo has been very sick but was in the shop yesterday. Isham is just getting out, looks very badly. Tom is laid up. Some of the women sick. [. . .] The sheep seem to be very unhealthy. For two days past they have brought me in a basket of wool from a dead sheep. I hear there was never anything like the sheep that are being killed and skinned (the carcass left) in the county. I wonder the farmers do not take some means to prevent the purchase of such things, as it is but an incentive to the negroes to steal.

Last week Sidney wrote us a note that [Hugh] Brent [the local provost marshall] said he must have the negroes for Camp Nelson, that should Kit not send them [. . .] he would certainly send a squad of soldiers and take several. Sidney advised Kit to telegraph you and compromise the matter by sending one rather than have the soldiers on the place. Kit refused however to do anything but that which you had directed him. Brent says many persons were complaining to him of your negroes being exempt and theirs taken and he did not think you should take advantage of your position, etc.

Kit says no one scarcely sent their slaves, and they have abandoned the impressment upon an order from [Gen. Ulysses S.] Grant, that no more slaves here to be impressed, but all hired and those sent back that were not at Camp Nelson. I tell Kit I know there is some abolition [mischief] [. . .] at the bottom of this very conciliatory measure. [. . .] I have just seen Henry. He thinks he is farming elegantly, he knows how you want things done and tries to have them done just as if you were here. [. . .]

We heard from Uncle Christopher through the Richmond friends, he was in Memphis. They seem to think he is afraid to go home as he writes the rebels harry a Union man on his place & threaten him upon his return there. Sidney says he has just now got his eyes open about the abolitionists' designs. Clay Smith seems to [be] held in great ridicule by his friends, etc. The baby is quite sick. Junius is well and says he knows now where Grandpa's big chair is, and is much pleased with his book and seed. He has been much bewildered about politics but after much talk concludes he is a "Union rebel." We look for Aunt Ann Saturday. Grandpa is very sick again. Mrs. Holloway, [Amelia] Burton will be here this week.

Affectionately,

your daughter

Ann got home that evening, a day earlier than planned.

ANN CLAY

At Home, Friday morning, 11 March [1864]

My Dear Husband,

I reached home safe last evening. The girls stopped with me to see Martha & will leave here tomorrow. We left Philadelphia on Tuesday night at 11 o'clock, reached Cincinnati on Thursday morning at half after 8. [. . .] I hope that you reached Washington without accident [Brutus had accompanied them to Philadelphia]. I can't tell when I have felt as bad as I did the day you left me & the next day when I heard that Papa was so ill again. I felt that it was quite probable he was not living but since I got home I hear that he is improving. [. . .] I found the sick at home better. Isham not yet well but Martha's baby sick with a violent cold and she very much afraid of his having croup. But Dr. Ray is here now to see him and does not think he is much sick and I am hurrying to finish this letter to send by him. [. . .] Please get Mrs. Tubman's pass as soon as is possible. Mrs. K. is like some one crazy about it. Met me at the cars to know if I had it for her. [. . .] Cit says he wishes you would come home so he can run somewhere to avoid the Lincoln draft. Joe came up today [. . .] to blame Mingoe [sic] with his affair. He was shot in the hip & through the left hand, is creeping about. In a few days I will tell you more about it as the Dr. is waiting to start. [. . .]

Yrs. devotedly,

Ann M. Clay

With Ann in Kentucky, husband and wife once again communicated by letter.

BRUTUS CLAY

Washington, D.C., March 12, 1864

Dear Ann,

I got home to Washington at ten o'clock [the] next day after I left you at that hotel at Philadelphia, did not get [a] sleeping car, sat up all night upon benches & [. . .] was much wearied for want of sleep. Have not heard from you since I left you. I hope you got home safe without accident. Upon reflection, I think you had better make sale soon of what wheat is on hand & have it delivered to the purchaser. Things is [sic] so uncertain we cannot tell whether or not we shall have a raid into Kentucky this spring. If it can be sold for a good price, sell at once & deliver it. [. . .] Also the cattle as soon as they are fat [and] through the winter. I would sell now but the pigs would have to be fed and cost as much as keeping the cattle. As soon as they can feed through let them be sold all together. [. . .]

I have so much to think about here I cannot think much about home. Christopher writes often and lets me know what is needed to be done. When my attention is drawn to any subject, I can then tell what is best to be done. I saw a call in the Commonwealth from [Brigadier] Genl. [Stephen] Burbridge [the recently appointed military commandant of Kentucky], ordering all negroes which [*sic*] have been impressed to be returned home to their Masters. I suppose I have none to be returned as I told Christopher not to send any under any pretense whatever. [. . .] I will take the consequences & tell the negroes to run off and get away if they attempt to take any. Tell the negroes what their object is, to put them in the war & have them all killed off under the pretense of giving them their freedom. They will win no liberty but all be killed off with hard work & exposure & in battle in place of the *cowardly scoundrels* from the North. Write often & give me the news at home & among the Neighbors so I may know every thing that transpires of note at Home.

Yours,

Brutus J. Clay

Brutus's constituents kept him posted on affairs in Kentucky, particularly with regard to the enlistment of blacks. On March 10, Colonel Frank Wolford denounced Negro enrollment in a speech in Lexington. Manly white soldiers from Kentucky did not want to march alongside Negro soldiers, he said, nor should they be expected to do so. Wolford was promptly arrested.

"We are in the midst of considerable excitement concerning the enlistment of slaves in Ky.," Joseph Bush of Winchester wrote Brutus. "Col. F. Wolford made a speech here on last Friday night on political topics. I was not present purposely as I had conversed with him only a few days previously & found him to be, to say the least of it, intemperate — Rumor says today that Wolford has been ordered under arrest — The tenor of his speech as reported was abuse of President Lincoln & his policy [. . .] [and] he defied the president to dismiss him from the service. The Secessionists seem to take some comfort from his position. They want resistance open and defiant, [are] not satisfied with the ground taken by the Legislature, protesting against negro enlistments. They desire the Executive of Ky. to defy the Government of the U.S. & bring the state into a collision with the Fedl. Government. [. . .] If Gov. Bramlette is made of the proper mettle we will pass through this ordeal unscathed. But if he hesitates we will have a time of it in Ky."

Louisa Keiningham's overwhelming preoccupation was her sister's pass. Brutus's memorandum book shows he sent one on March 7 (it never got there). In a letter to Brutus about the pass a week later, Mrs. K. added, "Ann & the girls reached here safely Thursday evening. She wrote me a note this morning that all were well. She has not been very well since her return but was much better this morning."

When she next wrote Brutus, Ann mentioned the Wolford incident.

ANN CLAY

At Home, Monday night [postmarked March 15] [1864]

My Dear Husband,

[. . .] I have been sick ever since I came home with Diarrhea. I thought it must be the water as it has tasted so mean to me. Sister Elizabeth & Amelia [Burton] came to Mr. Bedinger on Saturday & were here yesterday. They left Papa much better, sitting up some. James Miller came here tonight from Lexington Court, says he never saw so great a crowd [of] men and a good deal of excitement about the enrolling of the negroes. Christopher says that Bob Hearne is the enrolling officer in town & came to him on Saturday. He says he told him he was too grand a scoundrel for him to notice, but C. is so great a hand to exaggerate, I hardly think he talked so to him. He says that Hugh Brent [. . .] has resigned and a Michigan man is to be made Provost Marshall. I will try and find out what the people say & think & write you word. I have talked to Henry. He says he does not think any of our negroes will go willingly and said he would & did talk to them just as you wished. [. . .] It makes me sick to think about clothing them all at the present prices. I brought home about $220, did not buy what I expected after hearing Papa was so sick. I owe about 40 in Richmond, shall buy some groceries that we are now needing & other necessaries with the balance. Martha's child is much better. She is expecting Mr. Davenport if he can get a pass *any day*. I would not be surprised if you would have to get him a pass yet. I suppose he does not wish to take the oath. [. . .]

I find a great change in Martha since I left home. She gets much excited & talks a good deal, says she is a much greater rebel than she was when she came home. I suppose it is all to be attributed to her Secesh visitors. Whilst I was away, Aunt Liz, E. Bedford & even Molly Goodman came here, who was never in the house before. Aunt Liz told her that when Uncle Dug [Lewis] was fined, there was not a single Union man that would say one word to get him off [. . .] so you see you got no credit for anything you did. Christopher seems in a very bad humor about the enrolling of the negroes, says you began wrong by voting for Colfax & he knows you will come into this move. Martha says you have acted in such a way as to be abused by both sides, so write and give them your views. The report is that Wolford is under arrest for speaking against it [Negro enrollment] & Martha says if you do so they will hang you, that you will either have to run to Dixie or Canada for your life. [. . .] I dread to see Mr. Davenport come & hope he will not stay long. He has changed his mind quite soon as Martha says he said he never expected to come to Ky. again. They have a great contempt for the cowardly Kys. Ezekiel is now at Abington [Virginia] & the impression is that the rebels are collecting there to come into Ky. [. . .]

Yours,

A. M. Clay

A constituent wrote Brutus from Lexington on March 5, "Yesterday was our County Court Day — many citizens from the adjoining counties present. [. . .] A strong hope expressed that the Gov. [Bramlette] will do his full constitutional duty. They will stand by him. I hope the President will take counsel of his own good sense and at once correct the movement to enroll the slaves for military duty."

Meanwhile, another letter arrived for Brutus from Christopher Field.

CHRISTOPHER FIELD

Helena, Arkansas, March 15th, 1864

Honl. B. J. Clay

Dear Sir,

I have been here two days trying to induce some of C.'s & my own negroes to go home but I am now satisfied they have never intended going as this is the third time I have been here. Each time they knew I was not ready to take them and promised me if I would come about this time they would go. C.'s negroes say they are very anxious to go to Kentucky. I do not know that it is worth the effort but if you thought so and would write C. to come for them, I think they would go willingly. He has here Levi, Henry, Mary & 3 children and they say two other young women now gone off to the Army at Little Rock but will come here soon. He also has a small girl, Aga, the youngest daughter of old Fanny who died here ten days since. [. . .] I & David have about 15 here, all ages, but none have any idea of going home. [. . .] As time advances, I think stronger but little can be done in [the] planting of the River this year. I have just heard from home they have arrested some 15 or 20 citizens who have been trading in cotton and having the privilege of going into Federal lines too often as they say. I have been going about a good deal myself for 3 months but on legitimate business, have traded none in cotton. [. . .] I am now waiting for a Boat for home alone.

Yours,

[no signature]

As Ann had predicted, Henry Davenport contacted Brutus for a pass to visit Martha and the boys. "I am anxious to [. . .] go while there is comparative quiet along the line of the railroad, and shall hope to hear from you soon."

Kit wrote his father that the Federals were still enrolling blacks.

CHRISTOPHER CLAY

Paris, Ky., Sunday, March 19, 1864

Dear Pa,

[. . .] We have finished plowing all the stubble & commenced to sow the oats but the freezing weather has stopped us. The fat cattle are doing very well except one little fellow that is very poor & unhealthy. I think I will sell him to Jesse Kennedy for the soldiers to eat. We killed one for a beef, rather a small one. We have a great deal of fodder to feed out. The corn is quite light & we had to shuck a good deal to fill the crib. I expect to feed the cattle & cows until 20th April & left corn for that purpose. [. . .] We have had a few lambs, mule colts, & calves. All doing well, have not lost any stock of notice. We had to break a few mules to start our plows. Henry has sowed some clover seed, will finish when the weather will admit. We have had a good deal [of] sickness with negroes but no deaths. Some few cases of small pox in the county with the soldiers but no one seems to think much about it.

People here generally think that Lincoln's party will ruin them & is doing it as fast as they can. They are still going on enrolling the negroes. When people resist, [they] send soldiers to pick at them. They have not been to this place yet. I am getting all out of them [the slaves] I can as I think they will soon be no more. Some excitement about the negroes but *Lincoln bayonets* will quiet all, I suppose. [. . .]

Yours truly,

C. F. Clay

Ann continued to worry about the enrollment. Apparently, Brutus had told her not to give Federal officers the names and ages of the black men on the farm.

ANN CLAY

Paris, March 20, Sunday

My Dear Husband,

[. . .] Sidney [Clay] has just left here. [. . .] He seems quite sad & low down about the times and says the Secesh are bolder than he has ever seen them before and are confidently expecting the rebel army in. He is violently opposed to the enrolling of the negroes. But thinks it is no time [to resist] & [it] will only bring on more trouble to try to resist it or oppose it now. And says of course you know best what ought to be done, but he does not approve of your advice, for us to give no information in regard to the negroes, & asked me which I preferred to give in the ages & names of the negroes to some Bourbon man I knew or to refuse & have a dozen Michigan soldiers sent out here to go through the house helping themselves, insulting me, & to call up the negroes & tell them in my presence that they were free & better than their masters & etc. which if I refused would certainly be the case. [. . .] I told him I intended to act exactly as you had told me until I heard to the contrary from you, so please give this your serious attention & write me what I had better do. [. . .] Matt Clay told me yesterday that a week ago every one was all excitement, intending if Bramlette called out the militia to stand by him, but now they have quieted down, concluding that at best we lose only half the negroes [. . .] & he thought that was the conclusion the best Union Men had come to, that he thought a few weak-kneed Union Men like Sam Brooks was [sic] making a fuss who were always rebel sympathizers, & I suppose the Secesh are hoping the rebel army will come in before much is done. He said he heard that Charles Garrard was making a great fuss and talking a good deal. [. . .]

Mrs. Keiningham sends much love to you & says she has wanted to send you a good many papers but did not suppose you had time to read them but will now send you the Journal when she sees any pieces of interest. [. . .] She says the Journal had a very complimentary piece to you not long since. Sidney says that Clay Smith has made himself perfectly odious to his constituents & that he wishes he could hear a few things they say about him. [. . .] Lizzie Hickman was here a few days ago. She took Sister Elizabeth out & told her she would not have me for any thing say in Paris what I had said here, that was that I hoped the Governor would call out the Militia & they would resist this enrolling business. Said it was giving such encouragement to the Secesh & only hurting our course so I concluded that perhaps I had better say nothing. [. . .] Matt Clay told me that the impression here was that Bramlette had had some promises from the President, also that you had had some. Sidney says that Hugh Brent [the Provost Marshall] said it was strange you would refuse to send your negroes back to Camp Nelson, men were coming to him saying they did not know why they were [. . .] to send theirs when you had none there, said when this order of Burbridge's came out for the negroes to come back that he had positive orders to send soldiers here and take just double the number they had before & that that order was all that saved you.

Christopher took a sample of wheat to town yesterday. It was pronounced no. 1 wheat but he could only get $1.10 offered it. I told him we would take no such price unless you said so. [. . .] The fence goes on slowly; Henry is now sowing oats & the fields look very nice. All the negroes in usual health, some complaining. Joe going about but of course not able to work & I suppose his hand will never be as useful. He had a rock in his hand which caused the shot to wound more severely, was hit where his fingers join on to his hand, the three last fingers on his left hand. Also some shot in his head & some in his hip. Joe & all the negroes blame Mingoe [sic] with the fuss. He & Joe had not been friendly for one year. Mingoe in a very insolent way ordering him to use his Plumb line. Joe told him if he did not leave he would hit him with his hammer (he says he had no idea of doing it). Mingoe much excited, running off to Christopher. Joe says he is not conscious of hitting Christopher but only wanted to tell his story & be heard by Christopher, but I hope we shall have no more such fusses & regret extremely that it was the stone mason.

[. . .] Christopher has just come from town, says the 40th Ky. regiment is to be sent *away* & a Michigan regiment sent in its place. So do tell whether you are willing to have your negroes enrolled as the rest of the citizens are agreeing to, or whether we are to be insulted by them. Mr. Burton came here this evening on his way to Cincinnati, says every one submitted quickly in Madison. [. . .]

Yours, etc. etc.,

A. M. Clay

Brutus was annoyed that Ann and other members of the family were confused about his position on the enrollment of blacks. When I first read this and other harsh letters Brutus wrote during this period, I thought what a disagreeable person he must have been. I now realize that his awkward position in Washington was beginning to take its toll.

He also may not have fully appreciated just how upset his constituents were. On March 22, Governor Bramlette left for Washington, where he met with the president to discuss the situation. In the end, the governor assented to the enrollment if and only if Kentucky failed to furnish her quota of white soldiers for the draft.

BRUTUS CLAY

Washington, D.C., March 25, 1864

Dear Ann,

I wrote to Christopher yesterday. As I finished, I received your letter & last night I received Christopher's, after I received yours. I wrote a postscript [. . .] but this morning I concluded I would write again. Christopher is so anxious, when he gets a letter he is just as [likely] as not to never say any thing about it. I also received a short time ago one from Martha who gave me more satisfaction than any of your letters. You seem to think that of course I know a heap of things that I know nothing about and therefore leave me to grasp at your meaning. [. . .] In regard to the Draft, what do you mean when you say if we resist, they will send out a squad of men & take possession of the House & insult you all. What do you mean by resist? I did not tell you to resist anybody, but if I was at home & any man came to my house whom I did not want, without legal authority, I would put him out or kill him. A man because he is a soldier is not authorized to plunder any body's house. I am the head of the House and to me they ought to come & there is no body at home who is authorized to act for me in these matters. Now, if a man comes to see me upon business, if you don't know any thing about it, can't you tell him so & tell him to see me? Now I will ask you, do you know the ages of the negroes & if you don't, can't you say so if any body asks you, but if you do know about the matter you are asked about, is it your business to give an answer for me? & if you don't, is that resistance? I did not want you to do it because you might give in some wrongfully & I did not want my Books handled by any body. There are things in them I do not wish to be seen. I cannot recollect exactly myself about the negroes unless I examine my Book. I have endeavored to think who are of suitable age and enclose a list to you which you can give to the officer if he should call. The balance are too old or too young. Let nobody have my keys or go into my desk under any pretense whatever. My instructions to you & Christopher were not intended to be made public, nor my instructions about other matters, unless with those you have business with or trade to make. [. . .] You are too easily scared & too easily persuaded by others in opposition to what I tell you myself. Suppose you don't choose to give a list of negroes, the officer can only find out by other means, that is, inquiring about the farm, other sources such as they can. Your refusing is not like my refusing for I am the proper one to come to & you are not. You have no right to act for me unless specially instructed. I think the less you, Martha, and Christopher, tell the better it will be for us. [. . .]

Brutus J. Clay

Kit wrote a mild reproof to his father.

CHRISTOPHER CLAY

Paris, Kentucky, March 29th, 1864

Dear Pa,

[. . .] You have much complaint to make in regard to many things. I am trying to do the best I can in regard to all things on the Plantation. [. . .] If I fail I must still bear all blame. These are times that but few if any know what is the best to be done & but few know how to act toward the many Lincoln bayonets that now surround our immediate neighborhood. Troops of all kinds & character are here & I think the fair & beautiful fields of old Kentucky must soon be laid waste & annihilation must be the end. [. . .] Well, I will try & give you all news on the plantation. I will first commence with negroes. I am getting along with them at present without much complaint. [. . .] But negroes here are generally much demoralized by all doings, a great deal of stealing in the neighborhood. It seems as if every fellow is trying to see how much devilment he can do in that way. We are getting along, plowing very well. We have sowed all the clover seed in such fields as you wished, Kennedy field & rye field along the lane. We have also sowed the oats on the Kennedy place in the field near the pike. The stock of all kinds doing very well. We have had bad luck with the lambs. A good many came during the cool spell of weather we had not long since & good many froze to death. The mares are doing well. We have 6 young colts & I believe all the mares are in foal. We have several young calves. [. . .] The fat cattle are getting in fine order. The grass has commenced to grow a little. [. . .] There is some little excitement at present in regard to a report [General James] Longstreet invading Kentucky by way of Pound Gap. It is believed by many the rebels will certainly come soon. [. . .]

Yours truly,

Christopher F. Clay

Despite Kit's mollifying letter and others from Ann that no longer exist, Brutus remained angry with his family for not following his instructions and for asking "silly questions."

BRUTUS CLAY

Washington, D.C., Ap. 1st, 1864

Dear Ann,

[. . .] I have written several letters since you left here, more than I have received, & when I do receive them I am provoked when I read them. You ask such silly questions. You don't seem to understand what I write or what you read. You appear to be like children. Why is it you don't understand the simplest proposition? You write to me this morning to know if you had not better sell the Cattle & the Corn, as corn is worth 1$ per bushel. Now have you thought a moment upon the subject? If you have, you seem not to have a bit of sense upon the subject.

I wrote to you & Christopher to make arrangements to feed until the 20th of April. [. . .] As soon as you have warm weather, you will not lack grass but you must wait for it now. And I fixed the 20th of Apr. as about the average of [the] year to feed. Now you want to sell the cattle & the horses. Now I will ask you how will the hogs live? [Hogs ran in the field with cattle and ate their excrement.] Will they live on much? They can now feed from the cattle & if you sell the cattle won't you have to feed the corn to them to keep them alive until grass? [. . .] Are you like the worst of fools, sell now what you have & before another crop comes, get out & then have to run through the livestock to boot & buy more at double the price you sold them. This is the way many people do & they will always remain poor. [. . .] Now I have written so much about the cattle, corn & wheat & clover and I am tired & worn out in counting about these things to people who have no sense, goes in at one ear & goes out at the other, and as ignorant as before I wrote. If we had a surplus of these things, we might sell, but the first thing to ascertain [is] that we have a surplus. But this seems never to enter into your calculations. Do please have a little common sense and think a little before you act. I believe if you were left to yourself you would fool away what you have and starve. [. . .] Is Joe [. . .] so crippled that he cannot be of any service in the way of stonework? When he gets well, what is his condition? Put Joe with Milburn when not at work in the shop. [. . .] Tell Mingo I want some new gates made & painted to put up when I come home & tell Martha to write to me & give me all the news. [. . .]

Yours,

Brutus J. Clay

Cassius's daughter Sally alluded to the pressure under which Brutus was working in a brief note on April 1 to thank her uncle for sending on her pictures, described in Brutus's memorandum book as "Sally's photographs, 10 with hands clasped." "You say that you miss us," she wrote teasingly. "Ma wishes to know whether it is the trouble or the pleasure of having us. I tell her it is the latter, *of course*." She added a postscript, "Support Mr. Lincoln."

Ann wrote Brutus that everyone feared a Confederate invasion.

ANN CLAY

Paris, Ky., April 3, 1864

My Dear Husband,

[. . .] Christopher came home from town on Thursday in a very bad humor, saying the rebels were certainly coming, that our troops had all fallen back from Mt. Sterling, that there are about 7000 cavalry in & around Paris & that they will soon eat and destroy everything in the County & he is very anxious and uneasy about the cattle and the wheat & he seems to fear much that the rebels will come before there is any chance to sell and says now the cars would not ship cattle as they are so much engaged for the government. Last night he came from town in a worse humor, says he knows what they have come to Paris for, instead of going on to meet the Rebels, that it is to be *convenient* for running when the Rebels do get in sight & if I did not know him so well, it would make me crazy to hear him tell but I have seen him always before when the rebels were coming in this dreadful humor. [. . .] Christopher says 3 regiments stopped on the Kilmarnick farm [which Brutus owned] to camp but he bid them to leave there, and that they are now on George Bedford's farm slaying [stock] and destroying timber and everything. Mr. McClure's farm is occupied. Mr. Sam Brooks & some on the Georgetown Pike & more to come. [. . .] Christopher feels the responsibility of the place now very great, & is much troubled these uncertain times, but says he will obey your directions not to sell the wheat at the present low price nor the cattle till the corn is fed out. [. . .]

He says if the rebels come he will have to leave here. He says that Sidney [Clay] came from Camp Nelson yesterday quite a good rebel. Went for his negro man. Could neither get him nor any pay. Says the managers are all a set of *abolitionists*. They told him his man told them he was free and gave him his pay. [. . .] The report here is you have come out for [General George B.] McClellan [for president]. The Union people are quiet here because they are afraid to say anything but I hope they will do something to defeat an Abolitionist President, but I keep all this to myself rather than give the secessionists any encouragement. Martha seems rejoiced that the Rebels are coming. She is as bitter as any I have heard talk. She has not heard why Mr. D. did not come & has given out looking for him. One of the Union officers told Christopher that Ky. was invaded at 3 points & I was thinking it was quite probable you might be prevented from coming home when Congress adjourned. Have you given out the idea of coming this month as you promised? I saw John Kennedy at Concord at Church today & he says you had as well come home as you do not seem to be doing anything towards making peace.

We have had a heavy rain for a day & two nights & the grass begins to look a little green in the yard but very short everywhere, & if you were to come home you would be much disappointed to see so little done, but since I came home there have been only three days that we could work in the garden, either too cold or too wet & then so many of the negroes complaining. Isham still in bed, Sylvester done nothing since you left, his hand still running. Dansley cut or struck it with a piece of plank. Shelby complaining. I sent Joe to the Dr. last week & he told me it would be 6 months before his hand was well, a good many broken bones yet to work out of his two middle fingers & it is very much swollen. I have just received a letter from Sister Elizabeth. She is a good deal alarmed about the Rebels coming, says her trunk is packed, just ready to run at a moment's warning, says Pa is very feeble & low-spirited, mends very slowly. [. . .] Do write & let us know what you think about the rebels getting down here and what preparations we had best make for them. [. . .] I am in hopes it is not going to be so bad as Christopher seems to think. [. . .]

Yrs.,

A.M.C.

After receiving one of Brutus's angry letters, Ann wrote him back in a conciliatory tone.

ANN CLAY

Paris, April 6, 1864

My Dear Husband,

[. . .] I am sorry you did not appreciate our feelings. Our great desire about selling the cattle etc. was only because we could hear of nothing else but the rebels coming & *that very soon*. And as I had seen you so provoked once before about Christopher selling under just such circumstances, and he was disposed to obey your instructions though he seemed quite uneasy & troubled about it, we all doubted the propriety of his keeping them so long on an uncertainty when he was then offered such a good price for them. [. . .] We thought of the hogs & all that, and by no means wishing to convert everything to money mentioned if there was corn to spare we could sell for 5$ a barrel, and if you had been here a week ago, you would not have been surprised at our great lack of common sense. [. . .]

I have been sick for ten days, have seen no one scarcely [. . .] & hearing the roads & town was [sic] blocked up with soldiers & beggars I thought it best to remain at home. We have not been much annoyed with soldiers. A few been here to buy eggs & fowls. [. . .] Christopher says, that Jacobs & Woolford [sic] spoke in town yesterday to a crowd & *a delighted audience* though Christopher says, situated as we are, that he thinks such speeches are calculated to do much harm; but say what they will, these sentiments are the *sentiments* of the Ky. people if they were not afraid to speak, notwithstanding all this *blarney* you see in the papers about the attention that Clay Smith received. [. . .] Bramlette is much abused for *knuckling under as they term it*. Christopher says he never saw so much cheering or rejoicing as there was over the two speeches yesterday. [. . .]

I suppose you do not receive half of the letters I write or you would understand them better. If it stops raining, Martha will go to town this evening & if she can get any news, I will get her to write to you.

Yrs.,

Ann M. Clay

Meanwhile, Brutus received a discouraged note from Christopher Field, now back on the ruins of his plantation. "I signally failed in getting any of the negroes to come home," Christopher wrote on April 6. "They have lived such an idle life and supported by the Government that they are now and will ever be a worthless set, I think. [. . .] C. has 2 women, 3 children on my place. I intend him to have anything they may make or have made the past year. He has some mules & a few cattle which I am taking care of as well as I can, but we have Thieves & Marauders, deserters from both armies banded together and doing all they can to relieve the people of mules, horses and money, and I fear it will get worse. I think it will be years before this war is closed and can now see nothing favourable ahead."

It had been some time since Brutus heard from his nephew June

Holloway, who was no longer in the army. Out of the blue a letter, dated April 18, arrived from June's wife Laura, asking for $5,000 to enable June to start a dry-goods business in Huntsville, Alabama, now behind Union lines. She concluded, "For the sake of June, Uncle Clay, consider well before you reply and may the good angels hover round and tempt you to place a stepping stone for the young to climb." Within twenty-four hours, Laura sent Brutus a second letter withdrawing her request at June's insistence.

Ann wrote to reassure Brutus that the farm was progressing nicely.

ANN CLAY

Paris, April 9, 1864, Sunday

My Dear Husband,

[. . .] Things & the people seem to have quieted down a good deal. I was in town yesterday. There was one regiment of troops sent to Lexington, one to Mt. Sterling & another to Winchester. I do not know what it indicates. [. . .] But it is the general impression that the rebels will soon come & I heard that the Officers said let them come, that was why they had fallen back here. They would share the same fate [capture] that John Morgan did in Ohio. Mrs. Millerby Scott's place was sold yesterday. Sidney [Clay] the purchaser 3,515$. She had bought a place in Frankfort, gave 5000$ cash for it & expected her place here to sell for as much so she was much disappointed. Sidney is uneasy about the greenbacks, he also bought Tom Sadler's old place. [. . .] [Sidney was obviously buying up land cheaply during the crisis.] Mrs. Keiningham is almost well, says she would give a great deal to talk with you for one hour, says every body seems anxious to get clear of their money, for those that have been borrowing for some time have paid up, and she wants your advice about what she must do with her money, says she is more uneasy every day and particularly so when she hears of the Bank Officers buying land. Says C. [Charlton] Alexander [a local banker] has bought several tracts. [. . .] Mr. Burton bought me in Cincinnati 2 barrels of sugar & 1 sack of coffee. The bill was $160 which I paid the cash for. I also got him to purchase me a few cottons by way of a small beginning for the negroes' summer clothes. That bill was 220$. [. . .] Every thing is very high, butter 50 cts., eggs 30 cts. [. . .] and every thing else in proportion. [. . .] Have you heard from Green lately? & did you send him the money to travel on? I think if not that you had better do it. Whilst he is there, let him have all the advantages he can. [. . .] Mrs. Keiningham tells me as she was sick that Hugh Brent sent Mr. Whelan to check her negroes last Thursday. We have heard nothing more from the officers. I received your list in your last letter & if called on shall give the list. Write me if you intend to come home. We will be very glad to see you. We are all about wild.

Yours affectionately,

Ann M. Clay

Ann's account of land sales in Bourbon County describes the beginning of a process that continued after the war. Many Kentuckians sold their farms to wealthy men such as Sidney Clay, then moved west, often to Missouri, where land was still relatively cheap.

Brutus finally let out some of his pent-up frustration as he filled several pages to Ann about what was going on in Congress, a rare instance of his pouring out his feelings on paper. Perhaps because of this release, he no longer seemed as angry with her and Kit.

BRUTUS CLAY

Washington, D.C., April 11th, 1864

Dear Ann,

I have concluded this morning to drop you a few lines in answer to your letter I received a day or two ago. We are just dragging along here, doing little or nothing in the way of good to the Country. A good many of the members are coming and going home all the time. I would go home myself but there are one or two important measures [. . .] that these infernal *Rascals* are holding up to spring upon the House when we least expect it. One is a change of the Constitution [enfranchising freedmen] which they can not pass unless they can catch a very thin House [with] many of the Democrats away, & the other also in regard to the negroes, freeing all the family of the negro who should volunteer & go into the army. Every day I get more and more satisfied that these

Abolitionist Thieves don't want the war to stop until they accomplish their designs against all the slave states. On Saturday we had quite a scene in the House. The day before Mr. [Alexander] Long, a [Ohio] Democrat, made a peace speech, and [said] that he believed our trouble had narrowed down to 2 alternatives, that one was to recognize the Southern Confederacy, or to subjugate and exterminate the Southern people, and of the two he preferred the former. For this Speaker Colfax offered an expulsion resolution upon which a debate went on all day. [Benjamin G.] Harris [a Democrat] of Maryland made a very violent speech, and said very good things, & showed up the Abolitionists in [a] fine, able, sustained way & said he went further, that he hoped we would never conquer the South. For this, [Elihu B.] Washburne of Illinois [General Grant's principal supporter] introduced a resolution to expel him & called the previous question, & forced a vote, without debate, but the resolution failed 80 to 85, not having two thirds which it takes to expel a member. I voted against expulsion, for I have no notion that these vile rascals shall steal from & rob a man, & then gag him, and not allow him to say a word in reply. They then offered a resolution of censure against Harris, after they failed to expel him, which carried. I left the House before the vote was taken as it was late & the House [was] in a good deal of confusion & soon after the House adjourned. So today we have the same scene over again, as on Saturday, as today the resolution to expel Long will come up as first in [the] order. I would not be surprised if we get into a fight yet before the Session is over, as these abolitionists are very insulting & overbearing towards the opposition & particularly to slaveholders. I wish very much the session would come to a close, as I am tired of the business and anxious to return home.

In your last letter you seemed to be much alarmed about the Rebels. From what I hear from the Military Authorities, they don't seem to be uneasy about a raid from Pound Gap, & if there should be, there will be forces in Kentucky to drive them out. [Gen. Stephen] Burbridge who commands them thinks he has plenty of forces for the purpose. The object of moving the forces to Paris & neighborhood is to be close to the railroad to get supplies [. . .] although the troops will be a disadvantage to us, liable to plunder and steal from us, we must bear it. It is better than to be over-run by the Confederates. Christopher ought to be at all times at home to keep the negroes on the place and keep off straggling soldiers. Don't let them annoy you if you can help it. [. . .]

Yrs.,

Brutus J. Clay

Ann's next letter made it clear that she understood what was the matter with Brutus.

ANN CLAY

Paris, April 13, 1864

My Dear Husband,

I went to town today thinking all was quiet but much to my surprise found a good deal of excitement. The troops all getting ready to leave, some say to meet the rebels who are said to be in force at the Big Hill [southeast of Richmond]. [. . .] I asked Mr. Brent what he would give for the wheat. *Said nothing,* that he was giving 1.25 cts. this morning but was buying none this evening. That he knew the Rebels were coming in force, that we did not have the troops to keep them back, that he did not believe now we would be even able to hold Louisville. I asked Sidney [Clay] what I should do about the wheat. He said if the rebels should come I was fortunate enough to get clear of the wheat at 1.25, you would think I was very smart, but if the rebels should not come you would think it too low a price. So I shall go tomorrow & if I can get 1.25 cts., will sell it. It is the general impression that the rebels are near us and I have been much surprised that you have written as you have about their coming & treated our anxiety with so much *indifference.* [. . .] I send you a printed bill directed to you through the [provost marshall's] office. I was there today & promised Mr. Brent the list [of able-bodied blacks] tomorrow as he says he was directed to get your list in some way & had to report tomorrow at Lexington. [. . .] Zeke [Clay] is reported at the Big Hill today. If they [the Confederates] should come, Martha & me will do the best we can with everything. I suppose it is Christopher's intention to run if they should get here. There was not rock enough quarried at the pond for the fence & they are hauling today from the Kennedy quarry. So if you prefer them quarrying more at the pond you must write me word. [. . .]

[. . .] I hear of no disturbance with the negroes. They seem to go on as usual & I hear of no recruiting officers with them. Those troops that have been stationed near here are mostly Kentuckians. Martha says she appreciates your compliment about her letters as you so seldom pay one. [. . .] I know you must have a great deal to provoke you in Congress. I see from the paper there is a good deal of excitement about your friend Long. [. . .] It is a very free country that a man is not allowed to speak his sentiments & [I] hope you will remember all this at the next election. [. . .]

Yours,

A. M. Clay

Ann wrote Brutus again before a letter arrived from him.

ANN CLAY

Paris, April 16, 1864

My Dear Husband,

When I wrote you last there was a good deal of excitement about the rebels coming, citizens fleeing from Mt. Sterling & they are still afraid to go back. [. . .] Sidney [Clay] was here today & says the report is now that they are retreating and he does not feel uneasy for the present. But Christopher says they are coming & that very soon & will play the Devil with us. Yesterday Volney Bedford's Jepp, Andrew Lovely, young Hurley & 1 other Bourbon man was [sic] captured near Mt. Sterling and I suppose there is no doubt but Zeke and his regiment have been near West Liberty. [. . .] Christopher says the soldiers have broken your fence in a good many places at Kilmarnick. They did us no injury here. Matt Clay says he is afraid [. . .] you are sold to the Democratic Party, says are you not afraid of jumping from *the frying pan into the fire*, says the Union party is divided and he does not yet know which party is the most numerous. Patty [sic] Bedinger has just returned from Richmond, says her Papa [William Holloway] said your friends were down on you for voting not to expel Harris. I am glad you voted so. I will send you Matt's piece in yesterday's paper where he speaks of you dodging, etc. Have you ever said you were for McClellan? [. . .] I have been much surprised to see so little in the daily papers about the excitement about the Rebels. Can't tell why it is kept back. Christopher has some way of finding out & says he knows they are coming. [. . .]

Monday morning. I was sleepy & did not finish my letter & Christopher is waiting to start to town. As soon as I hear some news or any more, I shall write to you & hope to hear from you & would be so glad if you could come home.

Yours,

A. M. Clay

Kit continued to insist that the farm was in danger. He was fed up with soldiers no matter which side they were on. "We are at present in a good deal of commotion about the Rebel & federal troops," he told his father on April 18. "They are moving about in every direction. [. . .] From all I can see & hear, the Rebels are certainly coming into Kentucky. Some of the Federal troops camped near to us on Kilmarnick & pulled down our stone fence in twenty places, burned a good deal of fence for Uncle Douglas Lewis. Wherever they had a camp [they] ruined everything near them. I have been angered with soldiers until I hope I may never see another again. While they were camped on the Middletown road, they were at this place, night & day in the negro quarter, seldom came to white people's houses. Every body here in much excitement & don't know what to do."

Brutus's next letter to Ann was all business.

BRUTUS CLAY

Washington, D.C., April 18th, 1864

Dear Ann:

[. . .] I hope your fears in regard to the Rebels coming may prove unfounded. [. . .] The fat cattle I imagine could be driven to Cincinnati if the Rebels should come, therefore, do not sacrifice them through alarm. [. . .] Tell Christopher to put them on the best grass if he should have to graze them. If the Rebels should come it would be best to drive off all horses they would be likely to take. That would be mares & horses & mules old enough to ride or walk. There is some young stock of each kind [which] need not be moved. Tell Christopher to have all things ready to move the stock in case of necessity & not to leave anything to do when the rebels are upon you. [. . .] Has Christopher sold any of the Bull calves or not? Some of you wrote me he had sold & then again he had not. What has he done? How much rye was sold & to whom & at what price & did you get the money? [. . .] How much clover seed was bought & sowed, how much in each field, and what was the price & who you purchased it from, and does Henry think it is sowed thick enough? What is Christopher doing upon the creek? Has he finished the meat house and spring house and who has he put up there at work? Ask him if he has put the additional brick against the chimney I told him to.

Yours,

Brutus J. Clay

Another of Cassius's daughters, Mary, wrote Brutus in April about photographs taken in Washington. She added, "I am sorry to see Sallie's [sic] *lectures on politics* have done you no good, you are fast running toward the *rebs*. Who would have thought it *of you*? [. . .] Why didn't you vote against Long? I am afraid Cousin Mat [Martha] is making you all rebels at last."

Brutus's nephew Sidney sent his uncle information about the prevailing political sentiment in the district. Congress was busy hammering out a reconstruction bill that in its final form included the abolition of slavery. President Lincoln vetoed it because he did not believe Congress had the right to abolish slavery by statute.

SIDNEY CLAY

Paris, 18th of April, 1864

Mr. B. J. Clay

Dear Uncle,

[. . .] We are truly disgusted, mortified & humiliated at the proceedings of the Gov't. in relation to the Border States. The loyalists are & know not what to reply to the taunts of the Sympathizers, to whom we have been all along preaching that the Gov't. would protect us in our property & institutions if we remained loyal to it. They tell us now you see we were right. Lincoln has you in his power & [he] respects, as we told you he would, neither our laws, feelings nor property. They are jubilant over our betrayal, whilst the Unionists are almost despondent of the future, for if the Admin. persists in its monstrous policy, they think their cause must succeed whilst we the Border States Unionists will have no friends upon whom we can rely. Whilst the policy of his course is doubted, & even censured by some, the gallant Wolford is now the most popular man in our part of the State & the President universally condemned for his tyrannical course in dishonorably dismissing without a trial the Hero of *three hundred* battles & skirmishes, not for cowardice, not for treason, not for insubordination, but because he spoke in opposition to the policy of Mr. Lincoln & Co. Our *abolition* friends whose headquarters are at Lexington doubtless think it all right & that every measure is right & every act that tends to the suppression of freedom of speech in regard to our negro property. I have not been there & know nothing of the influence they exert over the public mind in their immediate vicinity. But here & elsewhere people have not yet apparently recovered from their surprise at the treachery of the Gov't. & the audacious villainy of the Republican Reps. in Congress. [. . .] Y'r. constituents of both parties so far as I can learn are extremely anxious to hear Y'r. views upon the state of affairs, & the loyalists especially to hear you upon the duty & the course of Ky. in the present crisis. And I *fully* believe yours will be the opinion of your constituents.

Much excitement prevailed about the time of Wolford's speech & his dismissal which has now subsided, & Ky. will submit to the enrollment & the draft I believe without even a riot. We are in daily fear of an invasion from Abingdon, Va. [. . .] I was at y'r house yesterday. All well. [. . .] Y'r negroes seem as contented & humble as usual. [. . .]

Sidney Clay

On April 16, Brutus wrote David Goodloe what must have been a very significant letter, judging from Goodloe's carefully veiled reply.

DAVID S. GOODLOE

Lexington, Ky., April 19/64

Hon. B. J. Clay

Dear Sir,

Yours of 16th has [been] received. I have not shown it to any one. And on your account *alone* prefer not doing so until I hear again from you. We held a large meeting here on the 3rd Monday of this month. The Union feeling was never more ardent. They passed resolutions denouncing the Chicago Convention [Democrats] and recommending the Baltimore Convention [Republicans]. I do not know any in this county that voted for you that are not in favour of sending delegates to Baltimore while those that voted against you, headed by Judge Buckner, are *unanimously* in favor of Chicago. I suppose one fourth of the state has held meetings and instructed delegates to go to Baltimore and have no doubt all the counties in the state will send delegates to Baltimore. And many of the mountain counties *will not allow* a meeting to be held to send delegates to Chicago. We are confident of carrying the state by a *large majority for the nominee of the Baltimore Convention*. I had a long chat with [Joshua] F. Bell [the 1863 gubernatorial nominee of the Union Party until he withdrew] as he returned from Washington. He says he will not go to Chicago and is opposed to going to Baltimore. But that *Ky. will certainly go for the Baltimore nominee*. I think your district will have every county represented in [the] convention at Louisville in favour of the Baltimore Convention whilst Buckner, Wickliffe, H. L. Duncan and others will get up meetings in favour of Chicago. Judge [William Cassius] Goodloe has just returned from Paris. Prall, Geo. Williams & others assured him that the county can be carried for the Baltimore nominee. [. . .] Many make inquiries for me every day saying that Wickliffe & Buckner insisted *that you are with them*. We deny. We are now threatened with a Rebel invasion and look to *Federal arms to sustain and defend us*. We can not see that the Democratic Party can do anything for us. [. . .] Hoping that you will stand by your old friends. Awaiting your answer. I am truly yours,

D. S. Goodloe

Unionists in Kentucky were positioning themselves for the upcoming presidential election. Should they continue to support Lincoln and the Republicans, or should they go for General George B. McClellan, commander of the Army of the Potomac until Lincoln got rid of him and now the probable Democratic nominee? The so-called Peace Democrats, who opposed Lincoln's continued prosecution of the war, had settled on McClellan as a symbol of opposition to the president's policies. In earlier letters, Ann mentioned rumors that Brutus had already come out for McClellan, but he hadn't. My guess is that Brutus wrote to tell Goodloe he was fed up with the Unionists.

David Goodloe mentioned Judge Goodloe's passing through Paris on the eighteenth, but he didn't mention the news the judge brought the Clays: that Zeke had been badly wounded in the eastern mountains. Since there had been earlier reports of his death, the family was at first skeptical.

ANN CLAY

Paris, April 19, '64

My Dear Husband,

Christopher says yesterday Judge Goodloe brought the news to town that Ezekiel Clay had been mortally wounded in the fight in the mountains [along the Licking River in Magoffin County] but Dan Bedinger has just come here from town saying that he heard [. . .] that he had been taken prisoner and was now in Lexington. Some man saw him there, but he heard none of the particulars & did not know who it was.

I sold the wheat yesterday to Mr. Shaw for 1.30 cts. No one else is buying at present. [. . .] Mr. Shaw complained at my asking him so much, sent me word in the evening that he had given so much that I must go to town & get me a fine dress with the extra price he had paid. [. . .]

Billy Gaines was here today. [. . .] He is as great an admirer as ever, says the world has produced but one *Brutus*, thinks everything you do is right, sends his love and says I must tell you he has *no abolition negroes*. He was a good deal annoyed at a Michigan regiment that was camped on Mr. Buckner['s] but now is in a very good humor as they have all gone. There is only a company or two in Paris at present [. . .] it is the impression here that Zeke [Clay] was acting as Brigadier in the absence of the General & had about 1500 men and it was the advance guard of a large force. Christopher saw a deserter yesterday that told him this. [. . .]

If Ezekiel is a prisoner I expect he is in need of clothing and if you are willing I would like to send him some.

Yrs. in haste,

A. M. Clay

Ann got infrequent letters from the family in Richmond during
this period. Her sister Belle Lyman wrote in mid-April that they had
heard Zeke was mortally wounded.

BELLE LYMAN

Richmond, April 19th, 1864

Dear Ann,

[. . .] Why is it that we hear so seldom from you? But perhaps you
make the same inquiry. I was thinking were it not for Pattie's [Bedinger]
letters that we should know but little about each other. [. . .] Pattie was
giving me the most glowing accounts of Martha, how much she had fat-
tened and improved. I said I knew she would holler when she saw me,
that I never was so thin and looked so old and ugly and toothless. I have
broken off one of my front teeth and will very soon have to have them
all extracted.

I received a long letter from Pattie [Field, then a student at the
Caldwell Institute in Danville] Saturday night. She had just received
the carpet bag of nice things I had sent her. I put the fan in. She was
very proud of it. Said she had no thought of your sending her anything,
but was very much obliged to you. [. . .] She has been much mortified
and distressed at that cruel slander that was circulated on her that she
had eloped. I received a letter from Miss Clarke, the head teacher in
the school. She wrote there never was anything more groundless and
false, that no girl in the school was striving harder than Pattie to discharge her duties more faithfully and that she felt that I had raised her
too well. [. . .] I have gotten a white girl on hire. [. . .] She seems to be
very good disposed, willing to do anything that may be required of her
[. . .] but does not wash or iron very well. [. . .] For weeks after Louisa
died, I thought I could not keep house without her, missed her so much
about everything and then we had so much sickness, but now I am
learning to do without her. Dr. Lyman wants to buy Mary but Mrs.
Johnson says no white women needn't expect to own her, that she has
no notion of such a thing, says Mary is making every arrangement to
buy herself. [. . .] Sallie's [Field] Millie has married a white soldier and
gone off with him. [. . .]

Dr. Lyman just came in, says Mr. Burton saw the dispatch from
[Colonel George W.] Gallup to [Brigadier General Edward] Hobson

Cassius M. Clay, the diplomat, age about 54, ca. 1864.

Bas-relief from the gravestone of Pauline Rodes Field and "little Pauline," Rodes burial plot, Richmond cemetery. October 1995. *Photograph by Berle Clay.*

Brutus J. Clay, age 55. Photograph taken in Washington, D.C., in 1864.

Ezekiel F. Clay, in his forties. Cabinet card, ca. 1880–90.

Cassius M. Clay Jr., age about 19.
Carte de viste taken in
New Haven, ca. 1865.

Louisa A. Keiningham, ca. 1865.

Auvergne, showing the lion gate. April 1966.
Photograph by Bradford F. Swan.

Mary Augusta Clay, 6,
Miriam Berle Clay, 46, and
Berle Clay, 4, in front of one
of the snowball bushes at
Auvergne. Summer 1944.
*Photograph by
Cassius M. Clay.*

Rebuilding the levees in
Bolivar County, Mississippi.
Tintype, 1860s.

Cassius M. Clay Jr.,
in his thirties.
Cabinet card,
ca. 1880.

Martha and Henry
Davenport's oldest sons.
Left to right: Henry, Junius,
and Ezekiel. Tintype, ca. 1870s.

Pattie A. Field, age about 14.
Carte de viste, ca. early 1860s.

Christopher Field's
tombstone in
the Field burial plot,
Richmond cemetery.
*Photograph by
Berle Clay.*

Field burial plot, Richmond cemetery. *Photograph by Berle Clay.*

Four surviving Clay siblings at the Paris railroad station, ca. 1905.
Left to right: Cash, 55; Green, 66; Martha, 73; and Zeke, 65.

Mahala Brent paring vegetables on the kitchen steps at Auvergne, ca. 1905. *Photograph by Cassius M. Clay III.*

Young Hamp Ayres with an armful of corn in The Lots, ca. 1895. *Photograph by Mary Harris Clay.*

that Ezekiel was mortally wounded. Oh! How sad and distressing yet I hope that it is false rumor. We have so often heard he was killed and it proved to be false. God grant that it may be so now. If you have heard anything more authentic, do let us hear immediately. [. . .]

Pa is improving slowly. [. . .] I wish he would go over and see you and Martha. If Martha has any pretty embroidery patterns, I wish she would let me have them. I am going to have a dress and casque worked for the baby [her daughter Pattie]. I am afraid you will think it a great piece of extravagance and nonsense when I had such a handsome one for David [her son], but it will be some time before she can wear that. I took a fancy to that lemon colored merino that has been in The Store so long and thought it would make her a pretty dress. I am crazy to put short dresses on her and will as soon as the weather gets warmer. I suppose Martha will too. Give my love to her and tell her she must come and see us as soon as the weather is favourable for taking the baby out. I feel so anxious to see her and the children. And you could get in the buggy and come any time and you must do it. [. . .]

Yours truly,

Belle

Brutus had also heard rumors about the capture of a Colonel Clay. "Can that be Ezekiel or not?" he wrote Ann on April 22. "I see nothing more in the paper today about it. If you know any thing about it, let me hear. If it should be Ezekiel, I am glad it has happened & hope he will be kept and not exchanged."

When Christopher Field next wrote, it was again about the cotton claims. "I was much in hopes you would have but little difficulty about our cotton claim. The others I confess I expected but little from at least during the war but thought as the Government had had the use of our money nearly a year now they would pay us back. I [. . .] was in hopes you would not have to go to the Court of Claims for such a transaction." He had been ill, he said, but was feeling better. While in Memphis, he had purchased two coats, a linen duster, vest, pants, and hat from R. Keiler and Company at a cost of $68.50, also an ounce of quinine from an apothecary.

At last Zeke's capture was confirmed. "I have just received a telegraphic dispatch from Col. Gallup at Louisa, Eastern part of Kentucky on the Big Sandy," Brutus wrote Ann, enclosing the telegram dated April 24. "Dear Sir, Your Son is at my Headquarters. He was wounded at Half Mountain. He is doing well. Will recover with loss of right eye. Your obt. servt., Geo. W. Gallup, Col. Comdg. Dist. Eastn. Ky."

On the same day Martha got word of Zeke's whereabouts.

MARTHA DAVENPORT

April 24, 1864

Dear Pa —

I have but time to write you a few lines as I am ready to start to see poor Zeke who is near Salyersville at a citizen's home, dangerously wounded if not mortally. We gained the first authentic information of him yesterday through Henry Howard. His right eye is shot out and nose shot through. I have hired a conveyance from Osland & Talbott [. . .], & Sidney [Clay] goes with me. We learn the road is quite good and no difficulty in getting there. Aunt Ann is I may say quite ill. I feel miserable about leaving her, but she is surrounded by friends and poor Zeke is among strangers. She has been endeavoring to keep the farm in the order you generally have it, cleaning up the trash. We rode out in the wagon for that purpose last Thursday and the jolting brought on one of her usual spells, except much worse than ever before. I am afraid it is also an inflammation of the bladder. We sent for Dr. Ray early after daylight and it is now 11 o'clock & he has not come. She has been trying so hard to attend to your business and also her garden, that she has broken herself down. She received your last letter asking about many things. I have not time to answer them all for you.

[. . .] I have just received by Dr. Ray a dispatch from General Hobson that Zeke's wound is not thought to be a mortal one. Mrs. Keiningham is now here, will stay with Aunt Ann while we are gone. Henry has finished planting our field of corn. [. . .] The boys are working along a little faster with the fence, one more stretch will carry them to the terminus, as you have directed. Henson is very sorry Kit has not sold the big steer as he is tired of feeding him. The grass is beginning to grow quite fast. Aunt Ann says the muskrats have impaired the far pond towards Ben Bedford very much, also the Rock pond dam. She says she intends to have them mended up as soon as the corn is planted. Kit is fishing so I know nothing of the rye. [. . .]

I never hear from Mr. Davenport. I don't know what is the matter. The children are well. The negro family are all well. [. . .]

Affectionately your daughter,

Martha C. Davenport

Christopher Field, who was in Cairo, Illinois, to expedite his claims against the federal government, wrote Brutus a letter of political advice.

CHRISTOPHER FIELD

April 26, 1864 [postmarked Cairo, Illinois]

Dear Sir,

[. . .] I have had access to the papers and speeches made in Congress and the general tone of sentiment in the North and have come to the conclusion that Union will never be restored, and I think you must come to the same conclusion after seeing and hearing what you have since you have been in Washington. I'm told you have lost position with your friends in Ky. I am not competent to advise you but were I in your place, on some suitable occasion I would make a speech in Congress [. . .], would state the feelings that activated me to wish a seat in Congress, i.e., your great opposition to secession, your love of the Union and desire to see its preservation and restoration, your desire to see the House organized without delay, hence your vote for the Speaker. I would tell them what I had seen and heard since I had been a member of the House, that the constitution had been thrown aside, no regard for it, the liberties of the people taken from them, free speech suppressed, & that I was still for crushing the rebellion and restoration, but it must be done in the pale of the Constitution. All these things I know you must have seen and that you must feel them. Make this speech and you will put yourself right with the people of Ky. and the whole Union, and the minds of your constituents are just right now to receive such a speech and with telling effects. [. . .] If you agree with me, prepare yourself for such. I want you to get my cotton claim all arranged if you can before you make this speech. I presume it is none too late to do so but I have been told if you had put the claim into the hands of a Mr. Risley who is in the Treasury Office and said to him you would pay him a fee, it would likely have been best and it might have passed without going before the Court of Claims, and I yet hope it may. [. . .] I am truly sorry to hear of E.'s capture and injury. He is a noble Boy and has made as much character and perhaps more than any young man in the Army. I have often heard of him during the war. You may have thought hard of him at first but you ought to be proud of him and forgive him. Burn this letter when read.

Yours,

[no signature]

Fed up, Brutus poured out his feelings to Ann.

BRUTUS CLAY

Washington, D.C., April 26th, 1864

Dear Ann,

[. . .] We are working day & night to try and get along & finish the session at as early a day as possible and will probably adjourn by the first of June. If so, I will not come home until the end of the session, but if I find it will be much prolonged I will come home soon.

We had quite a sight here yesterday. Gen'l. [Ambrose E.] Burnside marched through Washington with his whole army he has been collecting near Annapolis, said to be forty thousand, and among the crowd six thousand negroes said to have been principally stolen from the State of Maryland. I stood on the side walk near two hours and saw them pass. We took a recess in the House for the purpose. I got tired and did not stay to see them all pass. Burnside & the President stood on an elevated stand close by & they shouted as they passed, more particularly the negroes. It made me feel sad and depressed my spirits very much to see those poor, ignorant creatures deceived & flattered, with the hope of pardon, and then arrayed against our own people, and marching to their utter destruction, under the false plea of philanthropy, always in the mouths of these *infernal thieves*, who may endeavor to shield themselves from danger by putting the poor negroes in front of them. They will be put in front & in danger whenever it can be done, and shield the white men, and when it is spoken of they will give for an answer they would more rather have a negroe [*sic*] killed than a white man.

There is no telling what the fanaticism of the North will lead us to, and it seems our own people are catching the destruction. The other day [Lucien] Anderson [a Kentucky congressman] voted for negroe suffrage in the territory bill & Clay Smith looked like he voted against it with reluctance. His vote was very low as though he did not want any body to hear it. He is sold to the abolitionists body & soul. He is a vain creature & those abolitionists have flattered him & told him he was a great man. And I would not be surprised if he was not now thinking of being President of the U. States [Clay Smith did run for president on the Prohibition ticket in 1876] from his great devotion to the abolition cause, continually talking about willing to give up his negroes. One would think he is a great slave owner (& yet I know no negroes he owns). I reckon he don't own a negroe in the world unless it is some interest he may have in his mother's negroes, which he could get hold of to sell. I think about as little of him as any person I know. [. . .] The abolitionists saw his weak point, *vanity*, and made use of the knowledge. The abolition party here are the most unprincipled set of men I have ever met with in my life and don't suppose there will be such a set of *scoundrels* ever collected together again in this country. [. . .] The Constitution is nothing, law is nothing; their oath is nothing, their word is nothing; Nothing they won't do to carry out their designs. [. . .] All our legislation bad, the country will be overwhelmed in debt by the perjuring rascals & I fear ruined completely.

Yrs.,

Brutus J. Clay

Martha had delayed her visit to Zeke. "We were ready to start when Aunt Ann grew so ill I deferred going until the next day, she still grew worse, & I still delayed starting until today," she wrote her father on April 24. "The Dr. has just left, told me to tell you she is better. Of course she is quite ill yet, but feel assured the disease has begun to yield to medical treatment. Everything will be done for her that can be. Mrs. Keiningham, Amy and Eliza are her nurses while I [. . .] attend to all out-door matters to keep her from thinking of them, yet she will talk and regret not being able to have so and so done as you like to have it. She told me this morning she wanted to see Henry about the farming affairs. I told her never mind the farm. That that was going on very well. She is very nervous and cannot bear any noise or excitement. I will write to you every few days until she can write herself, told me to tell you she hoped to be able to write you very soon."

She enclosed a note from Sidney. "I had [sic] just seen a Gent. from Salyersville. He knows that Ezek was moved on Wednesday or Thursday last and advises you to go to Catlettsburg or Louisa. He is not mortally wounded. But better still *I do not believe he is wounded at all*. Will see you sometime tomorrow. I feel entirely easy about the matter tho not positively certain."

Meanwhile, young Cash sought his father's advice about college. "Mr. Sayre thinks I can certainly enter the Junior class at Yale, if I will go to New Haven early this summer, say about the middle of July. I wish you would allow me to do so for I desire to go to college. If I do not go on North this summer, I will perhaps have to enter a lower class, so by doing as I have before mentioned, I will both save money and time."

In Kentucky, Unionists were deserting the president in droves. George A. Robertson, a former Kentucky chief justice, wrote Brutus from Frankfort on April 28, "Mr. Lincoln's friends had a meeting here Monday week to appoint delegates to the Baltimore Convention and I assure you it was a small affair. The friends of Genl. Geo. B. McClellan had a meeting at the same time at the Court House. It did not hold more than one half of the people. It was the largest meeting I have seen in Frankfort for many years of the kind and [a] large number was appointed to the Louisville Convention."

All the anger that had been welling up in Brutus finally came to the surface on the House floor on April 30. The House was debating a Senate amendment to the Army Appropriation bill that would guarantee that black soldiers received the same pay, uniforms, arms, and equipment as white soldiers. This led to a discussion of black enrollment generally, as well as the "contraband camps" and the activities of the fledgling Freedmen's Bureau, which is recorded in the *Congressional Globe*. Representative William S. Holman of Indiana had the floor in opposition to the amendment. Thomas D. Eliot of Massachusetts was defending it.

Brutus rose to speak. "I wish to answer the gentleman from Massachusetts because he seems to be ignorant upon the subject. I will tell him that the agents of Massachusetts and other States and of the Government are not only in the western States drumming up recruits, but they are going about robbing and plundering—I may say stealing the property of my constituents, and yet he seems not to know it. I have certificates in my possession that troops of the United States have gone to plantations, the property of my constituents and others, and have swept away not only negroes, but stock, cotton, and everything else they could lay their hands upon of value, even household furniture and wearing apparel; a portion of the negroes having been put into the army and the balance of them, women and children, gathered in fields and supported at the expense of the Government of the United States."

He went on to say that Kentucky had supplied 57,000 men to the federal armies but that while they were fighting for the Union, their property was being seized by the federal government. "It is as true as that I stand upon this floor," Brutus declared. "I know it to be true. I have suffered myself. I know it to be true and I dare gentlemen to deny it."

Later, Eliot asserted that the contraband camps were not a drain on the U.S. Treasury because the people living in them were working for the government. In an Arlington, Virginia, camp, he said, former slaves had been given sewing machines upon which to work.

"I will say to the gentleman from Massachusetts that these servants are congregated in camps with no employment whatever," Brutus retorted. "They are brought together by thousands and are now dying with diseases of every description [. . .] and instead of being put to work they are lying there and literally rotting in their filth."

Eliot pointed out that the Freedmen's Bureau had been created just to prevent this sort of thing from happening.

"You are just murdering them by thousands," Brutus replied angrily. "I have information in my possession showing that on some different plantations more than one third of the negroes have died. This is the result of your system. Northern men are sending their agents to that country and by fraud and bribery are enticing away the able-bodied negroes — leaving the women and children to starve — and putting them in the armies of the United States to fill their quota, thereby saving themselves from having to serve. [. . .]"

Then Brutus launched into an anguished personal statement.

"Sir, as a slaveholder I have been scoffed at here and vilified for the last four or five months. I have held my tongue and refrained from answering, but my patience is worn out by this continual abuse. [. . .] I would rather be a slaveholder than one of you who sit here and legalize this robbery and stealing all over the country. That is what I think about it."

Brutus had taken the advice of Christopher Field "to put yourself right with the people of Kentucky." He had the dialogue reprinted for distribution to his constituents.

At home, Ann was no better. Mary, one of Cassius's daughters, wrote on April 30 to cheer her up. "I [. . .] regret *so much* to hear of your illness, but hope you'll be prudent and soon be well again. I was also delighted to hear [of] Zeke's wounds being no worse, though the loss of an eye is a very serious one and ever to be regretted." Clearly she did not understand how sick Ann was, for she added, "I know you are as busy as you can be in the garden. Sallie [Clay] is taking that off Ma's hands this year. She has a taste for such things. I have none, neither housekeeping [n]or gardening. [. . .] If I ever find any body suited to my mind, and that I consent to *throw myself* away upon him (the exalted opinion I have of the *masculine* gender) [he] is to be a lawyer and live in a city, so I'll not have any gardening to do except a few flowers and not much housekeeping."

Her relatives always thought Mary had a soft spot for her first cousin Green, the would-be lawyer, and she concluded her letter with comments about him. "I have almost fallen in love with Col. Adams of Woodford's command. He is a charming fellow, very handsome. Ma and Sal think him like your Green, but I do not. I had a letter from Green last night. [. . .] I shall expect some very interesting letters from him soon of his travels. Says he has not heard from home for a long time."

On May 1, Pattie Bedinger wrote Brutus that Ann was improving slowly. She added, "Cousin Martha and Sidney Clay started yesterday morning to see Cousin Ezekiel at Louisa. [. . .] She thought perhaps she would bring Cousin Ezekiel home, if he was permitted to come."

Meanwhile, Kit kept his father up-to-date on the farm. "I have had the last oats you sent here sowed. [. . .] We have but little grass yet, been so cold has not grown but little. The rye looks fine also the oats, the wheat not so well. The wheat on the Kennedy farm worth nothing. We are getting along planting corn very well, planted up to this time 4 fields. We have commenced to shear the sheep, are five fine cows that have calves and heifer calves. We are having good luck with all the stock on the place." He added, a little sadly, "I have tried to write you all about the place of any interest but seems I fail in every attempt to please you."

Sidney Clay wrote that he and Martha had finally located Zeke.

SIDNEY CLAY

Thursday — May — Ohio River at Ironton [May 1864]

Uncle Brutus,

While the boat is taking on freight I will write you a few lines. Cousin Martha & myself have been to Louisa on the Sandy to see Ezek. We found him with his right eye out & a small bullet hole through the nose. The ball did not touch the eye but the concussion from the nearness with which it passed I think burst the ball. He is out of danger now & except the eye, will be but little disfigured. At my request Col. Gallup sent him by same boat with us to Lexington to be given up to the Commander there. Ezek seems to be in only tolerable spirits. He lost in the battle, about 6 killed & near 100 prisoners & *deserters*. Col. Gallup 14th Ky., Commanding Dist. Eastern Ky. Louisa, is a gallant soldier, a fine lawyer and a noble gentleman. He treated Ezek with all the kindness he could have extended to a Maj. General. Placed no guard over him or his *surgeon* whom he permitted to attend him & in fact exceeded I have no doubt the rules of our army in extending favors & courtesies to him. He was much displeased with the conduct of his *surgeon* yet allowed him all the privileges of a loyal citizen simply "on account of the respect he had for Col. Clay's father." Of course he cared nothing for Ezek more than for an ordinary prisoner of same rank, & all his attentions, kindness, etc. to him, Martha and myself were on yr. account. Please write him a few words of thanks. [. . .] I will take it as a personal favor for I have no other way to repay him for his kindness to me & I know he would feel complimented by a letter from you. [. . .]

Yrs. Truly,

Sidney Clay

On May 5, Pattie Bedinger wrote Brutus that Ann had taken a turn for the worse. "Dr. Ray called this morning. I told him I would write to you this morning and what must I say to you about Aunt Ann. He said tell you she was very ill and he felt a great anxiety about her."

The next day, Kit told his father he thought Ann's condition "dangerous." He had additional news. "Mr. Davenport came to Paris two days ago." Cash had also come home from Frankfort.

A short time later, Martha arrived back at Auvergne. Martha and Sidney felt rebuffed by the commander of the military department of Kentucky, Brigadier General Stephen G. Burbridge, and his aide, Brigadier General Hobson. Burbridge repeatedly incensed Kentuckians with his tactless and often arbitrary treatment of them.

MARTHA DAVENPORT

Paris, May 8th, 1864

Dear Pa,

I reached home Friday evening from my visit to Zeke. He came with us on his way to Lexington, is doing very well, yet quite feeble. Sidney accompanied him to Lexington, sought an interview with Hobson & Burbridge, not only unsuccessful but felt himself insulted. Zeke was sent to Louisville yesterday evening to where no one knows. The authorities would give no information in regard to his destination. Poor Boy. I fear I shall never see him again. I found Mr. Davenport here when I came. Aunt Ann has been very ill in my absence but is mending. Still very weak and it will be a long time before she will be well again. She told me this morning to tell you she was better and did not want you to come home until the session ended. Mrs. Keiningham is in great distress about Mrs. Tubman. Says she believes she will not live through the summer if Mrs. Tubman does not come, looks very badly. She has a recent letter from her, says she has received no pass. [. . .] Aunt Ann says Mrs. Keiningham has been more than a sister to her, spent two weeks with her nursing her day & night, has just left, and she hopes you can do something towards getting her another passport. [. . .] Cash & Kit gone to the creek fishing. I know nothing of the farming operations and have not had time to send for Henry. [. . .]

Affectionately your daughter,

M . C. Davenport

Alarmed by Ann's illness and disgusted with the situation in Congress, Brutus returned to Kentucky in mid-May even though the House was still in session. Representative Holman wrote to tell him that copies of their "remarks" of April 30 were on their way to Kentucky and to fill him in on the latest political scuttlebutt. "The Baltimore Convention will of course nominate Mr. Lincoln. I firmly believe that on the nomination & election of a conservative statesman the fate of the country depends. If the extreme views of the New England politicians are to control the Government for four years longer, the fate of this Country is decided and the restoration of the Union rendered impossible."

Auvergne was fuller than it had been in years: Brutus, Ann, Kit, Cash, and all the Davenports. But Zeke was imprisoned at Johnson's Island in Ohio. And, despite his misgivings, Green remained in Italy.

ELEVEN

The Best of Fathers

As expected, the Kentucky Unionists split in 1864. The Union Democrats held their convention in late May and chose delegates to the Chicago Convention, instructed to support General McClellan for president and Kentucky governor Thomas E. Bramlette for vice president. On the same day, the Unconditional Union party also picked delegates to the Baltimore convention pledged to support Lincoln for president and Andrew Johnson for vice president. In a speech, Brutus denounced President Lincoln for using extreme methods to prosecute the war. He was an Unconditional Union Man no longer.

Although he still hoped to get to Kentucky in August, Christopher Field remained in the South. He wrote Brutus in July 1864 that he had heard that Brutus had failed to get the Treasury to pay their claims but was intending to pursue the matter before Congress. "This I was sorry to hear as I had some lingering hope that you would succeed. [. . .] I must ask you to try and get our claim through without any publicity to my name if you can do so, for I would subject myself or effects to confiscation at home, etc. I was thinking perhaps G. C. Smith might be able to accomplish now more than you could and would be perfectly satisfied with any arrangement you might make with him."

Christopher added, "I saw some extracts of a speech you made before leaving for Ky. and heard you had made one at home which has placed you right with your constituents at last which I think was wise from you and was glad to see it."

Ann's illness kept her a semi-invalid. Mrs. Keiningham, visiting

406

her brother and his family in Frankfort, wrote to cheer her up, then added these uncheerful comments, "[P]olitical matters seem to be in a much more excited state here than up at home. The feeling between the two parties much more bitter. I cannot but feel uneasy the whole time, and before the November election there may be an outbreak. I have seen but two or three abolition friends but all these *strong Union* men seem to be very much outraged at the way things have turned, and they do not hesitate to express their sentiments in the strongest language." Two days earlier, Lincoln had issued a proclamation establishing martial law in the state and suspending the writ of habeas corpus in order to prevent so-called secessionists from interfering with the upcoming elections.

By late July, Kentucky slaves were in an uncertain position. While many still remained with their masters, others had gotten a taste of freedom from their association with the Union army. Among Brutus's papers is a letter written to Miss Matilda Clay (a slave), care of Mrs. B. J. Clay. Matilda, twenty-one, was one of Amy's children and the mother of a four-year-old boy, Wallace. Her correspondent, Wallace Estill, who was not one of Brutus's slaves, appears to have been working for the army, though not yet a soldier.

WALLACE ESTILL

Castle Merion, July 30th,/64

Dear Cousin,

I now meet with the opportunity at last of writing you a few lines to let you know that I am well at present and doing first rate. I am also in hopes dear Cousin that this letter may find you enjoying the same blessing. I have been wanting to hear from you dear cousin the worse kind for a long time but could not hear a word from you. Dear Cousin I think you have a right to believe that I have forgotten you entirely. But it is not that way. You are ever on my mind as pleasant as my own dear sweet heart. You have no idea how often that I think of you and wish to be in your company. Often I sit and call to memory the happy moments that I spent while I was with you and wish them over again but I fear never. It looks to me as if it were impossible for me to live ever at home so you must excuse me for not coming over.

I am in hopes that you will not be so considerable [sic] as not to forgive me for not writing to you before now. The reason was that I have been out in the Army Department all the year. We are all generally well none of our boys has yet volunteered. I heard yesterday that Miss Ann Clay was very unwell. Mother & Sister sends their love to all. Give my love to all and except a portion for your self. I still remain your true & affectional [sic] Cousin.

Wallace Estill

[P.S.] Answer me.

One of Brutus's men, David Hill, who had left Auvergne to join the army, wrote his mother, Narcissa, from Russellville.

DAVID HILL

Russellville, Ky., Aug. 4th, 1864

My Ever Dear Mother,

I take my pen in hand to let you know that I am enjoying good health at present & I hope my lines may find you the same. We came from Bowling Green last Saturday & we are to march from here next Saturday. We drill twice every day, once in the morning & once in the evening. When we came from Bowling Green we left Charley & Jack Smith behind. They belong to another company. Shelby Richson sends his best love and compliments to his Mother [Edy], Father, Brother & Sister & especially his love to Miss Ellen Johnson. He is well and doing well. I eat when I get hungry & drink when I get dry. I joined the Union Army to live until I die.

A few lines to Miss Emma Turner. Miss Emma I wish that I could see you. What a good old chat we would have. But my Darling be patient & when this cruel war is over if God spares my life I will meet you again. I never knew that I loved you so well until I had to part from you. Forget me not Emma & my love for you shall never fail. I will send you my picture the first opportunity I have to get one taken. Give my respects to Miss Nany Clay also to Miss Bell Tillman. Tell her I have not forgot her yet. Tell Napoleon that we have all sorts of pleasure. I well remember when he lay at my feet in the same bunk with me. How he cried to go home. If he had known what good times I & the Sims boys have traveling around through the country money would not have hired him to run away from Camp Nelson. There is more pretty Ladies in this place than any town I was ever in. Camp is full all the time. Some remind me of a velvet rose before the dew leaves it in the morning on account of looking so fresh & Beautiful. Tell Isom Turner that I am well and give my compliments to him. Tell him I often think of the pleasant times we have spent together. I send my Respects to Father & should like to hear from him but 'tis impossible for me to hear from him until we get stationed. David Turner sends Respects to Isom Turner, also to his uncle, Harrison.

Respectfully Yours,

David Hill
Co. "B," 12th U.S.C.T.

[P.S.] Respects to all the Boys, Good Bye.

David Hill, along with Shelby Richson, were among the first young men from Auvergne to join the army. Both enlisted on July 21 in the Twelfth Heavy Artillery Regiment based at Camp Nelson in Jessamine County. David, at twenty-one the oldest of Narcissa's ten children, was articulate and educated. I don't know what happened to him, but his nephew George Brent grew up on the farm and became my grandmother's personal servant. Shelby, twenty-two, was one of Edy's sons. Charley and Jack Smith, also mentioned in David's letter, left Auvergne a couple of days after David and Shelby to join the same artillery regiment. Though David mentions that Napoleon ran away from Camp Nelson, Napoleon enlisted in the Fifth Cavalry Regiment there on August 29.

The previous March, Congress had passed legislation freeing the families of black soldiers, thus increasing the incentive for slaves to enlist. Seventeen young men from Auvergne joined the Union army between May 1864 and January 1865, according to Brutus's records: Napoleon Bonaparte, David Hill, David Ayres, Samuel Turner, Jack Smith, Israel Ayres, Charles Smith, Will Clay, Edmund Berry, Henson Clay, Isom Turner, John Zimmerman, Augustus Waters, Warrick Turner, Andrew Ayres, George Clay, and Richason Shelby (presumably Shelby Richson).

For many of them, joining the army meant assuming formal surnames for the first time. Mingo's son Henson took the name Clay, though there is no evidence to indicate whether Mingo also took that name. Will Clay, "Amy's Will," was probably not Mingo's son. Neither was George Clay, later murdered by Confederate soldiers while he lay wounded in a hospital, following one of General Burbridge's forays into southwestern Virginia to destroy a salt works there.

Brutus simply couldn't comprehend why these young men would want to leave the farm, since he believed the Union army intended them for cannon fodder. George Clay's sad end in Burbridge's ill-prepared army would support Brutus's belief. While Brutus cherished his own freedom, he simply couldn't understand that his slaves prized their newfound freedom enough to risk dying for it.

Hoping to be compensated for the loss of his slaves to the army, Brutus later filed claims of $300 per man for the seventeen listed above. He was never paid.

On the first of August, Christopher Field presented Brutus with an accounting of the expenses the Clay and Field plantation had incurred since 1862. These included items such as bacon, medicine, a midwife, the repair of two chimneys, and state and county taxes. On the credit side of the accounting, Christopher listed the sale of two mules, a cow, a heifer, and eighteen bales of cotton. By including what he calculated the government owed him for lost cotton and other injuries and outstanding notes, Christopher calculated that the expenses and the costs came out even, $4,600. Bills from various Memphis merchants at the same time show that Christopher had purchased staples such as salt, black pepper, oznaburg, red ticking, and flannel, as well as a silk hat and a cravat.

Despite his mother's continuing ill health, young Cash left for Yale in early August. His first impressions were not favorable. This letter in which Cash describes the college as being more suitable for "bats and owls" than boys is a favorite of my brother, a Yale graduate, and contrasts sharply with Green's first letter home.

CASSIUS CLAY JR.

New Haven, Aug. 11th, 1864

My Dear Ma,

I arrived here tonight about six o'clock. My trunk and carpet [bag] are both safely landed here. New Haven is a city of about 40 thousand inhabitants, being much larger than I supposed. The college buildings look old and gloomy, seeming as if they were abodes for bats and owls instead of boys, but perhaps this was the effect of the darkness which when I saw them was throwing her sable mantle over the face of the earth. Since leaving home, I have travelled incessantly until this period. I intended getting all my winter clothing in New York, but everything being so high I only bought a coat, intending to get what I needed when I wanted them at New Haven. Thus far I have not used any of my letters of introduction but will tomorrow make several calls.

Your son,

C. M. Clay Jr.

Young Cash wrote his father the following day, "If it were not for [the] expense I have incurred in coming here, I would return home. Thus far I have learned nothing as to board, tuition, etc. I am very homesick and you need not be surprised to see me any time."

A few days later, he again raised the possibility of returning to Kentucky. "If I don't enter the junior class," he wrote his father, "I shall come home and, if you permit it, will go to Dan. Col. [Centre College] but if you desire that I stay here then certainly I will remain." He added miserably, "I am very sorry that I show so much indecision of Char. [character] but I can't help it, and you must make some allowances for a homesick boy. Green, when he came here, was accompanied by several friends. I regret that I made up my mind to come here, but suppose, as I am here, I will have to remain." He concluded with the admonition, "Don't show this letter to anybody."

The following day, Cash wrote again.

CASSIUS CLAY JR.

New Haven, Conn., Aug. 15th, 1864

Dear Pa,

After calling at five or six boarding houses, the only room I could find was a poor one. I could get the room for three dollars and board for six, exclusive of fuel, washing, light, etc. Thus my board would be about 11 or 12$ per week and very poor at that. After the school commenced, I would have to give up my room. Thus boarding will be still higher, say

13 or 14$ per week. I can't get a room in College which I would now greatly prefer considering all circumstances.

A Tutor will charge over a dollar per hour. The college fee has doubled. Pa, I think I can go to other schools at much less expense which are fully as good as Yale, though they may perhaps not have an equal reputation. It seems as if the people try to take advantage of all circumstances to charge high for rooms, etc. etc. etc. I find to my surprise that the college is not using the text books that I supposed. I found a tutor today but as yet have made no definite arrangement with him. [. . .]

I hardly know whether I can enter college at all. I was introduced to one professor this morning but found him a fanatical abolitionist. But I am prudent and never intend to get into any dispute with them. I am dissatisfied with every thing but perhaps may be more contented after some time. [. . .]

Your son,

C. Clay Jr.

Reading Cash's first letters from New Haven, I am reminded of my own arrival at boarding school. I was four years younger than Cash. Like him, I had rarely left Kentucky, having never attended camp or indeed gone anywhere on my own. After a magical night at a Broadway performance of *The King and I*, my mother deposited me at the school where she had taught Latin and French for a number of years before marrying my father. Nothing in my life on the farm had prepared me for the give-and-take of living in a house with some thirty other teenage girls. During my first week there, I spent almost every evening in the wooden phone booth on the first floor having tearful conversations with my mother, who was still in New York.

Ann wrote immediately to reassure Cash.

ANN CLAY

Paris, August 17, 1864

My Dearest Child,

Oh, how much I feel for you but I knew exactly how you would feel & have thought of you hourly since you left. I hope you have received my letters written last week. Your Papa laughed at me for writing so soon. I told him I knew it would be acceptable. I [. . .] cannot say that I am so much surprised at your being so homesick [. . .] but am sorry to hear that you think of coming home but I sincerely hope by this time that you are better satisfied but I hope to see your Papa by tomorrow & shall consult with him & will write to you what he thinks best for you to do. I am now with Mrs. Keiningham & have been here for three days. Feel much better than when you left home & hope soon to be well again. Mrs. K. says I shall not go home for three weeks. I expected to go to Richmond next week but Dr. Lyman was to see me on Saturday and advises me not to take so long a trip yet awhile. [. . .]

Mrs. K. sends her love & says do you now feel just as she told you [you] would but to tell you you will soon get over that. She seems so anxious for you to remain at Yale so I hope you are now studying and are not so homesick. You will soon get over that and be contented. Nothing has happened since you left. [. . .] Zeke wrote he was suffering from his wound again. Kit has scarcely been at home since you left, so all is quiet. [. . .]

Yrs.,

Ann M. Clay

Ann was not the only member of the family who was ill. Eliza Smith wrote Brutus on August 17, "Mother has been very feeble for 10 days. She has shortness of breath and can barely walk about the room with assistance. [. . .] If Ann is well enough, I wish you would come over and see us." Mary Jane Clay wrote Brutus a short time later about her family's debts, adding, "Your mother is very feeble I understand and much desires to see you."

By late August, Cash wrote his mother in a more cheerful vein.

CASSIUS CLAY JR.

New Haven, Conn., Aug. 27th, 1864

Dear Ma,

[. . .] I am glad to find that you are a great deal better and write in a more cheerful tone. As for studying, I have been studying hard for the last week.

I was not as much surprised as you would suppose to hear that Henson and Isham had joined the army as I expect that we will lose them all that are able to go. Indeed the abolitionists are almost entirely to blame for it and if you would prevent it, we will have to do away [with] them.

I see that Chicago is crowded with Democratic candidates. Reading the New York World, you would suppose that McClellan would certainly [be] nominated. And in reality I find that all the Dem. in this part of the country are in favor of him. [. . .]

I am sorry to hear that Noah Alexander is a negro recruiting officer as I think that we Kentuckians should leave such work to the Northern fanatics.

The weather has been for several days very warm, even as much so as in Kentucky in the middle of summer. I have not as yet bought any winter clothes.

I have seen nearly all the wonders this city affords, which are not many.

Your affectionate son,

C. M. Clay Jr.

[P.S.] I suppose by the time I get through here I will be completely Yankeefied. [. . .]

After a long silence, a letter finally arrived from Green, dated August. He enclosed information about garden sculptures from Carrara, which Ann had apparently requested ("statues representing Europe, Asia, Africa & America, 5 ft. high in ordinary marble for [. . .] $250 each"). Possibly she was thinking of ordering some for Auvergne.

In the late 1850s, two handsome lions appeared on the gateposts in front of the house, one dozing, the other watchful. Brutus got the lions from someone in Paris, Kentucky, but it isn't clear whether this person carved them or simply procured them. According to family legend, a man leading a cow over to be bred to one of Brutus's bulls spotted the lions and, thinking them real, fled with the cow. As a child, I used to straddle the watchful lion for hours, daydreaming myself to faraway places as I rode.

Green sounded bitter. "In two successive letters to Pa I tried to impress upon him the constant rising scale of exchange. His long and absolute silence [. . .], I of course took for a refusal [to send money], and could not [but] think it strange that Pa should insist on me being brought up in a diplomatic life in the *most expensive* & *worst paid* of the whole public service and then not to allow me a sum the greater portion of which I had refunded to him. I don't gamble and at this age might be trusted yet I have no complaint to make. Pa's theory may be the wisest, tho it appears to me he must expect persons, like the fabled Mercury [*sic*] from the head of Jove , to leap full-grown into experience and business life. He must know I accepted this position mostly on his account. And that in order to serve honorably I have given up or at least suppressed political convictions [. . .] which were at variance with the policy of an administration of which I hold office. [. . .] Zeke was braver than I! I hope, the poor fellow, they will not kill him in prison."

He rambled on for several more pages about the abolition of slavery and the suspension of civil rights in Kentucky, concluding, "Whatever my fault may be, I hope the solicitude I sometimes show about some affairs will not be construed — even in such an hour — and how could it *reasonably* be any other time? — other than that of a patriotic heart — somewhat embittered at [the] ruin and the degradation of American Liberty."

In September, a letter arrived for Ann from Zeke in prison.

EZEKIEL CLAY

Johnson's Island, Ohio, Sept. 11, 1864

Aunt Ann —

Yr.'s of Sept. 1st was received a few days since. Was very glad to hear from you. By recent order we are limited to two letters a week, hence my delay in answering yr.'s. Have written to Sis several times since heard from her, can't account for her silence. [. . .] Have received one letter from Cash since he arrived in New Haven. Answered it in due time, but have not heard from him since — Felt very much disposed to write several times; insisting on his remaining with Mr. Sayre one more session — he would then find little or no difficulty in entering [the] Junior class and graduating in two years, but did not know whether it would be received kindly, and in the spirit in which it would have been written. [Cash did enter the junior class.] Am truly glad that he's willing to receive a thorough education. I deplore the present condition of affairs in Ky. very much. Sorry to hear of Uncle Cit's illness — hope he will soon be well — please remember me kindly to him. [Christopher Field was in Kentucky for the first time since 1861.] How are the ne-

groes getting along? Are Uncle Henry and Mingo still alive? Say to
Aunt Amy the butter she sent me was the best I ever ate. My wound
still suppurates very freely. Dr. thinks it will be a long time before it gets
entirely well. Remember me kindly to Mrs. Tubman and Mrs. Keiningham — Hope to hear from you often.

Aff'ly,

E. F. Clay

Brutus campaigned actively for McClellan, attending picnics and
making speeches. "[Curtis] Burnam is to speak [. . .] [in Nicholas
County] on Thursday next," Senator Garrett Davis wrote him on September 23, "and our friends are more than anxious that you should be
there to answer him. [. . .] Many in Nicholas have not yet decided how
they will go in the next election & I know you could do much good by
speaking to them."

The war dragged on throughout the summer. The Federal armies
were on the offensive everywhere. On September 1, General Sherman's
men took Atlanta. On the nineteenth, General Philip H. Sheridan defeated General Jubal Early's army in the Shenandoah Valley, thus open-
ing up an avenue from the North into the heart of the Confederacy.

The Kentucky war consisted mostly of guerrilla skirmishes. Robbers
stole horses and held up toll keepers. The military government grew
harsher and more arbitrary. Military authorities arrested men throughout the state and held them without hearings. Three days before the
state elections in August, General Burbridge ordered the name of
the Democratic candidate for chief justice of Kentucky stricken from
the ballots in order to ensure the election of the Republican candidate.
But the Democrats telegraphed the name of a well-known former chief
justice to all the polling places the morning of the election and he won.

The presidential campaign was a nasty one throughout the country. The Democrats resorted to racial slurs, calling the president "Abraham Africanus the First." A Catholic weekly claimed, "Filthy black
niggers, greasy, sweaty, and disgusting, now jostle white people and even
ladies everywhere, even at the President's levees." And a Copperhead
editor in Wisconsin published a parody of "When Johnny Comes
Marching Home": "The widow-maker soon must cave, / Hurrah, Hurrah. / We'll plant him in some nigger's grave, / Hurrah, Hurrah. / Torn
from your farm, your ship, your raft, / Conscript. How do you like the
draft, / And we'll stop that too / When little Mac takes the helm."

On October 17, Governor Bramlette sent a letter to election officials stating that all qualified Kentucky voters should be allowed into the polls and that their qualifications were not to be questioned by the military. He ordered local sheriffs to arrest any soldiers attempting to interfere with the election.

Senator Davis wrote Brutus that he had heard in Richmond that many voters, including old Ezekiel Field and another member of the family, probably William Holloway, were planning to vote for Lincoln. "Let me appeal to you most earnestly to go to Madison on Friday, make a speech on Saturday, stir them up, come home Sunday and be at the polls by the time they open Monday morning." He himself was speaking in Clark and Estill Counties, he told Brutus. "Let us strike radicalism to the heart in Ky."

In November, Lincoln was reelected. He carried every state except New Jersey, Delaware, and Kentucky. Brutus had been correct in assessing his constituents' views. Of all the counties he represented, only Fayette, a stronghold of Unconditional Unionism, went for Lincoln. However, 54,000 fewer votes were cast in Kentucky than had been cast in the presidential election of 1860. There were many reasons for this, but intimidation was one.

In October, Green wrote that he was thinking of returning to the United States. "I have written to Mr. Seward a private letter, asking permission to return," he told his father. "Before leaving home, you offered me the choice of two farms. If you are still so disposed, I would be very thankful to receive it on my return. Whether I shall seek to retain a position in the service depends upon what prospect & means of live[lihood] I may have. [. . .]

"In all events it is better for me, I think, to come home this fall. If I get a reappointment, can return in the spring. If not, to go to farming and will thank my stars to be able to do so."

Brutus continued to pursue the Field and Clay plantation claims, though avenues were gradually closed to him. Christopher, who had returned to the South at the end of the summer, wrote him in November with further suggestions about how to proceed. He added, "We are having a gloomy time this fall and winter. The lines are drawn very tightly on both sides. [. . .] And the restrictions are very great on both sides about cotton. I find I can do nothing in the way of shipping my own cotton and the Southern side are equally restricting, and between the two I fear a failure."

In December, a letter arrived for Brutus from his brother in Russia, expressing the hope that political differences would not alienate them. The letter also contained a family bombshell.

CASSIUS CLAY SR.

St. Petersburg, R., Dec. 9, 1864

My dear Brutus,

[. . .] I have just received a letter from Mary [Clay], dated Nov. 9th, in which she says, I wrote to you "not to answer my letters etc." My dear Brutus, you have certainly misconstrued my meaning. I am under such obligations to you that nothing you could do could put me against you! I knew that, like myself, you were of strong will; and that if I said anything likely to modify your views, the effect would be lost if you set about to answer it. Besides I did not write to discuss politics with you, feeling that argument of that sort never does any good. I felt very truly that you were about to take a wrong course, in my opinion, and felt that I ought to warn you against it. I hope that you may not have cause to regret that you were not on the side of the country in this her death-and-life struggle. But after your great tolerance of my opinions, I would not presume to dictate to you your course. Be assured that whoever else may blame you, I will not. For though I think you wrong in going for McClellan, I believe you conscientious — misled however by regard to slavery, which seems to have potent influence over men and nations where it exists.

Your son, Green, has asked my consent to marry Mary; I have given him my consent. He is a fine boy and I believe Mary is also of equal principles and character. I regretted that, as *cousins*, they should have made the match, but it is now too late to interfere. Give my love to Anne, & the family & [I] remain as ever

Your aff. brother,

C. M. Clay

The news that Green planned to marry Mary Clay sent reverberations throughout the family. "We heard *Green* has got home and is to be married in a few days to Mary, and will return immediately back to Europe," Brutus's sister, Eliza Smith, wrote at Christmas time. However, the young couple did not immediately wed.

In Richmond, Pattie Field had decided she did not want to go back to her boarding school. After Christmas, her grandfather wrote the headmaster to inquire what was wrong. "I did not know until after Patty [sic] left last Friday that she had thoughts of not returning," replied A. E. Sloan. "I have taken some pains to ascertain the *cause* of this, but can find out nothing except an expression from Patty that we did not *like* her. If Patty entertains any such feelings, they are *groundless*."

Cash spent his Christmas vacation in the north, then resumed college. He had revised his opinion of Yale.

CASSIUS CLAY JR.

New Haven, Conn., Jan. 2th, 1865

Dear Ma,

[. . .] I am very much surprised to hear that Pa talks about not letting me come back next year and graduate. It were certainly better for me not to come at all than not to graduate after having come. I certainly desire very much to come back next year. In reality, I had made up my mind to come back three more years. I think when the country is so unsettled that every man should study a profession for he knows not what the tomorrow may bring forth. Or, in other words, I had determined to graduate also in the Law School. I think that every man who can afford it should study law. As for staying away from home so long a time, I can bear it very easily — for the letters that I wrote when I first came on here and of which I am now heartily ashamed, expressed a great deal more than I ever felt of homesickness. Yale is certainly a fine college. There is a great deal more studying done there in proportion to no. of students than at Mr. Sayre's. Yale is certainly no humbug. From Mr. Sayre's representations I was expecting to find it nearly a humbug but I find that there is twice the application and study that was [sic] at his school. I labor under many disadvantages having entered the Junior Class. I would advise anybody to through the whole course. A boy can be far better satisfied here than at Mr. Sayre's for here societies, class honors, etc. etc. engross his attention and present worthy objects for his ambition. About Mr. Sayre's school there is a torpidity and inertness arising from want of competition and rivalry and from the want of societies and prize contests etc. To be at the head of your class here it requires herculean labor and unvarying at that and also a perfect memory and fair talents of which requirements I have none or perhaps very imperfectly the last. I do not believe the report about Green as yet, but perhaps it may be true. I see no impropriety in first cousins marrying, all other things being favorable. As to this case I express no opinion. This I wish to be distinctly understood. [. . .]

Your son,

C. M. Clay

A few days later, Cash again urged his mother not to take the possibility of Green and Mary marrying too seriously. "I think you trouble yourself about too many idle reports. It seems as if you give credence to every thing you hear. Recollect that rumor has had Cousin Sidney [Clay] on the point of marriage fifty times."

Early in the new year, Belle Lyman wrote Ann a long letter full of family news, from speculation about Green's engagement to an account of Pattie's distress at having to return to school.

BELLE LYMAN

Richmond, Jan. 6th, 1866 [sic]

Dear Ann,

[T]hank you for the exquisite bonnet you were so kind to send Pattie [her daughter]. She does look too beautiful in it. Dr. Lyman never desired or expected anything from you. It was a pleasure to him to have assisted you and would cheerfully do the same were it ever necessary, but I sincerely trust you may not in many *long years to come* require any more medical treatment. I felt so distressed to think you had gotten anything so expensive. It fits her beautifully. Dr. Lyman is equally as proud of it as I am and you would have been amused to have seen the little thing, how proud she was when we carried her to the glass to see it.

Well, as to the girl [servant]. I would not have had you and Mr. Clay to have sent her for any consideration as she was unwilling to come and if she was as delicate as represented she would have done me but little service. [. . .] We have hired a woman with a little boy, 10 or 11 years old, and is right handy about some things, but I find it a good deal of trouble to learn them everything. Well, Christmas is past and gone and they are not freed as they anticipated. I think it has been a great disappointment to them.

I write you with the hope of sending this by Green. [. . .] I believe we are none the wiser in regard to Green's marriage. [. . .] I asked him to tell me. He seemed to be inclined to deny it at first, but finally replied that he would tell us in time. [. . .] I had intended going to New York [to look at schools] with Pattie but I believe she has almost made up her mind to return to Danville in the morning. [. . .] Has Sue Clay [daughter of Ann's neighbor] gone back?

Uncle David [Irvine] has received a very gloomy letter from Brother. It is so strange that he is willing to stay there any longer when he can do no good.

Monday morning.

Pattie returned to Danville this morning and we all have felt pretty blue. David [Belle's son] was greatly distressed, thought to the last that he was going with her. I felt sorry to see her go back as she did so reluctantly. I was at a great loss to know what to advise, as she had heard nothing from her Pa. [. . .] Dr. Lyman received a letter from his cousin in New York with 3 catalogues of the most prominent schools there, said that [they] would not hesitate to place a sister or daughter at either of the 3. One was the Abbot Institute where Sallie Burnam is. A long letter came to her [Pattie] last night from Miss Lissa Clarke imploring her to return to the Caldwell Institute, complimented her on the most extravagant terms. [. . .] She [Pattie] wrote me that as she approached the Institute she grew heartsick and felt tempted to come back home. I told her if she found a letter from her Papa giving his consent, to come right straight back. She said her 2 weeks at home were so delightfully spent with me and the children. She visited very little, seemed to have no inclination. She says Miss Lissa fell perfectly in love with her visit to Sue Clay.

[. . .] I told Mary [Embry] that if we received invitations to Eliza Wornell's wedding we would accept and go to see you, but Cousin William says they have declined having a wedding. [. . .] I regret it so much. I felt so anxious to get out once more. I hadn't seen anything handsome on that line for so long. [. . .] You must not think of going to Washington. You could not undergo such a trip. Dr. Lyman says his impression is that you ought not to go, that the exercise you would take and *high living* would be very unfavorable to your disease and, to be candid with you, he has told me all the time that the trip would do you no good in his opinion.

I remain Yours Truly,

Belle Lyman

She enclosed a note from her physician husband containing prescriptions for "stopping the discharge of blood from your womb" (a pill of opium, ipecac, and sugar of lead) and "continual wasting" (cinnamon tea and elixir vitriol).

Brutus returned to Washington alone after New Year's, arriving on January 5, 1865, as he noted in his memorandum book, "by way of Columbus & Pittsburgh." There were two main orders of business as far as he was concerned. One was public — voting against the constitutional amendment to abolish and prohibit slavery. The other was private — freeing Zeke from Johnson's Island.

The previous year the Senate had mustered the necessary two-thirds majority to pass the Thirteenth Amendment to the Constitution. However, in June of 1864, it fell thirteen votes short of passing the House. In January 1865 the amendment again came up for debate on the House floor.

On January 9, the *Congressional Globe* records that Brutus rose to oppose it, arguing that the amendment applied only to Kentucky and represented a violation of the pledges made to the state when it agreed to remain in the Union in 1861. He said that most supporters of the amendment "commence their remarks against rebels [. . .] when in reality this is a movement, not against the rebellious States, but against a loyal State now in the Union."

He continued, "We have been told here, not only by the President of the United States, but by Mr. Seward, Secretary of State, as well as by Congress itself, that neither the people of the non-slave holding States nor Congress has any power over the subject of slavery. In this way the State of Kentucky has been led along, step by step, by the pledges you have given her, until she is now as it were, powerless in your hands. [. . .]"

Brutus estimated that "slave property" in the state before the war amounted to $150 million. "You have no right to take away that property," he argued, "unless for public use, and then only on making just compensation." How would New England mill owners feel if the Federal government were to seize the clothing they manufactured without paying them for it? he asked.

He described Kentucky under martial law. "At this time and at the last election the Federal soldiers were scattered all over the State. You could not go to a town or cross-road or railroad station without finding it bristling with bayonets. The soldiers were there at the last election, intimidating voters and driving them from the polls. And yet you propose the mockery of submitting this measure to the people [for ratification] under such circumstances."

Brutus then spoke of his own disillusionment. "When you declared that you would not perpetuate this outrage, we believed you — at least I did. When these troubles broke out I declared before my people that you would never interfere with the rights guaranteed to the States by the Constitution; that you would stand by your pledged honor, your plighted faith. I had confidence in your pledges, and I endeavored to infuse that feeling of confidence into those of my fellow-citizens with whom I had any influence. Sir, when I come again face to face with the men to whom I gave that assurance, many of them having taken opposite ground to that which I maintained, how shall I answer them when they say, 'Did we not tell you that when they got us in their power they would oppress us as they pleased?'"

Toward the end of his speech, Brutus waxed rhetorical in the manner of his more flamboyant brother. "You talk about slavery, and say you want to do us good by taking our slaves away from us. If you would march your armies into your northern cities, where men live in marble palaces, who make fortunes out of the people, and if you would seize the contents of their banks, and distribute it among the poor, you would do more good than you would by letting those nabobs have it who eat their sumptuous dinners and drink their fine wines. If you are going to revolutionize society everywhere and do the greatest good, seize upon that property and divide it among those who are poor and needy."

It was a speech for constituent consumption. Brutus knew very well he hadn't a chance of changing the mind of anyone in Congress.

I wish I could picture Brutus on the House floor more clearly. I know that he was about six feet tall and, while generally polite and affable, could on occasion be withering. He suffered few fools. Among Brutus's papers there is an undated clipping of dubious accuracy from the Baltimore *American* entitled "Etheridge Rebuked by a Kentucky Loyalist." Brutus was never a Democrat, of course, but I think the story may well capture Brutus's manner.

"A Washington correspondent of the New Hampshire *Statesman* says Emerson Etheridge [a former Tennessee congressman] was recently introduced to Brutus J. Clay, of Kentucky, and immediately began to denounce the Government. Mr. Clay, after hearing his tempest a few moments, replied: 'Well, Mr. Etheridge, this is pretty rough. Before the war, when I was a Democrat, I used to hear of you down in Tennessee as an abolitionist. You must have lately changed your views.' This was somewhat wilting to the retiring clerk [of the House], who supposed he had got a man after his own heart. He plucked up courage, however, and went into another tirade. Mr. Clay, thereupon, with calmness mingled with manifest indignation, rising to his full height, interrupted: 'Well, sir, this is our first meeting. Your language, sir, seems to me atrocious, and all I have to say to you is that when men talk thus down in Kentucky we regard them as Secessionists, and treat them accordingly.'"

A few days after Brutus's remarks on the floor, his nephew Clay Smith rose in support of the amendment. He claimed that the slave property in Kentucky belonged to only one-eighth of the people in the state and most of these were secessionists anyway. On January 31, 1865, the Thirteenth Amendment passed the House, 119 to 56. There was wild excitement on the streets of Washington. People cheered while cannon boomed a one-hundred-gun salute.

As all this was going on, Brutus was also working to get Zeke released from Johnson's Island. "I called to see the President today in regard to Ezekiel," he wrote Ann on January 12, "he treated me kindly, and gave me his promise to release him as a Prisoner of War on his parole to go home and remain, during the War, if I would get my colleagues to sign a petition to that effect. I have already got the names and have only to present it to the President to get him released. You may therefore expect him home soon." He added that he had not yet applied for a pass to allow Henry Davenport to visit Martha, who was again expecting a baby. Then he sent Zeke money to get home. The January 16 receipt from the Adams Express Company for "1 pcl. sealed and said to contain $35.00 addressed to E. F. Clay, Johnsons Island, O." can be found among his papers.

Ann wrote that she was no better and must seek medical assistance outside of Bourbon County. "I was in hopes you were getting well," Brutus replied on January 18, "and it would not be necessary for you to go to Louisville as you spoke of doing before I left home. If you think you can be benefitted, go. [. . .] Take any of the servants you wish and in whom you have most confidence and who will wait on you the best. Don't wait for my return home before you go. Your health is of more importance than anything else and nothing should weigh against it."

The same day, Special Order No. 14 was issued by the Office of the

Commissary General of Prisons for Zeke's parole to Bourbon County "on condition that he remain with said County during the continuance of the War." Zeke objected to the terms of this parole, as he told Martha. A version of his complaint reached Brutus, and Zeke hastened to set things straight.

EZEKIEL CLAY

Johnson's Island, Ohio, Jan. 18th, 1865

Dear Pa,

[. . .] I was very much gratified to hear from you, and feel exceedingly grateful for the effort you are making in my behalf. I infer that you are laboring under a misconception of what I intended to say in mine to Sister. Nothing would give me more pleasure than to return home in an honorable way, and I feel that perhaps I could be of some use to those who are so dear to me. I can accept, consistent with my views of honor, the parole you have been so very kind as to procure for me with a very slight alteration, instead of "during the continuance of the War" insert, until a *general exchange*, and if necessary report by letter periodically either to the Commandant of this post or elsewhere. This suggestion I feel assured will meet your views of propriety. To this parole I would most *strictly* conform to. [. . .]

I cannot tell you how much I regret that you misunderstood my letter to Sister. I fervently hope Pa that you will try and get the alteration suggested above. So far as the object of the two paroles are concerned, they are virtually the same, for don't believe there will be a general exchange during the War, but in one case in the eyes of the world I am a deserter, the very name of which would ever be a *brand of disgrace* to be pointed at with the finger of scorn of both and all parties, in the other case there is nothing inconsistent with my present obligations to the Confederate Government and nothing inconsistent with my views of honor. I hope you will consider this in the light in which I have set it before you, and will take a father's interest in my welfare. My health has not been very good. I yet suffer some with my eye. I hope you will write me very soon.

Affectionately Yr. Son,

E. F. Clay

Having not yet heard from Zeke himself, Brutus responded to Martha on January 31. "I have already arranged all matters in regard to Ezekiel and sent off the paper several days ago. I wrote in advance on Sunday before I sent his discharge, informing him what I contemplated doing. I have heard nothing from him. I do not know whether or not he will take your view of the subject. The whole of it was my proposition made to the President, and he granted it just as I desired it & I cannot go to him again upon the subject. [. . .] My proposition is, instead of keeping him in Prison, let him be paroled as a Prisoner of War and let him go home & the County be his prison [. . .] and of course if he is a Prisoner of War he will not leave the County nor again join the Confederates unless he was exchanged or his parole cancelled by the Government. [. . .] It never struck me until I received your letter that there could be any objection to the arrangement. [. . .] I certainly would not want him to do anything that was dishonorable or touch his high pride of duty. I hope he will not view it in the light you do. I certainly do not myself and acted as I supposed he desired. If he had not made the request, I should not have taken any action in the matter." Brutus added that he would apply for a permit to allow Henry Davenport to come to Kentucky again.

Zeke continued to object to the parole terms. "I still feel that you will agree with me, that the one suggested by myself is the much more preferable," he wrote on January 24.

Brutus got the parole altered to suit Zeke's sensibilities. In his memorandum book, Zeke's name is listed along with all the others, with an X beside it to indicate the parole had been granted.

As soon as the revised parole papers arrived in Ohio, Zeke left for home. "I just have time to drop you a few lines to tender my many, many heartfelt thanks for your great kindness in procuring my liberty," he wrote his father on January 31. "I cannot find words to express my gratitude so can only say I thank you a thousand times. The money has arrived, and I will start at once for home passing through Cincinnati."

Young Cash wrote his mother from New Haven that his father had agreed to let him graduate from Yale but wanted him to do so as quickly as possible, so Cash could help him on the farm. Law school was out of the question. He also defended Yale against an attack by Martha. "Tell Sister Martha that her notions about Yale are incorrect. There are fewer charity scholars than at almost any other college and besides they are only in the theological department. There are twice as many good students in proportion to the whole number here as are at B. B. Sayre's school. You can find 20 boys in each class better students than any Mr. Sayre has. The cause of this is evidently in the difference of the modes of teaching. Mr. Sayre [. . .] permits the memory to decay for the want of exercise. Here the boys are dependent alone on themselves to recite their lessons. Their memory is strengthened and their power of study increased." In a postscript, Cash inquired if Pattie Field were coming to New York to school and whether Kit had gotten any pointers (hunting dogs).

Brutus wrote Ann on February 3 that he had gotten Zeke's parole arranged although by the time she got the letter Zeke must have already arrived at home. Brutus was pondering which servant Ann should take with her when she consulted a doctor. "In regard to your going to Cincinnati I think you may care but little as to whom you take. I think that the indications are they will all be gone before the first of March. We passed the Constitution Amendment on the 31st of Jan'y. If it now passes 3/4 of all the State Legislatures, the thing will be accomplished & there will be an end of slavery in the U.S. Whoever you take you might say to her that I intend to free her when I return home & it is useless to run off, as it will be [in] her interest to remain, as they will be better off in Kentucky than in one of the Northern States."

Mary Jane Clay suggested Ann consult a doctor in Cincinnati. "Ma is not very well," her daughter Sally wrote Ann, "and is going to Cincinnati next week to see Dr. Ermine. She would be glad to have you go with her. If you go, meet us in Paris, Tuesday evening train."

Green stopped in Washington to visit with his father on his way back to Italy. Brutus noted in his memorandum book, "Feb. 9 Green Clay left for Newport for Europe from Washington." Although he did not record what was said, they must have discussed Green's marriage and career plans. Judging from comments Green makes in subsequent letters, his father questioned his marrying Mary Clay on the grounds that they were first cousins. However, marriages of the sort were not unusual. In their own family, Elizabeth and William Holloway were first cousins. But Green was as stubborn as Brutus. When he returned to Italy he was still engaged to Mary. As for his career, Brutus clearly wanted Green to remain in the foreign service, in spite of the expense. He didn't want another son in the army, fighting a war he could no longer support. Green continued to insist that he wanted to practice law, though he took no steps toward doing so.

Despite his preoccupation with business and political matters, Brutus was remarkably accessible to his children, whether they wanted to be released from prison or reassured about their future. However, he also bound them tightly to him, expecting them all to share the burdens of the family enterprise, the development and cultivation of his land. In the case of Kit, Brutus gave him the management of the Mississippi plantation but not the deed to it. In the case of Cash, Brutus insisted he forgo law school in order to join him at Auvergne.

Ann worried that General Burbridge, the military commandant of Kentucky, might attempt to interfere with Zeke. Burbridge was greatly feared throughout the state. Governor Bramlette had asked President Lincoln to dismiss him after the 1864 election and, on February 10, Lincoln did just that.

"I see no reason for Burbridge interfering with Ezekiel," Brutus reassured Ann. "We will [not] be troubled with him any longer [as] he is already dismissed from the District of Ky., and Genl. [John M.] Palmer takes his place who I am told is [a] good selection by those who know his deeds, Members of Congress from Illinois, from which state he comes. He left here yesterday for Kentucky."

Still searching for a doctor who could cure her of what seems to have been postmenopausal problems, Ann asked William Holloway to check on a Dr. Miller in Louisville. "From what I learn there is probably no foundation whatever as to Dr. Miller being insane," he reported back to her on February 14. "He has made a speciality of the treatment of such cases as yours and would no doubt prove as competent as any Dr. you would find."

Ann still could not make up her mind what to do. When Belle wrote her in mid-February, she had intended to go to Louisville with Holloway. (Though dated 1864, the contents of Belle's letter make it clear that it should have been dated 1865.)

BELLE LYMAN

Richmond, Feb. 14, 1864 [sic]

Dear Ann,

I have just read your letter this morning by Pattie [Bedinger] and am truly glad to find you are not complaining any more than when we last heard from you. [. . .] I must tell you that I felt a very great disappointment in your not meeting Cousin William Monday on one account alone. I had reserved some nice things for you, even saved some chicken salad and jelly. [. . .] I do hope Martha will now improve and will not have a backset. [Henry B. Davenport Jr. had been born on February 11.] I would like so much to see her and will go over as soon as she gets up. Would willingly have offered to have stayed with her if you should have gone, but knew Amy and the rest would wait on her so faithfully. I expect you will wind up going to Cincinnati which may be for the best. [. . .] Cousin Sarah White was here the other day, wondering why you did not go to New York and consult with some of those celebrated physicians, that she wouldn't think of Louisville & Cin. [. . .]

Wednesday morning.

Dr. Lyman has just come in after being gone all day and night and not gotten through yet. He says he knows nothing about this Dr. Mrs. Clay is under. [. . .] He would have more confidence in an allopathic or eclectic than a homeopathic Dr. He may benefit you for a while but, as to whether it will be permanent, we can't tell. Now make up your mind to go to some one and, if you are willing to try this Dr., don't regard anything that is said but act for yourself and the sooner the better. [. . .] Mary says she and me are crazy to go with you to stay a day or two, if you go to Cincinnati, but I can't go anywhere that I can't take the children, so the best place for me this winter is home with them. [. . .] Every morning Dr. Lyman says Pattie is to be weaned, that she is dragging at me so continually that I am as thin and as poor as I can be, but I can't give my consent. [. . .]

Yours truly,

Belle Lyman

Ann finally decided to consult Dr. Miller but postponed her departure in order to nurse Martha, who was having difficulty recovering from Henry's birth.

ANN CLAY

Paris, Tuesday night, Feb. 16, 1865

My Dear Husband,

[. . .] Martha has been quite sick for a few days and I feared much she would have a bad spell but she is now much better and in a few days I think she will be quite well enough for me to feel willing to leave her. She has a very large baby. And don't you feel sorry for poor little Zeke. [Neither] he nor June are either pleased with the idea of another baby. We are all so glad to hear that Green has gone and that you and him parted so pleasantly. I felt very sorry for him. He wrote a very affection-ate letter to Ezekiel that you were the best of fathers to all of them, and that you, in spite of temporary irritation at them at times, was [sic] ever their truest and kindest friend.

Annie [Holloway] was at Henry Clay's [a neighbor] yesterday, heard there that on Saturday last as Christopher [Clay] was going to the other place [the Green Creek farm], the *Guerrillas* stopped him & kept him all day, at Lafe Cunningham's, demanded his green backs & overcoat. They say he was much frightened but got off at night safe. They took possession of Lafe's house, let no one pass or leave there all day. We knew something had happened to him, but you know he keeps every thing to himself. I learn two of them were Archy Bedford's sons. They took nothing from Christopher.

[. . .] Elizabeth Bedford was here yesterday, said she was ready to go to Washington to see Mr. Lincoln to get her sons paroled or released [from Union prisons], but was sick and concluded to send her papers to you & Mr. [Garrett] Davis. I suppose they can't bear to have their chil-dren left as Zeke has come home but I was sorry that they were trou-bling you as I know it is but little rest you have. [. . .]

Every time Sidney comes he begs me to go some where to consult a Dr. and offered to go with me, but as Dr. Lyman has offered to go with me I think he will be more suitable than a single man. [. . .] I suppose it would be better if I were to leave Martha up, but Annie is so attentive that I think everything will go well. [. . .]

I am so thankful for your kind letter and wishes. Cow Lady Caroline [Brutus's champion] died yesterday. We have had but one calf since you left. [. . .]

Yrs. devotedly,

Ann M. Clay

One of the last things the hated General Burbridge did was to issue an order for the arrest of both Zeke Clay and Henry Davenport, who had arrived from Virginia to be with Martha and their children. Brutus protested, and Burbridge replied on February 27, "I have been informed by some of our mutual friends that you do not profess the kindliest feeling towards me that you have heretofore uniformly manifested, and that this change in your feelings was based upon my treatment to [sic] your son and son-in-law. While I regret that a damaging impression toward me should have been made upon your mind, I can but state that my motives in the transactions were pure and free from any personal feeling or animosity toward yourself or your sons. I was notified by the Provost Marshal of Bourbon County that your son and son-in-law were at home on a parole granted by the Commandant of the Prison at Johnson [sic] Island, that the papers did not state that they were here by any higher authority. I ordered them at once to be confined to their house till the proper information could come from the authorities at Washington. As soon as the answer to my Dispatch reached me I ordered them released at once. I feel that I did but my duty as a Federal Officer and am truly sorry that my action in the premises should have been construed by any one as savoring in the least of a personal feeling."

Ann left for Louisville before Brutus returned to Kentucky. On March 8, Louisa Keiningham, who had just returned from visiting in Frankfort, wrote Ann he had not yet reached home.

She added, "I met Dr. Lyman & Dr. Burns at the Frankfort depot and was much pleased to hear Dr. L.'s account of your situation & rejoiced you stayed to let Dr. Miller have time to do something for you. [. . .] Mrs. Massie says her sister Miller was considered hopelessly diseased for a long time, at last she had the resolution to go to Louisville to see Dr. Miller where she stayed either five or nine months, I forget which [. . .] and he made an entire cure of her, and that she now thinks him the *best* and *greatest* man living & thinks there is no womb disease he cannot cure. [. . .] It has cheered me up so much to think he can cure you in *four months*. These will soon roll by and then you will be a *Well Woman*, and won't we then have more pleasant trips to Cincinnati, Lexington, Frankfort etc. etc. than we ever had before? [. . .] I *command* you to take all care of yourself, *obey* implicitly all that Dr. M. tells you to do so that you may make haste to come home."

By the time Mrs. Keiningham next wrote, Brutus was at Auvergne.

In Paris, she had met Annie Holloway, who told her that Brutus had caught a cold on the way home. Ann was thinking of returning home herself. "If you are so *headstrong* and so regardless of my good advice as to come next week," Mrs. K. warned her, "I charge nay command you to get full explicit directions in writing from Dr. Miller how your case must be treated & you don't know but I may go out to your house, take the case in hand & *quack* on you to my hearts content."

She continued with a description of the things planted in Ann's garden ("potatoes, beets, salsify, carrots, parsnips, onions, peas & beans"). "So you see how far ahead [of me] you will be, but never mind I shall give myself no trouble about it for you know I have always gone on the principle that what ever was *yours was mine* and what is the use of my taking any trouble about the garden cabbage & *the vulgar things* when I have such grand fashionable associates as the Hon. Mrs. B. J. Clay, now living in grandeur at the finest Hotel in Louisville and who talked of getting a real fashionable landau & I now invite myself to turn out with you in it. What a sensation we will create, you a *well, well* woman, in your black silk velvet etc. and me a gay dashing widow with my moiré [. . .] but I must stop with this or you will think me crazy."

Not only were Brutus and Zeke living at Auvernge, but also Ann Holloway and Martha and her children. Kit lived mostly on the Green Creek farm near Sidney Clay's place. Henry Davenport had arrived to meet his namesake.

I once met the Henry Bedinger Davenport who was born at Auvergne that winter. Sometime in the mid-1950s, our family was returning to Kentucky from the East via Charleston, West Virginia, where he lived. Henry, who had been both an engineer and a lawyer, would have been almost ninety. My father suggested we stop as he had business to discuss with him. He had corresponded with Henry about the affairs of Henry's eccentric sister Amelia.

We pulled up in front of a porticoed house in downtown Charleston on a June afternoon. Henry, a tall man with a full head of white hair, was expecting us. While he and my father discussed family, my mother, my brother, and I sat in his dark cool living room. I could see barges moving up and down the Kanawha River across the street. That afternoon is like so many other times I now wish I could summon up at will. No doubt he and my father spoke of Brutus and Ann and Cit and Zeke and Martha and all the relatives from Richmond. But their words are forever lost.

In mid-March, Green wrote his father from Italy. He made no mention of their conversation in Washington. Instead he was full of advice for Cash. "I have just written to Cash," Green told his father. "He seemed becoming a little dissatisfied, though his stand in his class is a very fine one. [. . .] He is so much fonder of the mathematics than the classics and takes so little interest in the debates of the societies etc. that I suggested the idea of passing to the Engineering department. [. . .] We have only to think of the immense mineral resources, untouched, but which new railroads and rapid settlements are certainly bringing into demand. [. . .] He thinks there is a good deal of humbug about college. Granted! But where will you find better advantages, the same facilities for learning? [. . .] Colleges have stood the test of yrs. Wise men have founded them. The most civilized people have ever cherished them as a foundation of their greatness."

Christopher Field wrote Brutus once again about his cotton claims. "I see an important case has been decided in the Supreme Court in favor of a Lady on Red River who had cotton seized by the Navy. The court has decided that the Navy had no right to seize cotton on the inland river. [. . .] I of course have not heard from you in any way about it and felt an interest you should know of this decision if you had not seen it." He was discouraged about prospects for a crop in 1865.

Young Cash wrote his father in mid-March. He started out trying to convince Brutus that Yale was a fine college.

CASSIUS CLAY JR.

New Haven, Conn., March 14th, '65

Dear Pa,

[. . .] I am very well pleased with Yale. It exceeds my most sanguine expectations. [. . .] Our professors are all illustrious men in their professions. Indeed, I suppose no college in America can muster so much talent as Yale. [. . .]

But yet all the professors with perhaps one exception are fanatic abolitionists. We have our reading rooms in which there are none but the most ultra abolition papers. Sometime back some boys petitioned the faculty to allow some democratic papers to come into the reading room but the petition was refused and not even the New York Herald, such a vile sheet as it is, is allowed to enter. It maddens me every day to listen to the prayers that are offered up to the high theme of God. The students are even ahead of the faculty in fanaticism.

A man who has the least respect for his own feelings and honor cannot attend the societies. They declare all Southern men barbarians. They say ignorance and vice reign supreme in all the slave states and that we are not half as good as cannibals. The students not only say this, but also the professors.

The people up here are in perfect ignorance of our true character, civilization etc. They have been lied to so long by Wendell Phillips and others that they now believe no enormity is too hideous for Southern men to perform.

They believe that we are barbarians without the pale of civilization and to kill [. . .] [us] is doing service to God. They believe that all the evil passions in the world, that all the sin, vice and degradation reside in the South, covering that land in a cloud of barbarism blacker than that in which the ancient Scythians were enveloped. They declare that no man can be a Christian and at the same time be a slave holder. They hand out flags and ring bells for every scrimmage in which they are reported to be victorious but it is nonsense to write more, for it irritates me even to mention the vile slanders that are heaped upon our people. I am in very good health and am doing very well in my studies.

Your Afft. Son,

C. M. Clay Jr.

Ann wrote Brutus from Louisville on March 16. She was impatient with her cure. "I know I have improved very much & feel that I would still improve quite rapidly under Dr. Miller's care [. . .] but the great drawback with me is the enormous expense it is to remain at the Hotel (independent of the Dr.'s bill) which I had no idea of doing when I came here, but Mr. Holloway says he knows of no private boarding house but is filled & I have asked the Dr. several times and he says he knows of none, so I have been compelled to stay here. [. . .] Would you advise me to go home or remain here longer? If I leave here it was the understanding that I was to go to Richmond & place myself under Dr. Lyman's care for Dr. Miller thought to ensure a cure I would have to at least be under a Physician 4 months. I was feeling so sad & low down yesterday. I thought the Dr. did not think I was improving from some remark of his, but when I summoned up the courage to ask him, he said most certainly I was very much better, a decided improvement in my condition."

She enclosed a note to Martha which concluded, "Don't you think you had better sow some flower seed in [the] hot bed & tell Annie [Holloway] to look at the gladiola roots [. . .] in the pit [greenhouse] for fear they are damp. It is too soon to put them out but they may rot if damp."

Brutus wrote Ann at Louisville explaining why it had taken him so long to get home.

BRUTUS CLAY

Home, March 18, '65

Dear Ann,

[. . .] I had been very sick for several days before I left, confined to home, but felt better, & determined to start. I was nine days coming, stayed 4 days in Pittsburgh, Pa. My throat became so swollen I could not eat & drink for three days. As soon as I was able, I left Pittsburgh & got home last Monday. I am still quite unwell with [a] sore throat, but am getting better. I miss you much, & wish you were at home yet I do not wish you to come. I want you to remain as long as you can benefit. Health is every thing, never mind the expense. [. . .] If you have to stay long, I will come down to see you whenever I am well enough. This is a fine day & I can hardly stay indoors & yet [am] not well enough to get out, which makes me very restless as there is so much here that ought to be done & every body seems to move so slow. I believe we are all well here, but myself, the boys were fishing, they caught a fine mess [of fish] a few days ago [. . .] some very large. Martha seems to take most of her time in attending to her babies. Write often if you are able.

Yours,

Brutus J. Clay

Alarmed at the size of her hotel bill, Ann wrote Brutus that she wanted to come home as soon as possible. "Mr. Holloway has just left here, says the proprietor has just told him that my bill here on the first of March would be 315$. Did you ever in your life hear any thing to equal it? I told him there was certainly some mistake. [. . .] Said it was 4$ a day for me and the same for Eliza & extra for Jim [another servant]. [. . .] I told him that was 1100$ to board here a year, more than our Governor's salary."

She enclosed a note to Martha asking her to have the snowball bush near the pit moved to the lower part of the yard. Those snowball bushes, a kind of hydrangea, moved around the yard at Auvergne in every generation. When we got there, two of them grew at the base of the steps leading up to the front door. My father had the hydrangeas dug up and replanted at the end of the east wing, replacing them with boxwoods. He envisioned an avenue of boxwood leading up to the door, similar to those at the Larches, Uncle John's house on the edge of Paris which had once been Garrett Davis's place.

I used to play hide-and-go-seek in the bushes at the Larches with my cousins, huddling in the cool, sharply scented shade of their dense limbs as I waited for someone to call out, "Ally ally infree!" Whenever I smell the acrid odor of boxwood I am a child again, pigtails and sturdy brown oxfords, and I feel that combination of fear and elation that comes when you launch yourself toward home base.

My father's boxwoods never made a proper hedge though. Instead, they grew scraggly and birds nested in them. There was always a commotion among their branches at twilight as the residents settled themselves for the night.

Ann wrote a few days later to say Dr. Miller would soon decide whether she could come home.

ANN CLAY

Louisville, Friday morning [postmarked March 24]

My Dear Husband,

[. . .] Dr. Miller was here yesterday morning. I told him I wanted to go home. He said he would be here on Saturday & would then tell me whether I could go or not. If he insists on my staying I shall remain but will leave this house. [. . .] I have not felt quite so well for a day or two & believe it is only because I have felt so worried at the bad treatment of this Hotel keeper. Mr. Holloway thinks he has acted shamefully & is just as anxious for me to leave here as I am to go. [. . .] He came to tell me yesterday that the private boarding houses are full [. . .], but that he can get me boarding at the National Hotel much cheaper than here. So if the Dr. much prefers my staying I will move there tomorrow but if he is willing for me to go home, I will go on Monday. [. . .] I would like for the Rockaway to be sent to the Depot on Monday evening if I should possibly go.

I have just had a long sad letter from Belle. She says since the late order that the wives & children of the negro soldiers are free, that they are generally leaving their homes. A woman she had hired left without saying a word to them & [. . .] Mary Embry is in great trouble about her Daphne, says she tells her [. . .] she will go. [. . .] Mary is anxious to pay her to stay, but Mr. Embry is violently opposed to it and says he wishes they would all go. Belle is in great doubt whether she can stand the white servants or not, but is thinking of trying them. [. . .] I suppose some of ours will be leaving soon. I must give Eliza the credit whilst on the subject of behaving just as well as she can. She rarely ever leaves my room. Even does not leave to go to the table to get her meals but eats what I have in my rooms. But I have come to the conclusion there is not much confidence to be put in any of them. [. . .]

Yrs. devotedly,

A. M. Clay

Brutus sent Ann money to cover her hotel bill. He added on March 15, "I am much better, riding about some. All the balance well."

Green had returned to Italy hoping to take over the mission during his superior's leave of absence. When he learned the leave had not been granted, he wondered if he should not come back to the United States. At the time he wrote this letter to his father, he still intended to marry his cousin.

GREEN CLAY

Turin, March '65 26th

Dear Pa,

[. . .] Mr. M's leave of absence has been refused for the present. He thinks after the inauguration & press of office seekers is over it may be granted. But is at present advised there is no particular use of me remaining here. So after the coming quarter I think of resigning and go-

ing back to the law. [. . .] My three or four years abroad are not to be regretted. They have given me an insight into the working of different
systems of government, an intelligent survey of the politics of Europe
with a respectable knowledge of two foreign languages, all of which will
be of service to me in my profession. And, last though not least, have
kept me out of the army and the miserable passions of this war. Further
time here may now be a loss to my occupation in life. [. . .] I wrote you
from New York telling you I would find no difficulty in getting a place
in the office of Mr. Evans but could hardly expect it would yield me a
support for the first year at least. Of course before I give up a position
which has ceased to be one of more honor to me now — but will support me — it is natural I should wish to know what will be my circumstances afterwards — what you intend to give me, or what allowance
for me, & on what conditions, if any, in the commencement of a profession — where success, whatsoever abilities or application may be
employed, cannot be attained right off. [. . .] I think with the advantages of education you have given me, I could start with reasonable
confidence and hope of at least moderate success and a permanent
livelihood. I do not feel I have abused my advantages to such an extent
as to bar me from any further indulgence. [. . .] As to any preference I
may have shown or may show in regard to marriage. [. . .] I have at least
the weight of the moral as well as the loyal judgment on my side. There
have been some attempts to legislate on the subject of the marriage of
cousins (as you yourself remarked in Ky.) but I know of no country
where such is prohibited. On the contrary, the three great divisions of
law, which form the basis of legislation in all civilized countries, declare
the marriage of 1st cousins legal. "On this point, the canon, the civil
and the common law are in perfect harmony." And as being against the
moral law, no one has ever made a substantial argument. There waits
only the question of domestic policy — of which opinions differ almost
at hazard. Of course, if continued in for two or three generations there
can be but one opinion. [. . .]

Yr. affect. son,

Green Clay

Mary Jane Clay was dismayed to discover her family still owed Brutus money. "I thought Mr. Clay's indebtedness to you was closed," she
wrote him in April 1865, "so if you knew the trouble the debt has always given me you might judge my disappointment when I found out
there was still lacking some thousands of dollars." Hearing that Bru-

tus's recent illness was jaundice, she recommended "Tincture of Puccoon-root."

Green Clay Smith sent Brutus some of the interest he owed him on a loan in April, adding, "G. Mother [Sally Dudley] is quite feeble. She wants to go down to see Aunt Paulina [Rodes], but Mother thinks she is hardly able to stand the trip as the roads are so rough."

On April 9, 1865, General Robert E. Lee surrendered to General Ulysses S. Grant at Appomattox Court House. The terrible war was over. In many ways the war had ended almost a year earlier for the Clays and Fields. After Zeke's capture, they no longer had young men in either army. The final battlegrounds were far from Bourbon County, though guerrilla skirmishes continued in Kentucky even after Lee's surrender. No one, not even Christopher Field, reflected in a letter upon what the war had meant either to individuals or to the country; at least, no such letter has survived.

Five days after Lee's surrender, President Lincoln was assassinated in Ford's Theater by John Wilkes Booth. Young Cash's spring break from Yale coincided with the assassination.

CASSIUS CLAY JR.

New Haven, Conn. April 18th, 1865

Dear Ma,

[. . .] I have been in New York for the last two or three days. It is quite a pleasant trip to get on a steamer and go by water. While there I heard some of the best tragedians in the United States, visited Central Park and Barnum's Museum. I continued my trip no farther on account of the low state of my finances. Abe Lincoln is dead. The people here are mad with phrensy [sic] and hate. They cry out hang every rebel both north and south. They say, the preachers in the pulpit, that R. E. Lee is ten times as guilty as the assassin of Lincoln. One of the speakers here yesterday, a preacher of the gospel, said he was for calling out 2 millions of men and for exterminating the race. The most radical and they are all, say that it was a stroke of providence that Abe was killed as it enables [President Andrew] Johnson to punish the infernal traitors.

The cry is extermination of the traitors. Hang the leaders! Hang all! I will say no more. I had a very strong notion of coming home as we have three weeks and a half of holiday. [. . .] I am rejoiced to hear that you are much better and hope that by the time I come home you will be perfectly restored to health. [. . .]

Your devoted son,

C. M. Clay

Cash's comments can't possibly reflect what Brutus must have felt upon learning of the president's death. Lincoln had always treated him with deference. Brutus was, after all, a Kentuckian, and Lincoln had used his ties with his home state to keep it in the Union at the beginning of the war. Brutus was an independent who had chosen to align himself with the Lincoln administration in the troubled days of 1863. Time and again Brutus asked Lincoln for favors, and the president granted them — pardons for Zeke and many others, passes through the Union lines for Mrs. Keiningham's family, an arrangement to allow Christopher Field to operate his plantation.

However, Cash's words do echo the feelings of many white Kentuckians — that Lincoln had tricked them on the slavery question to keep the state in the Union at the beginning of the war. The deception rankled. Both the Emancipation Proclamation, even though Kentucky was exempted from its provisions, and the drafting of black soldiers had changed the social structure of the state forever. In February 1865, when the Thirteenth Amendment abolishing slavery had come up for ratification in the state, the Kentucky legislature had voted against it.

Kentuckians were also outraged by the harsh military government the Lincoln administration had imposed upon their state. To be sure, Kentucky's loyalty ebbed and flowed, but people there were imprisoned and even executed for treason, often on scant evidence. In December 1863, as a war measure, Lincoln had suspended the right of habeas corpus in Kentucky, Maryland, Delaware, West Virginia, and Missouri, but when his successor Andrew Johnson restored it in the other border states in late 1865, the suspension was continued in Kentucky as in the conquered South. Many people wondered which side the state had been on after all.

Ann completed her course of medicine with Dr. Miller and returned home in April. However, she was not yet cured. "I am sorry that you are not improving as fast as you expected since your return home," Dr. Miller wrote on April 28, acknowledging receipt of payment of his

$150 bill, "though your expectations were, perhaps, too sanguine. Amendment is always gradual in such cases as yours and I confidently expect that it will be so with you and that your health will finally be confirmed." He enclosed prescriptions and his photograph "according to your request."

Despite his unhappiness in Congress, Brutus decided to seek re-election. When a group calling itself the Conservative Union Party met on June 13 to nominate a candidate for Congress from the Seventh District, he let it be known that he was available. On the first ballot he received 19 2/3 votes to 40 2/3 votes for George S. Shanklin of Jessamine County and 19 2/3 for Richard Hanson. Shanklin went on to win the election, defeating the radical candidate.

A relative wrote Brutus a humorous account of what happened to the Clark County vote.

THORNTON LEWIS

June 21, 1865

Cousin Brutus,

I write to express my profound regret at the result of the Convention held in Lexington last week and inform you how the thing was managed in Clark County. At our May court Mr. Dick Hanson was here and he made a present of a fine Hat to Capt. R. Nicholas, a grocery man who keeps whiskey in the back room for those that are dry. We can guess what the Hat was given for. The good of the thing is this, while Nicholas was treating the soldiers and electioneering for Hanson, some one *stole* the *hat*. [. . .] Col. Charles Hanson was here and done [sic] what he could for his Brother. He took two delegates in his Rockaway to Lexington, both pledged for his Brother. There was great indifference about going to the convention. I tried hard to get men to go that I thought would vote for you. Several promised me that they would go and did go. I thought from what they said to me that they would vote for you, but when they got there voted for Hanson. My horse was lame. I made an agreement with Larry Flanagan. To make it more certain Mr. Redman told me he was going in his Buggy alone and would like to have my company. I promised to go with him provided Flanagan failed to call. In the morning Mr. Flanagan sent me word that his wife was taken suddenly sick and could not go. The man told me that Redman was in town. In the meantime the Stage passed, and I would have gone in it if I had known that Mr. Redman had gone before the Stage. So you see I was sorely disappointed in not being at the convention. If I had been there one vote would have been cast for you if no more. When Dick Hanson was here at May court, he was beastly drunk, staggering in the street, hardly able to get to the Court House, yet these delegates voted for this notorious drunkard. Is it not astonishing. [. . .] I have no doubt if the vote of Clark County was polled between Hanson and you, a very large majority of the conservative party would be for you. [. . .] I console myself with the conviction that you have not lost anything by the action of the party as expressed by the convention. [. . .]

Your relation and friend,

Thornton Lewis

Lewis's letter reminds me of the Kentucky election stories my father used to tell when he was a member of the legislature in the 1950s. His best election story was one he did not tell but participated in: the Bourbon County Vote Fraud. My brother and I were nine and ten at the time and what happened then erased the last vestiges of suburban Baltimore forever.

The night before the presidential election in 1948, when Thomas Dewey was challenging Harry Truman, someone stuffed some ballot boxes in Bourbon County so that they rattled when delivered to the polling place. When opened, it was discovered that the boxes contained ballots that had been cast in advance for Truman. Within forty-eight hours, everyone in the county knew who had done it, a promising young lawyer named Edward F. Prichard Jr., who had studied at Harvard Law School, clerked for Supreme Court Justice Felix Frankfurter, and recently returned from Washington, presumably to enter Kentucky politics. Why he did it is still a puzzle. Some people thought there was a bet involved. Whatever the reason, it was an act of great arrogance as it presupposed either that Bourbon Countians were such hicks that they would be unable to locate the perpetrator, or so inured to political corruption that they wouldn't try.

My father became the head of a committee that, against all odds, finally got the case prosecuted. Prichard had plenty of friends in high places, including the U.S. attorney general's office, and it is a tribute to my father's persistence and sense of outrage that the vote fraud case was ever resolved.

It was a harrowing time for all of us. My brother recalls Prichard's father pacing up and down in the local barbershop, ranting on and on about our father, while my brother, who had been dropped off there to get a haircut, shrank into the barber's chair and prayed he wouldn't be recognized. After our father accused the district attorney of dragging his heels, the D.A. sued him for libel, a case which was eventually thrown out of court but not before the anxiety it generated had demoralized my mother, a woman haunted by memories of finding herself without money during the Depression. I remember the excitement of those years, particularly the phone calls from Louisville *Courier-Journal* reporters. My brother remembers that our mother was always in tears.

In Italy, the government had moved from Turin to Florence, and the American mission had moved with it. This was a difficult period for the Italians who had hoped to make Rome their capital. In September 1864, the king had signed a treaty with Napoleon guaranteeing the existence of the papal states and the withdrawal of all French troops within two years. Moving the seat of government to Florence was supposed to convince Napoleon that the Italian government had no plans for Rome.

"I do not hear much about political matters in Ky.," Green told Ann in June, "but certainly we must pass through a severe ordeal in the reorganization [Reconstruction]. I was just writing to Cash [. . .] and telling him of my class. Mr. [Jefferson] Davis' private secretary, Col. Harrison, [. . .] is my old classmate. He was a gallant fellow & good friend and I cannot look upon him as a criminal though my government may."

In the limbo between the end of the war and the ratification of the Thirteenth Amendment, the status of former slaves in Kentucky was uncertain. General Palmer, who had replaced General Burbridge as head of the military district of Kentucky, wanted to make sure they were truly free before the military gave up control of the state. In July he ordered quartermasters to pay the wages earned by blacks to the men themselves and not to their "pretended masters."

The military also issued "passes" for former slaves that allowed them to travel at will in search of employment, so-called free papers. There are free papers among Brutus's letters, one issued on July 24 to

"Jack Clay & wife & child (colored)," another issued a couple of days later to "Harry Turner (colored)," and two more on July 27 to "Sylvester Ayres, wife & four child [sic] (colored)" and "River Wilkins & 1 child (colored)." All four men and their dependents were headed for Cincinnati.

In August, the conservative Shanklin won handily over the radical (Republican) candidate in the Seventh Congressional District. Within a short period of time, any candidate who was not a Democrat stood little chance of getting elected to office in the state. For almost a hundred years, Kentucky elections were decided in the Democratic primary.

In 1956, when I became eighteen and able to register to vote, I announced to my father that I intended to register as an Independent rather than commit myself blindly to one party or the other. "Don't be a fool," he told me. "You'd simply be disenfranchising yourself."

Only a short time before, Kentucky had decided to give eighteen-year-olds the vote, the second state in the country to do so. My father was a member of the legislature at the time and one of the few to vote against eighteen-year-old suffrage, a vote I felt was directed at me personally. Nevertheless, I carefully considered what he had said about registering as an Independent, then went to the courthouse and signed myself up as a Democrat.

In November 1956, I was one of the few girls in my house at Smith College to receive an absentee ballot. My friends, knowing I intended to vote for Adlai Stevenson, hid my ballot. I laughed and wept and threatened them with federal prosecution. The ballot turned up in my room just in time for me to use it.

In Kentucky, the 1865 election was conducted under military auspices. In some places, soldiers prevented voters from going to the polls. In Fayette County, a grand jury indicted five people, including Brutus's friend and kinsman David S. Goodloe, for election violations, but when their cases came up before Circuit Judge William Cassius Goodloe, David's brother, all were dismissed.

In August, Green wrote his father an oddly detached letter. Since his return to Italy, Green had become more distant than ever. He began with a subject that he doubtless knew would interest Brutus. "The cattle of Italy have some fine points. I think they are the foremost work oxen I ever saw, and the cows seem to be good milkers, but I cannot say much for the beef. Probably due to defective feeding and to a hard race of cattle. There is but one prevailing color — cream or dun. [. . .] Though the finest animal in this stable was a beautiful black red 3 yr. old and would have been considered a fine bull at our own fairs. Some of the cows did not come up, I thought, to the beauty of their names such as Guerissa, Gennia, Belfiona, Pomerania, Beatrice, etc. They are not as large as the Durhams and except in the neatness of horns are generally deteriorated on all fine points. I'm not sure their herdsmen would appreciate 'fair feeling' and 'flanking down' [show ring examination]."

After a rambling discussion of the relative merits of Italy and the United States, Green concluded, "The longer I observe & the wider my observations, the more I am convinced Americans are but the mass of humanity and God has given them no special preemptive claim [to] a short route to good government and national happiness."

In August, Christopher Field was once again in Richmond. His Mississippi plantation had been inundated by a massive flood in April that the damaged levees could not contain. "A Levee on the Vick place [immediately north of the Clay and Field holdings] was cut in 1863 by the Gun Boats to drown the people out," he wrote Brutus. "It [. . .] was the cause of great destruction this spring, nearly overflowed our whole country. Lake Bolivar which has never been entirely overflown before was entirely under, not a foot of land out. [. . .] I think something will be done to put up the Levees but not in time for a crop next year."

He told Brutus that he felt it was important for someone to live on the Clay and Field plantations so they would not appear to be abandoned. Northern men would be looking for "abandoned" land in the South to buy cheaply. It saddened him that neither Kit nor Zeke Field wanted to return to Mississippi. He also tried to interest Zeke Clay in living there, but without success.

Christopher was right about Northern men looking to acquire plantations. A month later, Brutus received a letter of inquiry from none other than General Burbridge. "I understand that you and your brother-in-law Col. Fields [sic] have two or three plantations for rent or lease in Bolivar Co., Miss.," Burbridge wrote. "Having made some arrangements to cultivate Plantations in the South, and having opportunities for obtaining labor to better advantage than persons generally engaged in the business, we are desirous of hearing your terms — how the lands are situated — and if they are subject to overflow etc. etc." Brutus referred him to Christopher.

Cash was at home during the summer of 1865 and, in September, returned to Yale for his senior year. He had a difficult trip, missing connections and staying overnight in unexpected places. He had traveled north with Christopher and Pattie Field and Belle Lyman, who were looking at girls' schools in New York. "We had a good many inconveniences arising from missing connections," he wrote Ann on September 16, "but I had as about as pleasant a trip as on either of the two other occasions. In reality more so. [. . .] I left Uncle Kit, Aunt Belle, and the girls all in good health."

Cash's letter crossed with one from his mother that was full of Bourbon County news.

ANN CLAY

Home, Sept. 21st, 1865

My Dear Child,

It has now been 11 days since you left home and not one word have I heard from you. I had hoped so much to get a letter from you today as your sister, the baby & me will leave in the morning for Richmond. I suppose your Uncle Cit will soon be there as he said he would only be gone 12 days. I could not help but be uneasy about you as you were not well when you left and there is so much sickness on the place, a great deal of measles & several new cases of Fever. [. . .]

I hear a great deal about cattle every day since you left and they were only weighed yesterday. Those your Papa bought weighing less than your Papa expected & also those that you & Zeke bought. [. . .] They have been squabbling about them for several days & I feel as Annie [Holloway] remarked today that she dreamed about cattle, hearing so much talk about them. [. . .]

I suppose we will be away two weeks if Martha's children do not get the measles but I do hope we will not be hurried back. Martha has just had a letter from Mr. D. tonight. [. . .] Said he had been to Baltimore and the city was crammed with Southerners all trying to get to business again!! Seen Capt. Hawes yesterday. He is looking quite well, said he had no trouble in getting his pardon at Washington. [Hawes had been the provisional Confederate governor of Kentucky.] It is late and I must close, hoping soon to hear from you, that you are well & doing well [. . .] do write to Green. He is truly neglected by all of us.

Yours devotedly,

Ann M. Clay

Ann and Martha had gone to Richmond so that Martha could say goodbye to her friends and relations before returning to Virginia, which had become the state of West Virginia in 1863.

ANN CLAY

Home, Oct. 11th, 1865

My Dear Child,

[. . .] Martha and me reached home from Richmond last Friday after spending two weeks very pleasantly there. [. . .] We found the Whites all well when we reached home but the negroes all sick, scarcely enough well to wait on us. Tom had to go to the Field & I have had no one to drive me as Scott died from measles on Sunday and all the other young ones sick. [. . .] A baby died last night, a small boy last week, & Anderson not expected to live. [. . .] Cit is now here looking for his Papa to get some money to pay for a lot of cattle he has bought & I will hasten to send this letter to town. [. . .]

Molly Garrard marries Edd Gayle on the 24th in the Christian Church. Charley Garrard marries Alice Jones in the Presbyterian Church the same day & they go north on a bridal tour. [Molly and Charley were Cousin Charles's children.] Sidney says he seen [sic] Mollie [sic] a few days ago on the street & she was certainly the most beautiful creature he has ever seen.

Lilia Lewis says Zeke and his lady love [Mollie Woodford] have had a quarrel. I suppose only a lovers' quarrel but I suppose they will soon become reconciled, but he looks sad about something. He & Cit speak of going to Madison hunting birds. On the night before we left Richmond, June Holloway reached there with his gun and two dogs, but the weeds are too green for hunting yet. Zeke Holloway is still there.

We spent a very pleasant day at your Uncle Cassius's when in Richmond. Mary Jane has built a splendid house. Every convenience but not finished. Mary [Green's fiancée] is very sad, not by any means her former self from some cause. [. . .]

Joe Embry's [Mary Embry's stepson] trial [for assault] comes off this week. Martha has taken quite a dislike to him, says he is the meanest roughest boy she has ever seen. He commenced wrong with her, called her baby a Norway *rat*.

Write often.

Yours devotedly,

A. M. Clay

Joe Embry was charged with assault and with carrying a concealed weapon. Joe had been a classmate of Cash's at Professor Sayre's school, and they had boarded together in Frankfort for a while. Judging from a letter he wrote Cash a short time after this, he was indeed a mean, rough person. Martha was right to dislike him.

Later in October, Ann wrote Cash of the changes taking place in their neighborhood and family. Always a restless man, William Holloway had caught the Westward fever. This did not surprise his relatives. Elizabeth, however, was heartbroken.

ANN CLAY

Saturday night, Oct. 1865

My Dear Child,

I received your last letter a day or two ago. [. . .] I went [. . .] to get your boots & he [the bootmaker] had sold them some time ago but he promised me most *faithfully* that he will have another pair made for you in a week. [. . .] [W]hen I packed your trunk I noticed that your studying gown was much soiled so I shall send you a new one as you are a senior and you must keep it nice. As for the *sheets* you said nothing about wanting any. [. . .] I suppose you have bought sheets by this time. [. . .] Joe Embry went to Frankfort but was not indicted by the grand jury so I suppose he feels relieved. I had a letter from Patty [*sic*] Field yesterday. She was delighted with her school, knew it is the best in the city, said she cleaned up her own room and conceited she did it very nicely and could give you some items if you would thank her. She is at the Abbot Institute, 38 Street corner of Park Avenue.

Your Papa consented for Zeke to sell the Kilmarnick farm if he could get 80$ [an acre] for it. He thinks he will sell to Billy Buckner [a neighbor]. [. . .] It seems that every one is crazy to buy & sell. Zeke is crazy to get *Charles Garrard's* place, thinks he can in a few years make the money to pay back to your Papa as it is more than he can afford to give him now & it would not surprise me much if your Papa buys it, though he says he has no notion of it, but is going tomorrow to see him [Garrard] about it. He will sell to your Papa for 120$ per acre. But Sam Clay [a neighbor] wants it to start for Matt's [his son] place. But say nothing about this or your Papa buying it to any one. Zeke says if it is sold at auction it will bring a good deal more than 120. [. . .] I suppose as soon as he can get a home he expects to marry which is very well though I do not care to be related to J. Woodford. [Brutus and Ann evidently considered Mollie Woodford's father something of an interloper. Also, he had been a Southern sympathizer during the war.] Your sister [. . .] is quite sad, had a letter yesterday from Mr. D., did not say when he was coming but is opposed to living any where except with his mother [his father had died at the end of the war] which is not agreeable to Martha and she says she will not go back if she has to live with her and your Papa says she can take the Kennedy house [a pretty stone house on the property Brutus had acquired from Jesse Kennedy]. Mr. D. knows her great opposition to living with his mother and I think it is mean & centering [*sic*] to insist on it. Annie [Holloway] has gone home as they have a sale next week & will soon go to Missouri. Her Mama wants her to go but her Papa thinks it is too cold for her to go this winter as her health is delicate. [. . .] [W]rite to Green. I feel for him. Keep the good resolution to write the essay. You lack confidence in yourself.

Yrs. devotedly,

A. M. Clay

Cash was looking forward to returning to Kentucky after graduation. "Time is swiftly flying by," he told his mother at the end of October. "I hope that at last when graduating day comes I may leave New England Never to return except perhaps on a transient visit."

Ann wrote him that Brutus had purchased the Garrard place.

ANN CLAY

Paris, Nov. 1st, 1865

My Dear Child,

I sent you today by Express a box containing a studying gown, pair of slippers, 1 pair of boots, your gold pencil I forgot to give you, and a few eatables. You must get some *sardines* to eat with the biscuits. [. . .] I wanted to put in a bottle of wine (though it was a bad example) but feared it would get broke & ruin every thing. [. . .]

Your Papa has gone to bed but sends his love & says make haste & get through & leave those abolition skunks. [. . .]

Your Papa yesterday bought privately Charles Garrard's place at 125$ per acre. It amounts to 52,000$. [. . .] I suppose he will some day give it to Zeke as Zeke thinks he can soon make 10 or 20,000 to pay back either your Papa or his children. I suppose it is well enough to commence in debt. [. . .] Sam Clay [the neighbor who had hoped to buy Garrard's place] says that is the secret of his success, always being in debt. He expected to buy it & exchange with Matt, & Hubbard [. . .] wanted it, and one of the Redmonds was trying to sell so as to buy [it] but Charles was satisfied with the price & feared to put it up for fear it would not get so high as he had so much land. Zeke is delighted but has been in bed ever since with boils, can't leave his room.

Your Papa sold the Kilmarnick farm for 75 per acre to little Billy Buckner and immediately sent Zeke down to tell Cousin Charles he would take his place, but quite early [the] next morning Sam & Matt were there & Zeke & your Papa are quite pleased [that] they were too smart for them. When they [Sam and Matt] found Zeke there & your Papa came soon after, Matt wanted to see the house *as he was going to build & Sam wanted a fine sheep*. The impression is that your Papa bought for Martha.

Yrs. devotedly,

Write soon,

A. M. Clay

From Joe Embry Cash learned that the Embrys would soon be leaving Richmond, too.

JOE EMBRY

Richmond, Nov. 7th, 1865

Dear Cash —

[. . .] I am as low down at this time as any fellow of common metier gets to be from the fact that I have been used to [the company of] so many boys and being taken from them all at once makes a vast difference.

Hunting is splendid this season, in fact, better than ever before from the quantity of birds on hand. Zeke Field and myself were out yesterday and found any quantity of birds; out of them we killed sixty-seven and would have done better though one dog got lame. There is [sic] no young ladies here at present and I am inclined to quarter in Bourbon this winter on account of Miss Alice Rogers. [. . .] I have some good dogs and occupy my time for the most part on the hunt. I know you would enjoy it so much but you are tied on at Yale for this year; and the next you will have such damn big notions in between your ears that you won't look at a Kentuckian, though I hardly think your head is one of the damn sort that will swell at any little stuck up idea you may have to enter it. I suppose you have heard that Pa [W. W. Embry] has bought a store in Cincinnati and will sell his residence on Saturday next at public auction and move soon to the city.

[. . .] I think I will remain in this town until Christmas and perhaps longer. I was cleared at the trial as the grand jury found no indictment except for carrying concealed weapons. [. . .]

There were twenty or thirty Negro soldiers passed through here three months ago robbing all the citizens in the county. They robbed one house [. . .] but there was one principal negro who did it all. So four of the negroes were met in the boat that leads to Lexington. The leader was shot down [. . .] by a young man whose parents had been robbed by them. The other negroes that were with him brought him through town in a wagon dead as hell. I went out and took a good look at the *son of a bitch*. [. . .]

I have not heard from any of the Bourbon boys since a *long time* but they are flourishing and on foot. [. . .]

J. C. Embry — C.M.C.C. [?]

The attitudes expressed by Joe in this letter speak volumes about the state of race relations in postwar Kentucky. As late as December

1865, Kentucky blacks were often still regarded as slaves. In October, the Kentucky Central Railroad ordered its conductors to stop transporting "slaves" unless they had written travel permits from their "owners." Blacks with military passes (called Palmer's passes, because they were issued in the name of the federal commander for Kentucky, General John M. Palmer) were simply thrown off the trains. In spite of this, thousands left the state in the months following the war. In late July, the roads to Paris were crowded with blacks going to town to get their "free papers" from the provost marshall. Most were headed for Cincinnati, but others crowded into federal military installations such as Camp Nelson.

The Freedmen's Bureau was established in June 1865 to help former slaves make the transition to freedom, but it wasn't very successful, both because of inadequate funds and because of attitudes such as those expressed by Joe Embry. The bureau did catalog innumerable murders, beatings, rapes, and other violent acts against blacks between the end of the war and 1870, when it was closed. Many were probably committed by members of the Ku Klux Klan, which was founded in Tennessee in 1866 and was especially active in Kentucky during the first two decades after the war. Few were ever brought to justice for these crimes, since law officers intimidated the victims and protected the accused regardless of the evidence. Until 1872, no black could testify against a white in a Kentucky court. Later, few dared to do so even with the law on their side.

In November, William Holloway wrote Brutus that he had left the army and would soon be departing for Missouri. "I have purchased a very neat comfortable residence in Independence and expect to commence business in the Spring. I have always had the faculty of making friends wherever I have been and I think we will all be eventually pleased with the change." The Holloways were moving to a part of Missouri so heavily settled by former Kentuckians that it became known as Little Kentucky.

Later in November, Ann wrote Cash that Martha and her little boys had finally left for West Virginia.

ANN CLAY

Paris, Nov. 20 [1865]

Dear Cash,

[. . .] I assure you the house seems quite lonely. And your Papa is still regretting that he did not keep Zeke [Davenport] & did propose it, but I told him I thought every mother ought to raise her own children. Mr. Davenport was quite indignant that there was such a difference made between June & Zeke, so much so that he was spoiling June by his indulgence & that he said Zeke was very ugly & the worst child he had ever seen. But Henry was the handsomest & best. [. . .] Mr. D. came ten days ago. His mother died a week before he left home & Martha went back quite willingly as she will now have the control of every thing & can have things her own way. Your Papa gave her 6 cows & a milk animal & Berry Bedford [a neighbor] took charge of them & started with them last Saturday to Virginia, drove them to Maysville & will there take a boat. He also gave her two mares, one of them the one you rode last summer. He consulted me about giving yours away. I told him I expected it would make no difference with you, as I knew he would give you a better one. I think he will give you the sorrel when you come home. Zeke has tried very hard to beg him [the horse] from him but he will not give him up. I know your Papa intends to do what is right for you so I hope you will come home determined to please him & willing to assist him in every way & if you do you will never regret it & it will be fully appreciated by him. He & Zeke go to the Garrard farm tomorrow to have it surveyed. Zeke bought the oil cloth on the floor, 4 waggons & other things at the sale last week. Stock sold very high. Some hogs at 50$, sheep near 30 & a pair of oxen 287. Yearling cattle were 60$. Mr. Davenport inquired consistently for you. He invited me to visit them in three or 4 years. I told him & laughed a good deal that I expected to go for you & then we would come by to see them but as he did not wish me I should hesitate about going so soon.

Your Aunt Belle, Mary [Embry] & Lizzie Miller [Patsey Miller's oldest daughter] came over on Saturday, spent yesterday & left today. Only came to see Martha. Belle complimented you continually which of course gratified me much. [. . .] Curt Burnam bought Mr. Embry's house last week for 15,600$. Mary is neither satisfied with the price [n]or the purchaser as she does not admire Mrs. Burnam. [. . .]

Yrs. devotedly,

Ann Clay

[P.S.] We have just heard from Green. He did not speak of coming home. Sid [Clay] has gone to Texas.

The Burnams named the Embrys' house Burnamwood. A curious hip-roofed building with a Gothic turret atop it, Mary's house is now retirement apartments. The Holloways' imposing home at the other end of town was for years a community center.

Cash sounded tired when he wrote his mother at Thanksgiving.

CASSIUS CLAY JR.

New Haven, Nov. 23rd, '65

Dear Ma,

[. . .] I have just eaten up the last of [the] biscuits that you sent me. I enjoyed the cakes, candies etc. very much. I am now looking forward impatiently to the end of the term which event will take place on the nineteenth of December. After this we only have one more term of study. I am very glad that this is the case or otherwise I would never perhaps enjoy the honor of being a graduate of Yale.

If facilities of traveling was [sic] so good that I could come home in much less time than it is now possible, I would look forward with far more anticipation of pleasure. As it is, perhaps, vacation will be hardly less disagreeable than term time, but in as much as the last three months have been three months of hard study I will welcome the change as merely relieving us for a time of onerous duties & early prayers.

[. . .] This is the most miserable climate I was ever in. The air is always damp. I really believe it rains or drizzles one half of the time. It would in a few years give any healthy man unacclimated the consumption. [. . .]

The weather (Nov. 28) is now intensely cold. The rooms in college are miserable, floors rough, very cold, floors never swept or beds made up but yet much more roomy as a general thing than those in town. [. . .]

I rec'd. your last letter a few days ago. I can imagine that it will be quite lonesome at home with only you and Pa there. I suppose Christopher keeps away from home or rather stays at *home* quite assiduously as it is his usual habit. What about the suit brought against Pa? I see a notice of it in the papers. [. . .]

Your son,

C. M. Clay

The suit to which Cash refers was one threatened by the Freedmen's Bureau against several prominent Bourbon County citizens, including Brutus and Garrett Davis. The military government of Kentucky claimed that they owed women whose husbands had served in the army wages accrued since March 3, 1865, when Congress passed legislation freeing the wives and families of black Union soldiers. Nothing came of it.

Kit wrote his brother the news of the county, mostly about hunting dogs and girls. Except for his references to "black white men" and "damn Yankees," Kit's letter could have been written before the war. Bourbon County was settling into a pattern that would continue largely uninterrupted until my childhood eighty years later.

CHRISTOPHER CLAY

Paris, Ky., Nov. 30, 1865

Dear Cash,

I have determined to write you a short letter & give you the little news in Bourbon. I presume a letter from the land of beauty would be of some interest if but a few lines. I hope you will not let the d — Yankees make you a black white man before you get back. Mr. D. & Martha left for [West] Virginia last week, took a few cattle & horses with them as stock of that kind quite scarce in their diggings. Little Zeke & June did not want to go & leave their Grand Pa. I suppose you heard Pa had bought [the] Charles Garrard farm for Zeke. [. . .] Zeke & myself are going over tomorrow to survey the farm. Everybody says Zeke & Miss Woodford are going to marry but Zeke says there is no truth in the report. [. . .] We are busy now killing hogs during this fine frosty weather. I have not hunted birds yet but think I will go to Mt. Sterling on a hunt next week. It is quite lonesome in Bourbon at present as all the boys are in the mountains hunting & fishing. There is a good many deer in the mountains. Birds & plenty in Madison [. . .] more than has been for many years. I have a splendid pointer [dog] gave [sic] to me by a friend. Your ma & all well. I see old [Zeke] Field & [Zeke] Holloway coming so I must close for the present. When at leisure I would be glad to hear from you. In haste,

Yours Very Truly,

C. F. Clay

After putting Pattie in school in New York, Christopher Field returned to Mississippi. He was having a hard time adjusting to free labor. The views he expresses in this letter to Brutus were typical of those held by many planters.

CHRISTOPHER FIELD

Bolivar, Miss., Nov. 30th, 1865

Dear Sir,

I have intended writing you for some time but have been so undetermined in what I would or ought to do that I did not know what to write, and even now I can't say. I am disgusted at the free labor and [the] heavy expense that we will have to pay. I think it will be at least two years before it will settle down or that the negro will feel himself under any obligation to return you labor for his hire. They shirk now just as much as they would have done when slaves if they had been permitted to do so, and I think labor will be very scarce and that many who wish to plant even under the present state of things will fail for want of labor. None of the negroes will contract for next year until after Christmas. They have been told by bad men that at that time the Government will give them lands, mules and farming tools & some negroes have said if they do not get it we will have trouble. [. . .] I myself have no fears of any insurrection but many have.

The condition of the levees is a serious matter in thinking of Planting. [. . .] Last spring [. . .] a very deep and ugly gully was washed out into Lake Bolivar and I find public sentiment is very much against crossing this wash with a levee and coming on down the River. They say it [the levee] must go around Lake Bolivar and come out some 5 miles below us, thereby throwing us outside! This route around the Lake is a very practicable route running on high ground all around to the River again and I now *have great* fears it will be adopted. If so, our property is ruined. I can only prevent it by being the Levee Commissioner for this county again, a position I have occupied. Whether I can get it again I can't say but I think from my character and position with the people I may get it. [. . .] All these facts I have given you had induced me to offer all three of our places for sale and [I] have so advertised them in Memphis, Vicksburg & N.O. [. . .] I will not make too great a sacrifice of any of the Land but if I can find a purchaser at any thing like what I think the property is worth I will sell. [. . .] If I fail in selling I am compelled to take a partner in each place except this one I [. . .] live on. This pricing of the negro has made many changes which I did not think of. I will have to rent some man at each place say 1/4 of the land, loan him 1/4 the capital, charging him interest, then give him 1/4 of the profits. [. . .] I wish you to hold yourself in readiness if I should call on you for means. [. . .]

Yours truly,

C. I. Field

Ann wrote Cash family news and local gossip. She urged him to visit Martha at Christmastime.

ANN CLAY

At Home, Dec. 3, 1865

My Dear Child,

I have just read your last letter received today [. . .] & in the first place will answer your questions. Your Papa has heard nothing more but what you saw in the papers about his being sued by the military. I suppose it is only newspaper talk. [. . .] Zeke will go to the Garrard place in March. I was a little surprised that he was so anxious to put his all in a high price home, knowing that he will have to work hard & pay back to your Papa for several years all he will make as it is more than your Papa is willing to divide out now with his children, but I expect it will be an incentive to him to work & economize from the start which will be of a great advantage. Your Papa & me made Cit a visit today. His farm was looking very well, but your Papa sees a good deal to complain of [Poor Kit! As usual he couldn't do anything right]. Both ponds ruining for a few days work. Latches off of gates, etc. He thinks Cit is too fond of going to town & has too little energy. He [Brutus] is so fond of keeping every thing in order he can not have any patience with any one who neglects it. Zeke is staying some at Sidney's whilst he is in Texas. [. . .] I received a letter yesterday from your Sister. She reached home the Saturday before, said tell Papa it seems such a Herculean task to get their farm in order she believed it would take them 5 yrs. hard work [. . .] and that she now regretted letting Zeke have the Garrard place. She thinks your Papa bought it for her & was very anxious for her to live on it. It is well enough for her to enjoy that belief, & says

Zeke will be so sick of his bargain that she can get it in a few years, but I think Zeke has so much pride & energy she will not have the chance. Mr. Davenport says when he moves he will go to Missouri where he can get cheap land. [. . .]

Martha wrote me though she had no business to offer she intended to write to you to spend Christmas with her. I expect it will be very agreeable to you, & if you had a gun you would have some sport hunting. If you would like to go, write me & I will get your Papa's consent & then you could spend a few days before Christmas in Washington whilst Congress [is] in session. Of course we miss the children & Martha much but I do not know but it is very agreeable to have a little quiet. Your Papa misses Zeke [Davenport] so much he says will have to send for him. I know he misses his Grandpapa & the kind attention of the negroes. He was a[n] affable pleasant boy & Junius a very good boy if Mr. D. does not spoil him. Your uncle William Holloway & family spent several days here this week on their way to Missouri, & I can assure [you] it was a sad parting with us — so disturbing to see them all except him so much opposed to going. Sister was in tears all the time, said she was being dragged off against her will. Annie said on account of her health she would spend the winter here but when the time came Sister was so anxious for her to go & told her she must but she was much opposed to it & could not make up her mind until dark to go. [. . .] Zeke H. will spend the winter with Patty [sic] [Bedinger]. [. . .] Patty & Dan went to Covington yesterday to see the spiritualist Dr. Newton & I suppose will come back tomorrow safe & sound by a mere stroke from his hand. David Irvine & Willis Benton are there waiting for him to cure them of their distress. Mr. Embry has bought a business house in Cin., a residence in Covington. I suppose his family will not go down before spring. [. . .]

[. . .] Mary & Sally [Cassius's daughters] expect to go to Washington. Sister told me that Mary told her that she & Green did not correspond now. [. . .]

Write soon. Yrs.,

A. M. Clay

On December 17, Martha wrote to invite Cash to Charles Town. "I have just read a letter from your Ma. She tells me you were anxious to go home during Christmas and that Pa says you may come to see us. Mr. Davenport says you must certainly come, and I will be much disappointed if you do not. I will look for you by Thursday as college is out your Ma writes on the 19th. [. . .] I know by this time you need some recreation. And a trip to this historic valley will please you and gratify us. Be sure to come. When you get to Charlestown [*sic*], just inquire the road and you can walk here, as it is only a mile & good walking."

She included some bad news. "We had a very sad accident two days ago. Poor little June caught fire and came near being burned to death. He is quite feeble now, but the Dr. thinks improving rapidly and I hope by the time you come will be able to sit up and enjoy your society some, as he talks very often of you."

Ann sent her Christmas letter to Cash in New Haven, not realizing that, after saying he did not want to visit Martha, he had gone to West Virginia after all. Her letter contained the not-unexpected news that Zeke planned to marry.

The Garrard house, which Brutus had bought for Zeke and his bride, is a large brick Greek Revival building of the same vintage as Auvergne. Zeke renamed it Runnymede and established a thoroughbred breeding and racing establishment there. Today a painting of Zeke's mare, Miss Woodford, hangs in the front hall of the house, where one of his grandsons lives with his family. The Runnymede Clays still breed horses.

Ann's letter also contains information about the former slaves' plans, including the financial arrangements some of them had made with Brutus. She seems quite sympathetic to Nancy's desire "to see something of the world" and even to Mingo's "airs." Perhaps the most telling comment of all is her remark that Brutus seems "loath to give any of them up" even now that he has to pay them for their work.

ANN CLAY

Paris, Dec. 28, 1865

My Dear Child,

I have just received your letter and [. . .] was surprised that you did not want to go to [West] Virginia. [. . .] I thought it would be a pleasant recreation for you & you would enjoy your sister & Mr. D.'s company. I wish you had have come home with Anderson [a classmate]. Your Papa & me would have been glad to have seen you. [. . .] Yr. Papa says he hopes when you come home you will not act the fool like his other boys & want to marry some common neighbor girl that he does *not even know* (do you think strange of that?). Zeke has informed us that if your Papa can furnish the money to buy him some clothes & a buggy, he wants to marry Molly [sic] Woodford in the spring. He also wishes his house furnished. It is quite a bitter pill for your Papa to swallow to have John Woodford's daughter for his daughter-in-law & at the same time Zeke says that Cit wants to marry if he has the money to fix up & furnish his house. So your Papa has just remarked to me that if [he] were to see either Molly Brooks [Kit's fiancée] or Molly Woodford he would not know them. Zeke told your Papa several months ago he wanted to marry but wanted his advice before he went too far. I told him he did not approve of it and considered John Woodford a dirty dog, but that after having his opinion if he still insisted on it he should not put any obstacle in the way of it, but I suppose they were engaged then & have been for some time. On Christmas Day, he & Cit were engaged in a deer chase. Jeff Grimes turned two loose, the first one Zeke says his dog caught, but, as there was a squabble about it, they chased others and Zeke lost it. He brought from Richmond two (he says) very superior hounds. [. . .] They started on Tuesday morning with Sam Clay to his Blue Licks farm to run Fox. [. . .] Your Papa is anxious for them to come home to see what servants they want as there are many changes going on. [. . .] All [former slaves] wanted to go to themselves to keeping house but I find them dropping in on home & quite anxious to make a trade with your Papa. Most of the old ones are remaining for reasonable [pay] with your Papa. Fleury 100$ but there is his family to support. Hamp & two boys for 100. Eli 120. Jordan & Woodson will leave. Milly has gone. Nancy left with a view of traveling, first will go to Lexington & Frankfort & then expected to go South to see her brother at Helena, but her mother is so opposed to it she has declined going South for the present but wants to see something of the world & then she will be willing to hire out. Maria & Matt will stay. Your Papa set out with the determination of clearing several of the houses [slave quarters] & certainly getting clear of Amy & family but has hired them & I find is loath to give any of them up. Altho Mingoe [sic] was the first to tell him he wanted to live here, he is putting on some airs and it is doubtful if he stays [ultimately he did]. Your Papa told him he could do head work [i.e., be headman]. [. . .] Harrison is looking out [for] a farm to rent & seems most provoked this evening that your Papa would not agree for them to stay until March, until he could get possession [of a farm]. Your Papa is constantly asking who I will have for a cook. I tell him so they are clean I am quite indifferent as there will be but little encouragement to learn one that will leave at any time. Eliza says she will not leave me alone [. . .] but still will not say how long she will stay, says she has been engaged to be married for 5 years to a free negro, a shoe maker in Cynthiana, so she may leave at any time. Emily will go with her father [Harrison] but I think it doubtful about his getting a farm.

Ellis Clay had a very handsome Christmas tree on Monday night. Zeke & me went. That is all the Christmas I have had. It was filled with candies & little fancy things, each numbered, then the corresponding numbers on pieces of paper were handed around to the company so each one had several numbers & it was quite amusing drawing the prizes & then we had a nice supper. When I have a house full of grand children I will prepare a Christmas tree. [. . .]

A. M. Clay

The reason Cash had been so unhappy the previous term may have been that he was not well, as Martha explained in a letter to Ann written shortly after Christmas. Martha had her hands full with a badly burned child and a sick brother.

MARTHA DAVENPORT

Dec. 29th, 1865

Dear Aunt Ann,

[. . .] The children were delighted with their present. June is very impatient that I shall write to return his thanks to you & Pa, and Zeke goes into perfect ecstasies over the idea of "riding in Grandpapa's buggy with his hat and walking cane and going to town to buy candy." I hung up their stockings Christmas Eve and filled them. They were delighted the next morning to empty them and have been enjoying the contents ever since. June is mending rapidly from his dreadful burn. He is able to sit up for several hours now. I should have written to you before but have been so constantly engaged waiting on him and the other children. All have been sick. For the first week after June's burn, he would not sleep without large doses of laudanum [tincture of opium] — and I lost so much sleep and was on my feet so much and as Mr. D. was unable to assist me, that I came near giving up. [. . .] I had at last to deny myself to every one. I have recovered some since he [June] has mended and am very well now. He has been a great sufferer and borne it with remarkable patience. We were delighted to have Cash walk in upon us on Thursday before Christmas. He says he read my second letter, looked at his watch, and found he had but 30 minutes to reach the depot. He threw in a few shirts and started, reached the cars just in time and got here the next evening. We enjoyed his company very much for two days when he began to complain of being sick, thought he had taken a violent cold. He and Mr. Davenport took a ride the day after he came and it was intensely cold, but Dr. Mason says he caught it before then. I told the Dr. I wanted him to see him & prescribe for him which he did. He seemed to get no better and is now in bed. Mr. D. accidentally saw the chamber [pot] I sent Amy to empty from his room and discovered indications of the gravel [kidney stones]. He made known his suspicions to Dr. Mason who upon examination pronounced it a disease of the kidneys and says if treated now and properly he will be well but if allowed to run on will terminate fatally. He also says he should quit college and go home until cured, but of course says he feels a delicacy in advising Cash to take such a step, as he is not acquainted with you or Pa and Cash is a minor. Cash tells me he has not been well for some time and said to me he did not want to go back as he was not well enough to study. [. . .] I thought I would write to you and Pa about it, as it is probable his modesty will prevent his representing his condition to you properly. [. . .] I think you should write for him immediately to go home, but of course you and Pa know best. [. . .] The negroes we have now are all anxious to remain and they are so trifling I do not want to keep them. Cash says today, Sis, you have so much to do. I replied yes but it is because the negroes are so filthy. I won't let them do anything for me unless I am looking at them all the time. I help to wash up every plate & dish else I would have nothing fit to eat out of, and I see every vegetable and piece of meat put on else they would use the same vessel for a week without washing it. They are all so lazy, standing in each other's way all the time, that they fret me to death. Mr. D. thinks I am very hard to please. I tell him I never saw a woman in my life who was any account that was easy to please [. . .] and that is exactly the opinion I want people to form of me, that I know the difference between neatness & filth, between comfort & discomfort, and have a fastidious taste. I do not wish any better trait of character. I hope you have finished your pork [hog killing] before the departure of the negroes. In my opinion all social pleasure in the South has departed, we are not to have much comfort & pleasure in our houses any more. It is so late I will close with my love to all. Tell Pa he can have Zeke whenever he wants him and he need not fear he will be neglected for I believe he has won his Pa so he is now his favorite. Dr. Mason is charmed with him. He accosts him every morning with, "Dr. Mason, did you bring me some candy apples and medicine?"

Affectionately,

Martha C. Davenport

The year 1865 ended on a familiar note, that of Martha complaining about her servants. She didn't care whether they were free or not. By December 18, twenty-seven of the thirty-six states had ratified the Thirteenth Amendment. Slavery was abolished in the United States, even in Kentucky.

TWELVE

Yours Truly in Distress

Soon after Lincoln's assassination, his successor, Andrew Johnson, met with the so-called Radical Republicans to work out a plan for the reconstruction of the conquered South. In 1865, the Radicals' principal goal was black suffrage, and they assumed that Johnson agreed with them. A one-time owner of five slaves, Johnson had supported emancipation, but he was not prepared to give the freedmen political equality.

In May 1865, the new president issued two proclamations that established the direction he hoped Reconstruction would take. The first granted amnesty and pardon — including the restoration of all property rights except the ownership of slaves — to all participants in the rebellion who were willing to take an oath of loyalty to the Union. (Certain categories of people, such as high military or political officials, had to apply individually for presidential pardons.) The second authorized the new provisional governor of North Carolina to call a convention to establish a republican form of government there. All loyal men who could have voted before secession were qualified to vote for delegates to this convention. White men, of course. No blacks. Thus the presidential Reconstruction restored the old Whig ruling class to power in the South, men such as Christopher Field who could prove they had been loyal to the Union when their states seceded even though they had followed their states into the Confederacy. In the fall of 1865, these men set about reestablishing the old order.

This upset the Radical Republicans in Congress, led by Senators Thaddeus Stevens of Pennsylvania and Charles Sumner of Massachusetts, whose aims grew out of the moral sensibility of abolitionism. The Radicals shared a utopian vision of a nation in which all citizens enjoyed civil and political rights upheld by a powerful central government. The most radical of them also advocated land reform, forty acres for every freedman (a promise General Sherman had made to freed slaves as he marched through the South), and public land to be made available to all. The Radicals' efforts led to congressional passage of legislation extending the life of the Freedmen's Bureau and the first civil rights bill ever, spelling out the rights of all citizens, regardless of race. Johnson vetoed both, whereupon Congress passed the Fourteenth Amendment to the Constitution, prohibiting states from abridging equality before the law and reducing a state's representation in Congress in proportion to the number of male citizens denied suffrage.

Although the Fourteenth Amendment was not ratified until 1868, the 1866 congressional elections became a referendum on it. When they were over, the Republicans dominated Congress with more than enough votes to override any presidential veto. The Radical Reconstruction followed.

For Brutus Clay, 1866 began with a letter from Christopher Field that reflects upon some of this turmoil. It also contains a clue to Christopher's state of mind. Before the war, he would never have forgotten the rate of interest he was charging someone.

CHRISTOPHER FIELD

Memphis, Tenn., January 4th, 1866

Honl. B. J. Clay

Dear Sir,

Before I left here I made an arrangement with an old overseer to work Christopher's place on the shares equally for the year. He had been to Texas during the War, had brought back 15 mules, 40 head cattle, oxen, goats, waggons etc. which he puts in the use of them for the year. I then gave him 1/2 the land free of rent for his services as manager. I [. . .] requested [him] to furnish the Capital necessary to run the place as the Yankees calls [sic] it, he paying me low interest (I have forgotten whether it was 6 or 8 per cent interest). I think the labor will cost 3000$ [. . .], say 5500$ in all. It may go to 6000$. This money need not all be advanced at once [. . .] say 1000$ every four months on your part, you advancing 3000$ and I [a] like amount either for myself or for Ezekiel [Field]. [. . .] I offered all three tracts for sale but found no purchaser and now have to prepare for planting it. [. . .] I have made a similar arrangement with all the places except my home place. I will try with the aid of Edmund [Field] to manage that one without any other partner than Col. Irvine. I have more to do now than any one man can attend to, but hope with health I will come as near doing it as any other man and have some confidence in succeeding. I think if we have no high water this man will make 150 bales of cotton and corn for another year. And should cotton be worth 200$ per bale [. . .], he will do well for himself and all interested. [. . .] Now the greatest difficulty is the labor and that is what I am up here for and tho the prospects look gloomy I think I will be able to get some hands before I leave. There is [sic] some 5000 of both sexes here idle, but the fools are unwilling to work or leave the city and some ever yet are fools enough to think the Govt. will give them land, mules and farming implements. [. . .] I am working through an old officer who has some influence with the [Freedmen's] Bureau and I have some more hope of success than others. I presume there is 500 persons here trying to get labor. My hotel in the city is full. I got here in the night and went to my hotel in the city. A *chair* in the office was my Bed the first night. [. . .] I have accepted the Presidency of the Board of Levee Commissioners for the River Counties. I had more business before than I could attend to, but it was a high compliment fully equal to a seat in Congress and I had some fears we might be thrown outside of the levee [. . .] but a *quietus* will be given to that now as long as I am President [. . .] and before that time runs out I will put another levee across the head of Lake Bolivar and thereby taking all 3 of our places in. [. . .]

Yours truly,

C. I. Field

A second letter followed in response to one from Brutus, who was apparently reluctant to invest more money in Mississippi. "I made the arrangement I did," Christopher explained, "because no man can work this free labor who is not interest[ed] in the crop and *living on the place* and [. . .] I thought it was nothing but due to C. & E. that they should have the privilege of having half the crop by advancing *half the money* but if you prefer not advancing the money I will do so and take the chances but I *advise you* to make the effort and the necessary advance. I do not think you can lose without we have the same flood water that we had last season."

Christopher next wrote Kit, who had asked him to check on some possessions left behind in 1862. "I examined your Box which had never been opened. It had but little in it, nothing you would have put any store upon. Nothing of the hunting apparel. I do not know what became of the Humphries' Horn [a hunting horn] which you valued."

Then he plunged into business. "I have partially succeeded by taking outside partners. [. . .] On your place I made a partnership with Childress, whom you knew. [. . .] Then to cultivate all the place I let a stranger in with 17 or 18 hands, giving the stranger one half the cotton his hands would raise. The stranger had no money. I agreed to furnish his share of the money, charging him 8 per cent interest for his share. I then charged him 10$ per acre for his portion of the Land. I did this to have all the land cultivated. I think a good crop will likely be made. Childress is a good planter but you see it takes two free negroes to make one hand. [. . .] If your Pa is willing to take your interest in the concern I will wish him to send to Thos. Anderson & Co. 2000$ at Louisville, Ky. If he thinks it best not to go any further, I will advance the money and take the interest, but I *advise him to do so*. I think he has a good show this year for fully 100 per cent upon the investment." Field Miller, Patsey's son, had been down, he added, and would return with mules to help run the old Anderson place.

Later that February a letter arrived for Brutus from June Holloway's wife, asking Brutus to help get her husband out of yet another scrape. June had been involved in a plan to cash fake army vouchers. Laura included copies of two incriminating letters written by June that were part of the evidence against him.

LAURA HOLLOWAY

Nashville, Tenn., Feb. 18, 1866

Hon. B. J. Clay

Dear Sir,

Nothing but [. . .] duty compels me to write you the sad news I now lay before you, hoping that you may do anything in your power for your unhappy nephew. June is imprisoned for forgery with five others. A man by the name of Masoner was arrested Thursday and on his person was found five letters from June, which will certainly convict him. One of the men has turned State's evidence and swears June was in partnership with him and knew he was buying forged vouchers. [. . .] The Judge Advocate says the lightest punishments will be imprisonment from three to fifteen years. June acknowledged the writing of the letters but declares he did not know there was anything criminal in the selling of these claims. He was put in prison but my Father signed a bond for $10,000 with one security and poor unfortunate June is at home. I enclose you copies of two of the letters. [. . .] We are all bowed down in sorrow. Pa has employed a Lawyer to defend him but June cannot find a witness. [. . .] For the sake of this broken down family, for the love you bear June and his Mother's family, come here and use your influence to save him from disgrace. We are doing all that can be done but I feel that the military commission will find him guilty certain and then perhaps influence may save him from oh, such a fate. I have telegraphed for Mr. Burton and Col. Holloway. The trial will come off in a week or ten days. Please come at once.

Yours in deep sorrow,

Laura Holloway

In Kentucky, Zeke married Mollie Woodford, but Kit clung to his bachelor life. After a period of convalescence at home, Cash returned to New Haven to finish his senior year at Yale. His father could hardly wait for him to return to help run the farm. Brutus viewed his sons' business concerns as extensions of his own. "I was at his [Brutus's] house on Saturday last for the purpose of purchasing a '*thoroughbred, short horn Durham bull*,'" a Lexington cattleman wrote Kit. "Desiring to obtain *a good red bull,* and he, having none of that *color, large enough*, and *old enough* for immediate service, he proposed to sell me one he had given you, and supply you with another."

Green's letters from Italy got shorter and shorter. In February, he informed his father, "The engagement with my cousin has been broken off. I need not say deference to your feelings and your kind manner in the matter had much to do with it. This, however, I do not wish to be talked about by the family & write only for your eyes."

He wrote Brutus again a few days later, asking for money and laying out his latest plans, which included visiting Rome during Easter week. "I am anxious now to get at my profession and feel some security for life. And still do not wish to miss my opportunities for seeing the Old World while here. During the summer, I should like to go through Germany and then return to N. York. But this will depend entirely upon you. [. . .] I do not feel justified in giving up this post until I have something sure & certain for the future. [. . .] Can I not hope to hear from you soon?"

In New Haven, Cash was having trouble catching up on his studies. In March he started off a letter to Ann unhappily, fearing that his weeks at home would lower his standing in his class, then swung into his characteristically optimistic rhetoric. "[T]he Republicans in college are all unanimous against [President] Johnson, although from all indications they are considerably divided in the state on the issue of reconstruction. But what Prentiss says, 'Public patronage like a huge magnet waves over the land and politicians like iron filings cluster around its poles' is at the present proven true, for the different wings of the Republican Party are at this moment held in close affinity by the cohesive power of public spoils. But we can have a firm reliance that better days are for us in the future. Political corruption can not in the present age last long. For it is not in consonance with the enlightment and wisdom of the nineteenth century that passion & prejudice having in their train fraud and corruption can long misrule a free country, a country remarkable for the wisdom of its statesmen & the moral sublimity of its government."

Green was also thinking about Reconstruction, but from a different point of view. "When Pres. Johnson came into the Presidential chair I must admit my opinion of him was not a favorable one," he reflected to his father in March, "but he has acted so well and shown such superior qualities that I think every True Friend of the Union should feel cause of congratulations."

Martha had more practical matters, such as interest rates, on her mind.

MARTHA DAVENPORT

Jefferson Co., [West] Va., March 26th [1866]

Dear Aunt Ann,

[. . .] I never saw anything like Mr. Davenport. He is run nearly to death some days, everything needs mending, everything to buy, and everybody wants cash down. I tell him I am dreadfully uneasy about his borrowing so much money. He borrowed from a Banker the other day $1000 for a year at 12 per cent, previous to that at 10. [. . .] He met the other day with a fine offer from a widow lady to take $3000 at 6 per cent for 5 years which just suits him exactly. So few people here have any visible property, the war having upturned every thing, that people are afraid to lend money to almost everyone. Mr. Gibson could not borrow here except at 15 per cent, as he says, a "bluff-off."

Mr. Davenport says it will require $7000 to start the farm in farming order and he knows with his land assessed at $67,000 he can soon pay the money. [. . .] I tell him I do not want any of Mrs. Sam Clay's nightmares of debt disturbing my slumbers [her husband was the one who said the secret of his success was always being in debt]. He has qualified as executor [for his parents' estate] and had the personal estate valued. What he retains amounts to $1,600 and nothing but old plunder except some good wagons and cows. Mrs. Gibson [her sister-in-law] took nearly everything in the house of any account in the shape of dry goods etc. etc. [. . .] The negroes tell many tales about the things that were hurried into boxes and trunks while Mr. Davenport was in Ky. They say she & Mr. Gibson began to pack up the day he left and never finished until the day he returned. I have always had a high opinion of Mrs. Gibson, but this thing stumps me. Mr. Davenport & I think it must have been his [Mr. Gibson's] influence over her. [. . .] I tell Mr. D. I never want anything in this world that does not come to me honestly and fairly, and I would never be caught playing the grab game. But I should like very much for him to have added to my supply of necessary household furniture and saved me the expense of buying such things until we were better able to do so. You know most of my bed linen, toweling etc. is too nice for everyday, so I will have to buy many such things. When I first came to [West] Va., I never saw such a quantity of sheets, pillow cases, towels, blankets & table cloths as the old lady had, and she had a great deal of material for making which was in the piece, that old-fashioned homemade flax linen which is so superior. They are all gone now, so I know the negroes do not lie. [. . .] Don't mention this to any one. They left us last week and we parted very amicably. We have never had a word on the subject and I suppose they are very well satisfied with their new home, as they were so well supplied with everything.

[. . .] I think Zeke is very foolish and extravagant. Why would not cotton clothes suit him just as well as linen [to get married in]? I think myself as good as anybody and Mr. Davenport got on without any linen shirts. I am sorry to hear of the fine bridal presents. I am afraid a comparison will be instituted and I am not abt. to give a very fine one myself, but what I do give I want it to be a useful one.

[. . .] I know of no one who should not better test the fruits of Abolitionism than Uncle Wm. Holloway. The pity is that his wife & girls have to share the evil with him. Just to think of Aunt E. washing. I know she has [had] many a cry. They had always the most competent servants in the world, did not have the trouble of most persons, but all the pleasure from good servants. The children are all well. My paper is full.

Yours affectionately,

M.C.D.

Green wrote from London that his minister now seemed about to get his long-awaited leave of absence, making Green chargé d'affaires. He was returning to Italy, which was preparing to go to war with Austria. "Please say to Aunt Ann I expect to return by the Rhine and may pass through Brussells [sic] and will make inquiries about her shawl," he wrote Brutus in April.

Once again, June Holloway managed to evade the charges against him. He wrote Ann what Green had already told Brutus, that his marriage was a sham.

JUNIUS HOLLOWAY

Nashville, May 9th, 1866

My Dear Aunt,

I arrived here on yesterday morning, and my attorneys informed me that the Grand Jury had refused to indict me upon the charges prepared by the military. I suppose the case will be thrown out of court. I wrote to Mr. Burton today to come here as it was necessary for one of my bondsmen to appear. I regret so much I was unable to attend your party [in honor of Zeke and Mollie]. I hope it was a success. I hope you did not think I was unsociable when at Pattie's [Bedinger]. While there I was very sad and unhappy and did not feel like visiting. I have been a very unhappy man for three years. My married life has been a "Hell on Earth" to me. I received three letters from Laura here. In one she states that she never did care anything for me and was unwilling to hear from me again. One of the letters I sent to Dan [Bedinger] and told him to show it to you. Laura has never treated me with respect, except [when] she wanted money. We are separated forever and I intend to apply for a divorce in the Fall. The letters I have from her will obtain one in any court. I imagine my relatives in Ky. thought it strange that I spent so much of my time in Ky. The reason was that Laura treated me so badly I could not live with her. [. . .] Aunt Ann, please take Laura's Photograph out of your Album and the Parlor. Remember me to Uncle Clay, Dan and Pattie. Do not show my letter to any one.

Very affectionately,

Your nephew,

Junius B. Holloway

Ann sent Cash all the family news.

ANN CLAY

Paris, June 10, 1866

My Dear Child,

I received your letter a few days ago and your Papa on Saturday got the check for you so I enclose it in this letter. I do not know but it would be best to let you do without awhile to give you a chance to get your money back you have loaned out. Now, do not loan one cent of this new. [. . .] Yesterday for a wonder your Papa proposed a visit to Christopher so he [. . .] & I went up & spent the day. I think it gratified C. though he told us when we got there he had no one to cook dinner for us as all had gone to church but [. . .] as I told him we had come to eat some of the numerous chickens he was bragging about having, so he gave us a very nice dinner & a chicken apiece, pudding etc. etc. [. . .] Your Papa's grass being rather short, he sent 23 of his cattle to Christopher to graze. I know he [Kit] will never get done bragging about it as our clover was a failure. Zeke is grazing our hogs on his, but with all Cit's bragging about his cattle being better fed, etc., ours are looking the best. [. . .]

I received a letter a few days ago from your sister, the first in a month. [. . .] I will have to scold her as I did you. She did not mention Zeke's wife. Now these young people are very touchy about their wives & want them noticed. Now when Zeke comes, he will want to see the letter and then will certainly remark on it. [. . .]

This morning whilst writing, Zeke and Mollie came to spend the day. She seems inclined to be quite sociable & pleasant. Your Papa, I think, likes her very well. They are going to spend the evening with Laura Hickman. I think a social party [is] given to them. [. . .] I was much surprised to hear on Saturday that Sid had offered his place for sale at 100$ per acre, 300 acres & the house. [This was his father's old place, Escondida, but Sidney didn't actually sell it until much later.] [. . .] I was under promise to Zeke Field to let him know if such a place was for sale. [. . .] I am under the impression that Zeke [Field] would take it for the price. [. . .] Zeke [Clay] says I must say to you he did not take your [fishing] poles to use them & that he will have them in fine order when you come.

Yrs.,

A. M. Clay

In July, Ann wrote from Richmond to tell Cash that his grandfather was seriously ill. "I was unexpectedly called here a day or two ago to see your Grand Papa [. . .]," she told Cash. "From the message I received I scarcely expected to find him living but when I reached here I found him a little better but quite weak & feeble, had a spell of cholera morbus and his bowels not yet checked. He has gone through so many spells that I cannot but feel hopeful but the Doctors & all the family think he cannot possibly recover and indeed think he will not last many days. [. . .] The family are all in great distress. [. . .] Your Uncle C. is still in Washington, has been telegraphed to. I left your Papa at home with a house full of painters, painting the shutters, roof & outside work, had not consented to having inside work except your room although I offered to pay the expense of the Hall. He is under the impression that Christopher and Sidney are both going to marry."

Ezekiel Field died a few days later. Born at Crow's Station, Kentucky, near Danville, in May 1782 — a few months after his father was killed at the Battle of Blue Licks — he was eighty-four when he died.

Cash remained in New Haven for the graduation ceremonies. He did well at Yale, graduating fifth in his class, and delivered a commencement oration, "The Permanence of England." "He was a fine classical scholar" wrote his friend, James K. Patterson, years later, as president emeritus of the University of Kentucky, "well versed in mathematics and more than ordinarily proficient in the natural science of the day. He was an indefatigable reader, an independent thinker, a profound student of History, Economics and Sociology, and flung himself eagerly into the controversial literature which rapidly grew up after the publication of Darwin's 'Origin of Species.'[. . .] He was thoroughly versed in the logic and political economy of John Stuart Mill, and became an enthusiastic adherent of the philosophical system of Herbert Spencer, based upon a modified Darwinian theory of Evolution."

I used Cash's interest in Darwin, Spencer, and Huxley when I modeled a character in a novel on him, a man of Cash's age and education named Nathan Lamont. Nathan was given to musing about Darwinian theory and I lifted his thoughts from my grandfather's writings. I imagined Cash/Nathan sitting in the front hall at Auvergne on a sultry summer afternoon, just as I had often sat, a book open on his lap. The same breeze made the heat bearable. Only our reading matter was different. Instead of Spencer's *Synthetic Philosophy*, I read *Anna Karenina*. I usually read novels. My father complained that I read too many. Biography and history would be better for my mind, he said.

Cash concluded his commencement address by insisting that the British Empire would last indefinitely. Even the English colonies would not seek independence except for a "great mistake in policy," as in the case of the United States. "If independent, they [the colonies] will be subject to insult, foreign domination and civil commotion," he told the commencement audience in New Haven. "As members of the empire, the British power avenges their wrongs; and they possess far more privileges than the Roman could boast when he exclaimed with pride, 'I am a Roman citizen'."

Not for the British the fate of the Roman Empire. English government and institutions would grow steadily stronger and wiser, Cash asserted. "We claim that in the future particular nations and civilizations will not be brilliant meteors that rise only to disappear and make more hideous the darkness that follows; but great planets that appear during the whole night, and at the dawn of the perfect day, [are] only dimmed by the great luminary from which they derive their radiance. We claim that these Christian nations shall disappear only when the lines that separate them one from another shall fade away in the brighter glory of the universal kingdom of perfect right and justice."

Cash's speech looks backward and forward simultaneously, with its insistence upon the superiority of the British Empire combined with a vision of a stateless world of universal justice — a curious mixture of nostalgia and idealism. I don't think Cash would have been willing to be a British subject, even if England hadn't made a "mistake" in its handling of the American colonies. However, Cash was an idealist and remained one throughout a lifetime of public service.

Cash wrote Ann that he would be in Paris on July 30 or 31. "I have not enough money to stop on the way, or to take a roundabout trip," he told her. "Staying here until commencement has cost quite dear. I have been forced to purchase a new suit and a pair of pants. And am obtaining my meals at seven dollars a week. A new pair of boots was also necessary in order to appear on the stage. "The temperature for several days has been above 100 degrees," he added. "The heat is unendurable. You cannot wear collars for half an hour. They become like wet rags."

Few letters from Green during this period have survived. By now he was acting chief of the mission in Florence. The Italians had begun their campaign to liberate Venice and the Tirol. "I have been quite busy — " he informed Ann in August, "a good deal of copying, indexing books, etc. enough to disgust the hand of the pen. And now I have to make up the dispatches for Washington which requires the latest & best information on the military status & peace negotiations, etc., besides other studies on financial [. . .] [matters], public sentiment, etc."

He continued, "I suppose you are in the dog-days of politics there. I am ashamed to say I do not know whether you have an election of any importance this year. Anyhow in Ky., I presume all support alike the policy of restoration & Union, and it would be a fight over names or rather bedfellows, [rather] than principles. The Secesh I believe are all pretty well amnestied and I would like to know what honorable right they would have gained by the success of rebellion — that they do not now enjoy? This is a fair test of the futility of their original cause and the moderation of the government — in fact some of them got more — gained their sweethearts & comfortable homes — while I — for one I know — on the other side, must pack up with an empty heart & a still emptier pocket."

Green was feeling sorry for himself. He was also dead wrong about the political situation in Kentucky. Few people supported the administration.

Martha wrote Ann, rejoicing in her bountiful garden. For the first time she was able to harvest what she had planted.

MARTHA DAVENPORT

Jefferson County, [West] Va., Sept. 8, 1866

Dear Aunt Ann,

I wrote to you immediately upon the reception of your last letter and enclosed some photographs of Zeke [Davenport]. [. . .] Henry has been sick again with bad digestion, looks very puny and pale and as sad as usual when he is sick. [. . .] Dr. Mason wants to perform an operation on June's face, cut out a chord which binds his lip to his chin, and is gradually turning his lip over and showing his teeth [the result of his burn] but we will not consent. I let him go to town to assist some little boys last week. When he came home, he told me he was playing on the street when a boy came up and looked at him and exclaimed, "What a chin" and ran off. He was much mystified, as he has never received anything but sympathy at home and was not aware that he was so much disfigured. I expect his feelings will be hurt very often when he goes in the world. As I have no idea of even sending him from home to school until he is ready for College. [. . .] Has Pa ever had the head and foot-stone put up at Nassa's grave? Did the man complete it according to promise and directions? He was to put the engraving and broken rose bud for $35. Ask Pa if he cannot find time to have it done before win-ter. [. . .] Mr. Davenport says I must tell Pa he has cut, hauled, and put up in 14 months 17 miles of fence, besides [. . .] putting up two large barns, dug two cisterns, and put up several outhouses for the different tenants, also moved and put up a corn house. He is some days nearly run to death, rides from 20 to 30 miles, sometimes for a week or more. I have scarcely a word with him except on Sunday. One of our cows has that throat disease, swollen jaws. What must we do for it? We have a young Bull which has gone crazy. It has eaten nothing for nearly a week, but still lives, plunging about all the time, sticks his head in the mud & remains for some time. [. . .] I have been busy putting up toma-toes, drying apples, corn and lima beans. I have the beans gathered green, shell them & put them in the sun. [. . .] I have used up in cans and catsup together about six bushels of tomatoes. We have some very fine apples and a good many pears, some grapes. [. . .] My love to Mrs. Keiningham and Tubman and to the family, to Cousin Mary Clay [Green's former fiancée] when you see her. I want to write to Mary soon.

Affectionately yours,

Martha C. Davenport

Christopher Field spent the summer in Kentucky. Although his relatives commented on his gloomy state of mind, they were used to his moods. Christopher was only fifty-one but his world had been shat-tered by the war. As had happened after the deaths of Pauline and David, he became deeply depressed. He might have pulled himself to-gether if he had had a supportive family around him when he returned to Mississippi, but the only person there was his brother Edmund, al-ways an ineffectual figure. The first letter Christopher wrote upon his return was to Brutus.

CHRISTOPHER FIELD

Bolivar, Miss., Oct. 8th, 1866

Dear Sir,

Enclosed I send you the note due the estate. It should have been sent earlier but I have failed to do it. I am very much discouraged at our prospects. We make a poor crop. I can't say how much but not enough to pay expenses. The negroes are very much demoralized and working very poorly. [. . .] You will have to raise money. I cannot do it. I have gone as far as I can. We have much sickness and cultivated the crop very badly and the yield is very poor. We have no cotton ready for shipment and require about 20$ on the bale before it goes, Revenue & Levee Taxes. I cannot raise it. [. . .] I have advanced a large sum and this cotton when sold will not pay me and I need the money for David's place etc. Money must be raised or crop mules and land will not pay. There is no money in the country. Land would not sell for 2$ per acre cash. It is a perfect failure with me. You must do something or everything we have will go and not stop at that. I am truly distressed and see no chances. My spirits are at desperation. [. . .] I confess I have managed very badly but it is now too late to remedy this. I fear it will get worse with us and should I get no relief all is gone. [. . .] I have no means left and have largely overreached myself and, I must be candid, if we were forced to sell everything we have here at what it would bring will not pay the debt. It is mortifying to me but it is done and the sooner I let you know it the better. I was much discouraged and gloomy when in Ky. but now I see it plainly. I wish I had never seen a Negro. They are ungrateful, no gratitude, and have robbed us. I am ruined and not myself. My life has been a failure. I see no chance to get through. In fact, I know I cannot. Now you have the stern facts which it is truly mortifying to me to relate. [. . .] You have often complained of my gloomy letters but I never had the same cause to feel as I now do. I have not supplies to last over six weeks, perhaps not that long. [. . .] You and others have or will think very hard of me but I had no idea when in Ky. but what I could go through but it was a foolish expectation tho I did not see it.

Yours truly in distress,

C. I. Field

Two days later, he wrote similar letters to his brother Zeke and his brother-in-law, W. W. Embry, as well as another to Brutus. I picture Christopher writing furiously at his desk, sheets of paper covered with his handsome script spilling onto the floor. By the time he got to W. W. Embry's letter, he could barely write. Chunks of it are illegible. Imagine signing a letter "Yours in gloom."

CHRISTOPHER FIELD

Oct. 10th, 1866

Dear Ezekiel,

You must immediately attach or garnishee my interest in Pa's estate [. . .] to secure yours[elf] & others, [for if] Mr. Burton endorses, everything here will go. You & Mr. Clay will have to do something to save your interest here. No crops can come in time. All will go to nothing very soon. I have been crazy for months. [. . .] Confer with Mr. Burton. I wish to save you all. God knows how it is to be done. I do not. I am ruined and will carry you all down. Write dear Mr. Embry. I fear I may injure him. This is all bad.

Your brother,

C. I. Field

In his letter to W. W. Embry, Christopher implies that he had kept himself afloat by borrowing against Pattie's inheritance.

CHRISTOPHER FIELD

Bolivar, Mississippi, Oct. 10th, 1866

W. W. Embry Esq.

Dear Sir,

I have overreached myself and will fail in crops and a debt down here that I cannot pay. I do not know what I was thinking about when I thought I had any means. I now find I had none. I am mortified to say to you you will have to pay the amt. in Mr. Green's bank or arrange his paper which he made. [. . .] [I]t will look like I have deceived you but it was ignorance of my situation. I did not know it and had great expectations for this year and all have failed me. [. . .] I fear Ezek [Field] will be [ruined]. [. . .] [I]f he has property it should be deeded to his wife. I am ruined and God knows how I have got in the situation. [. . .] I have never gambled or drank but have scattered my daughter's means every year without knowing it. I always thought my property would more than pay her. I now see different. [. . .]

Yours in gloom,

C. I. Field

The family decided someone must go south immediately. "I have just met with Uncle David [Irvine]," Zeke Field wrote Brutus on October 24, "told him of my interview with you. Says he is willing to go [to Mississippi] but he must have someone to go with him and, if Brother is in the state of mind that we fear he is, some one must go that can take charge of the business and remain with Brother two or three months [. . .] wants to know if Cit can go and how long he will remain. If he can't stay long, he says some man must be selected who can. [. . .] He wants to go early next week and Cit must come over here ready to go with the $500 you propose to send. If it will suit for Cit to go, I wish very much he would do so. I would willingly go if I had not first bought a home and have a large lot of troublesome mules to attend to. [. . .]"

"Uncle David left Wednesday morning," Zeke advised Brutus a few days later, "expecting to meet Mr. Stone at Louisville to accompany him. He seemed [a] good deal disappointed at Christopher not going, thinks if he can go upon his return from his hunt he had better come down as he [David Irvine] will only remain a day or two. [. . .] I received a letter from Edmund [Field] last night of date October 22cd. He says [. . .] that Brother is deranged, incompetent to attend to business, and is daily fearful he will destroy himself. Says the places are getting along badly, small crops and the negroes are refusing to gather the crop."

David Irvine returned from Mississippi in late November. "One week ago the information I rec'd. from him was not much as he said he could learn nothing from his [Christopher's] books," Zeke wrote Brutus, "only he is in a bad state of mind and health, but at the time he left he had been able to get him to take some medicine [. . .] and he seemed better. He left $500 of our money with Edmund. [. . .] He says you must come over and see him and we must have a man there by 1st January to settle up our business and rent or sell for the next year."

None of the men in the family were willing or able to leave their own businesses to go south, so Christopher's widowed sister Patsey and Dr. A. B. Lyman went, but, as soon as they left, Christopher became depressed again. Edmund was unable to rouse him. "Brother seems to be falling back again in his desperate condition," he told Zeke in December. "He seems to [be] getting worse all the time. He is in fact totally unfit for business of any kind. [. . .] I am at a great loss about what to do. It is time something should be done with the plantations and yet his mind is in such a bad condition that he will do nothing in the matter. I fear the longer he remains on the place he will grow worse all the time so you see how I am situated. While Patsey and Dr. Lyman stayed with me he seemed to improve, but since they left he has been getting more depressed in mind than ever. I have had quite a number of opportunities to rent the places but could do nothing on the matter owing to his condition. [. . .] I think if he remains in this country, he will lose his mind entirely."

Dr. Lyman sent Brutus his professional opinion. "His nervous system is very much deranged indeed rendering him entirely unfit for business at any time at present. [. . .] I think the only sure way for Col. Field to get well is to cut himself [. . .] [off] from business as far as possible for five or six months or a year. This present condition has been produced [. . .] by a diseased liver [and] overworked mind and body. [. . .] I had some difficulty in getting him to commence taking medicine but I succeeded while I was there [. . .] in getting him to commence a thorough course that he thought as well as myself had done him a great deal of good."

A few days later, Zeke Field again urged Brutus to send someone south. "Today I met with Uncle David. He says you must come over to see him, the time has come when we must do something and I think so myself."

Realizing at last that Kit had no intention of going, Zeke decided to make the trip. "It suits me badly [. . .]," he told Brutus right before Christmas, "but if no one else will go, I feel that my interest is sufficient to take me down [. . .] and if I can get any one to stay with my family and attend to the farm I will try and get off [the] first week in January."

Christopher Field's illness, despite Doctor Lyman's medical explanation of it, was rooted in his loss of identity and economic security, the very things that plagued men like him throughout the South. Christopher's life had not been a happy one, but the postwar depression that descended upon him in 1866 far exceeded his periodic "glooms." Trapped in the residue of a world that no longer existed, he could not make the new order work for him.

In his own way, Green Clay was just as lost as his uncle. Cut off from his roots and from participation in the most momentous event of his lifetime, the Civil War, he wandered aimlessly around Europe. Sometimes he wanted to come home; other times he didn't. He wanted to practice law, but he couldn't actually bring himself to begin.

In December, oblivious of what was going on in Mississippi, Green wrote his father his most recent plan. "Another year is about closing and the season of resolutions for the unsettled has come again. I find myself no nearer the actual practice of my profession. Indeed, our country has presented such an uninviting spectacle that I have had little heart to return. And, now the telegraph beings us the news that King *Caucus* [the domination of the Republican Party by its radical wing] has decided to put the Southern States under a territorial form of government. But another step and secession is justified!"

After some more political observations, he added, "My health too has been a drawback to me. And I am now just recovered from a spell of fever. My plan is, if you can spare me the expense, to make a trip to Constantinople by sea, up the Danube to Vienna, and then spend some time at the German Springs to drink the water [. . .] and stop in Paris for the great exhibition on my way home. I do not know yet exactly how much money I shall need but would like in the month of March $500."

Still at school in New York, Pattie Field began to receive troubling letters from home. Early in 1867, she wrote Ann, "It was a long time before I knew the real condition of Pa. Every letter I received from Ken. I hear of someone talking of going to see Pa or that some one has gone. I do not know that I could add to Pa's comfort or happiness but it seems so hard that I have to be separated from him. If his days are numbered, there certainly was reason that I should go. I do not know my father and I feel it deeply. O, Aunt Ann, it seems so hard, yet, I think I have stood it *well*. I have tried to take the right view of it."

But she wasn't sad long. She described her Christmas holidays with

Dr. Lyman's cousins. "I announced the fact that I was a boarding school girl and really sometimes I ate until I was ashamed. We had oysters twice a day.

"When I returned to the city, I found Clay Goodloe had passed Christmas with the Estills. He called on me once. [. . .] I rather think Mattie Estill thought she had made some impression on Cousin Sid [Clay]. I think he has turned out to be a regular flirt. His farewell call to Mattie was quite long. [. . .] She talks a good deal about Cousin Green [Clay]. She told me he was to be in the city this winter. She has his picture. Miss Mary [Clay] I reckon gave her a description of him. I sincerely hope he will remain in Europe till I go over [Pattie was planning a European trip in the spring]. It will be agreeable to meet with friends."

Kit finally had to go to Mississippi, as Zeke Field could not find anyone to look out for his farm. "I assure you everything in this country looks quite gloomy indeed," he wrote his father on January 20. "Our business here is quite complicated, so much so we will have a good deal of trouble to settle up. Mr. Childress before I came here shipped 15 bales of cotton without consent of the parties concerned. Childress has gone to New Orleans but will return very soon. So soon as he returns I will try to have a settlement & will come to some understanding. We only made 76 bales of cotton on the plantation and will make but little profit at all events. We have rented our place. [. . .] $10 per acre, that is choice land. I will start for Kentucky again as soon as I can settle the concern up. Col. Field is still in a bad state of mind."

Zeke Field wrote Ann a few days later with more Mississippi news gleaned from R. G. Burton, who had just returned from there. "He said Brother was [a] good [deal] better but still low spirited. [. . .] [I]t was the reason I was so anxious Cit or I should go down. Every man whom he was in partnership with has taken advantage of his illness and swindled him. Mr. Childress our man had shipped 15 bales of our cotton in his Name and had gone to New Orleans to see [to] it. Cit had landed then and was at a loss to know what to do but finally concluded it was best to await Childress' return & try and get a settlement paid. In fact he did not intend to leave without one. Burton said there would be nothing coming to Childress and that one might have our money back but if Childress would not settle fair all we invested was gone up. Truly am I now having a bad time. My first patronage gone and not by my bad management & [then] came to Ky., used energy & industry and supported my family, accumulated something & now it's gone. Well, some of us was born for misfortunes and it had as well be me as anyone else."

Pattie wrote Ann again in February. "As to Mr. Burton, he took it upon himself to write me a letter of *eight* pages and tell me I must write to Pa often. Aunt Ann, I have written to Pa *often* since Sept. Mr. Burton said when he mentioned my name, Pa seemed more desponding than at other times and that he said he could not write to me. When I read this I thought I was willing to give up life. It made me more sad than before. Mr. B. says it was by his begging that Pa wrote to me. I have had two letters from Pa. They were so sad when I think of them I cannot keep the tears back."

She had just learned that she would not be able to travel as planned. "What a great change a few weeks make! I had expected confidently to go to Europe & I was making all my plans that way and you have no idea what a shock it was when I found out I could not go. I dare not ask Pa if there is not any possible change. [. . .] He says he is so mortified that he cannot return the money & it grieves him to think he is the cause of my not being able to take such [a] [. . .] trip [. . .] I have not been the same 'being' since I received Pa's letters. I have not been able to study as well. I only wish I could take the world as it comes but such is not my disposition. I know I am young and I ought to be cheerful but I cannot. At times I am so sad. I sometimes think no one loves me."

Henry Davenport inquired if Brutus knew a reliable lawyer in Missouri (his father's estate included land there). "Tell Aunt Ann that Martha received her letter some two days since and will answer it soon," he added. "She and the children are all well with the exception of Henry who has some cowpox on his face and seems fitful and unwell for the last few days. We are very much excited over the proceedings of the Radical Congress. It may be fortunate for us that we have gotten into West Virginia for we may thus escape the domination of the Military Bill [legislation to impose military rule over the South] yet I do not doubt our loyal legislature will do for our humiliation whatever Congress fails to do." He concluded with the hope that Ann would visit them during the coming summer.

By March, Christopher had pulled himself together sufficiently to write a business letter to Kit. He sounded almost normal. "Things are pretty much as they were when you left. Mr. Childress has been to N.O. [New Orleans] but his merchant recommended his holding on to his cotton a while longer and he has not settled but I think there will be no difficulty with him. The River is up high again and I fear we will all suffer very much. The levee on the upper part of the Vicks place was cut or broke. [. . .] Lake Bolivar is filling very fast. [. . .] None of the new levees are completed and the construction has nearly all had to stop and some of the new levees will be lost. This I much regretted as my absence and failure to get funds delayed the work last fall. [. . .] I am not going about much but my health is about as usual. I have had a very bad cold and it has affected my hearing. My spirits are not good, despairing, but I hope I will overcome them by [in] time."

That same month, Green wrote Brutus again of leaves of absence and European travels. As usual, he asked for money. "In my letter to Mr. Seward, I say to him my health will not allow of another summer at Florence and, until the President finds it convenient to give me a transfer to a position at home, I must quit the service, that my expenses at this post are constantly in excess of my salary etc. upon which I must depend except the allowances you make me."

In April, Christopher again wrote Kit. Immersing himself in the details of leases and cotton sales, he sounded more like the man he had once been.

CHRISTOPHER FIELD

Bolivar P.O., April 6th, 1867

C. F. Clay Esq.

Dear Sir,

Your favor of *March 1867* came to hand our last mail which has been very irregular for a month. In consequence of the terrible high water for that length of time, we have done nothing. Our whole country is overflown. [. . .] The water is under your house. You have not 30 acres out. Mr. Mann is much discouraged & has offered to give up, land, hands & all. This, of course, I have refused. As you know I have worn myself out attending to the business of others. He went to N. Orleans two weeks after you left. He returned without selling his cotton and had no money to pay his rent. Some two weeks ago, I told him I was compelled to have money to pay your taxes. He a few days ago gave me a draft on N.O. for $515. [. . .] [T]his is all I think we will get. [. . .]

The Content place is badly overflown. Some 75 or 100 acres only out of water. They are anxious to give up the place. I am putting them off in the same way as I do Mr. Mann, but I have but little hope of my rent from them. [. . .] I fear Ezekiel [Field] made the larger purchase than his means will admit of [the farm Zeke Field had purchased in Madison County]. I think under all the circumstances you should be very lenient about your debt. [. . .] Edmund is in usual health and as usual in his notions etc. etc. [. . .] Ask your Aunt Ann if she knows of any suitable company for Pattie to go with to Europe. I want her to go. She has the means and had as well spend it in that way as any. [. . .]

Yours etc. etc.,

C. I. Field

[P.S.] Your cattle like our own and every body else's has done badly. E. [Edmund] sent them down to Cat Fish [sic] Point which is out of water. Many cattle have been drowned in the overflow but there is no money in the county for the people who have lost theirs to buy more. We had 2 mules caught out in the overflow back of your field. One will die, I fear, skin all off from standing a week in the water. E. to keep me from complaining told me all our mules were up, but a man, Mr. Myers, found them in the overflow and came by and told me. [. . .]

As he got better, Christopher became more and more determined that Pattie should have her trip to Europe. A possible companion was the daughter of his Louisville friend and agent Thomas Kennedy. "My daughter Sidney received a letter this week from Pattie in which she says Dr. Abbott [sic] is very secret about their trip to Europe and she does not know what they have decided on about it," Kennedy wrote Christopher in April. "I would suggest that you write to Dr. A. proposing that he will take charge of Pattie as far as London and then let her be taken charge of by Mrs. Ten Broeck. [. . .] She will be delighted to have Pattie with her."

Martha suggested Ann accompany Pattie.

MARTHA DAVENPORT

Jefferson Co., [West] Va., May 17th, 1867

Dear Aunt Ann,

I received your letter containing the receipt at a recent day and will sign it & return it. The additional $50 due me you can bring with you when you come. Do not think of such a thing as not coming to see me, it would be the greatest disappointment that ever happened to us. Mr. Davenport & myself, the children, & also the negroes have got their heart set upon you coming. Indeed I have not the least idea of going to Ky. and have no other idea than you coming here. So let the negroes and the garden go and take your pleasure & leisure. There is one condition however upon which I will release you from your obligation, that is that you go to Europe with Pattie. You are the very person of all others, and the one Uncle Christopher would prefer to go. I can't believe he would pay me such a compliment as June [Davenport] declares, nevertheless I would be delighted to go, for I have never relinquished the ardent desire I had in my girlhood of taking the trip, but I do not think I could [. . .] leave my children so young, for fear one of them might die — and then my whole life would be filled with remorse. Mr. Davenport says I can go and he will keep the children but I tell him I can't go without him as an escort. No, you must go. Uncle Christopher will pay your expenses and Pa and you together can pay Cash's to go as an escort — and if Pa is not willing for him to go, take Sidney Clay, he has nothing better to do with his money. But I do want Cash to go. I never had the privilege myself, but I feel anxious that my brothers should enjoy whatever privileges of information, pleasure, and benefit that come in their pathway. [. . .] Would not Amelia Burton be willing to go? Why won't Belle Lyman go? I expect Aunt Lucy [Field] would take her with great pleasure. [. . .] There are several other persons I might mention. Furthermore, it is not all important that Pattie should go right away. [. . .] There is great probability of war in Europe, and I should think it would be very disagreeable being there in that event. A stranger would be subject to constant annoyances, & espionage, and prohibitions frequently which would perhaps prevent one visiting the choicest spots of the old world. I will start to Baltimore in the morning. I had another disappoint[ment]. [. . .] I had June ready to take with me & Mrs. Gibson had Bettie, but Dr. Smith is in Europe and will not be back before September, at which time Mr. Davenport and myself hope to take him.

Dr. Smith tells us the entire burn will have to [be] cut out & will disfigure him very little. [. . .]

My love to Pa and the boys. Tell Zeke and Mary [his wife Mollie] I am looking for them certainly this summer. I shall write to Mary soon. We have still cold windy rainy weather. My tulips are in bloom and do look most beautiful. [. . .]

Affectionately yours,

M. C. Davenport

Martha's next letter to Ann was almost completely taken up with the details of a shopping trip to Baltimore: the types and prices of black silk sacques suitable for those in mourning, a description of a handsome new carriage, and the advantages of Brussels carpets. She concluded, "The weather still cool. We have had only a few hot days. It is said to be caused by a large quantity of icebergs which have become detached and are floating southward."

In late June, Christopher wrote to Brutus. Though still depressed, he seemed to be on the way to recovery.

CHRISTOPHER FIELD

Bolivar P.O., Miss. June 22cd, 1867

Honl. B. J. Clay

Dear Sir,

We have had a siege this spring, nearly entirely under water for four months. The River was at flood height for ten weeks in March, April & May, fell 7 feet. We all planted over three times before we could get a stand from the cut worms, had scraped the cotton out to a stand, and the water has again come [. . .] and drowned us out. We are much disheartened and discouraged and starvation to some will come. They have no crop, no money, no credit, heavily in debt, and their merchants have refused to advance them any further supplies in consequence of the second overflow. On your and Ezekiel's place Mr. Warren [. . .] has about 65 acres of land out of water. We have here at home almost 100, at David's place they have about the same out, at Mr. Estill's place they are entirely under water. I will have to reduce Mr. Warren's rent. I could not have the face to make a man pay 10$ per acre for Rent for 250 acres land and only 65 of it with any crop and he is a poor and honest man and a [. . .] Lady is planting with him who was ruined by the war. To effect a settlement with Mr. Childress on your place & E. for last year I bought him out. [. . .] I agreed to take the cotton at 28 percent less cost of sale. [. . .] You & E. must make your calculation to work your place yourselves another year as it cannot be rented again with the Levees [. . .] in their present condition. No place will be rented next year that has been overflown this year without the opening in the Levee is closed. [. . .] Edmund could work the place and would now have the means but I doubt the propriety of his doing so. He will never make any money, will only do as he has always been doing, eating up [. . .] the means which has been given him and I do not think he cares or thinks about anything ahead. He is of service to me tho he often fails to do as I wish and direct him to do [. . .] [H]e leaps without looking or thinking where he is to land, but if it will not suit you to work the place, I have no objection to your trying him. [. . .] Mr. Embry has written me he fears E. [Zeke Field] will not be able to pay for the Burnam [farm][. . .] I write him to do nothing about it (I mean Mr. E.) until I come up and I would see what could be done. I do not wish Ezekiel to know this. He is so sensitive. [. . .]

Politically we are very quiet. As sure as the water falls, the Registration [to vote] will commence for both white and black. As yet the negroes care nothing about it and take no interest. If we have no Radical Demagogue speakers among us, there will be no excitement. The negroes will vote as their employers dictate. [. . .] Genl. Ord our military commander offered me the chairmanship of the Registering Board but I refused to act. I enclose you a circular [about Levee Board bonds]. This levee is very important to [yours] & E.['s] interest as well as my own. If it is made the line of Levee is permanently established taking our places inside of the levee. The Engineer in chief is in favor of running the levee around Lake Bolivar [thus putting the Clay and Field property outside the levee]. [. . .] After reconstruction [. . .] the Government will take charge of the Levees and will make them permanent. The U.S. Engineer has been at my house and he told me if the Government took charge of the levees he would run around the Lake. [. . .] I think it behooves all property holders situated as your land [is] as well as my own & others to leave nothing unturned to get this line put up now. I am a subscriber for $10,000. I think the Bonds are a good investment and will be paid if *negroes quiet and have no disturbance with our military rule*. I called on him and was pleased with him. I think he is conservative and is strongly in favor of putting the levee up but said he did not know how he could aid us in any way but would do all he could. I will be in Ky. after the 11th July. [. . .]

Yours truly,

C. I. Field

Brutus's ailing mother had been urging him to pay her a visit. In her own hand, Sally Dudley wrote at the bottom of Eliza Smith's June 23 letter, "I am very old and you are young [. . .] in comparison with me." She was ninety-one.

This was her last letter to Brutus. Less than two weeks later, one of his nephews, Speed Smith, wrote, "Grand Ma has had a very severe spell of vomiting and diarrhea for the last two days and is very weak and low spirited. Mother is anxious you should come over to see her. She says herself she is sicker than she had been for years. Be sure and come."

Shortly after Speed's letter, his uncle Will Rodes sent word that Sally Dudley was dying. Evidently Brutus did not receive Will Rodes's letter, and neither saw his mother before her death nor attended her funeral on July 10. This caused considerable comment in the family. Everyone felt it necessary to explain that he or she was not at fault. This letter from Eliza Smith tells what happened.

ELIZA SMITH

July 14th, 1867 [mailed from Speedwell, Kentucky]

My dear brother,

On Monday night the 1st our dear Mother was taken with cholera morbus, cramped in her feet several times *Tuesday*. Wednesday I sent to Paulina [Rodes] and made Speed write to you. She was very sick. We thought you would be sure to get the letter and would be here as soon as you received it. You did not come and we wrote again Saturday. I sent to Mr. Rodes to send for you. Mr. Burton was going to Lexington and promised him he would telegraph you. We were looking for you every hour and I have not heard a word from you yet, have come to the conclusion you were not at home. I am very sorry now I did not send a boy for you, but thought at the time I was doing right. She did not suffer much after Wednesday, but we could not check her bowels, she had so much strength, Curran [Smith, a doctor] thought she would recover but Saturday morning at 2 o'clock she died. She was perfectly herself all the time, bore her sufferings with a great deal of patience and resignation, was ready and willing to go, she *said,* to her peaceful home. She was looking better than she had for a long time right up to the night she was taken. The weather was exceedingly warm and we have a great deal of Fruit, and vegetables, and she would eat everything and as much as she wanted, said she had allways [sic] done it, and it would not hurt her. We waited untill [sic] Monday for you. Her funeral was preached in the Baptist Church by Mr. E. Burnam, and she was buried in the Cemetery in the lot opposite mine and Mr. Rodes', selected by Cassius before he went away. She selected the clothes she wanted to be put on her, and the Hymn she wanted to be sung at her funeral. She was the youngest and most pleasant looking corpse I ever looked at. I regret so much you and Cassius did not see her. [. . .] I shall miss her more than any one. I have scarcely been from her a day since she has been living with me. [. . .] I hope you and Sister Ann will come over and see me.

Affectionately your sister,

E. L. Smith

A week later, Brutus's niece Sallie Watson sent him some things that had belonged to his mother. The picture she mentions has unfortunately vanished. Sallie had always been one of Brutus's favorite nieces and had written him cheeky notes ever since the summer he was courting Ann. On July 23 she tackled him on the subject of religion. "Dear uncle, this occasion is so suitable, forgive me, that I venture to say a word of admonition to you. You, who in *all other things* are so much *wiser* than I. The Lord has given you a large share of prosperity and influence in this life. He has blessed you in your family, in your children, in your home, with its pleasant surroundings in return for all these mercies, What have you done for Him? Read the parable of the unprofitable servant who hid his lord's torrent in the earth and tremble. Oh let me *entreat* you to seek His forgiveness, and mercy before it is too late. Delay not till those evil days of sorrow and affliction which finally come to us all arrive."

It took a good deal of nerve on Sallie's part to approach Brutus this way. While the women in the family were mostly believers, the men were, in the lingo of the time, "not united to the church." Brutus himself was a freethinker and a skeptic. The only church he ever enjoyed attending was the Universalist church near his farm.

I have always thought of Brutus as a deist, but that is a conceit on my part, reflecting my own views more than his. It is easy to be a deist in a place where every twisted walnut tree on the horizon seems a divine manifestation, particularly in the winter when the limbs are bare and the sky behind them pale, almost silver. Returning from school at Christmas time, I would take long walks across fields of dried grass and sort out thorny theological questions. The gaunt trees kept me company as I strode restlessly around the farm, tortured silhouettes on a bleak skyline, personal stations of the cross.

Sally Dudley's death was quickly followed by another. Again Will Rodes was the bearer of bad news. He told Brutus and Ann that Christopher Field was dangerously ill. "E. H. Field rec'd. a dispatch this morning from McGee, Bolivar, Miss. dated 15th inst. saying Col. Field was very ill and his physicians said he could not live. Ezekiel sent this morning to Estill for Edmund [who had come up to Kentucky for the summer] to come and this morning go to Lex. tonight and to the cars in the morning. Ed[mund Field] has not arrived yet from Estill."

Actually, Christopher had died the day before, July 18. He was not yet fifty-three. According to the death notice in the Richmond paper, the cause of death was "a long ride under a July sun solely to serve the interest of others." It was as if he had written his own obituary.

"How sad it is to think that your noble brother is dead," Dr. Lyman wrote Ann on the twenty-seventh, "Only think it is only one short year since your noble Father's spirit took its flight from earth and here it is in one short year and 3 days from that sad Sabbath evening when you all was [sic] called upon to bid your father a last earthly adieu. We are in mourning for one that you all said must take your Pa's place in the family." He added, "Belle wishes to see you all very much. She is not well and I fear that affliction will prostrate her in bed."

No letters describe Christopher's death, though the Field sisters must have rehashed it among themselves. Christopher's obituary makes his end sound eerily similar to his brother David's. Like David, his mind was reported to be "clear and calm." His last thoughts were said to be of Pattie, who arrived in Bolivar County with Uncle Edmund a few days later. He asked that Brutus, as her guardian, arrange for her to travel abroad. Like David, Christopher was buried at the edge of a field on his plantation until his remains could be exhumed and taken to Richmond, where he is interred beneath an enormous marble tree stump, an odd yet poignant tribute to a life spent taming the wilderness.

He left a huge estate in a jumble, naming Brutus as his executor. Brutus was reluctant to take on the job but finally agreed. Settling the family's affairs in Mississippi kept him busy for years, a task for which he was to enlist the help of several young relatives: June Holloway, Field Miller, and even the prodigal son returned home, Green Clay.

Field was the last member of the family to actually live in Mississippi, dying there in 1891. His executor was to have been Green Clay, who had been living nearby on Kit's old plantation, which he called Isole, but noting that Green had "given up on the country" and moved his family to Missouri, Field named a Mississippi neighbor as executor.

Reading Field's will in the dark high-ceiling clerk's office in the Rosedale, Mississippi, courthouse more than a hundred years later, my brother and I were surprised to see that he mentioned two sisters, Mary Belle Miller and Lucie M. Wooten. Until that moment, neither of us had been able to figure out how Cousin Lucie, who had conceived the Field family picnic, fitted into the family. Now we knew. She was the last of Patsey's many babies.

Christopher left the usual detritus of a human life, odds and ends. In his case, these included plows, harrows, grubbing hoes, scythes, and an assortment of mules. And a few more personal things: one bay saddle horse and one pair of saddlebags, a dozen chairs, a dining room table, a bookcase, a wardrobe, a pair of fire dogs along with a shovel and tongs. And some essentials that underline the loneliness of his life in Mississippi: four china plates; two knives, forks, and spoons; three cups and saucers; and a tablecloth.

Christopher's death marks the end of a way of life. The Civil War was over; slavery was abolished. The young Fields and Clays were scattered around the country. Theirs was a new and different world.

AFTERWORD

A Family Odyssey

The last time I am certain that the Field sisters were all together was in 1872, for the wedding of Christopher's daughter Pattie to one of Cassius M. Clay's sons. After her father's death, Pattie became what was called in Kentucky a *belle*. She was rich and self-assured, she traveled a lot (though she never got to Europe), and she frequently became engaged. She may or may not have been in love with Brutus J. Clay Jr., whom she married that February day in Richmond, since the wedding came only a few months after her rejection by her cousin Green. Pattie had often visited Green in Bolivar County, where he was running the old Clay and Field plantation — Isole — and it was clear that she found him attractive.

"His acts were as dishonorable as a man's possibly could be," Pattie wrote her Uncle Brutus in September 1871. "I give you mere outlines & I refer you to Aunt Ann for *particulars* as I told her all."

Green, of course, saw things differently. He was about to marry Janie Rhodes. "I think Pattie's aunts are wrong to encourage her in her tales of me," he complained to his father. "The idea of a girl not having delicacy enough to conceal her love for a man who, she knows, loves another better!"

Most of the relatives took Pattie's side. "I do think his affair with Pattie was as uncalled for and as unfortunate as anything that could have occurred in the family," Martha Davenport wrote Ann. Her husband amused himself by speculating that Green might install his new

494

wife on Pattie's plantation, which he managed. Henry said "he [Green] better look out, she will begin a duet of ejectment," Martha wrote.

It was a relief to everyone when young Brutus Clay asked Uncle Brutus, Pattie's guardian, for her hand. The aunts assembled to watch Pattie get married in satin and lace in the house in which they, too, had said their marriage vows.

The wedding, presided over by the Lymans, was "one of the grandest social events ever consummated in Kentucky," according to a gushing account in a Louisville newspaper. Belle Lyman gave the bride away, an odd departure from custom. The writer described Belle, who was dressed in black silk trimmed with Brussels lace and adorned with diamonds, as "a lady ever remarkable [. . .] for her extraordinary conversational powers" — the old "gift of gab" that Belle had noted in an early letter to Ann.

Her sisters surrounded and supported Belle: Elizabeth Holloway, "no one would have supposed that she had been a wife for forty years"; Patsey Miller, "a 'Florence Nightingale' in Richmond"; Ann Clay "looking most queenly"; and Mary Embry, white streaks showing in her black hair, "one would think it powdered." Martha Davenport was there, too, in lavender moiré, "still the glass of fashion and the mold of form."

Uncle Cash and Mary Jane, "most regal in appearance," were present. A year later they would separate, and, after five years of living apart, he would sue her for divorce. Uncle Cash lived on into the next century, a bitter, irascible old man. Try as he might, he could not find another political niche for himself. In 1872, campaigning for the election of Horace Greeley as president, he denounced the Radical Reconstruction in the South. Four years later, after failing to get the Democratic nomination for vice president, he retired to White Hall to write his memoirs. The last twenty-five years of his life were unhappy ones, for he was lonely in his big empty house. However, the night after Pattie's wedding, White Hall was far from empty. Uncle Cash and Mary Jane gave what Mary Embry would have called "an elegant dinner" for the newly married couple in its immense marble parlors.

The newspaper account doesn't mention any men except Dr. Lyman, Cassius Clay, and the bridegroom, but no doubt they were all there, including Brutus and his sons Kit, Zeke, and Cash, along with their wives. Kit had married his Molly shortly after Christopher Field died. Cash's wife, Sue, once Pattie's classmate at the hated Caldwell

Institute, even made the newspaper for "her sweet face" and "the naiveté of her manner." Cash was by then a rising political star, a member of the state legislature; his wife was the daughter of a neighbor who had made a fortune selling mules to the Union army during the war.

Green wasn't in attendance, of course, being persona non grata. He and Janie were living at Isole. But the other friends and relations attended, the Rodeses and the Smiths, the Bedingers and the Bedfords, the Goodloes and the Warfields. And Mrs. Keiningham, naturally.

In marrying Brutus, Pattie had selected a young man remarkably like Green. Sustained by his wife's fortune, Brutus farmed and practiced law in Madison County. Pattie built him an asymmetrical Queen Anne house in the west end of Richmond with fifteen rooms and an elevator. After she died in 1891, Brutus was often abroad. In 1905 President Theodore Roosevelt named him ambassador to Switzerland. He had become more like Green than Pattie could have dreamed he would be. He eventually remarried and returned to Kentucky, where he built himself another, simpler house.

The Field sisters went their separate ways after Pattie's wedding. The Holloways had already returned to Kentucky, their Missouri adventure having lasted only a couple of years. William Holloway went into business in Lexington, where he went bankrupt, ruining not only himself but also his daughter Pattie Bedinger's husband, Dan. Brutus, of course, came to the rescue. The Embrys, on the other hand, moved farther and farther west, from Ohio to Illinois and eventually to Missouri. Only Patsey Miller and the Lymans remained in Richmond. Patsey, long a widow, lived with her unmarried daughter, Mary Belle. Seven years after Pattie's wedding, Dr. Lyman came home from visiting a patient one evening, complained of feeling unwell, and died quite suddenly, making Belle a widow, too.

Despite her penchant for illnesses, Elizabeth outlived her sisters, as well as most of her children, dying in 1903 at the venerable age of ninety-two. Belle had died in 1887, Patsey a year later, and Mary ten years after that. In death, as in life, the sisters are only a short walk from one another in Richmond's ornate Victorian cemetery. Buried nearby are their parents, Christopher, David, Charlotte, Pauline, "the little Pauline," and many other members of the family.

Brutus Clay lived out his life in a pastoral idyll in Bourbon County, surrounded by luxuriant pastures and heavily laden orchards. He was a farmer to the end. The last entry in his daybook, dated September 27, 1878, reads, "Got of Matt Clay one Boar Shoat, price $10. In Home lots, 2 sows and 23 pigs."

Most of Brutus's children lived in Bourbon County, too: Cash and Sue at Auvergne with him, Kit and Molly a couple of miles away on Green Creek, and Zeke and his family on the other side of town at Runnymede. There were plenty of grandchildren to dote on, though Zeke Davenport seems to have remained his favorite. Visiting Martha after a tour of the Virginia hot springs in search of a cure for persistent rheumatism, Brutus offered Zeke a pony if he'd come back to Kentucky to live with him. Zeke said he'd rather stay at home.

In the fall of 1878, Brutus contracted typhoid fever, the first of several victims of Auvergne's polluted cisterns. He died on October 11 and was buried the next day in the corner of the garden where he had earlier interred both his first wife and Martha's Little Nassa. It was a secular ceremony, conducted by two members of the local Odd Fellows' lodge.

Brutus's real memorial service was the sale of his shorthorn herd the following spring. A hundred head of Durham cattle went on the auction block that June, advertised as being "from nearly all the distinguished families, including Blooms, Roan Duchesses, Goodnesses, Lady Carolines, Lady Littletons, Lady Elizabeths, and the purest and best Seventeens in America."

Ann outlived Brutus by three years, the first of the Field sisters to die since Amelia, thirty-eight years before. She was not yet sixty. Like Amelia and Brutus, she is buried in the garden. She had been happy living with her son and her daughter-in-law. Ann was fortunate in her daughters-in-law, "all clever girls and sociable," as Mrs. Keiningham once congratulated her. But Sue Clay died in childbirth in 1880 so Ann became mother as well as grandmother to Cash's four babies, just as she had once been mother as well as aunt to four other little Clays.

Martha and Henry Davenport settled in at Altona, his parents' house, which Martha ruthlessly modernized. They had two more children — Amelia who grew up to become the Cousin Amelia who intimidated my brother and me as children, and a second Braxton. In the curious way the Clay and Field families had of marrying back into themselves, Amelia became the wife of Uncle Zeke's business partner, Catesby Woodford, in 1889. They were married in front of the parlor mirror at Altona. I can imagine Martha hustling to and fro as she stage-managed the event. The pièce de résistance was a groom's cake topped by a racecourse (with a race in progress) in honor of Clay and Woodford, breeders of thoroughbred horses. Martha outlived the amiable Henry and died in 1908.

Kit had six children, but only three survived him. His teenage daughters Nannie and Sadie died in June 1893, within two days of each other, and his namesake was killed accidentally when he was twenty-nine. Kit himself died in October 1897 from a kidney infection. His obituary in the Paris newspaper described him as "a jolly kindly friend." His hunting companions would forever miss "the sound of his clear sweet voice as he cheered his hounds in the chase, the soft yet clarion-loud wind of his hunters horn as he called off the pack, and his entertaining companionship in camp and field."

Sometime early in the twentieth century, three men with gray beards, one of them wearing an eye patch, and a toothless old lady posed for a snapshot at the Paris railroad station. My father wrote on the back of this photograph, "My father, Uncle Green, Aunt Martha, Uncle Zeke, the last picture of the four together. [. . .]" Cash had the picture enlarged and framed. I imagine that he hung it in his office at the farm. It wasn't the sort of thing my grandmother would have wanted around; she liked contrived portraits — pensive children holding badminton rackets, and that sort of thing. But Cash knew better. If you could photograph brotherly love, this is what it would look like.

By the time the snapshot was taken, Green was living in Audrain County, Missouri, on land Brutus bought there just before the Civil War. Green inherited it at Brutus's death, along with the plantation in Mississippi, which he managed for his father after his return from Italy in 1867. Green thrived in Mississippi. Like Uncle Christopher, he served as president of the board of levee commissioners. He was elected to the legislature in 1875 and played a prominent role in the Redemption, a movement by whites to dismantle the freedmen's government in Mississippi, reduce the political power of blacks, and create a stable supply of cheap plantation labor. Redemption set the pattern by which Delta blacks were deprived of their civil rights for nearly ninety years. I don't know why Green left Mississippi. Perhaps the extravagantly desperate nature of the place finally got to him. He kept Isole for a while after he moved to Missouri, then sold it to a man named Box, who in turn sold it to the giant Delta and Pine Land Company, which eventually acquired Content and the family's other holdings in Bolivar County as well. In Missouri, Green again turned to politics, serving twice in the legislature, the second time to finish out the unexpired term of his son Rhodes, who was killed in a gunfight arising out of a debt of Green's. Another son died of a chronic illness shortly after his wedding. Green himself died in 1912.

Zeke was a stylish man in spite of his blind eye, neither as rough-hewn as Kit nor as self-important as Green. His farm, Runnymede, flourished first with shorthorn cattle, later with thoroughbred horses. He served as president of the Kentucky Racing Association. He also helped to found a bank and was its president for a while. And the descendants of his six children today seem to populate one-half of Bourbon County, from Cane Ridge to Ruddels Mills. Outside of my grandfather Cash's immediate heirs, it is Zeke's descendants I know best. I've even rummaged in Runnymede's attic for artifacts. Zeke outlived his sister and brothers, dying in 1920 at the age of eighty.

Cash had the most illustrious career of Brutus's sons, but, like his Uncle Cash, he never got what he wanted. From 1871 until 1890, he served in the state legislature, where he devoted himself to putting the brakes on the railroad interests, particularly the Louisville and Nashville, which then controlled commerce throughout the state. In 1890, he was president of the convention that wrote a new constitution for Kentucky. His fellow delegates awarded him a gold-handled cane, which is still kept in Auvergne's front hall umbrella stand. Twice Cash sought the Democratic nomination for governor and twice he was defeated by the L&N Railroad. After he lost in 1895, he retired from politics.

Cash's private life was bittersweet, too. After Sue died, he married Belle Lyman's daughter, Pattie. She died a year later and their child did not survive her for long. Then, in 1888, he married my grandmother, Mary Blythe Harris, the daughter of a Madison County politician. This couldn't have been an easy marriage for Cash. My grandmother was a tough woman, a bit like Martha Davenport actually. Moving to Bourbon County, she was appalled by antiquated, fusty old Auvergne. But she didn't let that faze her. She cut doors, built bathrooms, added an enormous stained glass window, laid down parquet floors, and repapered walls. All this left Cash and his children stunned and distressed. One gets the feeling that they were happy with their wood-paneled outhouse at the end of an avenue of cedars and daffodils.

The situation couldn't have been easy for my grandmother either.

I expect she thought she was marrying the next governor of Kentucky, and instead she got a beaten old man. And lame to boot, hence her disparaging remark in a letter to her mother about his ridiculous gait.

When my grandmother married him, Cash had four children: Junius, Henry, Anne, and Sue. The boys died around the turn of the century, Henry from typhoid (another victim of Auvergne's cisterns) and Junius from a gunshot wound inflicted by his wife. The second death particularly tormented Cash, who believed that it was not an accident. In the snapshots my father took as he was growing up, my grandfather never smiles.

His chief consolation was my grandmother's little boys, my father, Cassius Marcellus III, and my uncle John Harris. Cash took them everywhere with him, particularly my father, who was a carbon copy of him except for the limp, a serious little boy who usually had his nose buried in a book. Uncle John, more of a Tom Sawyer, was his mother's favorite.

Cash died in 1913. He had had a minor operation and seemed to be recovering when he developed tetanus. No one knows if it was the result of the operation, but he died horribly, clinging to a rope suspended from a hook in the bedroom ceiling whenever a spasm of lockjaw seized him. My father, a student at the Taft School in Connecticut, didn't make it home before he died.

My grandmother lived on for more than thirty years. All the energy she had intended to expend promoting her husband's political career she used to give elaborate parties, many of them for children. Once, when it rained on the day she planned to celebrate my cousin Norton's birthday with pony rides, she had the pony brought into the parlors so the children wouldn't be disappointed. The ubiquitous George Brent followed behind the pony with a shovel and a pail.

When my mother became engaged to my father in 1935, she went to Kentucky to meet her future mother-in-law. After one particularly interminable heavy meal, my grandmother assembled everyone in the front hall to watch the black children who lived on the farm do a cakewalk in honor of the bride-to-be. My mother was horrified.

I wish I knew what happened to all the black men and women who once lived at Auvergne. I can trace only a few. George Brent was the son of Mahala, the family cook when my father was a boy. We have a picture my father took of Mahala paring vegetables on the kitchen steps about 1905. From Brutus's records, I know that Mahala, the daughter of Narcissa, was born a slave. It was her brother, David Hill, who had written their mother triumphantly, "I joined the Union Army to live until I die."

Hamp Ayres, who picked collard greens in our garden in his old age, was one of a large family of Ayreses who once lived on the place. David, Israel, and Andrew all enlisted in the Union army, but their brother, Hampton, was too young to be a soldier. Using her wooden Kodak Two camera, my grandmother photographed Hamp with his dog Shep in the 1890s. At the same time, she took a picture of his son, Young Hamp, with an armful of corn.

The Ayres and Brent ancestors are buried in a graveyard in a corner of Brutus's orchard beneath slabs of unfinished limestone. There are no names.

When Ann Clay died, she left behind her Friendship quilt bearing the names of assorted friends and relations: the Green Clay who invited her to "grease a plate with him" before leaving for Texas; Willie Holloway, killed hunting deer in Bolivar County, and his father, the restless colonel; the lively Louisa Keiningham and her sister, Emily Tubman; Martha Clay as well as Martha Davenport; the beautiful Belle Rodes McDowell; Amelia Clay; Belle Field; Mary Embry; Amelia Burton; Pattie Holloway; Pattie Field; Zeke and Mollie Clay; and many more. Ann's quilted garden, pieced together some time after the Civil War, is a record in magenta and crimson petals of a family odyssey.

Sitting beside the quilt, I can hear the voices of these men and women. Sometimes they talk politics. Sometimes they speak of everyday events. They gossip about their neighbors. They tease and scold and laugh. Voices from the century before.

Selected Bibliography

Clay, Brutus J. The Brutus J. Clay Family Papers. Special Collections and Archives. Margaret I. King Library. University of Kentucky, Lexington.

Clay, Cassius M., *The Life of Cassius Marcellus Clay: Memoirs, Writings, and Speeches*, Vol. 1. Cincinnati: Brennan & Co., 1886.

Clay, Cassius M., Jr. *The Speeches, Addresses and Writings of Cassius M. Clay, Jr. (1846–1913)*. New York: Winthrop Press, 1914.

Clay, Cassius M., ed. *Letters from the Correspondence of Brutus J. Clay, 1808–1878*, Louisville: Filson Club, 1958.

Clay, R. Berle. Unpublished description of Brutus J. Clay's farm and its operation, 1830–1878.

Clay, R. Berle. "Landscape Change in the Bluegrass: 1830–1870." Paper presented at the 13th Annual Symposium on Ohio Valley Urban and Historic Archaeology, Greenville, Ohio, March 11, 1995.

Cobb, James C. *The Most Southern Place on Earth: The Mississippi Delta and the Roots of Regional Identity*. New York: Oxford University Press, 1992.

Coleman, J. Winston, Jr. *Slavery Times in Kentucky*. Chapel Hill: Univ. of North Carolina Press, 1940.

Collins, Lewis, and Richard H. Collins. *Collins' Historical Sketches of Kentucky*, revised and enlarged, 1874. Covington: Collins & Co., 1882.

Coulter, E. Merton. *The Civil War and Readjustment in Kentucky*. 1926. Reprint, Gloucester: Peter Smith, 1966.

Dorris, Jonathan Truman. *A Glimpse of Historic Madison County and Richmond, Kentucky*. Richmond: Richmond Chamber of Commerce and the Madison County Historical Society, 1934.

Everman, H. E. *The History of Bourbon County 1785–1865*, Paris, Ky.: Bourbon Press, 1977.

Foner, Eric. *Reconstruction: America's Unfinished Revolution 1863–1877*. New York: Harper & Row, 1988.

Fox, Minerva C. *The Blue Grass Cook Book*, intro. by John Fox Jr. New York: Scribner's Sons, 1930.

Fox-Genovese, Elizabeth. *Within the Plantation Household: Black and White Women of the Old South*. Chapel Hill: Univ. of North Carolina Press, 1988.

Hood, James Larry. "The Union and Slavery: Congressman Brutus J. Clay of the Bluegrass." *Register of the Kentucky Historical Society* 75 (July 1977): 214–21.

Kubiak, Lavinia H. *Madison County Rediscovered: Selected Historic Architecture*. Madison County Historical Society and the Kentucky Heritage Council, Richmond, 1988.

Langsam, Walter E., and William Gus Johnson. *Historic Architecture of Bourbon County, Kentucky*. Paris, Ky.: Historic Paris-Bourbon County, Inc., 1985.

Lucas, Marion B. *A History of Blacks in Kentucky*. Vol. I, *From Slavery to Segregation, 1760–1891*. Louisville: The Kentucky Historical Society, 1992.

McAboy, Mary R. T. *Roseheath Poems*. Cincinnati: Robert Clarke & Co., 1884.

Murray-Wooley, Carolyn, and Karl Raitz. *Rock Fences of the Bluegrass*. Lexington: Univ. Press of Kentucky, 1992.

Perrin, William Henry. *History of Bourbon, Scott, Harrison, & Nicholas Counties, Ky.* Chicago: O. L. Baskin & Co., 1882.

Sillers, Florence Warfield, and members of the Mississippi Delta Chapter, Daughters of the American Revolution. *History of Bolivar County, Mississippi: Its Creation, Pioneer Days and Progress*. Jackson: Hederman Bros., 1948.

Smiley, David L. *Lion of White Hall: The Life of Cassius M. Clay*. Madison: Univ. of Wisconsin Press, 1962.

Stampp, Kenneth M. *The Peculiar Institution: Slavery in the Ante-Bellum South*. New York: Vintage Books, 1956.

Whitley, Edna Talbott. *Antebellum Portraiture in Kentucky*. Louisville: National Society of Colonial Dames of America in the Commonwealth of Kentucky, 1956.

INDEX